Enterprise Cybersecurity

How to Build a Successful Cyberdefense Program Against Advanced Threats

Scott E. Donaldson

Stanley G. Siegel

Chris K. Williams

Abdul Aslam

Apress®

Enterprise Cybersecurity: How to Build a Successful Cyberdefense Program Against Advanced Threats

ISBN-13 (pbk): 978-1-4302-6082-0

ISBN-13 (electronic): 978-1-4302-6083-7

Managing Director: Welmoed Spahr
Acquisitions Editor: Robert Hutchinson
Developmental Editor: Douglas Pundick
Editorial Board: Steve Anglin, Mark Beckner, Gary Cornell, Louise Corrigan, James DeWolf,
    Jonathan Gennick, Robert Hutchinson, Michelle Lowman, James Markham, Susan McDermott,
    Matthew Moodie, Jeffrey Pepper, Douglas Pundick, Ben Renow-Clarke, Gwenan Spearing,
    Matt Wade, Steve Weiss
Coordinating Editor: Rita Fernando
Copy Editor: Ann Dickson
Compositor: SPi Global
Indexer: SPi Global

Distributed to the book trade worldwide by Springer Science+Business Media New York, 233 Spring Street, 6th Floor, New York, NY 10013. Phone 1-800-SPRINGER, fax (201) 348-4505, e-mail orders-ny@springer-sbm.com, or visit www.springeronline.com. Apress Media, LLC is a California LLC and the sole member (owner) is Springer Science + Business Media Finance Inc (SSBM Finance Inc). SSBM Finance Inc is a Delaware corporation.

For information on translations, please e-mail rights@apress.com, or visit www.apress.com.

Apress and friends of ED books may be purchased in bulk for academic, corporate, or promotional use. eBook versions and licenses are also available for most titles. For more information, reference our Special Bulk Sales–eBook Licensing web page at www.apress.com/bulk-sales.

Any source code or other supplementary material referenced by the author in this text is available to readers at www.apress.com. For detailed information about how to locate your book's source code, go to www.apress.com/source-code/.

To my growing family: Shelly, Melanie, Manoli, Nick, Stephanie, David, Jackson, Mason, Laura, and Ashleigh.

—Scott Donaldson

To Bena, my wife, and our grandchildren: Eva, Ezra, Avi, Raffi, Tal, Eli, Zoe, Sarah, and Emma.

—Stan Siegel

To Elisa, for joining me on these many adventures, and our children: Ryan, Brianna, and Rachael.

—Chris Williams

To Sharu SCube, my love, for inspiring the best in me and our three wonderful children: Zayd for making us laugh every day, Farhan for filling our home with music, and Ishaq for adding adventure to our lives!

—Abdul Aslam

Contents at a Glance

Contents

Foreword

Cybersecurity is a hot topic and deservedly so. Almost every day the newspapers carry stories about privacy violations, compromised computers, and stolen secrets. In the last few years, we have collectively learned about ransomware and revenge porn. We have been privy to secrets purloined from hacked systems. We have been stunned by huge data thefts and releases from supposedly secure government systems. We have seen nation-states victimized by cyberattacks and witnessed corporations, large and small, struggle to recover after being compromised. The security landscape has indeed become complicated. Making the situation even more complex is the continued explosion of interconnectedness and smart devices, which make enterprise boundaries increasingly porous.

If only the solution were to buy a technology, plug it in to your network, and sit back and relax while the technology takes care of the security challenges. Maybe someday some smart researchers will develop such a technology, but today it doesn't exist. The only rational way to approach enterprise security is as a complex systems engineering problem of conjoined systems. People, processes, and technologies must be considered; the systems dynamics in each component system must be considered; and the cascading behavior across the systems throughout the enterprise must be considered. Hard decisions must be made, both in terms of compromises for enterprise efficiencies and in terms of scarce resource allocations. Put in simpler terms, no enterprise can afford all the technologies, assets, controls, and processes for maximum security: There simply are not enough resources available. So compromises must be made. Making those decisions intelligently requires wisdom. Wisdom comes from education, experience, and analysis.

Enterprise Cybersecurity makes an enormous contribution to those striving to achieve the wisdom necessary in making the hard decisions needed to structure and manage an effective cybersecurity program in an enterprise. Structurally, a manager needs to start someplace. The enterprise cybersecurity architecture proposed and explained in this book is a great place to start. Through the lens of security, the book explores the architecture by way of 11 functional areas. The book then puts these functional areas into operational context through examination of the activities associated with the phases of security incidents. Finally, the book presents a practical approach to the long-term management of the problem space. This specific combination of material provides the reader with specific domain knowledge adapted to daily cybersecurity activities and long-term strategy.

This book may seem overwhelming or unnecessary to the small business owner or entrepreneur operating on shoestring budgets. And it is true: Not all enterprises can afford to have all the elements of a comprehensive security program. When the CEO is also the CFO, the secretary, and the IT help desk, the resources required to develop, manage, and maintain a full-scale cybersecurity architecture are clearly lacking. However, all enterprises can afford to have someone thinking about the subject, developing the wisdom needed to make the hard decisions and understanding the implications of the decisions. Real-world decisions lead to real-world complications. This book provides the structure and guidance for even the smallest organization to lay the foundations for growing a comprehensive enterprise cybersecurity architecture along with enterprise growth.

Cybersecurity is a problem area we can expect to grow—and it is everyone's concern. Simply knowing where to start is valuable knowledge. Understanding how to start, continue, and improve is even better. Here's to the hope that enterprises, large and small, benefit from this compilation of knowledge and strategy.

—Dr. Julie J.C.H. Ryan
Associate Professor
George Washington University

About the Authors

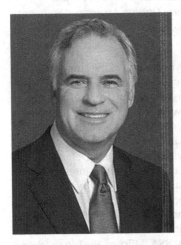

Scott Donaldson has more than 35 years of experience managing complex programs and applying expertise in systems development, business operations, process improvement, and technical cultural change. His experience spans both the federal and commercial marketplace. He is a Senior Vice President for Leidos, Inc., a Fortune 500 company that provides scientific, engineering, systems integration, and technical services. He is the Chief Technology Officer (CTO) and IT Director for its Heath and Engineering Sector.

Donaldson teaches software engineering, software process improvement, and information management courses at the Johns Hopkins University's Whiting School of Engineering. Johns Hopkins honored him in 2009 with an Excellence in Teaching Award. He has a BS in Operations Research from the United States Naval Academy and a MS in Systems Management from the University of Southern California.

Donaldson has co-authored three software engineering books: *Successful Software Development: Making It Happen, 2nd Edition*, (Prentice Hall PTR, 2001); *Successful Software Development: Study Guide*, (Prentice Hall PTR, 2001); and *Cultivating Successful Software Development: A Practitioner's View*, (Prentice Hall PTR, 1997). He has contributed to other software engineering books, including the *Encyclopedia of Software Engineering: Project Management—Success Factors* (CRC Press, 2010) and the *Handbook of Software Quality Assurance: Software Configuration Management—A Practical Look, 3rd Edition* (Prentice Hall, 1999). His most recent co-authored book, *CTOs at Work*, (Apress, 2012) is a collection of interviews with some of the best technical minds in the business.

Dr. Stanley Siegel has more than 40 years of progressive experience as a systems engineer, mathematician, and computer specialist. He started his career with the US government in the Department of Commerce and then the Department of Defense. After his government service, he was with Grumman for 15 years and Science Applications International Corporation (SAIC) for over 20 years. He helped SAIC grow to an $11 billion leader in scientific, engineering, and technical solutions with hundreds of millions of dollars in new business. He earned a nuclear physics doctorate from Rutgers University. While at SAIC, he served as a senior technical advisor and director on a wide spectrum of projects in areas such as software engineering methodology assessment, software requirements analysis, software testing and quality assurance, and technology assessment.

In the 1990s, Dr. Siegel and Scott Donaldson developed the Object Measurement methodology that appears in this book to show how this measurement methodology can quantify an enterprise's cybersecurity effectiveness in warding off cyberattacks. As the book explains, the enterprise can then use this effectiveness measurement to take corrective action to improve its cyberdefenses.

Siegel and Donaldson have jointly taught graduate courses since the mid-1990s. They teach both in-class and online software systems engineering courses at Johns Hopkins University's Whiting School of Engineering. Johns Hopkins honored them in 2009 with an Excellence in Teaching Award.

Siegel has co-authored four software engineering books including the seminal software engineering textbook *Software Configuration Management: An Investment in Product Integrity* (Prentice Hall, 1980). He has contributed to a number of books, including the *Encyclopedia of Software Engineering: Project Management—Success Factors* (CRC Press, 2010) and the *Handbook of Software Quality Assurance: Software Configuration Management—A Practical Look, 3rd Edition* (Prentice Hall, 1999).

Chris Williams has been involved in the cybersecurity field since 1994 in a combination of US military and commercial positions. He has been with Leidos (formerly SAIC) since 2003, focusing on enterprise cybersecurity and compliance and, before that, EDS (now HP) and Booz Allen Hamilton. He is a veteran of the US Army, having served five years with the 82nd Airborne Division and 35th Signal Brigade in Fort Bragg, North Carolina. He has worked on cybersecurity projects with the US Army, Defense Information Systems Agency, Department of State, Defense Intelligence Agency, and numerous other commercial and government organizations designing integrated solutions to protect against modern threats.

He holds a patent for e-commerce technology and has published technical papers with the Institute of Electrical and Electronics Engineers (IEEE). He has presented on cybersecurity at RSA, Milcom, the International Information Systems Security Certification Consortium (ISC)[2], the Information Systems Security Association (ISSA), and other forums. He holds a BSE in Computer Science Engineering from Princeton University and an MS in Information Assurance from George Washington University.

Abdul Aslam has 19 years of experience in devising risk acceptance and compliance frameworks, application security, security operations, and information protection. He is the Director of Cyber Security Compliance and Risk Management for Leidos, where he is in charge of delivering secure and scalable security solutions, policy governance, and strategic technology support. He has worked on numerous IT projects with a proven record of pioneering innovative systems analysis processes and secure application designs that improves availability, integrity, confidentiality, reliability, effectiveness, and efficiency of technology services.

Mr. Aslam has a MS in Systems Engineering Management and Information Assurance from George Washington University and a BS in Engineering in Electronics and Telecommunications from Osmania University (India). He also holds the CISSP certification.

Acknowledgments

Any book project cannot be accomplished without some impact on home life. To our family members, we express our gratitude for their patience while we took a lot of time away from them on evenings and weekends to write this book. Because this time can never be reclaimed, we are forever grateful for their understanding and support. Special thanks go to all of our families for their encouragement throughout the years spent making this book as good as we possibly could.

We thank Apress and Jeff Pepper for accepting this project and mentoring us through the authorship process.

We thank Robert Hutchinson, Rita Fernando, and Ann Dickson for helping to produce this book and for their untiring eyes looking over text and figures until we finally got them right.

We thank Dr. Julie Ryan at George Washington University for mentoring this project from the beginning and graciously agreeing to write the book's foreword.

We thank Scott Kennedy, Paul Rebeles, and Gib Sorebo for making time to read the manuscript cover to cover, catch omissions, and identify opportunities for improvement. Your feedback and insights helped make this book better than we could have done on our own.

We thank the business leadership at Leidos for encouraging and supporting us as we took on this project. In particular Jack O'Meara for listening to our ideas and providing us with real-world applicability and feedback.

Finally, we thank all our colleagues and friends who took time from their busy schedules to review, comment, listen, and advise. You helped us develop our ideas and put them on paper so that others can benefit from them as well.

—Scott Donaldson, Stan Siegel, Chris Williams, and Abdul Aslam

Introduction

Interest in cybersecurity is on the rise. As our world becomes more and more interconnected and more and more online, the damage cyberthreats can do to our cyberworld is increasing dramatically, day by day. For those of us old enough to remember life before personal computers—not to mention the Internet—it is staggering to consider how all of this connectivity has transformed our daily lives. Yet, as the online world developed in less than a generation, the ability to protect the online world has had even less time to develop and is still maturing.

Hardly a week goes by without an announcement of a cybersecurity breach or incident of some form or another, such as the following:

- Personal information compromised

- Credit cards stolen

- Medical records lost

- Companies hacked

- Governments targeted

The attackers perpetrating these crimes—and yes, most often these are criminal activities—seem to be acting with impunity compared to the defenders seeking to stop them. These hacks are occurring to major brand names, including Target, Home Depot, JP Morgan Chase, Sony, Apple, and many, many others. While many of the hacks hitting the headlines affect victims in the United States, the parties doing the hacking are in Russia, China, Korea, the Middle East, and elsewhere around the world. This problem is truly global.

If these hacks are happening to the biggest, most well-recognized and well-funded businesses and nations, then what chance do the *relatively smaller* cybertargets have at protecting themselves?

Anyone who is interested in cybersecurity or who is responsible for cybersecurity at an organization has certainly recognized that there is a long road ahead to achieving cybersecurity *success* against the threats mentioned here, however that success ends up being defined.

What Is This Book About?

This book is about achieving enterprise cybersecurity success. Does success mean computers never get compromised, malware never gets inside the enterprise, or breaches never occur? What success means depends on how an enterprise defines it. Cybersecurity professionals work with executive leadership to make business decisions on how *good* cybersecurity needs to be to defend the enterprise against cyberattackers. *Good* translates into various operational processes, cybersecurity capabilities, and information systems to protect the enterprise as needed to satisfy the business requirements.

Implementing a successful cyberdefense program against real-world attacks is what this book is about. Often in cybersecurity, everyone knows *what should be done*, but resources *to do it* are not sufficient. As shown in Figure I-1, the reality is that *the cybersecurity conundrum gets in the way of what needs to be done*. What cybersecurity professionals want to implement is more than what control frameworks specify, and it is far greater than what the budget allows. Ironically, another challenge is that even when defenders get everything they want, clever attackers are extremely effective at finding and exploiting the gaps in those defenses, regardless of their comprehensiveness. The challenge is to spend the available budget on the right protections so that real-world attacks can be thwarted without breaking the bank.

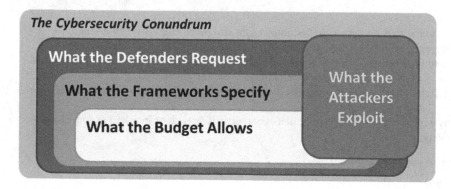

Figure I-1. Even though the cybersecurity conundrum presents significant challenges, this book is about implementing a successful cyberdefense program that works against real-world attacks, despite the challenges.

The cybersecurity business challenge is compounded by the fact that cyberthreats have to be looked at within the larger business context. The reality is cyberthreats are just one of *many* threats against the business and, from a budget perspective, are relatively small threats. Therefore, the enterprise has to prioritize limited resources to get the best possible security for the available budget.

Cybersecurity will *never* be funded to do everything that is desired, or even mandated by available *best practice* cybersecurity frameworks.

Cybersecurity professionals are frustrated, in part, because they request resources to fight threats that are, from a business perspective, a rounding error on the bottom line. In other words, the cyberbudget is a relatively small percentage of the organization's overall financial posture. Cybersecurity needs to be planned around the idea of achieving only partial security, rather than being resourced to do everything perfectly all the time.

Ironically, the major cybersecurity frameworks lay out what the *ideal* practices should be, but have little, if any, guidance on how to deploy a *partial* solution that is the best value for the cost when the funding is not adequate to achieve the ideal. Cybersecurity professionals must learn how to work with the business to find a new balance. Indeed, in a resource-constrained environment, cyberdefenders must consider how to build defenses that are only partially successful, but are wholly effective in the eyes of the business. This balance requires a new mindset, powered by the following axioms of cyberdefense:

Axioms of a "Next-Generation" Cyberdefense:

1. Assume an intelligent attacker will eventually defeat all defensive measures.

2. Design defenses to detect and delay attacks so that defenders have time to respond.

3. Layer defenses to contain attacks and provide redundancy in protection.

4. Use an active defense to catch and repel attacks after they start but before they can succeed.

With these axioms in mind, there is an acknowledged need for a framework that enables cybersecurity professionals to deploy balanced security with limited resources. Simply stated, cybersecurity professionals are not going to be able to implement the ideal solution.

This book presents a cybersecurity methodology for designing, managing, and operating a *balanced* enterprise cybersecurity program that is pragmatic and realistic in the face of resource constraints and other real-world limitations. In this book, the reader will learn the following:

- The methodology of targeted attacks and why they succeed

- The cybersecurity risk management process

- Why cybersecurity capabilities are the foundation of every successful cybersecurity program

- How to organize a cybersecurity program

- How to assess and score a cybersecurity program

- How to report cybersecurity program status against compliance and regulatory frameworks

- The operational processes and supporting information systems of a successful cybersecurity program

- How to create a data-driven and objectively managed cybersecurity program

- How cybersecurity is evolving and will continue to evolve over the next decade

Who Should Read This Book?

This book is for anyone interested in modern cybersecurity, as depicted by Figure I-2.

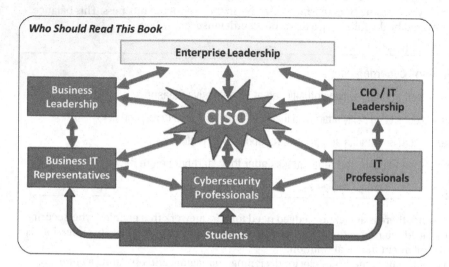

Figure I-2. *This book should be read by everyone involved in or interested in successful enterprise cybersecurity.*

Readers of this book include the following:

- *Enterprise Leadership* with oversight responsibility for information technology and cybersecurity concerns within an organization, business, or government agency.

- *Chief Information Security Officer (CISO)* or cybersecurity director who is responsible for overseeing a comprehensive cybersecurity program at his or her enterprise.

- *Cybersecurity Professional* who is responsible for managing, deploying, and operating effective cyberdefenses within the enterprise.

- *Chief Information Officer (CIO)* or *Information Technology (IT) Leadership* who are responsible for deploying information technology solutions to deliver business value while also complying with regulatory and security requirements.

- *IT Professionals* who are responsible for ensuring information technology solutions have adequate cybersecurity while also delivering value to the business or organization.

- *Business or Organizational Leadership* who are responsible for achieving business objectives while using information technology systems and protecting sensitive and valuable information.

- *Business or Organization IT Representative* who are responsible for delivering business capabilities using information technology and complying with cybersecurity requirements.

- *Students* who are learning about business, information technology, or cybersecurity and who need to understand the challenges of delivering effective cybersecurity solutions.

Why Did the Authors Write This Book?

The authors wrote this book based upon personal experiences fighting advanced persistent threats and other modern cyberadversaries. Using the *conventional* cybersecurity architecture of perimeter defenses and endpoint protections was not adequate against the adversaries. The authors realized they needed more resources than were actually available. Not only did they need a new cyberdefense architecture, but they also needed an architecture to coordinate an entire cyberdefense program that allowed them to explain to business leaders what they were doing and why.

The challenge to a cyberdefense program is about much more than buying cybersecurity technologies and deploying them. Without budget, those technologies will never be purchased. Without executive backing, the budget will never materialize. Without clear communications, executive backing will never be obtained. Without good organization, clear communications are impossible.

Figure I-3 delineates how a successful cybersecurity program needs to facilitate the coordination of policy, IT life cycle, cybersecurity assessments, and programmatics. The IT life cycle consists of strategy, engineering, and operation functions. Programmatics include the organization of people, budget, and technology. These major components work together to guide, build, and operate an enterprise cybersecurity program.

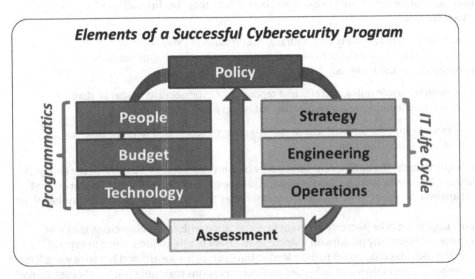

Figure I-3. *A successful cybersecurity program effectively coordinates cybersecurity policy and assessment with the IT life cycle and cybersecurity programmatics.*

A challenge is finding a single framework that can satisfy all these cybersecurity program needs. As the authors looked at major control frameworks and methodologies, they found themselves running into challenges that included the following:

- *Policy frameworks* did not align well with how people are typically organized or with how cybersecurity is usually assessed.

- *Programmatic frameworks* focus on business considerations and deal with cybersecurity at a high level of abstraction such that their guidance is not actionable, except in the most general of terms.

- *IT life cycle frameworks* deal with cybersecurity in broad terms and generally do not consider how cybersecurity needs to be decomposed for management and reporting purposes.

- *Assessment frameworks* tend to group cybersecurity controls and capabilities in ways that are not aligned with how people or budgets are typically organized.

An Enterprise Cybersecurity Architecture

As the authors looked at existing frameworks and methodologies, they developed a set of requirements for an effective enterprise cybersecurity architecture that addresses the cybersecurity program needs they encountered. They observed that an effective cybersecurity architecture needs to include the following requirements:

- It needs to tie together policy, programmatics, IT life cycle, and assessments using a single framework for delegation and coordination.

- It needs to break down enterprise cybersecurity into a number of sub-areas to communicate that there is more to effective cybersecurity than just firewalls and anti-virus software.

- Sub-areas need to align relatively well with real-world skills of cybersecurity professionals, budgets supporting those professionals, and technologies purchased and maintained with the budgets.

- Sub-areas need to enable quick and efficient reporting of cybersecurity status so that executives can understand the *big picture* of what is and is not working well.

- Sub-areas need to support the business decision-making process and help leaders define strategy and prioritization.

To satisfy these requirements, the authors envision a new framework that they simply call the *enterprise cybersecurity architecture*. This framework partitions enterprise cybersecurity into 11 functional areas and then focuses on 113 capabilities within those functional areas, rather than specific products, technologies, or processes.

When the authors organize a cybersecurity program in accordance with this architecture, they can show an entire enterprise cybersecurity posture on a single slide. Users of this architecture can express enterprise cybersecurity needs and challenges to their leadership in straightforward and intuitive ways. This information helps enterprise leadership make informed business decisions regarding how to allocate scarce resources to protect the enterprise.

Figure I-4 depicts an early, *simplified* cybersecurity status dashboard that came out of the analysis of various control frameworks. Figure I-4 lists the 11 functional areas of the enterprise cybersecurity architecture and then shows the overall status for each functional area along with a corresponding status of supporting capabilities. The figure shows the enterprise's entire cybersecurity posture on one slide. Showing this high-level, comprehensive status helps enterprise leadership envision areas for improvement. With this larger perspective, business leaders readily understand a single cybersecurity technology is not going to radically change the overall security posture. However, when the cybersecurity capabilities are taken in aggregate, they can make a significant difference.

Functional Area	Overall Status	Status by Capability
Systems Administration	O	◉ O O O ◉ ◉ O O O ◉
Network Security	◉	◉ ◉ O O ◉ ◉ ◉ ◉ O ◉ ◉ ◉ ◉ ◉ ◉
Application Security	◉	◉ ◉ ◉ O ◉ ◉ ◉ O O O
Endpoint, Server, and Device Security	◉	◉ O O O ◉ O ◉ ◉ O O ◉ O O ◉ O ◉ ◉
Identity, Authentication, and Access Management	◉	◉ ◉ ◉ ◉ ◉ ◉ ◉ O ● ●
Data Protection and Cryptography	◉	◉ O O ◉ O O ◉ ● O O O
Monitoring, Vulnerability, and Patch Management	O	◉ O O O O O O O O ◉ O O ◉ ◉ O O
High Availability, Disaster Recovery, and Physical Protection	◉	◉ O O O ◉ O O O ◉ ◉ ◉
Incident Response	●	● O O ◉ O ● O O
Asset Management and Supply Chain	◉	◉ O O ◉ ◉ O O
Policy, Audit, E-Discovery, and Training	●	◉ O O O ◉ O O ◉ O ● ●

Legend: O = Poor ◉ = Medium ● = Good

Figure I-4. *An enterprise cybersecurity architecture enables security leadership to manage and report on the status of the enterprise's cybersecurity program in a straightforward and intuitive manner.*

Figure I-4 lists all the functional areas and indicates which ones have the strongest capabilities and which ones have the weakest. Systems Administration and Monitoring, Vulnerability, and Patch Management functional areas are the weakest and most likely need investment for improvement. Incident Response and Policy, Audit, E-Discovery, and Training functional areas are the strongest and probably do not need significant focus for the moment.

For executives, being able to see inside a cybersecurity program without becoming buried in the details is important. For security practitioners, this dashboard provides actionable value as well.

Each dot in the capabilities section represents a security capability in the enterprise, such as protocol filtering, logging, or data analytics. Each one of these capabilities can be tracked and its status reported. Even here, with only three levels of status—perhaps aligning with *weak*, *medium*, and *strong*—practitioners can see which functional areas need the most work and which capabilities within those functional areas should be improved. The enterprise cybersecurity architecture supports all levels of the program.

A Complete Cybersecurity Program

Many frameworks describe the components that go into a cybersecurity architecture; however, few of them speak to the overall cybersecurity program process or cycle. Figure I-5 depicts the high-level cybersecurity program cycle consisting of a number of programmatic steps that occur in a cyclical manner to manage, assess, improve, and operate the enterprise's cybersecurity.

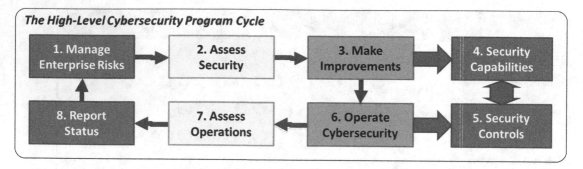

Figure I-5. *A successful enterprise cybersecurity program is an ongoing cycle of risk management, security assessment, improvements against security capabilities and controls, security operations and operational assessment, and finally reporting of status internally and externally.*

Figure I-5 shows this program cycle as a series of steps that are executed in the following cyclical manner:

1. *Manage Enterprise Risks* involves assessing risks to the enterprise and scoping enterprise IT systems to contain those risks and deploy mitigating controls and capabilities.

2. *Assess Security* involves evaluating the security that is currently deployed to assess its effectiveness and comprehensiveness compared to the negotiated business need.

3. *Make Improvements* involves planning improvements to enterprise cybersecurity by deploying or improving technologies and processes.

4. *Security Capabilities* are what are delivered by cybersecurity technologies and processes and what enable the enterprise to accomplish its cybersecurity objectives.

5. *Security Controls* apply those capabilities to address specific concerns, providing prevention, detection, forensics, or audit of the behavior that is of interest.

6. *Operate Cybersecurity* involves operating cybersecurity technologies, processes, capabilities, and controls to deliver cybersecurity to the enterprise.

7. *Assess Operations* involves measuring cybersecurity performance to understand what cybersecurity threats are occurring and how well defenses are serving to counter those threats.

8. *Report Status* involves reporting cybersecurity status both internally according to internally negotiated frameworks and standards, and externally to regulators, insurers, and other interested parties.

Combining these eight steps provides the major components of a complete cybersecurity program. This program and the cybersecurity architecture that enables it are valid for an organization of 100 people or a corporation or government agency of 100,000. The cybersecurity needs for this range of organizations are similar. The enterprise cybersecurity architecture described in this book can be used to develop an effective cybersecurity program for a wide range of corporate or government organizations.

Organization of the Book

This book contains 15 chapters and 9 appendices. The chapters and appendices are organized into six parts, covering different aspects of an effective enterprise cybersecurity program. The book describes the cybersecurity problem and how to implement a cybersecurity program tailored to an enterprise's needs. The appendices are designed to be companions to the chapters. The appendices explain the concepts introduced in the chapters in detail so an enterprise can design, implement, and run an enduring cybersecurity program.

PART I: The Cybersecurity Challenge

The first part of this book is about the cybersecurity challenge and how cybersecurity has changed over the past ten years. Due to this evolution, the cyberdefense methods that worked well in the past are doomed to fail in the future.

CHAPTER 1: Defining the Cybersecurity Challenge

Chapter 1 defines the cybersecurity challenge facing the modern enterprise and discusses the threats against those defenses and why those threats are succeeding at an alarming and increasing rate.

CHAPTER 2: Meeting the Cybersecurity Challenge

Chapter 2 describes how the cybersecurity challenge can be met and how cybersecurity controls and capabilities can be organized to prevent, detect, document, or audit malicious behavior.

PART II: A New Enterprise Cybersecurity Architecture

Part II introduces a new enterprise cybersecurity architecture that is designed to organize and manage every aspect of an enterprise cybersecurity program, including policy, programmatics, IT life cycle, and assessment.

CHAPTER 3: Enterprise Cybersecurity Architecture

Chapter 3 describes the new enterprise cybersecurity architecture and explores its 11 functional areas in terms of their goals and objectives, threat vectors, and underlying capabilities.

CHAPTER 4: Implementing Enterprise Cybersecurity

Chapter 4 discusses how to implement the new enterprise cybersecurity architecture by identifying security scopes, defining security policies, and selecting security controls to counter anticipated threats.

CHAPTER 5: Operating Enterprise Cybersecurity

Chapter 5 explains how to operate enterprise cybersecurity capabilities and processes, introducing the 17 operational processes and 14 supporting information systems essential to effective enterprise cybersecurity.

CHAPTER 6: Enterprise Cybersecurity and the Cloud

Chapter 6 discusses how cloud computing is different from the conventional data center and explains how the new architecture needs to be tailored to be used for cloud computing environments.

CHAPTER 7: Enterprise Cybersecurity for Mobile and BYOD

Chapter 7 describes the trends of mobile computing and Bring Your Own Device (BYOD), and how these two trends solve problems and introduce challenges for the new architecture.

PART III: The Art of Cyberdefense

Part III discusses the art of the cyberdefense, and how the new architecture is deployed and used to provide effective risk mitigation and incident response for cybersecurity crises.

CHAPTER 8: Building an Effective Defense

Chapter 8 examines why attackers have great success against legacy cyberdefenses, the steps of the attack sequence and how to disrupt them, and how to layer cyberdefenses so they effectively thwart targeted attacks.

CHAPTER 9: Responding to Incidents

Chapter 9 describes the incident response process in detail by considering what the enterprise needs to do on an ongoing basis to investigate, contain, and remediate cybersecurity incidents when they occur.

CHAPTER 10: Managing a Cybersecurity Crisis

Chapter 10 discusses how severe cybersecurity incidents become crises and how the enterprise must behave differently in a crisis situation while it struggles to restore normal operations.

PART IV: Enterprise Cyberdefense Assessment

Part IV establishes a methodology for quantitatively and objectively assessing cybersecurity using the enterprise cybersecurity architecture and then mapping those assessments against major frameworks for reporting purposes.

CHAPTER 11: Assessing Enterprise Cybersecurity

Chapter 11 explains the cybersecurity assessment and auditing process, and provides four worked-out examples using the new architecture to assess cybersecurity posture and effectiveness.

CHAPTER 12: Measuring a Cybersecurity Program

Chapter 12 provides a comprehensive method for objectively measuring an enterprise's cybersecurity by looking at risk mitigations, cybersecurity functional areas, and security operations.

CHAPTER 13: Mapping Against Cybersecurity Frameworks

Chapter 13 explains how to take the results of an enterprise cybersecurity assessment and map them against other cybersecurity frameworks for the purpose of evaluation, audit, or compliance reporting.

PART V: Enterprise Cybersecurity Program

Part V brings together the concepts of the rest of the book into a comprehensive enterprise cybersecurity program that combines assessment, planning, prioritization, implementation, and operations.

CHAPTER 14: Managing an Enterprise Cybersecurity Program

Chapter 14 explains the cybersecurity program management process and shows how the enterprise can use it to manage cybersecurity decision-making and prioritize improvements to get the best possible value for the investment.

CHAPTER 15: Looking to the Future

Chapter 15 concludes the book by discussing the evolution of generations of cyberattacks and cyberdefenses, and how enterprise cybersecurity architecture will evolve over time to support the enterprise's needs now and in the future.

PART VI: Appendices

The appendices provide greater detail than the chapters and provide important details and examples for cybersecurity practitioners who want to use the enterprise cybersecurity architecture described in this book.

APPENDIX A: Common Cyberattacks

Appendix A describes many of the cyberattacks that are common today, explaining their impact, methods and consequences, and potential defenses used to counter them.

APPENDIX B: Cybersecurity Frameworks

Appendix B describes a number of the major cybersecurity frameworks that are in common use at the time of publication, explaining some of the philosophy behind each framework and how each one *slices and dices* cybersecurity into components.

APPENDIX C: Enterprise Cybersecurity Capabilities

Appendix C details the 113 cybersecurity capabilities of the new architecture, organized into its 11 functional areas.

APPENDIX D: Sample Cybersecurity Policy

Appendix D provides a sample enterprise information security policy document, organized into the 11 functional areas of the new architecture described in this book.

APPENDIX E: Cybersecurity Operational Processes

Appendix E contains detailed flowcharts for the 17 operational processes of enterprise cybersecurity, and it also introduces the 14 supporting information systems.

APPENDIX F: Object Measurement

Appendix F introduces the Object Measurement methodology for objective assessment, and explains how to use it to measure and report enterprise cybersecurity architecture effectiveness.

APPENDIX G: Cybersecurity Capability Value Scales

Appendix G contains detailed, example Object Measurement value scales for measuring the performance of each of the 113 enterprise cybersecurity architecture capabilities, grouped by the 11 functional areas.

APPENDIX H: Cybersecurity Sample Assessment

Appendix H provides an example enterprise cybersecurity assessment using the methodology contained in this book, providing multiple levels of detail showing how different types of assessment can be performed.

APPENDIX I: Network Segmentation

Appendix I describes a simple methodology for network segmentation that is suitable for countering many advanced threats and provides a good balance between *containment and security* versus *complexity and cost*.

Glossary

The Glossary provides an explanation of the cybersecurity terms used in this book, expressed in *plain English* for the non-technical reader.

Bibliography

The Bibliography provides additional literature for readers who wish to explore extensions to material addressed in this book and who wish to explore alternatives to what this book addresses.

Index

The Index provides a means for the reader to locate concepts and other material the book addresses in a timely manner.

PART I

■ ■ ■

The Cybersecurity Challenge

CHAPTER 1

■ ■ ■

Defining the Cybersecurity Challenge

It appears that lately cybersecurity is in trouble, or at least going through a difficult time. If you are reading this book, you are one of the people trying to make cybersecurity work despite daunting challenges and information technology (IT) environments seemingly ill-suited to facing those challenges. The authors share your concerns.

This book is about building *effective cybersecurity* that works against advanced cyberthreats, despite the challenges. Effective cybersecurity works when you are faced with an adversary who is well-funded, intelligent, sophisticated, and who does not give up at the first sign of cyberdefense. Effective cybersecurity evolves over time to handle increasingly sophisticated adversaries in an increasingly interconnected world. Effective cybersecurity involves cybersecurity as a partner, coach, and scorekeeper for IT, rather than just a naysayer standing in the way of progress.

This book describes a comprehensive framework for managing an enterprise cybersecurity program that is pragmatic, realistic, and suited to battling today's cyberthreats. This book's field-proven framework has been used to run large-scale cybersecurity efforts against advanced nation-state adversaries and talented individual hackers. This flexible framework is designed to manage cyberdefenses against today's sophisticated cyberthreats, as well as tomorrow's next-generation cyberthreats.

The Cyberattacks of Today

Compared to today, cybersecurity used to be relatively simple. The major cyberthreats were viruses, worms, and Trojan horse. These cyberthreats randomly attacked computers directly connected to the Internet, but posed little enterprise threat. Inside enterprise networks with firewalls on the outside and anti-virus protection on the inside, the enterprise appeared to be protected and relatively safe. Occasionally an incident would occur and cyberdefenders would rally to fight it, but once the defenders understood the malicious code, detecting it and defeating it was straightforward.

Then, slowly but surely, a transformation started to take place. Cyberattackers started getting inside enterprise networks, and once they were inside they operated surreptitiously. Cyberattackers took control of infected machines and connected them to remote command-and-control systems. They captured usernames and passwords, and then used them to connect to systems for stealing data or money. Cyberattackers exploited vulnerabilities inside the enterprise to move laterally among computers on the network and capture the credentials of more and more people within the enterprise. Finally, cyberattackers escalated privileges and got control of the systems administrator accounts in charge of everything. Once these attackers got administrative control of the enterprise, they were able to do anything they wanted.

3

"We are using outdated, conventional defenses to guard against cutting-edge, innovative malware. We are no more prepared to do this than a 19th century army trying to defend itself against today's electronic weaponry." —FireEye.[1]

In recent years, this trend has played out in more and more spectacular breaches hitting the headlines. Just a couple of the severe intrusions include the following:

- In 2011, RSA's enterprise was breached and the security keys for many of its customers were believed to have been stolen. This breach prompted RSA to replace millions of its SecureID tokens to restore security for its customers. This breach is disconcerting because RSA is one of the oldest and most established cybersecurity brands.

- In 2013, Target's point of sale (POS) network was compromised, resulting in the loss of personal information and credit card numbers for over 40 million customers. The costs of this breach, particularly when reputational damage and lawsuits are taken into account, will likely be huge.

- In 2014, Sony Pictures Entertainment reported attackers had infiltrated its environment and disabled almost every computer and server in the company. This cyberattack brought the company to its knees and resulted in the public release of thousands of proprietary documents and e-mail messages.

- In 2014, a German steel mill was affected by a hacking incident that caused one of its blast furnaces to malfunction. This resulted in significant physical damage to the plant and its facilities.

- In 2015, Anthem reported its IT systems had been breached and personal information on over 80 million current and former members of their healthcare network was compromised, which included the US government's Blue Cross Blue Shield program.

These intrusions are but a handful of the myriad of cybersecurity breaches that have occurred recently. However, these breaches are indicative of some of the major trends. Cyberattackers are now targeting personal identities, financial accounts, and healthcare information and getting such information on millions or tens of millions of people in a single breach. Cyberattackers are taking control of industrial equipment and causing physical damage to plants and equipment. Thankfully, no one has been hurt so far, but given the current trends it may just be a matter of time.

These headlines seem to indicate that the attackers have gotten the upper hand, at least for now. The question is, "What has changed and how can the defenders recover?"

The Sony Pictures Entertainment Breach of 2014

In November 2014, Sony Pictures Entertainment employees got to the office to find themselves in the crosshairs of an IT horror story. Their computers had been taken over. Instead of displaying logon prompts, office productivity, and corporate web sites, they were completely nonfunctional and displayed a message from an organization claiming to be the Guardians of Peace. By the end of the day, most of the computers at Sony Pictures had been completely disabled, sharply impairing the company's business while they

---

[1]FireEye, "Advanced Malware Exposed," www2.fireeye.com/wp_advmalware_exposed.html, 2011.

recovered data and IT systems. The cyberattackers then went on to publish proprietary data from Sony Pictures, including salaries and personal e-mails of its senior executives. The breach caused a media sensation due to the salaciousness of the data published. The breach also caused earthquakes in the cybersecurity industry, as the IT community got a glimpse of what a devastating cyberattack could do.

Key lessons learned include the following:

- The Sony hack is significant, not because the attackers did something no one could do before, but because the attackers did what cyberattackers have been able to do all along, but have chosen not to. The security industry has been warning for years that cyberattackers could bring a company to their knees. The Sony hack put the reality of this possibility in full view of the press and the public.

- It is reasonable to expect that Sony's cyberdefenses were consistent with industry norms and reflected what is and is not being done at a myriad of other companies around the world. In fact, Sony Pictures was likely better defended than most enterprises due to its size and prominence. One has to ask, "Is this an indication of how vulnerable everyone is to a devastating cyberattack?"

- The effectiveness of the Sony hack was likely amplified by the consolidation of IT systems administration that has occurred over the past 20 years. In the past, a single systems administrator might manage a handful of servers providing, at most, one or two enterprise services. Today, the same administrator may have privileged access to a hundred systems, or even thousands. If attackers can get control of that one person's administrative credentials, the damage they can do is devastating.

- These types of attacks show how professional attackers, who understand how modern IT works and how it is managed, can effectively turn an enterprise's IT infrastructure against it. These infrastructures are largely designed for functionality, not security, and often lack compartmentalization to contain a breach and limit its damage.

- Finally, attacks like Sony's underscore the fear factor that devastating cyberattacks can have on an industry and the nation. What would be the political impact if an individual, an organization, or a nation-state could pull off a hundred Sony-style attacks, all simultaneously?

There is a mega-trend going on here. These types of cyberattacks are moving *down market* over time. In other words, the techniques nation-states were using a couple of years ago are being used by cybercriminals today. The techniques cybercriminals were using a couple of years ago are in commodity malware and viruses today. It is reasonable to expect what was done to Sony Pictures Entertainment will become more common in the future as cyberattack tools and techniques proliferate and become available to larger and larger communities. So, while these types of threats may only be of concern to a small group of top-tier players today, as these threats move down market, they will become more widespread.

The tools and techniques to fight these types of attackers exist today, but they are not cheap or easy to deploy. Also, fighting these cyberattackers requires re-thinking many aspects of IT so that security is *baked in* rather than *bolted on*. One cannot simply buy a widget and be immune to Sony-style attacks. Just as banks have to invest in alarms and security guards, enterprises have to invest in people doing the dirty, grunt work of cybersecurity, day in and day out. Enterprises have to be constantly evolving their defenses. Cybersecurity defense is an arms race and the attackers are smart, competent, and ill-intended. The attackers who hit Sony Pictures Entertainment are advanced, persistent, and very, very threatening.

Advanced Persistent Threats

In fact, these major breaches point to the rise of a new type of adversary, the advanced persistent threat (APT). These attacks are of great interest, not because they are mysterious or particularly advanced, but because they mark the widespread professionalization of cyberattacks. An APT attacker is skilled in the art of cyberattack and leverages IT technologies effectively to breach enterprises and systematically bypass all of their protections, one at a time. What makes APT different from earlier cyberattack types is the persistence of the attack. Back in the days of viruses and Trojan horses, cyberattacks were generally regarded as somewhat arbitrary. A software developer created a piece of malware and sent it out onto the Internet to propagate and spread. Either it propagated or it did not. Where it propagated was generally arbitrary, determined more by luck than by any specific direction from the developer.

APT makes cyberattacks much more focused and effective because now they are under the control of an intelligent actor who has an objective to achieve. If the attackers' goal is to break into a bank or a merchant, they persist in their attack and try multiple angles and approaches until they are successful. If their goal is to break into a company and steal corporate secrets, they persist in pursuing that goal until they succeed. If their goal is to break into a government and steal national security information, they persist in trying to find weaknesses in the government's networks and computers until they find them and exploit them.

In a conventional attack, defenses only need to block the malware, and it will move on to other targets. Simply having defenses is no longer effective when a single mistake can be exploited by an opportunistic attacker. An APT attacker constantly adjusts the attack to get past the latest round of defenses. *Given enough time, an APT attacker eventually gets through.* To stop the attacker from getting through the defenses, the defenses have to work perfectly and be maintained perfectly. Any mistake on the part of the defenders is promptly exploited by the attacker, who is waiting for mistakes to occur. APT requires a new type of defense method—one that adapts to the attack as quickly as the attack adapts to the defense.

Waves of Malware

Looking at the adversaries' techniques, tools, and technologies and corresponding cyberdefenses over the past 20 years, one can see there have been a number of generations, or *waves,* of malware technologies infecting computers and propagating on networks. These can be grouped into different categories based upon their characteristics and behaviors, including the following:

1. ***Static Viruses:*** The first malware wave is static viruses that propagated from computer to computer via floppy disks and boot sectors of hard drives. These viruses propagated themselves, but few of them actually impacted system operations.

2. ***Network-Based Viruses:*** The second malware wave is network-based viruses that propagated across the open Internet from computer to computer, exploiting weaknesses in operating systems. Computers were often directly connected to each other without firewalls or other protections in between.

3. ***Trojan Horse:*** The third malware wave is Trojan malware that propagates across the Internet via e-mail and from compromised or malicious web sites. This malware can infect large numbers of victims, but does so relatively arbitrarily since it is undirected.

4. ***Command and Control:*** The fourth malware wave includes command and control features that allows the attacker to remotely control its operation within the target enterprise. Compromised machines then become a foothold inside of the enterprise that can be manipulated by the attacker.

5. *Customized*: The fifth malware wave is custom malware developed for a particular target. Custom malware is sent directly to specific targets via phishing e-mails, drive-by websites, or downloadable applications such as mobile apps. Because the malware is customized for each victim, it is not recognized by signature-based defenses.

6. *Polymorphic*: The sixth malware wave is polymorphic malware designed not only to take administrative control of victim networks, but also to dynamically modify itself so it can continuously evade detection and stay ahead of attempts to remediate it.

7. *Intelligent*: The seventh malware wave is malware with intelligence to analyze a victim network, move laterally within it, escalate privileges to take administrative control, and extract, modify, or destroy its target data or information systems. Intelligent malware does all of these actions autonomously, without requiring human intervention or external command and control.

8. *Fully Automated, Polymorphic*: The eighth malware wave is fully automated, polymorphic malware that combines the features of the sixth and seventh waves. This malware takes control autonomously and dynamically evades detection and remediation to stay one step ahead of defenders at all times.

9. *Firmware and Supply Chain*: The ninth malware wave takes the eighth wave to its logical conclusion by delivering malware capabilities through the supply chain, either embedded in product firmware or within software products before they are shipped. Such malware is embedded in products when they are built, or at such a low level in the product firmware that they are virtually undetectable. By delivering malware in this manner, it is difficult for cyberdefenders to differentiate the supply chain malware from the other features *coming from the factory*.

Many people are familiar with the first three waves of cyberattacks, which represent the majority of consumer-grade cyberthreats and many of the attacks covered in the popular press. Enterprises are experiencing malware waves four, five, and six on a regular and increasing basis. However, these waves of malware are little-understood outside of specialized cybersecurity fields. Nation-state cyberattackers use malware waves seven, eight, and nine. Such waves require considerable resources and expertise. These waves are sophisticated malware packages designed to penetrate the most developed cyberdefenses.

All of these malware technologies are proliferating over time. Not too long ago, waves four, five, and six were solely in the domain of the nation-state attacker. Today these are in the hands of cybercriminals; the malware waves are moving *down market*. It is reasonable to expect in the future that such sophisticated tools will be in the hands of the casual attacker as well. The cyberattackers are not sitting still, and their tools are constantly evolving.

Types of Cyberattackers

Who are these mysterious cyberattackers hacking into systems and causing these headlines? Obviously, they are people, somewhere in the world, who choose to create, distribute, and use malware or other tools or techniques to do things on computers they shouldn't be doing. As depicted in Figure 1-1, these people can be grouped into five categories based on their intent and objectives.

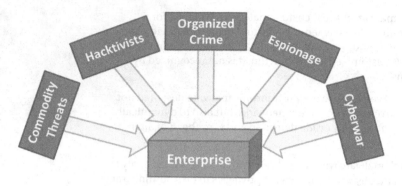

Figure 1-1. *Cyberattacker categories can be distinguished by their intent and objectives distinguishable by their intent and objectives.*

There can be significant overlap in the tools and technologies used by these groups. These five cyberattacker categories are described in the following sections.

Commodity Threats

Commodity threats are the random malware, viruses, Trojans, worms, botnets, ransomware, and other threats that are out propagating on the Internet all the time. Strictly by chance, commodity threats are undirected and may end up inside of the enterprise at any time. Commodity threats may exploit vulnerabilities or other cyberdefense weaknesses, but they do not adjust or adapt to work their way around protections that are in place.

Commodity threats can be destructive, although the amount of damage they can do is usually pretty limited. However, they can also be the starting point for more dangerous, targeted threats. Targeted cyberattackers may start their efforts by going to botnet operators and purchasing access to computers and servers that are already compromised inside the target environment. This purchased access can make the attackers' initial entry into the enterprise easier and save them valuable time and money.

For the purposes of this book, commodity threats are undirected and opportunistic. Defenders only need to block the threat's attack vector, and the defenders are safe. For the other cyberattack threat categories, simply blocking the initial attack vector is only a start.

Hacktivists

Activist hacking, or hacktivism, consists of targeted attacks. Hacktivists use hacking to make a public or political statement. Their goal is to use hacking to bolster their cause or embarrass their adversaries. Hacktivism may be used against individuals, enterprises, or governments, depending on the situation and the particular objectives of the hacktivists.

Hacktivists, because of their activist ideology, are seldom out to hurt anyone or do significant physical damage. Most often, hacktivists are simply looking to get their message out and draw attention to their cause. Hacktivists conduct their attacks with an explicit objective of getting it covered by the press, their message communicated, and their adversaries embarrassed.

Since hacktivists are frequently individuals acting alone or small organizations with only limited resources, hacktivists tend to use mostly commodity tools and techniques that are widely available on the Internet. The defenses to protect against these tools and techniques are also usually widely available. The hacktivists operate by taking advantage of vulnerabilities that are unpatched or otherwise open to exploitation. Hacktivists will try and try again until the defenders make a mistake that allows them to accomplish their goal.

Organized Crime

Like hacktivism, organized crime attacks are targeted. Criminals and criminal organizations have found there is serious money to be made on the Internet. There are a number of factors that make the Internet particularly attractive to criminal elements:

- *Easy Access:* On a global, interconnected network the so-called good neighborhoods and bad neighborhoods are just a click apart. Criminals can touch anyone in the world, without leaving their easy chair.

- *Lack of Attribution:* On the Internet, it can be notoriously difficult to track down attackers, especially when they take measures to cover their tracks. When the victims are in one country and the criminals in another country, it only gets harder to track down the attackers.

- *Wholesale Data:* Why steal money from one person at a time when, with only a little more effort, you can rob the bank instead? Criminals have found that with the consolidation of data into huge corporate databases, wholesale data theft can be shockingly easy to carry out.

These factors have turned data theft into big business. Big money can be made by those who get away with the big heists. When stolen credit cards or social security numbers go for $1 each on the black market and medical records go for $10 or more, the attacker who can steal a million records can make real money. This money, in turn, goes to support an entire shadow industry of players, suppliers, and supporting actors who are ready to help out and lend their services in exchange for a cut in the loot.

When considering cybercriminals, it is important to remember there are many ways to make money through cyberattacks. Many of those methods have nothing to do with stealing credit card numbers. Cyberattackers can get control of business banking accounts and use online banking to drain corporate accounts by wiring money to themselves. Cyberattackers can encrypt corporate data using ransomware malware and then blackmail the business to get its data back. Cyberattackers can compromise employee accounts and re-route payroll direct deposit to their own accounts. There is no limit to how creative cybercriminals get in monetizing the fact that they can compromise people, accounts, and computers at their victims' enterprises.

Espionage

What organized crime starts, espionage agents take to the next level. Cybercriminals are relatively easy to understand since their objectives are straightforward. Cybercriminals seek to gain access to computers, accounts, and networks and then exploit the access to either directly steal money or steal data that can then be quickly and easily turned into money. Cyberespionage, on the other hand, is a little more complex in its objectives and how it carries them out. Certainly, there is a financial driver, but other drivers are much less straightforward.

Cyberespionage centers on stealing trade secrets for commercial advantage or national secrets for political or military advantage. In the cases of international business, these two interests can be closely aligned, and multinationals can find themselves being targeted by national intelligence agencies working in close collaboration with their international competition. Whereas in the United States, business and government have an arms-length relationship, in many countries such a relationship is not always the case.

The secrets stolen may be surprising. All enterprises have the "crown jewels" of blueprints, formulas, or software code that are considered critical to success. However, there is plenty of other information such as organizational charts, budgets, project schedules, and even meeting minutes that are vitally useful to the competition. All of this information may be subject to espionage efforts on the part of adversaries, particularly multinational ones.

Cyberespionage practitioners frequently use APT-style methods, not because such methods are the only way to get the job done, but because they tend to be very effective against enterprises with legacy-style cyberdefenses. Why bother hacking the CEO's laptop when, for the same amount of effort, you can get control of every laptop in the enterprise? Once agents get administrative control, they can then steal proprietary data at will.

Cyberespionage campaigns can be conducted at the nation-state level, and these campaigns can be made up of multiple parts. Unfortunately for some enterprises, their cyberespionage experience may simply be because they are a stepping stone in a campaign focused on getting to other, unrelated objectives. For example, espionage agents may hack a hospital simply to get identity information on one of its patients who is of interest to them. A popular web site may be hacked simply because it is frequented by people at enterprises that the espionage agents are targeting. Cyberespionage is a serious issue, and the campaigns can involve complex webs of target individuals and enterprises as the agents work their way from their starting points toward their objectives.

Cyberwar

Whereas espionage is generally focused on stealing information, cyberwar is about damaging the ability of enterprises or governments to operate in cyberspace. This damage is done by overwhelming, overloading, disabling, or destroying the IT systems used by the victims, or even using those IT systems to cause physical systems to malfunction and damage themselves or their operators. The possibility of cyberintrusions causing physical harm, injuries, or death is a disconcerting one. Everything is increasingly computerized and networked—the damage that can be done from cyberspace continues to increase.

Cyberwar has a cousin, cyberterrorism, which is conducted using the same techniques but by unaffiliated individuals or terrorist organizations. While cyberwar is waged to support national interests, cyberterrorism is done for an activist agenda, or it may simply be performed for the sake of anarchy and destruction for its own sake. The effects, particularly the psychological effects, are the same either way. Both of these activities are done using similar tools and techniques, employing denial of service, data destruction, or control system manipulation to accomplish their goals.

There have been several instances of cyberwar in recent years. In 2007, Estonia's Internet infrastructure was targeted by a series of cyberattacks that interfered with telephone, financial, and government operations. The notorious Stuxnet worm infiltrated the Iranian nuclear program and ruined nuclear centrifuges required for enriching uranium. The 2012 cyberattack on Saudi Aramco resulted in tens of thousands of computers having to be replaced or rebuilt. Many nations have cyberwarfare capabilities, and it is an increasing factor even in conventional conflicts.

The Types of Cyberattacks

Regardless of the objective or techniques, there are generally three things that cyberattacks can do to an enterprise or its data, as shown in Figure 1-2. Cyberattacks compromise confidentiality by stealing data, compromise integrity by modifying data, or compromise availability by denying access to data, services, or systems. Some attacks may combine two or more of these types in a single attack, but these three cyberattack types are the building blocks for most malicious cyberactivities. Appendix A provides descriptions of common cyberattacks that have one or more of these effects on their victim enterprises. Cyberdefenses must focus on protecting the confidentiality, integrity, and availability of data and the IT systems that process it.

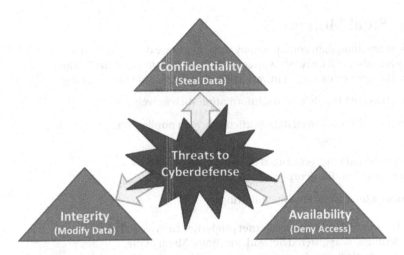

Figure 1-2. *The damage caused by threats to cyberdefense can be characterized by losses of confidentiality, integrity, or availability.*

Confidentiality: Steal Data

Confidentiality breaches are the ones most often making the headlines today. Social security numbers, credit card numbers, bank account information, electronic health records, and confidential corporate secrets and executive correspondence are just some examples of the data being stolen from enterprises and sold to the highest bidder. Attacks intended to steal data often focus on stealth, at least at first, to penetrate the target enterprise, get to the target data, and exfiltrate it without being noticed. On the other hand, once the victim enterprise is aware that a breach is in progress, the attackers may become significantly bolder, especially to finish an attack that is already ongoing.

Confidentiality breaches focus on getting access to the data where it resides, which can be any of a number of at-rest and in-transit locations:

- **Databases:** The most obvious place to find large pools of data is in the databases where it resides. However, these systems tend to be relatively well protected deep inside the enterprise architecture.

- **Backups:** Enterprise databases containing critical business and customer data should be backed up. Interestingly, these backups frequently end up being in a myriad of locations where data is replicated to disk, to tape, to non-production test systems, and to virtual machine snapshots, all on a regular basis. These secondary backup locations frequently do not get much security consideration and may be vulnerable to attack, particularly if they store their data unencrypted.

- **Application Servers:** Even the well-protected databases have to make their data available somehow, and the front-end application servers with access to that data are frequently directly connected to the Internet. Breaches of these systems can be used to get access to data through the applications, bypassing encryption and other protection methods.

- **Systems Administrators:** The Achilles' heel of most enterprises is the systems administrators and the credentials they use to administer systems. If attackers can get access to these credentials, they can bypass all other data protections and frequently do so with little or no audit trail to reveal their actions.

Integrity: Modify Data (Steal Money)

Integrity breaches are getting far less attention than confidentiality breaches these days. It is realistic to expect the prominence of integrity breaches will increase as attacks continue to gain in sophistication. Integrity attacks involve modifying data, which can result in various impacts to include the following:

- Reputational impacts if that data is public-facing information such as web sites

- Financial reporting impacts if it is financial data, particularly for a publicly traded corporation

- Losses of actual money if the data that is changed is bank routing numbers or financial commands to banks handling corporate accounts

Some integrity attacks of particular interest include the following:

- **Hijacking**: Altering infrastructure data about Internet properties such as domain names, social media identities, or registered network locations. Much of the Internet's *real estate* is purely electronic in nature and secured by nothing more than an e-mail address. Some of these properties can be worth thousands or even millions of dollars.

- **Sarbanes-Oxley**: In the wake of the Enron disaster, the Sarbanes-Oxley regulations were developed to protect the integrity of financial data published by publicly traded corporations. Unauthorized changes to financial data can have serious audit and regulatory consequences for the affected corporation.

- **Online Banking**: With the rise of online banking, enterprises have online access to business banking accounts that can include payroll, investments, stock funds, and other assets worth thousands or millions of dollars. Attackers who can get access to the credentials controlling these accounts can quickly steal large amounts of money. Moving the money through multiple intermediaries in multiple countries makes it impossible to trace or prosecute the attackers.

- **Direct Deposit**: Similarly, with payroll services Internet-enabled and providing online access to pay stub information and bank direct deposit settings, employees are vulnerable to thefts where their paychecks are re-routed to an attacker's accounts. If a single attacker can redirect paychecks of a number of highly compensated individuals all at the same time, it is possible to get away with a large sum of money quickly.

- **Vandalism**: Malicious actors deface web sites or other public materials with the intent of embarrassing the victim. Internet-facing systems can be hard to protect perfectly. A single vulnerability or configuration mistake can be all it takes to allow an attacker to strike.

Availability: Deny Access

The third type of cyberattack is to affect the availability of systems and deny access to them. Attacks causing denial of service can be difficult to diagnose, especially if systems are impaired but not disabled. Often the systems are impaired when the attack causes failures by overwhelming systems and infrastructure. In general, deliberate availability attacks can be grouped into three categories:

- ***Distributed Denial of Service (DDoS)*** attacks are used to effectively disable services in the victim enterprise or country. These techniques have been used in the past several years, and they can take significant portions of the victim's Internet capabilities offline for some time until they are mitigated.

- ***Targeted Denial of Service*** attacks involve hacking into the victim and then disabling systems so that they have to be rebuilt or recovered. Depending on the severity of the damage done, it can take some time for IT personnel to recover systems and restore service, particularly if backups are affected as well as the primary systems.

- ***Physical Destruction*** attacks involve using cyberattacks to cause physical destruction. Stuxnet is the most famous incidence of this type of attack, where a cyberattack sabotaged centrifuges used by the Iranian nuclear program. As more and more critical systems are computer-controlled, these types of attacks will become potentially more dangerous and destructive over time.

The Steps of a Cyberintrusion

How do these cyberattacks occur? For cyberintrusions, where hackers actually take control of computers and accounts inside of the victim enterprise, it is helpful to work out the steps required for the intrusion to succeed. If an enterprise can understand how cyberintrusions occur, then it can design defenses that disrupt, detect, delay, and defeat the attacks after they start, but before they can succeed. Each step in the attack is also an opportunity for defense. The following material delineates steps required for these cyberintrusions to be successful.

Attack Trees and Attack Graphs

In 1999, Bruce Schneier published an article in *Dr. Dobb's Journal* that introduced a methodology for analyzing attacks, called "Attack Trees." An attack tree begins with the objective of the cyberattack (for example, stealing enterprise data) and then works backward to consider the various ways that goal could be accomplished and the steps involved accomplishing the goal. Figure 1-3 depicts a notional attack tree that Mr. Schneier analyzed for the case of trying to break into a safe.

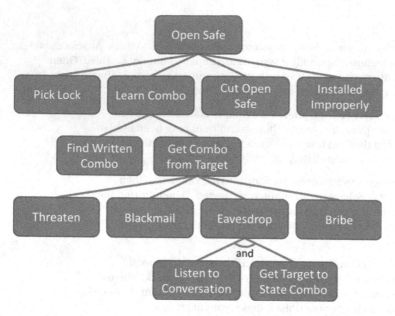

Figure 1-3. *Bruce Schneier introduced attack trees to help analyze the sequence of events involved in a successful attack, starting from the outcome and working backward.*[2]

"Attack trees provide a formal methodology for analyzing the security of systems and subsystems. They provide a way to think about security, to capture and reuse expertise about security, and to respond to changes in security."[3]

What makes this technique interesting from a defensive perspective is that each step in the tree is an opportunity to apply defenses and make the overall attack harder. Those defenses can make the individual step more difficult, expensive, or improbable. The defenses can increase the likelihood the attack step will trigger an alarm and cause the entire attack to be detected. Defenses can also add steps the attack must take before it can succeed. Just as putting the money in a safe means that the attackers then have to figure out how to get into the safe before they can get to the money, putting data into *virtual safes* can have the same effect. It does not make stealing the data impossible as no defense is perfect, but it can make the attack significantly more difficult, time-consuming, and expensive, and it can shift the odds in favor of the defense.

Significant academic research is ongoing using attack trees and a generalized version of attack trees called *attack graphs*. A graph is just like a tree, except that the dependencies can loop back on themselves. Attack graphs have been computed for massive networks. This research shows how vulnerabilities interconnect and how attackers can step from one compromised computer to another until they reach their target. While academically interesting, in practice, this research has shown itself to be of only limited use. Attack graphs of more than a handful of machines that consider more than a handful of potential vulnerabilities quickly become incredibly complex, and defenders have a very difficult time turning the data from these graphs into actionable intelligence that is helpful in designing cyberdefenses.

---

[2]Bruce Schneier, "Attack Trees," *Dr. Dobb's Journal*, December 1999.
[3]Bruce Schneier, "Attack Trees," *Dr. Dobb's Journal*, December 1999.

What kind of attack graph is useful? By using attack tree and attack graph methodologies, it is possible to come up with a generalized model of the cyberintrusion sequence of activities. Cyberdefenders can analyze multiple ways the attackers could accomplish an activity. Defenders can then focus their defenses on disrupting the activity across all potentially vulnerable computers, accounts, and networks. Consequently, the attack tree can be generalized into a model that is simpler to analyze, but almost as powerful in terms of providing specific, actionable results.

When simplified as described, the attack tree gets reduced down to a sequence. This sequence has been given many labels, including *Kill Chain* and *Attack Life Cycle*. For the purposes of this book, this sequence is called the *Attack Sequence*.

Lockheed Martin Kill Chain

In 2011, several researchers from Lockheed Martin published a paper, titled *Intelligence-Driven Computer Network Defense Informed by Analysis of Adversary Campaigns and Intrusion Kill Chains*.[4] This paper analyzed Advanced Persistent Threat (APT) attack campaigns and found there was a sequence of seven steps followed by all attackers, and defenses could be applied at each step of the process to attempt to thwart the attack. Figure 1-4 depicts the steps of this process.

Figure 1-4. *Lockheed Martin Kill Chain describes seven steps from reconnaissance through actions on the objective and recommends defenses be designed to align with each of the seven steps in the process.*

Here are the definitions of each of these phases, as described in the original Lockheed paper:

1. *Reconnaissance*: Research, identification, and selection of targets, often represented as crawling Internet web sites such as conference proceedings and mailing lists for e-mail addresses, social relationships, or information on specific technologies.

2. *Weaponization*: Coupling a remote access Trojan with an exploit into a deliverable payload, typically by means of an automated tool (weaponizer). Increasingly, client application data files such as Adobe Portable Document Format (PDF) or Microsoft Office documents serve as the weaponized deliverable.

3. *Delivery*: Transmission of the weapon to the targeted environment. The three most prevalent delivery vectors for weaponized payloads by APT actors, as observed by the Lockheed Martin Computer Incident Response Team (LM-CIRT) for the years 2004–2010, are e-mail attachments, web sites, and USB removable media.

4. *Exploitation*: After the weapon is delivered to victim host, exploitation triggers intruders' code. Most often, exploitation targets an application or operating system vulnerability, but it could also more simply exploit the users themselves or leverage an operating system feature that auto-executes code.

---

[4]Eric M. Hugchins, Michael J. Cloppert, and Rohan M. Amin, Ph.D., "Intelligence-Driven Computer Network Defense Informed by Analysis of Adversary Campaigns and Intrusion Kill Chains," www.lockheedmartin.com/content/dam/lockheed/data/corporate/documents/LM-White-Paper-Intel-Driven-Defense.pdf, 2011.

5. **Installation:** Installation of a remote access Trojan or back door on the victim system allows the adversary to maintain persistence inside the environment.

6. **Command and Control (C2):** Typically, compromised hosts must beacon outbound to an Internet controller server to establish a C2 channel. APT malware especially requires manual interaction rather than activity conducted automatically. Once the C2 channel establishes, intruders have "hands on the keyboard" access inside the target environment.

7. **Actions on Objectives:** Only now, after progressing through the first six phases, can intruders take actions to achieve their original objectives. Typically, this objective is data exfiltration that involves collecting, encrypting, and extracting information from the victim environment; violations of data integrity or availability are potential objectives as well. Alternatively, the intruders may only desire access to the initial victim box for use as a hop point to compromise additional systems and move laterally inside the network.

Mandiant Attack Life Cycle

Mandiant published a Lockheed Martin-like kill chain methodology called the *Attack Life Cycle*. Perhaps the best written reference on the attack life cycle process is contained in Appendix B of the Mandiant report *APT1: Exposing One of China's Cyber Espionage Units*.[5] This report describes the techniques Mandiant believes were being used by a Chinese espionage unit to spy on governments and corporations in the United States and elsewhere. The report was noteworthy at the time for rather blatantly calling out Chinese personnel alleged to be involved in this espionage. Mandiant published the names and photographs of specific individuals.

The appendix provides a detailed explanation of the Mandiant attack life cycle process. This process contains seven steps, like the Lockheed Martin process, but its step 1 starts at the initial compromise of a victim machine, which is step 4 of the Lockheed Martin process. The Mandiant process then breaks out the activities that occur after the initial compromise into additional detail. Figure 1-5 shows the high-level Mandiant attack life cycle.

Figure 1-5. *The Mandiant Attack Life Cycle contains seven steps that start at the initial compromise. The process breaks out the steps of accomplishing the mission in greater detail than the Lockheed Martin Kill Chain.*

---

[5]Mandiant, "APT1: Exposing One of China's Cyber Espionage Units," http://intelreport.mandiant.com/ Mandiant_APT1_Report.pdf, 2013.

According to the Mandiant APT1 report, here are the definitions of each of the life cycle steps:

1. ***Initial Compromise***: This first stage represents the methods that intruders use to penetrate a target organization's network. APT intruders frequently target individual users within a victim environment, or they look for technical vulnerabilities in public-facing infrastructure.

2. ***Establish Foothold***: Establishing a foothold ensures that APT threat groups can access and control one or more computers within the victim organization from outside the network. These back doors usually establish an outbound connection from the victim network to a computer controlled by the attackers. The back doors will give the APT groups basic access to a system, typically through a command shell or graphical user interface.

3. ***Escalate Privileges***: Escalating privileges involves acquiring items that will allow access to more resources within the victim environment. Most often this consists of obtaining usernames and passwords, but it may also include gaining access to Public Key Infrastructure (PKI) certificates, Virtual Private Network (VPN) client software, privileged computers, or other resources required to access data or systems of interest.

4. ***Internal Reconnaissance***: In this stage, the intruder collects information about the victim environment. Data of interest may take many forms, but it most commonly consists of documents, the contents of user e-mail accounts, or databases. Some APT groups utilize custom scripts in order to automate the process of reconnaissance and identification of data of interest.

5. ***Move Laterally***: In most cases, the systems that the intruders initially compromise do not contain the data that they want. Therefore, they must move laterally within a network to other computers that either contain that data or allow them to access it. APT groups leverage compromised user credentials or pass-the-hash tools (that steal user credentials) to gain access to additional computers and devices inside of a victim network.

6. ***Maintain Presence***: In this stage, the intruders take actions to ensure continued control over key systems in the network environment from outside of the network. They may install different families of malware on multiple computers and use a variety of command and control addresses, presumably for redundancy and to make it difficult to identify and remove all of their access points.

7. ***Complete Mission***: The main goal of APT intrusions is to steal data, including intellectual property, business contracts or negotiations, policy papers, and internal memoranda. Once APT groups find files of interest on compromised systems, they often pack them into archive files before stealing them. From there they use a variety of methods to transfer files out of the victim network, including file transfer protocol (FTP), custom file transfer tools, and existing back doors.

Enterprise Cybersecurity Attack Sequence

Based on the authors' experience building and operating defenses against real-world APT actors, they have adopted a simplified version of the attack sequence process called the *Enterprise Cybersecurity Attack Sequence*. Figure 1-6 depicts this process. This attack sequence is derived from the preceding work and simplifies it somewhat to align more closely with how and where defensive capabilities are often deployed in enterprise defenses. The process also includes iterative cycles among steps 2, 3, and 4, as those steps are frequently repeated many times as attackers move around the target enterprise in search of their objective.

Figure 1-6. *The Enterprise Cybersecurity Attack Sequence consists of a series of five steps involved in cyberintrusions. Steps 2 through 4 may cycle multiple times as attackers move around and obtain privileges in the target environment.*

Experience demonstrates that the initial attacker access and foothold are almost impossible to prevent completely. Consequently, defensive measures early in the process must be augmented by additional defenses in the later steps of the process. Interestingly, during the middle steps 2, 3, and 4, attackers often generate considerable telemetry activity that can be used to detect their presence and repel their attacks before they can succeed.

Here are the definitions of the five steps of the Enterprise Cybersecurity Attack Sequence:

1. ***Establish Foothold***: The attackers' first step is to establish a foothold with access to the target enterprise. They can accomplish this step in any of a number of ways including exploiting vulnerabilities in servers and applications, compromising end-user workstations, or even buying access through criminally operated botnet networks. This foothold consists of a compromise server, endpoint computer, mobile device, or simply a user account with access into the victim's enterprise network.

2. ***Command and Control***: For most attacks, the initial foothold is quickly followed by the establishment of remote command and control capabilities so attackers can manually run commands in the target environment. These connections can be made through inbound connections, outbound connections, or various forms of protocol tunneling.

3. ***Escalate Privileges***: Once command and control has been established, the next step is to gain control of user accounts with the privileges needed to accomplish the attack objective. In environments with username and password authentication, this step can be trivially easy to accomplish. In more complex environments, this process may take some time as attackers must identify and circumvent multiple layers of protections around the privileges they desire.

4. ***Move Laterally***: At the same time attackers are escalating privileges, they also move laterally from computer to computer. This lateral movement may involve transiting network zones, bypassing firewalls, compromising machines, and stealing credentials. This lateral movement may also then feed back into multiple rounds of privilege escalation and command-and-control establishment. In a complex environment, this cyclical process can take weeks or months to get from the starting point to the ultimate objective.

5. ***Complete the Mission***: Once the objective has been accessed, the attackers can complete their mission. If their objective is to steal data, they will then bundle the data up and exfiltrate it. If the objective is to change data, then they will make the desired changes or initiate the desired transactions. If the objective is to damage availability, they will disable the systems they are targeting. At the end of this step, the attackers may also take measures to cover their tracks, depending on how much stealth is a priority.

Why Cyberintrusions Succeed

Why are these cyberintrusions so successful? If it takes attackers six or seven steps from when they start an attack until they succeed and if there are defenses and defensive technologies at each of those steps, then why are cyberintrusions continuing to make the headlines?

While there is not a single or simple answer to these questions, there are a number of factors that, when taken together, are making it harder for today's cybersecurity defenses to succeed than in the past. This section describes these factors and considers the impacts they have on enterprises being able to protect themselves effectively.

The Explosion in Connectivity

The first factor is that network connectivity, Internet connectivity in particular, has simply exploded over the past ten years. Ten years ago, the enterprise architecture was fairly simple with a perimeter, a network, a data center containing servers, and desktop computers accessing those services from within a closed network. Today the architecture is mobile devices in coffee shops connecting to cloud services using federated credentials from corporate infrastructures operated by third-party providers. The complexity of the architecture has exploded—everything is interconnected in a myriad of ways. Understanding, protecting, and defending this complexity is extremely difficult, if not impossible.

Also, with the rise of mobile, cloud, and the "Internet of things", *everything* is connected. Even mobile devices have computing capabilities equivalent to the supercomputers of two decades ago. These complex and sophisticated devices are vulnerable to a myriad of glitches, bugs, and exploits that can turn them from useful appliances into malicious tools. In an all-connected world, the functionality is amazing, but the security challenges are daunting.

Consolidation of Enterprise IT

The second factor to consider is the consolidation of enterprise IT. IT functions that were performed by hand twenty years ago by highly trained and experienced administrators are now scripted and automated. Consequently, the same administrators can manage ten or a hundred times as many computers today than they did ten or twenty years ago. In turn, enterprise data centers that used to contain a hundred servers now contain a thousand, or even ten thousand or more. The effort required to keep thousands of computers properly configured, hardened, and defended is daunting. There are myriad opportunities for mistakes and glitches that could leave things wide open for an attacker.

The modern data center, with cloud services, virtual networking, virtual storage, and virtual computing only add to this protection challenge. Layers of virtualization and abstraction add complexity and specialized areas for administration that are difficult to understand, difficult to troubleshoot, and difficult to protect. In a legacy data center environment, the server administrator is the one point of contact for protecting a server and the services it provides. In a virtualized environment, successful cybersecurity depends on the network administrator, storage administrator, virtualization administrator, server administrator, and application administrator all collaborating successfully to achieve the proper configurations across all layers of the computing environment.

This consolidation of incredible IT power in the hands of a small number of IT professionals brings up another challenge. If attackers can get control of the computers and user accounts belonging to these personnel, the attackers can use the enterprise's own tools and infrastructure against itself. Why bother putting malware on computers one at a time if you can take control of the patching system and have it push the malware out for you? The same consolidation that enables fewer IT administrators to control huge enterprises and data centers over the network is being used by attackers to remotely take control and do with those enterprises and data centers whatever they please.

Defeat of Preventive Controls

The third factor to consider is the defeat of preventive controls. Up until now, most of cybersecurity involved blocking undesired activities and preventing them from executing. While this approach sounds good in principle, it has its challenges. Preventive controls are like putting up a network of fences and then assuming the fences are working as designed without ever checking on them.

APT attackers have shown a consistent ability to defeat or work around preventive controls and obtain the accesses they need. These attacks have shown that the preventive control systems enterprises rely upon are riddled with vulnerabilities, holes, bugs, and poor configurations. Enterprises must assume their preventive controls will, at best, only slow down an attacker. Eventually, even the strongest enterprise can and will be defeated by the skilled and patient attacker.

Does this reality mean preventive controls have failed altogether and are not to be relied upon? Of course not! However, it does mean preventive controls have limits to what they can do. A successful cyberdefense is going to need more than prevention alone.

Failure of Detective Controls

The fourth factor to consider is the failure of detective controls. While preventive controls are fighting and losing, detective controls have, in most cases, not even begun to fight. Perhaps the most telling example of this reality is how in the Target breach, which resulted in 40 million credit cards being compromised, attackers "...triggered alarms, which its [Target's] information security team evaluated and chose to ignore."[6] Sadly, this breach is unusual—not so much in that alarms were ignored, but by the fact there were even alarms to ignore in the first place. With regard to detective controls, two systemic failures are occurring:

1. First, in most cases, detection is not even occurring. While most IT systems can log activity, those logs are often in the form of cryptic text files or event codes stored in databases that require significant expertise to decipher. Consequently, most enterprises have little to no visibility of the activity taking place within their IT systems. Enterprises must tie these logs together, correlate across them, and then use that data to alert on activity patterns that are or may be malicious.

2. Second, even when enterprises have set up their systems to alert them on potentially malicious behavior, it is easy to become buried in alerts that no one has time to investigate. With terabytes of data and thousands of servers, it is easy to get into a situation where there are hundreds or thousands or even millions of events per day calling for investigation. The reality is an investigation team can actually investigate perhaps a dozen events in a day. When the people become overwhelmed with data, the enterprise is just as blind as they were when they had nothing.

Compliance over Capability

The fifth factor to consider is the focus on compliance over capability. One thing that many recent credit car breaches had in common was that the companies involved had been certified as complying with the Payment Card Industry Digital Security Standards (PCI-DSS). If this situation is in fact the case, then it appears standards compliance does not necessarily correlate with breach resistance.

---

[6]Matthew J. Schwartz, "Target Ignored Data Breach Alarms," www.darkreading.com/attacks-and-breaches/target-ignored-data-breach-alarms/d/d-id/1127712, 2014.

There are a couple of reasons why this situation may be occurring. First, standards must necessarily focus on the presence or absence of technologies or controls, but it is hard for standards to specify the resistance of those technologies or controls to deliberate attack by skilled attackers. One can ask if a firewall is present or if network traffic is being filtered. How does one expand these compliance specifications to determine if the firewall is properly configured to stop a deliberate attacker? Is the network traffic being filtered well enough to catch that attacker when they try to enter or leave the network? Unfortunately, the cybersecurity industry is still relatively immature compared to other security industries. These types of compliance specifications are still under development.

The second challenge is that, ironically, the presence of compliance standards can take enterprise resources away from *real* cybersecurity. Compliance standards incentivize leadership to focus on *checking the box* to meet standards and receive certification versus modeling cybersecurity threats and building effective defenses. Moreover, once an enterprise is certified as compliant, it can then fall back on the compliance certification if something goes wrong, shielding itself from liability or accusations of negligence.

This reality strongly suggests compliance frameworks are not having their intended effect. Cybersecurity certification frameworks and processes need to be upgraded to focus on certifying real-world cyberdefenses that are provably effective against real-world cyberthreats.

The Gap in Cybersecurity Effectiveness

As shown in Figure 1-7, one hypothesis is that perhaps cyberattacks are improving faster than cyberdefenses, resulting in a gap in effectiveness that means that cyberdefense is, unfortunately, losing ground over time.

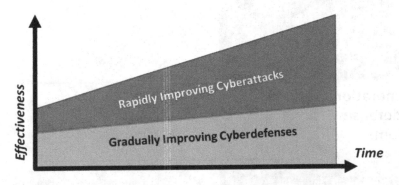

Figure 1-7. *If cyberattacks improve at a faster rate than cyberdefenses, then the attackers' advantage will grow even as defenses are improving.*

The modern cybersecurity architecture of secured networks, firewall protection, and anti-virus on endpoints does not seem to be holding up well against cyberattacks consisting of protocol tunneling, spear phishing, and zero-day attacks on endpoints and servers alike. In fact, given the complexity of modern devices, the exploding size of modern IT enterprises, the interconnections among partners, vendors, and customers, and the rise of bring-your-own-device (BYOD) and cloud services, even maintaining the defenses of ten years ago is an increasingly daunting task for systems administrators and cybersecurity professionals.

Given this increase in IT complexity and the fact that cybersecurity has to be applied to everything, one has to wonder if cyberdefenses are actually moving backward against these headwinds. The control over the enterprise that existed ten years ago is loosened up in the name of improving efficiency, increasing capacity and productivity, and reducing costs. Finally, cyberdefenders are often prohibited from talking to each other, so effective defensive techniques are not even being disseminated. Cybersecurity professionals are being squeezed on all sides.

"As cyberdefenders, we are not even allowed to talk to each other for fear of revealing our enterprises' weaknesses. Our adversaries, on the other hand, are all aggressively collaborating together so that they can hit us with everything they have." —Frustrated cybersecurity professional.

At the same time cyberdefenders are facing these headwinds, cyberattackers and the technologies they use are only getting better and better. As defensive technologies have been upgraded, experience has shown the development of cyberattacks capable of defeating defenses. The result is a consistent arms race between cyberattacker and cyberdefenders. The attackers have some important advantages in this race. Attackers are not subject to budget cycles or resource availability. Attackers are not competing for resources with other business priorities. Attackers can instantly share techniques and tools that work against specific defenses, while defenders have to upgrade defenses one at a time. Finally, attackers have the advantage of the initiative. In other words, attackers only have to succeed once, while the defenders have to succeed each and every time.

A New Cybersecurity Mindset

Now that the adversaries have been introduced and what they do, how they do it, and why they are successful have been explained, it is important to understand what cyberdefenders need to do to be more effective against these threats. Figure 1-8 lists four axioms of next-generation defenses.

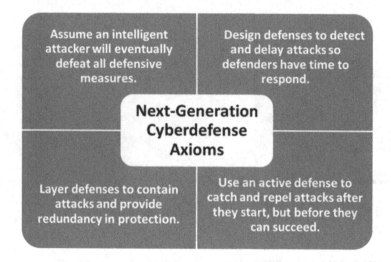

Figure 1-8. *The axioms of a next-generation cyberdefense focus on delaying and detecting cyberattackers.*

Intelligent attackers adjust their attacks to work around defenses. Attackers eventually penetrate any and all defenses defenders deploy. Consequently, enterprises must not overly focus defenses on *stopping* the attacker, because stopping the attacker is impossible. Instead, enterprises need to focus on delaying attackers enough so they can be detected. Defenders can then respond to the discovered attackers before they are successful. Enterprise defenses must value delay and detection. A detected attack can be stopped, while the non-detected attack will simply progress until it eventually succeeds. Finally, enterprise defenses must be architected around providing defensible areas where detection can occur after attacks begin but before attacks are completed. Active defenders patrol these areas searching for attacks on the enterprise. These defenders analyze the attacks to understand what the attackers are doing, the origin of the attacks, and so on. The defenders can then repel the attackers before they can succeed. Another way to look at this situation is to consider how defenses work in the physical world. Where physical security is concerned, no protection is ever considered to be perfect or impenetrable. Instead, the purpose of physical protections is simply to detect and slow down the attack until the authorities can arrive. For example, doors and locks are rated based upon how long they resist attack by an attacker with the proper equipment who knows how to defeat them. Even a bank vault, one of the strongest possible types of doors, is only rated to slow down an attacker by a matter of minutes. Those delay times assume the attackers have the blueprints to the door and know exactly what they need to do to defeat it. (Actually, we could argue if the attackers bring dynamite, even a bank vault won't last very long.)

With this analogy in mind, the most important element of a physical protection system is not the door, or even the vault. Instead, the most important part of a physical protection system is the alarm system, cameras, and security guards who are monitoring the facility and the authorities who can be called on when an incident occurs. Why should cybersecurity be any different? Why should we assume that cybervaults will be impenetrable when physical vaults have never been? Why do we blindly trust our cyberdefenses without even having the visibility when they fail?

Indeed, experience is starting to validate that perhaps enterprises should design its cyberdefenses in the same manner physical defenses are designed. Consider the axioms of a next-generation cyberdefense in a little more detail:

1. *Assume an Intelligent Attacker*: Enterprises must consider that an intelligent attacker is not going to walk into defenses as they are designed. Rather, the intelligent attacker is going to seek to find the easiest, fastest, and potentially the cheapest way to defeat the enterprises' defenses and achieve the attack objective. Enterprises must look at themselves from the attacker's perspective and design their defenses accordingly.

2. *Design Defenses to Detect and Delay*: While it is certainly nice to prevent attacks in the first place, prevention will inevitably fail or be defeated. When failure or defeat happens, the only hope is to detect the attackers and delay them long enough for defenders to respond. Detection must be designed so that it catches real attacks and does not overload defenders with *noise* from false positives that they do not have time to investigate.

3. *Layer Defenses to Contain Attacks*: Design defenses so that initial incursions, particularly in Internet-facing systems such as web servers or user endpoints, can be detected when they first occur. Have additional layers of protection around the databases, file servers, and security infrastructures the attackers are really targeting.

4. *Use an Active Defense to Catch and Repel Attacks*: The final critical component is the presence of an active defense. This component involves real people who monitor IT systems and respond to intrusions when they occur. This incident response team diagnoses the attacks and repels them before the attackers can defeat the enterprise's cyberdefenses and achieve their objectives.

An Effective Enterprise Cybersecurity Program

How is this new mindset turned into an effective enterprise cybersecurity program? To begin, an enterprise must pause and consider what the elements of an enterprise cybersecurity program are. There are policy, programmatic, IT life cycle, and assessment elements. For an enterprise cybersecurity program to be effective, all of the elements must be part of a common roadmap and have to be well coordinated and work effectively together. Otherwise, critical cybersecurity pieces *fall into the gaps* and are missed. For example, having the right policy is a necessary start. However, if the technology to implement the policy is not deployed, then the policy will not be effective. Having the right technology deployed is great, but if the operational processes are not in place to operate and maintain the technology after deployment, then it will not be effective. Finally, if the enterprise cannot constantly assess its status and cybersecurity effectiveness to keep up with rapidly changing threats, then even the best and most comprehensive program is going to quickly fall behind. Figure 1-9 shows eight elements needed for an effective enterprise cybersecurity program.

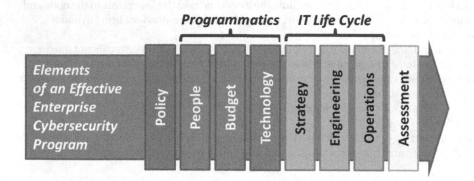

Figure 1-9. *An effective enterprise cybersecurity program contains a number of necessary elements that are well coordinated and work well together.*

Looking at each of these eight elements:

- **Policy:** The first element is policy. All cybersecurity measures, including staffing, budget, technology, and operations, must trace to written policy that directs what is to be protected, to what degree, and what the consequences are for violations of that protection. This traceability is the foundation upon which the entire cybersecurity program is built.

- **People:** The second element is the programmatic element of organizing the people responsible for cybersecurity in the enterprise. These people will often report to different areas of IT, operations, or compliance departments, and they must be carefully organized so their authority, responsibility, and expertise are all in synchronization with each other.

- **Budget:** The third element is the programmatic element of budget and allocating cybersecurity funding to pay for deploying, operating, and maintaining the cybersecurity technologies and operational processes making up the enterprise cybersecurity program. All of these elements cost money, and the amount of money allocated to each must be adequate for them to be effective.

- **Technology:** The fourth element is the programmatic element of cybersecurity technologies used to protect the enterprise. The size, complexity, and speed of modern IT dictate that cybersecurity cannot be accomplished manually. The right technologies, well deployed and properly maintained, are essential to success.

- **Strategy:** The fifth element is the IT life cycle element of strategy that ensures the technologies are well coordinated so they work together as integrated systems. This integration applies both to cybersecurity technologies themselves and also to ensuring cybersecurity technologies are well coordinated with the whole of the IT enterprise. Strategic disconnects can render technologies ineffective just as badly as if they were not present in the first place.

- ***Engineering:*** The sixth element is the IT life cycle element of engineering to ensure technologies are properly selected to meet requirements and then deployed and supported so they continue to meet those initial and new evolving requirements over their life cycle. Engineering ensures deployed systems are fit for purpose and fit for use for as long as they are needed and used.

- ***Operations:*** The seventh element is the IT life cycle element of IT infrastructure operations. Security technologies must be operated to stay effective, and other security operational processes such as policy exception management must also be performed. If cybersecurity is not maintained on an ongoing basis, it will be ineffective.

- ***Assessment:*** The eighth element is assessment to evaluate the effectiveness of the enterprise's risk mitigations, cybersecurity capabilities, and operational processes. This assessment includes reporting status against legal, regulatory, and compliance requirements, and ensuring enterprise cybersecurity measures up to the requirements of appropriate external guidelines.

The remainder of this book presents a new framework for managing an enterprise cybersecurity program that has been designed for managing all eight of these elements in a well-coordinated and integrated manner. This framework has been field-tested and field-proven for managing enterprise cyberdefenses against the most dangerous nation-state attackers. This framework organizes enterprise cybersecurity into 11 functional areas that allow policy, programmatics, IT, and assessment to be delegated and coordinated at the functional level. With this framework, cybersecurity leadership can spend less time on integration and more time on strategy. By using the framework in this book for their cybersecurity program, practitioners can build a cyberdefense that is flexible, cost-effective, comprehensive, and, above all, effective against today's modern cyberthreats and tomorrow's envisioned cyberthreats.

CHAPTER 2

■ ■ ■

Meeting the Cybersecurity Challenge

Chapter 1 discussed the challenges facing today's cyberdefenders. So how does an enterprise successfully defend itself against cyberattackers? This chapter discusses the challenges in building an effective cyberdefense, some of the major approaches that are currently available for addressing those challenges, and some of the difficulties with those approaches. Finally, it introduces a technique for dealing with those challenges.

What makes up an effective cybersecurity program? A cybersecurity program is not just about technology. It is not just about defenses. Nor is it just about people. Nor is it about compliance frameworks, checklists, or simply a passing grade on an audit.

An effective enterprise cybersecurity program protects the enterprise in a cost-effective manner that balances technology, processes, people, organization, budgets, and external compliance requirements, all while supporting the business mission as much as possible.

Protecting the enterprise requires a combination of business savvy, political acumen, technical knowledge, leadership, management, and good old-fashioned common sense. The enterprise's cybersecurity mission, in part, is to bring all these factors together effectively and make them work together to protect the enterprise. The good news is that unless the Chief Information Security Officer (CISO) is in a very small organization indeed, the CISO won't be alone in these endeavors. The CISO will have other people around who can help protect the enterprise, and these people should be leveraged.

Figure 2-1 shows one way of looking at the factors that must come together for an enterprise cybersecurity program to be successful. All of these factors are important and must be carefully considered.

Figure 2-1. *An effective cyberdefense framework represents the intersection of people, organization, and budgets, technologies, processes, and external compliance requirements.*

At the bottom of Figure 2-1, the block labeled "People, Organization, and Budgets" is the foundation of the cybersecurity program. Everything in an enterprise starts with people. People are the ones who make the program succeed or fail, and they look to the CISO to provide them with the vision and guidance to accomplish the mission to protect the enterprise. The most important thing a CISO can do to make cybersecurity people effective is to organize them so individuals and teams have clear responsibilities and "swim lanes" to accomplish the enterprise mission. The Control Objectives for Information and Related Technology (COBIT) and Information Technology Infrastructure Library (ITIL) offer excellent guidance on organizing people around different phases of the IT life cycle. COBIT and ITIL also provide clear guidance around RACI (Responsible, Accountable, Consulted, and Informed) so that everyone knows who has what responsibilities and accountabilities. The final element of this block is budgets. The CISO is responsible to make the business case for money for cybersecurity and to then utilize the budget so that it can be as effective as possible. If an enterprise does not fund cybersecurity, then it isn't important. The CISO guides the cybersecurity program and sets priorities by making difficult choices about what the enterprise does and does not fund.

In Figure 2-1, "Processes" and "Technologies" work together. An enterprise's processes and technologies go hand in hand and need to be carefully coordinated so the technologies are effective and the processes are manageable. These processes are in the diagram on opposite sides because, while they ideally work together, they can also be fundamentally opposed to each other as well. Frequently, a CISO can be tempted to deploy a technology without considering how people are going to operate that technology. Equally frequently, a CISO can be pressed to implement a procedure to compensate for a control deficiency without considering how to reconfigure the technology to close the deficiency once and for all. Both temptations must be balanced. Technology deployed without processes seldom stays working for long, while processes deployed without technology seldom endure. The CISO must manage cybersecurity process and technologies in lockstep, and not let one get ahead of the other.

In Figure 2-1, "Compliance Requirements" is a double-edged sword. On the one hand, the enterprise is always going to have requirements for external validation that the enterprise security measures are in place and functioning properly. These security requirements can be from external entities, the government, regulators, auditors, or the enterprise's own management. On the other hand, the reality is that there is only a loose correlation between compliance and security.

You can be secure without being compliant and compliant without being secure.

This compliant/secure challenge is important. Enterprise management wants to believe a clean compliance report indicates success. The CISO can help management understand this challenge is not so straightforward. Compliance is a good thing, but it must not be treated as the only cyberdefense objective. In many ways, a CISO's measure of success is related to how well the CISO can steer the cybersecurity program so it correlates compliance with actual real-world security. Compliance measures need to support the effectiveness of the security program, rather than simply being a check-the-box distraction.

Cybersecurity Frameworks

The cybersecurity literature presents excellent frameworks. Some of the major cybersecurity frameworks include the following:

1. (ISC)² Certified Information Security System Professional (CISSP) Common Body of Knowledge (CBK). (The International Information Systems Security Certification Consortium is also known as (ISC)²)

2. International Organization for Standardization (ISO) 27001 and 27002, version 2013

3. The National Institute of Standards and Technologies (NIST) Risk Management Framework (RMF) and special publication 800-53

4. The Council on Cyber Security Critical Security Controls (formerly known as the SANS 20 Controls)

A goal of these frameworks is to provide a methodology for talking about cybersecurity and ensuring that an enterprise's cybersecurity effort encompasses the most important elements of protection and defense. Each framework divides up cybersecurity in a slightly different way, and each framework has slightly different focuses and priorities. However, when looking at the frameworks, there are many commonalities and similar concepts. Figure 2-2 shows an overview of these four frameworks. Appendix B contains additional details on some of the major frameworks that are in widespread use.

(ISC)² Common Body of Knowledge 10 security domains	ISO 27001 / 27002 v2013 114 controls in 14 domains	NIST SP800-53v4 224 controls in 18 families	Council on Cyber Security Critical Security Controls - 20 controls
1. Access Control 2. Telecommunications and Network Security 3. Information Security Governance and Risk Management 4. Software Development Security 5. Cryptography 6. Security Architecture and Design 7. Security Operations 8. Business Continuity and Disaster Recovery Planning 9. Legal, Regulations, Investigations, and Compliance 10. Physical (Environmental) Security	1. Information Security Policies 2. Organization of Information Security 3. Human Resource Security 4. Asset Management 5. Access Control 6. Cryptography 7. Physical and Environmental Security 8. Operations Security 9. Communications Security 10. System Acquisition, Development, and Maintenance 11. Supplier Relationships 12. Information Security Incident Management 13. Information Security Aspect of Business Continuity Management 14. Compliance	1. Access Control 2. Awareness and Training 3. Audit and Accountability 4. Security Assessment and Authorization 5. Configuration Management 6. Contingency Planning 7. Identification and Authentication 8. Incident Response 9. Maintenance 10. Media Protection 11. Physical and Environmental Protection 12. Planning 13. Personnel Security 14. Risk Assessment 15. System and Services Acquisition 16. System and Communications Protection 17. System and Information Integrity 18. Program Management	1. Inventory of Devices 2. Inventory of Software 3. Secure Configurations for Computers 4. Continuous Vulnerability Assessment and Remediation 5. Malware Defenses 6. Application Software Security 7. Wireless Device Control 8. Data Recovery Capability 9. Security Skills Assessment and Training 10. Security Configurations for Network Devices 11. Network Ports, Protocols, and Services 12. Control of Administrative Privileges 13. Boundary Defense 14. Security Audit Logs 15. Need-to-Know Access Control 16. Account Monitoring and Control 17. Data Loss Prevention 18. Incident Response Capability 19. Secure Network Engineering 20. Penetration Testing and Red Team Exercises

Figure 2-2. *Different frameworks organize enterprise cybersecurity in different ways, but the major topics and categories are consistent across all frameworks.*

One commonality of these frameworks is they divide the enterprise and its protection into a number of functional areas. Sometimes areas are called domains, sometimes they are called families, sometimes they are called control areas, and sometimes they are called control objectives. Generally, there are between 10 and 20 of these functional areas that allow for logical organization and management of an overall cyberdefense program.

The second major commonality is almost all the major frameworks leverage risk management methodology. Risk management allows the enterprise to identify what protections are needed based on an objective evaluation of its assets, threats against those assets, vulnerabilities in the protection of those assets, and risks resulting from the threats being analyzed against the vulnerabilities. Once the enterprise identifies the risks, the enterprise can consider mitigations to reduce the risks, either by reducing their probability or their severity.

The third major commonality is all these frameworks talk about security controls. The purpose of a security control is primarily to reduce the probability or the severity of a risk, although some security controls can also serve to detect the exploitation of the risk or to collect forensic data to support later investigations.

The fourth major commonality is these frameworks provide a mechanism for auditing, evaluating, and validating the presence or absence of the controls described in the framework. Sometimes this mechanism is done through documented standards for evaluation, and sometimes it is done through checklists for auditing. Most of the frameworks contain such evaluation guidance, or the evaluation method is obvious or well-known.

The remainder of this chapter examines this cybersecurity process in more detail.

The Cybersecurity Process

All of the major frameworks contain some method of cybersecurity process that practitioners can use to implement their organizations' cybersecurity program. As shown in Figure 2-3, NIST has one of the more comprehensive documented processes and is freely available.

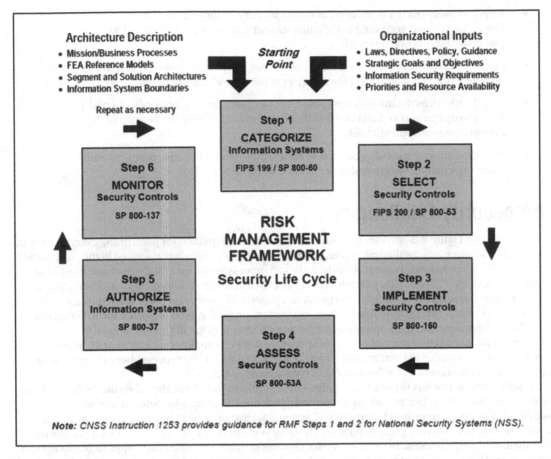

Note: *CNSS Instruction 1253 provides guidance for RMF Steps 1 and 2 for National Security Systems (NSS).*

Figure 2-3. *The NIST risk management framework security life cycle provides a process for implementing an enterprise cybersecurity program.*[1]

The NIST risk management framework consists of the following six steps:

- *Step 1* categorizes the information systems according to the "potential impact of loss." The method for doing this categorization is documented in FIPS 199 (Federal Information Processing Standard-Standards for Security categorization of Federal Information Systems) and then further detailed in SP 800-60 (Special Reports from the NIST Information Technology Laboratory) to include mapping both information and information systems to security categories.

- *Step 2* selects the security controls for each information system using the guidance in FIPS 200 (Minimum Security Requirements for Federal Information Systems) and SP 800-53 (Security and Privacy Controls for Federal Information Systems and Organizations). The security control selection process uses risk management methodology to identify risks and select the most appropriate security controls.

---

[1]Special Publication 800-53 Revision 4, National Institute of Standards and Technology, 2013.

- ***Step 3*** implements the security controls and security configurations for enterprise systems according to the guidance and methodology in SP 800-160 (Security Systems Engineering).

- ***Step 4*** assesses the security controls to ensure they were implemented correctly, operate as intended, and meet the security objectives and requirements.

- ***Step 5*** authorizes the information system for operation, based on the validation of the security controls and an overall risk assessment considering the benefits of the system against its potential risks.

- ***Step 6*** monitors the security controls to ensure they remain effective over time, and as the information system and information environment evolve.

Cybersecurity Challenges

The NIST process in Figure 2-3 provides practitioners a documented method for performing cybersecurity in the enterprise. However, this methodology runs into some challenges when it is exercised in the "real world."

The first challenge has to do with scalability. A six-step process is fine for a single computer, but what happens when a single IT system has a hundred computers in it? How does a single system administrator, who is trying to get everything set up, going to get all this paperwork done, especially when they are already over budget and behind schedule on their deployment project? All too often, the security process languishes until management ends up exempting the process simply to get things operational in time. The cybersecurity industry needs a streamlined security process that (1) actually gets implemented, especially for today's modern, complex IT environments, and (2) abstracts the security process above the level of single computers and single servers, to the "systems" and "systems of systems."

The second challenge has to do with the judgment calls that are involved. How does one "select" which controls are appropriate? When evaluating the controls, how does an enterprise determine what is "good enough"? All of us might agree to (1) protect our IT systems against unknown, but anticipated, attacks and (2) anticipate how attackers are going to operate. The issue is the frameworks give little or no guidance on what to do to achieve protection. In practice, the frameworks provide a "kitchen sink" approach, where even the smallest and least critical system is required to have the most onerous of security controls applied to it because no one wants to be seen as "skimping on security." In business, this approach is neither practical nor cost-effective, and the results are often ineffective. Equally common, these controls are arbitrarily applied and then incompletely implemented, resulting in crucial gaps in control protections that are hard to identify, prioritize, and remediate.

The third challenge is a lack of focus on detective controls. NIST SP 800-53 spends significant effort describing control measures to prevent attacks from being successful, but relatively little time talking about detecting and responding to attacks when they occur. Preventive controls are good, but they will not actually stop a determined attack. It's like having good locks on your doors. Realistically, a determined attacker will spend about five minutes playing with the lock, and then simply go and break a window. Greater attention is needed to what happens after the window has been broken, instead of simply installing all of the different kinds of locks that can be put on the door.

The fourth challenge is that security operations are also not given enough attention. NIST's "control monitoring" addresses some security operations aspects, but the six-step process primarily focuses on maintaining "preventive" controls, not "monitoring detective" controls to catch attacks in real time. As of the writing of this book, few of the mainstream frameworks focus on security operations to monitor security controls, capture events, detect incidents, investigate those incidents, and then respond to them and repel the attackers. Recognizing the importance of monitoring and detective controls is a transition that is still "in-progress" for the major frameworks and remains an area for improvement. Eventually, the frameworks will be updated to reflect a stronger focus on detective controls and security operations. This cybersecurity gap needs to be compensated for manually until the frameworks are updated to address this gap.

The fifth challenge is the security control frameworks frequently place requirements on products and technologies they simply cannot fulfill. In practice, this reality causes several things to occur, generally in sequence. First, there are awkward and uncomfortable meetings with the product vendor, where there is much hemming and hawing about how the product "can" be placed into a secure configuration. However, the secure configuration will result in many useful features being disabled (try configuring a cryptographic system for FIPS-140 [requirements and standards for cryptographic modules] compliant mode sometime). Next, there will be an investigation of third-party products to address the gap by enhancing the original product with additional protections, logging, or monitoring features. This investigation will likely be successful, but often results in a solution that is overkill for the need, excessively complex to maintain, and, ultimately unaffordable. Finally, there will be an effort to negotiate the security requirement in order to do the paperwork so it looks good enough to pass audit, but with the reality being the control is not actually effective as it was envisioned by the framework.

Although the mainstream security architectures represent an excellent body of work, the five challenges above leave room for some new ideas and a more pragmatic approach.

The Risk Management Process

Regardless of the cybersecurity challenges, there are fundamental elements on which all of the major literature agrees. The first fundamental element is the risk management process. There are entire books devoted to risk management; following is a summary of key points of the risk management process. The simplified risk management process can act as a starting point and can be adapted to specific enterprise needs.

The risk management process involves a systematic analysis to determine where an enterprise may have compromises, the consequences of those compromises, and ways to reduce the probability or severity of those consequences. As shown in Figure 2-4, the risk management process is simply represented below and can be adapted for specific enterprise needs.

Figure 2-4. *Simplified risk management process showing the analytical progression from assets to vulnerabilities to threats to risks to treatments of the risks and, finally, to controls to mitigate them.*

Risk management starts with "assets," which are things the enterprise wants to protect. Generally, there are four types of assets of interest: personnel, facilities, processes, and information. Personnel are the people in the organization and their knowledge and abilities. Facilities are the locations where people work, and the tools and equipment at those locations. Processes are the procedures whereby the organization operates and the systems it uses to accomplish its goals. Information is the data held by the enterprise, whether it is proprietary, customer, or business data. All these assets must be protected.

The next risk management step considers "vulnerabilities," which are ways the assets can be compromised. For example, a facility vulnerability may be where one side of the facility is adjacent to an abandoned building. A vulnerability for a business process may be that it relies on an IT system that is extremely unreliable. IT systems vulnerabilities can be further characterized in terms of the "CIA" of cybersecurity:

- *Confidentiality*, meaning protecting the secrecy of data

- *Integrity*, meaning protecting data from unauthorized changes

- *Availability*, meaning the availability of IT systems and the data the systems host to those who need the data when it is needed.

The next risk management step considers "threats," which are ways in which vulnerabilities can be exploited to cause damage to the asset. Threats may be natural or man-made, accidental or deliberate, random or deterministic.

Considering threats is one of the most creative steps in the risk management process. Considering threats involves a lot of "Murphy's Law" thinking (What can possibly go wrong?) and thinking like attackers (What vulnerabilities can be exploited?). It is helpful to think about threats in terms of how they would affect the confidentiality, integrity, and availability (in other words, CIA) of the enterprise's information and information systems.

The next risk management step identifies and evaluates risks. Combining threats with vulnerabilities, risks can be identified. A threat against a well-protected area generally produces a low level of risk, while a threat against an area where the enterprise is not well protected produces a risk that must be considered. Unfortunately, identifying and evaluating risks is fundamentally a judgment call. There are two challenges here: first, underestimating risk because vulnerability is underestimated, and second, missing a risk because a particular threat scenario is not considered. As will be discussed, identifying and evaluating risk challenges can be mitigated by using security scopes to group risks and handle them in aggregate.

Once risks have been evaluated, the next step is to address "risk treatment." There are a number of ways to handle risk, besides just trying to prevent the bad thing from happening. The first way to handle risk is to "avoid" the risk by eliminating the vulnerability or the threat. The second way to handle the risk is to "mitigate" the risk by reducing the probability that it will occur, or the impact when it does occur. The third way to handle the risk is to "share" the risk by introducing a third party—such as an insurance company—that will compensate the enterprise in the event that the risk occurs. The fourth way to handle the risk is to "retain" the risk, where the enterprise simply accepts the possibility that the risk may occur and deals with the consequences when they happen; self-insurance is a good example of this approach.

The next risk management step, especially if the enterprise chooses to reduce the risk, is to apply security "controls." Security controls can do four things. First, controls can reduce the probability the risk will occur or make it more difficult for attackers to execute on the risk. Second, controls can reduce the impact when the risk does occur, perhaps limiting the amount of damage that occurs. Third, controls can detect the occurrence of the risk happening, allowing for active responses to contain the damage and reduce the potential exposure. Fourth, controls can collect evidence that is used to show the operation of security controls, to detect failures of the controls, or to support investigations after an incident has occurred.

Considering Vulnerabilities, Threats, and Risks

Figure 2-5 presents the next level of detail of the risk management process first shown in Figure 2-4.

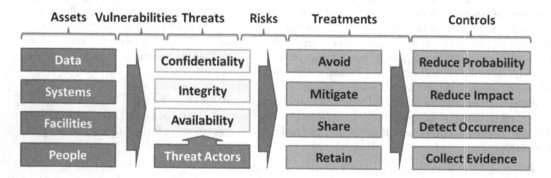

Figure 2-5. *Detailed risk management process showing the six steps from Figure 2-4, with additional detail showing the major considerations or alternatives for each step.*

Note the confidentiality, integrity, and availability (CIA) factors span the risk management assessments of vulnerabilities, threats, and risks. Also note that assets can be categorized as data, systems, facilities, and people. With regard to information assets, the enterprise should consider vulnerabilities, threats, and risks in terms of the CIA factors, rather than considering them separately.

First, consider confidentiality. Confidentiality is the protection of data that should be access-controlled and not widely disseminated. For confidentiality, the enterprise should consider what vulnerabilities there are: How can confidentiality be breached? What would be the resulting data loss? Next, consider the threats—either accidental or deliberate—that could cause data loss. Finally, combining the vulnerabilities and the threats, determine the risk with regard to confidentiality.

Next, consider integrity. Integrity involves data being consistent from when it is entered into a system and when it is later retrieved. Integrity does not sound very interesting, except when the data that is modified is about money or a transaction involving money. Once money is involved, integrity becomes critically important. Risk analysis surrounding integrity has to do, in part, with identifying where integrity is important, the consequences of an integrity violation, and the threats that could result in those consequences. Often, some people do not consider integrity much of a concern. However, integrity must be integral to the enterprise cybersecurity mindset.

Finally, consider availability. Availability involves information and information systems being available when they are needed. Threats to availability can range from systems being temporarily unavailable but otherwise unimpaired to systems being completely destroyed or corrupted beyond recovery. Generally, levels of concern about availability are driven by business considerations of negative financial impacts versus the costs of maintaining or recovering that availability in the face of adversity.

Risk Analysis and Mitigation

Once confidentiality, integrity, and availability risks have been identified—and they likely will not be the same levels of risk for each factor—risk mitigation can be considered. Risk mitigation is only one of the possible treatments, but it is the one that gets the most attention in the cybersecurity process.

Risk analysis is needed before risk mitigation can be implemented. Risk analysis characterizes risk in terms of its magnitude—high, medium, or low. However, risk could be broken out into more gradations or into a numeric scale. Risk can then be thought of in terms of its probability of occurring and the impact if it occurs. Figure 2-6 illustrates the first step to evaluate the risk in terms of its probability and impact. If the probability and the impact are both high, the overall risk level is probably also "high." If the probability and the impact are both low, then the overall risk is probably also "low." If the probability of a risk is low, but the impact is high, the overall risk level is most likely "medium." Similarly, if the probability is high, but the impact is low, the overall risk is most likely "medium."

Impact of an Incident

		Low	Medium	High	
Threat and/or Probability of an Incident	*High*	Medium	High	High	**Reduce Probability**
	Medium	Low	Medium	High	
	Low	Low	Low	Medium	

Reduce Impact

Figure 2-6. Simplified risk matrix showing how the impact and probability of an incident combine to generate an overall risk level. This matrix also shows how risk mitigation reduces the risk by reducing either its probability, its impact, or some combination of both.

With this framework as a context, one can see that risk mitigation has the effect of reducing either the probability of an incident or the impact of the incident. Mitigation that reduces both probability and impact is the most effective. Why? Such mitigation can take a "high" risk and move it to a "low" risk. However, risk mitigations that affect only probability or impact can still be effective. While risk analysis can be done at any level—using either more or fewer levels of detail—this general framework of "high," "medium," and "low" is robust and good enough for many purposes, such as prioritizing mitigations.

Cybersecurity Controls

The next risk management process component is the identification of cybersecurity controls to help mitigate enterprise risks. There are four ways these controls reduce confidentiality, integrity, or availability risks. Controls can (1) reduce risk probability, (2) reduce risk impact, (3) detect occurrences of incidents involving the risk, and (4) collect evidence to support evaluations of security and investigations of incidents related to the risk. Cybersecurity control types to mitigate enterprise risks include the following:

- *Preventive Controls*, which block the threat and prevent incidents from occurring altogether

- *Detective Controls*, which detect when the risk has transpired and generate alerts that can then be acted upon

- *Forensic Controls*, which collect records of activities related to the risk and can be used to produce artifacts to support the operation of detective controls, investigations of incidents, and audits of controls to verify their operation and effectiveness

- *Audit Controls*, which investigate for the presence of the risk, incidents associated with the risk, and the operation of controls that mitigate the risk

Figure 2-7 illustrates the operation of these four control types.

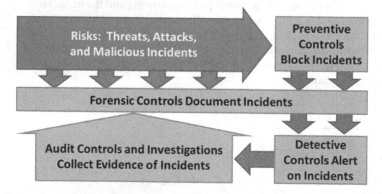

Figure 2-7. Interactions among risks and the different types of controls. While preventive controls are the controls that actually stop the risks, the other controls are critical to making people aware an incident is occurring so they can investigate, contain, and remediate the incident.

It is important to consider how the four cybersecurity control types interact with each other and how the four types serve useful purposes individually. Audit controls are frequently neglected, even though a simple audit can often find malicious activity that is otherwise missed.

Historically, disproportionate consideration has been given to preventive controls—for example, firewalls that block unwanted protocols—at the expense of the other control types. However, modern threats such as Advanced Persistent Threats (APTs) are designed to get around preventive controls and turn the enterprise against itself. Responding to the threat of APT attack by enacting more and more preventive controls can bring about its own set of problems.

Figure 2-8 depicts these four control types in terms of a number of different characteristics. This figure highlights some interesting results regarding each control type's strengths and weaknesses.

	Preventive	*Detective*	*Forensic*	*Audit*
Block Attacks?	Good	Medium	Poor	Poor
Detect Attacks?	Poor	Good	Poor	Medium
Operational Impact	High	Low	Low	Low
Investigate Attacks?	Poor	Medium	Good	Good
Cost to Implement	High	Medium	Medium	Low
Cost to Operate	Medium	High	Low	Medium
Flexibility	Poor	Poor	Medium	Good

Figure 2-8. *Comparison of security control types showing how each type of control represents a trade-off among multiple factors including cost of deployment, operation, and impact on continuing operations.*

Preventive cybersecurity controls generally get much of the attention because they block attacks and incidents, thus preventing a successful cyberattack. However, preventive controls have a number of shortcomings. Unless preventive controls have been configured in conjunction with corresponding detective controls, they are not generally good at detecting attacks. Preventive controls have a high operational impact because they may also prevent legitimate users from doing their jobs. Ever hear of people unable to do their jobs for weeks while they are waiting for accounts and permissions? People not being able to do their jobs is the operational cost of preventive controls. While it is difficult to track these costs, such costs can be considerable. Another preventive control shortcoming is while they are generally inexpensive to operate once they are operational, they can be very expensive to implement in the first place because of their complexity. Finally, preventive controls can be difficult to modify in response to rapidly changing situations.

The next cybersecurity control type is detective controls. These controls generally get shortchanged, but their prestige and importance in the enterprise are trending upward. What is interesting with detective controls is that, unlike preventive controls, they are cheap to implement and have little operational impact on the enterprise. While the control itself can be expensive to operate—alerts have to be investigated—the overall cost of detective controls can be significantly lower than the lost productivity from aggressive preventive controls. Essentially, it can be cheaper overall to let people do whatever they want, alert when they do wrong, and then deal with it. A real-world analogy is law enforcement trying to prevent crimes. Only a small range of potential crimes are actively prevented, while law enforcement is aggressive in pursuing and punishing crimes after they actually occur.

Next are forensic controls, which are not very good at actively detecting or blocking attacks, but they are absolutely critical to investigating attacks successfully after they have occurred. Forensic controls are relatively cheap to operate once they are in place and provide an economical way to implement parts of the security equation without significant investments.

Finally are the audit controls, which are almost the exact opposite of preventive controls. Where preventive controls are effective at stopping attacks, albeit at considerable operational impact, audit controls have almost no operational impact, but also don't stop much in the way of attacks. However, audit controls are low-cost, unobtrusive, and agile. Frequently, audit controls are the only way to find attacks that have defeated the preventive controls of the enterprise. So, while audit controls are not "exotic," these cybersecurity controls deserve respect and consideration in an enterprise's security architecture. A simple audit can often find problems that have been lurking for months or years, despite all the other controls.

Ideally, all four control types are designed and operated in parallel, supporting each other. For example, a firewall may block unwanted ports, detect a port scan, record legitimate traffic for correlation with other alerts, and, finally, perform packet captures for certain types of traffic, all from a single platform. When looking at security technologies, it is useful to evaluate them in terms of what types of control functionality they primarily provide. As described in the next section, when evaluating security technologies, it is also important to understand how the different control objectives are going to be achieved.

Cybersecurity Capabilities

Critically important to figuring out how to make security controls work is the concept of a security capability. NIST describes the idea of security capability as an abstraction:

… security capabilities can address a variety of areas that can include, for example, technical means, physical means, procedural means, or any combination thereof … it is important for organizations to have the ability to describe key security capabilities needed to protect core organizational missions/business functions … This simplifies how the protection problem is viewed conceptually. In essence, using the construct of security capability provides a shorthand method of grouping security controls that are employed for a common purpose or to achieve a common objective. This becomes an important consideration, for example, when assessing security controls for effectiveness. —NIST SP 800-53 Revision 4.

In this book, a "Security Capability" is defined, in part, as "a process or technology that enables the organization to perform a specific control." For example, a firewall capability makes it possible to implement (1) preventive controls for network access control, (2) detective controls for network traffic alerting, (3) forensic controls for network traffic logging, and (4) audit controls for validating network security and looking for intrusions.

A security capability may be as simple as a person following a procedure on a set schedule or in response to a predefined event. On the other hand, a security capability may be a sophisticated technological component that spans the enterprise and provides many features in support of many different controls. "Security Capability" is further defined, in part, as "providing for the auditing, logging, detection, or prevention of a particular type of malicious behavior." Simply stated, security capabilities can be either procedural or technological.

Procedural security capabilities are capabilities that are delivered by having a person follow a procedure on a set schedule, or in response to an action. Procedural capabilities are most likely an enterprise's most powerful ones. Even though procedural capabilities don't scale like a piece of technology, an enterprise's actual security against a professional attacker is almost entirely dependent on its people, not its technology.

Technological capabilities are provided by technologies that are installed into the enterprise's infrastructure. A single technology may provide multiple capabilities. For example, a single technology can block an attack and raise an alert that an attack occurred. Technologies may also provide security capabilities across multiple functional areas. Technological capabilities are powerful because once they are deployed, they tend to "just work" (at least until they break and stop working). Technologies are also interesting because they involve "buying stuff" and deploying "neat tech." However, technology needs to be engineered carefully, deployed, managed, and monitored if it is really going to live up to its potential.

An enterprise's security capabilities, both procedural and technological, form the foundation for its cybersecurity program.

Cybersecurity and Enterprise IT

Regardless of the specific technologies, enterprise IT provides services to deliver information to support the business. This fundamental principle is true whether (1) the business is large or small, or (2) the services are delivered using mainframes, microcomputers, servers, or cloud services. The information delivery can be from a single room, over a private network, over dial-up terminals, or over the Internet. For many enterprises today, this general IT architecture involves the Internet, which complicates cybersecurity protection. Unlike the physical world where there are good neighborhoods and bad neighborhoods, every host on the Internet is only one hop away from every other host, including the malicious hosts operated by potential attackers.

As illustrated in Figure 2-9, enterprise IT contains various components and is generally connected to the Internet. Obviously, real-world IT installations contain many more components, but Figure 2-9 depicts seven major components from architectural and strategic perspectives. Endpoint devices consist of customer, Internet organization, and internal organization devices. The enterprise infrastructure consists of application servers, database servers, and system administration and monitoring.

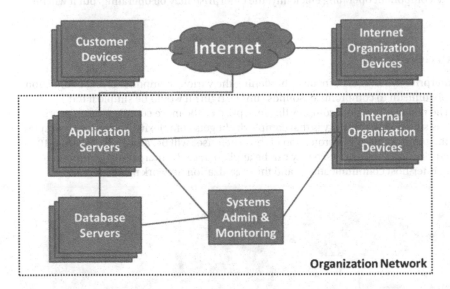

Figure 2-9. *Enterprise IT consists of infrastructure to provide services and data to enterprise users over networks and the infrastructure required to administer, manage, and monitor those services.*

A major endpoint component is customer devices. If a business involves interacting with customers over a network, then their devices are an important part of the overall IT architecture. Why worry about customer devices? What if every single customer devices is malicious and can attack the enterprise? From a cybersecurity perspective, how would an enterprise interact with their customers? If a customer's computer is actively using their data to attack the enterprise, would the enterprise trust the customer? Many people might say, "It depends." The point is that customer devices need to be considered when an enterprise implements its cybersecurity controls and capabilities.

Another endpoint IT component to consider is organization devices that connect to the enterprise over a public network—say, the Internet. Depending on enterprise policies, these devices may be company-owned computers, personal computers, mobile devices, or even Bring Your Own Device (BYOD). The range of organization devices is broad. The reality is the vast majority of organizations are going to allow at least some of their employees to connect to enterprise resources from devices connecting over an open network.

Organizational devices connecting to the enterprise over an internal network, such as the enterprise intranet, are also considered endpoints. The good news is the enterprise likely has more control over these devices than the myriad of customer and organizational devices that may connect over an open network. However, the bad news is, unless the enterprise tolerates a lot of operational headaches, the control is likely spotty at best due to personal devices, customer devices, vendor devices, and a myriad of other potential devices being connected to the enterprise network at least occasionally. These potential connections jeopardize the enterprise's efforts to control and protect the integrity of what is "internal."

The enterprise IT infrastructure consists of three components that should all work together as a coherent and coordinated system. The first component consists of the application servers delivering business applications enabling the generation of business value. The second infrastructure component consists of the database servers containing the business's data. In some cases, the data and the applications may actually be hosted on a single component, but most often the two are separate. It is helpful to look at the functionalities separately in terms of protecting the enterprise from attack and the various ways that attackers seek to penetrate the infrastructure and accomplish their goals. The third component is the systems administration channels for managing and monitoring the infrastructure. Without this infrastructure component operating efficiently, the enterprise may be operating, but it will be unmanageable.

Emplacing Cyberdefenses

At its most basic level, enterprise cybersecurity involves hardening the various components and connections so each component is more difficult to compromise. Sounds simple, right? It would be simple if the enterprise were simple. The reality is the more complex the enterprise is, the more complex the enterprise security is. What makes this situation really tricky is that complexity begets complexity, so the more complex enterprise defenses are, the more complex the protection of those defenses will be, and so on. Figure 2-10 illustrates a national enterprise and shows how security can be applied to each enterprise IT component, including accounts, hosts, inter-host communications, and the organization network perimeter.

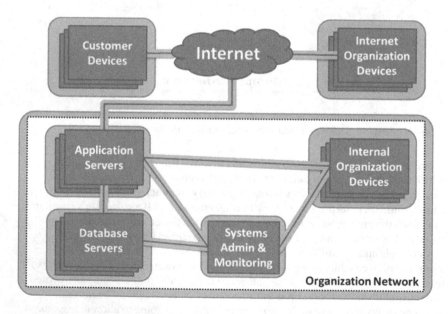

Figure 2-10. *Simply stated, enterprise IT security involves hardening the enterprise IT components so each component is more difficult to compromise or exploit.*

Going clockwise around Figure 2-10, consider the Internet organization devices that should be protected from compromise even while they are connected to the Internet and other trusted networks. Furthermore, note the highlighted line that connects to the organization network. This connection is another security boundary where cybersecurity protections can be applied. Inside the organization network, the internal organization devices, which are already inside the network, can be powerful attack vectors should they fall under the control of an adversary. The next component is the system administration and monitoring component. Protecting these components is probably the most important enterprise protection element because compromise of these components can be used to disable or bypass most of other cybersecurity defenses. On the left side of Figure 2-10, the database servers are where the enterprise data resides. These data must have its confidentiality, availability, and integrity protected. Also shown in Figure 2-10 are application servers that provide enterprise services. The challenge in protecting these servers is that they must be externally facing, while also providing access to enterprise data for legitimate and authorized users. The final component consists of the customer devices that access enterprise resources. These devices are almost impossible to protect, but whose security status must always be considered in an enterprise's security architecture.

An actual architecture will end up containing additional components beyond those shown in Figure 2-10. When an enterprise's basic security is faulty, advanced security is irrelevant. Attackers hit an enterprise where it is the weakest and easiest to attack. Therefore, keep this basic architecture in mind as the following sections explore how to put all these components together into a coherent whole. The final consideration here is that an enterprise's security infrastructure uses this same basic architecture—applications, databases, servers, clients—and protecting the security infrastructure itself requires use of these same techniques, albeit on a slightly different scale.

How Cyberdefenses Interconnect

Recall from Chapter 1, enterprise attack graphs illustrate how different IT components interact with each other and how their cybersecurity defenses depend on each other. An enterprise can use the attack graph methodology to envision conceptually what these interdependencies look like.

For example, an enterprise can construct an attack scenario statement such as, "To compromise organizational data, an attacker can compromise the (1) network and steal the data, (2) cryptography and steal the data in transit, (3) system administration and take control of the servers hosting the data, or (4) applications hosting the data and use them to obtain the data." Another scenario statement might be the following: "To compromise system administration, an attacker can compromise (1) the applications used for systems administration, (2) the endpoints used for performing systems administration, or (3) steal the credentials of the system administrators."

These example attack scenario statements are interesting because they cause an enterprise to step back and examine the big picture of how an enterprise really works. Figure 2-11 is an example of an attack graph that represents attack scenario statements for an entire enterprise.

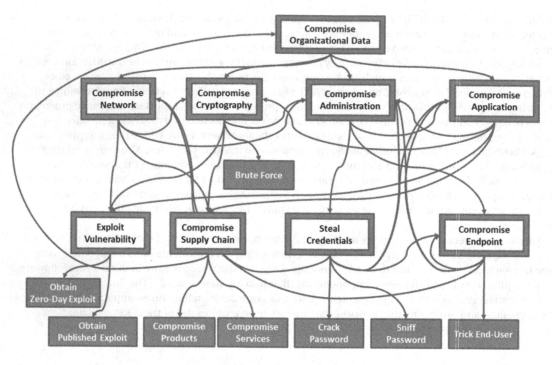

Figure 2-11. *Enterprise IT attack graph showing how enterprise security interconnects and how a compromise of one part of the enterprise can be exploited to eventually compromise the entire enterprise.*

While Figure 2-11 is a bit of a "spaghetti ball," this attack graph shows that all the enterprise security components connect with, and depend on, each other. Understanding this connectivity and dependency is important. Every aspect of the enterprise's security ultimately depends on every other aspect, and, consequently a breach anywhere in the enterprise can eventually be exploited to compromise the entire enterprise.

Due to the interdependency of enterprise IT and cybersecurity components, attackers can start with an exploit almost anywhere and eventually expand the initial exploit to get complete control. The best that defenses can do is make this process more difficult, expensive, and time-consuming, giving defenders time to detect and respond to the intrusion.

While disconcerting, this connectivity and dependency should not be dismaying. What it does mean is that an enterprise needs to appreciate the complexity of enterprise security as a system and understand how enterprise defenses actually stop attacks. The best enterprise cybersecurity defenses can do is to slow the attack down, add steps to the attack, and increase the enterprise's chances of catching the attack before it is completely successful.

An Enterprise Cybersecurity Architecture

Once one understands how the enterprise cybersecurity components fit together and depend on each other, one can start considering how to fit these pieces together into a coherent architecture. To be effective, a cybersecurity architecture should achieve the following objectives:

- Cover the full breadth of cybersecurity so that nothing is left out

- Align people, processes, budgets, and controls into a single framework so that all of them are well-coordinated

- Organize cybersecurity capabilities and controls into functional areas so that they can be managed more easily

- Account for the interdependence of controls and capabilities on each other across functional areas

- Be simple enough that it can be managed and briefed at a high level

With these objectives in mind, this book's authors created the enterprise cybersecurity architecture shown in Figure 2-12. This architecture organizes enterprise cybersecurity into 11 functional areas covering the technical and operational breadth of enterprise cybersecurity.

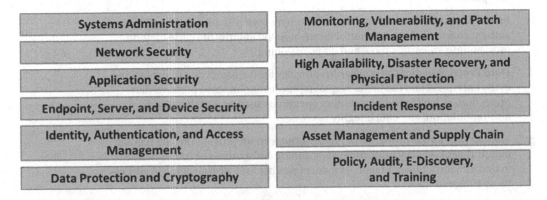

Figure 2-12. *This book organizes enterprise cybersecurity into 11 functional areas.*

The authors selected these functional areas for their relative independence from each other and because they align well with how staff, expertise, and responsibilities are distributed in an organization that utilizes ITIL (IT Infrastructure Library), COBIT (Control Objectives for Information and Related Technology), or similar IT management frameworks. These functional areas enable IT leadership to unify (1) technologies, (2) staff, and (3) corresponding budget into a coherent cybersecurity program.

Another reason the authors organize cybersecurity into these 11 functional areas is the enterprise's overall cybersecurity posture depends equally on the performance of each of the functional areas. In other words, if one functional area is deficient, targeted attackers will exploit it to undermine the security in the other functional areas. So, the enterprise's overall cybersecurity needs to be approximately equal in all 11 functional areas, and its overall security is only as good as the weakest functional area. So it is critically important to ensure all functional areas are covered equally in an enterprise cybersecurity program.

This enterprise cybersecurity architecture is used to manage the capabilities that deliver audit, forensic, detective, and preventive controls to the enterprise. This framework provides for consistent management of security capabilities and assists in prioritizing their deployment, maintenance, and upgrades over time. It also provides strong accountability and good alignment of strategy, staffing, budget, and technology to meet the security needs of the organization. It is designed to be flexible and scalable from a very small enterprise up to a very large one. It provides an extensible mechanism for adjusting cyberdefenses over time in response to changing cyberthreats.

The eleven functional areas of this book's enterprise cybersecurity architecture are as follows:

a. *Systems Administration*: provides for secure administration of enterprise infrastructure and security systems, and protects system administration channels from compromise

b. *Network Security*: provides for security of enterprise networks, their services, and access to them from the Internet and internally connected devices

c. *Application Security*: provides for the security of enterprise applications using security technologies that are appropriate to and tailored for the protection of those applications and their communications

d. *Endpoint, Server, and Device Security*: provides for the protection of endpoints, servers, and devices that access enterprise data, and protects them from compromise

e. *Identity, Authentication, and Access Management*: provides for identification, authentication, and access control throughout the identity life cycle including provisioning, re-certification, and de-provisioning

f. *Data Protection and Cryptography*: provides for the protection of data stored in the enterprise and the use of cryptographic technologies to perform that protection, as well as to support other operations such as authentication, non-repudiation, and data integrity

g. *Monitoring, Vulnerability, and Patch Management*: provides for the regular monitoring of security infrastructure, scanning and analysis of vulnerabilities in that infrastructure, and management of patches and workarounds to address those vulnerabilities

h. *High Availability, Disaster Recovery, and Physical Protection*: provides for the protection of availability in the enterprise, including making systems highly available, recovering from disasters, and physically protecting facilities, people, systems, and data

i. *Incident Response*: provides for the investigation, response, and recovery of incidents that are identified through monitoring of the enterprise

j. *Asset Management and Supply Chain*: provides for the accounting of enterprise assets, procurement information associated with them, their life cycles, changes, and ensuring orderly and secure disposal without compromise of enterprise data or security

k. *Policy, Audit, E-Discovery, and Training*: provides for policy oversight of controls and audit of their effectiveness, support for legal e-discovery activities, and training of staff in proper security policies and practices

The next chapter describes these functional areas in more detail. It is important to note that as the cyberthreat evolves, so will the enterprise cybersecurity functional areas and corresponding capabilities.

PART II

A New Enterprise Cybersecurity Architecture

CHAPTER 3

■ ■ ■

Enterprise Cybersecurity Architecture

This chapter describes the enterprise cybersecurity architecture in more detail. Figure 3-1 delineates the 11 functional areas this book uses to organize and manage enterprise cybersecurity.

11 Functional Areas of Enterprise Cybersecurity
Systems Administration
Network Security
Application Security
Endpoint, Server, and Device Security
Identity, Authentication, and Access Management
Data Protection and Cryptography
Monitoring, Vulnerability, and Patch Management
High Availability, Disaster Recovery, and Physical Protection
Incident Response
Asset Management and Supply Chain
Policy, Audit, E-Discovery, and Training

Figure 3-1. *The 11 functional areas of enterprise cybersecurity constitute a framework for managing a robust enterprise cybersecurity program.*

For each functional area, this chapter (1) defines it, (2) states its overall goal and objectives, (3) describes likely threat vectors, and (4) highlights corresponding capabilities. The capabilities in each of the functional areas are described in detail in Appendix C. It is important to note that as the cyberthreat evolves, so will specific functional areas and the corresponding capabilities within each functional area. By organizing its cybersecurity program around these functional areas, the enterprise has an extensible framework for adjusting its cyberdefenses to protect against evolving cyberthreats.

Systems Administration

Systems administration provides for secure administration of enterprise infrastructure and security infrastructure, protecting systems administration channels from compromise. Systems administration gets its own functional area because, if it is compromised, an attacker can easily disable and bypass the rest of enterprise security.

Secure systems administration is the foundation for enterprise security measures, and it needs to be airtight. If this functional area is compromised, the rest of enterprise security is rendered irrelevant.

Analysts have observed that systems administration channels have become increasingly popular with deliberate attackers. Here are a few reasons why systems administration is targeted:

1. Consolidation in IT over the past 15 years has placed tremendous power into the hands of a small number of systems administrators. Whereas 20 years ago one person might manage a dozen systems, now systems administrators have control of hundreds or even thousands of enterprise computers, often from a single console.

2. Systems administration security is frequently poor, relying on insecure protocols and username/password authentication. These insecure protocols are frequently used over the same networks that are used to conduct ordinary business, leaving them open to attack.

3. Systems administration technology is relatively immature, with few built-in checks and balances to detect malicious activity or prevent it in the first place. Many implementations lack protections such as detailed audit logs or two-party controls.

Due to these weaknesses, attackers can get into systems administration channels, allowing them unfettered enterprisewide access.

Systems Administration: Goal and Objectives

Systems administration's goal is to protect the enterprise's administrative channels from being used by an adversary. Systems administration major objectives include the following:

- The preventive objective is to make it harder for attackers to get systems administration control, to slow them down so that they are easier to catch, and to make it easier to catch attacks when they occur.

- The detective objective focuses on detecting (1) attacks on systems administration channels, and (2) malicious systems administration activity when it occurs. Detective controls need to be configured to alert on patterns associated with malicious systems administration activity. It may also involve manual review of certain systems administration activities to ensure that they are legitimate and appropriate.

- The forensic objective focuses on creating detailed audit logs of all privileged systems administration activities. These logs are then used to generate detective control alerts, facilitate regularly scheduled audits, and support investigations of incidents.

- The audit objective focuses on generating artifacts and evidence that systems administration is not malicious in the enterprise. Audits can be regularly scheduled, but unscheduled reviews of systems administration activities can also help ensure that they are legitimate. Audits do not have to be elaborate. An audit as simple as a review of what accounts logged onto what hosts at what times can be effective at catching malicious activity in a timely fashion.

Systems Administration: Threat Vectors

Systems administration protection involves keeping attackers (or insiders) from conducting malicious systems administration activities in the enterprise.

Systems administration threat vectors include the following:

- Attackers compromise the credentials used by systems administrators and then use those credentials from compromised machines inside the network.

- Attackers compromise the computers used by systems administrators and then use those computers to take control of systems.

- Attackers compromise the computing infrastructure such as virtualization, storage, or keyboard-video-mouse (KVM) and use the computing capabilities to take control of systems.

- Attackers compromise systems administration infrastructure such as enterprise computer management, patch management, or other systems and use the infrastructure to take control of the enterprise.

- Attackers compromise monitoring systems that have administrative access to the enterprise and use the access to take control of systems.

- Attackers use local computer administrative accounts to move from one personal computer to another with administrative rights.

Systems Administration: Capabilities

Systems administration capabilities make it harder for attackers to get administrative access to the enterprise or its systems, and they make those attackers easier to detect and stop if they do get control. Systems administration capabilities help (1) isolate command and control networks and protocols, (2) provide cryptographic protection for systems administration, and (3) allow for auditing of systems administration activities to detect attacks.

Some less-commonly considered systems administration technologies include power and environmental controls, Integrated Lights-Out (ILO) system consoles, KVM interfaces, and supporting infrastructures such as switches, routers, Storage Area Networks (SANs), and virtual machine management consoles. In this functional area, it is good to have redundancy in protection. For example, using network isolation along with strong authentication helps ensure that the breach of one protection mechanism alone will not be disastrous.

Following are some systems administration capabilities. Appendix C provides detailed descriptions for these capabilities.

- Bastion hosts

- Out-of-Band (OOB) management

- Network isolation

- Integrated Lights-Out (ILO), Keyboard Video Mouse (KVM), and power controls

- Virtualization and Storage Area Network (SAN) management

- Segregation of administration from services

- Multi-factor authentication for Systems Administrators (SAs)

- Administrator audit trail(s)

- Command logging and analytics

Network Security

Network security's purpose is to protect the enterprise network from unauthorized access. Network security examines data traversing the enterprise network to detect intrusions against the network and the computers connected to it. In addition, the network architecture and its defenses can be used to channel user and attacker activity, routing it toward sensors and defensive mechanisms and away from weaknesses and vulnerabilities.

Network security needs to be considered in terms of security controls that include the following:

- Preventive controls such as firewalls that block attacker activity and separate sections of the network from each other.

- Detective controls, such as Intrusion Detection, that detect attacker activity that cannot be blocked.

- Monitoring controls that capture activity that is input to correlation engines that support forensics, investigations, and more sophisticated attack detection that considers multiple variables and data sources.

Containment is another important capability that network security can provide. Containment involves isolating attacker activity in one part of the enterprise (for example, end-user workstations or Internet-facing web servers) from other IT functions such as financial systems in order to provide for a layered defense. Similarly, network security can be used to establish compartments in the enterprise that can be used to contain attacks and give defenders opportunities to catch them before they proceed too far.

Network security can also involve filtering and monitoring the network enterprise traffic to block malicious network traffic and to detect attacker network traffic when attacks occur. It used to be that network security was satisfied by simply having a network firewall; today network security includes a long list of services, devices, proxies, and other capabilities that are rapidly changing and evolving.

Network Security: Goal and Objectives

Verizon found that 92% of breaches involved activities perpetrated by outsiders entering an enterprise from the Internet.[1] Mandiant has observed that sophisticated attackers can work around multiple layers of network defenses, particularly when computers and servers in the enterprise have Internet access.[2] These two factors combine to make network security a central and critical component of successful enterprise IT defense. Network security is also a powerful defensive capability, particularly when it is integrated with other security functional areas creating an integrated defense.

Network security's goal is to protect the enterprise's network from use or attack by an adversary. Network security major objectives include the following:

- The preventive objective is to block malicious traffic from passing from one part of the network to another, or channeling that traffic so that it can be detected through other means.

- The detective objective is to monitor and analyze network traffic in order to detect malicious traffic while it is in transit.

- The forensic objective is to log information about network traffic, or possibly all of the network traffic itself, so that the network traffic can be analyzed by detective controls, or to support investigations and audits.

- The audit objective involves analyzing network traffic in order to identify malicious activity or to generate artifacts indicating the lack of malicious activity. This activity may be determined by a number of characteristics, including the source and destination addresses, protocols used, timing, or data contained within the traffic.

Network Security: Threat Vectors

Most targeted attacks utilize the network in some way and rely on the network to perpetuate their attack while it is in-progress. Network security threat vectors include the following:

- Attackers enter the enterprise through outbound network connections from servers or clients on the internal network.

- Attackers enter the enterprise through the network connections of Internet-facing servers.

- Attackers use internal networks to move laterally between computers inside the enterprise.

- Attackers use enterprise networks to extract data and remove it from the enterprise.

- Attackers take control of network infrastructure components and then leverage them to gain entry to the enterprise or to bypass other security measures.

---

[1] Verizon Data Breach Investigation Report, 2013.
[2] Mandiant M-Trends Annual Report, 2013.

Network Security: Capabilities

Network security includes a large number of capabilities that should be considered for deployment as part of an integrated security solution. Network security capabilities provide preventive, detective, forensic, and audit functions on the enterprise network. Network security technology or capability is not a "silver bullet" that will satisfy all cybersecurity requirements. However, an integrated set of capabilities can block, detect, and intercept many potential attacks.

Following are some network security capabilities. Appendix C provides detailed descriptions for these capabilities.

- Switches and routers

- Software Defined Networking (SDN)

- Domain Name System (DNS) and Dynamic Host Configuration Protocol (DHCP)

- Network Time Protocol (NTP)

- Network service management

- Firewall and virtual machine firewall

- Network Intrusion Detection/Network Intrusion Prevention System (IDS/IPS)

- Wireless networking (Wi-Fi)

- Packet intercept and capture

- Secure Sockets Layer (SSL) intercept

- Network Access Control (NAC)

- Virtual Private Networking (VPN) and Internet Protocol Security (IPSec)

- Network Traffic Analysis (NTA)

- Network Data Analytics (NDA)

Application Security

Network security involves protecting the enterprise at the network layer with little regard to the actual applications running on that network. Application security involves security measures that are specific to certain applications or protocols running over the network. Application security operates alongside network security. In examining these security technologies, though, it is helpful to think about them in terms of which of their capabilities are network general and which are application-specific.

Application security involves providing security capabilities that are specific to the applications used in the enterprise. The applications most needing additional security are the ones that communicate over the network and are accessible from the Internet. By this simple definition, application security technologies and capabilities include e-mail security, application-aware firewall features, database gateways, and forward web proxies.

Application security protects applications from cyberattacks by understanding the application and its protocols' inner workings, such as the HyperText Markup Language (HTML) used to create web pages or Simple Mail Transfer Protocol (SMTP) used for e-mail transmission. Application security helps prevent attacks that exploit application vulnerabilities or application communication protocols. Simply stated, application security is specific to the requirements of various application protocols and corresponding data types the protocols handle.

Application Security: Goal and Objectives

Application security's goal is to protect the enterprise's applications from use or attack by an adversary. Application security major objectives include the following:

- The preventive objective is to block exploitation of applications and application communications protocols for malicious use.

- The detective objective is to detect compromises of applications and attempts to exploit them for malicious purposes.

- The forensic objective is to log data about application activity that can be used for audits and investigations of incidents.

- The audit objective is for auditors to be able to collect evidence and artifacts that suggest that applications are safe and not being used or manipulated by attackers.

Application Security: Threat Vectors

Targeted and general threats utilize enterprise applications in some way, particularly the Internet-connected applications e-mail and web browsing. Many applications may be custom-built, and securing those systems can be particularly challenging.

Application security threat vectors include the following:

- Many attack vectors gain initial entry into the enterprise by leveraging e-mail to send malicious messages to users. These messages may then contain attachments or links that use vulnerabilities in other applications (for example, office productivity, picture viewers, or document viewers) to gain control of endpoint computing devices (such as personal computers, servers, and mobile devices).

- Other attack vectors leverage vulnerabilities in web browsers and web plug-ins (additional features) to gain control of users who go to malicious sites. These threat vectors can be particularly insidious when attackers compromise a legitimate web site and use it to serve up malware to unsuspecting visitors.

- Other attack vectors involve exploiting vulnerabilities in enterprise server applications (such as web application servers) to take control of those servers and use them to get into the enterprise.

- Once on the inside of the network, attackers leverage applications either to exploit their vulnerabilities and compromise additional machines or to use the applications themselves for malicious goals.

- With web applications and software developed in-house, such as productivity and mobile applications, attackers find and exploit flaws in the software to gain entry to the enterprise, compromise data stored in the application, or target the enterprise's employees or customers.

Application Security: Capabilities

While network security is focused on general network traffic, many enterprise applications can be given additional protections that are tailored to them specifically. Excellent examples of additional protection are e-mail filtering, web proxies, web application firewalls, and database firewalls. An important aspect of application security is procedural. Enterprise application developers need to use proven methodologies to ensure that custom business applications are not vulnerable to exploits such as buffer overflows, SQL injection, or cross-site scripting. Equally important, an enterprise needs to ensure that commercial applications are maintained and patched to address vulnerabilities that are discovered after their initial deployment into the enterprise.

Following are some application security capabilities. Appendix C provides detailed descriptions for these capabilities.

- E-mail security

- Webshell detection

- Application firewalls

- Database firewalls

- Forward proxy and web filters

- Reverse proxy

- Data Leakage Protection (DLP)

- Secure application and database software development

- Software code vulnerability analysis (including source code verification and bug tracking)

Endpoint, Server, and Device Security

Endpoint, server, and device security involves protecting endpoint computing devices (for example, personal computers, servers, and mobile devices) from attack and detecting when those endpoint defenses have been breached. Like most of the protections discussed, an enterprise can never assume that its endpoint security will be 100% effective.

In fact, the best an enterprise can hope to do is to reduce the probability that the enterprise's endpoints will be compromised. The number of compromised endpoints will NEVER be zero, no matter how hard an enterprise tries.

Given the fact that the number of compromised endpoints will never be zero, an enterprise needs the rest of its security functional areas to help compensate for these security shortcomings.

Paradoxically, an enterprise's security deployment strategy should consider endpoint, server, and device security somewhat separately. While the technologies' protection may be similar, an enterprise's deployment strategy will need to be adapted and tuned to the specific needs of each computing platform. Heterogeneous enterprise environments may also have different operating systems and hardware platforms to deal with as well. As a result, each environment has its own specific quirks and vulnerabilities. An enterprise should start with a general foundation, but not try to deploy a "one-size-fits-all" solution.

Another interesting consideration is that many of an enterprise's endpoints may be outside of its control and belong to enterprise partners, customers, and consumers. An enterprise needs to consider the security of these devices in terms of its overall risk analysis and consider how to compensate for their potential vulnerabilities through other means and protections.

Endpoint, Server, and Device Security: Goal and Objectives

Endpoint, server, and device security's goal is threefold: (1) prevent attackers from taking administrative control of computing devices that store organization data or process organizational transactions, (2) detect attempts to maliciously use these devices, and (3) facilitate investigation of incidents when compromises of systems or data are suspected.

Endpoint, server, and device security can NEVER be assumed to be 100% effective, as administrators will make mistakes, viruses will proliferate, and zero-day vulnerabilities (in other words, developers have had zero days to address and patch the vulnerability) will always be obtainable by well-resourced attackers. However, endpoint security represents a tremendous opportunity to (1) make it difficult for attackers to get into the enterprise, (2) set up alarms to detect attackers, and (3) improve the effectiveness of enterprise detection and response when attacks occur.

Endpoint, server, and device security major objectives include the following:

- The preventive objective is to make endpoints, servers, and devices harder to compromise in the first place. Endpoint security centers on "hardening" operating systems so that they are difficult to breach and exploit.

- The detective objective is to alert the enterprise on malicious software and attempts to exploit the operating system so that defenders can identify systems that are either compromised or under attack.

- The forensic objective is to log device activities securely so that there is an audit trail for investigations. These logs may include system configurations, administrator commands, and changes to sensitive areas of the operating system, such as security features and scheduled tasks. Forensics may also include complete imaging of systems for detailed forensic analysis.

- The audit objective involves analyzing logs to identify malicious activity or to create artifacts indicating the absence of malicious activity on audited systems. Auditing for endpoint, server, and device security involves analyzing the systems to gain confidence that they are operating properly and are free of malicious software.

Endpoint, Server, and Device Security: Threat Vectors

Attacks focus on taking control of endpoints within an enterprise. Unfortunately, there are countless ways to take control, and creative attackers are constantly coming up with new methods and new attack vectors. With that said, threat vectors include the following:

- Viruses proliferate across the Internet, exploiting operating system vulnerabilities to pass from machine to machine. This problem continues to be prevalent due to unpatched vulnerabilities (that is, not keeping up-to-date with latest security patches), particularly in application software that may not be centrally managed.

- Deliberate attackers exploit vulnerabilities in enterprise software products or operating systems, or even leverage zero-day exploits to take control of targeted computers.

- Advanced attackers obtain administrator credentials within an enterprise and then use those credentials to install malware and "backdoors" (in other words, unauthorized access pathways) on systems so that they can control them. This attack is challenging to defend against because it uses the same systems administration channels that the enterprise relies on for central control.

- Particularly on mobile devices, malware is embedded in software applications available through legitimate software stores and installed by unsuspecting users. This threat vector is particularly effective on mobile devices, but it will likely become more common as the application store paradigm becomes commonplace.

Endpoint, Server, and Device Security: Capabilities

An enterprise should consider a number of capabilities for protecting its endpoints, servers, and other devices. At the strategic level, these three practice areas may need to be considered separately due to the differences between how endpoints are used compared to servers. However, many technologies used to protect endpoints are common to all platforms.

Capabilities and technologies to consider include hardened computer images, computer policies, endpoint security suites (such as anti-virus, anti-malware, host firewall and intrusion detection), and policies for access controls, privilege management, and auditing and forensics. Mobile devices present an interesting twist since they use different operating systems that may not be as mature as those of personal computers and require their own sets of tools and technologies. Another endpoint challenge is the fact that many endpoints of interest are personally owned or consumer-grade devices that may not have the features needed for enterprise protection.

Following are some endpoint, server, and device security capabilities. Appendix C provides detailed descriptions for these capabilities.

- Local administrator privilege restrictions

- Computer security and logging policies

- Endpoint and media encryption

- Computer access controls

- Forensic imaging support for investigations

- Virtual desktop/thin clients

- Mobile Device Management (MDM)

- Anti-virus/anti-malware

- Application whitelisting

- In-memory malware detection

- Host firewall and intrusion detection

- "Gold code" software images

- Security Technical Implementation Guides (STIGs)

- Always-on Virtual Private Networking (VPN)

- File integrity and change monitoring

Identity, Authentication, and Access Management

Identity, authentication, and identity management supports all other security functional areas by providing answers to the following questions:

- Who is accessing enterprise IT systems?

- How are they identified?

- What can they access once they are authenticated?

When systems are isolated on corporate networks, the answers to these questions are often a matter of who has physical access to the enterprise facilities. It is expected that all who have access to corporate networks be cleared and authorized in some way. However, once systems are connected to the Internet, this connection becomes a tremendous problem, as billions of people are literally "one click and a password" away from accessing enterprise systems. This reality is where identity management and solid authentication mechanisms become critical to successful cyberdefense.

Identity management helps to ensure that accounts and accesses are provisioned, de-provisioned, and periodically re-certified according to enterprise policies. Authentication helps to ensure that appropriate technologies are used to positively identify users who are accessing enterprise systems so that there is a high level of confidence that the people are who they say they are. Access management helps to ensure that privileges on enterprise systems are provisioned and de-provisioned according to "least privilege" methodologies, and users do not have privileges that exceed their roles in the enterprise.

Identity, Authentication, and Access Management: Goal and Objectives

Identity, authentication, and access management's goal is to ensure that only authorized people can access resources in the enterprise. This goal would be straightforward, except for the fact that people, resources, and permission change over time. When there are large numbers of people, large numbers of resources, and huge numbers of potential access permissions, all of which are in constant flux, this goal can become extremely challenging.

Identity, authentication, and access management major objectives include the following:

- The preventive objective is to make it harder for attackers to gain access to enterprise resources by impersonating legitimate users, granting themselves inappropriate permissions, or using accounts that should not have been available to them.

- The detective objective is to alert the enterprise on credential or permission abuse within the enterprise and to identify when accounts are being attacked or have been compromised.

- The forensic objective is to log account activity, including the full life cycle associated with accounts, permissions, and logon activities. These logs can then be data-mined and correlated with other enterprise events to identify attack patterns.

- The audit objective involves analyzing logs to create artifacts and gather evidence that accounts and permissions are not being abused. To achieve this objective with a reasonable level of confidence requires a thorough audit trail and cross-correlation with evidence from other sources, such as the endpoints and applications.

Identity, Authentication, and Access Management: Threat Vectors

Credential abuse is one of the most common vectors for targeted attackers to gain enterprise privileges and accomplish their goals. Credential abuse is due to a few reasons. First, with username and password authentication, it is relatively easy for attackers to get ahold of credentials and then use those credentials in the enterprise. Second, once attackers start using legitimate credentials, many enterprise defenses are avoided because those defenses focus on activities other than those of "legitimate" enterprise users. Third, account and privilege management are extremely difficult to do well, and this area is a relatively "soft" area for attack, even in the most professional of enterprises. Threat vectors in this functional area include the following:

- Attackers use or abuse accounts that are no longer used or maintained, but have not actually been removed from the enterprise.

- Attackers obtain credentials to legitimate accounts and then use those accounts to gain entry to the enterprise. Once that entry is obtained, attackers escalate their privileges by exploiting vulnerabilities in endpoints, applications, or networks.

- Attackers exploit weak authentication methods or protocols to impersonate legitimate users and use their credentials over the network.

- Attackers leverage weaknesses in privilege management to take regular user accounts and grant them administrative or other super-user privileges within the enterprise.

Identity, Authentication, and Access Management: Capabilities

Identity, authentication, and access management capabilities center around managing the full identity and access life cycle, and making identities and authentication available to the full range of enterprise systems that would consume them. A major challenge is interfacing with the wide range of enterprise systems that need these services. Identity and access management technologies and deployments can easily become complex, multi-million-dollar undertakings. With regard to the identity life cycle, enterprises must manage a careful balance between automation and manual procedures to find the most cost-effective blend of capabilities.

Following are some identity, authentication, and access management capabilities. Appendix C provides detailed descriptions for these capabilities.

- Identity life cycle management

- Enterprise directory

- Multi-factor authentication

- Privilege management and access control

- Identity and access audit trail and reporting

- Lightweight Directory Access Protocol (LDAP)

- Kerberos, RADIUS, 802.1x

- Federated authentication

- Security Assertion Markup Language (SAML)

Data Protection and Cryptography

Data protection and cryptography is an increasingly important cybersecurity functional area. Cryptography has gone from the specialized niche of protecting military communications to protecting almost every aspect of Internet communications and commerce. Cryptography is also critical to the success of strong authentication technologies such as digital certificates, smart cards, and one-time password tokens. Cryptography protects data at rest and in transit, and provides for strong authentication and non-repudiation for messages and data, supporting message identity and authenticity. Even in the absence of such advanced technologies, it is important to remember that the simplest authentication mechanism (that is, username and password) employs its own cryptography in the form of a simple shared secret key, the password.

Data protection and cryptography must contend with the rapid rate at which cryptographic standards and technologies change. Enterprises must ensure that they only use cryptographic capabilities that are secure against attack, and that characteristic can change quickly over time. Cryptography that took a thousand years to crack a decade ago may only take weeks or days to crack today (or even less). Cryptography has many unique challenges that require specialized expertise to understand and evaluate effectively.

Data Protection and Cryptography: Goal and Objectives

Data protection and cryptography's goal is to protect the confidentiality and integrity of data using such techniques as encryption and digital signatures. Success of these techniques depends, in part, on enterprise *key management* that helps to ensure the cryptographic keys used for these operations are properly protected.

Data protection and cryptography has four major objectives:

- The preventive objective involves protecting the confidentiality and integrity of enterprise data by using cryptographic technologies. The effectiveness of these technologies generally revolves around the algorithms they use and the protection they provide for the cryptographic keys.

- The detective objective involves monitoring enterprise cryptographic use to detect weak cryptography or cryptographic breaches when they occur.

- The forensic objective involves tracking the cryptography used in the enterprise and logging what algorithms and keys are used where to support later investigations.

- The audit objective involves collecting information on the cryptography and keys that are used and their strengths, and ensuring that they meet the enterprise requirements for strength and protection.

Data Protection and Cryptography: Threat Vectors

It is important for enterprises to pay attention to cryptography and either have or obtain externally the expertise to ensure that it is utilized effectively. Cryptography is benign by itself, but how it is employed can serve either the defender or the attacker equally effectively. Unskilled attackers tend to be thwarted by it, while skilled attackers exploit it to protect themselves and their attacks. Making cryptography work effectively requires skill and finesse.

Data protection and cryptography threat vectors include the following:

- Attackers use encrypted web sessions either into or out of an enterprise to control computers on the inside so that those sessions are more difficult to monitor.

- Attackers encrypt enterprise data and then demand that a ransom be paid in order to get the keys to decrypt the data.

- Attackers crack weak cryptography to steal credentials, intercept encrypted sessions, or read encrypted data.

- Attackers use brute force to compromise passwords that have been encoded using weak cryptography.

- Attackers steal the keys to strong cryptography if those keys have not been well-protected.

- Attackers use "code signing" certificates to make malware appear to be a legitimate application or device driver.

- Attackers steal data at rest or in-transit while it is unencrypted, either through the application itself or at other vulnerable points in time.

Data Protection and Cryptography: Capabilities

Cryptography is notoriously difficult to get right because success requires three things all be accomplished properly. There is no such thing as "perfect" cryptography that will last forever, so any deployment involves making guesses and trade-offs. First, cryptographic algorithms must be chosen that are secure and expected to stay secure as long as will be necessary. Second, cryptographic keys must be chosen and protected from compromise as long as they will be needed. Third, the application of cryptography must be carefully coordinated with the overall life cycle of the data that is to be protected. Data needs to be protected, but also available when it needs to be used. When data is decrypted so that it can be used, it must be protected by other means.

Following are some cryptography and data protection capabilities. Appendix C provides detailed descriptions for these capabilities.

- Secure Sockets layer (SSL) and Transport Layer Security (TLS)

- Digital certificates (Public Key Infrastructure [PKI])

- Key hardware protection (Smart cards, Trusted Platform Modules [TPMs], and Hardware Security Modules [HSMs])

- One-Time Password (OTP) and Out-of-Band (OOB) authentication

- Key life cycle management (including key rotation)

- Digital signatures

- Complex passwords

- Data encryption and tokenization

- Brute force attack detection

- Digital Rights Management (DRM)

Monitoring, Vulnerability, and Patch Management

Monitoring, vulnerability, and patch management are about capabilities that monitor the status of the enterprise's security and maintain that security over time by identifying and patching vulnerabilities as they become known. The functional area's capabilities support operational processes by identifying and patching vulnerabilities, and by monitoring security systems so that security alerts can be detected and acted upon.

Monitoring, Vulnerability, and Patch Management: Goal and Objectives

Monitoring, vulnerability, and patch management's goal is to understand how security changes over time. When a system is deployed and everything is quiet, all is well. The problem is that the next day that system's security can become obsolete if things have changed and attackers have identified vulnerabilities in the original security design. This functional area involves maintaining security over time. Risk must be constantly re-assessed as yesterday's vulnerabilities that were not a concern may become a critical concern today.

Monitoring, vulnerability, and patch management major objectives include the following:

- The preventive objective is to ensure that vulnerabilities are compensated for and patched before they can be exploited by attackers.

- The detective objective involves monitoring all enterprise security automation systems to detect incidents so incidents can be promptly investigated and remediated.

- The forensic objective involves logging event and incident information that can be correlated, cross-checked, and investigated.

- The audit objective involves centrally collecting forensic data that can be analyzed by auditors and investigators.

Monitoring, Vulnerability, and Patch Management: Threat Vectors

This functional area is all about operational processes to catch threats before they can prove disastrous. Monitoring, vulnerability, and patch management threat vectors include the following:

- Attackers leverage attack methods that are not detected or that are detected by unmonitored systems and are invisible to defenders.

- Attackers exploit vulnerabilities during the time window between when they become known and before they can be patched enterprisewide.

- Attackers exploit vulnerabilities in software components that are not centrally managed or patched, or use zero-day exploits for which there is no patch or protection.

- Attackers target security and logging infrastructure to block or delete records of their activities so that their activities are invisible to defenders.

- Attacker activities are monitored and logged, but due to a lack of cross-correlation, defenders do not have a clear picture of everything that is happening in order to see the patterns and respond to them.

Monitoring, Vulnerability, and Patch Management: Capabilities

Monitoring, vulnerability, and patch management capabilities focus on maintaining the enterprise's security on an ongoing basis and actively detecting incidents against enterprise security systems.

Monitoring capabilities provide for the collection and analysis of logging data from the infrastructure, and then processing that data to identify events of interest. Given events of interest, the enterprise identifies specific incidents that require investigation and remediation. Vulnerability capabilities involve scanning enterprise infrastructure and computers to identify vulnerabilities in software or configuration so that identified vulnerabilities can be remediated. Patch management capabilities help ensure the ongoing patching of commercial products so that the products can be kept current with the latest security fixes and enhancements.

Following are some monitoring, vulnerability, and patch management capabilities. Appendix C provides detailed descriptions for these capabilities.

- Operational performance monitoring
- System and network monitoring
- System configuration change detection
- Privilege and access change detection
- Log aggregation
- Data analytics
- Security Information and Event Management (SIEM)
- Network and computer vulnerability scanning
- Penetration testing
- Patch management and deployment
- Rogue network device detection
- Rogue wireless access point detection
- Honeypots/honeynets/honeytokens
- Security Operations Center (SOC)

High Availability, Disaster Recovery, and Physical Protection

One cannot talk about security, even cybersecurity, without discussing the matter of physical protection. Within this book's framework, physical protection, disaster recovery, and high availability are grouped logically together because the greatest threat they protect against is availability. While there are other, easier ways to achieve breaches of confidentiality or integrity, there is no more effective long-term way to achieve a breach of availability than to gain physical access and destroy or disconnect the target systems.

With the rise of "all-hazards" risk management, it is helpful to think about all three of these capabilities together, as they can be integrated to increase enterprise security. An enterprise can balance disaster recovery with levels of physical protection to achieve cost-effective business continuity capabilities that are measured in terms of recovery point objectives and recovery time objectives (RPO/RTO).

RPO is the point in time that data is recovered through. For example, if the recovery point is nightly, then a recovery will not include transactions from the following day. Data and transactions generated after the recovery point are lost when a recovery has to occur. Recovery point is all about the data and how up-to-date it needs to be. For a financial system, the recovery point would need to be the most recently committed financial transaction, while for a data archive the recovery point might be the most recent reporting period.

RTO is how long it takes from when the disaster is declared until the system has been recovered and its data and transaction processing capabilities are available again. The range of acceptable recovery times may also range from minutes to months, depending on the specific system and its business requirements.

Generally, organizations should group systems by their RPO/RTO requirements to achieve the most cost-effective solution. Obviously, not all systems require immediate disaster recovery.

High Availability, Disaster Recovery, and Physical Protection: Goal and Objectives

High availability, disaster recovery, and physical protection's goal is to satisfy business requirements for continuity of operations in the face of adversity, which may range from mild, routine failures of computing devices to severe natural or man-made catastrophes.

Rather than discuss this functional area in terms of preventive and detective objectives, it is appropriate to discuss it in terms of the enterprise's reaction capabilities. The overall enterprise objective is to ensure it has the ability to respond to a wide range of potential adverse situations. Perhaps most importantly, an enterprise needs to consider how these reaction capabilities might serve the enterprise in the event of a cyberattack.

High Availability, Disaster Recovery, and Physical Protection: Threat Vectors

Primary threats to consider are potential adversities, whether adversities come from regular mechanical wear and tear, natural circumstances that are outside of anyone's control, or human-led activities that are either negligent or malicious. However, it is also useful to think "outside of the box" and consider how this functional area can work for or against the enterprise in the event of a cyberattack.

High availability, disaster recovery, and physical protection threat vectors include the following:

- Scheduled maintenance where systems administrators want to take systems offline for upgrades or patches without disrupting operations.

- Regular wear and tear or hard-to-predict circumstances that result in enterprise systems failing. Generally, systems failing is caused by hardware failures, but it can also come from software failures or even unpredictable factors such as cosmic rays that cause memory corruption (yes, cosmic rays actually can cause problems).

- As a result of a cyberattack, the integrity of certain IT systems is placed sufficiently into question so that restoring those systems, and possibly their data, using backups or disaster recovery systems is desirable.

- As a result of a cyberattack that is in-progress, it is desirable to activate contingency capabilities to provide either additional capacity or to allow for reconfiguration of primary systems to defend against the attack.

- A natural or man-made disaster results in the loss of a primary data center or other operational systems. As a result, enterprise services must be failed over (in other words, switched) to a secondary site. This transition is subject to recovery point objectives (RPO) and recovery time objectives (RTO) to stand up a secondary site.

- A deliberate attack (for example, either an act of war or a sophisticated criminal act) results in the physical destruction or impairment of facilities required for operations. In this type of situation, it is important to consider that attackers have likely targeted both primary and secondary sites. The most important considerations will likely be protecting confidentiality and integrity of data, even if that comes at the expense of availability.

High Availability, Disaster Recovery, and Physical Protection: Capabilities

High availability, disaster recovery, and physical protection capabilities center on making IT systems more robust, having the same data in multiple locations, and protecting the physical devices and storage containing enterprise data and systems. While this functional area primarily deals with availability, it considers data confidentiality and integrity as well. If an enterprise has made cyberattacks too difficult to be successful, physical attack may be the most attractive way to target an enterprise.

Following are some high availability, disaster recovery, and physical protection capabilities. Appendix C provides detailed descriptions for these capabilities.

- Clustering

- Load balancing, Global Server Load Balancing (GSLB)

- Network failover, subnet spanning

- Virtual machine snapshots and cloning

- Data mirroring and replication

- Backups and backup management

- Off-site storage

- Facilities protection

- Physical access controls

- Physical security monitoring

Incident Response

The incident response functional area is about responding to cybersecurity incidents. No matter how good or effective the rest of your defenses are, incidents will occur. The monitoring functional area is about having the capability to detect these incidents, but it does not address what happens once the incident has been detected. Transitioning from monitoring to incident response is a critical component of an enterprise's cyberdefense strategy.

While monitoring is continuous, incident response only occurs when monitoring has revealed that something of interest has actually occurred. Oftentimes, such an alert may not even be a certain indicator of malicious activity. Incident response consists of further alert analysis and investigation to understand what is occurring and its significance.

The incident response process is primarily procedural, with some technology supporting and facilitating it. Incident response does not protect the enterprise from attacks. Instead, incident response gives the enterprise the ability to respond to attacks. The incident response process is a multi-step process that consists of investigating, reporting, containing, and ultimately remediating the incident.

Incident Response: Goal and Objectives

Incident response's goal is to provide for timely response when security incidents are identified. Incident response includes: (1) operational disruptions, (2) security incidents, (3) deliberate attacks, (4) natural and man-made disasters, and (5) mistakes and accidents.

Incident response can be formal or informal, depending on the size of the enterprise. Incident response is more effective when the process is relatively formal. Before a crisis occurs, formal communication channels and lines of authority should be clearly defined. Processes for assessing the situation need to be defined so that the enterprise understands when a situation is "snowballing" and overwhelming the enterprise's initial response. It is also important for the enterprise to know the (1) limits of its crisis response capabilities, (2) points at which the enterprise is comfortable accepting disruption, and (3) potential losses of service due to exceptionally severe circumstances.

Incident response's overall objective is to understand what enterprise vulnerabilities deliberate attackers will attempt to exploit during the response. Attackers may try diversion or denial of service to cause confusion. Professional attackers know that an enterprise's reaction to operational problems may include disabling security capabilities to keep things running or as part of the troubleshooting process. Attackers may try to exploit those actions to penetrate defenses while the enterprise is distracted. To counter these attack strategies, layered security is an effective countermeasure. Even when the enterprise is operating in a degraded state, it is critical to have security reserve to protect the enterprise.

Incident Response: Threat Vectors

The incident response process is about the enterprise's response to threats against defenses and protections, rather than preventing those threats in the first place. However, there are some things an enterprise should worry about with regard to the incident response process itself. These threats can cause the incident response process to fail to be effective, not be as successful as it could be, or even make the situation worse.

Incident response threat vectors include the following:

- The enterprise does not have the incident response process coordinated ahead of time. This situation results in slow decision-making and response during an incident. To achieve incident containment, it is critical to be able to maneuver faster than the attacker. This maneuvering requires streamlined procedures, as well as clear decision-making authority and lines of responsibility.

- Poor coordination between operational and security staff. This situation results in operational staff not consulting security staff and inappropriately handling the incident.

- The enterprise's incident response process fails to coordinate with operational leadership before blocking networks or disabling computers or computers. This response is not well coordinated and causes operational failures. This situation causes organizational tension and potentially poor decision-making when trying to resolve the situation and restore operations.

- The enterprise's incident response process fails to feed indicators of compromise (IOCs) back to the monitoring and detection process. This situation causes defenders to believe falsely that they have containment.

- The incident remediation process fails to adequately strengthen defenses that were breached. This situation allows attackers to come back into the enterprise at a later date, repeating the same or similar attack over and over again.

- Deliberate attackers leverage the incident response process in their attack. For example, attackers force the enterprise into an incident response mode and then manipulate and disable security features.

- The incident remediation process fails to account for regulatory or legal requirements on reporting and disclosure. The result is the organization misses its regulatory requirements and potentially incurs financial, legal, or public relations penalties.

Incident Response: Capabilities

Incident response capabilities are about enabling the enterprise to respond to incidents effectively and efficiently. A lot of these capabilities are fundamentally procedural in nature. However, some technologies greatly assist with the forensic investigations that are needed to track down and catch stealthy attackers. In planning out an enterprise's incident response capabilities, it is useful to think "outside of the box" and consider how these capabilities can work for or against the enterprise in the event of advanced cyberattacks.

Following are some incident response capabilities. Appendix C provides detailed descriptions for these capabilities.

- Threat information
- Incident tracking
- Forensic tools
- Computer imaging
- Indicators of Compromise (IOC)
- Black hole server
- Regulatory/legal coordination

Asset Management and Supply Chain

Assessment management and supply chain involve tracking the assets in the enterprise, and understanding the supply chain from which those assets are obtained. This functional area is twofold in its intent: first, it involves being able to account for the IT assets in the enterprise throughout their life cycle, and second, it involves knowing where those assets come from and having an appropriate level of confidence that they are doing what they are supposed to be doing and nothing more or less. Supply chains have their own challenges and are a potential avenue for introducing vulnerabilities into the enterprise, either accidentally or deliberately.

Asset management is an essential prerequisite for endpoint and server security controls to be effective. Asset management helps to ensure enterprise assets (1) are accounted for during their life cycle, and (2) made compliant with enterprise policies when they are put into service (for example, comply with network security, endpoint security, and other enterprise policies). Asset management also helps to ensure enterprise data is properly disposed of or protected when assets are finally disposed of at the end of their useful lives.

An enterprise's risk management process should consider supply chain alongside other potential threat vectors. It may mean that some products are acceptable for use in some parts of the enterprise but not in other parts. It may mean that an enterprise applies other compensating controls so that it does not have to depend on a particular product to protect the enterprise. Having multiple sets of controls that interlock and compensate for each other is a good business practice.

Asset Management and Supply Chain: Goal and Objectives

Asset management and supply chain's goal is twofold: (1) ensure that the enterprise knows what IT assets it has, and (2) manage supply chain risks from acquisition through operation through disposal. Asset management and supply chain's overall objective is to ensure that operational staff follow proper procedures that are supported by various technical capabilities.

Asset Management and Supply Chain: Threat Vectors

Asset management and supply chain are about managing unknown threats to enterprise assets, what happens to those assets while they are in the enterprise, and where those assets came from and where they are going to when they leave the enterprise. This functional area protects against numerous unknown threats where some threats are obvious and some not so obvious.

Asset management and supply chain threat vectors include the following:

- The primary asset management threat has to do with the ability of an attacker to place components in the enterprise without those components being noticed. This threat can be physical devices that are connected to the network, or it can be software installed on enterprise computers.

- Another asset management function has to do with being able to detect unauthorized changes or reconfiguration of systems. Some of these capabilities may overlap with other functional areas, but it is often logical to have the overall supervision of change management centralized with the asset management department.

- Another threat to consider has to do with attackers compromising products through suppliers and then getting those compromised products into the enterprise. Such products may simply be of lower quality than expected, or they may be fully weaponized to attack the enterprise from within.

- Another threat that is not always as obvious has to do with attackers leveraging the supplier ecosystem to attack the enterprise. Frequently, suppliers are trusted with access to enterprise resources, but oftentimes their security protecting those resources is not as good as at the enterprise itself.

- Another threat to consider has to do with secure disposal. Just as "dumpster diving" can be used to obtain significant information about an enterprise, so can obtaining disposed electronics that have not been properly sanitized.

Asset Management and Supply Chain: Capabilities

Following are some asset management and supply chain capabilities. Appendix C provides detailed descriptions for these capabilities.

- Asset management databases

- Configuration Management Databases (CMDB)

- Change management databases

- Software inventory and license management

- Supplier certification processes

- Secure disposal, recycling, and data destruction

Policy, Audit, E-Discovery, and Training

This functional area deals with the governance of cybersecurity policy, audit, e-discovery, and training. This functional area groups together various security oversight functions, including mapping security controls to meet compliance requirements, along with some secondary functions regarding personnel security and privacy concerns.

- Policy sets the organizational strategy for all of the other functional areas.

- The audit function periodically reviews the other functional areas to ensure compliance with policy and effectiveness of preventive and detective controls.

- The CISO office oversees external reporting requirements (audit, e-discovery) and enterprise cybersecurity training.

- The CISO office oversees the audit program, which periodically reviews preventive, detective, and monitoring controls to verify their operation and effectiveness.

- The CISO interfaces with the legal department to support e-discovery measures as required by regulation, legislation, or litigation.

- This functional area oversees training for employees, IT, and security personnel to help ensure they are properly informed of their responsibilities and prepared to perform them on an ongoing basis.

This functional area is the home of the CISO executive, who would have authority and responsibility for the overall enterprise cybersecurity program. Generally, it makes sense for a single department to perform these functions, rather than having the functions spread across different departments.

Policy, Audit, E-Discovery, and Training: Goal and Objectives

Policy, audit, e-discovery, and training's goal is to address the people, policy, regulatory, and compliance aspects of enterprise cybersecurity. Policy, audit, e-discovery, and training's overall objective is twofold: (1) control of enterprise processes and capabilities, and (2) management of programmatic and personnel issues associated with process and capability deployment.

Policy, Audit, E-Discovery, and Training: Threat Vectors

This functional area is primarily about oversight, audit, and reporting, but it also has responsibility for the personnel aspects of security.

Policy, audit, e-discovery, and training threat vectors include the following:

- Gaps in security management that result in processes or capabilities being neglected, causing security risks

- Gaps in compliance management or reporting that result in external audit findings

- Gaps in personnel security that result in untrustworthy personnel in positions of enterprise trust (in other words, insider threats)

- Gaps in training and accountability that result in enterprise staff knowingly or unknowingly performing risky cybersecurity behaviors on a regular basis

Policy, Audit, E-Discovery, and Training: Capabilities

Following are some policy, audit, e-discovery and training capabilities. Appendix C provides detailed descriptions for these capabilities.

- Governance, Risk, and Compliance(GRC), with reporting
- Compliance and control frameworks (SOX, PCI, others)
- Audit frameworks
- Customer Certification and Accreditation (C&A)
- Policy and policy exception management
- Risk and threat management
- Privacy compliance
- E-Discovery tools
- Personnel security and background checks
- Security awareness and training

■ ■ ■

CHAPTER 4

Implementing Enterprise Cybersecurity

This chapter describes how to implement an enterprise cybersecurity program. It discusses how to:

- Organize personnel
- Integrate cybersecurity into the IT system life cycle
- Define security policies and scopes
- Select security controls and technologies
- Consider security effectiveness overall

The procedural and technological capabilities of the cybersecurity program deliver the security controls needed to mitigate risks, and can be organized into the 11 enterprise cybersecurity functional areas.

IT Organization

A first step in protecting an enterprise from cyberattacks is to organize people. Organization structure has a tremendous impact on what is easy or hard to accomplish, and where the functions and disjunctions exist in an organization. Based on IT management frameworks such as Information Technology Infrastructure Library (ITIL), there are three major IT functions that often report to the Chief Information Officer (CIO). There are also a number of security sub-functions that are generally organized within the cybersecurity department and report to the Chief Information Security Officer (CISO). Figure 4-1 depicts these functions and sub-functions (also known as teams or departments) in a notional organization chart.

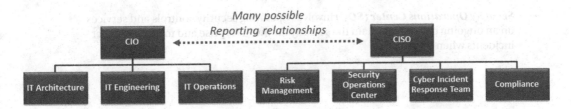

Figure 4-1. *This notional IT organization shows the major IT functions of architecture, engineering, and operations, alongside of the major cybersecurity functions of risk management, security operations center, cyber incident response team, and compliance.*

The exact reporting relationship between the CIO and the CISO is a complex question for which there is no one "correct" answer. In some organizations, the CIO and CISO are peers both reporting to senior leadership. In other organizations, the CISO reports to the CIO. In yet other organizations, the CIO reports to the CISO. In each of these reporting arrangements, there are tradeoffs with regard to how cybersecurity conflicts get escalated and at what level business decisions are made to accept cybersecurity risk or mitigate it in some way.

The *CIO* is the ultimate enterprise authority for IT, and they have authority over the other IT functions. Sometimes, one or more of the subordinate functions is in a separate organization. There may be multiple CIO levels where each CIO has some authority over an organizational component. Multiple CIOs often have dotted line relationships to an enterprise CIO with overall authority. Under the CIO are the following functions:

- *Architecture* is responsible for guiding the architecture and strategy of the IT organization. In smaller organizations, the CIO may perform this role itself; in larger ones, there may be an entire department dedicated to this role, which is often misunderstood or underutilized. The role of architecture is to coordinate the other departments to align the technology with the business through multi-year planning, high-level prioritization, and management of strategic vendor and technology relationships.

- *Engineering* is responsible for designing, deploying, maintaining, and retiring enterprise technologies. A key tenet of ITIL is a formal separation of engineering functions from operations functions in order to reduce costs and ensure accountability. This separation introduces its own challenges with regard to staff agility and career progression. Regardless of the actual organization structure, it is helpful to consider the functions of engineering and operation separately.

- *Operations* is responsible for operating IT technologies efficiently and cost-effectively according to formal service level agreements (SLAs). One of the challenges of separating operations from engineering is that it provides limited agility to "design solutions on the fly" or otherwise respond quickly to changing situations. On the other hand, this separation works well for managing operational costs, formalizing operational processes, and achieving high levels of system reliability and stability.

The *CISO*, like the CIO, is the ultimate authority for cybersecurity, and they have authority to direct cybersecurity policy and oversee compliance with that policy. The cybersecurity team, like the architecture team in IT, has a role throughout the IT system life cycle and has its own strategy, engineering, and operations activities. There are four major functions within the security organization:

- *Risk Management* includes (1) evaluating assets, vulnerabilities, threats, and risks; (2) defining policies to manage those risks; and (3) engaging with IT projects to identify and manage risks due to enterprise changes.

- *Security Operations Center (SOC)* involves operating security controls and services on an ongoing basis to maintain the security for the enterprise and to identify cyber incidents when they occur.

- **Cyber Incident Response Team (CIRT)** is responsible for responding to cybersecurity incidents and supervising their investigation and remediation. The CIRT function may employ outside experts for specialized skill sets and ramping up when an incident occurs and then ramping down when things are back to normal.

- **Compliance** is responsible for collecting security infrastructure and operations artifacts that provide evidence the security controls and policies are operating as intended. The compliance team is responsible for "mapping" the artifacts to external compliance requirements and regulatory standards to demonstrate enterprise compliance.

IT System Life Cycle

The IT system life cycle spans the stages systems go through over their lifetime. There are numerous frameworks for this life cycle; however, this section describes a notional life cycle that is adapted from ITIL. Figure 4-2 depicts the life cycle's seven stages, along with the IT departments responsible for the stages. The life cycle starts with the architect stage (also known as architecture) and then transitions to the design, deploy, operate, maintain, support, and retire stages. Note the engineering department's responsibilities span four stages (design, deployment, support, and retirement).

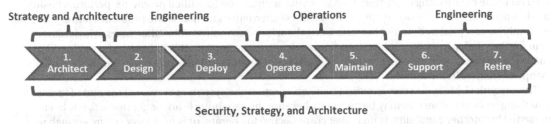

Figure 4-2. *IT system life cycle showing the seven major stages in the design, deployment, operation, and retirement of an IT system over its lifetime.*

The first IT life cycle stage is *architect*. The architecture department is responsible for (1) selecting preferred vendors and applicable technological standards, and (2) developing long-term technology roadmaps and high-level system architectures. Architecture engages the engineering department to ensure available technologies can work within the architectural guidelines with a high probability of success. As shown at the bottom of Figure 4-2, the strategy and architecture team stays engaged throughout the life cycle to monitor for significant architectural changes that might impact technology roadmaps.

The second IT life cycle stage is *design*. The engineering department is responsible for taking the defined system architecture and turning it into a functional system design. This stage involves (1) defining business and technical requirements; (2) working with vendors to get bids, evaluate proposals, and test technologies; and (3) determining the best balance of cost, schedule, and performance for the project. Engineering also works with the security department to identify security requirements and conduct risk analysis for the new system or service. It is critical that all necessary security features are included in the system design. The stage's end result is a "detailed design" document specifying what components are to be purchased, how they are to be configured, and how they are to be connected to the rest of the enterprise.

The third IT life cycle stage is *deploy*. The engineering department transforms the detailed design into a functioning system and then deploys the system into the enterprise IT environment. This stage involves (1) issuing purchase orders to procure components or services, (2) installing servers and software (if required), (3) configuring components and services, and (4) creating "as built" documentation, operating procedures, and manuals to get ready for operational use.

At the same time, security steps are performed to ensure system security configurations meet the specified requirements and the system or service is suitable for operation. This stage's last step is a formal transition to the operations department, which assumes responsibility for the maintenance and operation of the system or service. At this point in the life cycle, the engineering department transitions from a primary role to a supporting role.

The fourth IT life cycle stage is *operate*. Engineering staff is often involved at the beginning of this stage. Engineering supports the operations department to shake out procedures and ensure the system or service is performing as expected. Once the system is fully operational, the operations department is in charge and the engineering department is subsequently engaged through formally defined channels. During operations, the primary focus is on efficiency, meeting service level agreements, and managing and reducing operational costs over time. Operations collects extensive metrics to document the system or service operation, and it identifies opportunities for tuning and streamlining over time.

The fifth IT life cycle stage is *maintain*. The operations department keeps the system or service operating at a steady-state level on an ongoing basis. Operations can make minor system or service changes (also known as enhancements). Maintenance activities include patches, routine upgrades, hardware refreshes, and vendor service updates.

The sixth IT life cycle stage is *support*. Just because the system or service is operational, the engineering department is not completely off the responsibility hook. Beyond providing "warranty" service during the critical system stand-up stage, engineering is responsible for supporting the system or service on an ongoing basis. This engineering support involves a formal process, whereby "problems" are documented and then passed on to the engineering department. Engineering analyzes the identified problems, performs business analysis, and determines the best engineering/business alternatives to handle the problems. Some problems may simply be accepted or deferred because fixing them is not economical. In other cases, it is necessary to wait for the vendor to fix the problem in a future release. In these cases, it is important for engineering to manage the business decision and give the operations department guidance on how to handle potentially unhappy customers in the interim.

The seventh IT life cycle stage is *retire*. Engineering retires the system or service at the end of its useful life. Retiring a system or service may be necessary because the capability is no longer needed, has been superseded by another capability, is no longer cost-effective to operate, or is no longer secure enough to meet organizational standards. The decision to retire a system or service is made in consultation with all interested parties, including management, customers, architecture, operations and security. Retirement is a formal process where all components of the system or service are accounted for, and data and systems are archived and disposed of properly. Finally, enterprise records need to be updated so that the retired system or service is "off the books" and no longer supported.

Defining Security Policies

Security policies identify the assets to be protected and the protections afforded to those assets. Perhaps most importantly, security policies provide guidance on the consequences for noncompliance. Once security policies define what is to be protected, who is responsible for that protection, and what the consequences are for failures of that protection, then security standards can be written to provide guidance on how well the protection is to be performed. A sample enterprise cybersecurity policy organized using the 11 functional areas is contained in Appendix D.

Security standards provide specific guidance on protection levels and identify supporting technologies. In smaller organizations, it may be helpful to combine security policies and standards into a single document. In larger organizations, it may be helpful to separate policies from standards due to the administrative overhead involved in approving policy changes.

Once security policies and standards are defined, the next step is to specify guidelines and procedures for performing the security itself. Guidelines are used when subordinate organizations can set their own policy, standards or procedures. Guidelines leverage security expertise in the parent organization by assisting (in other words, guiding) security practitioners at subordinate organizations without impinging on their authority.

Security procedures define exactly how security is executed across the organization. Procedures are managed at the lowest organizational level (preferably at the level of the practitioners who follow the procedures) so senior IT leadership has confidence the procedures are actually being followed. Security leadership must periodically review and approve security procedures to ensure that practitioners adequately enforce the security policy and corresponding standards.

Defining Security Scopes

NIST SP 800-53 discusses the risk management process and SP 800-30 provides detailed guidance on performing risk management activities within the NIST Risk Management Framework (RMF). The six RMF steps are discussed in Chapter 2 and listed below:

1. Categorize Information Systems

2. Select Security Controls

3. Implement Security Controls

4. Assess Security Controls

5. Authorize Information Systems

6. Monitor Security Controls

The remainder of this chapter will focus on Step 1: *Categorize Information Systems*. NIST explains:

Conducting initial risk assessments brings together the available information on threat sources, threat events, vulnerabilities, and predisposing conditions—thus enabling organizations to use such information to categorize information and information systems based on known and potential threats to and vulnerabilities in organizational information systems and environments in which those systems operate. (NIST 800-30 rev 1)

While practitioners interpret this guidance as applying to a single server or computer system, it can be applied at a higher level of abstraction where a single set of analysis is applied to entire sets of computers and their networks. This book refers to such a grouping of systems and networks as a *security scope*. Figure 4-3 depicts the security scope concept.

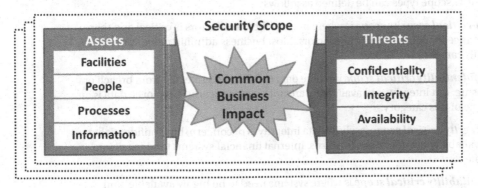

Figure 4-3. *A security scope groups together assets and controls around a shared business impact caused by a common set of threats against confidentiality, availability, or integrity.*

A security scope is a collection of IT systems, including computers and their associated networks, where the systems have similar risk profiles and share a common business impact due to a security incident. An IT organization defines a security scope by analyzing the security impact of a compromise or failure with regard to confidentiality, integrity, or availability, as well as examining the corresponding business impact. For example, a compromise of a corporate administrative system might result in a compromise of business data, while a compromise of a transaction processing system might result in a compromise of customer data. Since these compromises are fundamentally different and have different business impacts, these systems would be found in separate security scopes.

The Eight Types of Security Scopes

Security scopes are defined, in part, by the business impact due to a breach or failure. Business impact is the dominating factor when identifying security scopes. Figure 4-4 lists eight types of security scopes. The eight security scope types are distinguished by their posture with regard to the need for protection of confidentiality, integrity, or availability, or some combination of the three. Figure 4-4 shows these eight security scope types, based on priority of protecting confidentiality, integrity, or availability.

Security Scope Type	Confidentiality	Integrity	Availability
Non-Critical	Low/Med	Low/Med	Low/Med
Confidentiality Critical	High	Low/Med	Low/Med
Integrity Critical	Low/Med	High	Low/Med
Availability Critical	Low/Med	Low/Med	High
Confidentiality Non-Critical	Low/Med	High	High
Integrity Non-Critical	High	Low/Med	High
Availability Non-Critical	High	High	Low/Med
All Factors Critical	High	High	High

Figure 4-4. *The eight security scope types are identified by what security factors are critical. This prioritization ranges from scopes where no security factors are critical to scopes where all factors are critical.*

The eight security scope types can be defined as follows:

- A *non-critical security scope* is where none of the three factors is critical and there is tolerance for failures of all three factors. Most business administrative systems fall into this category.

- A *confidentiality critical scope* is where data needs to be protected from breach or disclosure, but integrity and availability are not major concerns. Employee data is an example of this category.

- An *integrity critical scope* is where data integrity is of concern, but confidentiality and availability are not major concerns. Internal financial systems tend to fall into this category.

- An *availability critical scope* is where systems need to be highly available, and confidentiality and integrity are not major concerns. Public-facing web sites tend to fall into this category.

- A *confidentiality non-critical scope* is where availability and integrity are critical, but confidentiality is not. An example of this scope is an enterprise directory that is used for authentication and access control.

- An *integrity non-critical scope* is where confidentiality and availability are critical, but integrity is not. This scope type is seldom used.

- An *availability non-critical scope* is where confidentiality and integrity are critical, but availability is not. An example of this scope is a customer account or application where data must be carefully protected, but temporary outages are acceptable.

- An *all-factors critical scope* is where confidentiality, integrity, and availability are all critical, and there is little tolerance for failures of any kind. Examples of this scope are online transaction processing systems (for example, amazon.com) and the security infrastructure that supports those systems. In particular, security infrastructure needs to operate at the highest security and availability levels because the scope enables other systems to operate at their desired levels of performance.

Considerations in Selecting Security Scopes

Selecting security scopes is an approximate process, and factors other than confidentiality, integrity, and availability factor into the process. Consider the following factors when identifying an enterprise's security scopes:

- Differing needs for confidentiality, integrity, and availability of systems and their data.

- The business impact of a failure or breach. This factor is an excellent way to analyze systems, as it can synthesize together numerous factors into a single comprehensive assessment.

- Distinct patterns with regard to vulnerabilities, threats that exploit those vulnerabilities, and the probabilities and impacts of exploitations.

- Production versus non-production environments. Note that non-production environments, if they host production data, may be subject to confidentiality requirements. Also, if non-production environments are part of an enterprise's high availability or disaster recovery strategy, the environments may also be subject to integrity and availability requirements.

Figure 4-5 provides NIST's graphical view of this analytical process.

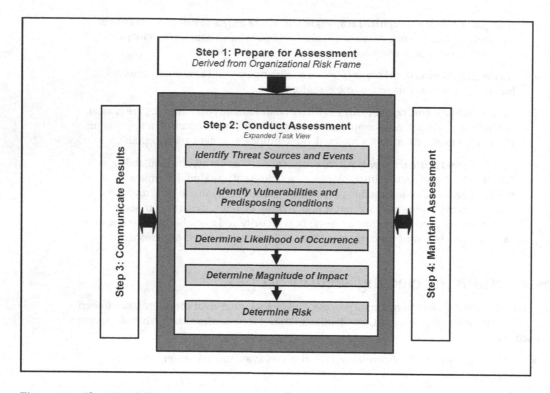

Figure 4-5. *The NIST risk assessment process as detailed in NIST SP 800-30 Revision 1.*

The NIST process considers most of these factors in its assessment process. One of the most important considerations when conducting this analysis is to keep the analytical process high level and not too detailed. An enterprise of 1,000 servers shouldn't have 1,000 security scopes; the enterprise should have about three to five scopes.

Identifying Security Scopes

Identifying security scopes establishes enterprise boundaries and compartments that are logical points for managing security. By using a security scope identification process and considering common business impacts due to security incidents, an enterprise is able to group IT systems into relatively few security scopes. As Figure 4-6 depicts, by simplifying things somewhat, the general process for selecting security scopes can be reduced to four steps: (1) business impact, (2) vulnerabilities/threats, (3) grouped assets, and (4) security scopes.

Figure 4-6. *Security scopes can be identified using a four-step process, starting with the business impact of a failure and working backward through the risk to group assets into a common security scope.*

This process provides an enterprise some simple statements of business impacts that characterize the consequences of a breach, compromise, or failure. These statements look something like the following examples:

- "If these systems fail, our business will be unable to generate revenue."

- "In the event of a breach, our customer data will be compromised and our entire business placed in jeopardy."

- "In the event of a failure, our business support operations will be disrupted, driving up costs and making us less efficient."

- "In the event of a failure, our security systems will be ineffective and unable to protect any of the rest of IT."

As the enterprise considers these statements, it intuitively identifies systems that have shared security postures and that are going to be commonly affected by a breach of confidentiality, integrity, or availability. Using this simple identification process, an enterprise also discerns how systems depend on each other, creating webs of interconnected systems that need to be treated similarly. Remember, this identification process is imperfect, so an enterprise should not expect the results to be clear-cut. The enterprise tries to identify the right scopes and keeps track of scope exceptions and gaps. As the enterprise designs the rest of the security program, the enterprise pays special attention to the identified exceptions and gaps.

Security Scopes for the Typical Enterprise

Figure 4-7 shows five typical security scopes that can be used as a starting point when using the above security scope identification process. Based on enterprise analyses, enterprises can add or remove security scopes as appropriate.

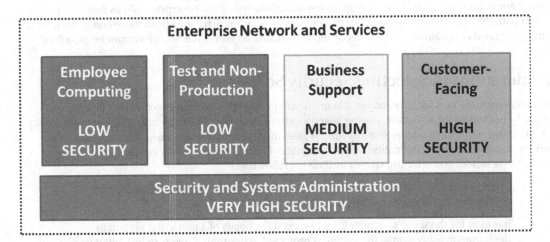

Figure 4-7. *Many enterprises will have approximately five security scopes to consider, covering their server, user, and security infrastructure environments.*

Security and systems administration is the first security scope to consider. In general, if an attacker gets control of an enterprise's authentication, network security, system management, or other security infrastructure, it is "game over" in terms of defending the enterprise. Because these systems are often shared across the entire enterprise and all systems (including customer-facing systems), this security scope needs to be secured to the same level as all security scopes depending on it, or higher. Multiple safeguards to protect against failures of confidentiality, integrity, or availability are recommended.

Business support is the next security scope to consider. This scope is interesting because it contains systems supporting the business operation that do not directly generate revenue, such as e-mail, collaboration, financial, or payroll. Consider the distinction between a credit card processing system and a payroll system. If the payroll system goes down, the enterprise cannot pay its employees. If the credit card processing system goes down, the enterprise cannot generate revenue. Both are critical systems, but the payroll system has a somewhat different business impact if it fails and, consequently, a slightly different risk profile. Therefore, these two systems may be in separate security scopes.

Customer-facing is the next security scope to consider. These systems are used to run the business and without these systems the business is unable to generate revenue. In an e-commerce business, these systems can be the majority of IT, while in a manual business there may be few or even none of these systems. Regardless, it is important to consider what IT systems result in an immediate loss of revenue and group them together into a scope, if practical.

Test and non-production is the next security scope to consider. These systems are the supporting systems that are critical in the long run, but non-critical in the short run. An enterprise looks at how these systems interact with production systems and weighs the benefits of simply putting them in the production scope with its more stringent security versus the benefits of having them in a lower-security environment. The enterprise also needs to watch out for the "gotchas" that occur when non-production systems are part of the path-to-production or when they are handling copies of production data.

Employee computing is another security scope to consider. If the enterprise allows its employees to surf the web from enterprise computers and receive e-mail from the Internet, then it is strongly recommended giving the employee computing its own security scope. The enterprise simply is not able to protect Internet-connected employees as well as the rest of the enterprise. Moreover, if the enterprise allows those employees to interact with the other security scopes (for example, systems administration) from these computers, then the enterprise needs to engineer protections carefully to ensure an employee breach cannot be exploited.

Considerations in Selecting Security Scopes

When an enterprise selects security scopes, it is important to find the number of scopes that is "just right"—not too many or too few. Having fewer security scopes simplifies an enterprise's security policy and engineering, while having more security scopes gives the enterprise more fine-grained control over its security policies and their application to different parts of the enterprise. Some general guidance on balancing these factors and selecting scopes include the following:

- Systems must be well matched with the policy of the security scope with regard to confidentiality, integrity, and availability protections.

- It is okay for the scope's security level to exceed the needs of a particular system in the scope (in other words, the system is protected better than it needs to be), but it is not acceptable for the system's needs to exceed the security of the scope.

- Security policies are applied to all computers in a security scope approximately equally. It does not make sense for half the computers in a scope to be exempted from the security policy. If half are exempted, then put them in a separate scope.

- It must be practical and acceptable to apply the security policy to all systems in the scope, and available technology must make it possible to implement that policy today.

- The operational trade-offs of the security policy must be acceptable to most of the computers in the scope.

- If there are a lot of operational requirements for greater agility, less configuration control, or lower cost operation and the security trade-offs are acceptable, consider segmenting those systems off into a separate security scope with a more relaxed policy.

- Interfaces between scopes become logical points for segmentation within the enterprise. These interfaces are both logical choke points for policy enforcement and also potential attack vectors.

Finally, understand that this process is imperfect. Enterprises have computer systems that bridge security scopes, and it is difficult to identify which scope such systems should reside in. Enterprises have situations where there are connections and dependencies among scopes. The enterprise needs to pay close attention to these connections/dependencies, as they are common vectors for threats propagating attacks across scopes. These connections/dependencies are where deliberate attacks gain footholds in less-secure scopes and then use those footholds to target the more-secure scopes. An enterprise's security architecture needs compensating controls to protect against these potential attack vectors and understand the attack sequence in order to detect and thwart the attacks before they succeed.

Selecting Security Controls

Once the enterprise has selected its security scopes, the next step is to identify the controls needed in those scopes. To do this, start by re-visiting enterprise assets and threats, and the attack sequence against those assets from the threats. Figure 4-8 shows the selected controls (that is, forensic, audit, detective, preventive) disrupting the attack sequence.

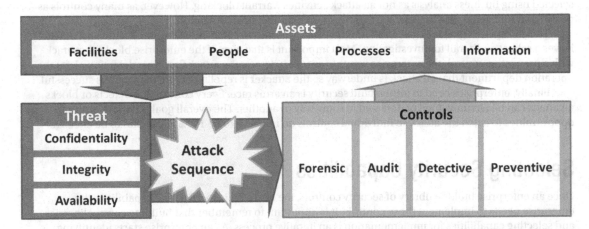

Figure 4-8. *Security controls (forensic, audit, detective, preventive) are selected to disrupt the attack sequence against confidentiality, integrity, or availability. The selected controls allow the enterprise to investigate, document, detect, and block attacks while they are in process.*

To select the best controls, the enterprise considers the following attack sequence:

1. Establish Foothold

2. Command and Control

3. Escalate Privileges

4. Move Laterally

5. Complete the Mission

A security control completes a sentence that goes something like this: "When an attacker ..., we respond by ..." Examples of security control statements are as follows:

- When an attacker sends a user a malicious e-mail message, we respond by intercepting that message and preventing it from getting to our users.

- When an attacker attempts to steal administrator credentials, we respond by thwarting the theft by requiring two-factor authentication.

- When an attacker installs malware on a server, we respond by blocking unauthorized software using whitelisting.

- When an attacker attempts to control compromised internal resources, we respond by intercepting and blocking the malicious command and control network traffic.

- When an attacker follows the attack sequence, we respond by having detective controls that detect attack patterns and alert us to their presence so that we can engage and defeat them.

Security controls are designed in sequence so that attacks leave a forensic trail, can be picked up by an audit, cause alerts that can be detected, and are blocked (where possible). The level of control protection is selected using business analysis as not all attack activities warrant blocking. However, as many controls as possible should generate a forensic log to be examined during an investigation.

The enterprise's goal is to give itself multiple opportunities to catch attackers and ensure any attack leaves a robust audit trail for investigation. Most important is that even if the enterprise blocks the attack with a preventive control, the enterprise wants to ensure it detects the attack first. This detection alerts the operation department that an attack is underway so the attacker is repelled before the attack is successful.

Finally, enterprises need to understand security is an arms race. Every control that detects or blocks an attack can be circumvented or defeated in some way or another. The overall goal is to have multiple opportunities to catch the attack so individual controls do not have to be 100% successful to be effective.

Selecting Security Capabilities

Once an enterprise builds a library of security controls, the next step is to select the capabilities the enterprise needs to implement those controls. It is important to remember that building control libraries and selecting capabilities for implementation is an iterative process. As an enterprise starts identifying capabilities, it will no doubt identify additional security controls related to those capabilities. Do not get bogged down trying to do a perfect job. The goal is to capture and record the high-level relationships among the most important components, without getting buried in minutia.

Figure 4-9 expands on Figure 4-8 to look at how the cybersecurity controls connect to the 11 enterprise cybersecurity functional areas. As the enterprise identifies the controls needed to disrupt the attack sequence, it should organize those controls and the capabilities that deliver them into the

11 functional areas so they can be managed and operated in a coherent manner. A key tenet of the enterprise cybersecurity architecture in this book is all functional areas are of approximately equal importance with regard to the controls and capabilities contained in them and their cybersecurity effectiveness. If an enterprise finds its control design results in one or more functional areas being largely ignored, then there are probably controls missing that should be considered so all 11 functional areas are equally represented.

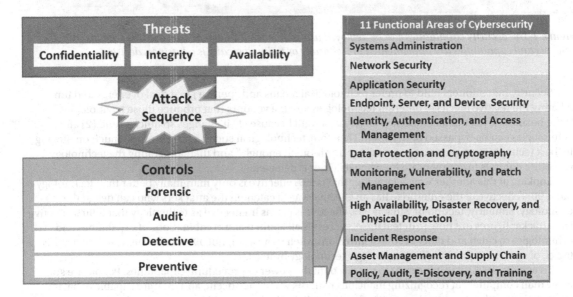

Figure 4-9. *Once controls have been selected, security capabilities from the 11 functional areas can be deployed to provide those controls. Note all 11 functional areas should be utilized to help ensure an effective and balanced overall security posture.*

As an enterprise evaluates capabilities, it examines those capabilities in terms of their deployment and operating costs, and the potential impact the capabilities have on enterprise IT operations and productivity. Some capabilities can support multiple controls. For example, anti-virus capabilities can block malicious software and also alert when malicious software has been detected. It can be beneficial to consider forensic, audit, and detective controls before simply deploying preventive controls, since detecting and investigating a targeted attack can just as important as disrupting it.

Also, remember that security controls can be achieved through technological means or through procedural means. In many cases, the cheapest way to achieve a security control on short notice is through a manual process that is consistently followed, not a sophisticated technology. Manual processes have their own issues and challenges, but they should not be discounted prematurely in favor of always trying to buy and deploy the latest and greatest technologies.

Selecting Security Technologies

Once an enterprise identifies the security capabilities that give it the controls it wants, the next step is to decide if the controls are achieved through procedural or technological means. If technological means are chosen, then the corresponding technologies need to be selected. Whether to use procedural or technological means to achieve security capabilities is a business decision.

Figure 4-10 shows security controls and capabilities can potentially be achieved by technological or procedural means.

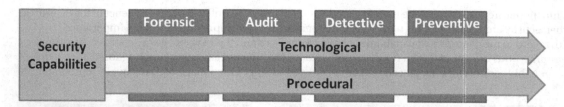

Figure 4-10. Security capabilities can be deployed using either technological or procedural means. Whether controls and capabilities are implemented procedurally or technologically is a business decision.

Security practitioners tend to prefer technological means and spend a great deal of energy and time debating the relative merits of different technologies and the vendors that produce those technologies. At the business level, the technology is largely irrelevant because (1) it changes so quickly, and (2) all technologies can be bypassed or defeated. Therefore, technological success hinges not so much on picking the best technology as on picking technology that is "good enough," and then integrating the technology with other controls to compensate for when it fails or is defeated.

Looking at this another way, technology that is 99% effective is only marginally better than technology that is 90% effective, if the enterprise has an effective way of catching the attackers who can defeat the technology. Similarly, technology that is 99% effective is just as ineffective as technology that is 90% effective if an attacker figures out how to defeat it. So, success is all about using combinations of capabilities and technologies to catch and defeat 100% of intrusions when they occur, not 90% or even 99%. Achieving this degree of success requires more than a single technology by itself.

To achieve 100%, it is important to not discount the power of procedural capabilities. People are still better than computers at recognizing malicious patterns when they occur, and they are capable of having conversations with other people to figure things out. Even the best machine-learning technology eventually relies on a person to look at the pattern and figure out if it is malicious or not. At small enough scales, it is far cheaper to have a person perform a manual review than to try to automate the review using a machine. Do not discount the power of people looking over things to provide detection, investigation, and response.

Considering Security Effectiveness

As an enterprise's security architecture comes together, it considers how effective security is going to be. To determine security effectiveness, the enterprise considers the overall attack domain and cyberattack threats against the enterprise security scopes. In the context of the attack domain, Figure 4-11 shows eight different classes of attacks.

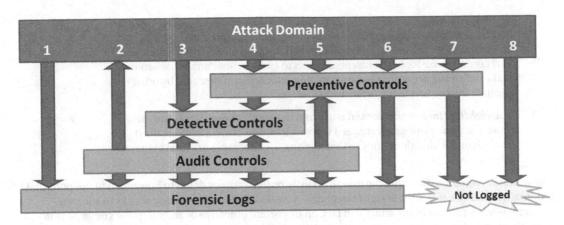

Figure 4-11. *Enterprise cybersecurity effectiveness can be evaluated by considering various attack scenarios.*

As illustrated by the following attack scenarios, an enterprise considers it security architecture effectiveness:

1. The ***first attack*** is not blocked by preventive controls or caught by detective controls, nor is it captured in security audits. However, it does leave a forensic trail that can be found during a careful investigation.

2. The ***second attack*** is not blocked by preventive controls or caught by detective controls. However, it is found during periodic security audits. Many insider attacks fall into this category.

3. The ***third attack*** is not blocked by preventive controls but generates alerts on detective controls. Defense against this attack relies on having a robust and timely incident response capability.

4. The ***fourth attack*** is blocked by preventive controls and alerts on detective controls, and it generates forensic logs picked up during audits. This attack is hitting the defenses at their strongest because they not only block the attack but also alert defenders to what is going on.

5. The ***fifth attack*** is blocked by preventive controls but does not alert on detective controls. It does, however, generate forensic logs used during audits that reveal when the attack occurred. These attacks are dangerous because attackers are blocked, but defenders are not alerted. This situation gives the attackers time to find ways around the preventive controls before audits reveal them.

6. The ***sixth attack*** is blocked by preventive controls and generates forensic logs, but it is not detected by detective controls nor is it picked up in security audits. Like the fifth attack, this attack type is dangerous because attackers eventually work around the preventive controls and are able to proceed without being detected.

7. The *seventh attack* is blocked by preventive controls and is otherwise not detected. Many attacks against Internet-facing firewalls fall into this category due to the sheer volume of logs generated off the firewall and the challenges in retaining those logs. An enterprise wants to ensure these attacks, when they make it past the preventive control, are then blocked and detected by other controls further inside the defensive perimeter.

8. The *eighth attack* is not blocked and is not detected. These attacks are the most dangerous since they succeed without leaving a trace. Defenses must be designed with redundancy so that this attack's success is not fatal to the enterprise.

These attack scenarios show that the overall security posture comes down to how much of the potential attack domain falls into each of these eight categories. A weak defense allows many attacks to succeed, while a good defense thwarts many attacks. In fact, an important objective of an enterprise's defense is to maximize the number of attack scenarios that are blocked, detected, audited, and logged while reducing the number of successful attack scenarios that are not stopped or detected. Figure 4-12 illustrates this security defensive objective.

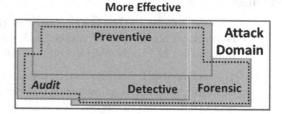

Figure 4-12. *Less effective security covers a smaller portion of the potential attack domain with preventive, detective, audit, and forensic controls, while more effective security covers the majority of the potential attack domain.*

An enterprise can use this risk analysis methodology to drive the control design process. An enterprise starts with the attacks that are of concern (focusing on the most likely and most dangerous attack scenarios) and identifies how it can catch those attacks. To catch the attacks, an enterprise starts with logging, auditing, and detection, and it ends with prevention so it can catch attacks even if it cannot block them. The enterprise creatively tries to envision attack scenarios where attackers defeat its preventive controls without being detected. Frequently, these scenarios fall into situations of insider attacks and credential abuse. Many enterprise defense architectures assume credentialed users on an internal network are legitimate users and not attackers. Experience has shown that these internal attacks on the enterprise are the most difficult types of attacks to detect, and the most difficult types of attacks to defeat.

■ ■ ■

CHAPTER 5

Operating Enterprise Cybersecurity

This chapter examines the enterprise cybersecurity operational processes. There are 17 major operational processes and 14 major information systems that support cybersecurity operations in the 11 functional areas of enterprise cybersecurity. This chapter explains how they all work together to operate an effective cybersecurity program. Additional detail on the operational processes and supporting information systems is in Appendix E.

If you do not monitor your cybersecurity systems and actively look for security incidents, you probably won't find many.

Organizationally, security does not have to be in charge of all cybersecurity operational processes and information systems, but it does need to have a role in ensuring they are present, operating properly, and satisfying enterprise security objectives. Enterprise security without security operations is unlikely to hold up long against a deliberate attacker, so security operations is critical to achieving successful enterprise cybersecurity.

Operational Responsibilities

Cybersecurity operations involves leveraging processes and technology to maintain the enterprise's security posture over time. Within the Information Technology Infrastructure Library (ITIL), the operations department is responsible for daily operations, but other departments provide necessary support. As shown in Figure 5-1, there are seven IT life cycle phases. Operations primarily entails life cycle phases four, five, and six; however, operations is consulted and coordinated within the other phases as well.

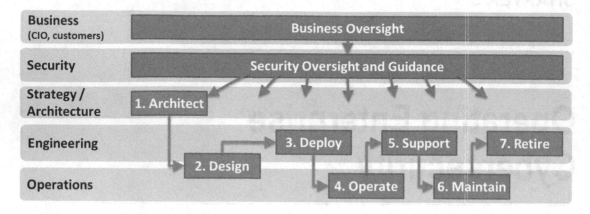

Figure 5-1. *All organizations have security responsibilities across the seven stages of the IT life cycle.*

Business (CIO, customers)

Figure 5-1 depicts the business leadership with the operational responsibility of providing business oversight with regard to cybersecurity operations. This responsibility involves adjudicating risk decisions and *security versus operations* trade-offs that involve tough calls on what level of risk is acceptable (in other words, best) for the business.

Security (Cybersecurity)

Cybersecurity, generally under the Chief Information Security Officer (CISO), is responsible for ensuring cybersecurity is operating within the enterprise. As such, cybersecurity has oversight responsibilities and provides guidance across all departments. For some security processes, cybersecurity initiates those processes, although such processes can be initiated from security operations instead. Most important is cybersecurity has the responsibility for ensuring security processes are in place and operating. Cybersecurity may either perform these processes itself or hold other teams responsible for them.

To support security operations and operational processes, the cybersecurity department often consists of teams to include the following:

- *Risk Management:* performs risk analysis and management

- *Security Operations Center (SOC):* provides for security monitoring and incident identification

- *CyberIntrusion Response Team (CIRT):* provides for incident response (CIRT may also stand for "Cybersecurity Incident Response Team")

- *Compliance:* performs reporting for external compliance requirements

These cybersecurity teams then work across the various IT functions to help ensure cybersecurity is properly considered throughout the IT life cycle. This collaboration includes the IT functions of strategy and architecture, engineering, and operations. Frequently, cybersecurity capabilities or functions reside in the IT teams, and then are "dotted line" accountable to the CISO office. An example of this situation might be IT architects who are expected to consider cybersecurity requirements in their architectures, or data center operators who are expected to comply with cybersecurity standards and operating policies in the course of performing their duties.

(IT) Strategy/Architecture

The strategy/architecture team is involved in a number of security operational processes to ensure system architectures are consistent with the enterprise strategy and overall architecture, including vendor and technology selections. From a strategy and architecture perspective, the team is also responsible for policy review and risk management.

(IT) Engineering

The engineering team has a significant role in security operational processes to design security capabilities and controls that are effective and cost-effective. The team ensures security is *baked in* to enterprise IT offerings before they are deployed. Engineering is consulted on cybersecurity policy and risk management activities to help ensure security solutions are practical and achievable.

(IT) Operations

The operations team has the overall responsibility for enterprise IT operations, including significant responsibility for security operational processes. However, it is important the cybersecurity department maintain oversight of the security operations performed by this team and ensure security is not compromised in the name of operational expediency. This separation of responsibilities ensures that when there is a conflict between cybersecurity operations and IT operations, the conflict gets escalated to the CIO level so it can be resolved as a business decision.

High-Level IT and Cybersecurity Processes

To maintain an effective cybersecurity posture, the CISO maintains a number of enterprise operational processes. This chapter describes four high-level IT and cybersecurity processes to set the context for introducing the more detailed 17 cybersecurity processes at the end of the chapter.

These four high-level IT and security processes are the following:

1. IT Operational Process

2. Risk Management Process

3. Vulnerability Management and Incident Response Process

4. Auditing and Deficiency Tracking Process

Appendix E contains a detailed description of the 17 cybersecurity operational processes that constitute a complete cybersecurity operational program.

IT Operational Process

Figure 5-2 depicts the IT operational process, which is the foundational process for IT. As shown, there are change drivers that influence the IT environment via business need, security, or strategy/architecture. The business needs drive the execution of two "loops" that operate and change the IT environment; namely, the *operations* and *engineering* loops.

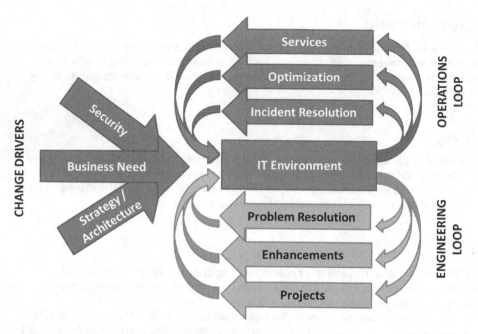

Figure 5-2. *The IT Operational Process is at the core of many IT functions, including many of the security functions supporting IT operations and engineering.*

The *operations* loop, shown in the top half of Figure 5-2, is led by the IT operations department, which manages the IT environment in accordance with service level agreements and other formal operational guidance. The operations loop involves three sub-functions that operate in parallel:

- *Services* involve delivering IT services, both on a continuous basis (for systems that are always operational) and on an as-requested basis (for services that must be requested). This function is most often associated with operations.

- *Optimization* involves performing relatively minor tasks and "tweaks" to improve the efficiency and effectiveness of IT operations. In an ITIL environment, there can be a fine line between optimization and engineering changes. Optimization usually involves changes that improve efficiency or performance without changing the service that is delivered, installing software, or adding or removing servers or computers.

- *Incident Resolution* involves solving problems with the IT environment where a deficiency occurs that must be resolved to restore normal operations. This incident may affect a single user (for example, someone whose account has issues), or it may affect an entire system or service. IT operations captures incidents and tracks them through to resolution.

In parallel with the IT operations loop is the *engineering* loop, which is centered on IT engineering activities to add or retire IT capabilities, as directed by the business leadership, cybersecurity, and strategy and architecture teams. The engineering loop involves three sub-functions that operate in parallel:

- **Problem Resolution** responds to IT infrastructure problems. IT operations identifies IT environment problems when a system does not perform as designed or flaws are identified in the design that require redesign or re-engineering to correct them. Problem resolution also addresses software bugs that impact operations and requires vendor support and correction.

- **Enhancements** are relatively minor changes to the IT environment to improve service quality, reduce cost, or enable new services. Enhancements are different from projects (see next bullet) because enhancements are generally performed within operations and maintenance budgets versus a dedicated budget or formal schedule. Enhancements are characterized as low-cost efforts that provide improvements without requiring significant resources or management oversight.

- **Projects** are major changes to the IT environment to deliver new services, retire legacy services, deploy new technologies, or make major upgrades to existing capabilities or services. Projects are distinct from enhancements because they have dedicated budgets, schedules, and management oversight to ensure they are accomplished successfully.

Risk Management Process

Risk management is one of the most fundamental processes of the cybersecurity effort. This process is a collaboration among cybersecurity and the other departments to identify risks to the business, the consequences of those risks, and appropriate mitigations to reduce the risks. Figure 5-3 depicts the risk management process.

Figure 5-3. *The Risk Management Process involves analyzing enterprise IT risks and determining appropriate responses to manage the risks.*

The risk management process starts with the IT environment and the business, and considers the IT environment assets with regard to risks to confidentiality, integrity, and availability. Cybersecurity, in concert with other departments, evaluates the identified risks with regard to their likelihood and level of impact and determines the overall risk level for a particular threat by combining likelihood and level of impact.

Once cybersecurity identifies the risks, it considers what to do about those risks. The first step is containment, where IT systems with similar risks are organized together into security scopes for subsequent protection. The second step is mitigation, where security controls are used to reduce either the likelihood or the impact of the risk occurring.

Vulnerability Management and Incident Response Process

This vulnerability management and incident response process is really two processes that operate side by side. There are some strong parallels between the two processes so it is advantageous to look at them together. Figure 5-4 depicts this high-level process.

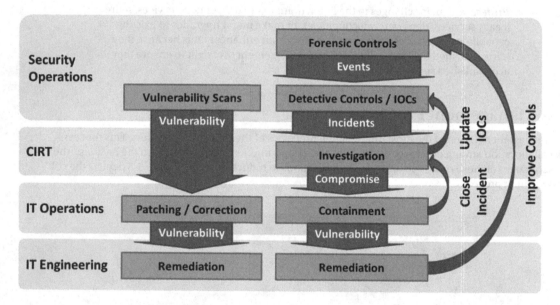

Figure 5-4. *The Vulnerability Management and Incident Response Process involves performing security operational tasks to find vulnerabilities and security incidents and remediate them in a timely fashion.*

The left-hand track in Figure 5-4 represents the vulnerability management process. This process is initiated by security operations although in some enterprises, it is initiated by IT operations. The security team ensures the vulnerability process is performed, and its quality and quantity are not compromised in the interest of other IT priorities. The vulnerability management process includes the following high-level steps:

1. ***Vulnerability Scans*** are performed by IT security against enterprise IT systems to identify vulnerabilities. Often, vulnerabilities are missing patches, but vulnerabilities can be configuration failures or other problems as well. Generally, this scanning is performed on as many IT systems as possible by using automated tools. Scanning priority should be given to production and public-facing systems that are connected to the Internet. The output of this process step is a list of enterprise IT vulnerabilities and remediation recommendations.

2.   ***Patching and Correction*** is performed by IT operations. This process step involves following guidance from the vulnerability scans to remediate as much vulnerability as possible. Sometimes compatibility issues, service level agreements, or other business considerations get in the way of timely fixes, or remediation involves non-trivial system changes. In these cases, IT operations passes such vulnerabilities to engineering.

3.   ***Remediation*** is performed by IT engineering when remediation requires redesign, re-engineering, or other engineering capabilities. IT security tracks vulnerabilities that require engineering actions until they are successfully mitigated, compensating controls are put in place, or the risk is handled by business leadership.

The right-hand track of Figure 5-4 represents the incident response process, which it is initiated by IT security. Incident response is passed on to IT operations and engineering until the situation can be resolved and remediated. Frequently, incidents identify vulnerabilities that need to be remediated—sometimes by patching and sometimes by re-engineering. The incident response process involves the following high-level steps:

1.   ***Forensic Controls*** log enterprise events and make them available for automated processing and review. These events are the starting point for the incident process since it is primarily from these events that incidents are identified.

2.   ***Detective Controls and Indicators of Compromise (IOCs)*** are applied to the forensic controls and logs to identify incidents from the events. There is no limit to the amount of sophistication involved in this identification (such as simple pattern matches, event cross-correlation, multi-variable analysis, and artificial intelligence). It is important to recognize the detective controls will have some measure of false positives (that is, where controls trigger incidents that are false alarms) and false negatives (in other words, where controls fail to trigger). The goal is to minimize both sets of negatives in a cost-efficient manner. The output of this process step is the incidents to be investigated.

3.   ***Investigation*** is performed by CIRT to determine the extent of the incident and to identify computers, accounts, and network addresses involved in the incident. This process step generates IOCs to feed back into the detective controls to identify more systems, accounts, and networks that are involved in the incident. The output of this process step is an assessment of the compromise and its impact on the enterprise.

4.   ***Containment*** is performed by the IT operations team to contain the incident and restrict it from spreading further. This process step involves denying the adversary the use of compromised machines, accounts, and networks so they can no longer operate in the enterprise and the actual cleanup process can begin. The outcome of this process step is vulnerabilities that were exploited by the attackers and need to be remediated to prevent the same attack from occurring again.

5.   ***Remediation*** is the final step in this process, and it is performed by IT engineering to harden the enterprise against future attacks. Depending on the extent of the incident and vulnerabilities revealed, the remediation can be quite significant. Remediation may involve strengthening preventive controls to make future attacks harder or improving forensic, detective, and audit controls to improve the detection, response, and remediation of future attacks should they occur. Remediation may result in cybersecurity projects that extend many months or years after the initial incident is resolved.

Auditing and Deficiency Tracking Process

The auditing and deficiency tracking process involves two tracks that run somewhat in parallel, one track in the security operations loop (a subset of the overall IT operations loop detailed in Figure 5-2) and one track in the engineering loop (also detailed in Figure 5-2). Figure 5-5 depicts this high-level process.

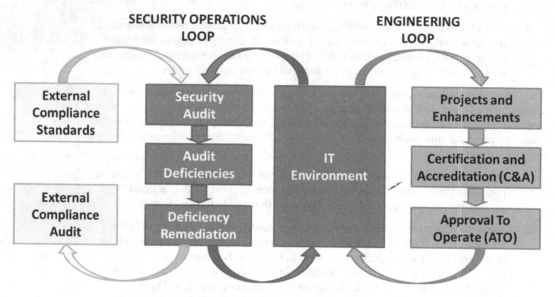

Figure 5-5. *The Auditing and Deficiency Tracking Process is used to conduct internal and external audits of IT operations as well as to perform formal security reviews of projects and enhancements.*

On the left side of Figure 5-5 is the security operations loop, which includes periodic audits of the IT environment to ensure security controls are present and operating as designed. These audits may be internally driven or externally driven. It is likely there may be multiple audits over the course of a year to satisfy different audit requirements, including general security maintenance. The audit process includes the following high-level steps:

1. ***External Compliance Standards*** are inputs to the audit for external compliance. Audits that are "internal-use-only" use either external standards and frameworks as guidance or internal documentation of the cybersecurity controls to be validated as guidance.

2. ***Security Audit*** is initiated by security operations to begin the process and examine the operation of cybersecurity controls. The audit is triggered by schedule (for example, regular monthly, quarterly, or annual audits) or by an event or external requirement. Regardless of the trigger, the audit examines cybersecurity controls to determine their effectiveness. For preventive controls, the audit involves testing to ensure behavior that is supposed to be blocked is actually blocked. For detective and forensic controls, the audit involves creating incidents to ensure incidents are detected or sampling logs to search for expected incident detections.

3. ***Audit Deficiencies*** are identified via the audit process and then formally tracked through to resolution. When identified by external auditors, deficiencies often require explanation or follow-on testing. Sometimes, identified deficiencies are not really defects or are the result of the control operating as designed, but not doing what the auditors expect.

4. ***Deficiency Remediation*** is the next process step to correct deficiencies so that controls function as designed. Sometimes audits reveal design deficiencies requiring engineering involvement or non-trivial investments to correct.

5. ***External Compliance Audit*** results are obtained from the audit process as required. With a well-designed control framework, it is possible to conduct a single internal cybersecurity audit that generates results satisfying multiple external compliance requirements, even when external audits use different control frameworks.

Operational Processes and Information Systems

The four operational processes described in the previous section present a high-level overview of some of the most important operational cycles involved in successful enterprise cybersecurity. Looking at cybersecurity operations in more detail, the authors have found that there are 17 operational processes and 14 supporting information systems that are necessary for effective cybersecurity operations. Appendix E provides a detailed description of these 17 processes and 14 supporting information systems.

Cybersecurity Operational Processes

To maintain an effective cybersecurity posture, the CISO should ensure the 17 operational processes described in this section are operating within their enterprise. These operational processes are above and beyond maintaining the various technologies and capabilities employed in protecting the enterprise. For example, if the enterprise deploys firewall technologies, operating those firewalls is an implied task and not considered to be an enterprise operational process.

The following 17 processes are considered essential to the proper operation of enterprise cybersecurity:

1. ***Policies and Policy Exception Management*** involves maintaining the cybersecurity policies and standards for the enterprise. It also involves tracking and managing exceptions to those policies and standards when they are required (in other words, for every rule, there is an exception).

2. ***Project and Change Security Reviews*** involve modifying the IT project and change processes to include security reviews and approvals prior to go-live. This process is tricky to get right so security is involved but does not become an obstacle to progress.

3. ***Risk Management*** involves identifying risks to the enterprise IT environment and its assets, and then identifying controls to mitigate those risks.

4. ***Control Management*** involves maintaining the enterprise security controls to ensure they stay relevant over time and effectively utilize available security technologies and capabilities.

5. ***Auditing and Deficiency Tracking*** involves auditing the IT environment to find cybersecurity controls' deficiencies and tracking those deficiencies until they can be resolved or remediated.

6. *Asset Inventory and Audits* involves inventorying enterprise IT assets to ensure IT properly accounts for all assets. This process is important from a security perspective because assets that are not tracked cannot be secured.

7. *Change Control* involves procedures to ensure enterprise changes are properly authorized and reviewed from a security perspective prior to implementation. This process results in formal approvals to operate new IT systems and tracking enterprise risks associated with vulnerabilities that are not remediated prior to deployment of operational systems. This process may also be able to detect unauthorized changes so they can be investigated.

8. *Configuration Management Database Recertification* involves periodically reviewing configuration documentation to identify discrepancies between enterprise records of system configurations and the actual configurations deployed and operating, and ensure those discrepancies are properly reviewed and remediated when they are identified.

9. *Supplier Reviews and Risk Assessments* involve reviewing the IT supply chain to assess cybersecurity risk from a supplier perspective and ensure mitigations are in place to protect against potentially compromised service providers or products.

10. *Cyberintrusion Response* involves responding to cyberintrusions when they occur and tracking them through to containment and ultimate remediation.

11. *All-Hazards Emergency Preparedness Exercises* involve testing emergency preparedness processes in the context of potential hazards, including natural disasters, man-made situations, accidents, and cyberincidents. This effort's goal is to have a robust set of emergency procedures that can be used to handle a variety of situations affecting enterprise information systems, facilities, or people.

12. *Vulnerability Scanning, Tracking, and Management* involves periodically scanning enterprise IT systems for vulnerabilities and then tracking those vulnerabilities until they are patched or otherwise remediated. Vulnerabilities that cannot be easily mitigated may result in enterprise risks that are tracked long-term.

13. *Patch Management and Deployment* involves patching enterprise systems to resolve security vulnerabilities, resolve operational problems, or stay current on vendor product patches. This process has two main tracks: one track for routine patch deployments and a second track for emergency patching to resolve urgent problems. The emergency patch process requires management oversight to adjudicate the risk of patching without adequate testing versus the security or operational risk of waiting for the normal process.

14. *Security Monitoring* involves monitoring security systems for alerts related to potential security incidents. These alerts feed into the incident response process when incidents are identified and confirmed. In this process, there is an important feedback loop where false alerts are identified and alerts are constantly tuned to minimize false alerts.

15. *Password and Key Management* involves managing enterprise keys throughout their life cycle, from creation through storage, rotation, recertification, and finally retirement. Organizational passwords, such as those used for service accounts and external cloud services, should be treated as keys and stored securely throughout their life cycle.

16. ***Account and Access Periodic Recertification*** involves managing accounts and accesses throughout their life cycles, from creation through assignment and removal of permissions, periodic recertification, and finally, retirement. Like with key management, it is important that recertification or a similar method be used to ensure accounts and accesses that are no longer needed are removed in a timely fashion.

17. ***Privileged Account Activity Audit*** involves manually auditing system administration activities for the most sensitive accounts. Not all administrative accounts need to be subject to this level of scrutiny, but accounts that have enterprisewide access and the ability to turn off or bypass security logging should be subject to audit and other controls to detect any attempt at misuse.

Supporting Information Systems

In addition to the 17 cybersecurity operational processes described in the previous section, there are 14 supporting information systems enabling the operational processes. These information systems may be simple or very sophisticated, depending on the needs of the enterprise and its level of complexity and maturity. At their simplest, these information systems may be spreadsheets or word processing documents, or even paper files in a file cabinet. In more sophisticated cases, they may be major enterprise applications with supporting databases and multiple interfaces. Exactly how they are maintained is not important as long as they are maintained somehow to support the enterprise cybersecurity effort.

The 14 cybersecurity supporting information systems are listed below. These information systems are described in greater detail in Appendix E:

- Enterprise Risks
- Security Policies
- Policy Exceptions
- Disaster Recovery Plan
- Approval to Operate (ATO) Records
- Security Controls
- Asset Database
- Configuration Management Database
- Incident Records
- Security Deficiencies
- Vulnerability Database
- Accounts and Permissions
- Password and Key Vault
- Administrator Audit Trail

Functional Area Operational Objectives

This section looks at the operational objectives of enterprise cybersecurity, grouped by functional area. Figure 5-6 illustrates how the enterprise cybersecurity functional areas, operational processes, and supporting information systems can all be unified to achieve successful enterprise cybersecurity operations. Each functional area's primary operational objective is to maintain its capabilities to deliver the enterprise's audit, forensic, detective, and preventive controls. In addition to this primary objective, most functional areas host one or more operational processes, and the operational processes are in turn supported by one or more of the supporting information systems. These operational relationships can be traced end-to-end.

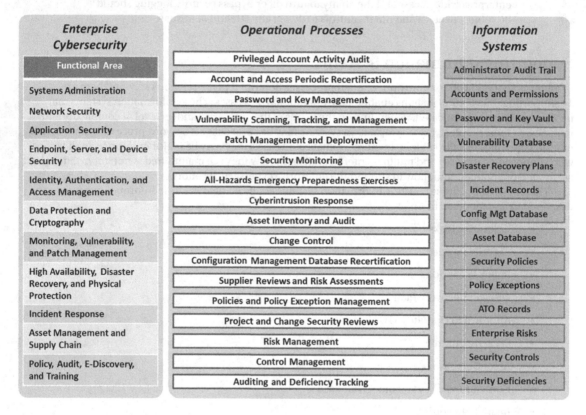

Figure 5-6. *The 11 functional areas, 17 operational processes, and 14 supporting information systems all work together to deliver enterprise cybersecurity.*

The remainder of this section describes the operational objectives for each of the 11 enterprise cybersecurity functional areas. Appendix E contains additional detail about the cybersecurity operational processes and supporting information systems.

Systems Administration

Systems administration's primary operational objective is to ensure that secure systems administration capabilities are operating to protect systems administration channels from exploitation by attackers who gain access to enterprise networks. This objective is achieved by using a combination of preventive, detective, forensic, and audit controls—all working together through automated and manual processes.

In addition to the primary operational objective, this functional area also hosts the following operational process:

- Privileged Account Activity Audit

It accesses the following supporting information systems:

- Administrator Audit Trail

- Incident Records

Network Security

Network security's primary operational objective is to prevent, detect, and document illicit activity targeting the enterprise. This objective is achieved by using a large number of capabilities to provide preventive, detective, forensic, and audit controls affecting communications among enterprise computers and the Internet. To accomplish this objective, network security needs to provide four main high-level capabilities:

1. A perimeter that connects the enterprise to the Internet while also protecting vulnerable systems inside the enterprise from external exploitation

2. Segmentation within the enterprise to protect business functions with different security needs from each other and to contain incidents

3. Inspection of external access to internal systems to identify unauthorized access or malicious network traffic

4. Support for incident investigation and response so incidents can be quickly analyzed, contained, and remediated when they occur

Operation of this functional area involves keeping all of these capabilities operational and delivering the required preventive, detective, forensic, and audit controls.

Application Security

Application security's primary operational objective is to prevent, detect, and document illicit activity in enterprise applications. Whereas the network security functional area is focused on network traffic in general, the application security functional area focuses on the capabilities, limitations, vulnerabilities, and security controls specific to particular enterprise applications, including e-mail, web servers, databases, and custom-built software. Operationally, this functional area involves operating these security controls so they can deliver the preventive, detective, forensic, and audit capabilities required to meet the enterprise cybersecurity posture.

Endpoint, Server, and Device Security

Endpoint, server, and device security's primary operational objective is to prevent, detect, and document attacks and compromises of enterprise computers and computing devices. This functional area focuses on the operating systems and software installed on these systems, hardening them so they are difficult to compromise, detecting compromises when they occur, and documenting compromises and security control activities so they can be investigated and audited after the fact. Operating this functional area involves keeping the capabilities supporting it operational and maintaining those capabilities according to vendor specifications and operational best practices. In this way, the enterprise is able to minimize the number of compromised endpoints, servers, and devices and rapidly detect and remediate the compromises that occur.

Identity, Authentication, and Access Management

Identity, authentication, and access management's primary operational objective is to manage identities and accesses within the enterprise throughout their life cycle. This objective involves tracking identities and accesses from their instantiation through to their retirement, and recertifying them on a regular basis so unused identities and accesses can be de-provisioned in a timely fashion. This functional area frequently uses automation (such as identity management technology and enterprise directories), but such automation is not necessarily mandatory for success, especially in smaller organizations. Successful operation of this functional area results in the enterprise having effective role-based access control and "least-privilege" provisioning with a minimum amount of unnecessary accounts and accesses lingering and posing a cybersecurity threat.

In addition to the primary operational objective, this functional area also hosts the following operational process:

- Account and Access Periodic Recertification

It accesses the following supporting information system:

- Accounts and Permissions

Data Protection and Cryptography

Data protection and cryptography's primary operational objective is to protect, detect, and document activities surrounding the data and keys of the enterprise. This functional area is data-focused and includes technologies such as digital rights management, digital watermarking, and pattern recognition to track data flows within the enterprise and what data is going where and how it is protected. This functional area includes cryptographic capabilities such as encryption, signature, authentication, key management, and password management (since passwords are also keys). Successful operation of this functional area results in effective use of data protection and cryptographic capabilities to protect enterprise data, detect misuse of that data, and document data and cryptographic activities for investigation and audit as required.

In addition to the primary operational objective, this functional area also hosts the following operational process:

- Password and Key Management

It accesses the following supporting information system:

- Password and Key Vault

Monitoring, Vulnerability, and Patch Management

Monitoring, vulnerability, and patch management's primary operational objective is to operate the enterprise security detective controls on an ongoing basis. Many of the major functions required to maintain and operate the security systems fall under this functional area. The major functions include maintaining enterprise information systems in a secure state (patch management), detecting and remediating vulnerabilities when they occur (vulnerability management), and monitoring the environment on an ongoing basis to detect and investigate security incidents when they occur (security monitoring).

Successful operation of this functional area results in the enterprise having effective monitoring and security maintenance on an ongoing basis that ensures its security posture and the ability to detect intrusions when they occur. This functional area includes scans for rogue computers and network connections, penetration tests if they are regularly scheduled, and advanced detection capabilities such as honeypots and honeynets. If the enterprise has a security operations center (SOC), its operation falls under this functional area.

In addition to the primary operational objective, this functional area also hosts the following operational processes:

- Vulnerability Scanning, Tracking, and Management

- Patch Management and Deployment

- Security Monitoring

It accesses the following supporting information systems:

- Vulnerability Database

- Incident Records

- Configuration Management Database

- Enterprise Risks

High Availability, Disaster Recovery, and Physical Protection

High availability, disaster recovery, and physical protection's primary operational objective is to be able to recover rapidly from operational disruption through redundancy, backups, and physical protection of data, equipment, personnel, and facilities. This functional area includes not only the IT technologies required to meet service level agreements, but also more dramatic capabilities required to recover from natural and man-made disasters. The operative term for this functional area is *resiliency* which makes the business resistant to all types of adversity and gives it tools and options when things go wrong and failures occur. The reason these capabilities are combined is that if they are designed in an integrated fashion, they can be leveraged to support each other through shared procedures, technologies, and common training. Disaster recovery capabilities are critical to robust incident response against advanced threats. It is important to remember the significance of physical protection in the overall security posture since physical access is an easy way not only to destroy information systems, but also to compromise them. Successful operation of this functional area results in the enterprise meeting its service-level agreements on an ongoing basis and also having robust capabilities to protect and recover from losses of data, systems, personnel, or facilities.

In addition to the primary operational objective, this functional area also hosts the following operational process:

- All-Hazards Emergency Preparedness Exercises

It accesses the following supporting information system:

- Disaster Recovery Plans

Incident Response

Incident response's primary operational objective is to prepare for and respond to security incidents when they occur. This functional area includes threat analysis to gain intelligence on what types of incidents should be detected and prepared for, as well as actually responding to the incidents themselves when they occur. Because it is difficult to staff a team against unknown incident volumes—and even small incidents can quickly overwhelm a fixed staff—it is important for this functional area to have methods for obtaining external assistance and "surge support" when it is required. Successful operation of this functional area results in security incidents being quickly identified, investigated, contained, and remediated within the enterprise environment.

In addition to the primary operational objective, this functional area also hosts the following operational process:

- Cyberintrusion Response

It accesses the following supporting information systems:

- Vulnerability Database
- Incident Records

Asset Management and Supply Chain

Asset management and supply chain's primary operational objective is to track the assets, configurations, technologies, and vendors used in the enterprise IT environment throughout the asset life cycle. This objective includes maintaining information to ensure the secure procurement of IT assets, track the assets throughout their life cycle, and ensure their secure destruction at the end of that life cycle. This functional area is responsible for a number of IT operational databases critical to not only enterprise security, but also to successful enterprise IT operations in general. Successful operation of this functional area results in the enterprise being able to track its vendors, technologies, assets, their configurations, and changes throughout their life cycle. This life cycle extends from selection through procurement, configuration, changes, and finally retirement and destruction.

In addition to the primary operational objective, this functional area also hosts the following operational processes:

- Asset Inventory and Audit
- Change Control
- Configuration Management Database Recertification
- Supplier Reviews and Risk Assessments

It accesses the following supporting information systems:

- Configuration Management Database
- Asset Database
- Enterprise Risks
- Security Controls

Policy, Audit, E-Discovery, and Training

Policy, audit, e-discovery, and training's primary operational objective is to operate the office of the CISO or director of cybersecurity and ensure the performance of the scheduled and unscheduled cybersecurity activities within the enterprise. This functional area includes risk management functions, development of security policy and architecture, performance of security screening and training for employees and contractors, reporting on security status and posture, audit of security functions, answering e-discovery requests, and external coordination and reporting on cybersecurity status, posture, and compliance. This functional area operates many of the administrative cybersecurity information systems that do not logically fit within one of the other functional areas, such as security awareness training, events, and activities.

Successful operation of this functional area results in the enterprise having a coherent cybersecurity policy, posture, messages and training, good coordination of the cybersecurity program across the other functional areas, and the cybersecurity program representing itself effectively to external auditors, evaluators, and regulatory bodies.

In addition to the primary operational objective, this functional area also hosts the following operational processes:

- Policies and Policy Exception Management

- Project and Change Security Reviews

- Risk Management

- Control Management

- Auditing and Deficiency Tracking

It accesses the following supporting information systems:

- Incident Records

- Security Policies

- Policy Exceptions

- Approval to Operate (ATO) Records

- Enterprise Risks

- Security Controls

- Security Deficiencies

CHAPTER 6

■ ■ ■

Enterprise Cybersecurity and the Cloud

Cloud is one of the major IT trends today, and it is transforming the way businesses everywhere approach building IT solutions. Rather than hiring technical staff to build data centers and configure servers, businesses are outsourcing these functions "to the cloud" and simply procuring applications, platforms, and computing capacity from mega-providers who operate them for hundreds or even thousands of other customers. Cloud enables new levels of business agility by giving a small startup access to computing and application capabilities that would have been described as "supercomputing" only a few years ago.

It is worth noting the transition to the cloud is not without its own sets of challenges. Cybersecurity practitioners still struggle to effectively secure on premise computers and servers. Having these systems "in the cloud" and outside of the corporate perimeter transforms cybersecurity protection from one of building high walls into something requiring more nuance and a new type of understanding. This chapter describes how an enterprise manages and operates cybersecurity when its computing and applications are in the cloud.

Introducing the Cloud

NIST provides an industry-recognized definition of the cloud in their special publication 800-145 and a discussion of challenges with cloud environments in their special publication 800-146. Figure 6-1 depicts a version of the NIST reference model.[1]

---

[1]National Institute of Standards and Technology Special Publication 800-145, Peter Mell and Timothy Grance, September 2011.

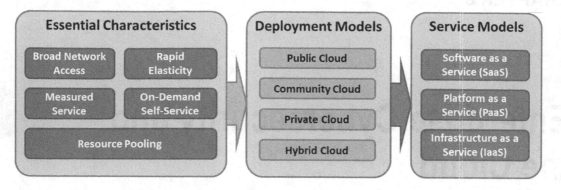

Figure 6-1. *The NIST reference architecture for cloud computing includes Software as a Service (SaaS), Platform as a Service (PaaS), and Infrastructure as a Service (IaaS) options that are delivered through public, community, private, or hybrid cloud deployment models.*

NIST defines cloud service by the presence of the five "essential characteristics":

1. ***Broad Network Access*** means services are delivered via a network—most often the Internet—and accessible from a wide range of network-connected devices, such as via a web browser.

2. ***Rapid Elasticity*** means resources and capacity can be increased or decreased quickly in response to changing demands, presenting what appears to be almost unlimited capacity to the end user.

3. ***Measured Service*** means all aspects of service delivery—including storage, bandwidth, computing capacity, and application activity—are measured for reporting and potential charge-back to both the provider and the customer.

4. ***On-Demand Self-Service*** means the customer of the cloud service can unilaterally provision capabilities and capacity without requiring significant human interaction or coordination.

5. ***Resource Pooling*** means all of these capabilities are delivered from a shared resource pool that supports multiple customers in a multi-tenant arrangement and with isolation among customers so individual customers only have visibility of the resources allocated to them.

NIST also defines four "deployment models" whereby service providers deploy cloud capabilities:

1. ***Public Cloud*** is a cloud solution provided by a service provider for the general public, with no restrictions on who may procure and use its services.

2. ***Community Cloud*** is a cloud solution provided for a restricted community of organizations, usually as a shared service or jointly contracted arrangement. A community cloud may be provided by a public cloud provider on its public infrastructure, but with certain restrictions on its configuration and authorized users.

3. *Private Cloud* is a cloud solution built and operated by a single organization for its exclusive use. The cloud infrastructure may be located on the organization's premises, or it may be provided by a third party via some sort of contractual arrangement.

4. *Hybrid Cloud* is a combination of two or more of the above arrangements, bound together using technology or standards so that they function as an integrated system.

The customer obtains cloud services from the service providers using one of three main "service models":

1. *Software as a Service (SaaS)* is the highest level of abstraction, where the entire software application—such as sales management, financial system, or database—is delivered to the customer over the network from the provider. The customer simply accesses the application using a web browser or other network client application.

2. *Platform as a Service (PaaS)* is a lower level of abstraction, where the service provider delivers the underlying computing platform and the customers have full control to install their own applications and data onto that platform.

3. *Infrastructure as a Service (IaaS)* is the lowest level of abstraction, where the cloud provider delivers the computing infrastructure—including storage, hardware, and network connectivity—and the customers have full freedom to install and configure whatever operating systems, application software, and data onto that infrastructure that they please.

Cloud Protection Challenges

Moving enterprise IT to the cloud may or may not improve cybersecurity compared to operating it in a private network and datacenter. In general, whether or not cybersecurity is improved by cloud computing depends on the enterprise size and security maturity versus the cloud provider size and security maturity. Cloud providers have the same challenges securing their systems that enterprises have. These challenges include: (1) shifting schedules and priorities, (2) resource constraints, and (3) finding and retaining talented security professionals. However, unlike their customer enterprises, cloud providers have the advantages of a consolidated, standardized infrastructure, the ability to "design once and replicate many" for security solutions, and simplicity due to standardized offerings and centralized management.

Figure 6-2 provides a summary of the high-level cybersecurity considerations based on customer enterprise size versus cloud provider size. Small cloud providers have many of the same strengths and challenges as small businesses. Likewise, large cloud providers have many of the same strengths and challenges as large businesses. However, large customer enterprises doing business with small cloud providers should be cautious, because the enterprise's cybersecurity may be better than the cloud providers' cybersecurity.

	Small Customer	*Large Customer*
Small Cloud Provider	When both organizations are small, security will likely be slightly better at the cloud provider than the customer, due to standardization across multiple customers and the provider's own motivation to protect its reputation and grow its business.	A small cloud provider likely will not be able to secure data as well as the customer can on its own. On the other hand, the cloud provider may be considerably cheaper and more flexible than customer's own services.
Large Cloud Provider	A small customer will most likely see a security increase with a large cloud provider, compared to the size and sophistication of the security controls they could build and maintain themselves.	Security is likely a toss-up between large cloud provider and a large customer. Both have the ability to secure data well. The provider has the advantage of scale and standardization, while the customer has the advantage of knowing which data is most critical and the motivation to protect it effectively.

Figure 6-2. *Security with cloud providers can generally be better than what the customers typically achieve on their own, except in the case of large customers using small cloud providers.*

When an enterprise decides to move to the cloud, there are a number of challenges that must be contended with, including: (1) developer operations and developer security operations, (2) scopes and account management, (3) authentication, (4) data protection and key management, (5) logging, monitoring, and investigations, (6) reliability and disaster recovery, (7) scale, and (8) contracts and agreements. These challenges apply to all cloud deployment models (public, community, private, and hybrid) and all types of cloud services (SaaS, PaaS, and IaaS).

Developer Operations (DevOps) and Developer Security Operations (DevSecOps)

One of the most interesting paradigm shifts that occurs when an enterprise embraces cloud services is the idea of DevOps and DevSecOps. Both of these terms refer to an agile, cloud-based environment where software developers need to be responsible for the lifecycle of their products from the development of the software through its path to production and ultimate operations. This paradigm shift turns the traditional enterprise IT paradigm on its side, and has the effect of dramatically increasing the speed and tempo of service updates and problem fixes. By using cloud computing, DevOps make server operating systems and system configurations "part of the code" and manages them in the same manner and with the same tools and procedures as the other software DevOps are maintaining.

In a DevOps environment, security becomes one more part of the software codebase, and changes to security configurations are coded into the scripts used to build the computing environment and configure the servers. In this type of environment, cybersecurity is achieved by modifying these scripts to include the security configurations and features that are desired. Cybersecurity staff champion security by meeting with the developers and reviewing system designs to ensure security is integrated as desired.

DevSecOps also means cybersecurity becomes more about code than it ever was before. Cybersecurity is integrated into systems in a cloud environment through: (1) scripts used to build the servers, (2) scripts used to configure the servers, (3) scripts used to install the applications, and (4) actual software code running on those applications. Cybersecurity team members may have to update their skillsets to understand how to script cybersecurity features and map traditional cybersecurity features into the system configuration scripts used for the cloud.

This paradigm shift also means cybersecurity team members may have to change their methods of incentivizing developers to comply with security policies. Since anyone with a cloud account can stand up a server, install an application, and start running code on the platform, cybersecurity may not be able to use traditional "gates" to review cybersecurity and enforce cybersecurity policies. Instead, the cybersecurity team may have to switch to a more passive method whereby they review cybersecurity after the fact and then provide feedback to developers and management on significant cybersecurity deficiencies. Rather than being a "gatekeeper," cybersecurity may need to be more of a "scorekeeper," giving cloud development teams feedback on their security in the form of "security scores" and "penalty flags" so business leaders can identify and consider cybersecurity concerns.

Scopes and Account Management

In a cloud environment, developers can access the cloud and create tens or hundreds of servers, platforms, or application instances quickly. If a developer's credentials are compromised, those same servers, platforms, or application instances can all be compromised or destroyed equally quickly. In a complex environment with hundreds of developers, thousands of servers, and multiple environments for sandbox, development, and production, questions of scope can become complicated rapidly. In response to this challenge, the enterprise should define a "blast radius" to ensure a single compromised developer account, or a single compromised server or endpoint, cannot result in disaster for the enterprise's cloud services.

The way the enterprise addresses this challenge is with a "network of trust" that organizes cloud accounts and services so a single compromise cannot bring down the entire enterprise. This approach provides the cloud equivalent of "watertight compartments" that contain compromises, breaches, and failures to provide the enterprise cloud environment with resiliency to resist incidents. These lines of compartmentalization may include:

- Isolation by business unit or development team

- Separation of sandbox, development, and production environments

- Separation of primary and alternate sites

- Isolation of high availability nodes.

By establishing scopes and ensuring that different people and different teams manage different scopes within the cloud, the enterprise can guard against a single breach or failure being disastrous.

Authentication

Authentication is a major challenge for customer enterprises using public cloud service providers. Since the service is often delivered over an open network, users and administrators *must* access the system and services through the network, and the only thing protecting their access is their authentication credentials. Consequently, the enterprise may be only one username and password away from the entire service being taken over by someone else, often with little protection or recourse. In fact, if someone takes over the enterprise's cloud service administrative account, it may even be impossible to prove the account was hijacked or prosecute the perpetrators. To protect against this possibility, the enterprise needs to put in place the strongest possible protection for administrative accounts, including network-based protections and multi-step or multi-factor authentication, if such protections are available.

Another authentication challenge is account life cycle and access management. Some cloud services offer federated authentication to enable users to use their enterprise credentials (username/password or even multi-factor authentication) to access the cloud service. Federated authentication can also allow the enterprise to manage permissions and access controls from within its enterprise directory, greatly simplifying the access management process, but adding risk in the event those enterprise credentials are compromised. Balanced solutions may involve using federation in conjunction with strong authentication to consolidate authentication and also increase its strength and resistance to attack.

Data Protection and Key Management

Data protection and key management is another major challenge. When using a cloud service data is residing on someone else's computer equipment in someone else's facility. The protection of the data is at the mercy of someone else's enterprise operational procedures and supply chain. It is possible to protect the data using encryption, but encryption must be carefully designed and deployed to be truly effective.

For encryption to be effective, the data must be encrypted when a possible attacker tries to access it, but decrypted when legitimate users need to access it. Enterprises need to have the encryption keys positioned so they are accessible only for legitimate users, and are not easily taken by attackers who compromise the cloud service or application. Positioning the encryption keys effectively is extremely tricky, because even small mistakes can negate the benefit of the encryption. When cloud providers talk about data being encrypted in their environment, they should be asked where the encryption keys are stored and how the keys are protected and made accessible. The cloud providers should be asked about key rotation plans, and the processes for key escrow and recovery in the event of contingencies or disasters. When the enterprise is the one holding the keys, administrators should take care to ensure the keys are properly protected, rotated and backed up within the enterprise's environment.

When analyzing cloud key management customers should ask the following questions:

- What cryptographic algorithms and key strengths does the provider support?

- Does the cloud provider have the ability to generate and store cryptographic keys for its customers?

- Does the cloud provider have the ability to use keys provided by the customer?

- What capabilities does the cloud provider have to rotate keys on an automatic or semi-automatic basis?

- What support does the cloud provider have for an enterprise re-key scenario?

Enterprises must design their key management strategy carefully. If the keys to encrypted data are lost, the data itself is as good as lost. Enterprises must design encryption solutions so the data is protected without being endangered. Balancing the risk of encrypted data loss with the risk of unencrypted data compromise is a significant challenge involving considerable specialized expertise and many difficult trade-offs.

Logging, Monitoring, and Investigations

Logging, monitoring, and investigations has to do with the ability of the enterprise to record, detect, and investigate cybersecurity incidents within their cloud services. Since cloud services host applications and data in someone else's IT environment, logging, detection, and incident investigation capabilities are determined by the cloud provider. This limitation is most significant with SaaS solutions, but it also exists to a lesser extent with PaaS and IaaS services. The potential lack of availability of logs sharply limits the enterprise's ability to create detective controls on its cloud services, and makes investigating incidents in those services difficult, if not impossible.

Incident detection and response start with logging of activity in the cloud environment so incidents can be detected. Enterprises should investigate to understand what logs are available and how those logs record activity. Some key attributes of cloud logs to consider include the following:

- Do logs record all activity in the cloud environment from the cloud provider's perspective?

- Are activities performed through application programming interfaces logged so that customers can match up calls made from their software with activities performed by the cloud provider?

- Do the logs differentiate activities that are performed programmatically through application interfaces from activities that are performed manually through consoles or web interfaces?

- Do the logs differentiate between activities performed on behalf of a server or application from activities performed on behalf of a person?

Frequently, good logging is an afterthought for cloud providers, and logging may be immature for the features the enterprise wants to use. Due to this potential limitation, an enterprise's cloud deployments may have to rely primarily on preventive controls for protection, and have limited recourse when those preventive controls are breached and incidents occur. Moreover, incidents originating with credential theft are extremely difficult to detect in the first place. Such incidents are more difficult to investigate when few logs are available. The enterprise should incorporate this fact into its risk assessment when adopting cloud services.

Reliability and Disaster Recovery

Reliability and disaster recovery are additional cloud service challenges to consider. On the one hand, cloud providers are highly motivated to provide the best possible service, and service outages can have dire consequences to their reputations and business. On the other hand, cloud services have complex, interconnected systems undergoing constant changes and upgrades, and are managed by a relatively small staff of people. Cloud service personnel are subject to the same challenges of human frailty and fallibility as any organization, and mistakes are bound to occur.

Cloud providers also have the IT challenges of a normal enterprise such as people changing roles, hardware failing, software patching and upgrading, and constant pressure to reduce costs and increase revenue. The difference for cloud providers is they manage these challenges on their schedule and not their customer's schedule. For example, an enterprise's cloud provider may have little to no awareness that their customer's quarterly close is coming up. Lacking this awareness, a cloud provider may upgrade its financial system hardware and create a major issue for the customer. In another example, a cloud provider may have little to no awareness that their customer's staff in Europe need systems to be fully available at midnight local time each week. Consequently, the best time for the cloud provider to perform system changes is in the middle of the day in North America. It is quite possible cloud providers could undergo risky changes at just the time when the customer needs systems to be the most highly available.

When a cloud provider does have an outage, customers may have limited recourse and there may be few penalties for the providers or compensation for the customers. Cloud provider contracts may provide little protection or remuneration in the event of service outages, and the customer's ability to negotiate such protections may be limited. Customers also need to think about what happens if the cloud service has an extended outage or the provider ceases doing business altogether. It is important for the enterprise to have solid contingency plans that protect against the full range of potential cloud provider failures, including disaster and default.

Scale and Reliability

Scale is a fundamental factor for cloud services, both on the part of the cloud service provider and on the part of the enterprise consuming the services. On the one hand, service consolidation into a cloud provider can be more efficient, just as a bus can transport people more efficiently than a car, and a train can transport people more efficiently than a bus. On the other hand, larger-scale systems are less agile than smaller-scale systems, which make it difficult to adjust the larger systems quickly in response to changing business circumstances. While a car can be started in seconds, starting up a bus can take minutes, and starting up a train can take hours.

Cloud providers deal with these scale challenges every day. Even when a cloud provider is significantly more efficient than a customer's legacy environment, it can still take the cloud provider longer to troubleshoot and repair simple problems, simply because they are solving them for tens, hundreds, or thousands of customers. Unplanned outages and failures that would result in only an hour of downtime for an enterprise on its own—hardly a business disaster—could result in ten times that much downtime for a cloud provider, simply because of the scale of the cloud provider's environment. In general, cloud providers are far more reliable and stable than on premise enterprise systems. However, when they fail they can fail spectacularly and businesses without considerable contingency capabilities may be dead in the water until the cloud provider restores its service. Compared to typical enterprises, cloud provider problems and failures are going to be much larger than they would be if the systems and services were for a single enterprise alone.

To contend with these challenges of scale and reliability, the enterprise must design its cloud architecture for resiliency at a fundamental level. Particularly when using IaaS and PaaS services, the enterprise should employ multiple providers at multiple locations, and design cloud-based applications to handle gracefully unexpected failures without losing transactions or data. Experts in cloud talk about the "Chaos Monkey" or "Chaos Gorilla" who randomly fail cloud components to ensure the overall service keeps operating smoothly. While designing for this level of resiliency drives up engineering and operating costs, the reputational value of reliability in the cloud can be priceless.

Contracts and Agreements

Contracts and agreements are challenges with regard to cloud services. By using cloud providers, the enterprise takes problems that are normally technical in nature—storage management, network configuration, application and operating system maintenance, high availability, and disaster recovery—and make them contractual in nature. What an enterprise gets with a cloud provider is no longer so much a function of what technology can deliver and engineers can deploy, as it is a matter of what is in the contract. Cloud providers write their contracts to provide their customers with the desired services while protecting themselves from liability to the greatest extent possible as allowed by the market and regulators.

Therefore, it is up to the enterprise to ensure its cloud service contracts provide the features and protections the enterprise needs to provide adequate protections against the many types of failures that can occur. The enterprise needs to perform risk assessments and consider contingency, insurance, and disaster recovery options to fill in the gaps between what the enterprise needs and what the cloud service providers provide. At the very least, the enterprise should consider the following questions:

- What happens if the cloud provider simply disappeared from the face of the earth tomorrow and we never heard from them again?

- Will the cloud provider have all of the enterprise's customer information, or all of its financials, or all of its billing?

- Will the enterprise be able to restore this data from backups to an operational system, or to another cloud service provider?

The enterprise needs to have some contingency plans without dependencies on the cloud providers. Cloud providers can fold up at any time, and an enterprise should be prepared in the event this situation happens to them.

Planning Enterprise Cybersecurity for the Cloud

Considering the cloud protection challenges discussed in the previous section, this section considers how an enterprise's cybersecurity program is affected by its use of cloud services. This section is organized by enterprise cybersecurity functional area.

Systems Administration

Secure systems administration may be severely impaired when using cloud services. Systems administrators frequently do their work using regular usernames and passwords, just like ordinary users. To compensate for this situation, here are some actions an enterprise can do to protect its cloud systems administration channels (if they are available from the cloud provider):

- Employ two-step or two-factor authentication for privileged accounts, if it is available. If these authentication capabilities are not available, change passwords frequently and review reports of failed logon attempts.

- Employ network protection where privileged accounts can only be used from certain IP addresses or address ranges, or via a virtual private network connection.

- Regularly audit privileged account activity logs for unusual patterns or malicious activity.

Network Security

With cloud providers, an enterprise's network security options are generally limited. Cloud providers often provide basic firewalling or load balancing for systems, but few additional network security services beyond the basics. The cloud provider has its own network security infrastructure that it uses for its own protection and detection. However, it is unusual for customers to get any visibility into the cloud provider's network security operations, or to be able to obtain provider events, alerts, or logs. These limitations may severely hamper an enterprise's ability to do investigations requiring analysis of network traffic or searching for specific patterns or signatures. Some key points for customers to consider include the following:

- For critical systems requiring network isolation, the lack of networking control, customization, and monitoring can make it challenging to use cloud services. Cloud service providers are seldom able to provide the type of custom network technologies and services required to achieve true isolation at the network layer.

- Cloud provider network security options with PaaS and IaaS services should be greater than with SaaS services because of the nature of how platforms and infrastructure are delivered as cloud services. In PaaS and IaaS scenarios, it should be possible for an enterprise to do some level of network security on the platform itself, including host-based firewalls, intrusion detection/prevention, and packet capture and signature detection (particularly in support of investigations). While using these features may consume considerable computing and storage resources, their availability may make cloud services acceptable for high-security needs.

- It may also be possible to do network-level access controls on hosts or through the service provider infrastructure (for example, restricting access to cloud services to only clients in certain countries). Such protections may not be documented in the cloud provider's documentation, but such protections may be possible if requested.

Application Security

With SaaS solutions, the application-level security configuration is up to the cloud provider configuring the applications to deliver the services. Because the cloud provider operates the application in a multi-tenant configuration, the provider will likely protect itself with some level of security, but the details of that application-level security will not be available to enterprise customers unless the cloud provider chooses to disclose them.

With PaaS and IaaS solutions, the customer has the ability to put in place whatever measures of application security they deem necessary, which can include extensive detection capabilities and secure software development methodology. Since the cloud provider has access to the customer's platform and storage, the customer should maintain tight control over the "path to production" so any unauthorized software changes in the cloud environment can be detected and investigated.

Another twist on application security in a cloud environment is that every aspect of system configuration can become a script managed by the developers (see DevOps). These scripts include network configuration, endpoint security, identity and authentication configuration, and so on. In this situation, an enterprise needs to consider how these aspects of its cloud cybersecurity are going to be managed under the umbrella of code management, code configuration controls, and the software path to production.

Endpoint, Server, and Device Security

With cloud services, this functional area is primarily about server security. With SaaS solutions, customers do not have control over how cloud providers configure and protect their servers. However, customers should use the contract negotiation phase to ask SaaS providers about their security capabilities and address any concerns.

With PaaS solutions, customers have more ability to configure server security. However, the available security options may still be limited. Customers should review what security options and capabilities are available, and consider the corresponding risks and attack vectors that are left open by the gaps in those capabilities.

With IaaS solutions, customer security options are almost unlimited with regard to hosts and operating systems. The major constraint is the servers reside on the Internet and may not be accessible from the customer's internal network and security services. The enterprise can compensate for this situation by connecting cloud systems to the enterprise network via a point-to-point, always-on, virtual private network. This connectivity will give these systems access to the enterprise's internal services, including security services, but must also be treated with care so that it does not become a backdoor into the internal network from a compromised cloud system.

Identity, Authentication, and Access Management

By their very nature, public cloud services are connected to the Internet and the protection of these services is primarily through the identity, authentication, and access management of the user accounts used to connect to them. Frequently, cloud services are procured by a single individual using a credit card to purchase them, and then authenticating to those services via a username and password. Enterprises frequently need more security than just a single individual or single-factor authentication. Multi-step or multi-factor authentication provides a dramatic increase in security, even if it is only used for privileged and administrative accounts. If the cloud provider supports federated authentication, then users can access the service using their enterprise credentials. Federated authentication dramatically simplifies the authentication and account management process, because accounts and accesses are managed inside of enterprise systems and subject to enterprise cybersecurity policies, but it can also add risk if those accounts are compromised.

Another significant security concern is identity life cycle and de-provisioning. When people leave the organization, who removes their accounts and permissions on cloud services? This removal can be a considerable identity management challenge, and is a major business driver for enterprises deploying identity and access management capabilities. In the absence of automation, the enterprise will have to rely on manual procedures. With manual procedures, periodic audits should be performed to clean up orphan accounts and excessive permissions.

Data Protection and Cryptography

Data protection is critical for cloud services, but it is incredibly difficult to "get it right." Enterprises must carefully review cloud provider cryptography standards, algorithms and key strengths to ensure encryption is not obsolete or inadequate. The review must then be updated annually to ensure the provider's cryptography and cryptographic settings remain up-to-date. Enterprises must pay close attention to key management and understand where encryption keys are stored, how they are protected, how they are accessed, and when they are rotated. Keys must be rotated on a periodic basis to protect against brute force attack, and this rotation must be carefully planned to avoid system outages related to cryptographic updates.

Some cloud providers have hardware security module (HSM) services for protecting cryptographic keys. Such capabilities can be extremely effective at ensuring physical protection of cryptographic keys and operations, but require significant expertise to deploy and maintain properly. Enterprises must ensure cryptographic keys are backed up as reliably as the data they protect so as to avoid a disaster recovery situation where the enterprise can recover the data but does not have the keys to decrypt it.

Another use of cryptography is digital signatures to protect data integrity. For some applications, the enterprise can use hashes and digital signatures to detect unauthorized changes to logs, transactions, or financial records. Digital signatures can protect the integrity of sensitive data effectively, although they cannot help with protecting the confidentiality of data that is private or should be protected from disclosure.

Monitoring, Vulnerability, and Patch Management

With cloud services, this functional area largely depends on whether it is a SaaS, PaaS, or IaaS solution, much like endpoint, server, and device security:

- With SaaS, monitoring, vulnerability, and patch management are entirely up to the cloud provider and should be transparent to the customer. Moreover, customers can expect to have few options in this area.

- With PaaS, customers have control over the applications running on the platform and have the ability and responsibility to monitor, scan, and patch the applications to maintain their security.

- With IaaS, customers have full control over the system at the operating system level and above, and have ability to monitor, scan, and patch the systems.

In all of these cases, customers need thorough logs of all activities against the cloud environment. These logs should include the user account, originating system, and whether the request is through a human-interface console or an application programming interface. Logs must provide a detailed audit trail of all activity on the cloud side, so those activities can be matched up with the corresponding activities on the customer side.

For monitoring, the cloud service provider may be able to feed some logs from their systems into their customers' systems for the sake of monitoring and incident response. In other cases, providers may make available application interfaces so that customers can connect to cloud service logs programmatically.

High Availability, Disaster Recovery, and Physical Protection

By the very nature of cloud computing, the physical location and protection of cloud resources is determined by the service provider and outside of the control of the customer. A customer may have the option to select cloud service provider facilities, if multiple facilities are available for use. In this functional area, there are several actions that the enterprise can perform do to protect itself:

- Most importantly, the customer MUST have a solid disaster recovery plan for the worst-case scenario of the cloud provider simply disappearing off the face of the earth and taking its infrastructure, software, applications, and data with it. While highly unlikely, this scenario is possible and the customer must take steps to ensure it does not prove fatal to the enterprise.

- This worst-case scenario plan must include (1) recovery point objectives (RPO) that state how recently data is backed up, and (2) recovery time objectives (RTO) that state how long it would take to stand up contingency operations.

- In addition to the worst-case recovery capability, the customer may also choose to implement high-availability solutions that span multiple cloud providers. While considerably more complex and expensive than simple backups and restores, high availability can handle contingency scenarios with minimal RPO and RTO constraints.

All of these actions are part of the customer designing its cloud solution so that *resiliency* is a central tenet. Since the cloud customer does not know the cloud provider's inner workings, the customer must assume that anything can go wrong at any time. Since the cloud customer does not know the cloud provider's business state, the customer must assume that anything can go wrong at any time. By adopting a resiliency mentality, an enterprise can ensure it is ready for any possibility and that none of the possibilities is fatal.

Incident Response

Even when using cloud services, there is still a need for an incident response capability. Monitoring and investigating cloud services for security incidents can be considerably more difficult than with a traditional network perimeter. The enterprise must ensure logs are recorded for all cloud service activities, regardless of whether they are performed manually or programmatically. The enterprise should design detection capabilities to cover the most expected attack scenarios against its cloud services. In particular, the enterprise should design detection capabilities to protect against stolen credentials and compromised servers.

The enterprise's security operations center (SOC) should have the ability to access cloud service logs for investigation and should practice common incident scenarios to ensure it has the data and investigation procedures that it needs. In addition, the enterprise should meet periodically with the cloud provider to discuss: (1) threat scenarios, (2) incidents the provider is seeing, and (3) protections that can be jointly put in place to defend against the threat scenarios.

Asset Management and Supply Chain

Fundamentally, cloud services transform a technology challenge—standing up and deploying storage, computing, operating systems and applications—into a supply chain challenge. The supply chain challenge involves the enterprise establishing a contract with a supplier so the supplier delivers a service and manages the assets involved in delivering that service. The enterprise needs to ensure the cloud service contract contains the cybersecurity needed to mitigate the enterprise's major risks. The contract frees up the enterprise's technical resources to focus on other important challenges in other functional areas.

The enterprise should treat the cloud service provider contract as a risk management exercise and consider the cybersecurity risks in terms of each of the 11 functional areas of enterprise cybersecurity. Enterprise functional area experts should ask the cloud suppliers what protections can be provided and consider how those protections fit into the enterprise's overall cybersecurity plan, including worst-case disaster recovery. The enterprise will need to perform a cost-benefit analysis on security tradeoffs. Such cost-benefit analyses include security tradeoffs involving increases in cloud provider costs, purchase of insurance or contingencies, or other investments in risk mitigation. When utilizing cloud services, the enterprise must also consider the potential costs associated with security breaches, loss of service, or necessity to change cloud providers on short notice.

Policy, Audit, E-Discovery, and Training

In the functional area of policy, audit, e-discovery, and training, the enterprise should consider the following key points when employing cloud services:

- When using cloud services subject to regulation or external standards, the enterprise must consider the cloud service with regard to those standards and consider the standards in the source selection process. There may be situations where one cloud service works better for one set of standards such as export control, while another cloud service works better for another set of standards such as healthcare. This situation can force the enterprise to make difficult trade-offs, or end up using multiple cloud providers for a single service, simply because of regulatory concerns.

- Cloud services may run afoul of other internal cybersecurity policies such as requirements for strong authentication, network protection, or use of encryption. In these cases, careful risk/benefit analyses should be performed. These analyses may result in a policy exception to allow the service despite the limitations, or the deployment of compensating preventive, detective, forensic, or audit controls.

- Just because a service is being provided by a cloud provider does not remove it from the enterprise's cybersecurity policies, procedures, or security capabilities. Procedures for audits, recertification, penetration testing, red-team exercises, and compliance reviews apply to cloud services just as they do for internally hosted IT capabilities. Enterprise cybersecurity leadership must ensure the policies requiring such activities include cloud services. Business leaders need to understand how to apply these policies to services sourced from cloud providers.

CHAPTER 7

■ ■ ■

Enterprise Cybersecurity for Mobile and BYOD

Mobile devices and bring-your-own-devices (BYODs) are major trends impacting how enterprises think about their own IT. Thanks to rapid developments in computing power and power consumption, a supercomputer from the 1970s can today fit into our pockets. With multi-processing, graphical user interface, and gigabytes of memory all at our fingertips, 24 hours a day, the face of IT is changing almost daily. These devices come in all shapes and sizes, including notebooks, tablets, sub-notebooks, "phablets," music players, and, of course, cellular phones.

This personal computing power arrives at the same time enterprises are moving their services onto the Internet and their computing into the cloud. Instead of working in a company office, connected to a company network using a company computer, employees can access the same data and capability from most any location by using the Internet from a network-connected device. At the same time, many people have one or more computing devices at home, and they also want to use those devices for work.

Put the impacts of these trends together and enterprises have little choice but to embrace the fact that their data is going to be accessed from mobile and personal computing devices. There are multiple drivers for this trend. Internet-savvy employees want to use the latest and greatest personal devices, which are often more capable than what an enterprise can economically maintain. Organizations want employees to be always connected and able to be productive at home and on the road. The costs of equipping employees with the "latest and greatest" technology rapidly become prohibitive, especially when most employees will gladly buy these devices themselves and the choices of what to buy are highly personal.

Given that mobile and BYOD are here to stay, it is important to figure out how to protect enterprise data in the face of this new reality. This chapter discusses the security challenges of mobile and BYOD, and how an enterprise cybersecurity program should manage the protection of these important devices.

Introducing Mobile and BYOD

NIST provides an excellent resource on security for mobile devices in their special publication 800-124,[1] and the Federal CIO Council has produced a helpful mobile security reference architecture that should also be examined.[2] For the most part, mobile and BYOD are just different types of endpoint computing devices that are not owned or managed by the enterprise.

---

[1]Murugiah Souppaya and Karen Scarfone, *National Institute of Standards and Technology Special Publication 800–124 Revision 1*, June 2013.
[2]*Mobile Security Reference Architecture, Version 1.0*, Federal CIO Council and Department of Homeland Security National Protection and Program Directorate Office of Cybersecurity and Communications Federal Network Resilience, May 23, 2013.

NIST defines a mobile device as having the following characteristics:

- A small form factor
- At least one wireless network interface
- Local built-in data storage
- An operating system that is "not a full-fledged desktop or laptop operating system"
- Applications available through multiple methods

In addition, mobile devices may have one or more of the following optional characteristics or features:

- Wireless personal area networking, such as Bluetooth
- Wireless interfaces for voice communications, such as cellular
- Global positioning system (GPS) for location
- One or more cameras or video recording devices
- Microphone or audio recording device
- Removable media storage capability
- The ability to act as removable media for another computing device
- Built-in abilities to synchronize local data with other devices, such as laptops, desktops, servers, or cloud services
- Biometrics or other strong authentication capabilities

NIST notes that mobile devices present the following concerns, from a cybersecurity perspective:

- Lack of physical security controls
- Use of untrusted mobile devices
- Use of untrusted networks
- Use of untrusted applications
- Interaction with other systems
- Use of untrusted content
- Use of location services

To address these concerns, the US Federal CIO Council created a detailed mobile security reference architecture that describes strategies for managing such protections in the federal computing environment. Figure 7-1 depicts the Federal CIO Council "mobile security reference architecture." The authors consider the components of the mobile device, the network that it uses to connect to the enterprise, enterprise mobile services that may manage and protect these mobile devices, and "internal" enterprise core services that may be accessed from these mobile devices.

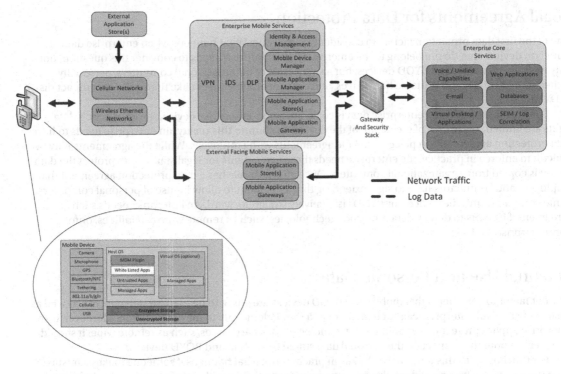

Figure 7-1. *The Federal CIO Council mobile security conceptual architecture shows the components of common mobile devices and how they might be managed by and interact with the enterprise IT systems.*

This architecture accounts for the challenges of mobile and BYOD security in great detail. If an enterprise already allows access to its resources from home computers, either through Internet-connected services, cloud services, or virtual private network (VPN), then the enterprise is already facing the challenges of having enterprise data on personal devices. Much of what people can do with mobile computing is exactly the same as what they can do with personal computers. The challenges of protecting enterprise data on these devices are just as great as if the devices were within the enterprise. Mobile computing only makes these challenges more poignant because the data is residing on devices that are going everywhere and getting dropped, stolen, misplaced, and misconnected from the enterprise more often than ever before.

Challenges with Mobile and BYOD

For the most part, mobile and BYOD are additional enterprise endpoints, which are not owned or managed by the organization. Enterprises need to plan for the protection of these devices as an integral part of their overall endpoint, server, and security functional area strategy.

There is no such thing as perfect endpoint security. All an enterprise can do is reduce the probability that any given endpoint, server, or device gets compromised, while increasing the probability that the enterprise will detect the compromised endpoint. Personally owned mobile and BYOD devices are no different than enterprise devices, except that the enterprise does not manage them, thus increasing the probability of such devices getting compromised. There are key factors to consider when an enterprise plans out its mobile and BYOD strategy.

Legal Agreements for Data Protection

One of the first data protection factors to consider is a legal one: What happens when enterprise data is stored on devices that do not belong to the enterprise? An enterprise needs to consider this question, not only in terms of mobile and BYOD devices, but also in terms of home personal computers, personally owned thumb drives, and portable hard drives, and even recordable media like floppy disks, compact disks, or DVDs.

For the most part, when enterprise data is copied to a non-enterprise device, the enterprise's data rights are limited, regardless of the nature of the device. To counter this reality, an enterprise needs to have data protection agreements in place to include agreements with employees. While the agreements may be difficult to enforce in practice, the enterprise needs these agreements for legal standing to protect the data after it is copied from organizational computers. Once an enterprise has a data protection agreement that employees and contractors have to sign, extending that agreement to allow for use of personal computers, home computers, mobile devices, or BYODs is relatively straightforward. An enterprise needs such an agreement if it wants to deploy data protection technologies, such as remote wipe capabilities, onto non-enterprise devices.

Personal Use and Personal Data

Another factor to consider is that mobile and BYOD devices are going to be used for personal use as well as business use, so an enterprise cannot treat them as if they belong only to the organization. Moreover, if an enterprise applies protection capabilities or technologies to these devices, such as remote wipe, it should consider the potential impact on the personal data stored on mobile and BOYD devices.

For the most part, this tends to work okay in practice, but what happens if someone makes a mistake? If a systems administrator accidentally wipes an organizational device, the organization is liable for the damage and ultimately bears the cost of it. On the other hand, what if that action accidentally deletes someone's personal information that is irreplaceable? What is the liability here? These are factors that need to be considered before accidents occur so that everyone's expectations are managed.

The Mobile Platform

A fundamental challenge with mobile is these devices do not run the common desktop operating systems. Consequently, an enterprise cannot use the same protection technologies, such as anti-virus, anti-malware, or intrusion detection, on mobile platforms. This distinction, however, is actually a double-edged sword that can improve security as much as it undermines it:

- *Strength*: Mobile operating systems are generally designed for the user to not have "root" access that would allow them to customize the operating system itself. This restriction actually makes these platforms more resistant to many types of attacks, although most platforms can be "jailbroken" either deliberately by the user or by malware that defeats this protection.

- *Challenge*: On the other hand, if the operating system privilege protection is defeated or if the user undermines it by "rooting" their phone, then there is not as much recourse to protect the device as there is with more mature desktop operating systems.

- *Strength*: With mobile, device vulnerabilities reflect badly on the carriers who sell these devices, so they are motivated to protect devices relatively well.

- *Challenge*: On the other hand, carriers "turn over" these devices at an exceedingly rapid rate and seldom provide patches or updates after the first year or so of release.

- *Strength*: Mobile devices use application stores that screen applications to ensure they adhere to a minimal level of security protection and non-malicious behavior. It is not as easy to accidentally install malware as it is on personal computers.

- *Challenge*: Application stores can lull users into a false sense of security. There are many documented cases of malware getting through and being downloaded by many thousands of users.

Put all of these factors together and mobile as a platform is fundamentally neither more nor less secure than the personal computers that we are all familiar with. It's just different.

Sensors and Location Awareness

A significant distinction between mobile devices and desktop computing is the multitude of sensors in most mobile smartphone devices. Light sensors, orientation sensors, fingerprint scanners, cameras, microphones, and, of course, GPS receivers give smartphones the ability to sense their environment wherever the devices are located. Moreover, it is not always easy to tell or control when these sensors are operating and what data they are collecting. Frequently, the sensors record and store data—particularly location data—whether individuals are explicitly using the sensors or not. All of this information is available to anyone who gets unauthorized device access.

From a security perspective, enterprises need to consider this unauthorized access possibility and the potential consequences, both to the safety of the enterprise data and the safety of enterprise employees. Because sensors might be active without individuals' knowledge, there might be some locations or facilities where enterprises simply do not want to allow these devices inside. Such devices might gain unintended access to proprietary information.

There may also be situations where an enterprise does not want its employees to carry these devices because of the possibility that sensor data may be recorded—either deliberately or accidentally. Such data may be used against the enterprise. While such sensors are extremely useful, protecting them from potential misuse is extremely difficult.

Always-On and Always-Connected

Unlike personal computers that are generally turned off or put into "sleep" mode when they are not used, or laptop computers that need to be connected to a wired or static wireless network, many mobile devices have cellular radios that enable them to connect from almost anywhere all the time. Because of this connectivity, consider them to be always-on and always-connected to the Internet, unless their radios have been explicitly turned off using "airplane mode" or a similar feature.

This connectivity poses some interesting security challenges. The robust mobile device sensor suite is able to transmit constantly what it sees and hears, as well as where it is to anyone who wants to know, without the device owner's knowledge or consent. So, a compromised mobile device becomes a rogue sensor that is always watching and listening and could be reporting to anyone, at any time. Since the mobile device is connecting through a public network, there is no way to compensate for this fact using network security capabilities or controls.

Multi-Factor Authentication

Another interesting challenge with regard to mobile in particular has to do with multi-factor authentication. There are two challenges here. First, many popular strong authentication technologies (for example, smart cards and USB tokens) are not directly compatible with many mobile devices. Second, there are a number of two-factor authentication technologies that use the mobile device as the second factor. What happens when the mobile device is both the endpoint and the authenticator?

For the first security challenge, multi-factor authentication strategies must be expanded to accommodate mobile endpoints. If the strong authentication strategy relies on smart cards or USB tokens, then it must consider alternative form factors, such as software certificates or one-time password (OTP) tokens that can be used with mobile devices and their smaller keyboards and screens.

For the second security challenge, an enterprise needs to consider how the mobile device, being both the security token and the endpoint, affects the overall multi-factor authentication. Frequently, if the mobile device is compromised, then the multi-factor authentication will be defeated as well. In some cases, this situation may be an acceptable risk. In other cases, an enterprise may be better off considering alternative forms of strong authentication or compensating in other ways, such as anomaly detection or adaptive authentication.

Mobile Device Management

Another mobile and BYOD security consideration is mobile device management (MDM) software. These software suites integrate with mobile devices to provide management and protection of the devices and enterprise data stored on them. Some of these suites are extremely powerful and include some or all of the following features:

- Device inventory and accounting

- Malware scanning and detection

- Encrypted storage of enterprise data residing on the device

- Protected "sandbox" for enterprise applications to run

- Secure application stores for enterprise-approved software

- Monitoring of device sensor use, including camera, microphone, and GPS

- Remote "wipe" capability if the device is lost or stolen

Looking at this MDM feature list, these are capabilities that an enterprise probably wants to have on all of its enterprise endpoints and computers, not just mobile devices or BYODs. Enterprises should strive to have these same protections for all of its endpoints—particularly the mobile ones—so that enterprise data is protected.

A key consideration is what happens if the enterprise deploys MDM to personally owned devices and its use or misuse results in personal data loss? The enterprise needs to balance the security choices and corresponding benefits. Also, the impacts to the enterprise and the employees need to be examined and understood. Some employees may not be willing to allow their personal devices to be managed in this way, regardless of the potential benefits.

Enterprise Cybersecurity for Mobile and BYOD

This section looks at the 11 enterprise cybersecurity functional areas, and considers how each functional area should be adapted to provide enterprise protection with mobile and BYOD endpoints.

Systems Administration

Ideally, most systems administration should be performed from enterprise-owned assets to fully protect and monitor those assets using endpoint protection capabilities. As a general rule, systems administrators should not performed their duties from mobile or BYOD devices. The potential benefits of allowing systems administrators, who are "on the go" or who need to be able to perform their duties at any time from any location, generally do not outweigh the security risks.

If an enterprise chooses to allow systems administration from unmanaged mobile or BYOD devices, it should consider that there is a greater possibility of these devices being compromised. If the devices are compromised, the potential negative consequences of systems administration from such compromised devices are significant. An enterprise can attempt to reduce these risks by leveraging other protection capabilities to include the following:

- Strong authentication for systems administrators using tokens that are separate from the mobile devices they use for administration

- Device recognition and fingerprinting for mobile and BYOD endpoints that are authorized for systems administration

- Virtual private networking (VPN) connections for systems administrator activities so that all traffic in and out of the device they are using can be monitored by the enterprise's network perimeter protection

- Increased logging and auditing of systems administrator activities to catch potential rogue or attacker activities

- Network-level anomaly detection to catch systems administration connections from unauthorized hosts or patterns and tools that are known to be malicious

Network Security

Mobile and BYOD devices generally get their connectivity from outside the enterprise. Consequently, these devices are not protected by the enterprise's network "perimeter" when they access the Internet. If the devices are compromised and are interacting with external command-and-control networks or botnets, the enterprise will not be able to see the traffic, nor detect that the devices have been compromised. With this scenario in mind, consider the following comments:

- An enterprise's network environment will be able to see traffic from mobile and BYOD devices when it comes in from the Internet. An enterprise will want to leverage this capability to watch for evidence of compromise, such as unusual connection patterns from unexpected locations or countries that indicate compromised credentials.

- For more privileged activities, an enterprise may want to force devices to create a VPN into its environment. This approach allows an enterprise to treat these devices as if they are on the inside of the network, and see all traffic in and out of them. Even though the devices are not enterprise computers, enterprise network defenses can monitor their network activity for malicious patterns and command-and-control traffic.

Application Security

Depending on specific use cases, an enterprise may be able to leverage application security capabilities to compensate further for the security challenges related to mobile and BYOD devices. For the most part, application security technologies that protect consumer-facing systems can apply just as well to enterprise users who are on mobile or BYOD devices.

Some of these techniques and capabilities can also be used on applications that would not normally be public-facing, such as e-mail or financial systems. These systems can be protected from potentially anomalous activities by enterprise users on mobile or BYOD devices. When an enterprise considers allowing enterprise users to access these applications from unmanaged and unprotected endpoints, the available application security capabilities may be able to reduce the security risk.

Endpoint, Server, and Device Security

This functional area is most impaired when users are on mobile or BYOD devices. With the exception of mobile device management (MDM) technologies, many enterprise tools are not applicable to personally owned computing devices. With that said, there are still some options that may be worth exploring:

- For mobile devices, MDM technology can provide outstanding protection of enterprise apps and data while still allowing personal use of the device. Enterprises need to make sure that any MDM technology used on personal devices is well understood in terms of the resources required and the consequences, particularly remote wipe.

- Enterprise endpoint security software, such as anti-virus, firewall, and intrusion detection, may be licensed for use on BYOD devices. Remote access systems can then enforce the presence of this software when machines connect to enterprise networks. While hardly perfect, this approach can reduce the probability of compromised or unprotected BYOD machines connecting to internal networks.

- Virtual desktops, thin clients, and "to-go" operating systems that boot from portable media are all ways of having users on mobile or BYOD devices connect to enterprise resources through mechanisms that provide secured, trusted endpoints. These capabilities can add considerable security, although they do so at the expense of a complex user experience.

- Don't underestimate the power of policy. Written policies should specify what activities and data can be performed on mobile or BYOD devices and what cannot. Policies should also specify endpoint activities like handling of removable media and encryption of data in transit and at rest. While these policies are hard to enforce, even limited adherence to them improves the security posture. Policies also provide a legal basis for punitive actions when negligent behavior occurs.

Identity, Authentication, and Access Management

This functional area's capabilities further compensate for the mobile and BYOD security challenges. Strong authentication, in particular, protects accounts from being compromised even when privileged credentials are used from compromised endpoints or mobile devices. However, it is important to remember that even strong authentication cannot protect against session hijacking attacks where attackers wait for the user to authenticate using their credentials and then send commands through that authenticated session. These attacks have already shown themselves to be very effective, particularly with applications such as electronic banking.

In this functional area, perhaps the most useful protection is logging and detection. When an enterprise logs authentications and activities, and then reports this information to the user after the fact, inappropriate logons and other activities can often be immediately recognized. Another effective protection is controlling accesses to minimize the potential consequences of compromised endpoints and compromised credentials.

Data Protection and Cryptography

This functional area has the most untapped potential with regard to securing personal computing devices used for enterprise purposes. In the future, secure elements on mobile and BYOD computers will store credit cards, payment information, and user identities in such a way that such information can be securely used over the Internet. Attackers will not be able to breach or compromise this securely stored information, even if they get control of the entire device.

Even though such a capability is still immature, it has tremendous potential for enterprise use of mobile and BYOD today. It is worth keeping an eye on this evolving technology. Today, enterprises can consider using the following capabilities:

- Using secure elements such as the trusted platform module (TPM) to store device certificates that authenticate "trusted" BYOD devices to enterprise resources.

- Using cryptographic tokens, such as smart cards or one-time password (OTP) generators to provide strong, multi-factor authentication, even from untrusted endpoints.

- Ensuring that all sessions are secured using secure sockets layer (SSL) and transport layer security (TLS) protocols to protect from snooping when using untrusted public networks such as cellular and Wi-Fi hotspots. Ensure that these protocol configurations are periodically reviewed to ensure that the cryptographic keys and protocols provide adequate security.

Monitoring, Vulnerability, and Patch Management

While an enterprise is not going to able to monitor mobile or BYOD endpoints for signs of attacks or intrusions, it can certainly monitor the enterprise infrastructure for signs of compromised mobile, BYOD, or even enterprise-managed endpoints. Such monitoring is *always* a good idea. Endpoints are going to be compromised no matter how well they are hardened and regardless of whether they are operating on protected enterprise networks or taken home and directly connected to the Internet.

With regard to mobile and BYOD, monitoring can take several forms:

- Systems that are Internet-facing, including VPN connections, should have monitoring in place that can detect unusual connection patterns, such as one set of credentials being used from different countries in a short period of time or large numbers of failed authentications or connection attempts.

- Internal networks should be able to detect and identify unmanaged computing devices connecting and, depending on the sensitivity of the network, send those devices to guest networks or otherwise isolate them from the most sensitive internal infrastructure.

- Guest networks, even though they may be isolated from corporate networks, should have the same level of intrusion and malware detection as any other network. The enterprise must make sure that when cybersecurity systems detect malware from guest, mobile, or BYOD devices, the corresponding response is fast enough to catch the devices before they leave the building.

High Availability, Disaster Recovery, and Physical Protection

Mobile and BYOD devices frequently have little to no physical protection. The potential loss and compromise of these devices is a reality that must be expected to occur. Because of this reality, mission-critical data and processing should never reside on such devices, at least not without strong contingency plans that can be activated when losses or disruptions occur.

An enterprise should consider the lack of mobile and BYOD physical protection alongside of the physical protection challenges it has with any type of personal computing device that is easily portable. Desktop computers are stolen from offices every now and then. Laptops are frequently lost or stolen. Personal computers and mobile devices are subject to the same situations. An enterprise should treat all of these possibilities as being on a continuum of physical protection challenges and use the same techniques and technologies to compensate for all of these potential loss scenarios.

Incident Response

When an enterprise introduces mobile and BYOD to its environment, it should be prepared for an increase in the number of incidents from lost or stolen devices, as well as potential data losses from unencrypted media and devices. An enterprise should update its incident response procedures to investigate potentially new anomalies stemming from mobile or BYOD access to corporate resources from internal networks or the Internet. An enterprise should have investigators consider the potential incident scenarios and make sure that the available monitoring and logs are adequate for them to perform effective investigations.

Perhaps most importantly, incident responders should be trained to understand where these devices are used and for what legitimate business purposes. Across the enterprise, *everyone* needs to be trained on enterprise policies for these devices to understand how they should and should not be using their vast storage and computing capabilities.

Asset Management and Supply Chain

Because mobile and BYOD devices are frequently personally owned, they are not going to be easily accounted for in normal enterprise asset management and supply chain processes. There are, however, several things that an enterprise can and should do to mitigate security risks in this area:

- Enterprise supplier managers should consider the mobile and BYOD device space, and identify if there are some suppliers that are unacceptable for certain purposes. This information needs to make its way into the appropriate policies and possibly be incorporated into and enforced by network and application controls.

- There may be some scenarios where personal devices are to be trusted for higher levels of access, such as systems administrators who will use mobile or BYOD for privileged systems administration. In these cases, such devices should be certified for use and tracked as if they were enterprise assets.

Policy, Audit, E-Discovery, and Training

With respect to mobile and BOYD, this function is probably the most important since it serves as the starting point for all other enterprise protection efforts, technical or otherwise. If an enterprise allows mobile and BYOD devices, then it needs to write a policy for these devices. This policy should include the following:

- What business activities and data are acceptable to be performed or handled from mobile or BYOD devices, without any limitations

- What business activities and data are acceptable to be performed or handled from mobile or BYOD devices, subject to limitations such as participation in MDM or installation of enterprise endpoint protection software

- What business activities and data are NOT acceptable to be performed or handled from mobile or BYOD devices, under any circumstances

- Policies for the protection of enterprise data stored on personal devices, at rest, in-transit, and on portable media such as thumb drives or recordable CDs or DVDs

- Guidance on the investigation of known or suspected breaches of the above mentioned policies

- Consequences for violation of these enterprise policies with regard to mobile, BYOD, and portable media

- Guidance on training related to these policies so that everyone understands his or her responsibilities and no one can "claim ignorance" when a violation occurs

These policies should apply to everyone who may be handling such data and using such devices, including temporary employees, vendors, and contractors. While training such personnel may not make sense, these policies can be incorporated into a "data protection agreement and end-user device policy" that they have to sign prior to beginning work.

PART III

The Art of Cyberdefense

CHAPTER 8

■ ■ ■

Building an Effective Defense

The cybersecurity architecture described in this book has been developed to be an excellent framework for running an enterprise cybersecurity program. However, a good framework alone is not going to stop cyberattackers who are targeting an enterprise and attempting to defeat its cyberdefenses. Well-organized cybersecurity capabilities are not going to protect an enterprise from advanced attacks by themselves. To be effective, those capabilities have to be applied in ways that disrupt, detect, delay, and defeat targeted cyberattacks.

This chapter describes the art of cyberdefense and explains how to apply enterprise cybersecurity capabilities to counter unknown, but anticipated, advanced attacks. To apply enterprise defenses effectively, an enterprise needs to understand the sequence of steps the attackers will take. At the same time, an enterprise needs to consider the practical challenges involved in deploying a program that is effective while also being cost-effective.

Attacks Are as Easy as 1, 2, 3!

The fact is, many enterprise cybersecurity attacks are ridiculously easy. Attackers compromise a single endpoint computer inside the target enterprise network. From that endpoint, attackers exploit one of a number of common vulnerabilities to gain administrative privileges over a large portion of the enterprise network. Attackers then use those administrative privileges to access, modify, or destroy whatever data they choose. As shown in Figure 8-1, attacks can be as easy as 1, 2, 3!

Figure 8-1. Frequently, cyberattacks are as easy as 1, 2, 3.

However, an enterprise cybersecurity goal is to make advanced attacks against the enterprise more challenging than 1, 2, 3. Effective controls deployed using the cybersecurity capabilities in the enterprise can make the attacker's job more difficult. To implement an effective cyberdefense, it is important to examine how attackers accomplish their goals and then design enterprise defenses that thwart cyberattacks.

The Enterprise Attack Sequence in Detail

For an enterprise cyberdefense to be effective, it has to protect against the attack sequence used for advanced and targeted attacks. In looking at this attack sequence, the enterprise needs to examine everything attackers might exploit as they penetrate the enterprise and seek their ultimate objective of removing, modifying, or destroying data or IT capabilities.

An enterprise conducts this examination by tracing the attack sequence backward and identifying the data attackers might want to steal, modify, or destroy. Then the enterprise thinks through the steps the attackers would have to take to accomplish their goals. To account for various attack scenarios, an enterprise considers the places where potentially targeted data replicates. Attackers might target enterprise data on servers, on endpoints, over the network, in backups, or on its customers' or business partners' systems. Generally, the data an enterprise is most concerned with doesn't reside on that many systems compared to the total size of its IT environment.

Figure 8-2 depicts a general five-step process many attackers use to penetrate an enterprise: (1) establishment of an initial foothold in the enterprise, (2) connectivity for command and control of that foothold, (3) escalation of privileges, (4) lateral movement to find the target, and (5) exploitation of the target data to exfiltrate, modify, or destroy data in the victim enterprise. Note this process does not deal with distributed denial of service attacks.

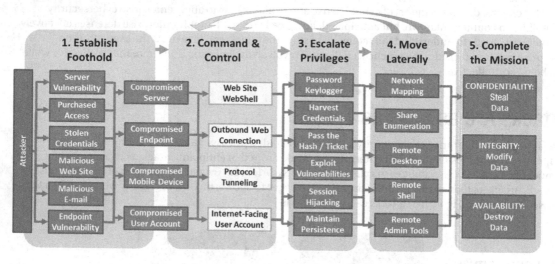

Figure 8-2. *The attack sequence, when examined in detail, reveals multiple paths that can be taken by attackers to accomplish their goals.*

Figure 8-2 delineates the attack sequence steps, details, and multiple approaches the attacker may take to get from the beginning to the end of the attack sequence. It is important to remember that these steps are not always executed exactly in sequence. Sometimes attackers escalate privileges before they establish command and control, or they move laterally before escalating privileges. Once the foothold is established, attackers go through multiple cycles of command and control, privilege escalation, and lateral movement between their initial foothold and the completion of their mission.

Attack Sequence Step 1: Establish Foothold

The first step in the attack sequence process is to establish a foothold in the victim enterprise. This foothold gives the attacker the ability to access resources belonging to the enterprise, whether those resources are in the enterprise computers, servers, or cloud-based systems. This foothold is often obtained by exploiting one of the following methods:

- A *server vulnerability* to gain control of an Internet-facing server. Generally, this server is a web server, but it may also be an e-mail server or other type of Internet-connected system belonging to the victim. Frequently, this exploit is due to a system misconfiguration where vulnerable services are left Internet-facing when they should have been firewalled off, or an application vulnerability due to a programming flaw or a missing patch.

- Attackers can *purchase access* to systems from botnet operators. There is a thriving black market in compromised machines, and attackers can purchase access to servers, endpoints, mobile devices and user accounts from multiple suppliers.

- Attackers can obtain *stolen credentials* for user accounts with remote access to enterprise systems, or with access to cloud services used by the enterprise.

- *Malicious web sites* can infect endpoints (or servers) that visit them, particularly if the victim machine is not properly patched or has other vulnerabilities. Sometimes this technique is used with popular web sites in a watering-hole attack; other times users are directed to sites via e-mail and other communications.

- *Malicious e-mail* messages may use a number of techniques to compromise victims. The most common techniques are executable malware attachments, malicious document attachments, and links to malicious web sites.

- *Endpoint vulnerabilities* can be exploited when one endpoint on a network is compromised and then exploits vulnerabilities or compromised network credentials to infect other endpoints on the same network. This technique is common on home networks and improperly configured public Wi-Fi networks.

Once the exploit has been invoked, attackers gain their initial foothold into the victim enterprise. This foothold generally consists of one of the following:

1. A *compromised server* where the attacker has control of the server or its application software and the ability to invoke commands against them.

2. A *compromised endpoint* where the attacker has control of an endpoint computer or device inside the victim network.

3. A *compromised mobile device* that connects to the victim network or handles data from the victim enterprise.

4. A *compromised user account* belonging to a user in the enterprise. This account then permits accessing Internet-accessible resources, such as web mail, employee portals, or virtual private networking.

From the foothold, the attacker then moves on to the next attack sequence step—command and control.

Attack Sequence Step 2: Command and Control

One the attacker has a foothold in the enterprise, the attacker maintains the foothold and the ability to execute commands in the target environment using command and control. The attacker may escalate privileges or move laterally before establishing command and control. It is important to note that attack sequence steps 2, 3, and 4 do not always occur exactly in sequence.

Generally, the attacker establishes command and control connectivity sooner rather than later so the attacker can manually control the activities within the victim systems. The main command and control methods include the following:

1. A ***web site webshell*** is a web page attached to an existing web site that allows attackers to execute commands on the web server. Because webshells are often buried inside of large and complex web sites, webshells can be notoriously difficult to find if their installation is not detected.

2. ***Outbound web connections***, otherwise known as "surfing the web," enables malware on compromised endpoints or servers to communicate with command and control servers outside the enterprise, request commands, and report back results. Frequently, these connections are encrypted using SSL or TLS so that they cannot be scanned, making them even more difficult to detect.

3. ***Protocol tunneling*** involves encoding command and control traffic inside of other protocols that are frequently allowed across firewalls, using extra fields or data payload space to encode commands and the results of those commands. Almost any protocol can be used for tunneling; common ones are Domain Name Service (DNS), Internet Control Message Protocol (ICMP) and e-mail's Simple Mail Transport Protocol (SMTP).

4. ***Internet-facing user accounts*** can be used for controlling web services that are Internet-facing. This technique is most commonly used for command and control of cloud services and web-based systems such as e-mail or Internet banking.

Once the attacker has command and control, the attacker can execute commands in the victim enterprise and install and operate additional malware and tools beyond those used to establish the initial foothold. The next attack sequence step is to obtain additional privileges and move laterally to get access to the desired target inside the enterprise and its systems.

Attack Sequence Step 3: Escalate Privileges

Once the attacker has command and control from the initial foothold, the attacker generally then needs to escalate his or her enterprise privileges to take control of additional servers and endpoints closer to the attack goal. In a modern enterprise with networked accounts, this technique can involve gaining control of system administration accounts that have permissions to log on to large numbers of machines in the enterprise. Frequently, these accounts include endpoint administrator, domain administrator, or enterprise administrator accounts. When these accounts are protected using username / password authentication, finding the accounts and getting control of them is generally a straightforward process. Common techniques for escalating attacker privileges include the following:

1. Using a *password keylogger* to capture the passwords of users and administrators when they log on from compromised machines. On compromised servers, this technique is particularly effective at capturing credentials of systems administrators who log on to these machines on a frequent basis.

2. *Harvest credentials* from applications, memory, and the hard drive on compromised machines. Modern operating systems provide for credential caching so that users do not have to type in their passwords every time they log on. This feature stores the credentials—frequently the username and an encoded hash of the password —where they can be extracted by malware. Also, servers such as e-mail servers can be modified to record the logon credentials of everyone who logs on to the server, rapidly capturing hundreds, thousands, or even millions of sets of usernames and passwords.

3. *Pass the hash or ticket* can be used with some network protocols to use credential hashes or authentication tickets over the network, even if the attacker does not have the original password or certificate used to initially authenticate. This attack method is particularly insidious because it allows attackers to defeat multi-factor authentication for network connections effectively. This method frequently gives attackers the same capabilities as if they had the full user account credentials.

4. *Exploit vulnerabilities* in the operating system or application software of computers to gain administrative control of those computers when they originally only had unprivileged access. This attack method is particularly dangerous inside the network because internal computers are seldom firewalled off from one another. Also, the numbers of potentially vulnerable services that are exposed from one internal computer to another are significantly greater than they are from outside the network.

5. Use *session hijacking* to take advantage of legitimate administrative sessions for malicious purposes, leveraging the user's authentication method to connect to the remote systems. This privilege escalation method is significant because it can be used to defeat multi-step and multi-factor authentication that are resistant to credential theft or password cracking.

6. *Maintain persistence* across server or endpoint reboots by migrating malware from the running session and embedding it into the operating system, hard drive, or device firmware. By doing this, the malware will be re-launched every time the computer restarts, making its presence in the victim enterprise persistent until it is found and removed.

The attacker generally goes through several cycles of privilege escalation and lateral movement by jumping from computer to computer and increasing network privileges with each jump. Starting from a regular user computer, the attacker may obtain endpoint administrator privileges and then use those privileges to get to a file server. From the file server, the attacker obtains the privileges of an e-mail administrator and jumps to an e-mail server. From the e-mail server, the attacker might obtain domain administrator privileges and then jump into the enterprise's domain controller servers. Going through several iterations of this process, the attacker can frequently get complete control of the enterprise and all of its endpoints and servers.

Attack Sequence Step 4: Move Laterally

As the attacker is gaining privileges inside the enterprise, the attacker simultaneously moves around from computer to computer to increase the footprint and get control of additional servers, endpoints, and user accounts, including privileged accounts. Strategically, the attacker likes to use system administration tools for this movement, as most enterprises permit system administration tools and protocols for their legitimate purposes with few safeguards to protect against their abuse. Some of the main attacker techniques used in this step include the following:

1. *Network mapping* to gain intelligence on the victim network, thus identifying subnets, computers, servers, exploitable vulnerabilities, and other aspects of the victim enterprise. An attacker will gain intelligence via scanning tools and by targeting network administrators and file shares containing enterprise administration documentation.

2. *Share enumeration* to identify major network shares containing data repositories shared by employees and other administrative information. This method can also be used to understand the enterprise's data sharing philosophy and its use of file shares, file transfer protocol servers, and other collaboration tools. From those tools, an attacker can escalate privileges to get administrative control of the shares and all of the data contained in them, frequently including enterprise documentation and administrative and service account passwords.

3. *Remote desktop* to obtain an administrator desktop interface on target systems using systems administration credentials. This method is the most robust method of lateral movement, as it gives attackers a full graphical user interface to work with on the target computer, and a robust and easy-to-use environment to do their work.

4. *Remote shell* to obtain a text-based command prompt using administrator credentials. This method generally runs using different ports and protocols from remote desktop, and it may be permitted when remote desktop is not (or vice versa). Command shells allow execution of arbitrary commands up to the permissions of the account used to connect.

5. *Remote administration* tools are also built into most modern operating systems and allow for executing a reduced set of commands compared to remote shell. However, such tools generally provide an attacker with the access needed to reconfigure servers and endpoints and install malware and toolkits on additional systems. Remote administration tools may use may use an entirely different network protocol from remote desktop or command shells and, as such, may be difficult to block compared to the other two attack vectors. Some tools allow for injecting software into the computer memory and running it. This situation allows for installing malware that may not be detectable by traditional anti-virus or other endpoint detection technologies.

Using these techniques, attackers will move around from machine to machine in the enterprise. Attacker may not install malware or back doors on all of the systems they touch. In fact, once attackers get control of privileged network accounts, they may switch to using systems administration tools already built into computer operating systems and permitted on the network. Attackers may go through several cycles of command and control, privilege escalation, and lateral movement before getting to the target. Frequently, by the time attackers get to the target, they have complete control over the enterprise, often without the victim's knowledge.

Attack Sequence Step 5: Complete the Mission

Once an attacker moves laterally to get to the servers and endpoints containing the desired data, the attacker attempts to complete the mission. This mission generally falls falls into three categories:

1. *Confidentiality: steal data* from the victim network. This common attack tries to compromise victim enterprises to steal logon credentials, credit card numbers or financial accounts, or healthcare information for identity theft. Enterprises are treasure troves of proprietary data, company secrets, personally identifiable information (PII), protected healthcare information (PHI), payment card data, or national secrets. This data can be stolen when attackers successfully penetrate the enterprise or its cloud-based services.

2. *Integrity: modify data* on the victim network. This attack is less common than a confidentiality attack, but no less destructive. In this attack, the attacker changes records in the victim enterprise. Often this attack method is used to steal money by either altering financial records or using compromised credentials to access financial institutions online and move money out of victim accounts. This attack may also be used in multi-phase attacks where one compromised enterprise is used as a stepping-stone to get access to another enterprise that is the real target.

3. *Availability: destroy data* in the victim enterprise. Disgruntled employees or other insider attackers frequently use this attack method, which can also be used for blackmail. Sometimes, the attacker uses ransomware that encrypts the victim's data and then charges the victim for the decryption keys. Furthermore, there is a class of distributed denial-of-service attacks that does not require successfully penetrating an enterprise. Such attacks render a victim's Internet services inaccessible for a period of time. An attacker may also use availability attacks as a distraction. For example, an attacker launches an attack to distract defenders or disable defenses while the real attacks on confidentiality or integrity take place. An attacker may also use the availability attack to cover up the attack after the real heist has been completed.

At the end of this step, an attacker has completed the attack mission. The victim is left to pick up the pieces and figure out what just happened. Most tragically, many victims do not even know that the attacks have taken place until weeks or months later.

Why Security Fails Against Advanced Attacks

But can't IT security simply stop attacks from gaining a foothold in the first place? Why can't computers be secure against attacks? The answer to these questions is complex, but it starts with the failure of endpoint security and other enterprise protection challenges. These challenges trace back to the fundamental challenges of operating complex systems and the fact that sufficiently complicated systems are impossible to secure perfectly for an extended period of time.

The Failure of Endpoint Security

A modern operating system is simply too large and too complex to ever be fully protected. Consequently, endpoints will always be susceptible to compromise. Security efforts make endpoints less likely to be compromised and statistically reduce the percentage of endpoints that are compromised, but such efforts can never ensure the compromise percentage goes to zero.

Figure 8-3 depicts experience-based *rules of thumb* for endpoint security. On average, 1 in 10 home computers, 1 in 100 enterprise personal computers, and 1 in 1,000 enterprise servers are compromised with malware of some kind.

Home Computers	Enterprise Computers	Enterprise Servers
1 / 10	**1 / 100**	**1 / 1,000**

Figure 8-3. *Experience shows that approximately 1 in 10 home computers are compromised, 1 in 100 enterprise computers are compromised, and 1 in 1,000 enterprise servers are compromised.*

These observations are due to the vagaries of living in a dangerous world and connecting computers to dangerous networks. It does not mean that people are fundamentally doing anything wrong. Rather these observations mean, in part, that attackers get lucky sometimes no matter how well security projection people do their job.

What is the origin of these numbers? First, consider that a *typical* enterprise allows its users to surf the web, get e-mail from the Internet, and take laptops home and on trips. Second, in a *typical* enterprise, the infection rate (in other words, the rate at which new computers get compromised) can be assumed to be approximately one-half of the compromise rate, per month. In an enterprise where 1 in 100 personal computers is compromised, it can be assumed that about half that many computers are infected every month. If the enterprise is in a steady state, about half that many computer infections are detected and cleaned up every month. So, for a typical enterprise of 10,000 personal computers, IT security is cleaning up approximately 50 compromised computers every month. And, at any given time, there are approximately 100 compromised computers on the network the enterprise does not know about or simply has not gotten around to cleaning up yet.

What has been observed regarding mobile devices? So far, mobile devices have proven to generally be more secure than home computers. For planning purposes, a rule of thumb is to expect that the mobile device compromise rate is somewhere between 1 in 10 and 1 in 100.

Experience shows these compromise numbers to be good rules of thumb for typical enterprises where web browsing and e-mail are allowed, and laptop computers are taken home and on trips.

Can cybersecurity defenses affect these numbers? Of course, they can! Enterprises with ineffective defenses with compromise rates that are ten times these rules of thumb have put effective defenses in place to reverse the compromise rates. There are enterprises with locked-down environments where compromise rates are one-tenth of these numbers. With additional mitigations and layers of defenses, it is entirely possible to not have any signs of compromise in an environment with thousands of endpoints. Endpoint protection is a numbers game that takes place across a number of computers over time. If an enterprise has a compromise rate of 1 in 100 and only has 50 endpoints, it is possible that none of the endpoints are compromised at a given point in time. If the enterprise is small but growing, the number of endpoints or servers increases over time. Eventually, one or more of the endpoints or servers will be compromised. These rules of thumb are for a point in time. Given enough time, it is inevitable that attackers will eventually breach enterprise defenses.

The "Inevitability of 'the Click'" Challenge

Verizon characterized this challenge nicely in a sidebar of their 2013 report, titled "The Inevitability of 'the Click.'"[1] Figure 8-4 depicts a key graphic adapted from the Verizon report.

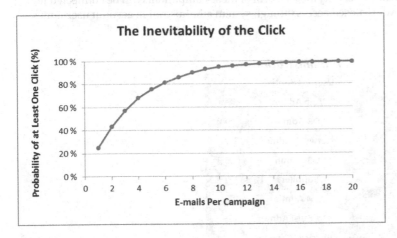

Figure 8-4. *ThreatSim found that the probability of at least one click in an e-mail phishing campaign increases significantly as more e-mails are sent during the campaign. Eventually, the campaign is almost guaranteed to succeed as the number of e-mails increases over time.*

In this sidebar, Verizon shared data collected by ThreatSim in their phishing-for-hire campaigns. ThreatSim found that with only six messages in an e-mail phishing campaign, there was an 80% chance one of the recipients would click on a link or open an attachment related to the message. The number only went up from there, exceeding a 90% probability with more than 10 messages in the campaign and approaching 100% as the number neared 20 messages.

In a large enterprise, sending thousands or millions of e-mail messages is trivial for an attacker. It's not like the attacker has to pay postage on e-mail messages. Since the attack is automated, what's the harm in a couple million extra messages, even if 95% of them get filtered out and discarded? The numbers mean the attacker eventually gets through and if the attacker gets through often enough, unsuspecting victims will eventually click on the link. If the attacker gets enough victims to click, then the odds further dictate that the attacker will be able to exploit and compromise at least one of the victims' computers. When the victim(s) then goes into the office, the foothold is established.

The conclusion is an enterprise *must* assume endpoints and servers are going to be compromised. The enterprise should be pleasantly surprised when endpoints and servers are not compromised. To protect against this type of compromise when it occurs, an enterprise must layer its defenses so that the endpoints and servers most likely to be compromised first are not the most critical ones. When compromise occurs, the enterprise then has opportunities to detect and respond to the breach before it proves disastrous.

Systems Administration Hierarchy

What happens when the endpoint gets compromised? Compromise gives the attacker a foothold into the enterprise and an opportunity to access the enterprise's systems administration channels. The security challenge here goes back to the complexity of enterprise applications and how the modern data center is built.

---

[1]"The Inevitability of 'the Click.'" Verizon Data Breach Investigations Report, 2013.

As depicted in Figure 8-5, the data center has many moving components layered on top of each other. The user accesses an application, the application uses a database, the database runs over the network, the computer runs an operating system, the operating system relies upon drivers, in a cloud environment the whole thing is virtualized, the virtualization runs on hardware with firmware and BIOS features, and finally cryptographic components use hardware security modules. All of these components can be connected to the network, and most of them allow privileged access through system administration account usernames and passwords.

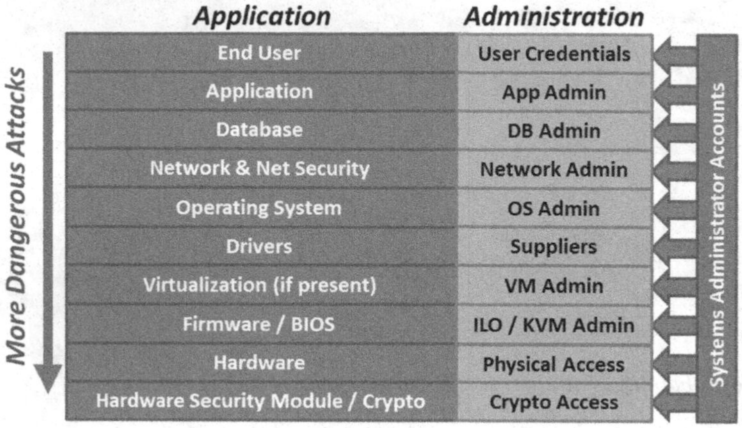

More Dangerous Attacks	Application	Administration	Systems Administrator Accounts
	End User	User Credentials	
	Application	App Admin	
	Database	DB Admin	
	Network & Net Security	Network Admin	
	Operating System	OS Admin	
	Drivers	Suppliers	
	Virtualization (if present)	VM Admin	
	Firmware / BIOS	ILO / KVM Admin	
	Hardware	Physical Access	
	Hardware Security Module / Crypto	Crypto Access	

Figure 8-5. The modern data center is built on layers of components, where components further down the stack can bypass the security of those components further up the stack and most layers are network-connected.

The challenge with these layers of components is twofold:

- *First*, the layers further down the stack can generally bypass the security of the layers above. For example, an *application* can bypass the security of *end-user* access because it can see all data for all users. Similarly, a breach of *hardware* can generally bypass all software protections because the hardware has direct access to the inputs and outputs of all software.

- *Second*, in the modern data center, most of these layers are network-connected. The fact that applications, databases, and computers are network-connected is obvious, but less well known is the fact that computer hardware integrated lights-out (ILO) interfaces are also network-connected, along with power strips, virtual machines, and cryptographic modules.

Putting these two facts together, if an attacker has connectivity to the right network and knows the right IP address, username, and password, the attacker can often run free in the enterprise computing environment. Many of these components are poorly designed, poorly secured, and poorly maintained, so successful attacks may be possible by just knowing the IP address and a little bit of information about the hardware connected to that port. It is trivial for many attackers to take advantage of these channels and bypass most of the enterprise security measures. An attacker does not have to defeat the defense. An attacker can simply go around defenses by using systems administration channels.

Escalating Attacks and Defenses

Looking at this challenge in another way, for every defensive capability, there is a corresponding attacker tool, technique, or procedure that can be used to defeat the defense. Figure 8-6 depicts attacks and defenses side by side. The figure shows an escalating chain of progressively more sophisticated and difficult defenses that are, in turn, defeated by progressively more sophisticated and difficult attacks. There is no "perfect" or "unbreakable" defense. Defenses need to be good enough to defeat the resources of the expected attackers. Finally, enterprises should focus on monitoring defenses throughout this spectrum to give defenders an opportunity to detect when attacks have breached each layer of the defensive perimeter.

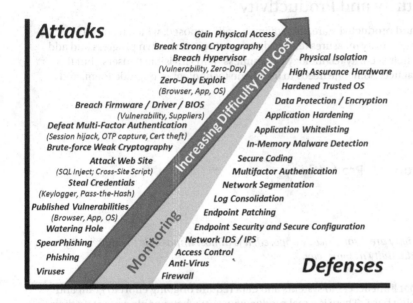

Figure 8-6. *Defenses and attacks are shown side by side along scales of increasing difficulty and cost, showing there is no such thing as a perfect defense—only a defense good enough to defeat the attacks that are expected against it.*

Most real-world attacks use relatively simple attack methods: spear phishing, published vulnerabilities, credential theft, and web site compromise. Attackers seldom use advanced attacks such as zero-day exploits, hypervisor breaches, and compromise of strong cryptography or gaining physical access. Attackers don't need to use these advanced methods because the basic methods work just fine and are much easier and cheaper to use. So, much of an enterprise's investment in advanced defenses—such as data encryption and high-assurance hardware—actually end up being wasted because the enterprise remains open to more basic forms of attack.

When designing enterprise defenses, make sure that basic defensive capabilities are operating properly before investing in advanced technologies.

Business Challenges to Security

In addition to the technical challenges of building effective defenses, what are the business challenges? While it is a significant challenge to get the technology right, security programs often fail because of business considerations rather than technical considerations. For an enterprise security program to be effective, it's critically important the enterprise understands its business and properly phrases its security needs in terms of business costs and business value.

Tension between Security and Productivity

As shown in Figure 8-7, security and productivity are often diametrically opposed, which results in significant tension between them. Security measures tend to drive up costs, slow down progress and add steps. Vendors always like to say their security technology is "seamless" and "invisible to users," but this situation is seldom the case in practice. Someone needs to install the technologies, upgrade them, and operate them while they are installed.

Figure 8-7. *Security and productivity are diametrically opposed; it is almost impossible to add security to an enterprise without impacting productivity in some way.*

In particular, technologies that limit access to systems and data require ongoing effort to grant and revoke those accesses on an ongoing basis. There is a real productivity cost when people cannot do their jobs while they are waiting for access. The cost can be fairly small, but if a company makes $1 billion a year in revenue, security measures reducing productivity by 1% cost the company $10 million a year in lost productivity. These costs add up fast.

The costs of security are offset by the costs of incidents that occur when security fails. However, the real value of such cost avoidance is subject to debate when compared to the significant costs of the security that is purchased. For example, if an enterprise is spending $1 million a year to mitigate a security risk that has a 10% chance of occurring and costs $10 million if the risk occurs, then it is probably a viable investment. The question becomes where the 10% chance came from, or the $10 million cost. These numbers are just estimates. Someone can argue for a 10% chance of a $10 million expense. However, there's always someone else who can argue it's really a 5% chance of a $5 million expense. Given the second set of numbers, the $1 million a year expense isn't such a good business decision.

Maximum Allowable Risk

As an enterprise manages its operational costs, it tries continually to minimize costs across its functional units to include security. Figure 8-8 depicts a range of potential security situations based on how much money is to be cut from the security budget.

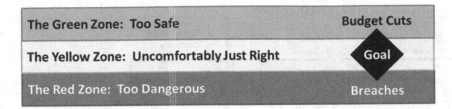

Figure 8-8. *Enterprises drive security to reduce costs and stay in a range where the program is operating uncomfortably close, from a cybersecurity viewpoint, to having a breach.*

The Green Zone implies the security budget is bloated and probably needs to be cut. At the other end of the budget spectrum, the Red Zone implies the security budget is cut too much and the enterprise is living on the edge of a security disaster consisting of multiple breaches. In between these two budget extremes is the Yellow Zone, which implies the security budget is about right; however, the enterprise feels somewhat uncomfortable regarding the security risks being managed.

Operational costs need to be reduced over time. Even when costs are mandated by regulations, the desire to reduce security costs pressures an enterprise to cut corners and flirt with noncompliance. Why is there such pressure to cut the security budget? Because money spent on security or high availability or other disaster avoidance is money that is being taken away from growth, profits, or shareholders. This budget cutting / security balancing act encompasses the concept of *maximum allowable risk*.

When the security program gets too far into the Green Zone, security investments are too great. The resulting security program is too good. There will be pressure to cut security budgets and free up that money for other purposes. When the security program gets too far into the Red Zone, security incidents happen, resulting in breaches and disasters that cause real costs of their own. The enterprise's goal is to keep the security program in the uncomfortable Yellow Zone. In the Yellow Zone, the security budget is not enough to do everything security thinks is necessary, but it is big enough to provide adequate security to prevent disastrous breaches and security incidents from occurring (in other words, cybersecurity disaster).

How does an enterprise measure and manage its security program to stay in the area of maximum allowable risk? In part, the answer is metrics. By collecting metrics on probes, attacks, and intrusions into the enterprise, security can show management what activities the cyberdefenses are stopping. Metrics help everyone understand better how close the enterprise is operating to cybersecurity disaster.

Security Effectiveness over Time

An enterprise's security posture effectiveness is not static, and it is subject to factors both within and outside of its control. Figure 8-9 depicts an enterprise's security posture over time, as it embarks on initiatives to improve its security, suffers setbacks and mistakes, and performs audits to measure its program and remediate deficiencies. The following bullets detail some of these hypothetical experiences.

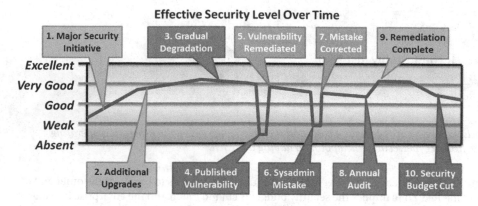

Figure 8-9. *Looking at security posture over time, effective enterprise security varies widely as vulnerabilities emerge and are remediated, mistakes are made and corrected, and audits / projects identify and remediate issues with the security program.*

1. ***Major Security Initiative:*** The enterprise has a weak security posture and then launches a major security effort to improve its security, bringing the level of security up to a good level.

2. ***Additional Upgrades:*** Prioritized upgrades to comply with various security standards (for example, NIST, PCI, or HIPAA) might further improve the security posture to a very good level.

3. ***Gradual Degradation:*** Once security projects end, security almost immediately starts naturally degrading due to losses of configuration control, cutting corners, and operational pressures to deliver services regardless of security.

4. ***Published Vulnerability:*** At any time, vulnerabilities can come up that fundamentally undermine the security program and render the enterprise vulnerable to potentially unlimited attacks. While the window of exposure time wise is generally short, these vulnerabilities are exactly what attackers look to exploit and gain footholds into enterprise IT systems.

5. ***Vulnerability Remediated:*** Just as quickly as a vulnerability appears, an enterprise can remediate it and protect itself from further attacks. When remediating a vulnerability, the enterprise needs to have the ability to catch attackers who were able to exploit the vulnerability in the first place. Catching the attackers is critical to protecting the enterprise on an ongoing basis.

6. ***Sysadmin Mistake:*** Systems administrators can make mistakes in security configurations and leave systems open to attack. This situation generally occurs when new systems are stood up, or when older systems are changed or upgraded. Once again, if attackers are standing by, they will be able to exploit the vulnerability and get into the enterprise. If the attackers are already in the enterprise, they may exploit the vulnerability to expand their reach.

7. ***Mistake Corrected:*** As quickly as a mistake is made, it can be corrected. However, the correction might not be fast enough to keep out attackers who are just waiting to exploit the smallest misstep. Catching the attackers is key to protecting the enterprise on an ongoing basis.

8. ***Annual Audit:*** If the enterprise's program is mature, it will have periodic audits to review its security posture and controls, as well as identify deficiencies and degradation when they occur. These audits generate lists of deficiencies needing remediation. The remediation efforts need to be a management priority.

9. ***Remediation Complete:*** Assuming an enterprise's security audit program is mature, the audit and remediation process should bring the enterprise back to its original security posture at the beginning of the current cycle (Figure 8-9, step 2). Then the process of maintaining the security program begins all over again.

10. ***Security Budget Cut:*** So, everything is going just fine and the enterprise's security program is going well. Of course, this situation means the enterprise must be in the Green Zone, so it's time to cut the security budget. Yes, this thought is cynical, but this reality represents the business challenges of operating a modern cybersecurity program.

Security Total Cost of Ownership

Another way to consider cybersecurity business challenges is to look at the security total cost. Security total cost consists of multiple components to include the following:

- The cost of installing, maintaining, and operating the enterprise security controls.

- The cost of responding to security incidents that occur and returning to normal operations after an incident. This cost includes any financial, reputational, or other costs related to the incident.

- Lost productivity cost across the enterprise due to employees, contractors, and guests interacting with security controls. Lost productivity can come from not having necessary privileges, time spent figuring out and requesting access, and time spent on policy exceptions required to conduct business.

Figure 8-10 depicts the total cost of ownership (TCO) for a notional security profile emphasizing *prevention* compared to a security profile emphasizing *detection and response*.

Total Cost of Ownership

Emphasize Prevention	Emphasize Detection and Response
Lost Productivity	Lost Productivity
Incident Response	Incident Response
Security Controls	Security Controls

Figure 8-10. *Looking at the total cost of ownership for security controls, incident response, and lost productivity, an emphasis on detection and response rather than prevention may in fact be cheaper to operate in the long run.*

The prevention profile suggests large numbers of preventive controls result in large amounts of lost productivity due to requesting permissions, recertifying accesses, and otherwise interacting with those security controls. On the other hand, the detection and response profile suggests the enterprise will have cheaper controls and less lost productivity. There is less of a need a need for personnel maintaining firewall rules or access permissions. However, this profile requires a greater investment in incident response, investigation, and remediation.

These notional security profiles help to make the point that it is important for an enterprise to consider such costs when evaluating its cybersecurity program. The lost productivity costs can easily add up to be many times the enterprise's overall cybersecurity budget. Decisions that reduce these costs (for example, relaxing restrictive and troublesome security policies or removing blocks that trip up legitimate users while not slowing down attackers) tend to be popular with employees and management alike.

Philosophy of Effective Defense

What makes up an effective cybersecurity program? This question is the billion-dollar question and can be answered, in part, by looking outside the IT realm. How do defenses work in the physical world, law enforcement, and warfare? In all of these areas, there are some commonalities. Nowhere outside of IT do people rely exclusively on technologies such as walls, doors, and gates to stop attackers. Perhaps this observation is a hint as to what an enterprise needs to do when implementing an effective cybersecurity program.

Mazes Versus Minefields

Looking at Figure 8-11, which is scarier, the maze or the minefield? Why do we keep building cybermazes, then?

Figure 8-11. *Most people love navigating a maze, but no one wants to walk across a minefield. [Photo credits: Floresco Productions/Getty Images (maze), Charlie Bishop/Getty Images (minefield)]*

Obviously, the minefield is scarier. Yet, enterprise IT defenses are often the cyber equivalent of mazes. An enterprise puts firewalls in place to block network traffic, network protocols to use accounts for authentication, and access controls to restrict who can see what within the enterprise IT systems. All of these methods and technologies block legitimate users from going outside of their permissions and accessing systems and data outside their job descriptions. But, just like neighborhood fences that keep backyard dogs in their place, these defenses are just an amusement for determined attackers who have tools and techniques to defeat just about every defense. To the attackers, the enterprise is a maze because attackers can see every obstacle clearly and generally have plenty of time to examine the obstacle and figure out a way around it.

Why is the minefield so scary? Because in a minefield, a person cannot see the obstacles and does not know which steps are the right ones versus missteps that prove fatal. From a distance, the minefield looks like a walk across a field. The mines cannot be seen and, if there are enough of them, the odds of walking across the minefield safely are slim. In physical security, the same principles are at work via cameras, sensors, and silent alarm systems. The goal of these defenses is to alert the defenders in such a way that the attackers do not know which steps are safe and which are not. This goal makes the attack significantly more challenging.

Figure 8-12 illustrates how to apply the maze and minefield concepts to an enterprise's security program. When an enterprise only contains preventive controls, attackers will eventually figure out a way to defeat each control in turn and eventually get to their target. However, by adding detection to the security profile, an enterprise will at least catch the attack in progress and have an opportunity to stop it. When an enterprise stops the attack, it can block the avenue of attack, close off the vulnerabilities the attackers were exploiting, and effectively send the attackers back to the starting point. Against determined attackers, the enterprise cannot stop attacks with preventive controls alone, no matter how many of them it has.

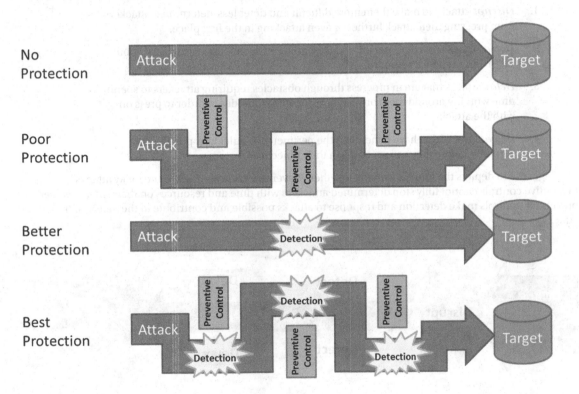

Figure 8-12. *By combining preventive and detective controls, an enterprise leverages the advantages of both mazes and minefields.*

For the best protection, an enterprise can combine preventive controls with detection to slow the attackers down and give itself more time to detect and respond to the attack before it is successful. Looking at protection from this perspective, an enterprise can see a defense consisting solely of detection capabilities can sometimes be more effective than one that consists only of prevention. At least the detection gives an enterprise an opportunity to respond to the attackers and repel them.

Disrupt, Detect, Delay, Defeat

According to the US Army *Field Manual 100-5, Operations*, the purpose of the defense is to "retain ground, gain time, deny the enemy access to an area, and damage or defeat attacking forces."[2] The manual further states, "A successful defense consists of reactive and offensive elements working together to deprive the enemy of the initiative. *An effective defense is never purely passive.*"

Army FM 100-5 states, "The immediate purpose of any defense is to defeat the attack."
How can an enterprise possibly defeat the attack if it does not even know it is being attacked?

In the context of this defensive philosophy, consider the four Ds of an effective defense:

1. ***Disrupt*** attacks to make them more difficult and deter less-determined attackers from pressing their attack further or even attacking in the first place.

2. ***Detect*** attacks that have penetrated the perimeter so defenders can learn about them and prepare a response.

3. ***Delay*** attacks that are in progress through obstacles requiring attackers to spend time working around them or searching for vulnerabilities in order to press on with the attack.

4. ***Defeat*** attacks that have penetrated the perimeter as quickly as possible and certainly before they can accomplish their objectives.

Figure 8-13 depicts the four Ds working together. Preventive controls disrupt and delay attacks. Preventive controls cannot fully stop determined attackers with time and resources on their side; however, preventive controls make detection and response to attacks possible and contribute to the defeat of the attacks.

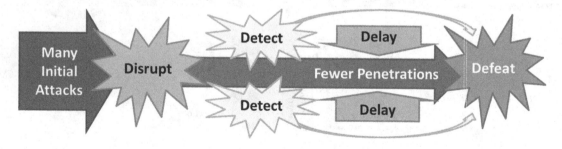

Figure 8-13. *The most effective defenses disrupt many attacks to dissuade less-determined attackers, detect the attacks that get through, delay the attackers before they can reach their objective, and ultimately give defenders the opportunity to defeat them.*

What does it mean to "defeat" a cyberattack? Unfortunately, an enterprise can seldom chase cyberattackers down and hand them over to authorities or send them to jail. Generally, the most an enterprise can do to its attackers is to eliminate their foothold within the enterprise and send them back to the Internet. Going back to the Internet sends the attackers back to "square one." At the same time,

---

[2]*Field Manual 100-5, Operations.* Washington, DC: US Army, 1986.

an enterprise seeks to close off the vulnerabilities the attackers exploited. The attackers have to wait for another "lucky break" to get into the enterprise and begin attacking again. Quite often, this cycle is the most an enterprise can possibly do with its cyberdefense, and it will have to do it over and over and over again.

Defeating cyberattacks involves removing the attackers from the enterprise and sending them back to their starting point. It is unlikely an enterprise will be able to catch them.

Cybercastles

When thinking about how enterprise defenses should work, consider the model of the medieval town in Europe. These towns can be viewed in terms of four major security zones: the fields around the town, the town itself, the castle within the town, and the tower within the castle. Figure 8-14 depicts this cybercastle analogy.

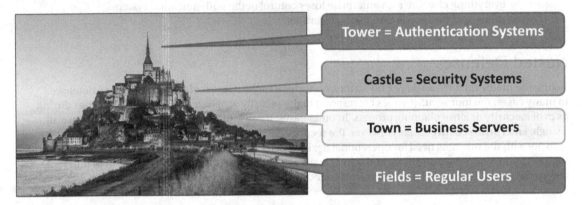

Figure 8-14. *A cybercastle provides progressively increasing levels of protection as you move further into the enterprise security infrastructure. [Photo credit: Jimmy Nilsson/EyeEm/Getty Images]*

In the medieval town, there are the following security *zones*:

1. *Fields:* The first zone consists of the fields around the town. Ironically, while the fields were where the food was grown and much of the town's economic productivity originated, fields were also almost completely indefensible. Attackers traveled across the fields at will, but simply sitting in the fields did not guarantee them success, either. Fields are like the regular user computers of most enterprises—they are where the productivity lies, but they are also almost impossible to defend.

2. *Town:* The second zone is the town itself. While the town was generally better protected than the fields, the typical medieval town was protected by a fence or perhaps a low wall that was easily scaled. Attacking the town is certainly more difficult than the fields, but still not too difficult. On the other hand, the town is where the commerce occurs. The town is like the business servers of the enterprise—they are where most of the key business occurs, but they are still difficult to protect from determined attacks.

3.   ***Castle:*** The third zone is the castle. The castle was designed for protection, with high walls and layers of defenses. Whoever controlled the castle protected the town. The attacker who controlled the town but not the castle was not successful in the long term. The castle is like the security systems of the enterprise. Whoever controls the security systems can potentially control everything else.

4.   ***Tower:*** The fourth zone is the tower. Even castles had layered defenses and just because an attacker penetrated the castle did not mean all was lost. The castle had its own enclaves, keeps, and towers where the weapons were stored and where battles were fought, even when the initial defenses of the castle were breached. As long as defenders controlled the towers, keeps, and enclaves, they could eventually retake the castle, town, and fields, and the battle was not lost. Moreover, attackers who controlled the fields, town, and castle did not truly win until they took the tower as well, and doing so may have cost them dearly. The tower is like the authentication systems of the enterprise. So long as the defender controls them, an enterprise can beat back attackers who have taken over everything else. Once an enterprise loses control of the authentication systems, though, its position is extremely precarious.

Nested Defenses

Taking the medieval town analogy a bit further, consider it in the context of nested enterprise defenses. In many cases, the four security zones correspond to the security scopes an enterprise establishes during its cybersecurity defense planning process. In other cases, these four zones are simply different parts of a single enterprise security scope. However, the security controls may be tailored to balance the need for security with the business need for operational flexibility. This approach integrates security policy, network segmentation, endpoint protection, and other capabilities to deliver appropriate protection to different enterprise zones. Figure 8-15 depicts this integrated approach in terms of a nested security perimeter.

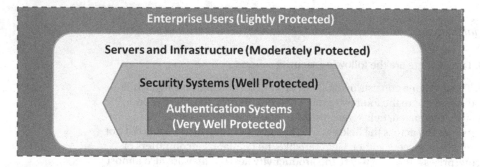

Figure 8-15.   *The cybercastle establishes nested security perimeter, where attackers have to penetrate progressively better protected perimeters to take control of the enterprise.*

In the cybercastle nested security perimeter, there are the following:

1. ***Enterprise Users:*** Like the medieval town fields, enterprise users are where most of the productivity in the enterprise lies, but are also the hardest to protect. Key protection challenges include users surfing the web, receiving e-mail, taking laptop computers home or on the road, and allowing mobile or BYOD devices. If any of these challenges exist, then securing the corresponding enterprise systems to make them impervious to attack will likely be a futile effort. Even if the management will exists to harden these systems, the operational costs of maintaining hardened endpoints can quickly become exorbitant. On the other hand, detecting compromised user endpoints and containing them before they can do significant damage may be significantly easier and cheaper than trying to harden them from compromise in the first place, and it may be easier in the long run.

2. ***Servers and Infrastructure:*** Like the medieval town, this area is where most of the business and commerce of the enterprise really lies. These systems are the ones most worth investing to protect. However, also like the medieval town, these systems are moderately difficult to protect because of the large amount of activity, upgrades, and connectivity. IT operations will be under pressure to compromise security in the name of doing more things faster, cheaper, and at a lower cost, and security will slow things down and make them more expensive. Still, this area is much easier to protect than enterprise users (that is, endpoint protection). Remember Figure 8-3's rules of thumb for endpoint security: On average, 1 in 10 home computers, 1 in 100 enterprise personal computers, and 1 in 1,000 enterprise servers are compromised with malware of some kind. For this analogy, assume the average enterprise has approximately one-tenth as many servers as endpoints. For every one compromised enterprise server, there will be 100 compromised endpoints. So, statistically speaking, protecting servers is easier than protecting endpoints.

3. ***Security Systems:*** Like the castle in the medieval town, the security systems protect the rest of the enterprise. The problem is when the security systems are running on the same operating systems, using the same accounts with the same network connectivity as everything else in the enterprise. At this point, they become no harder to hack than any servers or endpoints in the enterprise. If this situation is the case, then the smart attackers will focus their attention on the security systems, compromise them as quickly as possible, and then use the security systems to take control of the rest of the enterprise. If attackers want to put malware on an enterprise's computer systems with as little effort as possible, they take over the patch management system and let it do the job for them.

4. ***Authentication Systems:*** Like the tower of the castle, for enterprises with centralized authentication, the authentication systems are the keys to the kingdom, so to speak. With control of the authentication systems, attackers can issue themselves credentials, grant permissions to those credentials they have created, and take permissions away from the legitimate systems administrators. If attackers get control of enterprise authentication systems, the only fallback is to physically disconnect from the Internet and then slowly rebuild the enterprise's IT from scratch or backups. On the other hand, if an enterprise retains control of its authentication systems, it can remove attackers from the security systems and ultimately regain and maintain control of its enterprise. For this reason, authentication systems must be treated as if they cannot be permitted to be compromised, and any breach of their integrity must be detected and dealt with immediately.

Nesting enterprise defenses creates a perimeter defense with layers of protection ranging from easiest-to-penetrate on the outside to most-difficult-to-penetrate on the inside. From a security capability perspective, this approach means that with the outside layer, an enterprise may have fewer capabilities employed and more relaxed configurations and security policies. On the other hand, in the innermost layer(s), the enterprise will want to have the strictest security policies possible and deploy all of its available security capabilities.

Elements of an Effective Cyberdefense

What is the goal of an effective cyberdefense? Simply stated, the goal is to take the onus of perfection off of the defender and push it back onto the attacker, where it belongs.

With an ineffective cyberdefense, the defender has to do everything perfectly to protect the enterprise.

With an effective cyberdefense, the attacker has to do everything perfectly to attack it.

An effective cyberdefense pushes cyberattacks to be more like the bank heists in the movies, where the attackers have to do a hundred steps perfectly and where the slightest mistake results in the whole effort failing. Even though effective cyberdefenses cannot guarantee 100% success, such defenses certainly help to put the odds back in an enterprise's favor. Effective cyberdefense puts the onus of perfection on the attackers who are attacking an enterprise. Effective cyberdefenses make an enterprise's job much, much less stressful and the adversaries' jobs correspondingly harder.

There are five defensive techniques that the authors have found to be particularly effective at disrupting, detecting, delaying and defeating common advanced attacks: (1) network segmentation, (2) strong authentication, (3) detection, (4) incidence response, and (5) resiliency. Each technique is briefly described below.

Network Segmentation

Network segmentation is the oldest of these techniques. This technique has been used for decades to protect classified military and civilian networks from compromise via open and unclassified networks such as the Internet. While attacks such as Stuxnet have demonstrated that even isolated, *air-gapped* networks can be attacked, segmentation and network isolation make the attackers' jobs orders of magnitude more difficult than would be with monolithic, fully connected, and unmonitored internal networks.

In general, the network segmentation model should be nested (cybercastle analogy) and integrated into the enterprise security scope architecture (risk assessments). Systems in different security scopes should be segmented at the network layer. In between network segments, the enterprise should have its full range of network protection capabilities such as firewalls, IDS/IPS sensors, network recorders, and data leakage protection technologies.

Appendix I provides a detailed discussion of network segmentation, prioritization of segmentation efforts, and a notional architecture for doing network segmentation.

Strong Authentication

Strong authentication involves users proving who they say they are over the network or to enterprise computers by combining *something they have* with *something they know*. Traditional authentication consists of a username and a password typed into the console of a computer or typed into the logon screen of a web site or other application. It is relatively easy for an attacker to find out the username and password credentials. Once an attacker has the credentials, the attacker uses them to authenticate as the user, without the user's knowledge or consent.

With strong authentication, in order for the attacker to steal the user's credentials, the attacker has to physically steal the token used for secondary authentication or somehow figure out a way to clone it. Some tokens are more resistant to cloning or compromise than others.

When strong authentication is used effectively, the odds of a user's credentials being used without the user's consent or knowledge drop considerably. Is this method foolproof? Absolutely not! Even the strongest authentication is subject to an attack known as "session hijacking," where attackers take control of the user's computer and then wait for the user to log on before sending illicit commands. However, it makes all of these attack methods significantly more difficult than simply stealing usernames and passwords.

Strong authentication, when coupled with solid network segmentation, contributes to an effective cyberdefense. Networks are segmented to protect security scopes (and the business functions contained within them) from each other. Strong authentication is required for users to cross network segments and connect to more privileged systems from less privileged systems. Network security methods are used to protect these sessions from tampering and to detect attacker attempts to move laterally across the segmented network.

Detection

In many cases, an enterprise may not care if an attacker gains control of a single enterprise system or gains control of a single user account from the Internet or even inside the environment. There are serious limits to how much damage can be done in these cases, particularly over a short period of time. What makes these attacks insidious is if the attacks are allowed to progress for hours or days or weeks or months, undetected and unchecked. When attackers are able to operate undetected, there is little limit to what they can eventually accomplish. In particular, once attackers gain control of enterprise systems administration systems, they can largely move unfettered and appear to the security infrastructure to be legitimate, privileged systems administrators simply doing their jobs.

For these reasons, detection is the next technique to consider in protecting against advanced attackers. Blocking attackers is of little to no value unless the enterprise can also detect them. If the enterprise simply blocks attackers, they will continue to pound on enterprise defenses over time until they can get around the block. Given enough time, attackers will eventually defeat every obstacle the enterprise can put in their way. For this reason, an enterprise must give detection its focus. As this book's "Audit First Design Methodology" explains, an enterprise needs to design its controls around detecting adversary activity first, then preventing it second.

Interestingly, an enterprise's detective control framework does not need to be over designed. Just as a minefield is most effective when the mines are arranged in haphazard, unpredictable patterns, so an enterprise's detective controls are most effective when they are somewhat arbitrary and hard to predict as well. An enterprise can design its detection around specific attacks (for example, specific patterns like the running of particular commands, or the use of specific tools or protocols on the network) and should not hesitate to build whatever detection comes to mind. Detection rules can be fairly haphazard and still be effective. Simple, but effective, detection rules can include the following:

- On a segmented network, detect port and network scans that extend from one segment to another.

- On a segmented network, detect systems administration protocols such as secure shell or remote desktop when they originate from servers.

- For privileged accounts, send administrators a daily report showing all the computers where their accounts were used, along with an admonition to report any suspected account abuse.

- Alert when network administration tools or scanning tools such as ping or traceroute are used from workstations.

- Alert on the use of highly privileged network or service accounts on machines outside of the datacenter.

- Alert on changes to static web content on Internet-facing servers.

- Alert on outbound web connections other than patch downloads from Internet-connected servers.

- Alert on protocol anomalies in standard web protocols like domain name service or simple mail transport protocol.

Enterprise detection does not need to be thoroughly designed to still be effective. The goal is to look at the attack sequence and design detection to alert multiple times before an advanced attack can make it from the beginning of the attack sequence to the end. Then the rest of enterprise security controls can delay the attacker sufficiently so the enterprise can respond to the incident before the attacker can finish the attack. An enterprise does not need much in the way of detection for its defense to still be incredibly effective.

Incident Response

All the detection in the world is not going to save an enterprise if it does not have anyone responding to those alerts, investigating them to filter out false positives to identify the real attacks, and repelling those attacks so that business can continue. Without incident response, all the prevention and detection in the world is not going to make a difference against the most advanced attackers.

An enterprise needs to perform incident response itself using a team that is always on standby or a third party who is kept on retainer or otherwise engaged. It is critical the enterprise perform incident response to repel attacks when they occur and send the attackers back to their starting points. See Chapter 9 for a detailed incident response discussion.

Resiliency

Perhaps the most important property of an effective cyberdefense is resiliency. Resiliency is the enterprise's ability to withstand attacks that successfully compromise endpoints, servers, and accounts without those attacks resulting in the attackers gaining complete control. Resiliency means the enterprise has the ability to dynamically respond to those attacks by containing them, remediating them, or isolating them so the attacker's plan is disrupted and defenders have time and room to maneuver in response to the attack.

Some examples of resiliency include:

- The ability to rapidly rebuild servers or endpoints that have been compromised

- The ability to reset user credentials, and obtain detailed logs of user account activity of accounts that may have been compromised

- The ability to rapidly restore data or applications from backups that are known to be good and free of infection or malware

- The ability to isolate sections of the enterprise, or even the entire enterprise, from the Internet so that attackers lose the ability to control their foothold

Resiliency gives defenders options in an incident response, because the enterprise can be rapidly and flexibly modified in response to cybersecurity needs and to thwart the plans and tools used by cyberattackers. This agility makes it possible for defenders to outmaneuver their adversaries, even when the adversaries are skilled and moving quickly. By outmaneuvering the attackers, cyberdefenders can take control of the situation, achieve rapid containment, and remediate incidents before the attackers can gain administrative control and complete their objective.

CHAPTER 9

■ ■ ■

Responding to Incidents

Some cyberattackers penetrate enterprise cyberdefenses no matter how well the defenses are designed, implemented, and maintained. Responding to these incidents (in other words, incident response) and the related costs are facts of life in the modern cyberenvironment. Enterprise endpoints and servers are destined to be compromised. It benefits the enterprise to embrace this reality and simply deal with these compromised systems as quickly and as cheaply as possible. Generally, an enterprise can accept a number of *minor* cyberincidents provided the incidents are contained before significant damage is done.

Figure 9-1 delineates a high-level sequence of events associated with a detected cyberattack and the resulting enterprise response, including: (1) the attack itself, (2) incident investigation, (3) containment, (4) remediation, and (5) post-incident activities.

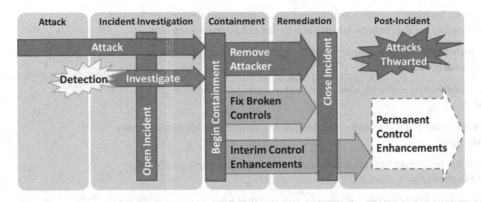

Figure 9-1. *The incident response process extends from the initial attack investigation, containment, remediation, and a post-incident IT environment with permanent security control enhancements to prevent a recurrence.*

The high-level sequence of events related to enterprise incident response consists of the following:

- **Attack:** The incident starts with a cyberattack on the enterprise or its systems. The attack may be as simple as a computer getting infected with a virus, or it may be an elaborate, multi-phase attack by cyberintelligence agents working from another country. The enterprise cyberdefenses eventually detect the attack with a detective control or sensor.

- **Incident Investigation:** After the attack is detected, defenders have an opportunity to begin responding. The response starts with a preliminary investigation to filter out false positives. Corroborating evidence is collected to verify that the sensor reported an active cyberattack. Once the cyberattack is verified, the defenders formally start the enterprise's incident response process.

- **Containment:** After the incident is investigated and the extent of the attack is understood, the enterprise's response moves to containing the attack. The response objectives include removing the attacker from the enterprise, fixing broken cybersecurity controls that permitted the attacker to get into the enterprise in the first place, and emplacing interim security fixes. These security fixes should make it more difficult for the attacker to get in again, or should detect of the attacker succeeds in getting in again.

- **Remediation:** After the attacker is contained, the defenders remediate the damage that was done, rebuild affected systems, clean up defaced web sites, and restore the enterprise back to normal operation. At the conclusion of remediation, the enterprise formally closes out the incident.

- **Post-Incident:** After the initial incident has been remediated, follow-on attacks by the same attacker using the same tools, techniques, and procedures should be thwarted, or at least rapidly detected and defeated. Additional security controls put in place as a result of the attack may lead to long-term permanent security enhancements or strengthened controls.

The Incident Response Process

At the next level of detail, incident response can be represented as the following ten-step process that begins with identifying an incident and ends with resuming normal IT operations:

1. *Identify the incident* through alerting from monitoring and sensors, or through an event occurring that brings the incident to the enterprise's attention.

2. *Investigate the incident* to understand the extent of the compromise and the attacker's methods.

3. *Collect evidence* from the incident if law enforcement or other parties will need it.

4. *Report the results* of the incident to enterprise management for its awareness and oversight.

5. *Contain the incident* so that attackers and malicious software can no longer operate in the environment.

6. *Repair gaps or malfunctions* in security controls that permitted the incident to occur in the first place.

7. *Remediate compromised accounts, computers, and networks* so that they are restored to normal operations.

8. *Validate remediation and strengthened security controls* to ensure that the situation has been fully resolved.

9. *Report the conclusion of the incident* to enterprise management.

10. *Resume normal IT operations.*

These incident response steps are described in the following sections.

Incident Response Step 1: Identify the Incident

How does an enterprise know a security incident has occurred? Generally, an enterprise finds that a security incident has occurred in one of four ways (most preferred to least preferred):

- Enterprise security monitoring system generates an alert.

- Users notice something wrong with enterprise IT systems.

- An external party notifies the enterprise of an issue.

- The enterprise name shows up on the front page of the news!

Regardless of how the enterprise finds out about an incident, the incident response process needs to be engaged. Incident response is a formal process, and an enterprise needs to have a mechanism for declaring an incident and initiating the process. Everyone involved in the incident response process needs to know that a security incident is taking place. Everyone needs to understand how the incident response process should be prioritized in relation to other responsibilities. While many people think handling the incident should be a "drop everything" top priority, the reality is usually somewhat more nuanced. Generally, supporting security incidents should be a close second priority behind maintaining normal operations and services, but ahead of system improvements, upgrades, or audits. This can be challenging, because operations staff members are normally 100% engaged supporting operations. Incident response may need to be prioritized ahead of serving customers, which may result in service degradation.

Another key consideration is the question of who is in charge. Notionally, with the full backing of the enterprise CIO, IT Security is in charge of incident response. The CIO makes the tough calls allocating limited resources when IT Security impacts enterprise operations. Trade-offs need to be made between security response effectiveness and the delivery of IT services. Frequently, the CIO makes these difficult decisions and accepts the business consequences and impacts of such decisions.

When a security incident is declared, IT Security goes from having an enterprise-supporting role to having a leading role. Resolving the incident will likely have operational impacts. For example, IT systems may have to be isolated, disconnected, or disabled; user accounts may have to be disabled; services may have to be shut down; or networks may have to be reconfigured. These operational impacts need to be carefully negotiated with impacted parties throughout the incident handling process.

Incident Response Step 2: Investigate the Incident

Once the incident handling process is initiated, the enterprise incident response team begins investigating the incident. The simplest investigations involve a single computer, account, network address, or piece of malware. The most complex can include hundreds of systems and can take months to complete. During the investigation process, it is critical that the investigation team maintains four lists to track the following *Indicators of Compromise* (IOCs):

- **Computers** in the internal IT environment that were compromised, including regular personal computers, servers, and infrastructure systems.

- **Network Accounts** on the internal network that were compromised or used by attackers, including regular user accounts, privileged system administrator accounts, and service accounts used by applications to communicate with each other.

- **Tools, Techniques and Procedures (TTPs)** used to conduct the attack, including viruses, malware, remote controller programs, and operating system tools such as secure shell and remote desktop.

- **Internet Locations** used by the attackers to control systems on the inside or to receive data that has been exfiltrated.

Figure 9-2 notionally depicts the IOC cycle where the enterprise incident response team investigators use IOCs to identify the full scope of the incident. The bullets below the figure describe each of these four investigative actions.

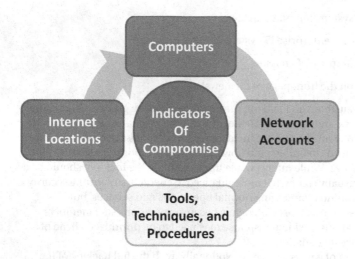

Figure 9-2. *The incident response team uses the IOC cycle to identify the resources and techniques being used by the attackers.*

1. ***Computers:*** Investigators often start the IOC cycle by inspecting a single computer that generated an alert from anti-virus or some type of malware activity.

2. ***Network Accounts:*** Investigators analyze the computer and identify user accounts that were used from that computer. They then track the use of those accounts across the network. They identify uses of those accounts on the network that are not legitimate. Investigators also identify other computers that were accessed using the identified accounts.

3. ***Tools, Techniques, and Procedures (TTPs):*** Investigators analyze the malware and identify hash signatures of the files involved or specific strings in the software. Using these analytic results, investigators then search the rest of the enterprise for the malware. They can also look for network communications patterns that are distinct to the software involved. Such patterns are particularly useful when attackers are using operating system tools that are already built into the system.

4. ***Internet Locations:*** Investigators further analyze the computer and its network connections. They look for web connections to the Internet or evidence of protocol tunneling to Internet addresses.

Each time the IOC cycle is performed, more computers, network accounts, TTPs, or Internet locations related to the incident may be found. The incident response team continues performing this cycle until all leads have been followed up and no new IOCs can be found. At this point, the scope and the effects of the attack are known. Investigators should have a better understanding of the attackers' goals (for example, data exfiltration, modification, or deletion).

Incident Response Step 3: Collect Evidence

Frequently, incident response team investigations do not occur in a vacuum. More often than not, the systems involved in cyberincidents are governed by laws, regulations, or industry standards that require formal reporting or other procedures. During the investigation, it may be necessary to formally collect evidence and maintain chains of custody for the evidence. Investigators often collaborate with internal auditors, external auditors, or law enforcement authorities. Investigators need to understand these potential legal or regulatory requirements. Investigators also need to understand their own capabilities and limits regarding investigating potential cybercrime, international nation-state espionage, or other illegal activities.

Some regulatory frameworks that might trigger formal evidence collection requirements in the United States include the following:

- *Payment Card Industry (PCI):* regulates data including credit card numbers and sometimes online banking information

- *Personally Identifiable Information (PII):* regulates data regarding personal identification and identity, regulated by US privacy laws

- *Health Insurance Portability and Accountability Act (HIPAA):* regulates data containing personal health information

- *International Traffic in Arms Regulations (ITAR):* regulates technologies that are export-controlled by the US Department of State

- *Sarbanes-Oxley (SOX):* regulates financial data for public companies related to company finance and financial results reporting

It is important to remember that the scope of the investigation can change as more information becomes available. An incident that starts out as a small affair in an obscure part of the enterprise can easily expand to encompass sensitive operational systems. Investigators and enterprise management must be constantly aware of how their procedures need to be modified (if at all) when doing regulated investigations and conscious of at what point auditors and legal or law-enforcement authorities need to be briefed and involved in the investigation process.

Incident Response Step 4: Report the Results

Investigators report to enterprise management on what is going on and what the plan is for going forward. Investigators can certainly report earlier or later as well, but it is absolutely essential that a report be issued following the investigation and collection of evidence. If investigators engage external services to assist in the investigation, then they will likely issue a formal report outlining what malware they found and evidence they collected.

The report should contain the following information:

- *Timeline* of what is known about the attack, including the first infection, lateral movements, and the time of discovery

- *Regulatory impact* of affected computers and data so that enterprise management understands evidence collection and regulatory reporting requirements

- *Business impact* of the attack, including how current business is being affected and how future business may be affected by the remediation process

- *Incident resolution plan* to remove the attackers from the enterprise, strengthen defenses, and restore normal operations

- *Technical data* about the attack, including computers, accounts, network addresses, and malware involved in the attacker activities

The report needs to be action-oriented so that enterprise management is aware of needed decisions and corresponding actions. At the conclusion of the report, investigators ask management to provide guidance on executing the incident resolution plan.

Incident Response Step 5: Contain the Incident

Containment is the first step in the incident remediation process. Containment blocks computers, tools, accounts, and network addresses from being used by attackers. Containment must be carefully thought through to prevent a "whack-a-mole" scenario where the attack continues spreading at the same time the enterprise is trying to contain it. An enterprise wants to avoid a situation where attackers know that they have been detected and are being contained. If attackers know, they can change their methods and tools and become invisible again.

Containment generally consists of the following actions:

- *Computers* that have been compromised are disconnected from the network or malware is removed from them so that it can no longer run.

- *Attacker software tools* are detected and blocked from running on enterprise computers.

- *User and service accounts* that have been compromised are disabled or their credentials changed so that they can no longer be used by the attacker.

- *Internet locations* being used by the attackers are blocked so that they can no longer be used to communicate with computers inside the network.

Containment must be performed swiftly to regain control of the enterprise and deny attackers access to its networks, computers, and user accounts. At the same time, the operational impact of containment must be carefully managed so that the business can continue functioning while the attack is being dealt with. Generally, breakdowns in containment occur when the need to continue IT operations gets in the way of the containment effort. When investigators detect that containment and IT operations are coming into opposition with each other, they need to immediately bring this situation to management's attention so that the trade-offs involved can be carefully managed. These decisions are difficult and leadership needs to make them with full understanding of the consequences involved.

Incident Response Step 6: Repair Gaps or Malfunctions

Once the incident has been contained, the enterprise can breathe a sigh of relief, but the enterprise is not out of the woods yet. The next step—and perhaps the most important step—is to identify enterprise security deficiencies that allowed the incident to occur and close those deficiencies before getting too far along with the rest of the remediation. While the enterprise may not be able to fix every identified security deficiency, the enterprise needs to strengthen security enough so that the original attack is not going to succeed if the attackers come back and try it again. If the enterprise does not strengthen its controls, it runs the risk of having the same incident over and over again.

Some key steps in repairing enterprise security controls include the following:

- *Analyze attack sequence* to understand how the attack occurred, what steps were involved in it, and where the enterprise can disrupt, detect, delay, and defeat future attacks.

- *Identify controls* that are in place or can be put in place quickly to catch the attack should it occur again.

- *Emphasize detection* to ensure that the enterprise can detect future attacks while they are in progress and before they can be completed or cause significant damage.

- *Consider training* to protect against attack vectors and methods that rely on user behaviors and mistakes—such as clicking on links in phishing e-mails—to succeed.

In the course of this effort, the enterprise will identify security enhancements that it would like to perform, but that will take more time or money than is available. In such cases, the repair process needs to focus only on what can be performed immediately. Improvements that take more time and money than are immediately available need to be managed and prioritized as longer-term projects. The residual risk of not having these improvements needs to be managed as an enterprise risk until it can be remediated.

Incident Response Step 7: Remediate Compromised Accounts, Computers, and Networks

Once security controls are repaired, the enterprise can proceed with remediating affected computers, accounts, and network components to bring them back to normal operation. Remediation must be carefully planned to ensure that malware is thoroughly eradicated, and potential backdoors are cleaned up and closed off.

Following are some key steps in the remediation process:

- *Change account credentials* and passwords so that they are no longer available to attackers.

- *Wipe and rebuild* affected computers, where possible. Take care that the rebuild process does not end up moving the infection from the old system to the new one.

- *Manually clean up* systems where wiping and rebuilding is too labor-intensive or disruptive to be practical.

- *Restore Data* from backups, where necessary.

The remediation process can require considerable negotiation with business leadership regarding the impact of the remediation process and the costs of resulting business disruption. For example, what happens when security wants to have a compromised server rebuilt, but that server is already slated for retirement in a few months? Or what if remediating service accounts is going to take critical enterprise applications offline? In all of these cases, security and the business must work together to ensure that the incident is adequately remediated while keeping the business impact within an acceptable range.

Incident Response Step 8: Validate Remediation and Strengthen Security Controls

Security personnel need to validate the remediation activities to ensure such activities were performed correctly so that future attackers are kept out of the enterprise. This step is important because often security directs IT to take remediation actions, but before they can be completed, another crisis comes up and the remediation gets put on the back burner or forgotten. It's important to make sure that the remediation is completed to an acceptable degree before the incident is closed out.

The validation process involves the following:

- ***Checking computers*** to ensure affected computers are remediated. Generally, this involves rebuilding or cleaning up computers to remove malware and tools used in the attack.

- ***Checking user accounts*** to ensure affected user accounts are remediated. For most user accounts, this requires simply changing the password.

- ***Checking network configurations*** to ensure network blocks or other changes are properly documented so that they can be sustained.

- ***Checking security controls*** to ensure a future attack of the same type will be detected and disrupted.

- ***Checking regulatory requirements*** to ensure necessary regulatory and legal requirements are complied with and reports filed, if necessary.

- ***Identifying future actions*** to be done after the incident as part of long-term strengthening of the enterprise security posture.

- ***Conducting an after action review*** to understand what went well with the incident response and what went poorly, and how the incident response process can be improved going forward.

Incident Response Step 9: Report the Conclusion of the Incident

The incident response team should provide enterprise management with a final report to close out the incident. This report documents the major details of the incident and supports future incident responses and investigations. It is not uncommon for a single group of attackers to come back again and again. The returning attacker may use slightly different malware or techniques. Having documentation of previous attacks helps the enterprise understand the attack vectors and scenarios (the big picture of what is going on), and it provides valuable input to future cyberdefense planning efforts.

The final report can follow the same basic outline as the initial report, except that at this point all known facts about the attack are documented and reported. Key elements in the final report include the following:

- ***Major differences*** from the initial report, including initial "facts" that later turned out to be incorrect or assumptions that turned out to be false.

- ***Timeline*** of the attack and remediation sequence including the dates and times for the attacker initial activity, initial discovery of the breach, and major incident response activities including the beginning and completion of containment, remediation, and validation activities. Make sure that times are referenced against an appropriate time zone to prevent confusion.

- ***Incident resolution activities*** should be documented, so the reader understands what actions were taken to remove the attackers from the enterprise, strengthen defenses, and restore normal operations.

- ***Business impact*** of the attack and remediation process, and whether the business impact is temporary or permanent. Potential long-term impacts of security control changes should be considered and documented for senior enterprise leadership.

- ***Regulatory impact*** of the incident, as well as any changes in regulatory impact and reporting that occurred during the course of the investigation. It is not uncommon for an incident to start out unregulated and then become regulated as the investigation progresses. In cases where the incident's regulatory status changes, the reason for the change should be clearly documented for potential regulatory or legal review.

- ***Technical data*** about the attack, including lists of computers, accounts, network addresses, and malware involved in the attacker activities. This information should be retained with the final report for use in subsequent investigations, where necessary.

- ***After action report*** describing what went well with the incident response and what went poorly, and what lessons learned the enterprise can take away from this incident to prevent future incidents and improve the response should similar incidents occur in the future.

It is okay if the final report contradicts the initial report in many places. Quite frequently, initial reports contain inaccuracies due to the challenges of collecting good information during a crisis. The incident response team needs to understand that this reality does not reflect poorly on their efforts; it's just a matter of fact caused by the realities and confusion of the crisis.

Incident Response Step 10: Resume Normal IT Operations

By this point in the process, things should be back to normal and systems should be fully operational. It is not uncommon to get to this point and still be performing *temporary* risk mitigation activities (such as manual security controls, manual audits and checks, or strengthened security procedures in anticipation of technology upgrades). Just as a pothole may be temporarily patched for a period of time until it can be permanently repaired, these temporary risk mitigation activities are the realities of operating in a resource-constrained world. An enterprise needs to be cautious that such temporary measures do not become permanent. Alternatively, if these measures are supposed to be permanent, the enterprise needs to be cautious of them falling apart when management moves on to the next crisis.

Supporting the Incident Response Process

Incident response involves performing many steps that are difficult at best and often are impossible without many supporting cybersecurity capabilities. The incident response team relies on the following enterprise cybersecurity capabilities to support the enterprise's response to incidents, in particular the following:

- ***Detection:*** If an enterprise cannot detect intrusions, it will not be able to start the incident response process. Some key detection capabilities include privileged activity monitoring, network intrusion detection, traffic analysis and data analytics, data leakage protection, anti-virus, in-memory malware detection, rogue network device detection, honeypots, honeynets, and honeytokens, change detection, and event correlation.

- ***Investigation:*** Investigation requires solid forensic capabilities across a wide variety of systems. Some key capabilities supporting the investigation process include endpoint logging policies and forensic imaging support, network packet intercept and capture, firewall and IDS logging, administrator audit trails, forensics and e-discovery tools, and threat intelligence and indicators of compromise. In the investigation process, it is critical to be able to find malware instances across large numbers of enterprise systems and also to search for network activity patterns across the entire network's critical connectivity links.

- ***Remediation:*** Remediation requires the ability to move faster than the attackers and remove them from the enterprise faster than they can maneuver to avoid removal. Key capabilities to support this function are multi-factor authentication for administrators, network service management, application whitelisting, identity life cycle management, rapid computer imaging, and patch management and deployment. High availability and disaster recovery capabilities can also be helpful in the remediation process, as they can allow for remediation without having to cause operational outages.

Incident response is not just about a single enterprise cybersecurity functional area or capability. Rather, it involves leveraging all functional areas and appropriate capabilities to mount an effective response when incidents occur.

CHAPTER 10

■ ■ ■

Managing a Cybersecurity Crisis

When does a cybersecurity incident become a crisis? Generally, when it has enterprisewide impact or when it requires activation of disaster recovery plans, it's a crisis. It's when a single compromised server becomes ten compromised servers, then a hundred, and pretty soon the entire data center is infected, damaged, or worse. Over the past several years, there have been several public instances of massive IT crises including Saudi Aramco in 2012 and Sony Pictures Entertainment in 2014. Smaller incidences occur every day, outside of the public eye. This chapter describes how things change when a crisis occurs and how enterprises behave under the duress of a crisis situation. The chapter also describes techniques for restoring IT during a crisis while simultaneously strengthening cybersecurity to protect against an active attacker who may hit the enterprise again at any moment.

Devastating Cyberattacks and "Falling Off the Cliff"

A cybercrisis begins with a devastating cyberattack that impacts an enterprise's ability to function or to deliver revenue-generating services. For example, if attackers could force the Amazon.com web site offline, that would be a devastating cyberattack. The cyberattack that disabled computers at Sony Pictures Entertainment is an excellent example of a devastating cyberattack. Similarly, the Stuxnet attack that impaired the Iranian nuclear program could also be characterized as devastating. A less well-known attack in 2014 caused a German foundry's blast furnace to malfunction and resulted in extensive physical damage. Fortunately, the malfunction did not cause serious injuries or loss of life. These real-world incidents are examples of devastating cyberattacks.

Appendix A describes some of the most common cyberattack types in terms of their impact, methods, and consequences, as well as potential enterprise defenses. Any cyberattack can be devastating if its business impact is severe enough. Many devastating cyberattacks involve attackers gaining complete administrative control of the victim network. Once the attackers have control, they can do whatever they want. The victim is truly at their mercy. Unfortunately, many enterprises structure their security in a manner that attackers can gain administrative control relatively easily. With this control, the attackers have tremendous advantage and freedom to conduct whatever attacks they choose.

The Snowballing Incident

For the victims of a devastating cyberattack, the true magnitude of the incident may not be visible initially. The devastating cyberattack often starts with an incident like any other incident, perhaps an anti-virus alert or a failed logon with an administrator credential. As investigators analyze the incident and start correlating it across the enterprise, the incident's impact expands:

- An administrator account is being used inappropriately throughout the enterprise.

- Malware is discovered on critical application servers, systems administration servers, or authentication servers containing large numbers of user credentials.

167

- A piece of malware—once it has been identified as such—is present on a significant portion of the enterprise's computers.

- A large number of enterprise computers are communicating with an external command-and-control server.

- Once the right signatures are loaded into network security systems, the enterprise realizes malicious communications are taking place throughout the enterprise network.

Falling Off the Cliff

As the investigation proceeds, the enterprise realizes this incident is not a small incident to be cleaned up in a day. This incident is a *big deal*, and the enterprise is in *big trouble*. This situation is what incident responders refer to as "falling off the cliff." All of a sudden, this situation isn't an incident anymore—it's a crisis.

As the crisis snowballs, the enterprise's ability to respond to it diminishes. At first, the incident appeared to be limited to just a server; now the incident includes most, if not all of the servers in the system, along with the consoles used to control them. At first, it was just one network; now it is most, if not all, of the enterprise networks. At first, it was just a couple of personal computers; now it is most, if not all, of them. As the incident becomes more visible, the enterprise realizes most of its disaster recovery plans (which assume the enterprise has control of its servers, networks, and computers) are not going to work in a situation where an attacker is in control. Furthermore, the enterprise is still uncertain as to what the attacker can or cannot do.

Another thing that happens is the enterprise realizes it needs to be careful in order to avoid tipping its hand to the attacker. More specifically, an attacker with administrative control of the enterprise is dangerous. If the attacker believes the enterprise knows what is going on and is about to kick the attacker out, the attacker might do something extremely destructive before the enterprise is able to take back control. The enterprise needs to be very, very careful and not make any sudden or poorly thought-out moves.

At this point, it may become necessary to establish out-of-band communications. There is no point in e-mailing senior executives to ask for a meeting to discuss the cybersecurity crisis if the attackers have control of the e-mail server and are reading executives' messages. At this sensitive time, cybersecurity staff should be cautious and prefer face-to-face and telephonic communications over messages or other collaboration tools that could be compromised and easily tip off the attackers.

Reporting to Senior Enterprise Leadership

As the enterprise gains an understanding of the cyberattack's magnitude, it is time to report the situation to senior enterprise leadership. The initial reports were most likely incorrect and did not accurately portray what it will take to resolve the situation. With a better understanding, reporting needs to accurately characterize what is taking place. In business terms, reporting needs to present clearly the magnitude of the knowns, unknowns, threats, and risks. Key reporting points include the following:

- **What is known so far**

  - Date and time of initial incursion (if known)

  - Numbers of computers and accounts that are compromised

  - Business capabilities linked to those computers and accounts

  - What the attacker *has done* with those computers and accounts so far, if this can be determined

  - What the attacker *could do* with those computers and accounts in the future if they are unchecked

- **What is not known so far**
  - What are the limits of the investigation to date
  - Extent of what still needs to be investigated
- **What is understood about the attacker**
  - Who the attacker appears to be, if known
  - What the attacker's motive *appears to be*, based on available evidence
  - What is the most likely thing the attacker has done or will do, given the extent of penetration
  - What is the most dangerous or destructive thing the attacker could do, given the extent of penetration
- **What will be required to stabilize the situation**
  - Remove the attacker from the environment
  - Adequately shore up defenses to keep the attacker out
  - Deny the attacker access long enough for the defenses to take effect
- **What will be required to resolve the situation**
  - Fully investigate and identify attacker activities and compromised accounts, computers, and network traffic
  - Change credentials for compromised accounts
  - Rebuild or clean up compromised computers
  - Intercept and block malicious network traffic
  - Repair or restore damaged or compromised data
- **What help should be called in immediately to start the response**
  - Surge staffing
  - Incident response
  - Forensics investigation
  - Legal counsel
  - Regulatory reporting

Calling for Help

As soon as senior enterprise leadership understands the magnitude of the situation, leadership and employee channels are going to become consumed just keeping organized around the situation and maintaining accurate status for senior leadership. Enterprises that are staffed properly for "normal" operations seldom have the extra bandwidth present to do all of this reporting while simultaneously actually doing the remediation work. There simply isn't enough time or resources. *Calling for help* takes pressure off regular employees so they can stay focused on staying in control of the situation and making decisions.

Without help, employees at all levels can become quickly saturated and the quality of the response will suffer. Areas where enterprises may need help include the following:

1. **Strategy, Architecture, and Planning:** Advising leaders on the *big picture* strategy, architecture, and planning for the crisis. Providing leaders with templates based on experience at other enterprises so leaders do not have to create them from scratch.

2. **Investigating the Incident:** Doing the investigation to understand the magnitude of the crisis, affected accounts, computers, networks and malware, and collecting the information necessary for remediation.

3. **Strengthening Cybersecurity:** Reinforcing security capabilities so attackers will not be able to counterstrike while they are being removed or get back in quickly after remediation.

4. **Rebuilding IT:** Reconstituting affected IT systems and restoring impacted business operations. Tightly coordinating rebuilding with cybersecurity improvements so restored IT systems are not open to counterattack.

5. **Tracking Status:** Keeping track of crisis activities and accurately reporting them to leadership. Facilitating the discussions required to understand and make risk-based decisions trading off operational risk with cybersecurity risk.

Keeping Calm and Carrying On

Once the enterprise knows it is in crisis, the first concern is to, as the British say, "keep calm and carry on." (See Figure 10-1.)

Figure 10-1. *The original "Keep Calm and Carry On" poster from 1939.*[1]

As the magnitude of the crisis unfolds, people will be afraid—afraid for their jobs, their careers, and their livelihoods—and many people will be looking to find mistakes that may have led to the situation becoming a crisis. During this time, it is critically important for leadership to keep calm and hold the second-guessing in check so that everyone can stay focused on the problems and finding potential solutions.

---

[1]This poster was developed in Great Britain as part of the preparation for World War II, but was not widely distributed at the time. The British government kept it in storage for use in case of a devastating German attack. It was rediscovered in 2000 and has since become quite popular.

Playing Baseball in a Hailstorm

Of course, keeping calm is going to become increasingly difficult for everyone at all levels. One of the first things that happens when the situation becomes a crisis is that established communications channels become overloaded, along with the leaders in those channels.

A cyberattack crisis is like playing a game of baseball while it is hailing baseballs.

Using the baseball analogy, everyone becomes quickly overwhelmed by all of the activity going on, and traditional communications channels become saturated. Leaders spend most of their time in meetings, and little of their time synthesizing reports, setting up assignments, or delegating tasks. Consequently, "the ball gets dropped" everywhere in the organization and the normal processes of reporting and delegation become ineffective in the face of overwhelming workloads. In the face of these challenges, the usual organization and communication channels of e-mails, voicemails, meetings, and to-do lists break down.

In short, normal operational methods simply do not work in a crisis situation. In a crisis, the enterprise needs to change its method of operation if it is to manage the crisis effectively. The enterprise's supporters and contractors need to go along with these operational changes if they are to succeed as well.

Communications Overload

As the situation becomes a crisis, regular communications channels become saturated and managers in particular become overloaded by status information, requests for support, and guidance from leadership. As depicted in Figure 10-2, communications overload seriously undermines their ability to accurately assess the situation, synthesize reports from subordinates, and distribute guidance to staff to keep them moving. Often managers are reduced to handling the people and the situations standing in front of them with no bandwidth available to check e-mail, listen to voicemail, or deal with anything that is not urgent and immediate.

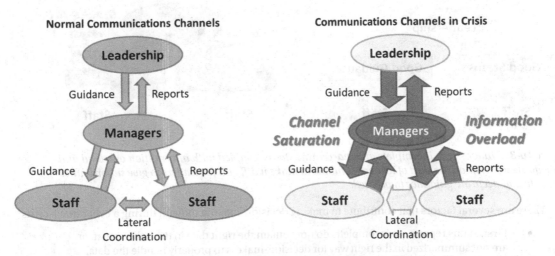

Figure 10-2. *Information overload occurs when managers become saturated with guidance and reports, placing greater importance on lateral coordination between staff and subordinates.*

In this situation, there are several actions to help reduce the impact of management overload and improve the flows of information and the quality of manager decision-making.

- **First**, staff and contractors can rely more on lateral communication to coordinate among themselves rather than on managers to move information among teams. This approach takes pressure off of managers who do not have time for lateral coordination.

- **Second**, staff and contractors can spend more time synthesizing their reports into the formats that managers are going to need rather than simply giving the managers the raw data. This processing may be work that is normally done by managers. However, in a crisis the managers simply do not have time to do it. The key point is giving the managers less information, not more, and ensuring the information given to them is just the information they need and in the format in which they need it.

- **Third**, staff and contractors can elicit the guidance and requirements they need from managers rather than waiting for the managers to provide such information to them. This action is important because saturated managers seldom have time to work out the guidance they need to give to subordinates, while the subordinates often know exactly what they need to do but need management's support to get started. If subordinates and contractors go to managers with a proposal of what they intend to do, then it is relatively easy for the managers to simply adjust the proposal into the desired guidance, rather than trying to create the guidance from scratch.

Decision-Making under Stress

As the crisis situation unfolds, confusion in reports and status information can have an extremely detrimental effect on management effectiveness. Incomplete and inaccurate status can dramatically impede decision-making and can result in incomplete and inaccurate management guidance, as depicted in Figure 10-3.

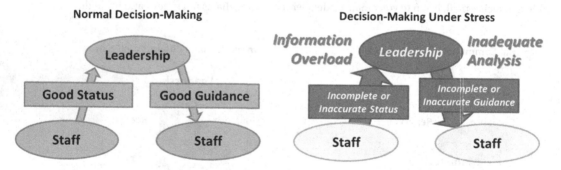

Figure 10-3. *Under stress, incomplete and inacccurate status, coupled with information overload and inadequate analysis on the part of leaders, combine to make it difficult for leaders to give subordinates complete and accurate guidance to proceed.*

There are several factors that contribute to making decision-making difficult during a cyberattack crisis:

- **First**, status reports are incomplete, do not contain the right data in the right format, or are not summarized in the right way for decision-makers to properly handle the data.

- **Second**, some status reports are inaccurate or get distorted as the reports get passed through multiple layers of management; the reports may be summarized or condensed or embellished with hearsay or conjecture, resulting in an inaccurate status picture at senior leadership levels.

- **Third**, overwhelmed leadership misses important facts or performs inadequate analysis or synthesis of the facts, resulting in faulty decisions. The guidance resulting from this process can have the same problem traveling back down the management chain, resulting in guidance that is incomplete or inaccurate by the time it reaches staff for execution.

To assist decision-makers in getting the best possible status and making the best possible decisions, it is important to remember the following factors:

- Accurate decision-making requires accurate data regarding the status, *not* opinions about the data or the status. Intermediate managers and leaders must resist the temptation to summarize by replacing data with opinions, going from "four out of five servers have been rebuilt and the fifth one will be ready tomorrow" to "most of the servers are done and we will be done soon." Opinions do not synthesize well into combined reports for leadership.

- Accurate data will not always be available—collecting status takes work as well—and frequently decisions will have to be made with incomplete information. This reality is one of the most difficult situations for managers. Talented leaders will shine in these situations by making the right *gut choice* in the absence of data or guidance. Inevitably, though, these decisions will be reconsidered after the fact, especially when such *gut decisions* do not work out well. To support after-action review, it is helpful to understand the assumptions the leaders made in the absence of accurate data. Leaders need to capture and document their assumptions and other related documentation when they make key decisions.

- On the other hand, inaccurate status information—or status that becomes distorted as it passes through multiple layers of management—is absolutely toxic to good decision-making. When different enterprise departments are each maintaining their own status and the two statuses do not match, senior leadership must spend valuable time de-conflicting between the two reports to figure out what is really going on. Bad status can result in wasted time and delays in decision-making as the enterprise must go back and forth to get accurate information. Worst of all is when leaders make decisions and give guidance that is wrong because it is based on inaccurate situational awareness.

Asks Versus Needs: Eliciting Accurate Requirements and Guidance

Staff and contractors can compensate for some of the previously mentioned challenges by understanding the difference between *asks* and *needs*. Staff and contractors should think and ask intelligent questions to ensure the status they are giving is the status that is actually needed, and the guidance they are receiving is actually the appropriate guidance. It is not unusual for staff members to send up a situation status report and expect to get certain guidance based on that status, only to get guidance that is totally contradictory to the status and does not make sense. This situation occurs because the original status was distorted going up the chain of command, or the resulting guidance got distorted coming back down. Staff and contractors who recognize these disconnects can question the communications and address the distortions to help ensure the enterprise makes smart decisions. To help with this clarification, staff and contractors should take the following key actions:

- **First**, when reporting status, staff and contractors need to have a conversation with management about what status management is looking for and what the resulting status actually *means*. Management may say, "I want you to tell me how many servers are built." However, when talking to management, staff and contractors realize what management is really looking for is how close a key business application is to being operational, and getting the servers built may be only one of several phases of activities related to getting the application operational. In this specific example, when 90% of the servers are built, management reports that they are 90% of the way to having the application operational, when the actual result may be more like 25%. By having a conversation with management to understand what it is they are trying to measure, staff and contractors can define and collect metrics that accurately reflect the goal to be achieved and the corresponding progress toward the goal. Staff and contractors can waylay misinterpretations ahead of time and avoid situations where last-minute heroics are required to close the communications gap.

- **Second**, staff and contractors need to have conversations with management when they receive guidance for action. These conversations can address the same type of disconnects that occur when reporting status. Such disconnects include management giving guidance based on incorrect assumptions about the situation, the staff or contractors' capabilities, and so on. Management can say, "Get me an airplane," but it is up to staff to ask the follow-up questions to understand if it's a model airplane or a jumbo jet that is actually needed. Even guidance that seems to be unambiguous—such as requests for plans or architectures—can actually be satisfied by a wide range of deliverables, and getting clarification is better than wasting time doing the wrong thing.

- **Third**, staff and contractors should elicit accurate deliverable requirements. This activity is related to clarifying guidance, but it has to do specifically with the requirements process. It particularly affects contract situations where requirements are at the heart of the contract and satisfaction of those requirements is necessary for the contractor to be paid. In these situations, overloaded and overwhelmed customer management will not necessarily have the time to thoroughly think through what they actually need, and contractor requests for requirements can be met with deaf ears and silence. Rather than being paralyzed by this type of situation, contractors can often keep things moving—and *help the customer*—by writing their own version of the requirements based on their understanding of the customer situation. For example, "I know that you are looking to rebuild x, y and z. Therefore, I believe that you need me to do a, b, and c." By giving the customer sample requirements to approve, disapprove, or correct, contractors can make it easier for management to give them concrete guidance and accelerate the process of getting everyone "on the same page" and working effectively.

The Observe Orient Decide Act (OODA) Loop

US Air Force Colonel John Boyd (1927-1997) captured the challenges of effective decision-making under pressure when he documented the OODA loop shown in Figure 10-4.

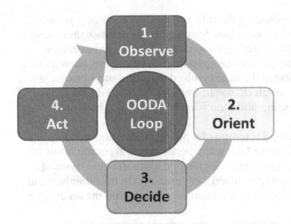

Figure 10-4. *The OODA loop is a decision-making cycle that involves four steps: observe the situation, orient based on those observations, decide what to do next, and act to carry out the decision.*

The OODA loop consists of four steps that are repeated iteratively. While Colonel Boyd developed this theory to describe how fighter pilots perform in combat, this model is also relevant when it is applied to how enterprises make decisions. The four steps are as follows:

1. ***Observe:*** The enterprise observes its situation by collecting status from personnel "on the ground" and synthesizing the status into a coherent picture for decision-makers.

2. ***Orient:*** Based on observations, the enterprise analyzes the situation and prepares to make decisions. This step may involve processing status data into "actionable intelligence" and having staff members prepare plans and alternative courses of action for decision-makers.

3. ***Decide:*** The decision-makers decide on a course of action. Staff members break those decisions out into their contingent parts for subordinates and subordinate teams so that they may take action based on the decision.

4. ***Act:*** The enterprise executes the decisions that were made by repositioning resources and executing procedures. In other words, the decision is turned into action. The results of those actions and their impact on the situation are then observed (along with the actions of adversaries and allies) and the cycle begins again.

A key OODA tenet is that each of these steps takes time. If an enterprise can operate faster than the cyberattacker's OODA loop, then the cyberattacker will be forever "one step behind" and unable to respond effectively to the enterprise's actions.

Establishing an Operational Tempo

Colonel Boyd's OODA loop theory maps directly to enterprise crisis operations in terms of information collection and decision-making. OODA theory states that reports and decisions have to be synchronized so there is time to observe the results of decisions before making new decisions to continue moving forward. If the enterprise wants to make decisions at an accelerated rate, then reporting, meetings, and coordination all need to take place at an accelerated rate as well. This synchronization, in turn, defines the enterprise's operational tempo.

The pace of decision-making is dependent on understanding the time required for each step of the OODA loop. For example, operational changes can be made on an hourly or daily basis because they involve simply changing operational parameters. On the other hand, staffing changes can take weeks to execute because of the delays inherent in changing personnel and training new personnel. Engineering changes can take days, weeks, months, or even years to execute because of the time involved to re-tool components, test and integrate systems, or obtain regulatory approval for design changes. Strategy shifts can take months or even years to observe and orient before making key decisions, and then years to execute on those decisions once they are made.

Normal business operations often revolve around a weekly tempo of reports and decision-making. Staff and teams set up weekly meetings to coordinate the members of the team, perform lateral coordination with other teams, and collate and send up reports to management. At higher and more strategic layers of management, the reports and meetings may become monthly, quarterly, or annually. On the other hand, at lower levels there may be daily, or even hourly, "huddles" to make sure that everyone is working on the right tasks and problems are dealt with quickly.

In a crisis situation, these cycles tend to become compressed due to the urgency of the situation and the desire of leadership to ensure every hour of every day is used to its maximum potential to make progress against the threat. In normal enterprise circumstances, the most common operational tempo is the week. In a crisis, the most common operational tempo tends to be the day. Daily status reports and daily operational guidance become the norm. Even with a daily operational tempo, there are delays as information moves up the enterprise hierarchy, decision-makers orient and decide on courses of action, guidance moves back down the hierarchy, and technical staff execute against the guidance. Figure 10-5 shows this operational tempo.

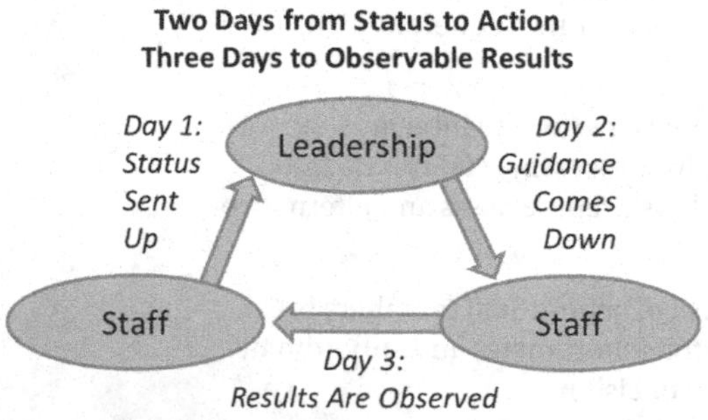

Figure 10-5. *Even with daily reporting and guidance, it can still take several days for status to travel up the hierarchy, decisions to travel down, and the impact of decisions to be observed and reported back up.*

It is important for leaders to understand the operational tempo and keep up with it as the enterprise moves forward. When a situation starts deteriorating, it will take time for the enterprise to understand the situation and start responding to it. If the situation comes up in daily operational meetings, then such a response may take several days to manifest itself. Situations that come up in weekly meetings may take three or more weeks from the emergence of the situation to the impact of the response. Depending on the situation, these response rates may or may not be acceptably fast to handle rapidly changing circumstances.

In a crisis, the enterprise may need to be able to operate on even faster OODA loops than days or weeks, with the ability to respond effectively within minutes or hours. To achieve this type of speed, regular meetings are no longer effective and the enterprise must use alternative methods such as war rooms and crisis operations centers, where observers, analysts, and decision-makers are all co-located and able to interact with each other in real time. The bottom line is that an enterprise needs to consider these factors to identify the appropriate processes, procedures, and tools required for effective decision-making for day-to-day and crisis operations.

Operating in Crisis Mode

To sum up how the enterprise should operate in a crisis, it is helpful to think about *planning, process, prioritization, parallelism,* and *sequencing*. These five factors should be considered as follows:

- **Planning:** First, it important for an enterprise to have a plan for the crisis recovery effort. The plan does not have to be elaborate, but there needs to be some agreement on where to go and how to get there. An initial plan may be as simple as identifying the high-level goals and approximate timelines for recovery, reconstitution, and protection against counterattack. A single page of information, if it gets everyone "on the same page," helps to manage the chaos. This initial plan can be refined and detailed as the situation unfolds so that everyone gets the information that they need to stay organized and coordinated. As nice as it would be to have a complete plan standing by when the crisis occurs, most crises are unique and recovery plans must be created once the extent of the crisis is understood. Consequently, planning must occur "just in time," along with everything else in the recovery process.

- **Process:** Next, an enterprise needs to establish some process for the recovery effort. A handful of processes can do wonders to reduce ad hoc communications and permit teams to interface with each other smoothly. Processes should include the following elements to help people coordinate effectively and take the stress off of saturated communication channels:

  - Regularly scheduled meetings for reporting, coordination, and issue discussion

  - Standardized formats for reports and requests

  - Supporting capabilities such as telephone bridges, document repositories, request trackers, or workspaces

  - A room that people can go to for information, a whiteboard containing important announcements, or a telephone bridge or request line staffed by support personnel

- **Prioritization:** With some processes in place, the next challenge is to prioritize recovery efforts. Prioritization tends to be difficult because everyone wants everything recovered immediately, and the IT systems that are nonfunctional have critical business consequences. The reality is there seldom are enough resources to do everything simultaneously. The enterprise is going to have to make some tough decisions. IT leaders need to turn discussions about technical priorities and dependencies into discussions about business priorities. If there are two IT systems that need to be brought back online and only enough resources to do one at a time, the enterprise will need to decide which system to do first. The enterprise will need to accept the consequences of delaying bringing the other system online. Conversely, if one of those IT systems is dependent on the other, then the order in which they come online may be decided by technical considerations, regardless of the business priorities. An enterprise needs to understand these factors so leadership can make informed decisions.

- **Parallelism:** In a crisis, and especially after help is obtained, the enterprise may have a lot of resources at its disposal. These resources will be able to accomplish many activities quickly. The challenge is going to be keeping the resources organized so they are working at maximum efficiency. Their effectiveness is going to be limited by how well the enterprise can coordinate parallel activities and avoid having the resources tripping over each other while waiting for interdependencies among teams and systems. This coordination challenge is difficult because *normal* project planning is done around technical interdependencies while *crisis* project planning should be done around resource constraints. With resource-driven planning, the goal is to keep available resources fully utilized at all times, thereby avoiding time spent waiting on interdependencies. Resource-driven planning turns into managing a delicate balance between parallelism and prioritization. Sometimes lower-priority items get pushed up in implementation order simply because resources are available to do them and would otherwise be idle. Leadership needs to shift its mindset to use resource-driven planning to help get the recovery done as quickly as possible.

- **Sequencing:** Sequencing helps to ensure recovery happens in the right order to keep the recovery effort moving forward and to avoid having critical resources sitting idle while they are waiting for other pieces of the enterprise to recover. In a modern IT system, there are many layers of technology that interact to deliver capability (for example, networking, storage, computing, operating systems, applications, Internet connectivity, and clients). The order in which these systems are built is important. Often systems cannot be tested end-to-end until late in the recovery process due to the time required for all the pieces to be integrated. During planning, it is important for the system owners to understand how quickly they can establish an initial operating capability (IOC) versus full operating capability (FOC) so recovery can continue in parallel across multiple tracks. For many low-level capabilities such as networks and storage / computing, an enterprise may want to establish IOC quickly so other teams can start working on rebuilding while simultaneously working on the FOC for those systems. Planning the sequencing so that all available resources are fully utilized is of paramount importance to a successful recovery.

Managing the Recovery Process

What does an enterprise need to do in a cybersecurity crisis to regain control of the situation, rebuild impaired systems, and recover lost business functionality?

The CIO looked around at his staff as the gravity of the situation sank in.

The attackers had complete control, and the enterprise was entirely at their mercy.

"So, what do we do now?" he asked, looking around the room.

The CISO leaned forward and replied, "Now we fight!"

Cyber Hand-to-Hand Combat

The beginning of a cyberattack crisis is not be the end of the cyberbattle. In fact, the cyberbattle can take days, weeks, or even years to conclude. Some days the defenders gain ground, and other days the attackers gain ground. Generally, a cyberbattle consists of the following phases:

- **Stealth:** In the beginning, attackers often have stealth on their side, and are attacking systems and moving through the enterprise unseen. In this phase, attackers move slowly and carefully to avoid setting off enterprise defenses.

- **Discovery:** After the enterprise defenders discover the attack, they should also move carefully to avoid tipping their hand and letting the attackers know the enterprise is aware of the attack. During this phase, defenders carefully analyze the attack sequence to understand the extent of the attack and consider defensive and remediation options.

- **Containment and Remediation:** Now the game is on. Defenders attempt to contain the attack and remediate affected systems so the attackers are repelled from the enterprise. Mistakes and oversights in this phase allow the attackers to retain their foothold inside the enterprise, or retake it after they are first repelled.

- **Counterattack and Battle:** After the initial remediation, attackers may attempt to regain control of the enterprise. At this point, attackers know the defenders are on to them, so they often switch tactics. Speed and tenacity are all-important now, as defenders are watching and responding to attacker moves as they occur. This cyberbattle may wage back-and-forth for days, weeks, months, or even years, as attackers and defenders move and counter-move against each other.

- **Entrenchment and Stabilization:** Eventually the situation stabilizes, with one party emerging victorious. Generally, defenders regain control of their enterprise. Sometimes, attackers out-maneuver the defense and disappear inside of unmonitored IT systems, retaining their foothold on an ongoing basis. Other times, the business disruption required for complete eradication may be too great for the enterprise to accommodate and an "uneasy truce" emerges where attackers continue to have access, but such access is relegated to non-critical systems that are not cost-effective to fully remediate.

For cybersecurity personnel in the midst of the battle, it feels like cyber hand-to-hand combat. Attackers take over accounts, computers, servers, and networks, while defenders scramble to retake control of these systems. The process is grueling and exhausting, and few outside of the cybersecurity department understand or appreciate what is happening.

Often, this cybersecurity battle will be raging at the same time the IT recovery effort begins. Frequently, IT personnel who are recovering systems are not aware of the cybersecurity struggles going on alongside them, or of the threats to themselves, their accounts, and their computers as they begin the rebuilding process.

"Throwing Money at Problems"

In a crisis, money may be the only lever the enterprise really has to deal with the problem. Throwing money at problems can rapidly take pressure off of overburdened staff and teams by bringing in additional resources. Money can be used to obtain expertise, services, software, and equipment to give the recovery effort options and flexibility. Some of the ways the enterprise can use money to its advantage include the following:

- *Buy Expertise:* Money can be spent to bring in service providers to help with planning, investigation, cybersecurity improvements, IT rebuilding, and status tracking. Often, it is smart to bring in outsiders to do these jobs even when there are employees who would normally do them. By bringing in outsiders, the employees are freed to use their expertise and enterprise knowledge to provide leadership and strategy.

- *Buy Services:* While enterprise IT systems are offline, it can be advantageous to buy services to supplement those systems during the recovery process, even if it is on a temporary basis. This approach can enable the enterprise to get key capabilities, such as e-mail, telephones, trouble ticketing, and financial systems operational again while the primary systems are being rebuilt.

- *Buy Capacity:* During the rebuilding process, the enterprise may need excess capacity on a temporary basis. This need may be because primary systems are being held as evidence for criminal investigations, or it may be because parallel rebuilding efforts can proceed faster if there is extra infrastructure capacity to support them. Simply stated, money can be spent to purchase, lease, rent, or borrow the additional capacity that is needed.

- *Buy Capability:* During the rebuilding and cybersecurity strengthening process, the enterprise will not know exactly what long-term products and features are needed. Personnel will want to be able to rapidly test and discard options without having to get bogged down in contract and licensing negotiations with vendors. The enterprise can negotiate with vendors for *sampler platter* licensing contracts that enable the enterprise to use the vendors' full range of products, and then only keep long-term the capabilities that are ultimately needed.

- *Buy Contingencies:* Finally, not everything in the rebuilding process is going to go according to plan. Business leadership will want to hedge against the failures and uncertainties that will undoubtedly occur. Money can be spent to line up contingency options and alternatives to guard against such failures and ensure big problems do not become showstoppers.

Identifying Resources and Resource Constraints

An early step in the recovery process is identifying the resources available for the recovery effort. These resources can be internal, external, hardware, software, intellectual, or time. An important activity is identifying which resources are going to be critical and which are going to be overtaxed as the cybersecurity effort and recovery processes unfold. Resources likely to be overtaxed during a major recovery effort include the following:

- *Leadership and Project Management:* Leadership and management quickly become saturated in a crisis situation and need whatever useful relief they can get.

- *Incident Response and Forensics:* Few enterprises have in-house incident response teams that are staffed to handle an incident of any magnitude.

- *Cybersecurity Engineering:* Efforts to shore up cyberdefenses in the wake of a breach will likely exceed the capacity of the existing team. The crisis makes almost everything that is desired "essential" and places these desires on the critical path for proceeding.

- **IT Infrastructure and Backups:** As rebuilding efforts get underway, critical infrastructure such as networking, firewalls, storage, computing, and backup systems become bottlenecks to progress and system recovery.

- **IT Support and Help Desk:** If major changes are performed to endpoints or enterprise applications, IT support staff quickly become overwhelmed supporting employees who are impacted by the changes and unable to work effectively.

As these resource constraints are identified, planners can hedge against them by obtaining additional resources, lining up contingency resources, or exploring alternative approaches.

Building a Resource-Driven Project Plan

The result of the recovery planning effort is a *resource-driven* project plan. A resource-driven plan is different from a *normal* project plan because the resource-driven recovery plan is designed around the primary constraint, which is time and available resources. The goal of the recovery planning process is to ensure all resources are gainfully employed to the maximum extent possible so the overall rebuilding process goes as quickly as possible.

In developing the resource-driven recovery plan, availability of critical resources will likely be the bottleneck driving the overall sequence of events and the prioritization of the rebuilding effort. The highest-priority project should be overlaid onto the resources first, so the resources (people) can proceed in executing the project's critical path. Lower-priority projects will be sequenced later with the understanding they will spend time waiting for the resources needed to execute successfully. In this manner, high-priority, mid-priority, and low-priority projects are laid out and sequenced. Low-priority projects are worked on an "if-time-is-available" basis until higher priority efforts have been completed. This planning process can be very challenging to accomplish, especially under stressful circumstances. Figure 10-6 depicts how five projects can be overlaid onto the available resources so the highest-priority project completes first and all the projects are executed at the maximum efficiency. Even though Figure 10-6 depicts the projects as progressing linearly, the reality is much more complex and iterative.

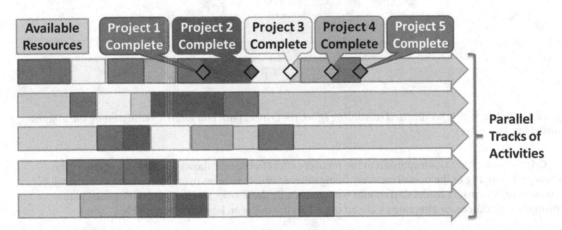

Figure 10-6. *In a resource-driven plan, projects are overlaid across the available resources and sequenced so the most important projects are completed first while utilizing all available resources to the maximum extent possible.*

"Keep calm and carry on" while remembering that in a crisis you never have the resources you need to do *everything* you want.

Project planners need to be creative when developing the overall resource-driven plan. Often, projects can be performed out of sequence. Software development can be performed at the same time the infrastructure is being set up. Non-production systems can be tested while the production systems are being built. Such out-of-order execution is uncomfortable to project planners and technical staff, and it increases overall project risk. However, in a crisis situation, out-of-order execution can result in significant time compression of the overall process, which saves precious time for other priorities. Risk added by this process can be mitigated through additional testing or simply accepted as a consequence of the crisis situation.

Maximizing Parallelism in Execution

A resource-driven plan strives to optimize available resources to get the most important recovery activities done first and help the business recover as quickly as possible. As this plan is executed, the *critical path* jumps around among the different teams as each team's activities become critical to the progress of the rebuilding effort. Most likely, the same teams identified as being resource-constrained early on in the planning process will also be the teams disproportionately on the critical path. These resource-constrained teams include leadership, incident response, cybersecurity, IT infrastructure, and IT support teams. These critical resources need to be watched carefully so relief can be obtained when it is needed, or preferably before it is needed. Figure 10-7 depicts a notional pattern of how the critical path can jump around.

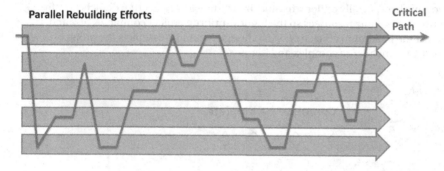

Figure 10-7. *In a highly parallelized rebuilding effort, the critical path can jump around among the different parallel tracks.*

Critical path analysis is important to the recovery effort because it shows where there is risk of the critical path slipping or the overall recovery being delayed due to failures in critical teams or of critical personnel or systems. IT leadership should work to identify these risks and line up contingency plans, contingency resources, or alternatives ahead of time so the risks can be kept manageable.

Depending on the severity of the crisis, delays in recovery can cost *thousands or even millions of dollars per day in lost productivity*. Business leaders should calculate the cost of lost productivity so that they can make smart investments to minimize the real or potential costs of such delays.

Taking Care of People

In a crisis, there usually is a brief period where everyone dives in and gives up their nights and weekends to deal with the crisis. As encouraging as this sudden burst of adrenaline is, it is seldom sustainable in the long run, especially when setbacks inevitably occur. After this initial surge of adrenaline wears off and everyone starts to get an idea of the magnitude of the effort ahead of them, leadership needs to step in and establish a sustainable pace for the overall effort. Most likely, the pace is going to be for a marathon, not a sprint.

Establishing a pace includes identifying critical personnel, getting them backups, and arranging shifts. When recovery is going on seven days a week and 24 hours a day, key decision-makers like the CIO, CISO, and other staff are needed to make critical decisions at critical times. However, this reality does not mean they need to be available 24 hours a day, seven days a week. A little bit of planning and scheduling, especially utilizing deputies and senior direct reports, can make it possible for these critical personnel to get the rest and breaks they need to be able to stay on top of things.

Ironically, this situation can be more difficult for key technical personnel, whose importance is well-known to their colleagues and subordinates, but perhaps not as well-known to IT leadership. Management should watch out for the technical people who are consulted on *every project* or who are the *sole source* of institutional knowledge on key systems. There are usually a few such individuals and their importance to the recovery process cannot be understated. When such people are identified, leadership should consider a few key steps to include:

- **First**, leadership should ensure these people are incentivized to stay with the enterprise through the recovery process, even though it may be difficult and stressful.

- **Second**, leadership should ensure these people have some relief, either internally through colleagues who are assigned to assist them or externally through consultants who are assigned to shadow them and back them up.

- **Third**, leadership should watch their work schedules and ensure they are given breaks when the opportunities arise. Often, the same high performance that makes these people critical also precludes them from giving themselves the breaks that they need, even when the opportunity presents itself.

Another thing leadership should do is to establish work schedules to ensure everyone gets time off and days off with some regularity. Even though there is a crisis, houses still have to be fixed, kids have to be taken to school, elderly parents have to be cared for, and doctor's appointments have to be attended. Teams should set schedules for work to accommodate the realities of people's personal lives and include reasonable amounts of time off for everyone involved. It may make sense to shift work schedules. For example, if IT systems are to be repaired during the evenings, then perhaps staff should come in at noon each day and stay late, with the mornings available as personal time. Weekend breaks should be planned around people's personal and religious needs. Not everyone in the department is on the same schedule or needs the same days off. Finally, religious and national holidays should not be discounted if they occur during the recovery period. Even if it delays the recovery, these breaks should be protected so employees understand people are more important than recovery.

Furthermore, there are inexpensive things leadership can do to support morale and help everyone stay productive. If teams are co-located and working nights and weekends, bringing in catered food can give everyone a welcomed break and an opportunity to think and talk about something other than work for a few minutes. Personal services like laundry, haircuts, and daycare assistance can also be a treat for stressed employees. Compared to the costs of flagging morale, waning enthusiasm, or accidents caused by mistakes or carelessness, none of these actions is terribly expensive and they can help the team stay together through a difficult time.

Recovering Cybersecurity and IT Capabilities

As the recovery process gets moving, there will likely be two parallel tracks occurring simultaneously: one track to remediate and strengthen the cybersecurity situation, and a second track to restore damaged IT capabilities. Figure 10-8 highlights the reality that cybersecurity improvements in controls (particularly preventive controls) can often interfere with the rapid rebuilding of compromised IT systems. As a consequence, these two tracks may be in tension with one another.

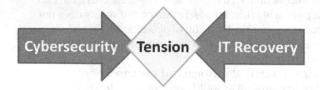

Figure 10-8. *During the crisis and recovery process, cybersecurity and the IT recovery effort may be in constant tension.*

Leadership must carefully manage this tension to ensure IT does not jeopardize the recovery process by undermining cybersecurity protections. Conversely, cybersecurity cannot jeopardize the recovery process by imposing controls that devastate productivity at a time when efficiency and speed are critical.

Building the Bridge While You Cross It

In 2000, Electronic Data Systems (EDS), a US multi-national IT services company, had a television advertisement, entitled "Building Airplanes in the Sky." In the advertisement, construction workers build an airplane while it is in flight, and then parachute off of the completed airplane at the end. The whole thing is rather tongue-in-cheek, but they make an important point about the challenges of building and deploying complex systems that are needed immediately when they are ready, or are operational throughout the project.

A similar analogy for the relationship between cybersecurity and the IT recovery might actually be "Building the Bridge While You Cross It." In an extensive rebuilding effort, the cybersecurity team needs to protect IT. At the same time, the cybersecurity team also relies on IT to provide the enterprise with networks, storage, and computing needed to deliver cybersecurity protective capabilities. If the cybersecurity team gets too far out ahead of IT, it will deploy security capabilities that IT cannot use, and get in the way of the IT recovery process. If the cybersecurity team falls too far behind IT, then IT systems will be deployed without the cybersecurity protections the systems need to be safe. The key is to keep the two carefully synchronized throughout the recovery process.

Cybersecurity needs to protect IT as systems are built, but it also relies on those systems to support it. IT and cybersecurity construction efforts need to be carefully synchronized so IT functionality and cybersecurity protection both come online together.

Preparing to Rebuild and Restore

Before starting the rebuilding process, leadership should come together and consider the following questions in order to define a balanced strategy for rebuilding:

- What will it take to disrupt the attackers, deny them the ability to operate in the IT environment, and regain cybersecurity control?

- What will it take to recover impaired business IT capabilities?

- What is the minimum amount of cybersecurity necessary before proceeding with the IT recovery process?

- How can cybersecurity enhancements be phased so cybersecurity and business recovery can proceed together?

- What if the attackers counterattack in the middle of the recovery process?

- What is at risk if cybersecurity gets defeated while the recovery is in progress?

- What is the business's tolerance for risk in the overall recovery effort, balancing the factors of business impairment, IT recovery, and cybersecurity?

The answers to these questions help set the strategy for the recovery and allow it to proceed with an agreed-upon balance of business, IT, and cybersecurity risk. Generally, the resulting plan will use a phased approach to start the recovery without making the situation worse:

- First, critical cybersecurity controls are shored up enough to remove attackers from the enterprise, or at least deny them administrative control.

- Second, interim IT capabilities are established so the business can continue functioning. These capabilities may come from "cloud services" or other external providers so internal IT personnel can focus on rebuilding.

- Third, more extensive IT recovery is performed in parallel with more extensive cybersecurity improvements. These two tracks run in parallel, "building the IT bridge while cybersecurity crosses it." This approach is used to establish initial operating capabilities for IT and cybersecurity functions in parallel.

- Fourth, as the situation stabilizes and the business regains functionality, initial operating capabilities are matured into full operating capabilities, with full capacity, high availability, redundancy, and disaster recovery as needed by the business.

Closing Critical Cybersecurity Gaps

A first recovery step is to repel the attackers (if they are actively inside the environment) and close critical cybersecurity gaps so the attackers cannot interfere with the recovery process while it is taking place. While it is not realistic to think cybersecurity can be immediately brought *up to par* (particularly if cybersecurity had serious shortcomings before the attack), there are usually small, incremental steps that can be easily taken to deny attackers administrative control, or to keep them out of critical infrastructure. This approach may involve the use of *air-gapped* systems and networks, or establishing multi-factor authentication on critical system accounts.

Since the rest of the recovery is waiting on this initial step, it should be done as quickly as possible and only to close critical gaps. Key things to consider at this point in the recovery process include the following:

- Disrupting attacker communications channels so attackers cannot control malware inside the enterprise that might be left over from before the attack

- Protecting critical systems administrator accounts with multi-factor authentication, rapidly changing passwords, or extensive auditing

- Protecting critical security servers through patching, hardening, network isolation, or monitoring

- Isolating key infrastructure onto separate network segments with restrictive firewall rules

- Using application whitelisting or monitoring to detect unauthorized changes on key and/or vulnerable systems

- Establishing 24x7 monitoring and alerting to detect and respond to future attacker activity

Establishing Interim IT Capabilities

While cybersecurity gaps are being closed, IT can simultaneously start preparing interim IT capabilities to replace those capabilities lost during the attack and to support the recovery process. Depending on the severity of what was lost and the long-term strategy for the IT functions involved, there are a number of options here:

- Transitioning production IT data and services to development or staging systems that were unaffected by the attack

- Recovering IT servers from backups and bringing them back to operation as they were before the crisis

- Recovering IT data from backups and rebuilding affected servers as they were before the crisis

- Migrating IT functions to cloud services, either on a temporary or a permanent basis

- Accelerating otherwise planned upgrades to IT systems and rolling out upgraded systems (Note that this option can be risky if the upgrades are significant.)

- Proceeding to use manual workarounds, such as pen and paper or personal computer tools rather than enterprise applications.

If the crisis is severe and affects multiple IT services, a combination of these approaches can be used on a case-by-case basis for each IT service and system. Do not underestimate the value of manual workarounds; as pen and paper or personal computing can work fine on a temporary basis for many functions and free up critical IT talent to focus on recovering the most important IT systems and functions. The other important point is these approaches are *interim* IT capabilities to buy time while the full IT recovery takes place. These approaches only need to last long enough to bring the full production capability back online during the next phase of the recovery.

Conducting Prioritized IT Recovery and Cybersecurity Improvements

Once critical cybersecurity gaps are addressed and interim IT capabilities are established, the recovery effort can begin in earnest. This effort should be prioritized based on business need, with recovery efforts coordinated to use all available resources to the greatest extent possible to deliver business capabilities in the order they are needed. These efforts are often broken up into multiple phases of IT capabilities so initial operating capability can be delivered as quickly as possible and full operating capability achieved at a later time. By breaking recovery up in this manner, limited resources can be used to deliver the greatest amount of IT functionality in the least amount of time.

In parallel with the IT recovery, the enterprise will also most likely be making improvements to cybersecurity capabilities as well. These improvements will help ensure recovered IT systems are adequately protected from the current attackers returning or other more advanced attackers striking in the future. These improvements must be carefully planned so they do not get in the way of the IT recovery process and excessively hold up progress. Like IT capabilities, cybersecurity improvements may also be broken up into initial operating capabilities and full operating capabilities in an effort to efficiently utilize limited engineering, deployment, and support resources.

Establishing Full Operating Capabilities for IT and Cybersecurity

With the completion of the above phase, IT and cybersecurity should have initial operating capabilities for the majority of the functions damaged or lost due to the crisis. The enterprise should be able to resume *normal* operations as it conducted before the crisis occurred. However, these initial capabilities mean the IT work is not done. Usually, initial operating capabilities have significant limitations in terms of capacity, redundancy, high availability, disaster recovery, or security. In the final phase of the recovery effort, these shortcomings should be addressed so full operating capability of all systems is achieved.

Due to schedule, budget, and resource constraints, this last phase may end up taking place over a lengthy period of time—extending months or even years after the initial restoration is completed. In the event of budget constraints, full recovery may be deferred to future fiscal years. Systems may be operated in a "high-risk" configuration until the recovery budget becomes available. While uncomfortable, these decisions and trade-offs are appropriate, provided such decisions are made as business decisions accurately considering the business, IT, and cybersecurity risks that are involved.

Cybersecurity Versus IT Restoration

Throughout the recovery process, there will likely be an active tension between cybersecurity and IT. Cybersecurity controls to protect against counterattack or future breaches will inevitably get in the way of IT personnel recovering systems and rebuilding IT capabilities. When the balance between these two factors needs to be adjusted to either improve cybersecurity at the expense of the IT recovery process or to speed up the IT recovery process at the expense of cybersecurity, it is important the enterprise embraces this tension and maintains open channels of communication on what is working and what is not working. There is no right answer here—only a delicate balance that must be carefully maintained.

The enterprise can take several actions to maintain this balance:

- Educate IT staff on the purpose of cybersecurity controls that interfere with their work and let everyone know that management understands how the controls impact productivity.

- Ensure cybersecurity staff understands thoroughly the operational impact of cybersecurity controls and plans ahead for alternatives should this impact become untenable at a critical time.

- Have leadership regularly monitor the productivity impact of cybersecurity controls and be prepared to execute contingency plans if necessary.

Cybersecurity can be very helpful by being proactive about these challenges and engaging regularly with IT staff to understand the impact of security controls and discuss the trade-offs and alternatives. IT staff will be much more supportive of security controls if they have had the opportunity to discuss them with cybersecurity, consider the alternatives, and come to their own conclusion that the chosen security controls are the *least bad* alternative from among the possible approaches.

Cybersecurity should also remember the security value of speed. Relaxing some security controls on a temporary basis may be warranted if it causes a critical recovery action to proceed twice as fast, or even faster. Getting key infrastructure operational may be more valuable to the business if it is done sooner, even if considerable security risk is accepted to get there. To support this type of improvisation, cybersecurity can compensate for relaxing preventive controls by being more aggressive with detective or audit controls to achieve the same levels of security with a lower operational impact.

Maximum Allowable Risk

In balancing all of these factors, business, IT, and cybersecurity leaders need to remember the concept of *Maximum Allowable Risk*. As shown in Figure 10-9, leadership needs to ensure all aspects of the recovery are performed at the same overall risk level.

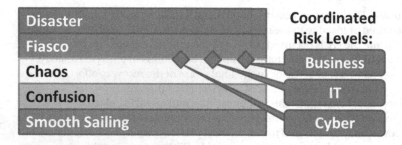

Figure 10-9. *In a crisis, business, IT, and cybersecurity risk levels must be synchronized at an agreed-upon maximum allowable level until service can be restored.*

Depending on the severity of the original crisis, the enterprise's tolerance for risk may be quite high. If the crisis was minor, then the enterprise appetite for risk in the recovery may also be low. If the crisis was catastrophic, then the enterprise appetite for risk in the recovery could be very high.

During the recovery effort, business leaders must constantly monitor the business, IT, and cybersecurity risk levels for the recovery effort, and they must ensure these risk levels stay as well coordinated as possible. The primary business driver is going to be speed, and business leadership will likely push IT and cybersecurity to move at the maximum speed possible to get the recovery done in a secure way without resulting in spectacular failure. The business impairment caused by the criss may be worth thousands or even millions of dollars each day. When these costs are high, the business appetite for risk in the name of speed will likely be quite high. The challenge is translating these risk factors into business decisions so leaders can make the best-informed decisions possible.

Ending the Crisis

As the expression goes, "This too shall come to pass." The enterprise will eventually reach a point where it is no longer operating in crisis. This transition generally happens at different times for different teams, with some personnel—particularly cybersecurity personnel—staying in crisis mode long after most employees have gotten back to business as usual.

Resolving the Crisis

Generally, a crisis winds down through four distinct phases of business recovery, as different parts of the enterprise return to *normal* operations:

- *Regular Employees*: The first recovery phase is when basic enterprise functions are restored, often using interim or contingency capabilities. This phase may occur relatively quickly after the crisis first occurs, and it allows the enterprise to continue operating even while IT and cybersecurity are recovering systems. Interestingly, for most regular employees, this first milestone marks the conclusion of the crisis since the impact to their ability to do their jobs is largely mitigated.

- *Corporate Staff*: The second recovery phase occurs when the most important enterprise IT systems are recovered to an initial operating capability since, at this point, business personnel (also known as corporate staff) are able to get back to work using their normal processes.

- *IT Staff*: The third recovery phase occurs when IT systems are fully restored back to full operating capability. At this point, IT staff can get back to a regular schedule of system maintenance, updates, and improvements.

- *Cybersecurity Staff*: The fourth recovery phase occurs when cybersecurity improvements are completed and cybersecurity staff can "relax" and get back to their business as usual.

Declaring the Crisis Remediated and Over

At some point in these four recovery phases, enterprise leadership is able to declare the crisis remediated and over. Why is it important to declare the crisis remediated and over? Reasons for this include the following factors related to morale and business considerations:

- First, it is important for employees to understand the crisis is over and the expectation for them *to go the extra mile* is no longer present. Employees can get back to a normal work-life balance, take care of families and households, and enjoy vacations, as they would have otherwise planned. It is important to explicitly state this situation to employees, as what is obvious to managers and leaders in staff meetings may not be so apparent to IT staff on the ground.

- The second reason for declaring the crisis complete is there may be policies and procedures put in place specifically for the crisis that need to either be returned to *normal* or permanently adjusted into part of the *new normal* enterprise culture. These temporary arrangements need to be taken out of limbo and either dismantled or made permanent.

- The third reason for declaring the crisis complete has to do with funding. Often, crisis situations are funded and accounted for separately from normal business operations so that they can be tracked as *one-time events* or may even paid for separately by insurance. In these cases, the costs associated with the crisis need to be accounted for and the end of those expenses must be clearly delineated.

There is no hard-and-fast rule when the crisis is declared remediated and over, but generally it is some time between the third and the fourth recovery phases. Generally, once IT systems are fully restored, cybersecurity strengthening that occurs afterward is characterized separately as a *cybersecurity improvements* project.

After Action Review and Lessons Learned

When the crisis is declared complete, it is very helpful for leadership to come together and make a list of lessons learned regarding the crisis experience. This list should not be huge, but it should candidly review what went well and what went poorly with the crisis response, and what lessons the enterprise should learn in order to handle the next crisis a little better or at least with a little more collective wisdom than it had before. These lessons learned can then form the basis for strategic culture shifts that will persist long after the original crisis has been declared resolved. The after action review can include lessons in successes and failures regarding:

- Balancing of operations versus cybersecurity and recovery

- Task organization and coordination

- Performance of technologies, procedures, and techniques

- Performance of teams and organizations

- Performance of partners and contractors

- Recovery costs and cost-savings opportunities

Establishing a "New Normal" Culture

Every crisis has a lasting impact on an enterprise. The leadership challenge is to leverage the crisis to make strategic adjustments to enterprise culture and translate those cultural changes into a *new normal*. Cybersecurity crises can translate into cultural changes that emphasize computer and information security more greatly than they were in the past. This new emphasis can translate into a number of concrete and visible changes to how the enterprise does business:

- Greater willingness among business leaders to trade-off cost and productivity in the name of cybersecurity

- Greater security of enterprise endpoint devices and computers at the expense of functionality

- Restrictions on the use of personal computing devices and conduct of enterprise business from home or other locations

- Greater emphasis on using enterprise devices inside of controlled facilities to do critical work

- Greater discipline among IT staff to focus on protecting enterprise systems and servers

- Employee awareness training on cybersecurity concerns and potential threats

Being Prepared for the Future

Inevitably, one of the most important crisis situation lessons learned is that going forward the enterprise needs to prepare better to prevent or reduce the impact of future cyberattacks. Figure 10-10 depicts how such preparations can accelerate the OODA loop process in future crisis situations.

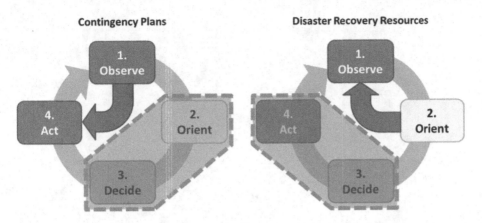

Figure 10-10. *Contingency planning can increase the performance of the OODA loop by preparing contingency plans to specific scenarios or arranging disaster recovery resources ahead of time.*

The left-hand side of Figure 10-10 depicts how enterprise contingency planning prepares the enterprise for potential situations by spending a minimum amount of time in the "Orient" and "Decide" phases of the OODA loop. When contingency scenarios are well defined ahead of time, subordinate staff can go straight from observations to execution, without having to waste precious time with leadership orienting them to the situation and getting decisions on how to proceed. This contingency planning is critically important for incident rapid response scenarios, where very specific attack scenarios can be worked out ahead of time along with response procedures to isolate affected accounts, computers, networks, and servers so attacks can be stopped before they get out of control.

The right-hand side of Figure 10-10 depicts how enterprise disaster recovery resources can be brought to bear quickly in a future crisis. These resources may be offsite backups, contingency systems, or cloud services that are pre-coordinated and prepared ahead of time (the "Decide" and "Act" phases of the OODA loop). By doing this work ahead of time, the enterprise is able to quickly go from the "Orient" phase through to decision and action by activating the emergency resources and getting back to the "Observe" phase to see if the resources have the intended effect.

In addition to these two types of general preparations, the enterprise can also gain a great deal of institutional knowledge about how to operate in a crisis and what capabilities are needed (for example, reports, meeting formats, decision-making processes, and contingency task organization). These capabilities can be built ahead of time through realistic training and tabletop exercises. The value of practicing these skills cannot be understated.

Disasters happen, and they happen to everyone … eventually.

PART IV

Enterprise Cyberdefense Assessment

■ ■ ■

CHAPTER 11

Assessing Enterprise Cybersecurity

This chapter discusses several things related to assessing an enterprise cybersecurity program. First, it discusses the audit process and how auditing is used to evaluate enterprise cybersecurity. Second, it discusses how audits can and should be used to drive the cybersecurity control design process. Third, it describes how enterprise cybersecurity can be systematically evaluated using four different levels of assessment detail. Finally, it describes deficiency tracking, which is an integral component of any formal auditing or assessment process.

Assessments and audits can be conducted by internal or external assessors, and they can be risk-based, threat-based, framework-based, or control-based. It is critical that assessments and audits be a formal part of a successful enterprise cybersecurity program. Without periodic and objective assessment, the cybersecurity program will eventually suffer due to the atrophy that naturally occurs over time and the demands of competing IT priorities.

Cybersecurity Auditing Methodology

What is a cybersecurity audit? For the purposes of this book, an *audit* is a process whereby a person checks an automated system or operational process to ensure that it is operating properly. As illustrated in Figure 11-1, these checks involve looking at the *records* generated by the system or the process, and collecting from those records *evidence* that indicates the proper operation of the automated system or operational process. This evidence is then compiled into *artifacts* that are collected to support the audit process. The artifacts and the conclusions drawn from them are then compiled into the *audit results*, which are stored as formal records that the cybersecurity audit occurred. The audit results document what was done during the audit and what was found from the audit, including identified deficiencies and their eventual remediation.

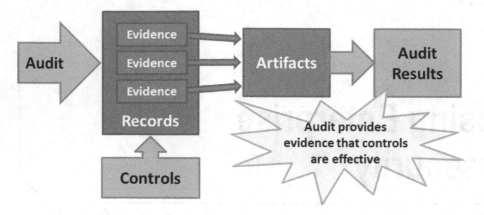

Figure 11-1. *Cybersecurity audits analyze records generated by security controls and obtain evidence regarding automated system and process operations. They then compile those artifacts together into formal results that are retained for presentation to interested parties.*

The Challenge of Proving Negatives

The fundamental challenge with a cybersecurity audit is *proving negatives*, where the goal of the auditor is to collect evidence that proves nothing bad or unexpected occurred during the audited period of time. Inductive reasoning suggests it is not possible to prove the absence of something, but that collecting evidence of its absence gives us basis for reasonably concluding that it may not exist.

To phrase this thought another way, if it can be reasonably assumed malicious or negligent activity generates records of its occurrence, then checking those records can be used to gain confidence if the negligent activity took place or not. The question then becomes how thorough does the checking need to be. In the case of financial records, it may be necessary to check every transaction because fraud may only be in a single transaction. For other records, spot-checking may be sufficient to achieve a high degree of confidence that all is well.

In general, audits work fundamentally the same way by collecting evidence from the available records to indicate the proper operation of the automated system or operational process.

Cybersecurity Audit Objectives

The cybersecurity audit planning process starts with the audit objective. The objective is phrased in terms of a sentence that goes something like the following:

> *I want my audit to indicate that ___ is occurring, or*
> *I want my audit to indicate that ___ is NOT occurring.*

Following are example cybersecurity audit objectives:

- I want my audit to indicate that my web servers are functioning properly and serving up the correct pages.

- I want my audit to indicate that my IT systems are compliant with Sarbanes-Oxley regulations.

- I want my audit to indicate that payment information stored on my systems is being protected as required by Payment Card Industry (PCI) standards.

- I want my audit to indicate that attackers are NOT abusing my systems administrator accounts.

Threat-based cybersecurity audits focus on threats to confidentiality, integrity, or availability of IT systems. Example threat-based audit objectives include the following:

- I want my audit to indicate that my confidential customer data is not being inappropriately accessed.

- I want my audit to indicate that the integrity of financial transactions in my system is being maintained.

- I want my audit to indicate that the availability of my front-end web applications is not being impaired.

Cybersecurity Audit Plans

The second step in the audit process is to create a plan for conducting the audit in order to indicate the desired outcome. Many audits involve *proving a negative*. Logic theorists will state that this is an impossible task, but that it is possible to show evidence supporting a negative hypothesis, even if it cannot actually be proven beyond a doubt. Consequently, the best the audit plan may be able to do is establish a high degree of confidence that the undesired activities are not actually occurring.

The cybersecurity audit planning process starts with the audit objective and then identifies what evidence is helpful to prove the audit objective. This desired evidence must then be compared to what evidence is available from IT systems' audit trails and logs, or manual processes' records. Figure 11-2 illustrates this high-level process.

Figure 11-2. *Starting with the cybersecurity audit objective, this audit process is followed to identify the evidence necessary to satisfy the audit objective. The audit process may involve modifying IT systems or manual processes to log additional data.*

The cybersecurity audit planning process is a six-step process:

1. The auditor(s) analyzes the *audit objective* to understand what information is needed to satisfy the objective(s).

2. The auditor determines the *desired evidence* that supports the audit objective(s).

3. The auditor analyzes the *available records* to see what logs and information are available for analysis.

4. The *available evidence* comes from the available records. The auditor analyzes the available evidence to determine if it will be adequate for satisfying the audit objective(s).

5. If the available evidence is not adequate, *system changes* (automated or manual) may need to be made to increase or change the available logs and evidence.

6. Finally, the auditor constructs *audit procedures* to analyze the available evidence in order to satisfy the audit objective(s).

Audit Evidence Collection

Audit procedures direct how the available records and evidence are to be analyzed to satisfy the audit objectives. The procedures document (1) what records are to be analyzed, (2) the analysis processes, and (3) key information such as record sources, points of contact, and sample sizes.

Often, the audit does not look at all records and instead relies on statistical sampling. In these cases, the audit procedures specify sample sizes and statistical analysis methods that are to be used. Sample sizes are selected so they provide reasonable evidence of compliance or non-compliance, and are tailored based on experienced failures, control deficiencies, and other issues.

Audit Artifacts

When the auditor reviews records for evidence, the records become artifacts that are attached to the audit. The purpose of artifacts is to answer the "because" question regarding the audit. For example, an audit states:

> *We believe systems administrator accounts are not being compromised BECAUSE we looked at systems administrator activity for 50% of the administrators over a two-week period and did not find any anomalies.*

This audit's artifacts are the data behind the second half of this sentence. What makes an artifact different from the original logs is that an artifact is copied out of the logs and then stored with the audit, subject to the data retention rules that apply to the rest of the audit. Generally, audit artifacts are kept longer than the underlying data records due to their smaller size and the need to review them after the original logs are deleted.

Audit Results

The final step in the audit process of Figure 11-1 is to compile the results together for reporting to management. These results will identify what was audited and the findings that resulted, including deficiencies to be remediated. Audit results should be summarized to management in terms of their business impact or level of concern, while also containing enough supporting information to be used by security practitioners to respond to and remediate the deficiencies. To be effective, audit results must be actionable—security practitioners must be able to turn the audit results into an action plan that is executable and will produce tangible and measurable improvements on the next audit.

Deficiency Tracking

Cybersecurity audits frequently identify deficiencies in security controls that need to be remediated. While tracking and remediating the deficiencies is generally outside of the audit process of Figure 11-1, it is important that deficiencies be formally tracked and associated remediation documented when it occurs. If a particular deficiency occurs over and over again or if a deficiency is identified but never remediated, these issues should be brought to management's attention.

Sometimes it may not make sense to remediate deficiencies. Remediation may be too expensive or less important than other business priorities. Consequently, remediation may be deferred for an extended period of time. Deficiencies that cannot be remediated, or are not cost-effective to remediate completely, should be treated as enterprise risks and handled using the enterprise's risk management process.

Reporting and Records Retention

Audit results and deficiency remediation should be reported to management and retained for subsequent review and analysis. A couple of rules of thumb regarding audit record retention:

- Audit records should include the audit report and all supporting artifacts. Artifacts that stem from IT system logs should be copied from those logs so that the artifacts can be retained after the original logs are deleted or recycled.

- How audits are reported and records retained depend, in part, on the type of audit. Required audits for regulatory compliance should be retained as per the requirements of the regulations, or as required by the independent auditors attesting to regulatory compliance. In the absence of specific regulatory guidance, audit records can be retained like other enterprise business and financial records.

- Often, it does not make sense to report on deficiency remediation as part of the original audit report since it can take weeks or months to complete remediation after the original audit is completed and reported. In this case, the remediation team could conduct a follow-up briefing to cover remediation. If the audit is a regularly scheduled one, the remediation team could brief the deficiency remediation at the start of the next regularly scheduled audit.

Cybersecurity Audit Types

Various cybersecurity audits follow a consistent methodology that starts with audit objectives and ends with an audit report. Figure 11-3 depicts three main cybersecurity audits described in this book.

Figure 11-3. *Among many audit types, there are three main cybersecurity audit types: threat, assessment, and validation.*

A ***threat audit*** involves analyzing cyberthreats and then auditing for evidence that those threats are occurring in the IT environment. Threat audits are specifically focused around looking for evidence of the threat targeting the confidentiality, integrity, or availability of the enterprise's IT systems and data. Another cybersecurity term for this audit is *hunting* where auditors actively search for intruder and attacker activities. The hunting effort factors in the latest intelligence on intruder/attacker tactics, techniques, and procedures (TTPs). The threat audit report includes an evaluation of which attacks are actively being conducted against the enterprise and the outcomes of those attacks.

An ***assessment audit*** involves analyzing a set of requirements and assessing the cybersecurity controls pertaining to those requirements. In general, assessments are conducted against regulatory requirements, external standards, industry frameworks, or with regard to defenses against specific cybersecurity threats. Unlike a threat audit, the assessment audit is concerned with (1) determining if controls are countering the threats or complying with the regulations or standards, (2) identifying which controls pertain to which threats, regulations, or standards, and (3) evaluating the effectiveness of those controls in satisfying the requirement or countering the threat. Often, the assessment audit output (1) is organized by the regulation, standard, or threat under consideration, and (2) documents the applicable controls (for example, control type), and (3) details the evaluation of the controls' effectiveness.

A ***validation audit***, unlike the other two cybersecurity audit types, starts with the enterprise security controls and evaluates each control's effectiveness compared to its design and documented requirements. Whereas an assessment audit identifies which controls apply to the satisfaction of a particular regulation or requirement, the validation audit evaluates if those controls are actually performed effectively. The validation audit report is used to improve cybersecurity control operation and design. The report can also be mapped back to external regulations or standards to demonstrate compliance.

Figure 11-4 summarizes the three types of cybersecurity audits in terms of their inputs and outputs. It is possible to combine different audits into a single audit activity, although it is important to understand the different inputs and outputs that need to be considered.

Audit Type	Input	Output
Threat	List of threats and attacker tactics, techniques, and procedures (TTPs).	For each threat, evidence of the threat being conducted against the enterprise or not.
Assessment	List of regulatory requirements to be complied with, standards to be adhered to, or threats to be countered.	For each requirement, standard, or threat, identification of the controls that pertain to them, whether they are preventive, detective, forensic, or audit in nature, and analysis of their status and efficacy.
Validation	List of enterprise IT security controls.	For each control, a report on its nature and effectiveness compared to its documented requirements.

Figure 11-4. Each type of audit has specific inputs and outputs for evaluating different aspects of enterprise cybersecurity.

"Audit First" Design Methodology

All too often, security practitioners jump straight to preventive controls (versus audit, forensic, or detective controls) when they are designing cybersecurity defenses. Preventive controls are frequently cheap to operate, use exciting new technology, and allow the practitioner to answer questions about enterprise security with definitive statements of "We block that behavior" or "They won't be able to do that." The reality is enterprise cybersecurity is never as simple as a point solution or collection of point solutions. Every preventive control technology has vulnerabilities or dependencies on other systems to do its job. Smart attackers target those vulnerabilities and dependencies to defeat the controls. A preventive-control-first approach results in a set of complex interdependencies that are often poorly understood, yet represent the foundation of the enterprise's security. All too often, the actual enterprise cybersecurity ends up simply being *security by obscurity*, until an attacker comes along and figures out how to bypass everything.

To address this reality, security practitioners should design controls by thinking about preventive controls *last* instead of *first*. Figure 11-5 delineates an *Audit First Methodology* for thinking about preventive controls last, after considering the other control types.

Figure 11-5. The Audit First Methodology involves starting from the threat analysis and then designing controls to counter those threats, beginning with audit controls, then forensic controls, detective controls, and finally preventive controls.

Threat Analysis

The Audit First Methodology starts with the threat analysis that was used to determine the enterprise's various security scopes. Remember, a security scope groups together assets and controls around a shared business impact caused by a common set of threats against confidentiality, integrity, or availability (CIA). Therefore, the threat analysis identifies CIA threats to the enterprise's data and IT systems in terms of threat impacts and indicators.

It is important to note that an enterprise does not have to consider *every* single possible threat—such consideration will quickly become overwhelming. An enterprise starts by considering the threats that are *most likely* and *most dangerous*, or a combination of the two. As the enterprise has time and resources, it should consider additional threats and less-likely risks. It is important to prioritize, just as an enterprise does with physical security considerations by addressing the greatest risks first.

Audit Controls

After the threat analysis, the next step is to design threat audit controls that search for threat activities.

- If an enterprise's concern is a loss of confidentiality, then how would the enterprise manually search the IT systems to identify that a confidentiality breach had occurred? What evidence would the attacker leave?

- If the enterprise's concern is a loss of integrity, what evidence would be left when data was changed inappropriately? How would the enterprise investigate a data change incident to prove that data had been changed?

- If an enterprise's concern is a loss of availability, how would the enterprise differentiate an availability loss due to system failure from one caused by malicious attack?

Interestingly, most of these questions *cannot* be answered easily. In many enterprises, the available instrumentation and monitoring does not collect enough information to make it possible to answer the threat audit questions. However, the proper exercise is to start with these questions and then use them as a starting point for determining what types of information should be collected so attacker activity can actually be found when it occurs.

Forensic Controls

When conducting a threat audit, an enterprise generally discovers that little of the information needed to find confidentiality, integrity, or availability breaches against its systems is available. However, going through a threat audit provides the enterprise with insight regarding the information it *needs to collect* to protect itself against such breaches. This insight leads an enterprise to consider forensic controls, where it configures its systems to log the data that is needed to search for attacks.

Generally, an enterprise finds the forensic control effort requires significant upgrades to enterprise IT systems to increase logging, enable correlation between system logs, and enable effective investigations. This reality is common, as many real-world environments are deficient in logging the *right* data. However, it is also important to resist the temptation to *log everything*.

Logging efforts should collect the information necessary to investigate likely threat scenarios first. Then the enterprise can evaluate the usefulness of the logs by conducting simulated attacks or actual investigations. Logs that are less likely to be needed in an investigation do not need to be as easily accessible as other logs. So that potential attacker activities can be successfully investigated across the IT security environment, data logging should extend across all of the 11 enterprise cybersecurity functional areas.

Detective Controls

Once effective logging is in place and can support actual investigations that find attacker activity, it becomes possible to detect attacker activity when it occurs. In this step of the Audit First Methodology, the enterprise designs detective controls that alert on suspected attacker activity. The challenge here is that if the detective controls are too noisy and generate lots of false positives that have to be investigated, the detective controls are not useful. In this situation, a security information and event management (SIEM) system may be helpful to do cross-correlation and enable more sophisticated alerting. An alternative to SIEM is a *big data* logging system to conduct complex multi-dimensional queries and alerts. It is important to design detective controls to ensure they alert seldom enough so that every alert can be investigated, or at least checked, to identify if the alert is malicious. Alerts that are consistently ignored are of little use.

Detection does not need to be perfect to be effective. The goal with detective controls is to ensure the most dangerous attacks trigger an alert when the attack occurs, and ideally trigger more than one alert. The alerts themselves can be somewhat arbitrary as long as they have a high probability of indicating an attack. For example, there is no point in alerting on port scans against Internet-facing firewalls since those scans occur all the time and do not necessarily correlate with a successful attack. However, port scans against internal firewalls should generate alerts since there are few legitimate business reasons for such scans to occur during normal business. In other words, an alert on internal firewalls has a high probability of indicating an attack, a compromised machine, or employees or contractors who are poking around in areas where they shouldn't be. Thinking creatively and analyzing the attack sequence, an enterprise can find that there are many activities it can recognize (in other words, alert on) to identify attacks when they occur.

Another important detective control consideration is the cost and business impact of deploying detective controls. Detective controls tend to have a small impact on business operations, while preventive controls tend to be high-impact. Therefore, an enterprise can be more aggressive in deploying detective controls versus preventive controls. An enterprise can deploy detective controls and remove them as desired with a minimum of business impact. This agility is critical when responding to fast-evolving threat scenarios.

The greatest advantage of focusing on forensic and detective controls is these controls give an enterprise the ability to know when attacks occur and stop them. If an enterprise only blocks attacker activity, then attackers simply try something else and wait until the enterprise makes a mistake to allow them to bypass the controls. On the other hand, if an enterprise detects attacks while they are still in progress, it gets an opportunity to catch and repel the attackers.

Preventive Controls

The Audit First Methodology final step involves preventive controls that block undesired activities and prevent them from occurring. Enterprises often primarily consider preventive controls, to the detriment of audit, forensic, and detective control types. However, it is these other control types that fill in the gaps when prevention fails. Also, preventive controls are frequently the most disruptive to the business to emplace and operate.

For every preventive control, there must be a process for getting access or bypassing the block when required by the enterprise. This access may be a firewall exception process, an account request process, or an access management process. In practice, enterprises frequently have access control processes that are complex and cumbersome for all employees. At the same time, attackers frequently find the vulnerability in the access control system and bypass it altogether. Consequently, an enterprise can have a preventive control that is expensive, disruptive, and largely ineffective against a determined attacker. This situation is not a good use of limited security resources.

If an enterprise focuses on detection first, it may find that it can use fewer preventive controls to obtain the same amount of security effectiveness and specifically target them to deliver the greatest value. Useful preventive controls have the following characteristics:

- They block behaviors that would be *noisy* with detection alone, reducing investigation costs.

- They do not cost too much to deploy or operate, particularly in terms of business disruption caused by the block.

- They do not introduce significant new vulnerabilities, either in the preventive control itself or through dependencies on supporting services such as enterprise authentication or directories.

- They not only block attacks, but also detect attacks in progress so the attacks can be thwarted before the attackers figure out how to bypass the block.

Letting Audits Drive Control Design

As shown in Figure 11-6, the Audit First Methodology helps an enterprise design controls that effectively detect attacker activities while reducing the disruption to the enterprise's business operations.

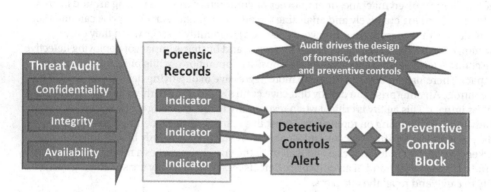

Figure 11-6. *Using the Audit First Methodology, an enterprise analyzes the threats to be countered to identify attack indicators. The enterprise then builds detective controls to alert on the indicators and, finally, blocks the most concerning threat activity with preventive controls.*

A threat audit identifies the most likely threats to enterprise IT confidentiality, integrity, or availability. The threat audit is designed to search for attacks that have occurred and collect the necessary supporting evidence. Based on the threat audit, the enterprise identifies what forensic records are needed to log incidents and give the enterprise indicators of compromise (IOCs) when attacks occur. From those IOCs, the enterprise creates detective controls that alert on attacks and bring them to the attention of the enterprise defenders. Finally, preventive controls block the attack patterns that are most destructive, hardest to detect, or otherwise of greatest concern. The preventive controls are supported by robust business processes for control operation and exception management.

Enterprise Cybersecurity Assessments

The enterprise cybersecurity architecture presented in Chapters 2 through 7 lends itself well to a hierarchical cybersecurity assessment model that generates measurable results quickly and detailed results progressively. This approach is directly tied to the risk assessment process and the 11 functional areas this book uses to organize an enterprise cybersecurity program. The remainder of this section describes how to do a multi-level enterprise cybersecurity assessment organized around the 11 functional areas of enterprise cybersecurity.

This top-down assessment approach differs from control-based cybersecurity assessments because it looks at cybersecurity functional areas and capabilities, rather than focusing on the individual controls. Often, traditional assessment approaches produce results containing dozens or hundreds of recommendations, but contain little guidance on how to manage the remediation at a strategic level or prioritize the remediation activities. The top-down assessment approach described in this section addresses the traditional assessment problem of *finding the forest for the trees* by organizing assessment activities and results into the 11 enterprise cybersecurity functional areas. By grouping results into functional areas, it is easy to compile, report, and delegate the remediation activities among cybersecurity staff so that assessments can be turned into improvements.

This section's top-down approach uses four levels of assessment to examine enterprise security in increasing levels of detail: (1) Risk Mitigations, (2) Functional Areas, (3) Security Capabilities, and (4) Controls, Technologies, and Processes. Each assessment level produces results that are useful and actionable, while the lower level assessments produce results that are more detailed and more specific. Figure 11-7 illustrates the four enterprise cybersecurity assessment types. An example assessment at three of these four levels of detail for a notional enterprise is contained in Appendix H.

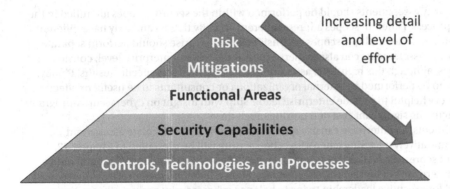

Figure 11-7. *An enterprise cybersecurity program organized into functional areas lends itself well to an assessment methodology that can be executed at different levels of detail.*

The four levels of enterprise cybersecurity assessment described in this section are as follows:

1. ***Level 1 Focus on Risk Mitigations:*** This assessment level involves analyzing the risks to the enterprise and the threats against the confidentiality, integrity, and availability of enterprise IT systems and data. It identifies the *most likely* and *most dangerous* threat vectors. This assessment level examines the attack sequences for those threats and enterprise defensive capabilities to disrupt, detect, delay, and defeat those attacks.

2. ***Level 2 Focus on Functional Areas:*** This assessment level builds on the Level 1 assessment to include evaluating the 11 enterprise cybersecurity functional areas, as well as security operations, at a high level. This assessment quickly identifies the functional areas that are most likely to be exploited by targeted attackers to compromise enterprise cybersecurity and should be prioritized for improvements.

3. ***Level 3 Focus on Security Capabilities***: This assessment level involves assessing in detail the 113 enterprise cybersecurity capabilities and 17 operational processes described elsewhere in this book. It looks at the capabilities and operational processes to assess their effectiveness in protecting the enterprise. This level aggregates the results into an overall enterprise cybersecurity assessment that can be used to prioritize areas for focus and improvement.

4. ***Level 4 Focus on Controls, Technologies, and Processes***: This assessment level involves assessing the controls, technologies, and manual processes that deliver the enterprise's cybersecurity capabilities. It is usually used to identify specific recommendations for tuning, adjustment, or remediation to improve their operational effectiveness.

Enterprise cybersecurity assessments should be performed within the security scopes identified in the cybersecurity planning process. Different scopes address different security threats and may have different protection postures. When there are multiple scopes to consider, the enterprise should perform separate assessments for each scope. Assessments can also be performed at the whole-enterprise level, considering the aggregate of all scopes, although this high-level assessment type can yield less specific results. Finally, assessments do not have to be performed by external organizations or consultants to be useful or effective. Self-assessment can be very helpful to provide enterprise leadership with insight on cybersecurity program effectiveness, without incurring significant cost or requiring much time.

In all of these assessments, an enterprise can use quantitative methods to calculate assessment scores. A method for quantitatively assessing enterprise cybersecurity will be presented in Chapter 12. Cybersecurity assessment scores, if calculated appropriately, can be combined into measurement indices that indicate the entire enterprise's cybersecurity effectiveness. Such a "combined enterprise cybersecurity score" can be very useful for executive leadership trying to balance cybersecurity against other enterprise business risks and challenges.

Level 1 Assessment: Focus on Risk Mitigations

In the context of Figure 11-7, the highest-level enterprise cybersecurity assessment is a Risk Mitigations Assessment. This assessment starts by using the risk management methodology described in Chapters 2 and 4 to identify the most likely and most dangerous threats to the security scope. The assessment then considers those threats in terms of their attack sequence steps and security measures that log, detect, or prevent each step. If possible, assessors may also audit system logs to find if attacks have occurred in the past or are actively occurring at present. This assessment includes the following activities:

1. Identify threats to the security scope and their business impacts on confidentiality, integrity, and availability of enterprise IT systems and data

2. Consider the threats in terms of *most likely* and *most dangerous* so that the most important threats are considered

3. Analyze the threats to understand the attack sequences that attackers would follow

4. Assess security controls that log, detect, or block those attack sequences in terms of their ability to reduce the probability or the impact of the attack occurring

5. If possible, investigate security control logs to see if attacks have occurred or are occurring and may be escaping detection

The risk mitigations assessment outcome includes the following:

- A list of the highest-level risks and the threats that they pose to the security scope

- Documentation of the attack sequences associated with those risks

- Identification of the security controls that apply to those attack sequences

- Scoring of the impact those controls have on reducing the probability or the impact of the attacks occurring

Level 2 Assessment: Focus on Functional Areas

The second level of enterprise cybersecurity assessment focuses on the functional areas. This assessment builds on the Level 1 Assessment by considering not only risk mitigations but also the cybersecurity posture with regard to the 11 enterprise cybersecurity functional areas, as well as security operations. In this assessment, the security scope is examined to estimate its security effectiveness by using expert judgment to evaluate and score each of the 11 cybersecurity functional areas. This assessment measures each functional area's effectiveness to determine which functional areas are the strongest and which are the weakest. Like the Level 1 Assessment, this assessment is performed for each security scope and may have to be performed multiple times if there are different cybersecurity scopes within the enterprise.

A key tenet of the enterprise cybersecurity architecture in this book is that the 11 functional areas of enterprise cybersecurity are of approximately equal importance. This means the functional areas that are weakest are the ones most likely to be attacked successfully in a targeted attack and should be prioritized first for strengthening. When risk mitigations and security operations are considered alongside of the 11 functional areas, there are a total of 13 characteristics of enterprise cybersecurity that should all be considered and should all be of approximately equal levels of effectiveness.

This assessment builds upon the Risk Mitigations Assessment and also considers the 11 enterprise cybersecurity functional areas and a high-level evaluation of security operations. The assessment includes the following activities:

1. Use the Level 1 Assessment to identify security scopes and evaluate risk mitigations against the enterprise cybersecurity attack sequence.

2. For the security scope to be evaluated, consider the 11 enterprise cybersecurity functional areas in terms of their comprehensiveness and effectiveness at delivering security capabilities to the enterprise. Use expert judgment to assess the functional areas at a high level.

3. For the security scope to be evaluated, consider security operations in terms of comprehensiveness and effectiveness at effectively operating the scope's cybersecurity. Use expert judgment to assess security operations at a high level.

4. Capture results for all 11 enterprise cybersecurity functional areas and security operations, identifying which functional areas are strongest and which are weakest.

5. For the weakest functional areas, identify how they could be improved considering people, organization, budgets, processes, technologies, and capabilities.

6. Finally, consider the overall security posture compared to the security requirements of the scope. A high-security scope requires that all functional areas deliver effective security, while a lower-security scope does not require the functional areas to be as mature.

For each security scope considered, the Level 2 Assessment outcomes include an evaluation of each functional area and an identification of the weakest functional areas, which can then be prioritized for strengthening and improvement. Finally, this result is combined with the Level 1 Assessment focusing on risk mitigations and the high-level evaluation of security operations to get the full Level 2 Assessment results.

Level 3 Assessment: Focus on Security Capabilities

A Level 3 Assessment goes into greater detail by considering the individual capabilities within each functional area, as well as examining each of the 17 operational processes. For each capability and operational process, this assessment evaluates their maturity and utilization.

This level of assessment supplements the Level 2 Assessment by replacing the high-level expert judgments with more detailed evaluations based on individual security capabilities and operational processes. Its evaluation steps can replace the Level 2 Assessment altogether, or they can be combined to assess some functional areas at a high level and then only go into detail on the functional areas that require additional attention.

In a Level 3 Assessment, individual capabilities and operational processes are evaluated in terms of their maturity and utilization within the evaluated security scope. When used to "drill down" into functional areas of interest, this assessment can be used to develop action plans for improving specific functional areas or to confirm and refine the higher-level Functional Areas assessment.

The Level 3 Assessment focusing on cybersecurity capabilities represents an excellent balance of assessment effort versus actionable results. It is comprehensive enough to provide specific, actionable results, while still being simple enough that it can be performed quickly as a self-assessment. This assessment includes the following activities:

1. Use the Level 1 Assessment to identify security scopes and evaluate risk mitigations against the enterprise cybersecurity attack sequence.

2. Identify the functional areas to be evaluated and the corresponding enterprise cybersecurity capabilities for those functional areas. For a complete assessment, all capabilities in all functional areas should be evaluated, along with all operational processes. However, a partial assessment that focuses on only one or more functional areas is possible and can also be useful, particularly as a supplement to a Level 2 Assessment.

3. For each of the functional area capabilities considered, examine the technologies and processes that deliver the capability. Its maturity should be analyzed to understand how well it works, and its utilization should be analyzed to understand how consistently it is being used. This examination evaluates how well the capability delivers security to the enterprise.

4. For each of the operational processes considered, the operational process should be analyzed to understand its maturity and utilization. Maturity should be analyzed to understand how well it works, and utilization should be analyzed to understand how consistently it is being used. This examination evaluates how well the operational process helps the enterprise operate its cybersecurity.

For each capability considered, the capability assessment evaluates its maturity and utilization within the scope. This capability assessment identifies which capabilities are strongest and which are weakest. Capabilities that are weakest can then be prioritized for strengthening.

It is important to note there is not a perfect correlation between the presence of capabilities and a functional area's overall security effectiveness. A functional area can be effective without having all of the enterprise cybersecurity capabilities. Similarly, a functional area can have many of its security capabilities present and utilized; however, if they are not configured properly, they can still be ineffective or neutralized by a deliberate attacker.

Level 4 Assessment: Focus on Controls, Technologies, and Processes

The fourth level of enterprise cybersecurity assessment focuses on controls, technologies, and supporting processes. The Level 4 Assessment builds on the Level 3 Assessment by evaluating the specifics of the security controls, technologies, and processes that deliver the risk mitigations, security capabilities, and security operational processes to the enterprise. This assessment examines controls, technologies, and processes to identify and prioritize areas for improvement to deliver better security to the enterprise.

It may be the case that a complete Level 4 Assessment is not necessary. Instead, the assessment can be limited to a single functional area or even just a set of cybersecurity capabilities, their supporting technologies and processes, or the security controls that they support. A Level 4 Assessment can be useful when evaluating deficient functional areas in order to identify tuning opportunities and cost-effective capability improvements. The assessment includes the following activities:

1. Identify the functional areas, capabilities, or operational processes that are of interest and the controls, technologies, and/or processes that are related to them. Because of the level of detail and amount of work involved in this assessment, it is generally helpful for this assessment to focus only on a small set of controls, technologies, or processes that are of greatest concern.

2. For the controls, technologies, or processes to be considered, examine them in detail to identify issues with their effectiveness, configuration, or operation. This analysis should be specific to the control, technology, or process and any third-party products involved. Resulting recommendations should be doable actions to address effectively the identified issues.

3. At the end of the assessment, resulting recommendations can be aggregated together into comprehensive change proposals for updating controls, technologies, or processes to make them more effective at delivering enterprise security risk mitigations, capabilities, or operations.

The outcome of this assessment is specific recommendations to improve the effectiveness of each control, technology, or process that was considered. These recommendations should be technology-specific and actionable.

Audit Deficiency Management

Deficiencies and deficiency tracking are important parts of the auditing process and must not be short-changed or ignored just because the audit is over. All too often, enterprises identify important security shortcomings and then those shortcomings persist because the audit is completed and attention shifts elsewhere.

Deficiencies are important because they undermine, or even completely nullify, the enterprise security that should be present through the various security architecture controls and capabilities. Deficiencies are the *fine print* that needs to be appended to any discussion of the business value of the security controls and capabilities found to be deficient. Tracking such deficiencies is one of the 17 processes that are important to a successful cybersecurity operation.

What is a deficiency? Formally, a security deficiency is a situation where a capability, process, technology, or control does not function as it was designed and documented. A deficiency indicates overall enterprise security is not as effective as one would expect based on a simple review of the documentation. For example, an enterprise's documentation may state that firewalls block all inbound traffic except a, b, and c, but then an audit reveals that d, e, and f are also allowed. This situation is a security deficiency. This deficiency undermines the value of simply looking at the documentation to understand the enterprise's security posture. Audits reveal deficiencies when the actual performance of capabilities, processes, or technologies is not what was expected when they were tested.

When deficiencies are identified, a simple process is followed to track the deficiencies until they are resolved or accepted. An enterprise does not *have to* remediate all deficiencies, but an enterprise shouldn't simply *ignore* them either. An enterprise should formally track deficiencies as part of its overall risk management process so that deficiencies do not slip through the cracks. Figure 11-8 depicts a process for tracking deficiencies over their life cycle.

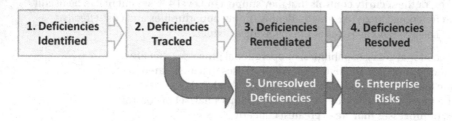

Figure 11-8. *Deficiencies found during audits should be formally tracked until they can be remediated. If deficiencies are not going to be remediated, they should be tracked as enterprise risks.*

The figure shows six main steps, which are in turn part of the larger auditing and deficiency tracking process.

1. The first step is to identify the deficiencies through an audit or other formal test of security capabilities, processes, or technologies. Deficiencies are situations where things do not work the way the enterprise claims they should, where reality does not match up to documentation, or where the enterprise's security does not meet a required standard.

2. Once deficiencies are identified, they should be tracked via a list, spreadsheet, or a database. Deficiency tracking should be robust enough to keep track of deficiencies over time and to keep track of deficiencies that remain unresolved for weeks, months, or years. While tracking does not need to be fancy, the tracking mechanism should be robust enough that employee departures, lost laptops, or other routine changes do not result in the deficiency list being lost. Also, the deficiency list must be reported to management on a regular basis until deficiencies are remediated, converted to enterprise risks, or otherwise closed out.

3. Ideally, identified deficiencies should be simply remediated so things go back to working as expected. In practice, remediation is seldom this simple. First, there may be back-and-forth between technical staff and the auditors arguing the deficiency does not really exist or is not as bad as it appears. Ultimately, management may have to adjudicate such situations and make a final determination. Second, there may be delays or resource constraints involved in the remediation. Management should decide what constitutes *reasonable* in terms of timeliness for remediation, especially if that remediation is delayed waiting for staffing, budget, or other limited resources.

4. Remediated and resolved deficiencies should be documented and reported, just like deficiencies that remain open. This documentation is helpful for two reasons. First, it gives credit where credit is due to the people working hard to fix these types of problems. Second, the documentation provides visibility into deficiencies that are discovered and resolved repeatedly. This repetitive deficiency situation is particularly common for manual processes, where deficiencies are often found every time the process is audited and then remediated every time as well. Such patterns of repeat deficiencies and remediation should be tracked and recognized as the enterprise risks that they really are.

5. Unresolved deficiencies are deficiencies that are not remediated in a timely fashion, possibly due to resource constraints or enterprise priorities. Deficiencies that are open for more than a year should probably be considered unresolved, unless there is an enterprise-approved mitigation plan.

6. If a deficiency is left unresolved, typically there are two consequences. First, the capability, process, technology, or control that contains the deficiency is not as effective as it should be. For security controls, this situation may be entirely acceptable provided that there are compensating controls to fill the gap and limit the overall risk. In such cases, the key is to update documentation to reflect the fact that this capability, process, technology, or control is imperfect and that future audits of it should expect to find deficiencies, up to some threshold. For example, a manual account de-provisioning process that is 75% effective is still much better than a fully automated process that is broken and does not work at all. The key is documenting the fact that the enterprise only *expects* it to be 75% effective. Consequently, when the de-provisioning process is audited in the future, the auditors should expect 75% effectiveness. Second, unresolved deficiencies must be considered in the context of overall enterprise risk. If security controls expected to mitigate enterprise risks are not as effective as planned, then the residual enterprise risk may be higher than was previously expected. Often, this risk may be acceptable, but it is important that the auditors engage and inform enterprise management. There is nothing worse than a CISO believing enterprise risk is effectively handled only to find out the control the enterprise was relying on is deficient and ineffective.

Whether the audits are regularly scheduled control validations, externally performed assessments, or internal threat audits, it is critical the audit findings, deficiencies, and recommendations be tracked through to completion. With tracking, follow-up, and timely remediation, an enterprise can benefit from the value of the overall audit process.

CHAPTER 12

■ ■ ■

Measuring a Cybersecurity Program

Measurement for measurement's sake is a waste of time and money. It is not unusual for people to measure things simply because somebody—some edict or some policy—stipulates that things should be measured. Yes, measurement certainly has a role to play in making successful cybersecurity happen. But unless this role is thought through, measurement can degenerate into a meaningless exercise. This chapter describes a measurement approach that can help an enterprise assess the effectiveness of its cybersecurity program.

In the measurement world, the term *meaningless* has a number of nuances. Consider the following comments:

- It is meaningless to try to measure lengths down to the nearest sixteenth of an inch with a ruler that contains only quarter-inch marks.

- It is meaningless to try to measure things in a vacuum. There are many ways to set measurement context. In this book, measurements are taken for the purpose of answering specific questions.

- It is meaningless to express measurements in language the intended audience cannot understand—in effect, a *foreign* language. It makes no sense for someone to listen to a presentation in, say, Latin, if that person never studied Latin. Likewise, it makes no sense to communicate measurements in a language that may be foreign to an intended audience. For example, if the intended audience is conversant with the language of statistics, it is appropriate to use statistics to express measurements. If, on the other hand, statistics is a foreign language for the intended audience, using terms such as *mean*, *mode*, and *standard deviation* will be meaningless.

The preceding discussion leads to the following fundamental measurement principle that underlies much of the discussion in this chapter:

Measurement needs to be expressed in everyday terms that are familiar to the enterprise—otherwise, the measurements may, at best, be of little value.

Measurement, like many of the other cybersecurity techniques in this book, is an exercise in effective communication among the parties responsible for defending an enterprise against cyberattacks. Understanding how to define, collect, use, and communicate measurement is a significant contributor to making successful enterprise cybersecurity happen. This chapter describes how to measure the effectiveness of ongoing enterprise risk mitigation and security operations. Furthermore, this chapter offers guidance on how to measure the effectiveness of cybersecurity functional areas and their associated capabilities in everyday terms familiar—and therefore meaningful—to the enterprise.

An enterprise can use various measurement approaches to measure cybersecurity. For example, an enterprise can use *expert judgment* to measure the nuances and complexities of cybersecurity, subject to the judgment, knowledge, and experience of the evaluator. A challenge with expert judgment evaluation is that different evaluators can produce widely different results. Consequently, results are not always reproducible across different environments or at different times.

On the other hand, an enterprise can use *observed data* associated with cybersecurity processes or security controls. The advantage of using observed data is the results are generally more objective, more reproducible, and less subject to individual opinions, knowledge, experience, or judgment.

Regardless of expert judgment measurement, observed data measurement, or some combination of measurement approaches, an enterprise measurement program needs to produce results that support smart business decisions. If an enterprise's measurement approach tells it to do things that the enterprise knows are incorrect, then its measurement approach needs to be reworked.[1]

Cybersecurity Measurement

How does an enterprise measure cybersecurity? Despite the significant challenges cybersecurity practitioners face on a daily basis, there is no shortage of assessment frameworks that can be used to evaluate an enterprise's cybersecurity program. Today, the most popular of these frameworks focus on business processes or security controls. Ironically, while the major frameworks include guidance for evaluators on how to judge whether business processes or security controls are present or compliant, assessment frameworks generally do not include guidance on how to *score* or *measure* the effectiveness of the security controls.

For example, an enterprise can end up with the following situation. An enterprise evaluates its cybersecurity program against a control framework and finds 80% of the controls are present and functioning. So, is the cybersecurity good? Or are the 20% of the controls that are missing the ones that attackers are exploiting to steal the enterprise's data?

Using control frameworks to measure cybersecurity programs poses a number of challenges to include the following:

- Frameworks are often designed around cybersecurity programs achieving 100% *compliance*. Programs less than 100% compliant may be considered deficient.

- Frameworks do not provide much guidance on how to prioritize remediation of security controls for cybersecurity programs that are found to be deficient (in other words, noncompliant).

- Frameworks do not provide much guidance on how to prioritize maintenance of security controls to ensure the most important controls stay operational.

---

[1]See Appendix F - Object Measurement for a more detailed discussion regarding expert judgment and observed data measurement approaches and associated steps.

Another framework challenge has to do with quantifying cybersecurity measurements. How does an enterprise score itself when it is trying to determine the *effectiveness* of it security controls?

- When using frameworks with lots of controls, an enterprise can count how many controls are effective, ineffective, or absent, and score the cybersecurity program based on various ratios. Defining *effective* and *ineffective* can be a measurement challenge.

- When there are fewer controls, the enterprise may need to consider some shades of gray and give partial scores to controls based on how well they are implemented or how effectively they are employed.

- Finally, when some controls are more important than others, the enterprise may need to weight scores to account for more important controls carrying more weight in the overall evaluation.

These challenges are non-trivial and contribute to the uncertainty in trying to get useful, actionable results from a cybersecurity program evaluation.

Cybersecurity Program Measurement

For the purposes of this book, a cybersecurity program includes enterprise policies, personnel, budgets, security capabilities organized into functional areas, security controls, technologies, IT systems, and supporting processes.

The functional areas and their security capabilities are at the core of a cybersecurity program and can be used, in part, to measure a program's effectiveness. Measurement provides enterprise leadership with insight into functional areas' strengths and deficiencies, and provides a direct correlation between an enterprise's risk analysis and its level of protection. If the risk analysis requires an *excellent* level of protection, then all 11 functional areas need to be excellent, along with enterprise security operations and risk mitigation. If the risk analysis requires only a *good* level of protection, then all 11 functional areas can be good, along with enterprise security operations and risk mitigations. Leadership can then prioritize remediation activities and corresponding budgets. Measurement needs to flex with morphing cybersecurity threats and enable an enterprise to adjust dynamically its security posture.

Measurement acts as a focusing agent to help point the enterprise to potential weaknesses that cyberattackers can use as attack vectors. Rather than wading through lists with dozens of security controls, enterprise leadership can focus on functional areas needing improvement and empower the next level of leadership to worry about the security controls, and so forth. This layered management approach lends itself to the realities of delegation, budgeting, and shared management.

Figure 12-1 depicts a cybersecurity program measurement approach leveraging the connectivity among an enterprise's risk mitigations, functional areas, and security operations. This connectivity also encompasses the corresponding security controls, security capabilities, and technologies and processes.

Figure 12-1. *A cybersecurity program measurement approach considers enterprise risk mitigations, functional areas, and ongoing security operations.*

Object Measurement (OM) is a methodology that can be used to measure an enterprise cybersecurity program and produce actionable results. Object Measurement for cybersecurity uses the following six-step process. This process is explored in the remainder of this section using an example cybersecurity program assessment.

- Step 1: Define the question(s) to be answered.

- Step 2: Select appropriate objects to measure.

- Step 3: For each object, define the object characteristics to measure.

- Step 4: For each characteristic, create a value scale.

- Step 5: Measure each characteristic using the value scale.

- Step 6: Calculate the overall Cybersecurity Program Assessment Index using Object Measurement.

OM Step 1: Define the Question(s) to Be Answered

The remainder of this section walks through an example *expert judgment* assessment. For this example assessment, the question is:

> *For the selected scope, how effective is the enterprise's cybersecurity program against cyberattacks?*

OM Step 2: Select Appropriate Objects to Measure

Measurement can be done with different levels of detail and fidelity (in other words, various assessment scopes), allowing for *quick, high-level* assessments or *thorough, detailed assessments*. For example, assessment scope could be defined with different levels of detail as follows:

- ***Level 1—Focus on Risk Mitigations***: Measure Risk Mitigations

- ***Level 2—Focus on Functional Areas***: Measure Risk Mitigations + Functional Areas + Security Operations

- *Level 3—Focus on Security Capabilities*: Measure Risk Mitigations + Security Capabilities + Security Operations

- *Level 4—Focus on Controls, Technologies, and Processes*: Measure Security Controls + Technologies + Processes

Assessment scope can be a portion of the enterprise's environment where a security compromise will have a business impact. Within well-defined scopes, systems work together to maintain a particular security posture to defend against the business impact. Scope is frequently defined based on regulatory, statutory, or liability requirements. Note that there can be multiple cybersecurity program assessments performed against corresponding assessment scopes.

OM Step 3: For Each Object, Define the Object Characteristics to Measure

This example assessment focuses on *Level 2-Functional Areas*. Figure 12-2 depicts the scope for this example, shown as a *measurement map*.

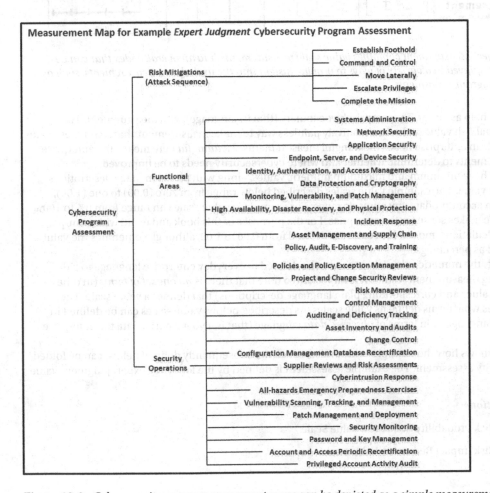

Figure 12-2. *Cybersecurity program assessment scope can be depicted as a simple measurement map.*

OM Step 4: For Each Characteristic, Create a Value Scale

This step establishes value scales the enterprise can use to measure cybersecurity program effectiveness. Often, people think of cybersecurity effectiveness from a single perspective (such as a manager or cybersecurity expert) or in terms of a function (such as a systems administration or network security) or a security operation (for example, control management or cyberintrusion response). However, measuring effectiveness often involves multiple dimensions.

Appendix F: Object Measurement (OM) provides a detailed explanation of how to define assessment value scales. Simply stated here, OM defines almost any object (for example, risk mitigation, functional areas, and security operations) in terms of *value scales* that help tie measurement activities to familiar enterprise language. Figure 12-3 depicts OM combining multiple *value scale measurements* into an overall index (in other words, overall score).

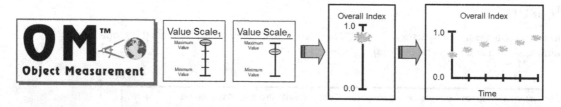

Figure 12-3. *Object Measurement combines value scale measurements into an overall index that can be "unfolded" and displayed in a variety of ways to provide insight into the underlying measurements, such as cyberseucurity program assessments.*

Value scales help associate an enterprise's vocabulary (that is, language) with measurement. The challenge is to establish value scales in a relatively painless way to make measurements based on these value scales. In the end, an enterprise needs meaningful measurements. *Meaningful* here means the enterprise uses the measurements to determine whether and where cybersecurity needs to be improved.

Value scales have minimum and maximum numeric values, along with plain language descriptions for each numeric value. The example value scales described below range from zero (0.00) to one (1.00), but the scales can accommodate any numeric range. For example, a value scale can range from 0% to 100% or whatever range makes sense for the enterprise. For the purposes of this book and to aid with example measurement calculations, most value scales are defined from 0.00 to 1.00, although sometimes the values may be displayed as percentages.

Furthermore, the numeric value labels need to be defined in everyday enterprise language to aid in communicating measurement results. It is important to note that there is *no one set of terms* (in other words, numeric values and corresponding plain language descriptions) that defines a value scale. The enterprise decides what terms define its value scales. As described below, value scales can be defined in *expert judgment* language or in terms of *observed data* language (that is, cybersecurity data the enterprise observes).

Figure 12-4 shows how the example value scales, which are subsequently defined below, can be folded into a cybersecurity assessment. The example assessment is defined by the following expert judgment value scales:

Risk Mitigations

1. Risk Probability Reduction Value Scale

2. Risk Impact Reduction Value Scale

- *Functional Areas*
  1. Effectiveness Value Scale
  2. Comprehensiveness Value Scale
- *Security Operations*
  1. Maturity Value Scale
  2. Utilization Value Scale.

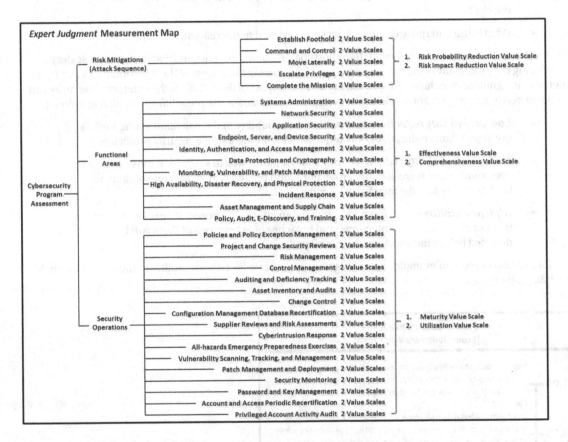

Figure 12-4. *Expert judgment or observed data value scales define how a cybersecurity program assessment is measured. For this example, the value scales are defined in expert judgment terms.*

Risk Mitigations Value Scales

Within each cybersecurity program scope one of the first measurement challenges is to see how well the enterprise mitigates cybersecurity-related risks. The enterprise needs to list out the business consequences associated with the risks and then consider the attack sequences if those risks occurred. Consider the following example risks:

- Intruders steal customer financial data.
- The business loses regulated data.

- Attackers steal money from the business.

- The business suffers reputational damage from a breach.

The list of risks should not be too long, nor should it be too specific. The list should be specific enough so the enterprise can apply the attack sequence to the risks, at least for the risks driven by intrusions. The enterprise could ask itself the following questions:

- What is the enterprise doing to prevent the risk from happening in the first place?

- What is the enterprise doing to reduce the amount of damage that can be caused by the risk?

- What is the enterprise doing to detect and respond to the risk when it happens?

An enterprise can grade its *risk mitigation* efforts based on two dimensions (that is, two value scales): (1) reducing the probability of the risk occurring, and (2) reducing the impact of the risk should it occur. If an enterprise is significantly reducing the probability and the impact of the risk, then the enterprise's security can be considered to be very good or excellent. An enterprise can evaluate *risk probability reduction* as follows:

- ***Low probability reduction*** means that the probability of the risk manifesting itself is not significantly reduced, or only requires overcoming a single security protection.

- ***Medium probability reduction*** means that for an attack to succeed, it must overcome two or more security protections, and breaches of at least one of them will be detected before the attack can be completed.

- ***High probability reduction*** means that for an attack to succeed, it must overcome three or more security protections, and breaches of at least two of them will be detected before the attack can be completed.

Figure 12-5 depicts an example expert judgment value scale for risk probability reduction based on the preceding descriptions.

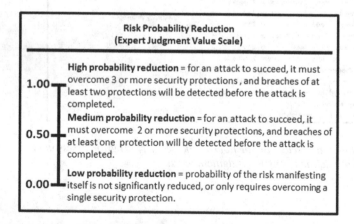

Figure 12-5. *Expert judgment risk probability reduction value scale related to risk mitigation.*

An enterprise can evaluate *risk impact reduction* as follows:

- *Low impact reduction* means that the impact is not reduced.

- *Medium impact reduction* means that successful attacks are detected and the impact and cost of the risk are reduced some, but not significantly.

- *High impact reduction* means that successful attacks are detected and the impact and cost of the risk are significantly reduced.

Figure 12-6 depicts an example expert judgment value scale for risk impact reduction based on the preceding descriptions.

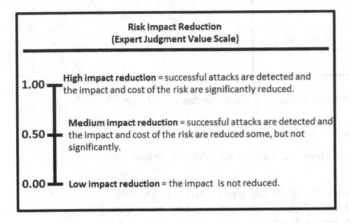

Figure 12-6. Example expert judgment risk impact reduction value scale related to risk mitigation.

Functional Area Value Scales

Within each assessment scope, the next measurement challenge is to evaluate functional area effectiveness. An enterprise can grade these items based on two dimensions (that is, value scales). Consider the following questions:

- Is the functional area effective or ineffective?

  - *Effectiveness* measures how effective the functional area is in protecting the enterprise and mitigating cybersecurity risks.

- Is the functional area used in a comprehensive manner (in other words, everywhere consistently or only sporadically)?

  - *Comprehensiveness* measures how comprehensively the functional area is used to protect the security scope.

An enterprise can evaluate functional area effectiveness as follows:

- *Low effectiveness* means the functional area is not very effective in protecting the enterprise and has significant issues or capability gaps.

- *Medium effectiveness* means the functional area is effective, but has moderate issues or capabilities gaps that impair the functional area.

- *High effectiveness* means the functional area is effective and has few issues or capabilities gaps that impair that overall functional area effectiveness.

Figure 12-7 depicts an example expert judgment value scale for functional area effectiveness based on the preceding descriptions.

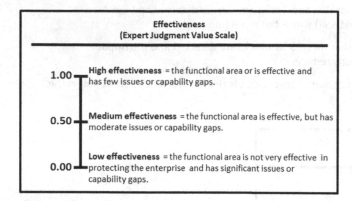

Figure 12-7. *Example expert judgment effectiveness value scale related to functional areas.*

An enterprise can evaluate functional area comprehensiveness as follows:

- *Low comprehensiveness* means the functional area is used for 25% or less of the areas where it could be used.

- *Medium comprehensiveness* means the functional area is used in many of the places where it could be used. Measured quantitatively, this usage amounts to approximately 25% to 75% of potential utilization.

- *High comprehensiveness* means the functional area is used in most of the places where it could be used. Measured quantitatively, this usage amounts to greater than 75% of potential utilization.

Figure 12-8 depicts an example expert judgment value scale for functional area comprehensiveness based on the preceding descriptions.

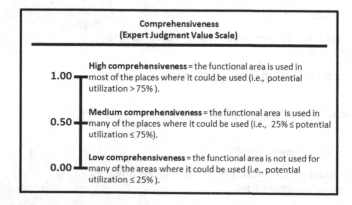

Figure 12-8. *Example expert judgment comprehensiveness value scale related to functional areas.*

Security Operations Value Scales

Within the assessment scope, the next measurement challenge is to evaluate the elements of security operations. An enterprise can grade an individual security operations element based on two dimensions (in other words, value scales). Consider the following questions:

- Is the security operations element mature (that is, well-developed and well-proven, or it still under development and relatively untested)?

    - *Maturity* measures how well implemented the security operations element is.

- Is the security operations element utilized everywhere it can be and should be utilized, or is it still in a pilot or limited-rate deployment?

    - *Utilization* measures how much the security operations element is used in the enterprise.

An enterprise can evaluate the maturity of security operations elements as follows:

- *Low maturity* means the security operations element is barely or partially operational. There is little operational documentation and procedures are ad hoc. There are severe limits on its functionality, durability, reliability, or scalability.

- *Medium maturity* means the security operations element is partially operational but unproven. Documentation and operational procedures are not complete or are untested. There are minor limitations on functionality, durability, reliability, or scalability. It has not been tested for durability, scalability, or security.

- *High maturity* means the security operations element is fully operational and proven. Its configurations and operational procedures are fully documented, and performance specifications for functionality, durability, reliability, and scalability have been defined and validated by third-party experts.

Figure 12-9 depicts an example expert judgment value scale for security operations maturity based on the preceding descriptions.

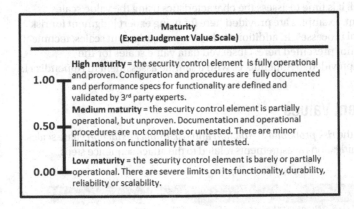

Figure 12-9. *Example expert judgment maturity scale related to security operations.*

An enterprise can evaluate the utilization of security operations elements as follows:

- **Low utilization** means the security operations element is in pilot or only used by a small group. Total utilization is less than 25% of its potential.

- **Medium utilization** means the security operations elements is being utilized for many of its intended purposes. Total utilization is between 25% and 75% of its potential.

- **High utilization** means the security operations element is being utilized for most of its intended purposes. Total utilization is above 75% of its potential.

Figure 12-10 depicts an example expert judgment value scale for security operations element utilization based on the preceding descriptions.

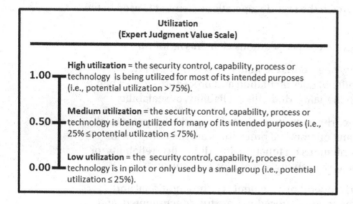

Figure 12-10. Example expert judgment utilization value scale related to security operations.

OM Step 5: Measure Each Characteristic Using the Value Scale

Now that the characteristics to be measured have been identified and the measurement values for those characteristics have been determined as well, it is time to assess the characteristics using the value scales and determine the raw data of the assessment. Examples are provided here for using expert judgment for risk mitigations, functional areas, and operational processes. In addition to these expert judgment scales, technical data observations can also be used, but are not presented here. Observed data value scales for the 113 enterprise cybersecurity capabilities are provided in Appendix G, with a sample assessment in Appendix H.

Risk Mitigations Expert Judgment Values

Attack sequence steps are measured by using the *risk probability reduction* and *risk impact reduction* value scales. Figure 12-11 lists the following example risk mitigation measurements related to the attack sequence steps.

Risk Mitigations/Attack Sequence	Risk Probability Reduction	Risk Impact Reduction
1. Establish Foothold	Low Risk Probability Reduction = 0.00	Low Impact Reduction = 0.00
2. Command and Control	Low Risk Probability Reduction = 0.00	Medium Impact Reduction = 0.50
3. Move Laterally	Low Risk Probability Reduction = 0.00	High Impact Reduction = 1.00
4. Escalate Privileges	Medium Risk Probability Reduction = 0.50	Medium Impact Reduction = 0.50
5. Complete the Mission	Medium Risk Probability Reduction = 0.50	High Impact Reduction = 1.00

Figure 12-11. Example expert judgment risk mitigations measurements.

Functional Area Expert Judgment Values

Functional areas are measured by using the *effectiveness* and *comprehensiveness* value scales. Figure 12-12 lists example functional area measurements.

Enterprise Cybersecurity Functional Areas	Effectiveness	Comprehensiveness
Systems Administration	Low Effectiveness = 0.00	Low Comprehensiveness = 0.00
Network Security	Low Effectiveness = 0.00	Medium Comprehensiveness = 0.50
Application Security	Medium Effectiveness = 0.50	Medium Comprehensiveness = 0.50
Endpoint, Server, and Device Security	High Effectiveness = 1.00	Medium Comprehensiveness = 0.50
Identity, Authentication, and Access Management	High Effectiveness = 1.00	High Comprehensiveness = 1.00
Data Protection and Cryptography	High Effectiveness = 1.00	Low Comprehensiveness = 0.00
Monitoring, Vulnerability, and Patch Management	High Effectiveness = 1.00	High Comprehensiveness = 1.00
High Availability, Disaster Recovery, and Physical Protection	High Effectiveness = 1.00	Medium Comprehensiveness = 0.50
Incident Response	High Effectiveness = 1.00	High Comprehensiveness = 1.00
Asset Management and Supply Chain	Low Effectiveness = 0.00	Low Comprehensiveness = 0.00
Policy, Audit, E-Discovery, and Training	Medium Effectiveness = 0.50	Medium Comprehensiveness = 5.00

Figure 12-12. Example expert judgment functional area measurements.

Security Operations Expert Judgment Values

Security operations elements are measured using the *maturity* and *utilization* value scales. Figure 12-13 lists example security operations elements measurements.

Enterprise Cybersecurity Operational Processes	Maturity	Utilization
1. Policies and Policy Exception Management	Low Maturity = 0.00	Low Utilization = 0.00
2. Project and Change Security Reviews	Medium Maturity = 0.50	Medium Utilization = 0.50
3. Risk Management	High Maturity = 1.00	Medium Utilization = 0.50
4. Control Management	Medium Maturity = 0.50	Medium Utilization = 0.50
5. Auditing and Deficiency Tracking	Medium Maturity = 0.50	Medium Utilization = 0.50
6. Asset Inventory & Audits	High Maturity = 1.00	Medium Utilization = 0.50
7. Change Control	Medium Maturity = 0.50	Medium Utilization = 0.50
8. Configuration Management Database Recertification	Medium Maturity = 0.50	Medium Utilization = 0.50
9. Supplier Reviews and Risk Assessments	High Maturity = 1.00	Medium Utilization = 0.50
10. Cyberintrusion Response	Medium Maturity = 0.50	Low Utilization = 0.00
11. All-hazards Emergency Preparedness Exercises	Low Maturity = 0.00	Low Utilization = 0.00
12. Vulnerability Scanning, Tracking, and Management	Medium Maturity = 0.50	Low Utilization = 0.00
13. Patch Management and Deployment	High Maturity = 1.00	Medium Utilization = 0.50
14. Security Monitoring	High Maturity = 1.00	Low Utilization = 0.00
15. Password and Key Management	Medium Maturity = 0.50	Medium Utilization = 0.50
16. Account and Access Periodic Recertification	Medium Maturity = 0.50	Low Utilization = 0.00
17. Privileged Account Activity Audit	High Maturity = 1.00	Medium Utilization = 0.50

Figure 12-13. Example expert judgment security operations element measurements.

OM Step 6: Calculate the Overall Cybersecurity Program Assessment Index Using Object Measurement

Once the risk mitigations, functional areas, and security operations elements have been measured, the measurements can be aggregated into corresponding summary ratings (also known as the three overall indices). As shown in Figure 12-14, the three expert judgment indices (RiskMitigations*Index*, FunctionalArea*Index*, and SecurityOps*Index*) and the overall expert judgment index (CybersecurityProgramAssessment*Index*) are calculated using the calculated using the **OM Index Equation** (explained in detail in Appendix F).

$$\text{RiskMitigations}\textit{Index} =$$

$$= \frac{\sqrt{0^2 + 0^2 + 0^2 + .5^2 + 0^2 + 1^2 + .5^2 + .5^2 + .5^2 + 1^2}}{\sqrt{10}}$$

$$= \frac{1.73}{3.16} = 0.55; \text{ where number of Attack Sequence Steps measurements} = 10$$

$$\text{FunctionalArea}\textit{Index} =$$

$$= \frac{\sqrt{\begin{array}{c} 0^2 + 0^2 + 0^2 + .5^2 + .5^2 + .5^2 + 1^2 + .5^2 + 1^2 + 1^2 + 1^2 + \\ 0^2 + 1^2 + 1^2 + 1^2 + .5^2 + 1^2 + 1^2 + 0^2 + 0^2 + .5^2 + .5^2 \end{array}}}{\sqrt{22}}$$

$$= \frac{3.28}{4.69} = 0.70; \text{ where number of Functional Areas measurements} = 22$$

$$\text{SecurityOps}\textit{Index} =$$

$$= \frac{\sqrt{\begin{array}{c} 0^2 + 0^2 + .5^2 + .5^2 + 1^2 + .5^2 + .5^2 + .5^2 + .5^2 + .5^2 + 1^2 + .5^2 + \\ .5^2 + .5^2 + .5^2 + .5^2 + 1^2 + .5^2 + .5^2 + 0^2 + 0^2 + 0^2 + .5^2 + 0^2 + \\ 1^2 + .5^2 + 1^2 + 0^2 + .5^2 + .5^2 + .5^2 + 0^2 + 1^2 + .5^2 \end{array}}}{\sqrt{34}}$$

$$= \frac{3.32}{5.83} = 0.57; \text{ where the number of Security Operations Elements} = 34$$

$$\text{CybersecurityProgramAssessment}\textit{Index} =$$

$$= \frac{\sqrt{.55^2 + .70^2 + .57^2}}{\sqrt{3}}$$

$$= \frac{1.11}{1.73} = 0.64; \quad \text{where number of Expert Judgment Indices} = 3; \text{ all weighting factors} = 1; \text{ all value scales range from 0 to 1.}$$

Figure 12-14. *The overall CybersecurityProgramAssessmentIndex combines the expert judgment indices for the risk mitigations, functional areas, and security operations elements into a single index, which can be tracked over time as the enterprise makes changes to its cybersecurity program.*

At this point, the enterprise needs to decide whether the question "How effective is the enterprise cybersecurity in protecting against cyberattacks?" has been answered. The appropriate people in the enterprise should meet to examine the measurements and discuss how to address the corresponding results. This measurement approach helps the enterprise focus on what cybersecurity areas need to be addressed.

As a result of reviewing the above measurements, enterprise leadership can focus its attention (and, potentially, resources) on those areas that may need improvement or questions that need to be answered. The decision might be to take more measurements and review them carefully. Perhaps the cybersecurity program needs to be more rigorously enforced, maybe the program needs to be changed, or maybe leadership is overcommitted and resources are scarce. Regardless, these measurements need to be expressed in everyday terms that make sense to the enterprise so leadership can make informed decisions.

Visualizing Cybersecurity Assessment Scores

As illustrated with various measurement maps, there are numerous assessment scopes ranging from a specific portion of the enterprise cybersecurity program to the entire program. Correspondingly, there is an equal number of methods for visualizing the measurements, which need to be tailored to the intended audience. When an enterprise sets out to establish a measurement program, it is important to think ahead of time how the measurements are going to be used. With this purpose in mind, the measurement program can be based on what enterprise stakeholders view as important or needed to make informed decisions.

Figure 12-15 depicts alternative ways to visualize expert judgment value scales.

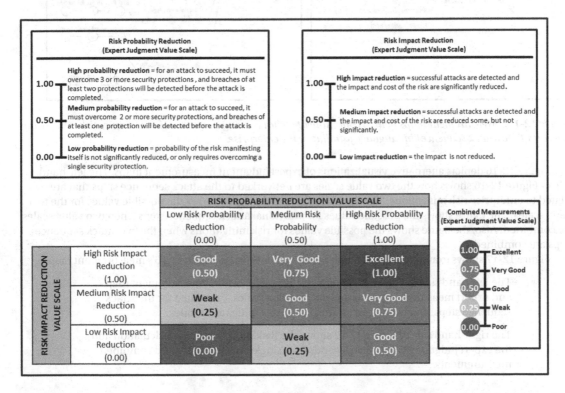

Figure 12-15. *Cybersecurity assessment measurements can be visualized in a number of ways, but enterprises need to decide what makes the best sense for their organizational culture.*

The upper half of Figure 12-15 shows example risk mitigation expert judgment value scales for risk probability reduction and risk impact reduction. These value scales are expressed in everyday enterprise language to aid in communication measurement results. The enterprise determines what terms define its value scales. Once agreed upon within the enterprise, these terms help to increase effective measurement communications within the enterprise.

The left-hand, lower half of Figure 12-15 shows an alternative visualization of the upper-half value scales. Furthermore, the intersections of the two value scales present nine combinations that provide additional insight to the meaning of potential measurements. The right-hand, lower left of Figure 12-16 shows another way to depict the combination or interaction of the two value scales.

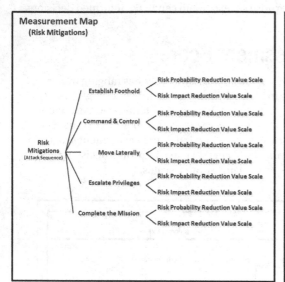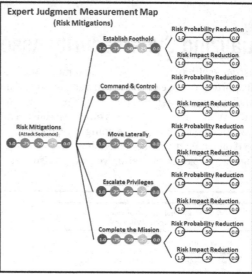

Figure 12-16. *Measurement maps help to communicate what is being measured (for example, risk mitigation in terms of the attack sequence) in language familiar to the enterprise.*

Figure 12-16 depicts alternative visualizations of expert judgment measurement maps. The left-hand side of Figure 12-16 shows how the two value scales are networked to the attack sequence steps that are related to enterprise risk mitigations. The right-hand side of the figure shows the possible values for the two value scales. The figure shows the possible values for individual attack sequence steps when two value scales are combined. Also, the figure shows the possible values for risk mitigations when the five attack sequence steps are combined.

Figure 12-17 shows example risk mitigation measurements using Figure 12-16's measurement map.

- The left-hand side of Figure 12-17 depicts the corresponding measurement map and expert measurements recorded on the value scales, calculated for the attack sequence steps, and calculated for the overall risk mitigations index.

- The right-hand side of Figure 12-17 shows the RiskMitigations*Index* calculation and the expert judgment value scale legends for a single measurement and combined measurements.

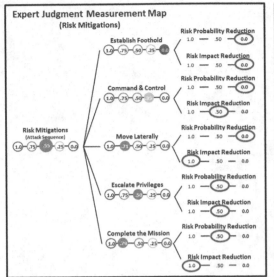
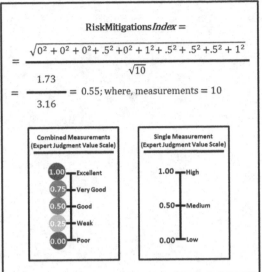

Figure 12-17. *This figure shows, in part, what expert value judgments are recorded in terms of risk probability and impact reductions (indicated by circled values), the resulting attack sequence step metrics (indicated by solid circles with a numeric value), and the overall combined risk mitigation metric (that is, indicated by a solid circle with a numeric value = 0.55).*

Cybersecurity Measurement Summary

This chapter demonstrates how to quantify the extent to which an enterprise is defending itself against cyberattacks. This demonstration proceeds from the following measurement principle:

Measurement needs to be expressed in everyday terms that are familiar to the enterprise—otherwise, the measurements may, at best, be of little value.

This chapter focused on showing how cybersecurity experts, using their experience, can assess an enterprise's cybersecurity posture. This chapter uses example calculations to show how a collection of expert judgments can be combined into a single number called an "index" that gives enterprise management the means to chart a corrective-active course to improve this cybersecurity posture.

Appendix F extends the measurement approach discussed in this chapter. In the appendix, worked-out examples show how observed data measurement (versus expert judgment measurement) can be quantified to provide insight into an enterprise's cybersecurity behavior. When tracked over time, such measurements can serve to help focus the enterprise's cybersecurity improvement activities.

CHAPTER 13

■ ■ ■

Mapping Against Cybersecurity Frameworks

While designing an effective enterprise cybersecurity architecture is an admirable goal in and of itself, no architecture lives in a vacuum. Being able to map to other cybersecurity frameworks is an important part of making sure the enterprise's cybersecurity program is complete and demonstrating that completeness to outside observers. This chapter details how an enterprise cybersecurity program can be mapped against other cybersecurity frameworks, some of which were introduced in Chapter 2. Reasons for mapping an enterprise cybersecurity program against other frameworks include the following:

1. Parts of the industry are regulated and cybersecurity programs must be designed so they comply with regulatory cybersecurity requirements and that compliance can be demonstrated to independent auditors and regulators.

2. Enterprises need to report on the status of their cybersecurity programs against external frameworks to satisfy their own auditors or other internal business purposes.

3. Enterprises wish to cross-walk their cybersecurity program against an external framework to generate ideas for strengthening the enterprise's cybersecurity posture.

Why not simply run an enterprise's cybersecurity program according to one of these frameworks? In the authors' experience, while these frameworks are designed for organizing cybersecurity information or cybersecurity controls for compliance purposes, they are not generally designed for running a comprehensive cybersecurity program. The enterprise cybersecurity architecture described in this book, on the other hand, was designed from the beginning to be a complete framework unifying all aspects of an enterprise's cybersecurity program into coherent functional areas useful for day-to-day cybersecurity operations.

Specifically, the 11 enterprise cybersecurity functional areas are designed to group together the following aspects of enterprise cybersecurity into a single framework:

- Cybersecurity policy
- Staffing and expertise
- Budgets and resource allocation
- Technology, capabilities, and controls
- Processes and operations
- Auditing and reporting

For cybersecurity operations, the 11 functional areas provide: (1) clear lines of responsibility and accountability, (2) alignment of enterprise technologies and capabilities with the people skill sets, and (3) efficient engineering, deployment, operation, auditing, and reporting of enterprise security capabilities. These combined features make this an easy-to-understand and practical cybersecurity architecture that adapts to the real world of evolving threat vectors.

In addition to day-to-day operations, enterprises need to respond to regulatory requirements and resulting compliance activities. The 11 functional areas lend themselves to the type of cross-walking needed for cybersecurity reporting against multiple regulatory requirements. For example, a publicly traded company doing business with the US government may be subject to Sarbanes-Oxley regulations for their financial systems and NIST guidance for their customer-serving systems. A healthcare provider may be subject to HIPAA or HITRUST for their medical systems and PCI DSS for their payment processing. An energy company may be subject to NERC CIP regulations for their energy generation systems and ISO 27001 for their general IT security. There are many regulatory reporting combinations. It is not uncommon to find an enterprise reporting against two, three, or more cybersecurity frameworks. As described in the following section, an enterprise cybersecurity program organized using the architecture described in this book lends itself well to these regulatory reporting scenarios.

Looking at Control Frameworks

Figure 13-1 presents a side-by-side comparison of this book's enterprise cybersecurity architecture alongside of some of the major control frameworks.

Enterprise Cybersecurity Architecture 11 Functional Areas	(ISC)² Common Body of Knowledge (CBK) 10 Security Domains	ISO 27001 / 27002 Version 2013 114 Controls in 14 Domains	NIST SP800-53 Revision 4 224 Controls in 18 Families	Council on CyberSecurity Critical Security Controls Version 5.1 20 Controls and 182 Control Activities
1. Systems Administration 2. Network Security Application Security 3. Endpoint, Server, and Device Security 4. Identity, Authentication, and Access Management 5. Data Protection and Cryptography 6. Monitoring, Vulnerability, and Patch Management 7. High Availability, Disaster Recovery, and Physical Protection 8. Incident Response 9. Asset Management and Supply Chain 10. Policy, Audit, E-Discovery, and Training	1. Access Control 2. Telecommunications and Network Security 3. Information Security Governance and Risk Management 4. Software Development Security 5. Cryptography 6. Security Architecture and Design 7. Security Operations 8. Business Continuity and Disaster Recovery Planning 9. Legal, Regulations, Investigations, and Compliance 10. Physical (Environmental) Security	1. Information Security Policies 2. Organization of Information Security 3. Human Resource Security 4. Asset Management 5. Access Control 6. Cryptography 7. Physical and Environmental Security 8. Operations Security 9. Communications Security 10. System Acquisition, Development, and Maintenance 11. Supplier Relationships 12. Information Security Incident Management 13. Information Security Aspect of Business Continuity Management 14. Compliance	1. Access Control 2. Awareness and Training 3. Audit and Accountability 4. Security Assessment and Authorization 5. Configuration Management 6. Contingency Planning 7. Identification and Authentication 8. Incident Response 9. Maintenance 10. Media Protection 11. Physical and Environmental Protection 12. Planning 13. Personnel Security 14. Risk Assessment 15. System and Services Acquisition 16. System and Communications Protection 17. System and Information Integrity 18. Program Management	1. Inventory of Devices 2. Inventory of Software 3. Secure Configurations for Computers 4. Continuous Vulnerability Assessment and Remediation 5. Malware Defenses 6. Application Software Security 7. Wireless Device Control 8. Data Recovery Capability 9. Security Skills Assessment and Training 10. Security Configurations for Network Devices 11. Network Ports, Protocols, and Services 12. Control of Administrative Privileges 13. Boundary Defense 14. Security Audit Logs 15. Need-to-Know Access Control 16. Account Monitoring and Control 17. Data Loss Prevention 18. Incident Response Capability 19. Secure Network Engineering 20. Penetration Testing and Red Team Exercises

Figure 13-1. *This book's enterprise cybersecurity architecture alongside the (ISC)² Common Body of Knowledge, ISO 27001/27002, NIST SP800-53, and the Council on CyberSecurity Critical Security Controls.*

As shown in the figure, the five frameworks have some commonalities. All five frameworks include access control and network or communications security; four of the five include physical security, and so on. A detailed examination reveals the frameworks more or less cover the same topics, just "slicing and dicing" the various aspects of enterprise cybersecurity slightly differently.

However, unlike the other frameworks, this book's enterprise cybersecurity architecture is designed not only for organizing controls, but also for running an entire cybersecurity program. The 11 functional areas of enterprise cybersecurity have been selected so they are of approximately equal importance. Effective enterprise cybersecurity requires an enterprise to have an approximately equal level of capabilities in all 11 functional areas. This principle means functional areas that are weaker than other functional areas should be prioritized for improvement, thus dramatically simplifying the enterprise cybersecurity strategy and prioritization challenge.

Another interesting aspect of this book's enterprise cybersecurity architecture is that it does not require an enterprise to do a "perfect" job in every area, nor does it "check the compliance box." Instead, the architecture focuses on the enterprise identifying the capabilities that it has compared to the capabilities that it needs in order to be successful in thwarting attack patterns that are of concern.

In addition to the frameworks shown in Figure 13-1, Appendix B contains high-level summaries of the following other frameworks that are likely to be encountered in real-world enterprise cybersecurity:

- (ISC)^2 Common Body of Knowledge (CBK)

- ISO 27001 / 27002 Version 2013

- ISO 27001 / 27002 Version 2005

- NIST SP800-53 Revisions 3 and 4

- NIST Cybersecurity Framework (2014)

- Department of Homeland Security Cyber Resilience Review (DHS CRR)

- Council on CyberSecurity Critical Security Controls (SANS 20)

- Australian DSD Strategies to Mitigate Targeted Cyber Intrusions

- PCI DSS Version 3.0

- HIPAA Security Rule

- HITRUST Common Security Framework (CSF)

- NERC CIP Cyber Security Version 5

- NERC CIP Cyber Security Version 3

Clearly Defining "Controls"

An examination of some of these external cybersecurity frameworks reveals there is some confusion over exactly what is meant by an "IT security control." This confusion results in considerable room for interpretation and judgment with regard to auditing against these frameworks. Sometimes, what the frameworks call a "control," this book would call a "capability." Other times, the frameworks talk about "requirements," and it is up to individuals to identify what capabilities and controls would be needed to satisfy the requirements. So, for the sake of clarity and purposes of this book, a security control is defined as follows:

A security control consists of security capabilities or audit activities that are applied to an IT system or business process to prevent, detect, document, or investigate specific activities that are undesirable, and incident response to react to those activities when they occur.

Figure 13-2 depicts this security control definition and shows how enterprise cybersecurity controls fit in with security capabilities and the various types of audits into an operational cybersecurity program that reacts to malicious activity and responds to incidents.

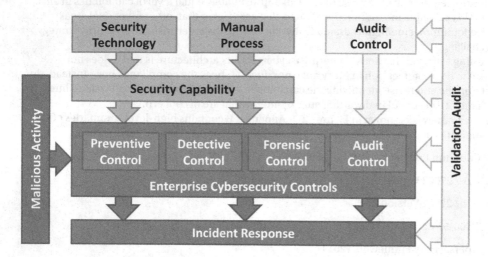

Figure 13-2. *Security controls result when security capabilities or manual audits are applied to IT systems or business processes to restrict, delay, detect, or document activities that may potentially be malicious.*

Starting from the top of the figure, security technologies or manual processes deliver security capabilities to the enterprise, and the enterprise security program is managed around those capabilities. When those capabilities, along with manual audit controls, are applied to enterprise IT systems or business practices, the capabilities result in four types of security controls: preventive, detective, forensic, and audit. These controls can then trigger incident response when potentially malicious behavior occurs. Finally, there are audit activities that deliver enterprise audit controls and periodic validation audits to ensure that everything is operating as designed.

For a security control to be effective, these five elements should be present:

1. A specific **IT system** or **business process** must be identified that contains information where the enterprise is concerned about its confidentiality, integrity, or availability.

2. A specific **malicious activity** against an IT system or business process must be identified. This activity attempts to compromise the confidentiality, integrity, or availability of the IT system or business process.

3. A **security capability** or **audit control** must be applied to an IT system or business process to restrict, delay, detect, or document the specific malicious activity that is of concern.

4. **Incident response** must occur when malicious activity is detected. This incident response must investigate the malicious activity, repel the attacker (if necessary), and restore systems back to normal operations following the attack.

5. **Validation audits** must occur periodically to ensure that controls are effective and functioning properly. These audits must thoroughly test the controls and underlying capabilities, technologies, manual processes, and audit activities to provide evidence of the controls' proper operation.

As an enterprise looks at its enterprise cybersecurity in the context of external frameworks, the enterprise wants to ensure that all five elements are present so its security controls are effective, even if the controls are not specifically called out in the framework itself.

Remember, the enterprise control list, as discussed in Chapter 5, is one of the 14 cybersecurity information systems of a successful enterprise, and the cybersecurity control management process is one of the 17 operational processes. So, for an enterprise's overall security program to be effective, it is very important that it tracks and maintains its controls over time.

Mapping Against External Frameworks

An enterprise can use external cybersecurity frameworks in the following three ways:

- To help design an enterprise's cybersecurity program to comply with specific external standards

- To validate an enterprise's cybersecurity program against those external standards

- To give an enterprise ideas for cybersecurity capabilities and controls that may be of interest

Figure 13-3 combines the these usage scenarios with the Figure 13-2 control model and the Chapter 11 audit types (threat, assessment, and validation audits) into a process for selecting appropriate security scopes and controls for defining an enterprise cybersecurity program.

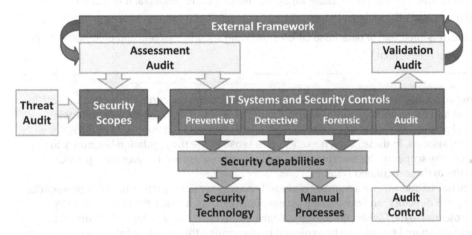

Figure 13-3. *External frameworks feed into the selection of security scopes and security controls in the enterprise that are delivered by security capabilities, technologies, manual processes, and audit controls.*

Assessment Audit and Security Scopes

The first step in the Figure 13-3 process is the assessment audit. In the assessment audit, the enterprise takes the controls and requirements of the external framework and analyzes how it applies to the enterprise. Key to this analysis is identifying the scope of the framework and deciding if the enterprise wants a *narrow scope* or *broad scope* application of the framework:

- In a "***narrow scope***" assessment, only IT systems and processes that are primarily involved in the external framework's scope are considered to be in-scope for assessment. Supporting systems and processes that are only indirectly involved in the assessed function are considered to be out-of-scope.

- In a "***broad scope***" assessment, IT systems that are primarily involved in the external framework's scope, as well as supporting IT systems that are only indirectly involved, are all considered to be in-scope for assessment. This scope choice can result in a large number of systems to be considered in-scope.

An example of the difference between the two assessment scope choices has to do with how supporting security systems, such as authentication and network security, are handled. Since these systems are general cybersecurity systems that frequently support the whole enterprise's security, they may or may not be considered in-scope for a specific assessment such as the Payment Card Industry Digital Security Standards (PCI-DSS) or Sarbanes-Oxley (SOX) for financial systems.

If an enterprise security program is going to be validated by internal or external auditors, it is recommended that the cybersecurity team meet with the auditors to mutually agree on whether a "narrow scope" or "broad scope" approach is appropriate. It is important to determine which supporting security systems and processes are to be considered in-scope for an assessment.

Regulatory frameworks, in particular, will lead to an enterprise identifying certain systems that are in-scope for regulation and others that are out-of-scope. Examples of these situations involve financial systems, payment card processing systems, healthcare electronic health record systems, or energy production and control systems. In these cases, it likely makes sense to use the regulation boundary to define one or more security scopes in the enterprise and segment the enterprise IT systems to provide isolation and protection to these regulated systems.

Similarly, enterprises frequently use a number of shared security services, such as network protection, authentication, enterprise directory, and centralized access control. In such cases, the shared security services have to be protected to the highest level of all systems and security scopes dependent on them, since a compromise of the shared service can be exploited to undermine the security of all dependent systems. Enterprises can have situations where the regulated systems themselves are locked down nicely, but then rely on supporting security systems that are poorly secured and easily exploited.

IT Systems and Security Controls

The next step of the assessment audit is to identify the security controls appropriate to meet the external framework's requirements. These requirements may be general guidance such as "you shall have a firewall" or "credit card data will be encrypted," or it may be very specific such as "application whitelisting technology will be used on servers." The mandated controls depend upon the specifics of the framework being considered and the capabilities available to implement them.

In the case of frameworks with general requirements (for example, ISO 27001 and the HIPAA security rules), there may be considerable leeway for an enterprise to select the specific controls that meet the spirit of the framework requirement. Other frameworks, like the Council on CyberSecurity 20 Critical Controls and HITECH, are more specific in their guidance. When using the frameworks where there is leeway, an enterprise can take advantage of the opportunity to select controls that work well in its environment and are economical to procure, deploy, and operate.

Balancing Prevention with Detection and Response

Many of the popular frameworks focus primarily on preventive controls that block undesirable activities and give far less attention to detective, forensic, and audit control alternatives. This prevention focus can lead to both a false sense of security and controls that are highly disruptive to legitimate business activities. When an enterprise delivers the same level of security "in the background" without disrupting people's normal activities, it can be a significant win compared to the situation of security being a constant disruption to people doing their jobs.

Enterprises should look at security control alternatives with an open mind and consider audit requirements when selecting controls or control alternatives. This "audit first" consideration helps to minimize procurement, deployment, and operational costs and limit the impact of security on business operations.

If an enterprise opts for detective, forensic, or audit control alternatives versus preventive controls, then some negotiation between the cybersecurity team and the auditors may be required with respect to how the enterprise protects itself. The auditors may be thinking only of preventive controls and not give credit for other controls that are in place. The enterprise may need to describe its other security controls in preventive terms, using phrasing like the following:

- Unauthorized users are not able to get access to protected data because the data access logs are reviewed daily and unauthorized accesses are identified, investigated, and remediated.

- Network access is restricted to authorized devices only. Unauthorized devices are detected and removed from the network within one hour of their connection.

- All administrator activity is logged and audited the next business day to detect and remediate unauthorized or inappropriate systems administration.

- Server configuration files are monitored to detect unauthorized or inappropriate configuration changes hourly, with systems administrators investigating and remediating problems by the next business day.

An enterprise may be able to show that detective, forensic, and audit controls are just as effective as preventive controls and may even be more effective. Perhaps most interesting about this exercise is there are many areas—such as systems administration—where intelligent and effective prevention is almost impossible. In such cases, detective and audit controls are in fact an enterprise's only viable protection, and they are more effective at catching actual rogue activities than layers of preventive controls alone. An enterprise needs to work with its auditors to consider how passive controls (detective, forensic, and audit) can provide effective protection of IT assets and data.

Security Capabilities, Technologies, and Processes

Once an enterprise identifies the security controls to satisfy the requirements of the external frameworks it supports, the next step is to identify the security capabilities, technologies, manual processes, and audit processes necessary to deliver those controls. It is often faster and cheaper to set up a manual detective control or audit process than to install a new security technology. In situations where speed is of the essence, an enterprise can stand up "quick and dirty" controls to give it some protection until more permanent solutions can be put in place. In fact, don't underestimate the power of manual processes to protect an enterprise on a temporary basis. It is important to remember a temporary fix can serve for months or years until funding for long-term solutions is obtained. Such an approach is normal and acceptable, provided the protection works well enough to satisfy the enterprise's needs, the requirements of the frameworks, and the judgment of the auditors.

The next component is manual processes and audit controls. Some of an enterprise's controls are manual in nature. Such controls consist of personnel manually doing certain procedures on a regular basis, maintaining paper or digital logs of activities, and auditing system logs to identify and investigate malicious activities. These controls are no less valid than automated preventive and detective controls, and they can be just as effective. For these manual activities, an enterprise should document what they are, who should be doing them, and who is responsible for overseeing and maintaining them. If these activities deliver the same functionality as an automated technology, then the enterprise should give itself credit for having that capability, even if it is through manual procedures.

Validation Audit and Reporting

Given that an enterprise's controls are in place, an enterprise can conduct validation audits of the cybersecurity program and report the results of the validation to internal and external auditors and regulators. Figure 13-3 shows the validation audits parallel to the initial assessment audits because they should be conducted in a similar fashion. Once an enterprise's cybersecurity program is in place, the validation audit from one time period can serve as the assessment audit for the next time period. This audit sequence provides the enterprise with the inputs needed to make adjustments to the cybersecurity program over time.

There are two validation audit reports, one external-facing and one internal-facing:

- The *external-facing audit report* presents the results of the validation audit to external auditors and regulators. It lists the requirements of the framework to be audited against and explains how the cybersecurity program satisfies the requirements of that framework, any deficiencies identified during the audit, and the results of remediating those deficiencies.

- The *internal-facing audit report* is an addendum to the external-facing report and contains internal-use-only recommendations for improving security and audit results in the future. There are cases where internal controls satisfy external audit requirements but are not as effective as they should be, or where significant "tap-dancing" was involved in the audit process. These "almost-a-deficiency" cases should be tracked and remediated where possible, albeit at a lower priority than the actual deficiencies.

One Audit, Many Results

Enterprises are often required to report to multiple external frameworks where a number of controls are common to more than one framework. Figure 13-4 depicts an approach for auditing the controls and then reporting the results of those audits against the separate frameworks.

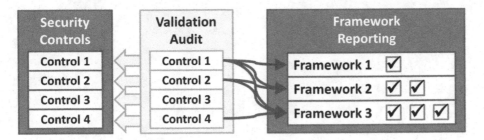

Figure 13-4. *Once controls are in place, validation audits can verify the control framework as it was implemented, and then the results of those audits can be mapped and reported against multiple frameworks.*

The key to this reporting approach is separating the audit process from the security frameworks so that the audit covers all controls and a superset of the framework requirements.

Audit Report Mapping

Once the audit has been conducted, the audit results can be reported against the various frameworks involved. It is straightforward to track results to various frameworks if the enterprise's control database includes cross-references connecting controls to the applicable framework requirements.

Using such cross-references, a single control can be referenced by multiple frameworks, and it can even be referenced from different parts of a single framework. When the audit is completed, the enterprise follows these cross-references to build the report against the structure of each framework to be reported against. A simple database is able to show results against multiple frameworks across multiple audits.

Deficiency Tracking and Management

Similarly, an enterprise's audit deficiencies should be tracked against the controls they apply to and cross-referenced against the external frameworks for reporting purposes. This tracking and cross-referencing allows an enterprise to report on its deficiencies against the frameworks. Furthermore, these results provide input to substantial discussions about the materiality of deficiencies against framework compliance.

Interestingly, an enterprise may have cases where a single deficiency is material (in other words, substantial) against one external framework, and immaterial and unsubstantial when measured against another external framework. While uncommon, this situation is to be occasionally expected.

The key deficiency tracking challenge is properly handling the delay between reporting the initial results of the audit and actually remediating the deficiencies identified in the audit. An enterprise's best bet here is regularly scheduled audits that look at the same controls on a regular basis—say quarterly or annually. When an enterprise does not have regularly scheduled audits, the deficiencies from the previous audit may become a part of the kickoff for the next audit. By doing this reporting, enterprise management can pay particular attention to deficiencies that are not remediated between audits, or that show up as recurring problems across multiple audit cycles.

PART V

Enterprise Cybersecurity Program

CHAPTER 14

■ ■ ■

Managing an Enterprise Cybersecurity Program

Once the enterprise has its cybersecurity controls and capabilities, and can quantitatively assess its cybersecurity posture and operate its cybersecurity processes, it is time to engage with the business at a programmatic level and operate a comprehensive cybersecurity program. This chapter describes how the enterprise can use iterative assessments and prioritization to select, plan, resource, and execute progressive improvements to its cybersecurity posture. This cybersecurity program utilizes all the management tools described in this book, including: (1) a framework for managing a cybersecurity program, (2) a quantitative method for assessing the program and identifying strengths and weaknesses, and (3) ongoing operations and cycles of improvements.

Enterprise Cybersecurity Program Management

Enterprise cybersecurity program management ties together risk management, control management, deficiency tracking, process improvement, and measurement processes into a single overarching programmatic cycle. Figure 14-1 depicts this high-level process.

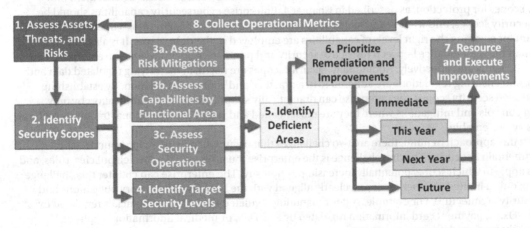

Figure 14-1. *The enterprise cybersecurity program management process involves an ongoing cycle of assessing threats and risks, making progressive improvements to mitigate them, and collecting metrics from security operations.*

The enterprise cybersecurity program management process consists of the following major steps:

1. Assess assets, threats, and risks

2. Identify security scopes

3. Assess risk mitigations, capabilities by functional area, and security operations

4. Identify target security levels

5. Identify deficient areas

6. Prioritize remediation and improvements

7. Resource and execute improvements

8. Collect operational metrics

9. Return to Step 1

Each of these process elements is summarized in the following sections.

Cybersecurity Program Step 1: Assess Assets, Threats, and Risks

Step 1 involves assessing enterprise assets, threats, and risks and its IT systems, as outlined in Chapter 4. This step involves considering the missions of potential attackers—whether they are to to breach confidentiality, compromise integrity, or disrupt availability. Well-defined cybersecurity scopes simplify the defensive process by ensuring that defensive measures focus on the needs of the security scope, rather than trying to protect everything from every possible threat simultaneously.

This step's output is an understanding of the enterprise assets to be protected and the threats against those assets. These assets might be corporate data, customer data, or critical services such as power generation or healthcare delivery. With an understanding of the assets, how they interconnect, and how attackers might target them, the enterprise can ensure that the defensive measures applied to each scope are appropriate and the most economical way to achieve the desired protection.

Cybersecurity Program Step 2: Identify Security Scopes

Step 2 is to group the previously identified enterprise assets and the threats and risks against them into security scopes for protection, as described in Chapter 4. Enterprise cybersecurity capabilities should be tied to security scopes, and while many scopes may use the same security capabilities, scope boundaries are important for ensuring the right levels of capabilities are employed in the right places. It is also important to maintain the right balance between restrictive security and permissive operations so the enterprise can operate efficiently and effectively. Additionally, security scopes are useful in identifying regulated data and systems, and ensuring regulations are adhered to in a practical and economical fashion. By establishing well-bounded security scopes, the enterprise can dramatically simplify the cybersecurity effort by only applying controls and mitigations where they are most needed and where the operational trade-offs of those controls are acceptable.

With this approach in mind, there are two challenges that occur when using scope boundaries to compartmentalize security. The first challenge is the enterprise must keep track of which policies, rules, and controls apply to which scope, potentially increasing complexity. The enterprise can counter this challenge by having only a limited number of scopes, clearly aligned with the business's regulatory obligations and cybersecurity architecture. For example, systems handling regulated data such as financials regulated by Sarbanes-Oxley, payment card information regulated by PCI-DSS, or medical information regulated by HIPAA might be placed into separate scopes to ensure their protection.

The second challenge has to do with systems that cross scope boundaries, such as data interconnects and systems administration consoles. In these cases, compensating controls may be necessary to ensure the interconnections do not become security vulnerabilities. A common example of this situation involves systems administration workstations, which typically are nothing more than regular personal computers that are used with very powerful systems administration credentials. Allowing these systems to receive e-mail, surf the web, and run office productivity applications may open them up to targeted attacks that would give the attackers significant administrative permissions.

Cybersecurity Program Step 3: Assess Risk Mitigations, Capabilities by Functional Area, and Security Operations

With an understanding of the assets, threats, and risks within each security scope, the next step is to assess the security of the scope. This assessment can be performed using the methods described in this book, looking at risk mitigations, the 11 functional areas of cybersecurity capabilities, and security operations. Using this book's methodology, assessment results include Object Measurement scores for the cybersecurity functional areas and can also include an aggregate score for the complete enterprise cybersecurity posture.

Looking at risk mitigations, the enterprise uses the attack sequence to evaluate its ability to disrupt, detect, delay, and defeat attacks against its assets. This evaluation considers each potential attack scenario and then aggregates the results together. Looking at security capabilities, the enterprise examines the 11 functional areas and calculates scores for each of the functional areas. One area of focus involves looking out for functional areas that are deficient when compared to the other functional areas. Finally, looking at security operations, the enterprise examines the 17 security operational processes. The enterprise assesses its ability to perform these processes to operate its cybersecurity systems.

Once the enterprise has scores for these areas, the scores can be aggregated and compared for evaluation and further analysis. The overall enterprise cybersecurity program assessment score can be tracked over time to show quantitatively how the cybersecurity posture evolves as improvements are implemented. The overall score can be evaluated within the security scope to determine if the scope is adequately or inadequately protected. If the security scope is inadequately protected, then specific activities can be implemented to reach a stated improvement goal or target assessment score.

Cybersecurity Program Step 4: Identify Target Security Levels

With an idea of the assets, threats, risks, and effective security in each scope, the next programmatic goal is to use risk assessment methodology to identify the target security levels and understand if the scope's current security is adequate, inadequate, or even excessive. Generally, it is not cost-effective or practical to deliver "perfect" security to every part of the enterprise. Various parts of the business require different security postures to satisfy business needs while giving employees the freedoms they may desire. Various parts of the business require different preventive, detective, forensic, and audit controls.

Security scopes accommodate these realities by limiting the number of systems and people who are subject to the most stringent security protection. Security scopes help prioritize limited cybersecurity resources toward the areas where they will deliver the greatest enterprise benefits. Security scopes also simplify the cybersecurity process by reducing the attack surface of vulnerable systems and increasing cybersecurity's ability to succeed through that simplicity.

For each security scope and associated assets, this step involves identifying threats, risks, and a target security level. The identified security level represents the business tolerance for potential compromise within the scope. Furthermore, the security level is used to balance the severity of the threats with the business desire for flexibility and unobtrusive security that does not impede business agility. Different parts of the enterprise require different levels of protection, but the security infrastructure requires the greatest level of protection so that it can successfully protect the rest of the enterprise.

Cybersecurity Program Step 5: Identify Deficient Areas

Once the enterprise has identified its security scopes, actual security within the scopes, and established target security levels, the next step is to identify which areas are deficient and require improvement when compared to the targets. Identifying deficient areas produces results to include the following:

- First, the target security level for the security scope might be too high or too low. In this situation, when the enterprise considers what additional security capabilities might be necessary, the associated costs, and potential operational trade-offs, the business may determine that a different security posture is more appropriate. When a different security posture is required, the target security level can be adjusted either up or down, and the evaluation can be reconsidered.

- Second, during the assessment, some functional areas are likely to stand out as being considerably weaker than other areas. These weaker areas should be prioritized for improvements first. Shoring up the weaker functional areas with improvements addresses the cybersecurity gaps that are the most likely to be exploited by potential attackers.

- Third, after the most deficient functional areas are addressed, the next improvement phase involves bringing all areas up to the target level of security. This phase often involves a comprehensive effort to improve risk mitigations, security capabilities, and security operations.

Cybersecurity Program Step 6: Prioritize Remediation and Improvements

Once the enterprise understands its "as-is" cybersecurity posture, as well as its security needs for each scope, the next step is to prioritize remediation and improvement efforts. This prioritization is influenced by the following factors:

- Bringing deficient functional areas up to target levels of security

- Improvements that rely on other improvements as prerequisites

- Availability and skill levels of available staff and contractors

- Costs of improvements

The goal is to address deficient enterprise cybersecurity functional areas first, then work on bringing all functional areas up to the target cybersecurity level in a balanced manner.

As improvements are prioritized and sequenced, they can be logically grouped into four different categories. This categorization is based on practical assessments of what should be done in what order and when different efforts can realistically be resourced. These categories can be maintained across all security scopes provided the scopes of improvements are clearly identified within each project. Improvements should be grouped into the following categories:

- *Immediate* improvements that can be done starting immediately using readily available staff and budget

- *This Year* improvements that can be done within the current year using resources that are obtainable in the year or after minor prerequisites or other dependencies have been addressed

- *Next Year* improvements that should be done next year, after completing the immediate and this year projects, and obtaining budgets, approvals, or satisfying other prerequisites

- *Future* improvements that are lower priority or will require obtaining budget, hiring staff, completing prerequisites or satisfying other non-trivial requirements before they can begin

Within each of these categories, improvements can be further prioritized and sub-grouped, but at the highest level this grouping is helpful to start aligning cybersecurity priorities with business financial cycles so that work can be resourced and executed. Obviously, projects and tasks will move around on these priority lists and get moved forward or back in the sequencing as priorities change and time passes. Having a "big picture" story to tell leadership about where the enterprise is, where it is going, and how it is going to get there is important. Business leadership wants to understand that such prioritized improvements are not just spending money or buying new *cybertoys*. Maintaining the cybersecurity strategy grouped into these four categories simply makes it easier for security to manage and explain its priorities and plans to enterprise leadership.

Cybersecurity Program Step 7: Resource and Execute Improvements

Once improvements are prioritized, the enterprise can begin resourcing and executing them. This resourcing process generally involves the following tasks that are conducted in parallel against each category grouping of improvements:

- For *Immediate* improvements, cybersecurity leadership directs the work and supervises its progress.

- For *This Year* improvements, cybersecurity leadership works on lining up resources, shuffling priorities, or completing prerequisites so the actual improvement can start work within the current year.

- For *Next* and *Future* improvements, cybersecurity leadership starts framing project plans and resource requirements so they can be considered and budgeted in future fiscal years. Many times, improvements are pushed back because they are too big or expensive to execute in a foreseeable time frame. In such cases, it is helpful to consider creative ways to break these projects up into smaller pieces that are more manageable and potentially fundable. Alternatively, it may help to link their benefits to other business needs so they have business support from multiple departments.

Cybersecurity Program Step 8: Collect Operational Metrics

As the enterprise executes its improvements and operates its security program, the next step in the programmatic sequence is to collect metrics from cybersecurity operations. These metrics should span all functional areas, with particular emphasis paid to metrics that measure signs of security incidents and near-incidents, or indicators of attacker activities indicating the presence of anticipated threats. These metrics give enterprise leadership visibility into what the threats are, where they are coming from, and what can result if the threats are not stopped before they can succeed. Even relatively crude metrics, like "The enterprise was scanned a million times last month," can be useful if metrics are tracked and trended over time. For example, tracking and trending threats could show that the million scans are an increase from only ten thousand from the previous month. Security takes on a whole new urgency if enterprise leadership has a mental picture of attackers who are just waiting to pounce at the slightest mistake or vulnerability.

Cybersecurity Program Step 9: Return to Step 1

After collecting metrics, the cybersecurity program management process returns to the assessment phase and the cycle repeats. This *assess* ➤ *prioritize* ➤ *execute* ➤ *operate* cycle should go through a complete iteration multiple times each year. During each cycle, the enterprise updates its threat assessment, takes stock of completed security improvements, identifies new security improvements to implement, and lines up future security improvements for execution when resources become available.

As this cycle iterates, security projects move through the various priority categories until they are executed. A project might start out on the *Future* category, then get moved to the *Next Year* category, then to the *This Year* category, and finally to the *Immediate* category for execution. In addition to this natural flow, projects get inserted into the categories due to incidents, new threats, or IT projects requiring additional protections. This insertion provides the enterprise a flexible framework for managing its overall cybersecurity program. The framework also provides the ability to report on both immediate activities and the *big picture* strategy at any time. Moreover, this overall strategy helps to balance effectively cybersecurity with business needs in a cost-effective manner.

Assessing Security Status

Once an enterprise has assessed its assets, threats, and risks (Enterprise Cybersecurity Program Management Step 1), and identified security scopes to contain those risks (Step 2), the third step is to assess the overall security posture and status within each scope. Figure 14-2 depicts the next level of detail for assessing the enterprise's overall security posture.

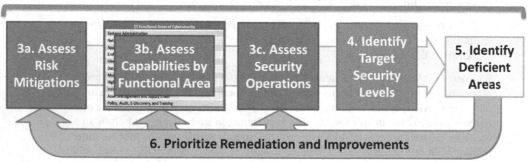

Figure 14-2. *The assessment process involves looking at each security scope from a perspective of risk mitigations, security functional areas, and operations, as well as considering progressive improvements into all areas on an ongoing basis.*

For each scope, the enterprise can consider if it needs to protect primarily confidentiality, integrity, or availability. Also, the enterprise needs to consider the appropriate balance of preventive, detective, forensic, and audit controls to deliver that protection.

Complementing these considerations, it is important for the enterprise to have substantive discussions with business leaders to understand, for each scope, the proper balance of cybersecurity versus business utility to deliver the most appropriate and cost-effective protection. The discussions need to include what costs and trade-offs the enterprise is willing to accept to achieve agreed-upon cybersecurity protection. This next level of assessing the security status, per security scope, is summarized below.

Cybersecurity Program Step 3: Assess Risk Mitigations, Capabilities, and Security Operations

Step 3a: Assessing Cybersecurity Risk Mitigations

What is the effectiveness of risk mitigations within the security scope? What are the abilities of the risk mitigations to disrupt the attack sequence of the anticipated attack? This step considers the attacks to be countered, the controls being deployed against those attack sequences, and the effectiveness of the resulting risk mitigations. This step can use Object Measurement methodology detailed in Chapter 12 to measure these mitigations and calculate an aggregate score across all anticipated attack sequences. If risk mitigations are deficient compared to the other aspects of the cybersecurity program, improving the mitigations to the baseline standard should be a top priority.

Step 3b: Assessing Cybersecurity Capabilities by Functional Area

The next step assesses the cybersecurity functional areas using Object Measurement methodology to calculate enterprise cybersecurity program assessment scores for each functional area. These functional area assessment scores are evaluated alongside the risk mitigations and security operations to determine, in part, the enterprise's overall cybersecurity posture.

Step 3c: Assessing Security Operations

The next step is to consider security operations by considering the utilization and effectiveness of the 17 security operational processes and the 14 supporting information systems. Objective Measurement can be used to score the security operations processes and/or information systems separately.

Cybersecurity Program Step 4: Identify Target Security Levels

The next step is to identify the target cybersecurity levels for the scope, based on the risk assessment process detailed in Chapter 4. This risk assessment process considers the assets, threats, and risks to the scope, and the potential attack sequences against its assets. It considers the balance between restrictive cybersecurity needs versus flexible business agility needs to determine if preventive, detective, forensic, or audit controls are most appropriate for mitigating the considered risks. One output of this step can be an enterprise cybersecurity program assessment score that represents the target cybersecurity level for the scope.

Using Object Measurement, the target security level can be represented as a *single* number for the entire scope. A comprehensive enterprise cybersecurity program assessment evaluates risk mitigations (per attack sequence), the 11 functional areas, and 17 security operational processes. For enterprise cybersecurity to be effective, all of these assessments should be at approximately the same level of effectiveness, since they are all of approximately equal importance in delivering overall enterprise cybersecurity. So, the target cybersecurity security level for the scope can be represented as *a single value that applies to the risk mitigations, functional areas, and security operations.*

Figure 14-3 depicts one way to visualize this step's output. This figure shows the measured enterprise cybersecurity program assessment scores for risk mitigations (aggregated score), the 11 functional areas (individual scores), and security operations (aggregated score). Finally, the target cybersecurity program assessment score is shown on the chart as a dotted line at the 80% level.

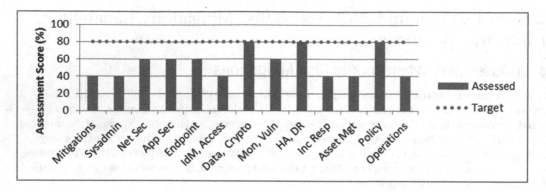

Figure 14-3. *The enterprise can depict the side-by-side results of its enterprise cybersecurity program assessment of the risk mitigations, the 11 functional areas, and security operations, along with the target cybersecurity level for the security scope.*

This figure becomes the baseline assessment for the enterprise cybersecurity program and shows which areas are strongest and which areas are weakest. In addition, this assessment can be used to calculate an overall enterprise cybersecurity program assessment score for the enterprise. In this example, the overall score for the evaluated scope is 55%, and the target score is 80%.

Cybersecurity Program Step 5: Identify Deficient Areas

Once the scoring is complete and the results plotted or otherwise displayed, the areas of the cybersecurity program that are most deficient should be apparent. In Figure 14-3, the following areas stand out as being deficient relative to the overall average cybersecurity level:

1. Risk Mitigations (40%)

2. Functional Area: Systems Administration (40%)

3. Functional Area: Identity, Authentication, and Access Management (40%)

4. Functional Area: Incident Response (40%)

5. Functional Area: Asset Management (40%)

6. Security Operations (40%)

Based upon the enterprise cybersecurity program assessment, the above enterprise cybersecurity areas are most likely to be related to security failures leading to successful attacks. The fact that risk mitigations and security operations are two of the weaker areas indicates the attack sequences are most likely not disrupted as effectively as they should be. Also, the enterprise's overall cybersecurity program is likely not being operated with adequate rigor to protect against deliberate or targeted attacks.

A recommendation coming from this assessment might be that these six areas should be designated for improvement. These improvements should address the greatest known weaknesses in the overall cybersecurity across the enterprise. Remember, a tenet of the enterprise cybersecurity architecture in this book is that risk mitigations, functional areas, and security operations are all of approximately equal importance in delivering overall enterprise cybersecurity.

Cybersecurity Program Step 6: Prioritize Remediation and Improvements

Once the enterprise assesses its cybersecurity posture, identifies a cybersecurity target level, and identifies the most deficient areas for improvement, the next step is to prioritize the remediation and improvement efforts. Unlike the assessment steps, which are done on a per-scope basis, this step should be executed as a single process across *all* security scopes within the enterprise. Also, this step integrates improvements across all scopes to come up with and manage a single list of cybersecurity improvements for the entire enterprise. These cybersecurity improvements can be performed in two phases. The first phase involves addressing deficient functional areas and bringing them up to the same cybersecurity level as the other areas, making cybersecurity effectiveness consistent across all functional areas. The second phase involves bringing all the cybersecurity functional areas up to the target level together.

Considering the example from Figure 14-3, this first improvement phase should focus on the areas identified as deficient. These improvements should bring the following cybersecurity areas up to a consistent score of approximately 60%: (1) risk mitigations, (2) systems administration, (3) identity, authentication, and access management, (4) incident response, (5) asset management and supply chain, and (6) security operations. These improvements are shown in Figure 14-4. Calculating the overall enterprise cybersecurity program score, the phase-one improvements change the scope's overall cybersecurity assessment score from 55% to 65%.

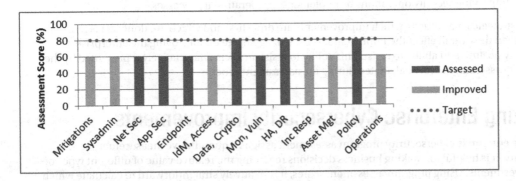

Figure 14-4. *In this enterprise cybersecurity program assessment example, the first phase of cybersecurity improvements brings the most deficient areas up to the same level as the others.*

The second phase of cybersecurity improvements would be more comprehensive, bringing all cybersecurity areas up to the target 80% level. As shown in Figure 14-5, every area needs to be improved except for the following three functional areas that were already at the target level:

- Functional Area: Data Protection and Cryptography

- Functional Area: High Availability, Disaster Recovery, and Physical Protection

- Functional Area: Policy, Audit, E-Discovery, and Training

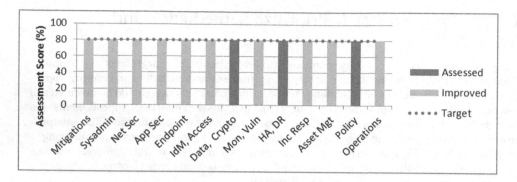

Figure 14-5. *Once the deficient functional areas are brought up to baseline, the second phase of improvements brings all cybersecurity areas up to the target level.*

These phase-two improvements might be accomplished by the following:

- Improving risk mitigations by addressing projected attack sequences

- Improving functional areas by adding security capabilities or improving their utilization

- Improving security operations by implementing operational processes

At the strategic level, exactly which improvements are done first and which are done last is less important than the overall effect the improvements have in aggregate on improving the enterprise's cybersecurity posture and ability to resist. This ability to resist attack is quantitatively represented by the cybersecurity assessment score calculated during the assessment process.

Analyzing Enterprise Cybersecurity Improvements

Because the enterprise cybersecurity program assessment assigns a quantitative measurement to cybersecurity, it is helpful for making business decisions regarding the relative value of different types of security investments. Using program assessment scores, it is relatively straightforward to calculate which improvements will provide the biggest "bang for the buck." Dividing projected program assessment score changes (delta score changes due to the improvements) by the estimated improvement cost helps to provide insight into which cybersecurity improvements will generate the greatest security improvement for the lowest potential cost.

One cybersecurity improvement challenge is related to the fact that there are multiple scopes in most enterprises. An enterprise cybersecurity program assessment focuses on the security scope as the basic platform for analyzing security and security capabilities. When considering security improvements, it is important to remember that a single risk mitigation, capability, or operational process may be shared across multiple scopes. Consequently, the benefit of security improvements should be considered across multiple scopes as well. This section explains this calculation process in more detail and provide some helpful examples of how it can work in practice.

Considering Types of Improvements

In general, security improvements fall into three categories, depending on the specific security area to be improved. These categories are the following:

- **Risk mitigations** should be the top improvement priority if it scores poorly compared to the other categories. Risk mitigations focus on disrupting, detecting, delaying, and defeating known threats and their attack sequences. To achieve effective risk mitigations, certain levels of security capabilities and security operational processes are required.

- **Security capabilities** is the next category for improvement. After risk mitigations are addressed, the overall security capabilities (and their utilization) will address unknown threats, unanticipated attacks, defender mistakes, and attackers who use new technologies or innovative approaches.

- **Security operations** is the third category for improvement. When risk mitigations and security capabilities are all in place, effective security operations is required to make them work in repelling attacks on an ongoing basis.

Cybersecurity improvements in all these categories improve the enterprise's cybersecurity posture. However, it is very useful for the enterprise to do some modeling to calculate which improvements will generate the greatest security improvement for the lowest investment and in the least amount of time.

Considering Threat Scenarios

When considering attacker scenarios and corresponding risk mitigations, it probably makes sense to take a moment and consider the value of *red-team exercises* and *penetration testing*. Red-team exercises and penetration tests analyze enterprise defenses from the attacker's perspective to identify gaps in protection and vulnerabilities in defenses. The enterprise should consider conducting exercises involving the following threat scenarios elements:

- What asset would be endangered (for example, credit card numbers that could be stolen)

- Where the asset resides and when

- Who has access to the asset

- When and how an attacker might access the asset (for example, via the operating system, database, application, or user account levels)

- Attack sequences for attackers to obtain access

- Audit controls to find the attacker's access point, if the scenario occurred

- Forensic controls to log the access, if the assess occurred

- Detective controls to alert the enterprise when such access occurred

- Preventive controls to block such access from occurring

At the same time, after the enterprise works out threat scenarios on its own, it is useful to bring in third parties who might look at the situation more creatively and find attack vectors the enterprise never considered. This type of red-team exercise is useful to identify faulty enterprise cyberdefender assumptions and gaps in cyberdefense thinking that might undermine the overall security posture.

Once attack scenarios are identified, another useful exercise is to have penetration testers actually exercise the scenarios, utilizing the tools and techniques attackers might be expected to use. These exercises can then be used to understand how preventive controls should block the attacks. Such exercises can also test detective, forensic, and audit controls to help ensure that even if the attack is not blocked, it could still be successfully detected and investigated after the fact.

Examining Cybersecurity Assessment Scores across Multiple Scopes

If the enterprise is using enterprise cybersecurity program assessment scores to evaluate its cybersecurity posture and quantitatively establish its cybersecurity target levels, it is important to remember that assessment scores are calculated within a single security scope. Most enterprises will have multiple security scopes to contend with, representing different aspects of the business and different balances of flexibility versus security. This reality adds complexity to the cybersecurity management effort. In an enterprise cybersecurity architecture, security scopes represent the following:

- Separately managing the security posture of each scope, including:

  - Assets, threats, and risks

  - Risk mitigations applied to defend against attacks

  - Cybersecurity capabilities and controls used to deliver risk mitigations

  - Operational processes used to operate capabilities

- Separately calculating cybersecurity assessment scores and target scores for each scope

Frequently, there will be significant sharing of cybersecurity capabilities across multiple scopes. This sharing is fine as long as the cybersecurity capabilities do not themselves become a vulnerability that attackers can exploit to get from a lower-security scope to a higher-security scope.

Figure 14-6 depicts one way to visualize enterprise cybersecurity program assessment scores and targets across multiple scopes. The figure shows how a hypothetical publicly traded enterprise might have data regulated by Sarbanes-Oxley (SOX), Payment Card Industry (PCI), and the Health Information Portability and Accountability Act (HIPAA).

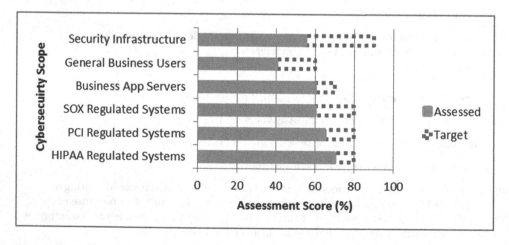

Figure 14-6. *Using enterprise cybersecurity program assessment scores, an enterprise can track cybersecurity assessment scores and targets across multiple scopes.*

Considering the cybersecurity requirements typically associated with these regulations, the example enterprise might have the following six security scopes:

1. ***Security infrastructure*** that protects the data in the other five scopes. This infrastructure must be hardened to resist attack, detect breaches or failures of security, provide a forensic trail for all security-related activities, and be aggressively audited to ensure its ongoing integrity.

2. ***General business users*** who primarily use e-mail, desktop productivity tools, and web-based business applications for conducting general business. Such users should not have significant or privileged access to business systems, and the amount of damage that could occur if a single user or a group of users' computers is compromised should be limited.

3. ***Business application servers*** that support the enterprise's business operations. These servers might include e-mail, file servers, collaboration servers, and other secondary business systems.

4. ***SOX regulated systems*** that support the business's reporting of financial results to the public stock markets and are subject to the Sarbanes-Oxley regulations regarding financial reporting integrity. These systems, because of their regulatory importance, must be well protected and audited for cybersecurity by external auditors.

5. ***PCI regulated systems*** that support the business's processing of credit cards and other payment mechanisms and are subject to the regulations of the payment card industry (PCI). These systems must be protected and their security audited according to PCI guidelines.

6. ***HIPAA regulated systems*** that handle medical and personally identifiable information for the business and are regulated by the Health Information Portability and Accountability Act (HIPAA). These systems must be protected according to HIPAA regulatory requirements.

Figure 14-6 shows how the security posture of these six scopes might be visualized. As illustrated, the assessed scores for each scope are overlaid on the corresponding cybersecurity target scores. The enterprise's cybersecurity program objective would be to ensure regulated security scopes are operated according to the specific regulation requirements, and to gradually improve all the security scopes to achieve their target security levels.

Considering Improvement Opportunities across Multiple Scopes

When looking at cybersecurity scores across multiple scopes, it is worthwhile to model and visualize the cybersecurity value of potential improvements. To assess the cybersecurity benefits to be had from a cybersecurity improvement project, the enterprise simply calculates its cybersecurity program assessment scores for the enterprise *before and after* the improvements, and determines the amount the assessment scores change between the two assessments. Figure 14-7 provides an example before-and-after calculation showed graphically. In this example, the proposed improvement impacts five of the six security scopes. The total improvement value can be calculated by adding up its impact across all of the scopes.

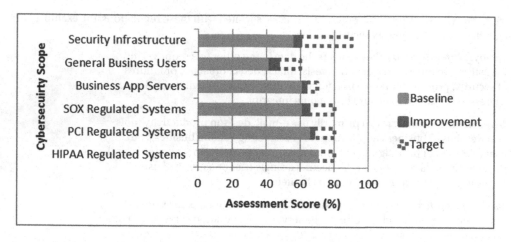

Figure 14-7. *Using enterprise cybersecurity program assessment scores, the enterprise can calculate quantitatively the impact of cybersecurity improvements across multiple scopes.*

Considering "Bang for the Buck"

It is important for leadership to make well-informed decisions regarding possible cybersecurity investments. Every cybersecurity investment must be considered in terms of its cost and the time involved in deployment and operations, compared to the impact the capability will have on the enterprise cybersecurity posture once it is deployed and operational. One management challenge that frequently occurs is the enterprise embarks on a major cybersecurity initiative—for example, to upgrade core firewalls or to deploy identity management technology—and then spends thousands or even millions of dollars on the deployment. However, at the end of the day, this huge investment only delivers one of the 113 enterprise cybersecurity capabilities. While certainly some capabilities are more valuable than others, there is a cautionary tale here: There are no "silver bullets" in cybersecurity and the deployment of a single capability will seldom make the difference between overall cybersecurity success and failure against targeted attackers.

A single capability will seldom mean the difference between cybersecurity success and cybersecurity failure. In fact, capabilities should back each other up so that the failure or defeat of a single one does not prove disastrous.

This book's enterprise cybersecurity architecture, by focusing on the *big picture* of risk mitigations, the 11 functional areas, and security operations, de-emphasizes the value of a single cybersecurity capability and instead focuses on the value of having many capabilities all working together in an integrated fashion. In this framework, the *value* of an investment in cybersecurity is represented by how much it increases the enterprise's cybersecurity program assessment scores across all scopes. Investments that improve multiple capabilities, deploy capabilities across multiple security scopes, or increase the utilization of deployed capabilities result in the greatest increase in the enterprise's assessment scores, and are the most likely to improve the enterprise's cybersecurity overall.

By looking at security benefits compared to cost and complexity, potential improvements can be considered based on whether the cost or the benefit is low or high. Figure 14-8 depicts a matrix of possible results when combining these two variables.

Cost / Complexity	Security Benefits	
	Low	High
Low	Tweaks	Quick Wins
High	Poor Investments	Good Investments

Figure 14-8. *Security strategy should consider the cost and benefit of desired improvements and prioritize "quick wins" and "good investments" for leadership focus. Lower-value "tweaks" should be delegated to technical staff and "poor investments" should be avoided altogether.*

This simple matrix shows potential improvements falling into four general categories, as examined in the following list. These categories are based on whether the security improvement benefit is low or high, and whether the security improvement cost/complexity to deploy/operate is low or high:

- ***Quick wins*** have high security benefits and low cost and complexity. Enterprise leadership should be on the lookout for these opportunities and should give them high priority for implementation.

- ***Good investments*** have high security benefits, but also high cost and complexity. Leadership must carefully consider and manage these investments to ensure they are successful. Making multiple *good investments* in a single fiscal year may require significant resources.

- ***Tweaks*** have low security benefits, but also low costs. Tweaks can be a time sink for enterprise leadership as they distract leadership from the high-value activities and investments. Technical staff should be empowered to implement tweaks on their own, with minimal leadership oversight.

- ***Poor investments*** have high costs, but low security benefits. Unless these investments can be carefully managed to control the costs and ensure the potential benefits, these projects should be avoided. In particular, poor investments can be a significant drain on leadership bandwidth, taking attention away from other opportunities with greater security value.

One interesting note regarding the preceding matrix is the scenario of the *partially implemented good investment*. This situation can be a large project (for example, an identity management effort, public key infrastructure, or core firewall upgrade) that is finished or stopped before its full security benefits are realized. In these situations, it is easy for the *good* investment to turn into a *poor* investment that delivers little value or a marginal improvement in capability, simply because the project was never fully completed. Cybersecurity leadership should watch out for these situations and try to prevent or minimize their occurrence.

Prioritizing Improvement Projects

Once the enterprise identifies the most valuable cybersecurity improvement projects, the next cybersecurity program management step is to prioritize projects for execution. As much as everyone would like to, it is seldom possible or practical for the enterprise to do all the improvements at once to improve the enterprise's security posture. Tasks have to be prioritized based on value and cost, sequenced based on dependencies, and ultimately resourced from limited available resources. Furthermore, there are often other internal and external constraints. These projects can be grouped into the following general categories depending on the effects of the cybersecurity improvements:

- They directly thwart anticipated attacks or address known risks to improve risk mitigations

- They deliver capabilities that improve cybersecurity functional areas

- They strengthen cybersecurity operational processes

For each intended cybersecurity project, leadership should consider the following questions related to what it will take to successfully complete the project:

- **Risk Mitigated:** What is the risk to be mitigated by the project or its capabilities? Expressed in business terms, what is this project going to do to improve the enterprise's cybersecurity?

- **Resources:** Are the resources required for the project within both the budget and personnel expertise?

- **Duration:** What is the duration for the project? A quarter? A year? Multiple years? Can it be broken up into phases that are manageable and enable iterative success?

- **Prerequisites:** What are prerequisites for the project? Is the project loosely or strictly dependent on other projects or tasks being completed beforehand?

- **Constraints:** Does the project account for other constraints? Particular attention should be given to security controls or information systems that are regulated or subject to external scrutiny or audit.

As the enterprise analyzes and prioritizes cybersecurity projects, they can be sorted into four groups for easy management. Figure 14-9 depicts these groups in terms of time frames: immediate, this year, next year, and future.

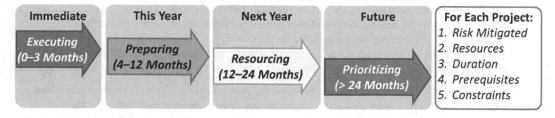

Figure 14-9. *Cybersecurity improvement projects can be divided into four groups based on when they might take place. These groups can be characterized as "executing," "preparing," "resourcing," or "prioritizing."*

When combined, these four groups and their improvement projects constitute the enterprise's long-term cybersecurity improvement program and strategy. Using enterprise cybersecurity assessments and calculated assessment scores, cybersecurity leadership can show quantitatively how the enterprise's cybersecurity posture is going to change as projects are completed and improvements are made.

Immediate: Executing

Immediate or *executing* projects are projects to be executed now. Early in a cybersecurity program, these improvements are generally *quick wins* that deliver new/improved/enhanced capabilities at low cost. Later in the improvement program, immediate executing projects will also include larger investment projects that focus on project execution for success to help ensure the desired cybersecurity capabilities are obtained in a timely and cost-effective manner.

This Year: Preparing

This year or *preparing* projects are projects to be completed within the current fiscal year. These projects are often low-cost in nature but may require an investment. When these projects are ready to execute, they will be moved to the *executing* list and tracked for successful completion. In the meantime, the business needs to focus on preparatory tasks that need to be completed so the project can start. These tasks include technical prerequisites, vendor selections, or contract negotiations. Cybersecurity leaders need to carefully track these tasks to ensure all preparations are completed so the projects can start on time, execute on schedule, and stay within budget.

Next Year: Resourcing

Next year or *resourcing* projects are projects that cannot be queued up within the current fiscal year and must be deferred to next year for one reason or another. Generally, projects are deferred because of limited resources to include financial, personnel, or some other constraint. For these projects, the focus is on refining plans and estimates to ensure they are accurate and ready to execute if needed. It is also important to take care of prerequisites so the projects can be lined up to actually execute during the following year.

In addition, projects in this category should prepare for two possibilities that may result in their acceleration. The first possibility is the situation may change and new or emerging cybersecurity threats may warrant accelerating these projects and executing them sooner than was originally planned. The second possibility is budgets and available funding change during the course of the year, and sometimes extra funding becomes available for projects that are prepared and ready to be accelerated to the current year.

Future: Prioritizing

Future or *prioritizing* projects are projects that do not make sense to execute in the current fiscal year and where resources are not available to plan them for the following fiscal year. These projects are characterized as *prioritizing* because they are competing for priority alongside other business concerns and strategic investment opportunities. For these projects, the focus is on clearly understanding the costs associated with the projects and communicating to business leaders the benefits once the projects are completed.

Projects in this category are usually deferred because they are expensive and complex, or they depend on a number of other things being completed first. Because of these reasons and others, such projects are seldom pushed up to immediate execution, but they may be accelerated if the situation changes and the business need becomes more urgent or critical.

Cybersecurity leadership should remain aware of the risks mitigated by the projects and watch those risks carefully. Leadership should ensure that addressing these risks can really be deferred to future years, and should monitor the associated risks in case the situation changes and the risks need to be addressed more urgently.

Updating Priority Lists

Over time, cybersecurity projects naturally migrate from one list to another. Executing projects are completed, projects planned for this year move into execution, and, as fiscal years transition, what was planned for next year transitions into executing for the current year. Each year the enterprise updates its plans and projects get shifted. Some projects are perennially in the *deferred until next year* category until they become critically needed. Other projects are planned for the future and then pulled forward due to changing circumstances or shifting priorities.

Figure 14-10 depicts this process of updating the enterprise's priorities. In general, as time marches on, projects shift to the left on these lists, although sometimes shifting business priorities and limited available resources can cause them to be deferred to later times as well.

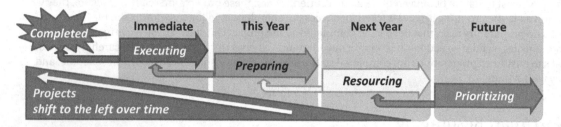

Figure 14-10. *Cybersecurity improvement projects naturally shift to the left over time as executing projects are completed and future planned projects move closer to execution.*

Tracking Cybersecurity Project Results

Because the enterprise cybersecurity program assessment score is a quantitative measurement, it is well suited for managing cybersecurity status over time and visualizing that status graphically to inform leadership decision-making. As a quantitative method, these program assessment scores are well suited for tracking results over time and aggregating results for functional areas and scopes into combined scores that can then also be tracked and reported over time.

Visualizing Cybersecurity Program Assessment Scores

Earlier in this chapter, cybersecurity program assessment scores were visualized as column charts showing risk mitigations, the 11 functional areas, and cybersecurity operations side by side. An alternative method for visualizing these aspects of the enterprise cybersecurity program is a Kiviat diagram or spider chart format, as shown in Figure 14-11. This figure shows the same data as Figures 14-3, 14-4, and 14-5, except in this depiction the data is visualized using a circular format, with zero at the center of the circle.

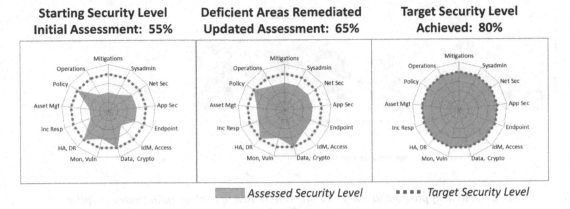

Figure 14-11. *A Kiviat diagram or spider chart format is useful for showing the assessment scores for a scope as cybersecurity is improved from the initial assessment through to the target security level.*

The advantage of this format is that the shape of the filled-in area reflects nicely the relationships among all of the plotted assessment scores. If all of the assessment scores vary widely in their values, then the shape of the filled-in area is irregular, as can be seen in the left-hand *Initial Assessment* chart. If all of the assessment scores are at similar levels, then the chart is more circular in shape, as can be seen in the center *Updated Assessment* chart. When all of the assessment scores are at the same level (and also match the target security level), then the resulting chart is circular, as can be seen in the right-hand *Target Security Level Achieved* chart. Achieving this right-most chart should be the objective for the enterprise's cybersecurity program.

There are other formats that can also be used, such as bar charts, column charts, and line charts. Bar and column charts can be particularly helpful when looking at the security of multiple scopes side by side, as was shown in Figures 14-6 and 14-7.

Measuring Cybersecurity Program Assessment Scores over Time

Enterprise cybersecurity program assessment scores also lend themselves well to measurement and trending over time. Using these scores, the security posture for a cybersecurity scope can be reduced to a single number. The resulting number can be tracked over multiple time periods (for example, quarterly, semiannually, or yearly) to observe its trends upward and downward, and show quantitatively the impact of security investments in terms of improved enterprise cybersecurity. Recalling the example of the six security scopes used earlier in this chapter, the scores for these security assessments can be plotted over time to show trends and to measure quantitatively if the enterprise's cybersecurity posture is improving or degrading over time, as shown in Figure 14-12.

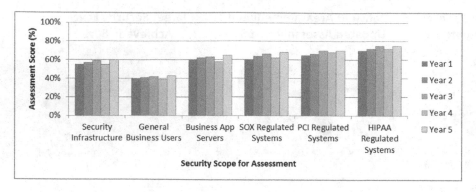

Figure 14-12. *Cybersecurity program assessment scores can be used to track quantitatively enterprise cybersecurity posture over the course of multiple years. This chart uses columns to show the assessment scores for multiple security scopes on a single chart.*

While investments in cybersecurity will generally result in the enterprise's cybersecurity assessment scores increasing over time, it may also be possible for scores to decline from assessment to assessment. The following are some potential causes for such a downward trend when it occurs:

- First, it is possible the enterprise may deliberately choose to dismantle cybersecurity capabilities to reduce operational costs, simplify the enterprise architecture, or because cybersecurity systems reach end-of-life and are retired without deploying replacements.

- Second, cybersecurity capabilities may degrade over time due to neglect or lack of upgrades, or due to products not keeping pace with the level of capability required to be effective.

- Third, scores for risk mitigations may go down as new attacker threats and risks are identified and left unmitigated, thus reducing scores for risk mitigation.

- Fourth, staffing changes and reorganizations may result in security operational procedures languishing or falling apart, thereby reducing scores for operational processes.

Regardless of the cause of downturns, a well-run enterprise cybersecurity program has the ability to identify these downturns, diagnose their causes, and work with cybersecurity, IT, and business leadership to address them quickly, before they prove disastrous. Using quantitative assessment methods and the functional areas of enterprise cybersecurity, the enterprise has the tools it needs to delegate and manage its enterprise cybersecurity program so that its overall posture improves more often than it degrades.

■ ■ ■

CHAPTER 15

Looking to the Future

This book describes a pragmatic framework for managing a comprehensive enterprise cybersecurity program. This architecture uses 11 functional areas to organize all aspects of an enterprise's cybersecurity, including policy, programmatics, IT life cycle, and assessment. While this framework may provide a successful cyberdefense today, attackers and defenders are not standing still. Cybersecurity challenges and technologies continue to evolve quickly. How will this book's framework hold up over time? Only time will tell for sure. This concluding chapter examines how the authors expect that this book's enterprise cybersecurity architecture may evolve in the future.

The Power of Enterprise Cybersecurity Architecture

Figure 15-1 illustrates how the enterprise cybersecurity architecture in this book provides a single framework that encompasses all aspects of an enterprise's cybersecurity program.

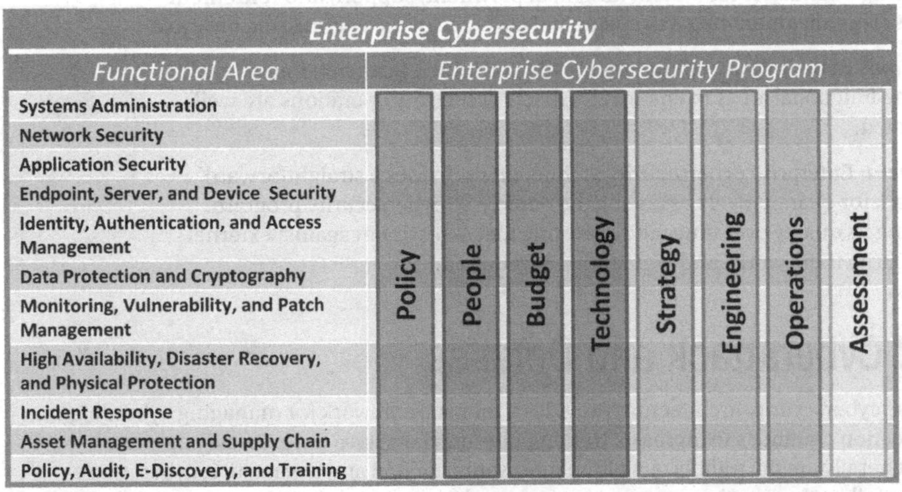

Figure 15-1. This book's enterprise cybersecurity architecture is a single framework for organizing all aspects of a comprehensive enterprise cybersecurity program.

As shown in Figure 15-1, the 11 cybersecurity architecture functional areas align with the eight aspects of a cybersecurity program to produce a comprehensive enterprise cybersecurity solution. Looking at each of these aspects in sequence:

- **Policy:** Cybersecurity policies can be organized using the 11 functional areas, helping to ensure comprehensive coverage of enterprise cybersecurity with clear policy statements.

- **People:** Enterprise cybersecurity functional areas align closely with actual skill sets of technical staff and team leaders. By aligning responsibilities with skills, technical staff and cybersecurity leadership are positioned for success in their areas. Cybersecurity functional areas also align well with typical organizational boundaries for matrixed teams where cybersecurity policy and enforcement might be separated from technical implementation and operations.

- **Budget:** Enterprise cybersecurity functional areas align well with policy and organizational structures. Cybersecurity leadership can allocate operational and project budgets along functional areas, ensuring that money, people, and technology are coordinated.

- **Technology:** Enterprise cybersecurity functional areas align well with the capabilities of many security technologies. Enterprise technologies can be organized by functional areas to establish clear organizational accountability of all cybersecurity technologies and the capabilities they deliver.

- **Strategy:** Enterprise cybersecurity functional areas were designed with the IT Infrastructure Library (ITIL) framework in mind. IT strategy and architecture can be planned using the 11 functional areas to help ensure a well-integrated overall solution.

- **Engineering:** Enterprise cybersecurity functional areas align well with typical engineering boundaries for system design, deployment, support, and retirement activities. This alignment helps to ensure full coverage of the engineering life cycle.

- **Operations:** Cybersecurity operations can be performed in an integrated fashion across the functional areas to ensure all aspects of security operations are well coordinated.

- **Assessment:** Enterprise cybersecurity architecture provides a straightforward framework for quantitatively assessing the enterprise cybersecurity program, measuring its quality over time, and reporting that assessment against external cybersecurity frameworks and regulations as required.

Evolution of Cyberattack and Defense

This book's enterprise cybersecurity architecture provides a robust framework for managing cyberdefense, but attacker sophistication continues to increase. Nation-state attackers have the greatest amount of sophistication and generally are the trailblazers of the most sophisticated and devastating cyberattacks. Professional attackers follow these nation-state leaders, taking their techniques and commercializing them for use on industrial scales to conduct espionage, blackmail, larceny, and identity theft. Casual attackers take these capabilities when they become mainstream and use them for opportunistic ends to disrupt operations, explore private enterprises and their data, and make political statements for the world to see. Figure 15-2 depicts generations of cyberattacks increasing in their sophistication and proliferation over time.

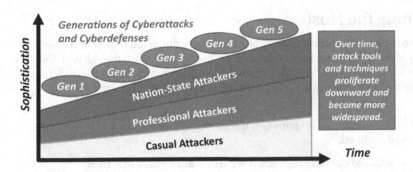

Figure 15-2. *Over time, attacks are continuing to become more capable and sophisticated across all levels of potential attackers.*

Looking at this pattern over the past 20 years, one sees a cyberattack and cyberdefense evolution that can be grouped into discrete generations of cybersecurity. Military scientists characterize generations of weapons systems as a group of improvements that, when taken together, effectively render the previous generation of weapons obsolete. Historically, the tanks, planes, and aircraft carriers of World War II rendered the Maginot Line, guns, and battleships of World War I obsolete. More recently, the American F-15 fighter plane, a fourth-generation fighter, has *never* been shot down in combat because it has always faced third-generation opponents.

Each generation represents such a leap forward in capability that it is virtually invulnerable when facing the previous generations. Cyberweapons work the same way. Newer cyberattack tools and techniques are almost completely effective against previous generation cyberdefenses. To remain effective against newer generations of cyberattacks, defenses must be constantly upgraded to include the capabilities of newer generations of cyberdefense.

Applying this generational theory to cybersecurity, cyberattacks and cyberdefenses can be grouped into the following distinct generations:

- Generation 1: Hardening the Host

- Generation 2: Protecting the Network

- Generation 3: Layered Defense and Active Response

- Generation 4: Automated Response

- Generation 5: Biological Defense

The next section will describe each of these generations, how they can be identified, and how cyberattacks and cyberdefenses are changing with each succeeding generation of capability improvements.

Before the Internet

Before the Internet, there was the Advanced Research Programs Agency network (ARPANET). Back in the ARPANET days, there was little cybersecurity since the network was small and everyone on it was essentially trusted. As the community got larger, ARPANET users started putting passwords on computers and networking protocols. However, ARPANET was not designed with security in mind. This earliest security did not provide robust cyberdefenses. Essentially, it was good-fences-make-good-neighbors security that was good enough to keep honest people honest, but it was not designed to withstand the onslaught of a determined attacker. At the same time when ARPANET had little to no security, neither did disconnected personal computers. Early viruses ran rampant propagating from machine to machine via floppy disks and other media. On the other hand, since none of this personal computerization was interconnected and was essentially being used as advanced typewriters and calculators, not much was at stake, either.

Generation 1: Hardening the Host

As the ARPANET evolved into the Internet, more and more computers were connected from enterprises outside of the initial community of military researchers and academic institutions. Even though ARPANET was still a select community, the community was becoming more diverse. The opportunities for malicious activities were increasing. First-generation cyberattack and cyberdefense challenges included the following:

- The community of Internet-connected systems and the people operating those systems expanded and diversified.

- Internet-connected systems did not have significant security features built into their operating systems and were open to external connections.

- Internet communications protocols, such as Telnet, File Transfer Protocol (FTP), Simple Mail Transfer Protocol (SMTP), and Simple Network Management Protocol (SNMP) provided only rudimentary security features and lacked protection against many types of deliberate attacks.

- Network service authentication was almost exclusively single-factor using usernames and passwords.

Generation 1 Attacks: These attacks center on directly attacking computers connected to the networks via authorized network connections. Attacks against unprotected systems (in other words, systems that had not been hardened) were almost always successful. Following are some key characteristics of these attacks:

- Network connections originate *from* attacker machines and connect *to* services running on victim machines.

- Attacks exploit insecure protocols to obtain credentials or send false commands.

- Attacks exploit unpatched vulnerabilities to take control of victim machines.

Generation 1 Defenses: Because Generation 1 attacks consist of directly targeting network-connected computers, the corresponding generation of defenses must focus on protecting network-connected computers from attack. Some key characteristics and capabilities of these defenses include the following:

- Security Technical Implementation Guides (STIGs) for installing and configuring operating systems in a secure fashion

- Regularly scheduled installation of vendor patches

- Host firewalls and intrusion prevention / detection to reduce network attack surfaces

- Disconnecting critical systems from the network altogether (air-gapping and air-gapped networks)

The Resulting Generation 1 Environment: After Generation 1 protections are applied, most computers are still directly connected to the Internet, but hardened so that they are resistant to attack. Unfortunately, those security configurations have to be constantly maintained to ensure continued protection, setting the stage for the next cybergeneration.

Generation 2: Protecting the Network

As networks continued to grow in size and complexity, the number of hosts connected to them exploded. Whereas before, a single administrator might manage a dozen machines, now the same people were trying to manage ten times the number of machines, or even a hundred times the number of machines. Faced with this proliferation of network-connected systems, administrators struggled to maintain the security protections of their Generation 1 defenses. Second-generation cyberattack and cyberdefense challenges included the following:

- Numbers of Internet-connected machines increased by one to two orders of magnitude, overwhelming manual systems administration methods.

- System communication and administration protocols remained insecure and were being deliberately targeted over open networks.

- Personal computers and Internet-connected services were becoming mission-critical and unplanned downtime became a leadership and business concern.

Generation 2 Attacks: First-generation cyberattackers practiced the art of exploitation on a single victim machine at a time. By the second generation, scripting and automated tools turned such exploitation into a science. Some key characteristics of these attacks include the following:

- Attackers use automated tools that scan for vulnerabilities and exploitable protocols across hundreds or thousands of victim systems in a matter of seconds or minutes.

- Automated tools work fast enough that even minor vulnerabilities or mistakes in configurations can be exploited before they are remediated.

- Automated tools can then take control of vulnerable machines and add them to centrally managed communities of remotely controlled *zombie* machines (botnets).

- From these compromised systems, attackers steal files, databases, and user account information such as online identities and passwords.

- Botnets can also be used to overwhelm Internet-connected systems through Distributed Denial of Service (DDoS) attacks.

Generation 2 Defenses: To defend against these newer, faster Generation 2 attacks on ever-growing IT environments, defenders rely on their own automation to stay ahead of the attackers. Most importantly, defenders rely on the network perimeter to protect the majority of the enterprise's machines from remote attack. Some key characteristics and capabilities of these defenses include the following:

- A strong network perimeter uses network address translation to protect user workstations and secondary servers from direct network connections originating from the Internet.

- On the network perimeter, centrally managed firewalls, intrusion prevention and detection, and other features protect the Internet-connected systems using a small group of centrally managed security appliances.

- Within the perimeter, enterprise management systems enable automated endpoint management and patching, centralized user accounts and passwords, and single-sign-on authentication.

- Since only a small number of systems are directly connected to the Internet, the Generation 1 challenges of hardening endpoints are kept manageable. Endpoint and server protection inside the perimeter can be imperfect without tremendous risk.

- Internet services can be protected from DDoS attacks through network perimeter protections, high-performance infrastructure, connectivity diversification, and content delivery networks.

The Resulting Generation 2 Environment: The Generation 2 environment is one where strong network perimeters shield the majority of endpoints and servers from direct Internet-based attack. This shielding reduces the attack surface of most enterprises by 90% or more. The remaining Internet-facing servers can be manageably protected using Generation 1 techniques to harden them from attack and make them difficult to compromise, especially when the servers are positioned behind the network perimeter in demilitarized zones (DMZs). However, the central automation that is critical to the Generation 2 defense has its own vulnerabilities. Central automation becomes the enterprise's Achilles' heel against the next generation of evolving cyberattacks.

Generation 3: Layered Defense and Active Response

At this point in cyberhistory, Generation 2 enterprises have a great wall protecting them and isolating specialized areas such as the DMZ. However, inside the wall there is a very soft interior filled with haphazardly protected endpoints and servers. An attacker who establishes a foothold on the inside has numerous options to propagate the attack from the initial foothold. The Generation 2 defense of central management and security infrastructure is itself nothing more than servers and endpoints delivering services inside the network. Those servers and endpoints are themselves attackable from the inside. The use of cloud services, Bring Your Own Device (BYOD), and vendor network connections has contributed significantly to increasing perimeter complexity. Third-generation cyberattack and cyberdefense challenges include the following:

- Inside the perimeter, enterprises have the same Generation 1 cyberdefense challenges of hardening endpoints and servers against attack but with tens or hundreds of times as many systems to protect.

- IT consolidation has put administrative control of hundreds, thousands, or tens of thousands of systems and servers in the hands of a small group of highly privileged systems administrators and the tools they use.

- Systems administration protocols and technologies used inside the network are vulnerable to attack and exploitation that can give attackers administrative control.

- Security servers on the enterprise network are vulnerable to the same Generation 1 attacks as any other system.

- Enterprise perimeters have become more complex than ever before, protecting regulated data while enabling remote connections from employees, vendors, customers, and partners.

- Network resources, tools, and services are frequently protected using single-factor username and password authentication.

- In this complex and sprawling IT environment, operators have limited visibility or auditing of activities to be able to detect potentially malicious activity going on inside.

Generation 3 Attacks: The IT challenges described above set the stage for a whole new generation of cyberattacks. These Generation 3 attacks focus on getting inside the perimeter and then using the enterprise's centralized infrastructure and administration systems against itself. Attackers get control of security systems and privileged accounts, and then use them to obtain complete enterprise control, all with a minimum of effort. Some key characteristics of these attacks include the following:

- Attackers target end-user personal computers through viruses, compromised web sites, and malware delivered inside the perimeter via targeted e-mail (phishing).

- Professional attackers buy access inside the enterprise from botnet operators, who maintain catalogs of systems *for sale* inside of compromised enterprises.

- From an initial foothold *inside* the enterprise, attackers target the security infrastructure and its accounts, tools, and protocols to gain administrative control over the entire enterprise.

- Attacker activity inside the victim network is remotely controlled using network connections from compromised machines, or from *command-and-control* systems installed in the victim's network perimeter.

- Once administrative control has been obtained, attackers then can do whatever they want to do, including stealing, modifying, or destroying intellectual property and data.

Generation 3 Defenses: The Generation 3 attacks pose a conundrum to cyberdefenders, as attackers exploit a decade of IT consolidation and centralized management trends against the very enterprise they are meant to serve. Enterprises with thousands of Internet-connected systems cannot go back to the "good old days" of having a few expert administrators maintaining, by hand, a small number of hardened systems. Combating Generation 3 attacks requires an equally powerful generation of defenses designed to enable the business while providing the enterprise with multiple layers of cyberdefenses. Some key characteristics and capabilities of these defenses include the following:

- The enterprise architecture is re-evaluated with cybersecurity as a central objective. Security is designed from the inside-out to protect critical systems first. This approach is in contrast to second-generation defenses that were designed starting with the perimeter and then implemented from the outside-in.

- Cybersecurity perimeters are established inside the enterprise to protect servers from users and to protect cybersecurity infrastructure and protocols from the rest of the enterprise.

- All systems with Internet connectivity—whether inbound or outbound—are treated as *demilitarized zones* with security protections surrounding them and protecting the rest of the enterprise from them.

- Multi-factor authentication is employed both to protect privileged accounts on the inside of the enterprise and to protect access to enterprise resources from outside the enterprise on the Internet.

- Enterprise cybersecurity central administration systems are treated as critical infrastructure and *armored* to make them difficult to attack, raise alerts when such attacks occur, and log activities so attacks can be investigated.

- Incident detection and response is established to catch cyberintrusions that occur in Internet-connected systems, and repel those intrusions before they can be extended further into the enterprise.

- Cybersecurity systems are monitored full time, 24 hours a day, 7 days a week, 365 days a year (24×7×365).

The Resulting Generation 3 Environment: The Generation 3 environment is significantly different from the Generation 2 environment. The entire enterprise's IT environment has been remodeled around cybersecurity, with multiple layers of defenses that attackers must breach before they can succeed. Consequently, cyberdefenders have multiple opportunities to detect and repel attacks before they are successful. Still, this environment is far from invulnerable; it will just take a new generation of cyberattacks to defeat it.

Generation 4: Automated Response

Generation 3 cyberdefenses, if properly deployed, present a dramatic improvement in the enterprise cybersecurity posture and make an enterprise considerably harder to attack than it was with just a Generation 2 defense. However, Generation 4 attacks will defeat the Generation 3 layered defense by moving faster than the defenders can respond, and overwhelming the defenses at machine speeds. Key Generation 4 cyberattack and cyberdefense challenges include the following:

- Whereas before, enterprises only had a single perimeter to consider, with a third-generation cyberdefense there are multiple perimeters protecting different areas of the infrastructure, and all these perimeters must be maintained using limited staffing and expertise.

- Numbers of network-connected systems continue to increase, with the addition of the *Internet of things* with devices, appliances, and accessories all becoming network-connected. Often, these devices have only limited security features and are vulnerable to a myriad of attacks.

- External business relationships continue to increase as cloud services are employed for more and more business functions. All these services require complex interconnections to permit authentication, identity management, data sharing and synchronization, systems administration, and operational monitoring.

- Mobile computing and Bring Your Own Device (BYOD) make endpoint security policy enforcement more complex and increase the possibility of enterprise data and credentials ending up on potentially compromised devices.

- Incident responders must be constantly vigilant to investigate alerts and repel attacks before they can break through all layers of defenses and complete successfully.

Generation 4 Attacks: Generation 4 attackers must design a new generation of attacks to overwhelm and defeat the Generation 3 defenses. These attack methods target the weaknesses of the Generation 3 defenses. Such weaknesses include the challenges of managing a complex network environment, the explosion in network-connected devices, the challenges of securing unmanaged endpoints, and the limited bandwidth of incident responders who must manually investigate alerts and events. Some key Generation 4 cyberattack characteristics include the following:

- Attackers leverage social media and data analytics to target enterprise employees and their online accounts to establish targeted initial footholds inside the enterprise, focusing on executives and systems administrators with privileged account access.

- Once an initial foothold is obtained, customized malware (to evade initial detection) automatically exploits vulnerabilities and escalates privileges to jump from the foothold network into more protected parts of the enterprise.

- Automated malware is scripted to execute the detectable portion of the attack so quickly that defenders do not have time to investigate and repel it before it is successful.

- Scripted attacks generate so much security event activity that incident responders are overwhelmed and unable to respond effectively.

- Attackers compromise the enterprise so completely that defenders are unable to clean it up, enabling the attacker to maintain a persistent presence.

Generation 4 Defenses: The hallmark of the Generation 4 cyberattack is speed. Attackers hit the defenders' manual incident response teams with automated attacks that overwhelm and distract them. The remainder of the attack can be executed while the defenders are ineffective. With this attack approach in mind, a Generation 4 cyberdefense must use defensive speed to repel the attackers before they can succeed. Some key Generation 4 defense characteristics and capabilities include the following:

- IT environments provide containment so high-speed attacks are limited in the amount of damage they can do before automated defenses are engaged.

- Automated technologies detect, disrupt, and remediate attacks by cleaning malware, disabling compromised accounts, or blocking malicious network traffic—all automatically and without human intervention.

- Well-rehearsed manual procedures are developed to enable rapid manual response to attacks that cannot be stopped by automated technologies.

- Systems are monitored 24x7x365, with the ability to investigate, contain, and remediate cybersecurity incidents in real time.

The Resulting Generation 4 Environment: A Generation 4 defensive environment looks similar to a Generation 3 defensive environment. However, these looks are deceiving because a Generation 4 environment is able to detect, contain, and remediate cyberintrusions many, many times faster than its predecessor. While a Generation 3 environment might become overwhelmed by a dozen cybersecurity investigations per day, a Generation 4 environment might be able to handle a hundred times more attacks due to the power of automated detection and response, freeing up incident response personnel to watch the big picture and spot-check the systems. This ability to repel attacks automatically in real time is game-changing.

Generation 5: Biological Defense

If an enterprise can achieve a Generation 4 cyberdefense, one would think the job would be done and all would be well. However, as with all things biological, and especially when there is a talented adversary involved, nature finds a way to defeat even the most determined defense. Since attacks can be contained, and rapid attacks can be contained rapidly, the attacker must change tactics once again. Key Generation 5 cyberattack and cyberdefense challenges include the following:

- Complexity continues to be a problem because enterprise IT architectures continue to increase in the numbers of connected devices, the size of connected networks, and the amount of traffic and activity taking place over those networks.

- With complexity, visibility and detection inside the environment is an ongoing challenge. Cybersecurity controls require constant maintenance to keep up with rapid IT changes to support the business.

- Automated detection and response can only detect what it can see and can only respond in predetermined ways.

Generation 5 Attacks: Generation 5 cyberattacks focus on stealth and intelligence to avoid detection and work around automated defenses. The malware powering these attacks is almost biological in nature, constantly morphing its code and techniques to avoid detection. Malware moves quickly through target environments and stays one step ahead of automated defenses trying to target it. Following are some key Generation 5 attack characteristics:

- Professional adversaries will obtain security technologies and thoroughly analyze them to understand their weaknesses and limitations. Malware is designed to specifically target defensive technologies and avoid or defeat them.

- The resulting malware is stealthy and polymorphic, covering its tracks and constantly changing so that it cannot be identified and targeted by defensive systems or incident responders.

- Malware uses built-in intelligence to analyze its target environments, find targets, move laterally, escalate privileges, and perform its objectives. This built-in intelligence does not require external command-and-control connections that could be detected and blocked.

- Professional and nation-state attackers use social engineering and good old-fashioned spying to obtain access to IT systems protected by organizational personnel and secured facilities. Attackers target network-connected physical security systems to defeat facilities using coordinated attacks that cross cyber and physical boundaries.

Generation 5 Defenses: Since the hallmark of the Generation 5 cyberattack is stealth, the hallmark of the Generation 5 cyberdefense is visibility. Defenses must be designed to catch attacks specifically trying to evade detection and thwart those attacks before they can succeed. Detected attacks can be brought into the crosshairs of legacy Generation 3 and Generation 4 defenses, and be disrupted, contained, and remediated. Some key Generation 5 cyberdefense characteristics and capabilities are as follows:

- Defensive technologies are distributed rather than centralized, making them harder for attackers to target and easier for attacks targeting the defensive systems to be detected, contained, and remediated.

- Protection is tied to data with data rights management, data leakage protection, and data integrity validation. These technologies are used to monitor sensitive data flows and detect inappropriate transfers or data modifications.

- Logging and analytics are used to observe account, network, and computer software patterns to identify and trace anomalies. To minimize false positives, behavioral analysis is used to track suspect activities before flagging them as being potentially malicious. Intelligent incident detection uses complex triggers created via machine learning.

- Analytics are integrated with automated response systems to disrupt detected attacks and contain them at machine speed.

- Generation 5 defenses take place 24×7×65, under the watchful eyes of trained staff at an equipped security operations center (SOC).

The Resulting Generation 5 Environment: A Generation 5 defensive environment has the biological capability to detect and respond to sophisticated and stealthy cyberattacks. Detection and response are mostly automatic. This environment's behavior is almost biological in nature, as attacks adapt to evade the defenses and the defenses adapt to keep up with attacks. Exactly how Generation 5 defenses behave in practice is yet to be seen. The technologies to deliver Generation 5 defenses are cutting-edge at the time of this writing and largely unproven in practice. Much evolution of the technologies is required before these attacks, and the defenses to thwart them, achieve what could be called *maturity*.

Cybergenerations Moving Down Market

At the time of this writing, Generation 5 cyberattacks and Generation 5 cyberdefenses represent the pinnacle of what can be done using existing cyberattack and cyberdefense technologies. There have been relatively few known Generation 5 cyberattacks, which have been almost exclusively in the realm of nation-state actors. As for Generation 5 cyberdefenses, while many of the technological pieces exist today, the authors are not aware of any operational installations satisfying the entire Generation 5 defense criteria previously described (except for very specialized or limited environments).

With this said, cyberattack generations move *down market* over time. *Down market* means that cyberattack techniques become cheaper and more widely used over time. For example, whereas Generation 5 cyberattacks are solely in the domain of advanced nation-state attackers, it is realistic to expect five years from now that these techniques will be used by other nation-state attackers. Ten years from now, these Generation 5 techniques might be used by everyday professional cybercriminals. As another example, the Generation 3 cyberattacks that are causing so much trouble for commercial industries today were being commonly used by nation-state attackers only five years ago. Looking forward five years from now, these Generation 3 cyberattack tools and techniques will likely be in the hands of casual hackers. Over time, cyberattack technologies proliferate. Cyberattacks that are niche problems today will likely be widespread problems tomorrow. Enterprises must be aware of these trends and try to stay ahead of them.

Future Cybersecurity Evolution

As has been discussed, cyberattacks and defenses can be grouped into generations that provide strategists a convenient way to group and characterize attacker methods and defender abilities. Furthermore, newer generations of attacks will be extremely effective against older generations of defenses. Moreover, defenses cannot simply *skip a generation* and jump straight to advanced defensive techniques. These generations are cumulative, and each successive generation of defenses requires the previous generation of defenses be present and functioning properly to support the protections of the next generation of defensive technologies.

At the time of this writing, enterprise cybersecurity is at a crossroads. Most enterprises have Generation 2 cyberdefenses while nation-state attackers, professional cybercriminals, and advanced hacktivists have adopted Generation 3 targeted cyberattack methods. These cyberattacks are extremely successful against legacy cyberdefenses. Consequently, there is an explosion in breaches and incidents affecting almost every industry segment. A whole-scale adoption of Generation 3 cyberdefenses will help the IT industry catch up to these attackers and once again regain defensive parity. Many of the cybersecurity techniques described in this book, particularly in Chapters 8, 9, and 10, have to do with deploying effective cyberdefenses against these Generation 3 and later cyberthreats. By keeping defenses up to the levels of the anticipated attacks, defenders will be able to keep up or get ahead.

A second-generation cyberattack will almost *always* succeed against a first-generation cyberdefense, and a third-generation cyberattack will almost *always* succeed against a second-generation defense. Cyberdefenses must keep up if they are to remain effective over time.

These challenges are made more acute because the compliance frameworks used by industry, regulators, and government to assess *effective* cybersecurity were largely designed around the model of Generation 2 cyberdefenses. The compliance framework language used to describe effective cyberdefense tends to focus on establishing strong perimeters to keep attackers on the outside and prevent malicious behavior. Such models can only go so far in thwarting determined, professional attackers using advanced Generation 3, 4, and 5 cyberattack techniques and technologies to accomplish their goals. Upgrading these frameworks to reflect the capabilities needed to disrupt, detect, delay, and defeat advanced attacks is fundamental to confronting today's cybersecurity challenges.

Another key cybersecurity challenge is balancing the trade-offs in cost, protection, and agility versus prioritizing cyberdefense deployment speed and convenience. Balancing these trade-offs requires translating security considerations into business consideration and translating security trade-offs into business trade-offs. Few business or cybersecurity leaders have the skills to do these translations, so there is a lot of work to be done.

Evolving Enterprise Cybersecurity over Time

Since cybersecurity is constantly and rapidly evolving, is it realistic to expect an enterprise cybersecurity architecture to sit still as well? Of course not! While this book's enterprise cybersecurity architecture is designed to be relatively enduring, the authors harbor no false illusions about this framework and its ability to stand the test of time. However, this book's framework was designed to hold up over time reasonably well as a framework for managing a cybersecurity program. Over the past five years of using this framework, it has proven itself to be effective while also evolving. In the future, this book's enterprise cybersecurity architecture and the cybersecurity environment in which it is used will continue to evolve and mature.

Enterprise Cybersecurity Implementation Considerations

This book's enterprise cybersecurity architecture is a framework for cybersecurity practitioners to organize and measure real-world cyberthreats, cyberdefense capabilities, and day-to-day cybersecurity operations. This framework is designed to accommodate a wide spectrum of enterprise cybersecurity configurations so that practitioners can manage and communicate the challenges they deal with on a daily basis. Like all frameworks, this book's framework is only an approximation and will never be able to capture all the richness and nuance of the underlying reality. A major goal of this architecture is to provide a framework to help enterprise leaders and practitioners summarize this complexity effectively so that they can make informed strategic and tactical decisions.

As an enterprise incorporates this book's cybersecurity architecture into its cybersecurity program, there are implementation considerations that include the following:

- This book's enterprise cybersecurity architecture is designed to be a simple framework for organizing policy, programmatics, IT life cycle, and assessment into a coherent program of 11 functional areas. These functional areas were selected so they apply well to a wide range of enterprise types, but may need to be adapted or modified to meet an enterprise's particular needs. This customization can be performed without diminishing the value of the overall framework.

- A key tenet of this book's enterprise cybersecurity architecture is the idea that all functional areas are *approximately equal in importance*. This tenet means that a key strategic goal for the enterprise is to keep all functional areas at approximately equal levels of effectiveness. This tenet helps cybersecurity leaders ensure their program stays balanced over time and they are not relying too much on a single set of cybersecurity capabilities for enterprise protection.

- The list of enterprise cybersecurity capabilities in this book, while comprehensive, is not and will never be perfectly *complete*. New technologies and capabilities are being developed all the time. Each enterprise should treat this list as a starting point and add, remove, or tailor it to suit its needs.

- This book's enterprise cybersecurity architecture groups cybersecurity capabilities into functional areas so they can be managed with regard to policies, programmatics, life cycle and assessment. This alignment will never be perfect, and some technologies and capabilities will bridge functional areas or blur the lines between them. If an enterprise needs to move capabilities around to make them align better with how it prefers to operate, then this framework can be tailored to accommodate the enterprise's needs.

These implementation considerations should be kept in mind when using this book's enterprise cybersecurity framework to support a cybersecurity program. No framework is perfect. An enterprise will need to adapt this book's framework so it makes sense and works as effectively as possible.

Tailoring Cybersecurity Assessments

Entire books have been written on the cybersecurity assessment process. Entire volumes exist for assessing cybersecurity maturity against the many published frameworks and regulations. This book's enterprise cybersecurity architecture works well for conducting a cybersecurity assessment, because of the following strengths:

- By considering risk mitigations, cybersecurity capabilities (grouped into functional areas) and security operations side by side, this book's cybersecurity assessment results align closely with an enterprise's real-world cybersecurity effectiveness.

- By using a hierarchy of risk mitigations, functional areas, capabilities, and underlying technologies, enterprise cybersecurity assessments can be performed at numerous levels to provide high-level results quickly and detailed results progressively. This multi-level assessment process provides the enterprise with flexibility for choosing what to assess and to what depth.

- When an enterprise cybersecurity program is organized into functional areas, assessment results are already aligned with the way policy, programmatics, IT life cycle, and operations are organized. This organizing principle enables immediate delegation and assignment of the resulting recommendations to the appropriate teams for execution.

With these strengths in mind, enterprises considering this book's enterprise cybersecurity architecture for conducting assessments will need to tailor it to make sure the results accurately reflect reality and make sense. When tailoring cybersecurity assessments, enterprises should consider the following:

- The cybersecurity capabilities presented in this book are meant as a starting point only. New technologies and capabilities are coming out all the time and should be incorporated into the enterprise cybersecurity framework for assessment and evaluation.

- This book's cybersecurity assessment methodology uses Object Measurement to quantitatively measure cybersecurity program effectiveness. This measurement approach provides a direct correlation between an enterprise's risk analysis and its level of protection. Value scales used for performing assessments necessarily summarize many aspects of complex cybersecurity technologies and the capabilities they deliver into quantitative metrics. Such metrics act as a focusing agent to help point the enterprise to potential weaknesses that cyberattackers can use as attack vectors.

- The enterprise cybersecurity assessment framework presented in this book rates all cybersecurity capabilities equally within each functional area. This is a deliberate simplification to help clarify the explanation and examples. Tailored assessments may choose to apply weighting factors to capabilities and functional areas based on their strategic cybersecurity power and value.

There is no harm in tailoring a framework like this one to meet the needs of the enterprise. The only key is to track the customizations so that subsequent assessments are performed using a consistent methodology, and valid comparisons among assessments can be made.

Evolution of Enterprise Cybersecurity Capabilities

Considering that cybersecurity technology is evolving at a rapid rate, the enterprise cybersecurity capabilities presented in this book will evolve significantly over the next ten to twenty years. Just as it would have been hard to conceive ten years ago of the myriad of advanced firewalls, intrusion detectors, multi-factor authentication, and other capabilities that go into the modern cybersecurity architecture, it is difficult to envision today what such capabilities might look like a decade from now. This book's enterprise cybersecurity architecture will continue to evolve with the strategic challenges of managing complexity in an increasingly interconnected world. Enterprise cybersecurity capabilities may change in a number of ways that include the following:

- Valid security capabilities available today may not have made it onto the lists contained in this book. While the capabilities list is comprehensive, winnowing down all of enterprise cybersecurity to a single set of capabilities means capabilities had to be omitted. Capabilities not listed in this book, but useful for an enterprise, should be considered and added to the framework as necessary.

- New security technologies may provide capabilities that simply did not exist before. Such technologies may be added to the list over time. These capabilities may fit into the existing functional area framework fairly well. Sometimes, a single technology will provide multiple capabilities that might fall into different functional areas. In these cases, the enterprise will want to choose which functional area makes the most sense to be the owner and operator of the technology.

- Security capabilities this book's list shows as separate may, over time, merge into what is effectively a single, integrated capability. Alternatively, single capabilities may split into multiple sub-capabilities over time. In either of these cases, the lists may need to be updated to reflect the proper separation of the capabilities.

- Capabilities on the current list may, over time, be superseded by other capabilities, fall out of favor, or simply become obsolete. In these cases, these capabilities should be removed from the list.

Evolution of Enterprise Cybersecurity Functional Areas

While this book's enterprise cybersecurity architecture may need to be tailored for assessments, the 11 functional areas, along with risk mitigations and security operations, were designed to be relatively stable and require little adjustment over time. The key point is that *all* of an enterprise's cybersecurity should be divided up into the functional areas, and capabilities within those functional areas, so everything is accounted for and nothing is missed.

Over time, the enterprise cybersecurity functional areas may evolve as follows:

- First, as capabilities are added to the architecture, the new capabilities may strain the original definitions of the different functional areas, prompting adjustments. It is important that the functional areas provide clear lines of delineation for organizing policies, people, programmatics, IT life cycle, and assessments. Over time, it may make sense to adjust the definitions of one or more of the functional areas so their core functions and the lines separating them are as clearly defined as possible.

- Second, as cybersecurity technologies and practices evolve, there may be a marked shift in the importance of different functional areas to overall enterprise cyberdefense. The enterprise cybersecurity framework was designed to address the needs of Generation 3, 4, and 5 cyberdefenses. However, this architecture is already being challenged by the rise of cloud and BYOD and how they strain enterprise cybersecurity methodologies, technologies, and practices. There is no reason to think other innovations and paradigm shifts might prompt additional future adjustments. Over time, the architecture will need to evolve so the overall framework remains balanced and maintains its relevance and effectiveness.

Final Thoughts

This book has presented a number of ideas for dealing with the challenges of modern enterprise cybersecurity. It has attempted to frame these challenges in a logical and coherent manner that enables cybersecurity practitioners to succeed despite determined adversaries and internal struggles for priority and resources. This book includes the following key ideas and methodologies:

- A characterization of modern cybersecurity challenges

- A management approach for facing those challenges

- A coherent, integrated cybersecurity program framework suitable for an enterprise ranging from a few dozen employees to hundreds of thousands

- Techniques for applying this cybersecurity program framework against modern adversaries

These ideas are not theoretical, but represent the authors' own experiences within our own enterprises and our clients' enterprises. These clients include the US federal government, US Department of Defense, and commercial customers ranging from small nonprofits to huge multinationals. Organizing cybersecurity into the 11 functional areas of enterprise cybersecurity makes it possible to manage most aspects of a cybersecurity program (including policy, people, budget, technology, architecture, engineering, operations, and assessment) in one convenient and coherent framework. This book's enterprise cybersecurity architecture works—and it works well—across a wide range of enterprise situations.

The different generations of cyberattack and cyberdefense provide a context for considering cyberthreats at a strategic level. While technology evolves on a continuous basis, it is helpful to use generational groupings to simplify the different attack waves and the sets of defensive capabilities required to counter those waves. At the time of this writing, the cybersecurity industry is in the throes of a generational shift going from Generation 2 defenses to Generation 3 defenses. Within the next decade, a similar shift will need to occur to get to Generation 4 defenses, and then Generation 5 defenses. Of course, by the time Generation 5 defenses are commonplace, there will be sixth- and seventh-generation attacks to defend against. What those generations will look like is difficult to articulate now, but in ten years these next steps in cyberevolution will be clearer.

Finally, the authors want to leave you with some thoughts on the larger context of the cybersecurity journey we are all embarking on together. As computers have risen in power and capability, and the capability has been multiplied through networking, the threats against these systems have risen as quickly as the capability. As reliant as people are on computers and networked systems, it is only today they are becoming truly *mission critical*. For example, in the airline and financial industries, when their computers go down, the businesses stop. It is reasonable to expect that over the next 20 years, this *mission critical* reliance on computers and networks will occur in almost every area of business and government. In the next few decades, our computers and computerized systems will have to achieve a level of resilience where they do not go down, even in the face of severe crises from adversaries, criminals, or natural disasters.

Looking back on the past 30 years of information technology, it is mind-boggling how information technology has transformed our lives. Nothing makes this observation clearer to us as authors than to talk to our children about technology. Our children cannot conceive of televisions that aren't large and flat, of typewriters that only put words on paper, or of mobile devices that do not have instant access to all of the knowledge on Earth. Even for those of us who remember the past, it is hard to conceive of what life would be like today without these amazing machines at our fingertips. Let's work together to keep these machines, and ourselves, safe for the next 30 years.

PART VI

■ ■ ■

Appendices

APPENDIX A

■ ■ ■

Common Cyberattacks

When people talk about cyberattacks, they generally think about the solitary hacker, penetrating computers in far-away countries and stealing data, changing records, or doing other dastardly deeds. In reality, there is a veritable smorgasbord of cyberattacks out there using various techniques to get into the enterprise, maintain a presence, and move around within the enterprise to accomplish the attackers' objectives.

While hardly an exhaustive list, this appendix describes some of the most common cyberattacks in terms of their impact, methods and consequences, and potential defenses, as listed in Figure A-1.

1. Phishing / Spearphishing	9. Distributed Denial-of-Service	19. Sniper / Laser / Smart Bomb
2. Drive-By / Watering Hole / Malvertising	10. Identity Theft	20. Smokeout / Lockout
3. Code Injection / Webshell	11. Industrial Espionage	21. Infestation / Whack-a-Mole
4. Keylogging / Session Hijacking	12. Pickpocket	22. Burndown
5. Pass-the-Hash and Pass-the-Ticket	13. Bank Heist	23. Meltdown
6. Credential Harvesting	14. Ransomware	24. Defamation
7. Gate-Crashing	15. Webnapping	25. Graffiti
8. Malware / Botnet	16. Hijacking	26. Smokescreen / Diversion
	17. Decapitation	27. Fizzle
	18. Sabotage	

Figure A-1. List of common cyberattacks.

1. Phishing / Spearphishing

Phishing and spearphishing are some of the most effective ways of getting into an enterprise's network. Attackers send e-mail to the victims (targeted e-mail to a specific person if it's spearphishing), and the e-mail takes control of the victim's computer.

- *Impact:* The impact of this attack is the attackers gain control of a personal computer inside the enterprise's network. In the case of spearphishing, this control includes a computer belonging to a specific person, such as an executive or systems administrator.

- *Methods and Consequences:* There are three techniques commonly used for phishing and spearphishing attacks.

  - The first, and most straightforward, technique is for the e-mail message to contain a malicious attachment that takes control of the victim's computer when it is opened.

- The second technique is for the e-mail to contain a link to a web page that exploits a vulnerability to take control of the victim's computer.

- The third technique is for the e-mail to contain a link to a web page that asks for the victim to type in his or her logon credentials, giving the attackers the victim's username and password.

Attackers can dramatically increase their probability of success by launching a campaign of many e-mails that are all related, increasing the odds that the victim will click on one of them.

- *Potential Defenses*: The first round of defense against these attacks is user training to help users recognize when they are being phished, and educating executives and systems administrators on the threats specifically targeting them. Additional protection can be provided through e-mail and web gateways that block or strip malicious attachments and links, and by hardening endpoint computers so they are harder to compromise.

2. Drive-By / Watering Hole / Malvertising

A drive-by or watering hole attack involves compromising a victim's web site and then configuring that web site to deliver malware to people who visit the site. When unsuspecting users visit the site, their computers are infected with malware and the attackers are able to move their attack forward.

A malvertising attack has the same effect, but rather than directly compromising the site, attackers deliver malware through advertising feeds displayed on the web page alongside the victim's content.

- *Impact*: This attack is interesting, in part, because the victim enterprise is just an intermediary in an attack that is really targeting the people who visit the victim's web site, not the victim enterprise. The victim is simply "collateral damage," although the enterprise's reputation can certainly be damaged when the story comes out.

- *Methods and Consequences*: Attackers perform this attack by compromising the victim's public-facing web site, either directly (watering hole) or through advertising feeds on the site (malvertising). Watering hole attacks are generally done through one of two methods:

  - Web sites with vulnerabilities are exploited to get control of the site directly from the Internet.

  - Attackers compromise the victim's enterprise to get access to the computers and accounts with administrative control over the site. Once they have control, the attackers configure the site to deliver its malware payload.

  Malvertising attacks, on the other hand, are performed through advertising web networks, using rich media functionality that can be modified to deliver malware.

- *Potential Defenses*: To protect against web site attacks, web site operators need to have strong configuration control over public-facing web sites. Strong control means that changes are difficult to perform in the first place, and unauthorized changes can be easily identified and analyzed. Malvertising attacks are more difficult to prevent since they require advertising networks to filter their content and prevent unexpected and unacceptable behavior. Either way, potential victims can protect themselves by surfing the web carefully using non-administrative credentials on fully patched and hardened endpoint computers.

3. Code Injection / Webshell

Servers are potentially just as vulnerable as endpoint computers, and they can be compromised using some of the same techniques. Two attacks unique to servers are code injection and webshells. Code injection compromises a vulnerable web site by modifying requests to the site so they contain either scripting code or SQL code that is executed by the server without checking it. If the server executes this code using administrative privileges, then the attackers can use the attack to take control of the server. Once the attackers get control of the server, they can place a webshell into the server's web site. The webshell is a back door that allows attackers to come back to the server's web site and execute commands directly on the server.

- *Impact*: These attacks give the attackers administrative control over an Internet-facing server just like they might get control of a personal computer. Because the server is always on and operating, it gives the attackers a back door into the enterprise that is always open and operational. If the server is running web applications, the attackers can then use this access to compromise the data and account information of all the users of those applications.

- *Methods and Consequences*: Attacker toolkits contain exploits designed to test Internet-facing web sites for a large number of potential code injection and scripting vulnerabilities. They can re-scan sites periodically to catch these vulnerabilities should they occur due to a bad patch or coding mistake. Once the attackers identify the vulnerability, they can move quickly to exploit it, compromise the server, and install a webshell or other permanent back door for access.

- *Potential Defenses*: Strict configuration control of Internet-facing servers is the best defense against these types of attacks since the attackers must change the configuration of the server and the site to make their incursion permanent. Web servers should be carefully configured so even if they are vulnerable, attackers are not able to exploit the vulnerability. Sites should then be scanned frequently to catch vulnerabilities if they occur.

4. Keylogging / Session Hijacking

Once attackers gain control of a victim's endpoint computer, they can use a variety of methods to gain use of the victim's online accounts. Keylogging can be used to capture usernames and passwords of accounts with single-factor authentication, while session hijacking can be used to exploit accounts protected by multi-factor authentication.

- *Impact*: The impact is the attackers gain control over the victim's online accounts and can do anything the victim can with the accounts. This control can include accessing the victim's address book and e-mail, social networking accounts, or even financial accounts and money.

- *Methods and Consequences*: Once attackers gain administrative control over the victim's computer, they can see everything the victim sees and record everything the victim does. Common malware packages interface with the operating system to be able to recognize computer logons and authentication to common web sites, including multi-factor authentication logons. Once these logons occur, attackers can impersonate the user and make use of the accounts.

- **Potential Defenses:** The easiest way to protect against these attacks is for the user's endpoint to never be infected in the first place. This situation can be accomplished by having users use unprivileged accounts that are unable to modify their computers and having endpoint protection, such as anti-virus, anti-malware, and intrusion prevention and application whitelisting capabilities. Multi-factor authentication is also effective since it forces attackers to use session hijacking, which is usually more difficult than keylogging.

5. Pass-the-Hash and Pass-the-Ticket

Pass-the-hash and pass-the-ticket are attack techniques that enable attackers to exploit credentials on an enterprise network. These credentials are stored in computer memory and on hard drives. These attacks effectively bypass the authentication mechanism of certain enterprise applications.

- **Impact:** These attacks can be extremely effective in allowing attackers to move laterally within enterprise IT environments from computer to computer.

- **Methods and Consequences:** To use these techniques, attackers must gain administrative control of the victim's computer. They then scan the memory and hard drives of the victim's machine for hashes and tickets belonging to the user, as well as other users who have logged onto that system. For large multi-user systems, such as virtual desktop or e-mail servers, there can be hundreds—or even thousands—of credentials that are accessible in this way. Once attackers have the hashes and tickets, they use them to connect to other computers on the enterprise network and move laterally.

- **Potential Defenses:** There are a number of specific techniques to reduce enterprise vulnerability to these attacks. Such techniques reduce the numbers of hashes and tickets stored in memory and on hard drives, and make the use of these hashes and tickets over the network more difficult. These techniques are readily available online.

6. Credential Harvesting

Credential harvesting is a technique whereby attackers compromise systems that a large number of users visit. They then harvest user credentials from those systems. In this way, attackers can get the user credentials for a large portion of the enterprise, all in a single step.

- **Impact:** This attack gives attackers access to a large number of user credentials in a single step, and it may also afford them access to administrator credentials as well.

- **Methods and Consequences:** There are two general approaches for conducting credential harvesting attacks:

  - The first approach is to target public-facing systems with large numbers of users (such as e-mail, web portal, or virtual desktop systems), exploit a vulnerability to gain control of them, and then start capturing user credentials from them.

  - The second approach is to get inside the enterprise and target vulnerabilities in authentication systems. Once authentication systems can be compromised, attackers can get access to credential hashes, tickets, and often the usernames and passwords themselves.

- *Potential Defenses*: Protecting against credential harvesting involves understanding which enterprise IT systems collect large numbers of user logons. The enterprise should protect those systems so they are difficult to compromise. Attempts to compromise the systems, or successful compromises, should be detected and responded to in a timely fashion. Since most multi-factor tokens are resistant to credential harvesting attacks, multi-factor authentication can be extremely effective against credential harvesting.

7. Gate-Crashing

Gate-crashing attacks involve attackers positioning themselves so they can exploit a vulnerability or a defender mistake to get past a particular security defense. Due to the realities of security technology maintenance and human errors, almost every preventive defense gets disabled sometime, either intentionally or by accident. The gate-crashers make sure they are there to take advantage when it occurs.

- *Impact*: Gate-crashing enables attackers to slip past defenses when the opportunity arises and get deeper into the attacker's IT systems. In well-defended enterprises with layers of defenses, attackers may have to wait multiple times for just the right vulnerability or mistake to occur so they can slip past each layer of defense.

- *Methods and Consequences*: Gate-crashing can be done either manually or automatically. When it is done manually, attackers must have active command-and-control connections to systems inside the victim's network so they can probe for and exploit the vulnerabilities or mistakes they require. When it is done automatically, intelligent malware watches the victim network for openings and then exploits those openings when they occur.

- *Potential Defenses*: The best protections against gate-crashing are defense layering so a single successful exploit is not disastrous, and active monitoring so gate-crashing activity can be recognized and stopped before it is successful. In addition, security administrators must be educated on the gate-crashing possibility so they understand that turning security off "just for a minute" can be just the opportunity the smart attackers need and can be a far greater vulnerability than one might think.

8. Malware / Botnet

Malware is a generic term for malicious software, and it can include viruses, worms, Trojans, and others. There is an extensive malware industry with commodity and custom toolkits that can be integrated together to perform remote control, session hijacking, credential harvesting, maintain persistence, and other functions. It's also important to consider remote control functions built into most modern operating systems as well since, with the right administrator credentials, those functions can be used for malicious purposes as well. Once computers are infected with malware, they may be tied into a botnet so they can be accounted for and access to them can be sold to the highest bidder. Botnets can contain hundreds, thousands, or even millions of compromised machines that can then be used for any attacker purpose.

- *Impact*: Once installed, malware can be used to monitor all activity on the victim computer, record any credentials and accounts used by the victim, and allow the attackers to use the computer, either on its own or in conjunction with other machines in a botnet.

- **Methods and Consequences:** Malware is installed once a computer has been exploited via a vulnerability, or by the user of the computer willingly (but most likely unwittingly) allowing it to be installed from a malicious web site, e-mail attachment, or web link. Malware may be custom-built or morphed so it is not recognized by signature-based anti-virus software. Once compromised and joined to a botnet, the computer and its data become available to the botnet operators for whatever purpose they chose.

- **Potential Defenses:** There are a number of ways to protect against malware being installed in the first place, including hardening the operating system, anti-virus and anti-malware, user privilege limitation, and application whitelisting. All these techniques involve operational trade-offs, and none of them will make computers "invulnerable" or reduce malware infections to zero in a large enterprise. When computers are compromised and added to botnets, enterprises may be able to catch botnet command-and-control traffic using advanced network defenses.

9. Distributed Denial-of-Service (DDoS)

DDoS involves flooding the victim's computers with so much web traffic—generated from a distributed network—that the victim is unable to continuing delivering services over the Internet.

- **Impact:** The impact of DDoS is the targeted web site is often rendered unusable. If this site is a business capability, such as an e-banking or a government web site, the capability is effectively neutralized and made unavailable to customers or partners.

- **Methods and Consequences:** There are massive networks of thousands and thousands of compromised computers available for hire on the Internet. Attackers only need to hire one of these networks and point it at the desired target.

- **Potential Defenses:** There are two approaches to defend against DDoS:

  - The first approach is to utilize content distribution networks that are hard to target and have the distributed capacity to resist all but the largest DDoS attacks.

  - The second approach is to respond quickly to block DDoS traffic at the network layer, thus mitigating its impact and allowing services to stay operational.

10. Identity Theft

Identity theft is one of the most common professional cyberattacks since stolen identities—particularly social security numbers, credit card numbers, and medical records—can be easily sold on the black market for cash. Such attacks tend to focus on centralized IT systems and databases, and hacking into point-of-sale (PoS) and other critical systems to obtain identity information.

- **Impact:** The impact of these attacks can be severe for victim enterprises. The data involved is frequently regulated and such breaches can have severe disclosure requirements, compensation to victims, and possibly penalties as well.

- **Methods and Consequences:** Attackers use a number of techniques to gain access to victim networks and get privileged access to victim data. These techniques take advantage of victims who do not have good visibility into their environments for detecting or protecting against attackers who have penetrated the outermost defensive layers.

- *Potential Defenses:* Protection against these attacks hinges on protecting the data involved, whether it is financial, medical, or identity data. Defenders should think through the life cycle of the data involved from capture to disposal, and consider the steps an attacker would need to take to intercept that data. Security revolves around making these steps both difficult for attackers to perform and easy for defenders to monitor. Some systems, such as point-of-sale networks and backups, are often assumed to be secured, but such security is not actually tested or looked at from an adversary's perspective.

11. Industrial Espionage

Industrial espionage is a common attack performed by professional and nation-state attackers to gain advantages in international business. In the international marketplace, such advantages can be big business, indeed, with billions of dollars and entire market segments at stake.

- *Impact:* The impact of these attacks can be difficult to measure since it is often difficult to differentiate "healthy" open-market competition from competitors who are reading each other's playbooks clandestinely. At the same time, the economic impact of players who gain the advantage of knowing their competitors' every move can be difficult to understate. Recent industrial revelations have shown it isn't just the "crown jewels" data that is stolen. Often, benign business information, such as meeting schedules and enterprise processes, can be just as useful in defeating competitors in the international marketplace.

- *Methods and Consequences:* To conduct espionage attacks, attackers generally target victim networks to achieve an initial entry, and then exploit the entry to move laterally and gain privilege within the victim networks. Once attackers have administrative control of the victim's environment, or at least the data they are targeting, attackers can steal business information with impunity.

- *Potential Defenses:* Protecting against industrial espionage generally revolves around defeating the targeted cyberattack sequence through preventive and detective controls, and layering those controls so targeted attacks cannot succeed without tripping multiple alarms and detectors.

12. Pickpocket

A "pickpocket" attack involves hacking victim systems to steal relatively small amounts of money across a large number of transactions. Some common examples of this attack include redirecting direct deposit accounts, payroll, or accounts payable accounts to send money to the attackers' accounts instead.

- *Impact:* The impact of this attack is the attackers quickly get away with a large amount of money when the many transactions involved are added up. When this money is transferred via wire transfer or direct deposit, it can be difficult or even impossible to trace and recover.

- *Methods and Consequences:* Attackers target victim enterprises and target systems with a large number of financial transactions that can be intercepted and redirected. This attack often involves employee payroll and accounts payable systems. Attackers get into these systems—or intercept credentials to them if they are "cloud" services—and redirect the accounts involved. By the time the victim enterprise catches the redirection, the money is often long gone.

- *Potential Defenses*: This attack involves rapidly changing online payment destinations to redirect funds to the attackers. When these functions are provided by cloud providers, detecting such changes can be difficult. Defenders must make account destinations difficult to change, with rapid alerting and auditing to catch unauthorized changes before money is moved. Financial institutions can help with this defense by imposing time delays between when account information is changed and when the change becomes effective.

13. Bank Heist

While a pickpocket attack involves changing financial destinations and intercepting the victim's money, a bank heist involves simply getting direct access to the victim's bank accounts and stealing it.

- *Impact*: The impact of this attack is that victims can find their bank accounts partially or completely drained in an instant, with little recourse. Business banking and checking accounts do not have many of the safeguards afforded to consumers so, in many cases, the money may simply be gone.

- *Methods and Consequences*: Attackers conduct this attack by compromising victim computer systems with privileges to access business financial accounts. Once attackers get access to these systems, attackers transfer large sums of money out via hard-to-trace methods such as wire transfer.

- *Potential Defenses*: Protecting against this attack involves closely guarding the computers and credentials used to manage corporate financial accounts. Allowing financial personnel to manage these accounts from their personal computers used to surf the web and do e-mail may not be adequate. Such systems can be easily compromised, and once compromised there is little protecting those accounts.

14. Ransomware

Ransomware compromises victim computers and encrypts the data stored on them, and then charges a ransom to get the keys to decrypt the data. While this attack can be an expensive nuisance for an individual, it can be devastating at an enterprise level.

- *Impact*: In highly collaborative enterprises, large amounts of corporate data are accessible by large numbers of employees. An employee who has write access to that data and who is infected can end up encrypting it for everyone.

- *Methods and Consequences*: Ransomware is a common type of malware that is out on the Internet and constantly used to get into victim computers and enterprises. More sophisticated ransomware is even aware of common backup methods, such as shadow copies. Such ransomware will take steps to ensure online backups are rendered useless as well.

- *Potential Defenses*: Fortunately, ransomware vendors tend to have good customer service, so victimized enterprises can usually "pay up" and get their data back. Preventing this attack from happening in the first place requires hardening endpoints and training users to not get infected in the first place. Containing outbreaks when they occur requires having good segmentation and access controls to contain the damage, plus good backups for data recovery.

15. Webnapping

In the cloud-connected environment, many enterprise IT assets are web intangibles that are only protected by an online account. These assets include domain names, online accounts at popular sites such as Facebook and LinkedIn, and services such as Twitter. In a webnapping, attackers steal enterprise account credentials with these services, or enterprise assets such as domain names, and then hold the credentials or assets hostage until the enterprise pays to get them back. Since Internet real estate can be costly—domain names have been sold for thousands to millions of dollars—getting things back to normal can be quite expensive.

- *Impact:* The theft of a domain name can be extremely destructive to a business, while the theft of enterprise e-mail or other communications channels can cause tremendous damage, even if it only occurs for a short time.

- *Methods and Consequences:* Attackers intercept the credentials used to set up and operate these accounts online. Unfortunately, these accounts are Internet-based, attackers can easily control these accounts, and enterprises may or may not have recourse to get the accounts back.

- *Potential Defenses:* Enterprises can protect themselves from webnappings by tightly controlling the credentials used to manage web accounts and the computers where those accounts and credentials are used. Critical accounts to the enterprise's public Internet presence should be carefully protected to the maximum amount possible, and enterprises should inquire with providers on additional protections, such as auditing, alerts, and multi-factor authentication.

16. Hijacking

Hijacking is similar to webnapping, except attackers use the compromised web resources to suit their own malicious goals. Attackers may use compromised accounts to send out malware or malicious links, hurt the victim's reputation, or simply to make a political statement.

- *Impact:* The impact of a hijacking is almost always reputational in nature, as the victim enterprise is used to serve the attacker's goals and left "holding the bag" for the damage done. Fortunately, hijacking attacks are generally easy to remediate, once hijacking is identified as what is happening.

- *Methods and Consequences:* Like webnapping attacks, hijackings generally start with getting control of computers inside the victim enterprise where web resources are controlled, and then using those computers to intercept credentials for web systems and take control of them. Unlike webnapping attacks, attackers generally do not take measures to prevent the victim from re-taking control of the accounts once they know what is happening.

- *Potential Defenses:* Once again, the best defense is to carefully lock down administrative access to web resources and the people, accounts, and computers with such privileges to these systems.

17. Decapitation

A decapitation attack involves targeting an enterprise's senior leadership and neutralizing its computer assets so leadership is sharply limited in its ability to lead the enterprise.

- *Impact*: By rendering most of the senior leadership ineffective for a period of time, the enterprise is sharply impaired in its ability to respond to circumstances. If this technique is used against an enterprise that is already in the middle of a crisis or in the middle of a significant business event (such as a merger or divestiture), it can have a dramatic psychological impact and affect the conduct and outcome of negotiations.

- *Methods and Consequences*: Attackers perform this attack by targeting senior personnel. Frequently, these people can be identified from corporate publications and social media. Once identified, senior personnel can be easily targeted directly with phishing or spearphishing attacks. They can also be targeted on the internal corporate network from other compromised computers. A single compromised computer or account may be enough to get access to enterprise directories and organization charts, thus making it easy to identify and target senior personnel. If attackers can get administrative control of the victim's network, conducting a decapitation attack is relatively trivial.

- *Potential Defenses*: Educate executives on the cyberrisks posed to them by being senior, publicly visible representatives of the company and help them understand the threats posed by that visibility. Configure security and monitoring systems so their computers are better protected, or at least better monitored, than average employees. In particular, pay attention to supporting administrative staff members who may have many of the same privileges as the executives they support. Administrative staff members may not believe they are targets as well.

18. Sabotage

The purpose of sabotage is to deliberately cause damage to the victim's systems or infrastructure. This type of attack can be performed in the cyberworld just as easily as it can be performed in the real world.

- *Impact*: Perhaps the most famous incidence of sabotage was Stuxnet, where malware affected centrifuges used by the Iranian nuclear program, ultimately destroying them. Pure cyberdamage is also possible. Corruption of data or destruction of IT systems can take months and cost millions to rebuild, depending on the extent of the damage and the robustness of recovery capabilities.

- *Methods and Consequences*: Sabotage attacks are usually conducted in a targeted fashion, with a specific objective for destruction. As physical security, control, and monitoring systems all go online and get interconnected, the amount of damage that can be done by sabotage attacks only increases.

- *Potential Defenses*: Isolate mission-critical applications and control systems on the network. Require tight restrictions on all data going into or out of these systems. Conduct monitoring to detect anomalies on the network that might indicate an attack or attempt to penetrate into the protected networks. For cyberassets that might be damaged, have robust backup and disaster-recovery capabilities that can be quickly brought to bear to repair or replace damaged systems should they be affected.

19. Sniper / Laser / Smart Bomb

These are all targeted attacks designed to have a significant impact with a small amount of cyberdamage that is difficult to trace and investigate. In a sniper attack, a single person's accounts and computers are targeted. In a laser attack, a single critical computer or infrastructure component is targeted. In a smart bomb attack, a single IT system is targeted.

- *Impact*: These attacks are designed to have strategic impact with a small footprint of damage. Impacts might include taking out an enterprise's financial system or timekeeping system, or neutralizing their general counsel or a critical executive in the midst of important negotiations.

- *Methods and Consequences*: These attacks can be conducted over the Internet through targeted campaigns such as spearphishing. Such attacks can also be conducted from inside the enterprise once an initial foothold is established through control of one or more computers on the inside. If attackers can establish administrative control of the victim's network, these attacks are trivial to conduct. Because this attack is highly targeted with a minimum of collateral damage, it may be difficult to determine if the damage was actually caused by malicious activity, and not simply a random failure or bad luck.

- *Potential Defenses*: Layered security and cybersecurity training for key personnel are essential for recognizing and mitigating these types of attacks. Robust recovery capabilities can dramatically reduce their impact when they occur.

20. Smokeout / Lockout

In this type of attack, attackers take administrative control of the victim's enterprise or its infrastructure and lock the enterprise out of its own IT systems.

- *Impact*: This attack can be highly disruptive, generally without causing significant permanent damage. It can be particularly effective as a diversion since it buys attackers considerable time to steal information, change data, or move money while IT personnel are trying to get back into their systems.

- *Methods and Consequences*: Attackers conduct this attack by penetrating systems administration and privileged systems, and then using those systems against the victims. A good channel for conducting this type of attack is "lights-out" data center infrastructure systems that are network-connected, such as keyboard-video-mouse, storage subsystems, and virtualization control consoles. If attackers can take control of these low-level systems, they can power down the data center virtually or even physically. Bringing things back up again will be difficult and time-consuming.

- *Potential Defenses*: When this attack occurs, remediating it may require physical access to equipment, which can take time when the equipment is in "lights-out" data centers or cloud services. Preventing this attack vector involves protecting low-level supporting infrastructures and ensuring that their administrative channels are isolated, protected, and monitored for intrusions.

21. Infestation / Whack-a-Mole

An infestation attack spreads malware so thoroughly around the victim's IT infrastructure that it is infeasible to remove it without having an unacceptable business impact. The other objective is to give the attackers enough leverage in the enterprise so any attempt to remove the attacker's foothold results in a futile exercise in removal and re-infection (whack-a-mole).

- *Impact*: While this attack may not have business consequences, it gives the attackers tremendous leverage on the enterprise and makes the attackers difficult, or even impossible, to remove without dramatic business consequences. This situation, in turn, can put the business in an untenable risk position because of the vulnerability of data and systems to breaches of confidentiality, integrity, or availability.

- *Methods and Consequences*: Attackers conduct this attack by gaining partial or complete administrative control of the enterprise, and then using that control to distribute malware to large numbers of servers and endpoints. More sophisticated versions of this attack may use multiple versions of malware, or malware that dynamically modifies itself, to make it more difficult to find and remove the malware after the fact. This attack can then be used as a precursor to a more serious attack in the future, such as a lockout, meltdown, or even a burndown attack that destroys the victim's entire IT enterprise.

- *Potential Defenses*: There are a number of defenses against this attack:

  - The first line of defense against an infestation attack is robust protection around administrative accounts and systems, including authentication, patch management, and enterprise endpoint security systems.

  - The second line of defense is application whitelisting to block and alert on attempts to install malware onto protected systems.

  - The third line of defense is robust detection and response capabilities so an outbreak can be caught and stopped quickly.

  - The final line of defense is auditing of system activities so an outbreak can be analyzed and cleaned up after the fact.

22. Burndown

A burndown attack destroys the victim's entire IT infrastructure, or a major portion of it, rendering the business unable to use its computer systems. Effectively, this attack pushes the victim back to the age of pen and paper. The most famous publicly disclosed instance of a burndown is the Sony Pictures Entertainment attack of 2014.

- *Impact*: If the attack is successful, a burndown renders the victim's entire IT infrastructure unusable, thus having to be replaced or rebuilt. A thorough burndown can even damage equipment firmware to the extent that firmware has to be reprogrammed or equipment—such as hard drives—has to be replaced altogether. A burndown can cause considerable business disruption during the recovery period. When used as a diversion, a burndown attack can completely cover up the actual crime and make it difficult or impossible to investigate.

- *Methods and Consequences*: A burndown requires extensive administrative control of the victim's enterprise at multiple levels of systems administration (for example, application, operating system, and data center infrastructure layers). The attack requires careful planning to ensure systems are destroyed in the correct order for the full sequence to complete.

- *Potential Defenses*: A tiered and layered security defense with extensive monitoring is an effective way to protect against a burndown attack. A robust backup and recovery capability is the best way to recover from a burndown attack. Compartmentalization in the enterprise can help contain a burndown attack and reduce the amount of damage that can be done all at once.

23. Meltdown

Similar to a burndown, a meltdown attack disables a significant portion of the enterprise's IT capabilities. Unlike the extensive nature of a burndown, a meltdown targets just the core enterprise infrastructure, causing an enterprisewide outage, but without necessarily causing enterprisewide damage. A meltdown may take out just a handful of components, such as the network or virtual environment, or it may take out the entire data center or enterprise applications.

- *Impact*: Because a meltdown attack takes out key infrastructure, this attack can have an extensive impact on enterprise business operations by disabling web sites, stopping assembly lines, or other dramatic effects. Depending on the extent of the damage, a meltdown may take a considerable amount of time to recover disabled servers and restore deleted data.

- *Methods and Consequences*: Attackers conduct this attack by gaining administrative control of all or part of the enterprise's data center infrastructure, and then use that infrastructure to disable a large portion of the enterprise's IT systems and applications. Low-level access to data center hardware and virtualization layers may make it possible to do this attack without having to compromise systems at the operating system or application layers. A meltdown may also occur as a result of a burndown attack that fails or is disrupted before it can complete.

- *Potential Defenses*: To protect against meltdown attacks, data center systems and infrastructure must be well protected. In particular, low-level infrastructure that can bypass application and operating system protections must be isolated, protected, and monitored for anomalous activities. In the event this attack occurs, robust disaster recovery and reconstitution capabilities can reduce the business impact.

24. Defamation

A defamation attack is intended to damage the reputation of the victim, either by releasing embarrassing information from within the victim's environment—such as executive memos, e-mails, or voicemails—or by publishing false and defamatory information through authoritative channels such as the press.

- *Impact*: A defamation attack—particularly when it involves the release of true, but embarrassing information—can cause extensive public relations damage that can take a long time to repair. Even when it involves false information, a defamation attack can disrupt public confidence in the enterprise in significant ways.

- **Methods and Consequences**: There are multiple ways this attack type can be conducted:

  - First, attackers can compromise press channels external to the enterprise and use them to publish false or misleading information.

  - Second, attackers can compromise critical public relations components, such as enterprise web sites or Twitter or Facebook accounts, and then use them to distribute false or misleading information.

  - Third and perhaps the most destructive, attackers can compromise key internal IT systems such as e-mail or voicemail, and then publish embarrassing information from those systems.

- **Potential Defenses**: Enterprises must stay constantly vigilant of their reputation in public and in cyberspace. There are monitoring services that watch press and other channels to stay abreast of what information is being published and its truthfulness. Internally, executives and employees must be aware that every message they write, send, or record can be stored and may be publicly released outside of its original context. Finally, key collaboration and communications systems—particularly telecommunications, videoconferencing, and voicemail systems—must be carefully protected and defended from cyberattack.

25. Graffiti

Graffiti is a common attack by politically motivated organizations and cyberactivists, and it involves defacing victim web pages to make political or ideological statements.

- **Impact**: Impact is generally reputational in nature since having one's web site defaced can be publicly embarrassing and possibly require political damage control after the fact.

- **Methods and Consequences**: There are two main methods for conducting these types of attacks:

  - The first method is to compromise the user accounts or computers of web site authorized administrators. In the case of smaller enterprises, this attack can be easily done using information publicly available in domain name service (DNS).

  - The second method is to find and exploit a vulnerability in the web site itself, and use the vulnerability to take control of the site and/or its servers. Once control is established, modifying the site tends to be straightforward.

- **Potential Defenses**: Several methods to reduce exposure to this type of attack include having tight configuration control of web site content, the ability to quickly "roll back" unauthorized changes, tight control of web site administrator credentials and permissions, and aggressively testing the security and protection of web site servers and applications.

26. Smokescreen / Diversion

Attackers use a smokescreen attack to disguise another attack that is taking place simultaneously. For example, attackers might use a DDoS to distract defenders while they are conducting a bank heist and draining the victim's accounts. The purpose of the smokescreen is to keep defenders busy enough so they do not notice the real attack until it is too late.

- *Impact*: While the smokescreen itself may or may not do much damage, the underlying attack it is covering up can be as damaging as the attackers wish. In cyberspace, attackers can use a very destructive attack—such as a burndown—as the smokescreen, and effectively cover their tracks for quite some time.

- *Methods and Consequences*: To use a smokescreen, attackers plan out the primary attack and then consider what type of diversion attack will be most effective. The diversion attack can serve to distract attackers while the real attack takes place, or it can also serve to cover up the evidence after the real attack is conducted.

- *Potential Defenses*: Cyberdefenders should be educated on the concept of diversions and the possibility of multiple attacks taking place simultaneously. Leadership should be trained in how to watch for multiple sets of anomalies taking place at the same time and understand that what they are seeing may not be the attacker's primary objective. Finally, it is useful to have contingency plans to allow for "locking down" both physical assets and cyberassets when cyberattacks are taking place, even if those assets appear to be unrelated to the attack in question.

27. Fizzle

Not all attacks succeed. However, a potentially disastrous attack can still be highly disruptive even if it fails before it can be completed. An example of this attack might be a burndown attack that fails because it disables key infrastructure too early in the attack, resulting in a meltdown instead of the intended burndown. Even when the attack does not succeed in accomplishing its full objective, it can still be highly disruptive to the business and disconcerting for defenders.

- *Impact*: A fizzled attack can still be extremely destructive, even though the impact is less than what was originally intended by the attackers. Defenders should analyze attacks to understand what the attackers were intending to accomplish and to understand why the attack fizzled and failed to achieve its full objective.

- *Methods and Consequences*: Attacks fizzle because something goes wrong before the attack can realize its full intent. This situation may be because the attackers fail to properly plan the attack sequence, or it may be because they make a mistake in their execution. An attack can also fizzle because defensive measures catch it and disrupt it before it can complete.

- *Potential Defenses*: Sometimes attacks fizzle because defensive controls worked as intended and disrupted the attack before it could complete. When this situation happens, the enterprise can count it as a defensive win, which is great. Other times, attacks fizzle because of mistakes made by the attackers. Defenders should always remember the attackers will learn from their mistakes and the actions of the defense, and they will try to improve their attack so it is able to completely succeed the next time around.

APPENDIX B

■ ■ ■

Cybersecurity Frameworks

Many cybersecurity frameworks have been established over the past two decades and are in common use today. It is interesting to place these frameworks side by side and observe quite clearly how all of them are *slicing and dicing* the cybersecurity pie in different ways. This appendix provides an introductory overview of the following major cybersecurity frameworks that an enterprise may need to comply with or assess against:

- (ISC)² Common Body of Knowledge (CBK)
- ISO 27001/27002 Version 2013
- ISO 27001/27002 Version 2005
- NIST SP800-53 Revisions 3 and 4
- NIST Cybersecurity Framework (2014)
- Department of Homeland Security Cyber Resilience Review (DHS CRR)
- Council on CyberSecurity Critical Security Controls (SANS 20)
- Australian DSD Strategies to Mitigate Targeted Cyber Intrusions
- PCI DSS Version 3.0
- HIPAA Security Rule
- HITRUST Common Security Framework (CSF)
- NERC CIP Cyber Security Version 5
- NERC CIP Cyber Security Version 3

(ISC)² Common Body of Knowledge (CBK)

The International Information Systems Security Certification Consortium, Inc. (ISC)² created the CBK as a core knowledge base for training Certified Information Systems Security Professionals (CISSP). CISSP is one of the most widely used cybersecurity certification programs today. While not a security framework per se, this training curriculum for CISSP professionals is one way of organizing a comprehensive enterprise cybersecurity program, and it aligns closely with the cybersecurity functional areas described in this book.

The CBK consists of 10 security domains, as shown in Figure B-1.

(ISC)² Common Body of Knowledge (CBK)   10 Security Domains
1. Access Control
2. Telecommunications and Network Security
3. Information Security Governance and Risk Management
4. Software Development Security
5. Cryptography
6. Security Architecture and Design
7. Security Operations
8. Business Continuity and Disaster Recovery Planning
9. Legal, Regulations, Investigations, and Compliance
10. Physical (Environmental) Security

Figure B-1. (ISC)² Common Body of Knowledge (CBK).

ISO 27001/27002 Version 2013

The International Organization for Standardization (ISO) created the ISO 27000 series of standards. ISO 27001 is the specification for an enterprise information security management system (ISMS), and ISO 27002 is the code of practice for information security controls. Enterprises can be accredited for ISO 27001 by following a formal audit process that requires independent accreditation by an outside auditor. The 2013 version of this standard reduces the number of controls, but it adds additional domains for cryptography, operations security, and supplier relationships.

ISO 27001/27002 version 2013 consists of 114 controls in 14 domains, as shown in Figure B-2.

ISO 27001 / 27002 Version 2013   114 Controls in 14 Domains
1. Information Security Policies
2. Organization of Information Security
3. Human Resource Security
4. Asset Management
5. Access Control
6. Cryptography
7. Physical and Environmental Security
8. Operations Security
9. Communications Security
10. System Acquisition, Development, and Maintenance
11. Supplier Relationships
12. Information Security Incident Management
13. Information Security Aspect of Business Continuity Management
14. Compliance

Figure B-2. ISO 27001/27002 Version 2013.

ISO 27001/27002 Version 2005

The International Organization for Standardization (ISO) created the ISO 27000 series of standards. ISO 27001 is the specification for an enterprise information security management system (ISMS), and ISO 27002 is the code of practice for information security controls. The 2005 version of this standard focused on a core *Plan-Do-Check-Act* cycle for continuous improvement of cybersecurity practices and controls.

ISO 27001/27002 version 2005 consisted of 133 controls in 11 domains, as shown in Figure B-3.

ISO 27001 / 27002 Version 2005
133 Controls in 11 Domains
1. Security Policy
2. Organizing Information Security
3. Asset Management
4. Human Resources Security
5. Physical and Environmental Security
6. Communications and Operations Management
7. Access Control
8. Information Systems Acquisition, Development and Maintenance
9. Information Security Incident Management
10. Business Continuity Management
11. Compliance

Figure B-3. ISO 27001/27002 Version 2005.

NIST SP800-53 Revisions 3 and 4

The US National Institute of Standards and Technology (NIST) has responsibility for setting standards used by the US federal government. Such standards are frequently adopted in private industry as well. Special Publication (SP) 800-53 is titled "Security and Privacy Controls for Federal Information Systems and Organizations" and contains a catalog of security controls to be used for US federal IT systems. Revision 4 is an extensive revision that focuses on the risk management process and dramatically expands the control catalog.

NIST SP800-53 revision 3 and 4 are organized into 18 control families. Revision 3 contains 171 controls while revision 4 contains 224 controls, as shown in Figure B-4.

NIST SP800-53 Revisions 3 and 4
171 Revision 3 Controls; 224 Revision 4 Controls in 18 Families
1. Access Control
2. Awareness and Training
3. Audit and Accountability
4. Security Assessment and Authorization
5. Configuration Management
6. Contingency Planning
7. Identification and Authentication
8. Incident Response
9. Maintenance
10. Media Protection
11. Physical and Environmental Protection
12. Planning
13. Personnel Security
14. Risk Assessment
15. System and Services Acquisition
16. System and Communications Protection
17. System and Information Integrity
18. Program Management

Figure B-4. NIST SP800-53 revisions 3 and 4.

NIST Cybersecurity Framework (2014)

The US National Institute of Standards and Technology (NIST) has responsibility for setting standards used by the US federal government. Such standards are frequently adopted in private industry as well. The NIST cybersecurity framework was created in response to Executive Order 13636, which requested a "prioritized, flexible, repeatable, performance-based, and cost-effective approach" for enterprise cybersecurity. This framework complements the more established SP800-53 framework in that it focuses on the cybersecurity operations and response process. To date, NIST has not yet provided detailed guidance on how to use these two frameworks together in concert.

The NIST Cybersecurity framework contains 5 functions, 22 categories, and 98 subcategories, as shown in Figure B-5.

NIST Cybersecurity Framework (2014)
98 Subcategories in 22 Categories and 5 Functions

1. **Identify**
   - A. Asset Management
   - B. Business Environment
   - C. Governance
   - D. Risk Assessment
   - E. Risk Management Strategy
2. **Protect**
   - A. Access Control
   - B. Awareness and Training
   - C. Data Security
   - D. Information Protection Processes and Procedures
   - E. Maintenance
   - F. Protective Technology
3. **Detect**
   - A. Anomalies and Events
   - B. Security Continuous Monitoring
   - C. Detection Processes
4. **Respond**
   - A. Response Planning
   - B. Communications
   - C. Analysis
   - D. Mitigation
   - E. Improvements
5. **Recover**
   - A. Recovery Planning
   - B. Improvements
   - C. Communications

Figure B-5. *NIST Cybersecurity Framework (2014).*

DHS Cyber Resilience Review (CRR)

The Department of Homeland Security (DHS) created the CRR as a "no-cost, voluntary, non-technical assessment to self-evaluate operational resilience and cybersecurity capabilities within Critical Infrastructure and Key Resources sectors."[1] The CRR framework focuses on enterprise assets and understanding how resources are allocated to ten domains of cybersecurity. It is designed for performing self-assessments and on-site sessions facilitated by DHS representatives.

The DHS CRR is organized into 10 domains, as shown in Figure B-6.

DHS Cyber Resilience Review (CRR) 10 Domains
1. Asset Management
2. Controls Management
3. Configuration and Change Management
4. Vulnerability Management
5. Incident Management
6. Service Continuity Management
7. Risk Management
8. External Dependency Management
9. Training and Awareness
10. Situational Awareness

Figure B-6. *DHS Cyber Resilience Review (CRR).*

---

[1]Cyber Resilience Review web site: www.us-cert.gov/ccubedvp/self-service-crr.

Council on CyberSecurity Critical Security Controls

The Council on CyberSecurity manages the Critical Security Controls, which is an international cybersecurity control framework. The Council is an "independent, expert, not-for-profit organization with a global scope committed to the security of the open Internet."[2] The Council published a set of 20 "critical" security controls that it has found to mitigate a majority of real-world cyberthreats. This framework was originally publicized by the SANS Institute as the "20 Critical Controls" before it was put into the public domain as an open standard.

The Council on CyberSecurity Critical Security Controls consists of 20 controls and 182 control activities, as of version 5.1. (See Figure B-7.)

Council on CyberSecurity Critical Security Controls
Version 5.1: 20 Controls and 182 Control Activities
1. Inventory of Devices
2. Inventory of Software
3. Secure Configurations for Computers
4. Continuous Vulnerability Assessment and Remediation
5. Malware Defenses
6. Application Software Security
7. Wireless Device Control
8. Data Recovery Capability
9. Security Skills Assessment and Training
10. Security Configurations for Network Devices
11. Network Ports, Protocols, and Services
12. Control of Administrative Privileges
13. Boundary Defense
14. Security Audit Logs
15. Need-to-Know Access Control
16. Account Monitoring and Control
17. Data Loss Prevention
18. Incident Response Capability
19. Secure Network Engineering
20. Penetration Testing and Red Team Exercises

Figure B-7. *Council on CyberSecurity Critical Security Controls.*

---

[2]Council on CyberSecurity web site: www.counciloncybersecurity.org/about-us/.

Australian DSD Strategies to Mitigate Targeted Cyberintrusions

The Australian Defense Signals Directorate (DSD) publishes a list of strategies to mitigate targeted cyberintrusions. The strategies are informed by the DSD's experience with serious cyberintrusions against Australian government agencies. This list was first published in 2010 and was revised in 2014. This framework emphasizes the "Top 4" mitigation strategies (that is, Application Whitelisting, Patch Applications, Patch Operating System Vulnerabilities, and Restrict Administrative Privileges) they believe thwart more than 85% of cyberintrusions.

The Australian DSD Strategies to Mitigate Targeted Cyber Intrusions consists of 35 controls, as shown in Figure B-8.

Australian Defense Signals Directorate (DSD) Strategies to Mitigate Targeted Cyber Intrusions: 35 Controls	
1. Application whitelisting	18. Web content filtering
2. Patch applications	19. Web domain whitelisting for all domains
3. Patch operating system vulnerabilities	20. Block spoofed e-mails
4. Restrict administrative privileges	21. Workstation and server configuration management
5. User application configuration hardening	22. Anti-virus software using heuristics and automated Internet-based reputation ratings
6. Automated dynamic analysis	
7. Operating system generic exploit mitigation	23. Deny direct Internet access from workstations
8. Host-based Intrusion Detection/Prevention System	24. Server application configuration hardening
9. Disable local administrator accounts	25. Enforce a strong passphrase policy
10. Network segmentation and segregation	26. Removable and portable media control
11. Multi-factor authentication	27. Restrict access to Server Message Block (SMB) and NetBIOS
12. Software-based application firewall, blocking incoming network traffic	28. User education
13. Software-based application firewall, blocking outgoing network traffic	29. Workstation inspection of Microsoft Office files
	30. Signature-based anti-virus software
14. Non-persistent virtualized sandboxed trusted operating environment	31. TLS encryption between e-mail servers
15. Centralized and time-synchronized logging of successful and failed computer events	32. Block attempts to access web sites by their IP address
16. Centralized and time-synchronized logging of allowed and blocked network activity	33. Network-based Intrusion Detection/Prevention System
17. E-mail content filtering	34. Gateway blacklisting
	35. Capture network traffic

Figure B-8. Australian DSD Strategies to Mitigate Targeted Cyber Intrusions.

PCI DSS Version 3.0

The Payment Card Industry Digital Security Standard (PCI DSS) version 3.0 was published in 2013 as a "minimum set of requirements for protecting cardholder data"[3] for enterprises handling credit card data on their IT systems. It is a set of straightforward security controls that must be employed by all certified entities. For PCI certified entities, compliance must be re-certified at least annually by an independent assessor.

PCI DSS version 3.0 contains 12 core requirements and a 13th that applies to shared hosting providers, as shown in Figure B-9.

PCI DSS Version 3.0
12 Core Requirements; Plus 1 Shared Hosting Requirement
1. Install and maintain a firewall to protect cardholder data
2. Do not use vendor-supplied defaults for system passwords and other security measures
3. Protect stored cardholder data
4. Encrypt transmission of cardholder data across open, public networks
5. Protect all systems against malware and regularly update anti-virus software or programs
6. Develop and maintain secure systems and applications
7. Restrict access to cardholder data by business need to know
8. Identify and authenticate access to system components
9. Restrict physical access to cardholder data
10. Track and monitor all access to network resources and cardholder data
11. Regularly test security systems and processes
12. Maintain a policy that addresses information security for all personnel
13. Shared hosting providers must protect the cardholder data environment

Figure B-9. *PCI DSS version 3.0.*

---

[3]From PCI DSS web site: `www.pcisecuritystandards.org/documents/PCI_DSS_v3.pdf`.

HIPAA Security Rule

The Health Insurance Portability and Accountability Act (HIPAA) of 1996, in addition to providing for health insurance coverage for workers and their families, established national standards for the use and protection of electronic protected health information (EPHI). The HIPAA security rule specifies requirements for protecting the confidentiality, integrity, and availability of EPHI at healthcare providers, clearinghouses, insurance plans, and drug dispensers. NIST provides an excellent introduction to the cybersecurity requirements of HIPAA through their SP800-66 document, "An Introductory Resource Guide for Implementing the HIPAA Security Rule."

The HIPAA Security Rule contains 22 cybersecurity standards, as shown in Figure B-10.

**Health Insurance Portability and Accountability Act (HIPAA)
Security Rule: 22 Requirements in 5 Areas**

Administrative Safeguards
1. Security Management Process
2. Assigned Security Responsibility
3. Workforce Security
4. Information Access Management
5. Security Awareness and Training
6. Security Incident Procedures
7. Contingency Plan
8. Evaluation
9. Business Associate Contracts and Other Arrangements

Physical Safeguards
10. Facility Access controls
11. Workstation Use
12. Workstation Security
13. Device and Media Controls

Technical Safeguards
14. Access Control
15. Audit Controls
16. Integrity
17. Person or Entity Authentication
18. Transmission Security

Organizational Requirements
19. Business Associate Contracts or Other Arrangements
20. Requirements for Group Health Plans

Policies and Procedures and Documentation Requirements
21. Policies and Procedures
22. Documentation

Figure B-10. *HIPAA Security Rule.*

HITRUST Common Security Framework (CSF)

The Health Information Trust Alliance, or HITRUST, is an industry organization "born out of the belief that information security should be a core pillar of, rather than an obstacle to, the broad adoption of health information systems and exchanges."[4] HITRUST created the Common Security Framework (CSF) as a "certifiable framework that can be used by any and all organizations that create, access, store, or exchange personal health and financial information."[5] The HITRUST CSF was informed by the other major cybersecurity frameworks, including HIPAA, PCI, and NIST.

The HITRUST CSF contains 13 security control categories with 42 control objectives and 135 control specifications, as shown in Figure B-11.

Health Information Trust Alliance (HITRUST) **Common Security Framework (CSF)** 13 Security Controls; 42 Control Objectives; 135 Control Specifications
1. Information Security Management Program
2. Access Control
3. Human Resources Security
4. Risk Management
5. Security Policy
6. Organization of Information Security
7. Compliance
8. Asset Management
9. Physical and Environmental Security
10. Communications and Operations Management
11. Information Systems Acquisition, Development, and Maintenance
12. Information Security Incident Management
13. Business Continuity Management

Figure B-11. HITRUST Common Security Framework (CSF).

---

[4]HITRUST web site: http://hitrustalliance.net/about-us/.
[5]Ibid.

NERC CIP Cyber Security Version 5

The North American Electric Reliability Corporation (NERC) is a not-for-profit international regulatory authority "whose mission is to ensure the reliability of the bulk power system in North America."[6] The NERC Critical Infrastructure Protection (CIP) program includes a number of cybersecurity standards, numbered CIP-002 through CIP-011. These standards are mandatory for energy providers and distributers involved in the generation, transmission, and delivery of energy in North America. Version 5 is a significant update to the control framework with a focus on effective security rather than just regulatory compliance. Instead of referring to "critical cyber assets," it refers to "Bulk Electric System (BES) cyber systems," with a new categorization of these systems into "high," "medium," and "low" criticality levels. This categorization is intended to simplify certification, as computer systems can be considered in aggregate rather than as individual assets. Version 5 is scheduled to be fully enforced starting in 2015.

NERC CIP version 5 contains 32 cybersecurity requirements organized into 10 areas, as shown in Figure B-12.

North American Electric Reliability Corporation (NERC) **Critical Infrastructure Protection (CIP) Cyber Security Version 5** 32 Cybersecurity Requirements in 10 Areas
CIP-002 Critical Cyber Assets
CIP-003 Security Management Controls
CIP-004 Personnel and Training
CIP-005 Electronic Security
CIP-006 Physical Security
CIP-007 Systems Security Management
CIP-008 Incident Reporting and Response Planning
CIP-009 Recovery Plans for BES Cyber Assets
CIP-010 Configuration Changes and Vulnerability Assessments
CIP-011 Information Protection

Figure B-12. *NERC CIP Cyber Security version 5.*

---

[6]NERC web site: www.nerc.com/Pages/default.aspx.

NERC CIP Cyber Security Version 3

The North American Electric Reliability Corporation (NERC) is a not-for-profit international regulatory authority "whose mission is to ensure the reliability of the bulk power system in North America."[7] The NERC Critical Infrastructure Protection (CIP) program includes a number of cybersecurity standards, numbered CIP-002 through CIP-009. These standards are mandatory for energy providers and distributers involved in the generation, transmission, and delivery of energy in North America. Version 3 went into effect in 2010, and was superseded by Version 5 in 2015.

NERC CIP version 3 contains 43 cybersecurity requirements organized into 8 areas, as shown in Figure B-13.

North American Electric Reliability Corporation (NERC) Critical Infrastructure Protection (CIP) Cyber Security Version 3 43 Cybersecurity Requirements in 8 Areas
CIP-002 Critical Cyber Asset Identification
CIP-003 Security Management Controls
CIP-004 Personnel &Training
CIP-005 Electronic Security Perimeter(s)
CIP-006 Physical Security of Critical Cyber Assets
CIP-007 Systems Security Management
CIP-008 Incident Reporting and Response Planning
CIP-009 Recovery Plans for Critical Cyber Systems

Figure B-13. *NERC CIP Cyber Security version 3.*

---

[7]NERC web site: www.nerc.com/Pages/default.aspx.

APPENDIX C

■ ■ ■

Enterprise Cybersecurity Capabilities

This appendix describes 113 of the major enterprise cybersecurity capabilities that should be considered in an enterprise cybersecurity program. While hardly an exhaustive list, the authors believe this list reflects the most important capabilities available at the time of writing. These capabilities are organized into 11 functional areas to make them easier to track, manage, and delegate. As new capabilities emerge and become important, they can be added to this list or incorporated into an enterprise's own cybersecurity architecture. These capabilities are outlined in Figure C-1 below and on the next page.

Functional Area	Capabilities	
Systems Administration (SA)	• Bastion hosts • Out-of-Band (OOB) management • Network isolation • Integrated Lights-Out (ILO), Keyboard Video Mouse (KVM), and power controls • Virtualization and Storage Area Network (SAN) management	• Separation of administration from services • Multi-factor authentication for Systems Administrators (SAs) • Administrator audit trail(s) • Command logging and analytics
Network Security (NS)	• Switches and routers • Software Defined Networking (SDN) • Domain Name System (DNS) and Dynamic Host Configuration Protocol (DHCP) • Network Time Protocol (NTP) • Network service management • Firewall and virtual machine firewall • Network Intrusion Detection / Network Intrusion Prevention System (IDS / IPS)	• Wireless networking (Wi-Fi) • Packet intercept and capture • Secure Sockets Layer (SSL) intercept • Network Access Control (NAC) • Virtual Private Networking (VPN) and Internet Protocol Security (IPSec) • Network Traffic Analysis (NTA) • Network Data Analytics (NDA)
Application Security (AS)	• E-mail security • Webshell detection • Application firewalls • Database firewalls • Forward proxy and web filters	• Reverse proxy • Data Leakage Protection (DLP) • Secure application and database software development • Software code vulnerability analysis
Endpoint, Server, and Device Security (ESDS)	• Local administrator privilege restrictions • Computer security and logging policies • Endpoint and media encryption • Computer access controls • Forensic imaging support for investigations • Virtual desktop / thin clients • Mobile Device Management (MDM) • Anti-virus / anti-malware	• Application whitelisting • In-memory malware detection • Host firewall and intrusion detection • "Gold code" software images • Security Technical Implementation Guides (STIGs) • Always-on Virtual Private Networking (VPN) • File integrity and change monitoring

Figure C-1. The 113 enterprise cybersecurity capabilities grouped by functional area.

Functional Area	Capabilities	
Identity, Authentication, and Access Management (IAAM)	• Identity life cycle management • Enterprise directory • Multi-factor authentication • Privilege management and access control • Identity and access audit trail and reporting	• Lightweight Directory Access Protocol (LDAP) • Kerberos, RADIUS, 802.1x • Federated authentication • Security Assertion Markup Language (SAML)
Data Protection and Cryptography (DPC)	• Secure Sockets Layer (SSL) and Transport Layer Security (TLS) • Digital certificates (Public Key Infrastructure [PKI]) • Key hardware protection (Smart cards, Trusted Platform Modules [TPMs], and Hardware Security Modules [HSMs])	• One-Time Password (OTP) and Out-of-Band (OOB) authentication • Key life cycle management • Digital signatures • Complex passwords • Data encryption and tokenization • Brute force attack detection • Digital Rights Management (DRM)
Monitoring, Vulnerability, and Patch Management (MVPM)	• Operational performance monitoring • System and network monitoring • System configuration change detection • Privilege and access change detection • Log aggregation • Data analytics • Security Information and Event Management (SIEM)	• Network and computer vulnerability scanning • Penetration testing • Patch management and deployment • Rogue network device detection • Rogue wireless access point detection • Honeypots / honeynets / honeytokens • Security Operations Center (SOC)
High Availability, Disaster Recovery, and Physical Protection (HADRPP)	• Clustering • Load balancing, Global Server Load Balancing (GSLB) • Network failover, subnet spanning • Virtual machine snapshots and cloning • Data mirroring and replication	• Backups and backup management • Off-site storage • Facilities protection • Physical access controls • Physical security monitoring
Incident Response (IR)	• Threat information • Incident tracking • Forensic tools • Computer imaging	• Indicators of Compromise (IOCs) • Black hole server • Regulatory / legal coordination
Asset Management and Supply Chain (AMSC)	• Asset management databases • Configuration Management Databases (CMDB) • Change management databases	• Software inventory and license management • Supplier certification processes • Secure disposal, recycling, and data destruction
Policy, Audit, E-Discovery, and Training (PAET)	• Governance, Risk, and Compliance (GRC), with reporting • Compliance and control frameworks (SOX, PCI, others) • Audit frameworks • Customer Certification and Accreditation (C&A)	• Policy and policy exception management • Risk and threat management • Privacy compliance • E-Discovery tools • Personnel security and background checks • Security awareness and training

Figure C-1. (*continued*)

Systems Administration (SA)

Systems administration provides for secure administration of enterprise infrastructure and security infrastructure by protecting systems administration channels from compromise.

SA-01: Bastion Hosts

A bastion host is a dedicated, isolated system that is only used for systems administration and is only accessible by authorized systems administrators. Generally, applications, services, accounts, and ports not required to perform administration tasks are removed, thereby reducing the attack surface of the host. Ideally, bastion hosts enforce additional protection methods such as strong authentication.

SA-02: Out-of-Band (OOB) Management

Out-of-band management, or lights-out management, utilizes a dedicated channel to manage and administer critical systems. This approach protects these administration channels from potential attack or compromise.

SA-03: Network Isolation

Network isolation is segmentation of a network located between protected and unprotected segments. Network isolation is used to protect systems administration by isolating systems administration network communications from unprotected network segments. A demilitarized zone (DMZ) is an example of network isolation.

SA-04: Integrated Lights-Out (ILO), Keyboard Video Mouse (KVM), and Power Controls

These capabilities enable a "lights-out" data center. ILO manages servers even when they are turned off, and can be used to power up, power down, and manage systems at the hardware level. KVM connects to computers and enables their keyboard, video, and mouse to be controlled from a central console, frequently over a network. Power control involves connecting power strips and power distribution systems to the network so they can be controlled remotely. All these capabilities require careful protection to ensure they cannot be abused by attackers.

SA-05: Virtualization and Storage Area Network (SAN) Management

Virtualization allows a single physical host to run multiple virtual machines simultaneously, while SAN provides shared storage to a large number of client machines. Systems administration channels to these systems can access hardware and storage at a very low level, bypassing the security protections of the computer system running on top of this virtualized hardware and storage.

SA-06: Separation of Administration from Services

When services and systems administration can be done over a single interface—as in with a web application where the privileges you have depend on the account you use to logon—anyone who has access to the service can do systems administration if they have access to the right credentials. By separating administration and service channels, then only those with access to the administration channel can get privileged access. This separation dramatically reduces the attack surface of systems since the number of users who need privileged access is generally very small.

SA-07: Multi-factor Authentication for Systems Administrators (SAs)

Multi-factor authentication makes successful authentication dependent on having multiple factors of authentication. Generally, these are physical tokens, out-of-band or one-time passwords, or biometrics. Multi-factor authentication is significantly harder to compromise than single-factor authentication such as usernames and passwords.

SA-08: Administrator Audit Trail(s)

An audit trail documents activities performed by system, database, or application administrators. The audit trail should be designed in a way so it is not under the control of administrators. Also, the audit logs should be frequently reviewed to validate the changes performed. An audit trail provides accountability of the activities performed by the administrators.

SA-09: Command Logging and Analytics

Command logging or keystroke monitoring is a type of monitoring where a system records every keystroke entered by a user during an interactive session. Analytics uses the keystroke data to attempt to identify malicious systems administration or credential abuse. This type of monitoring generates prodigious amounts of logs and is recommended for a short duration of time and should be limited in scope.

Network Security (NS)

Network security makes a network safe from cyberattacks. More specifically, this functional area provides for the security of enterprise networks, their services, and access to them from the Internet and internally connected devices. Network security needs to be considered in terms of preventive, detective, and monitoring controls.

NS-01: Switches and Routers

Switches and routers are the building blocks of an information technology network. Protection of these critical infrastructure components (logical and physical) is one the important capabilities of a security framework.

NS-02: Software Defined Networking (SDN)

Software Defined Networking provides a greater flexibility in deployment and management of the networking devices (routers, switches, and so on). Along with these operational benefits, it provides better control over data flows, helping administrators thwart various denial of service attacks.

NS-03: Domain Name System (DNS) and Dynamic Host Configuration Protocol (DHCP)

The domain name system translates hostnames to IP addresses so names can be used when referring to unique addresses on the Internet. Protection mechanisms to protect against internal and Internet DNS attacks (for example, DNS poisoning) are required in a network.

NS-04: Network Time Protocol (NTP)

To record timestamps in security audit logs and systems logs, all information systems must synchronize their clocks to a master clock. This synchronization helps to ensure accuracy of the audit logs and aid in event correlation. Network time protocol can be utilized for this purpose.

NS-05: Network Service Management

Network management infrastructure frequently uses secure shell (SSH) and simple network management protocol (SNMP) to manage networking components at the enterprise level. These components must be hardened to protect them from attack and abuse.

NS-06: Firewall and Virtual Machine Firewall

Firewalls are utilized to restrict access from one network to another and enforce enterprise specific policies of acceptable actions on the network. A common firewall application is to separate an enterprise's internal network from the Internet. There are various types of firewalls (for example, packet filtering, stateful firewalls, and application proxy firewalls). As more and more information systems are virtualized, host-based or VM-based firewalls are used to isolate various VMs running on the same host.

NS-07: Network Intrusion Detection / Network Intrusion Prevention System (IDS / IPS)

Network intrusion detection systems (IDS) continuously scan the network and incoming data traffic for malicious activities. IDS logs malicious events in a security log to investigate a malicious session after the fact. Network intrusion prevention (IPS) enforces predefined network policies to prevent malicious events from taking place. Some of the commercially available products combine IDS and IPS into a single system referred to as intrusion detection and prevention system (IDPS).

NS-08: Wireless Networking (Wi-Fi)

Wireless technology enables devices to connect to a private network or the Internet without needing physical cables. Because wireless communications can be listened to by anyone within range, wireless networks are vulnerable to snooping, monitoring, and unauthorized connection. This capability involves securing wireless networking against potential attack.

NS-09: Packet Intercept and Capture

Network packet intercept and capture is a process of capturing and examining traffic on a network segment. This process examines protocols and their content for appropriateness. The captured information is logged for further analysis by users or tools. There is a wide variety of packet interceptors available in the market. Network engineers can use network protocol analyzers to understand network performance or read information contained in the data packets.

NS-10: Secure Sockets Layer (SSL) Intercept

With the advent of sophisticated cyberattacks, new products were developed to fill the gap identified in detection of outgoing encrypted traffic. It was long assumed that encrypted traffic originating within the boundaries of an enterprise must be necessary and not warrant further examination. Attackers have taken advantage of this false sense of security. There have been many security incidents where critical data was transmitted to the hacker's machines via an encrypted channel using a rogue digital certificate. SSL interceptors fill this security gap by examining encrypted connections for malicious traffic. To work, the interceptor needs the current digital certificate from the host to decrypt the traffic.

NS-11: Network Access Control (NAC)

Network access control is a technology that verifies security posture (for example, patching level, malicious software, anti-virus, encryption strength, and so forth) before it grants network access permission. This technology is commonly used in an enterprise's internal network to keep unauthorized computers from connecting to the enterprise's network. In some cases, NAC is used as part of a remote access solution, such as virtual private network.

NS-12: Virtual Private Networking (VPN) and Internet Protocol Security (IPSec)

VPN is a technology that provides the ability to extend an enterprise's internal networking resources to external or remote users in a secure manner. There are two commonly used protocols to deploy this technology: secure sockets layer (SSL) and IPSec. Both protocols may be combined with two-factor authentication (for example, smart card or public key infrastructure [PKI] token) for authentication and encryption of the communication channel.

NS-13: Network Traffic Analysis (NTA)

Network Traffic Analysis is the examination of the volume of traffic generated. There is no need for in-depth packet inspection. The goal is to monitor the network to determine if there a significant event happening or going to happen based on the network traffic patterns.

NS-14: Network Data Analytics (NDA)

Network Data Analytics analyze network traffic trends, network availability, planned outage impacts, and network traffic. NDA is utilized in combination with other analysis tools to create a comprehensive model of various network threats. NDA's goal is, in part, to predict the next big network-based attack.

Application Security (AS)

Application security provides for the security of enterprise applications using security technologies that are appropriate to and tailored for the protection of those applications and the protocols they utilize. Application security is focused on protecting those applications by understanding the application and its protocols inner workings (such as HyperText Markup Language (HTML) used in web pages or Simple Mail Transfer Protocol (SMTP) used for e-mail). Application Security helps protect applications from attacks that exploit (1) vulnerabilities in the applications to take control of servers delivering those applications, or (2) communications of web application protocols to deliver malicious payloads into an enterprise. An important aspect of application security is procedural. For example, developers need to use appropriate development methodologies to help ensure custom business applications are not vulnerable to known exploits such as buffer overflows, structured query language (SQL) injection, or cross-site scripting.

AS-01: E-mail Security

E-mail is one of the most common forms of business and personal communication. It is relatively easy to compromise an e-mail message by spoofing, tampering, phishing, and so on. A good security program deploys security capabilities to protect e-mail systems and the messages they carry. Some of the e-mail security protection capabilities deployed include spam filtering, e-mail block, e-mail redirect, custom malware detection signatures, scanning of attachments for viruses or malware, e-mail encryption, e-mail authentication, content filtering, and e-mail archiving.

AS-02: Webshell Detection

A webshell is a special web page that attackers install on a compromised web server to give them a back door to execute commands inside the enterprise. With a webshell, attackers can perform reconnaissance, run commands, transfer files, connect to databases, and exfiltrate data. Because it is only a single web page buried in a site that may contain hundreds or thousands of pages, a webshell can be very difficult to find. Webshell detection involves monitoring web servers to catch the installation or operation of a webshell back door.

AS-03: Application Firewalls

Application firewalls are sometimes known as application-level proxies. These firewalls inspect data packets and make decisions based on the contents of the data packets. As the name suggests, the firewalls work at the application layer. One proxy is usually required per application.

AS-04: Database Firewalls

Database firewalls allow application servers to connect to database servers on specific structured query language (SQL) ports. To detect and prevent malicious code executions like SQL injection attacks or cross-site scripting/forgery attacks, database firewalls can be programmed to inspect the content of the packet at the SQL code level.

AS-05: Forward Proxy and Web Filters

Forward proxy handles outgoing requests from internal computers accessing the Internet. For example, a forward proxy masks and handles web request traffic on behalf of internal web browsers. Web filters (or web proxies) are utilized to enforce web content filtering. Simply stated, web filters enforce an enterprise's acceptable use policies while browsing or using the Internet.

AS-06: Reverse Proxy

Reverse proxy masks the internal network from direct access by Internet users. It handles requests for internal resources from the Internet. Reverse proxy is typically placed between internal web servers and the Internet. Reverse proxies can also handle content filtering and some load balancing. Reverse proxy protects internal web servers from being directly accessed and possibly attacked by Internet-based clients.

AS-07: Data Leakage Protection (DLP)

DLP ensures data in the enterprise is protected from unauthorized access and, ultimately, theft and exfiltration during an attack. Once the sensitive data (enterprise propriety or regulatory) is identified, DLP tools can alert if it transits the network in an unauthorized manner.

AS-08: Secure Application and Database Software Development

A robust software development methodology using secure development practices (such as Microsoft's Security Development Life Cycle and Threat Modeling) is required in security programs. No matter how fortified an enterprise's perimeter is, if the application has known vulnerabilities, it is easy for a malicious actor to bypass the security controls. Common security standards exist to guide software developers on how to create secure applications.

AS-09: Software Code Vulnerability Analysis

As part of secure application and database software development (see AS-08), the enterprise should also consider code analysis tools. Application, database, and operating system-level vulnerability scanners are available in the marketplace. Some of these tools have built-in code review and code library capabilities.

Endpoint, Server, and Device Security (ESDS)

Endpoint, server, and device security involves protecting endpoint computing devices (for example, personal computers, servers, and mobile devices) from attack and detecting when those endpoint defenses have been breached. These security areas may need to be considered separately due to the differences between how endpoints are used compared to servers. However, the technologies used to protect endpoints and servers are common to all platforms, including hardened computer images, computer policies, endpoint security suites (such as anti-virus, anti-malware, host firewall, and intrusion detection) and policies for access controls, privilege management, and auditing and forensics.

Mobile devices present an interesting twist on endpoint security since they use different operating systems that are different from those of personal computers and require a different set of tools. In addition, they are frequently personally owned, which makes allowing mobile devices very similar to allowing employees to connect to enterprise systems from non-corporate home computers. Regardless of whether the endpoint is mobile or personally-owned, the goal of endpoint security is to prevent attackers from taking administrative control of endpoints that store enterprise data, detect attempts to take administrative control, or maliciously access data through such devices, as well as to facilitate investigation of incidents when compromises of systems or data are suspected.

Endpoint security can NEVER be assumed to be 100-percent effective, as administrators make mistakes, viruses proliferate, and zero-day vulnerabilities are obtainable by well-resourced attackers. However, the goal of this functional area is to make it harder to compromise systems and to improve the effectiveness of detection and investigation of breaches when they do occur.

ESDS-01: Local Administrator Privilege Restrictions

Malware and viruses often require local administrator rights to install their payload (malicious code) on to a user computer. Restricting local administrator privileges to a computer helps reduce the threat exposure. Restrictions also protect the credentials from getting compromised should the user have systems administration privileges to other sensitive systems. Losing control of local administrator credentials puts an enterprise's infrastructure at significant risk.

ESDS-02: Computer Security and Logging Policies

Computer security and logging is the method where computer systems' activities are recorded so malicious activities can be potentially identified and investigated. Security audit logging performs two critical functions. First, it is the method whereby malicious activity is detected, usually with pattern matching, correlating indicators of compromise, or other analytical intelligence. Second, it is the record that is used for investigating an incident and understanding the full extent of the activities that were performed and damage that was done.

ESDS-03: Endpoint and Media Encryption

Endpoint and media encryption provides a logical protection of the data stored on a computer or external storage media such as thumb drives. To protect sensitive regulatory data, encryption is required by law (for example, Health Insurance Portability and Accountability Act [HIPAA]). Encryption can render media unreadable to a malicious actor.

ESDS-04: Computer Access Controls

Computer access controls are the capabilities that protect users, systems, and related resources from unauthorized access. Access controls provide an enterprise the ability to manage access to protect confidentiality, integrity, and availability of resources. Computer access controls include identification, authorization, authentication, and accountability.

ESDS-05: Forensic Imaging Support for Investigations

Computer forensics is an art where electronic data (at rest or in transmission) is recovered and analyzed to support digital criminal investigations. There are specific guidelines for handling digital data so it can be admissible in the court of law. To help with evidence collection, forensic imaging support can provide for the scanning and recovery of files and data from enterprise computers.

ESDS-06: Virtual Desktop / Thin Clients

Virtual desktop (sometimes known as thin clients) makes it easy for an enterprise to secure endpoints without having to connect privately owned desktops or laptops to its enterprise network. This capability provides higher performance and availability of the desktop resources to end users. The virtual image is transportable across various devices and is kept current with latest security patches and updates.

ESDS-07: Mobile Device Management (MDM)

Mobile device management provides a secure method to access corporate e-mail, calendaring, and contacts on a personally owned mobile device, and it protects that data from malicious/non-secure mobile applications. This capability leverages a secure application that creates a protected container on the devices for storage of e-mail data and prevents data from moving from the protected container to other untrusted mobile applications.

ESDS-08: Anti-Virus / Anti-Malware

Viruses and malware are disruptive software designed by malicious actors to harm users' computers and the network infrastructure. This disruptive software has the potential to make an enterprise's network unavailable for considerable periods of time, thereby impacting business. Typically, anti-virus / anti-malware capabilities are installed on endpoints (for example, desktops and laptops) and servers (such as e-mails and file shares) to scan and destroy infected files.

ESDS-09: Application Whitelisting

Application whitelisting is a capability whereby an enterprise locks down key systems at the file-system level by not allowing the installation of any software; only pre-approved applications and programs are allowed to run. It contains a database of all the programs authorized to run on the computer and rejects all others.

ESDS-10: In-Memory Malware Detection

This capability involves special software to detect malware that is installed in the memory of the computer but not actually stored on the hard drive, where it might be caught by conventional anti-virus software. Malware may be installed into memory by special operating system functions that allow executable programs to be loaded directly into memory over the network, or may be injected into the operating system by malware exploiting an operating system vulnerability. In-memory malware detectors may rely on heuristics, pattern matching, or anomaly detection to notice when the computer operating system has been modified in an unauthorized or inappropriate manner.

ESDS-11: Host Firewall and Intrusion Detection

Host firewalls and intrusion detection systems are software applications installed on a host to restrict and inspect incoming and outbound traffic. These firewalls provide more insight into the data packet crossing the wire than a network-based firewall. Host firewalls and intrusion detection systems make decisions based on the contents of the packet. Often, host-based firewalls include the functionality of intrusion detection as well.

ESDS-12: "Gold Code" Software Images

Enterprises use master images of software to install operating systems onto endpoints and servers, and they distribute software for installation on enterprise computers when requested. These "gold code" software images and the processes for updating them must be protected, lest attackers modify them to include malware or vulnerabilities.

ESDS-13: Security Technical Implementation Guides (STIGs)

Out-of-the-box software and hardware is often unsecured. Before it is put into production, it has to be hardened by applying vendor recommended patches and configuration changes. Defense Information Security Agency (DISA) STIGs or Center for Internet Security (CIS) hardening guides can be utilized for this purpose.

ESDS-14: Always-on Virtual Private Networking (VPN)

Always-on VPN is an operating system feature where the client computer always connects to the enterprise network via VPN. This connection takes place even when the client is directly connected to the Internet, like from a home network or coffee shop. This feature ensures that the client is always protected by the enterprise's network security perimeter.

ESDS-15: File Integrity and Change Monitoring

File integrity and change monitoring periodically scans the file systems of protected computers and detects when files in those file systems have been modified. This protection is useful for detecting unauthorized changes that might be made by malware, inside attackers, or careless systems administrators.

Identity, Authentication, and Access Management (IAAM)

Identity, authentication, and access management provides for electronic identities of enterprise users throughout their tenures as authorized enterprise users from provisioning, re-certification, and ultimately de-provisioning, along with management of access controls and enterprise reports for audit and compliance.

IAAM-01: Identity Life Cycle Management

Identity life cycle management is the management of user identity (for example, user accounts, digital certificates, roles, profiles, user groups, user memberships, and physical access cards) in an enterprise to ensure that user identity is provisioned, de-provisioned, and re-certified in a timely fashion. It is important that an enterprise has a robust audit trail validating this life cycle at each step of the process.

IAAM-02: Enterprise Directory

Enterprise directory provides administrators with the ability to manage identification, authorization, and access control for information technology resources available on the enterprise network. Enterprise directory can centrally manage user access across the enterprise's digital resources.

IAAM-03: Multi-factor Authentication

Multi-factor authentication is also referred to as strong authentication. Multi-factor authentication means that more than one type of authentication factor is required to access a resource. Authentication factors include something you know (for example, password, pin, pass phrases), something you have (such as a token device or smart card), and something you are (for example, biometrics). Two Factor Authentication (also known as 2FA) means that two of the three factors listed above are required for authentication.

IAAM-04: Privilege Management and Access Control

Privilege management and access control capabilities enforce "least access" required to perform a function. By providing on-demand privilege access and restricting it from regular use, an enterprise has better assurance and control over its sensitive access. Tools with this capability can perform automated password changes per enterprise's policy, keep the sensitive passwords in a secure vault, and release the password to pre-approved users or applications.

IAAM-05: Identity and Access Audit Trail and Reporting

An audit trail provides security professionals and law enforcement personnel with a capability to trace the interaction of a user with an information system. It is important to have audit trail of user actions to support regulatory compliance and support investigations. Many application, appliances, databases, and operating systems provide auditing and reporting capabilities. It is prudent to review those capabilities and turn on auditing per enterprise's policies, report anomalies on a regular basis, and design protection mechanisms to save audit trails from accidental deletion or tampering.

IAAM-06: Lightweight Directory Access Protocol (LDAP)

The LDAP protocol is the most common enterprise directory protocol (see IAAM-02), and is required by many enterprise application systems and network operating systems. LDAP identifies users and other objects using text strings called distinguished names, and then associates additional data with them using attributes. User attributes can store a wide variety of identity data, including account names, authentication credentials, group memberships for access control, and personal data like phone numbers, e-mail addresses, and photographs.

IAAM-07: Kerberos, RADIUS, 802.1x

Kerberos is an authentication protocol. It works based on shared secret or keys (symmetric keys). It is a common authentication method in a client / server model. Remote authentication dial-in user service (RADIUS) is a network protocol providing authentication, authorization, and auditing services to remote users. This protocol is used to assign various profiles and respective networking resources to remote users. Most Internet service providers use this protocol to authenticate their subscribers. 802.1x is an IEEE standard for port-based network access control (PNAC). It provides authentication and authorization services until full connectivity is established with a remote user.

IAAM-08: Federated Authentication

Federated authentication provides identity portability to integrate seamlessly across multiple companies or networks. It provides flexibility to integrate different directory services (see IAAM-02) without the need for replicating the directory contents. E-commerce and business-to-business (B2B) sites typically utilize this capability.

IAAM-09: Security Assertion Markup Language (SAML)

SAML is the authentication technology behind Federated Authentication (see IAAM-08). SAML makes it possible to exchange authentication and authorization information among various domain services (see IAAM-02). SAML provides a single sign-on user experience.

Data Protection and Cryptography (DPC)

Data protection and cryptography is an increasingly important functional area, as cryptography has gone from the specialized niche of protecting military communications to the general purpose realm of protecting almost every aspect of Internet communications and commerce through secure sockets layer (SSL) and strong authentication technologies (for example, digital certificates, smart cards, and one-time password tokens). Even in the absence of such advanced technologies, it is important to remember that the simplest authentication mechanism—username and password—employs its own cryptography in the form of a simple shared secret key, the password. This functional area oversees the rapid changes in cryptographic standards and technologies, ensuring enterprises only use capabilities that are secure against rapidly changing threats. In addition, it protects enterprise keys through secure databases, access controls, and the deployment of specialized cryptographic technologies like smart cards, trusted platform modules, and hardware security modules to ensure critical cryptographic keys cannot be lost or stolen.

DPC-01: Secure Sockets Layer (SSL) and Transport Layer Security (TLS)

SSL provides encryption capability to secure client / server communication. A common use case is securing web server connections with users (for example, online banking, stock brokerage web sites, and web e-mail).

TLS is the open standard version of SSL. TLS can also be utilized to encrypt a communication channel between client (user) and server.

DPC-02: Digital Certificates (Public Key Infrastructure [PKI])

PKI provides e-mail message protection, authentication, non-repudiation, digital signature, remote access authentication, and so forth. PKI uses multiple components (including certificate authority, digital certificates, registration authority, keys, and users) that work in concert to provide these listed services.

DPC-03: Key Hardware Protection (Smart Cards, Trusted Platform Modules [TPMs], and Hardware Security Modules [HSMs])

Key hardware protection aligns with the multi-factor authentication described in IAAM-03. A smart card is a credit-card-sized card with a built-in microchip that provides identification, authentication, data storage and low-scale processing capabilities. Such cards are usually used as a second factor in the authentication process. TPM is a microchip installed on the motherboard of computers to provide dedicated security-related processing. They are designed to hold sensitive passwords, process keys, and perform cryptographic functions. HSMs are devices or appliances that are designed from the ground up to preform critical cryptographic functions and to safeguard digital keys for an enterprise's authentication service. HSMs are commonly used to support PKI service.

DPC-04: One-Time Password (OTP) and Out-of-Band (OOB) Authentication

OTP is a one-time use password that is set up during initial password reset or new account creation. OTP is a safety mechanism to protect misuse of user accounts. Another common OTP use case is a token that generates OTPs for logging into an enterprise's network or web sites. OOB authentication mechanisms utilize two different channels to verify the identity and password of a user. OOB reduces the risk of "man-in-the-middle" attacks. OOB also meets the requirement of two-factor authentication as discussed in IAAMC-03.

DPC-05: Key Life Cycle Management

Cryptographic key life cycle management is the heart of any enterprise's program. Key life cycle management provides capabilities to generate, store, and destroy cryptographic keys.

DPC-06: Digital Signature

Digital signature is a cryptographic signature identifying individual users or processes for achieving non-reputation and authentication. Digital signatures are commonly used in electronic signing of financial documents or e-mails.

DPC-07: Complex Passwords

A user credential used for authentication commonly has two pieces of information: (1) user ID (in other words, user identifier) and (2) password. The user ID is considered public information—hence, the password must be secured. Password complexity policies and enforcement are required to protect passwords from brute force attack (see DPC-09).

DPC-08: Data Encryption and Tokenization

Data encryption is used to protect data at rest from being read by an attacker who does not have the encryption key. Tokenization involves replacing data with a scrambled version that uses the same format and can be handled by the application even though it has been scrambled. For example, a social security number might be 123-45-6789 and then gets tokenized to produce 759-54-6134. While the result looks like a legitimate number, it is actually an encrypted value.

DPC-09: Brute Force Attack Detection

Brute force attack is frequently performed on passwords. A malicious actor tries different password combinations until a correct password is found. Simple detection mechanisms include intrusion detection systems (IDS) and monitoring system security logs for incorrect logins.

DPC-10: Digital Rights Management (DRM)

Digital rights management can be used to protect sensitive data. It works by encrypting the data contained within files. Users who wish to read the files must authenticate with a central server to obtain the decryption key.

Monitoring, Vulnerability, and Patch Management (MVPM)

This functional area is operational in nature. It focuses on maintaining the enterprise's security on an ongoing basis and actively detecting incidents against security systems. Security monitoring frequently involves cybersecurity systems feeding their security log data into a central Security Information and Event Management (SIEM) system for tracking and analysis. This tracking needs to include not only security alerts, but also change management, as many security incidents result from or result in unauthorized changes to system configurations. Vulnerabilities against the enterprise and patches / fixes to address those vulnerabilities must be constantly managed and responded to, sometimes quite quickly. Perhaps the most interesting capability of this functional area is a management one. Events and vulnerabilities should be constantly evaluated and managed against operational impacts. Using risk management techniques, responses should be designed to minimize disruptions to the enterprise.

MVPM-01: Operational Performance Monitoring

Operational performance monitoring protects information technology resources by ensuring systems are operating properly, and detecting when operational anomalies occur that may be security-related. There are various tools to monitor the health and security of network resources and critical systems. Some enterprises have a security operations center (SOC) and performance-monitoring (for example, system up / down check) teams performing this function.

MVPM-02: System and Network Monitoring

System and network monitoring observes the enterprise's security on an ongoing basis and actively detects incidents against those security systems. Since alerts can only be detected from systems that are monitored, this monitoring is the first step to detecting attacks in real time.

MVPM-03: System Configuration Change Detection

One of the clear indications of a system security posture change is an unauthorized change to a system's configuration. File integrity monitoring or file system baseline monitoring provide the ability to detect suspicious changes that are not related to legitimate patching or system update activities.

MVPM-04: Privilege and Access Change Detection

Privileged access to applications, databases, and operating systems are the most sought cyberattack targets after user accounts. Protection of these privileges should be included in any security program. Any changes to privileges must be monitored and followed up with a validation check (audit).

MVPM-05: Log Aggregation

A system log captures a wide variety of information and events related to system security and health. Since typical IT environments have many systems supporting various applications and databases, a significant quantity of logs are generated. These logs should be collected centrally for analysis and troubleshooting. Typically, tools in this space have data indexing capabilities for faster searches, reporting, and plug-ins to other monitoring tools.

MVPM-06: Data Analytics

Cybersecurity data analytics is a method to organize data related to threats, vulnerabilities, and security logs so such data is easy to find. Data analytics help with the categorization of security relevant data in a structured form. This structured data can be used for predicting the next wave of attacks, analyzing trends in various attacks, or analyzing changes in the security posture of various systems. Data analytics can sometimes be performed by a SIEM (see MVPM-07).

MVPM-07: Security Information and Event Management (SIEM)

SIEM, also known as security event management (SEM), gathers logs from many of the enterprise's servers and security infrastructure to facilitate security incident detection and investigation. SIEM provides tools to correlate the collected data for analytics capabilities. Capabilities MVPM-05 and MVPM-06 are often part of the SIEM solution. One of SIEM's major goals is to provide correlation capability, whereby a cybersecurity analyst can see the complete picture of a cybersecurity incident from a single integrated console.

MVPM-08: Network and Computer Vulnerability Scanning

Network and computer vulnerability scanning are processes that identify vulnerabilities in an enterprise's IT environment. These processes can be automated to perform the scans on a periodic basis or executed on an ad hoc basis. Administrative or privileged credentials are recommended when scanning an environment to get the complete vulnerability results. Usually, vulnerability scanning is coupled with patch management (see MVPM-10) to complete the scan and patch cycle.

MVPM-09: Penetration Testing

Penetration testing (also known as pen testing) is a user request-based security assessment of a network, server, database, or web site with the intent to find the vulnerabilities, exploit them to demonstrate real-world hacking, and recommend remediation actions. Pen testing differs from vulnerability scanning because no prior system information is provided to the tester. A pen tester thinks and works like a hacker to find the vulnerabilities. Typically, the scope of this testing is limited to a few critical systems as it is time-consuming and may disrupt the business.

MVPM-10: Patch Management and Deployment

Patch management is part of the remediation for the vulnerability scanning program/process. Note that a security program is incomplete without a robust patch-management process. Many software vendors periodically release patches to address issues related to performance and security. However, it is up to the enterprise's security program to take advantage of these critical patches and apply them to their systems in a timely manner.

MVPM-11: Rogue Network Device Detection

Every network device is assigned a media access address (MAC) and often an IP address. These addresses are the primary means whereby a network communicates with various devices. There are network detection and authorization capabilities (for example, network access control [NAC]) that work with other authentication services to allow or disallow certain devices on the network. These systems can also detect the connection of unauthorized or rogue devices, such as from publicly-accessible kiosks or conference rooms.

MVPM-12: Rogue Wireless Access Point Detection

Wireless access points take an enterprise's private network beyond the protection of its building's walls. Like detecting hardwired network devices discussed in MVPM-11, some network infrastructures also include features to detect rogue wireless access points. Security uses the term "war-driving" to describe its activities to detect rogue wireless access points in a building.

MVPM-13: Honeypots / Honeynets / Honeytokens

Honeypots, honeynets, and honeytokens are mechanisms used to entice would-be malicious actors to a dummy vulnerable computer or network segment to study the actors' behavior. Analyzing this behavior helps security administrators tighten critical systems or network segments to repel real attacks, and it also aids in finding the origins of attacks. Honeynets consist of an entire subnet of honeypot systems connected together to detect network-level attack traffic. Honeytokens are data stored in applications that are used to detect an unauthorized release or abuse of application data. For example, a dummy social security number may be placed in a database and then network sensors are configured to detect that dummy social security number traveling over the network or if it is placed on the Internet.

MVPM-14: Security Operations Center (SOC)

SOC is a function of an enterprise's security team to monitor the configuration, performance, and security posture of an enterprise's information technology environment in order to satisfy regulatory compliance, contractual requirements, and enterprise policies. It is typically configured for 24/7 operations with clear responsibilities and escalation paths defined.

High Availability, Disaster Recovery, and Physical Protection (HADRPP)

High availability, disaster recovery, and physical protection (HADRPP) makes services highly available, even in the event of unforeseen disasters. HADRPP also provides physical protection of IT assets, which is critical to availability as well as confidentiality and integrity of enterprise data. To be available, IT services must serve the enterprise user community in accordance with the business needs, and must be robust enough to continue delivering that service when disasters occur.

HADRPP-01: Clustering

Clustering is a logical grouping of servers that provides for failover in the event that one of the servers fails or has to be taken off line. Clustering, also known as a server farm, can also provide for load balancing and increased compute capacity.

HADRPP-02: Load Balancing, Global Server Load Balancing (GSLB)

The concept of load balancing is to distribute the computing load across multiple computers or servers joined in a cluster (see HADRPP-01). Load balancing provides greater redundancy and availability of services by distributing the load when the demand increases. GSLB takes the load balancing concept to a larger level and applies it to geographically separated data centers. This capability is very commonly used by e-commerce web sites or social media sites to achieve high availability of their sites.

HADRPP-03: Network Failover, Subnet Spanning

Network failover capability provides network redundancy by switching to a redundant network if the primary network fails. Most of the network switching is done via automated tools. Subnet spanning involves configuring networks so that a single Ethernet subnet spans across multiple locations. Subnet spanning is a valuable high-availability technique since it allows computers at multiple sites to act like they are in a single site and protects against loss of one or the other site.

HADRPP-04: Virtual Machine Snapshots and Cloning

The virtual machine snapshot capability takes a digital, in-time snapshot of a virtual machine and reverts back to that state when needed. This capability functions as a recovery tool and provides users with the ability to discard corrupt system image(s) and restore back to the last clean image of a machine. Cloning is a process of taking an image of a live virtual machine to create another machine with a very similar configuration. This capability is frequently utilized in server farms where a pool or cluster of servers with similar configuration is required.

HADRPP-05: Data Mirroring and Replication

Data mirroring is a concept of duplicating the data exactly from its primary site or machine to a remote or secondary site. Primary and secondary sites are usually separated geographically. If the primary site goes down, the secondary site is able to continue to function and provide service without disruption. Replication copies data from the primary site to the secondary site. Depending on the type of replication (synchronous or asynchronous), there can be a lag in the data copy and service availability.

HADRPP-06: Backups and Backup Management

A backup is the process of copying data with the intent of making it available in an event of data loss. Backups provide insurance against system corruption due to user error or malicious actors. Backup management oversees the life cycle of backup data from when it is created until it is destroyed, including cryptographic keys that protect backup data at rest. It manages the shelf life of backed-up data including scheduling, testing, and quality checks for the backup media and data stored on it.

HADRPP-07: Off-Site Storage

To reduce the risk of losing all data due to a catastrophic event, most enterprises maintain an off-site storage site to store backed up data. These sites could have a link to the primary site to keep the backed-up data as real-time as possible or a low-tech solution of storing backed-up tapes in a fireproof safe in another facility. In either case, the key is to have geographic distance between the primary site and the off-site location.

HADRPP-08: Facilities Protection

Facilities protection has its own set of challenges with regards to man-made (for example, intrusion, theft, and sabotage) and environmental threats (such as fire, flood, and earthquake). A comprehensive facilities protection plan includes consideration for neighborhoods, crime rates, proximity to fire, police and medical centers, major highways, and the facilities' natural disaster area ratings.

HADRPP-09: Physical Access Controls

Physical access controls are deployed to protect against, malicious actors gaining access to a protected facility. The access controls are also deployed to monitor and manage the flow of visitors and employees. Locks (such as electronic locks and manual locks), fences, lighting, and presence of an on-duty guard play an important role in a secure physical access control design.

HADRPP-10: Physical Security Monitoring

Access control monitoring systems, closed-circuit TV, intrusion detection systems, sensors, and access control audit logs are all parts of a good physical security monitoring system.

Incident Response (IR)

Incident response involves responding when monitoring reveals evidence of malicious activity in the enterprise. Unlike ongoing monitoring, incident response is event-driven and only occurs when monitoring reveals that an incident has actually occurred. When an incident response process is invoked, a number of activities need to occur in order to identify the activity, contain it, and ultimately remediate the breach and restore normal operations. Incident response then feeds back into the monitoring process using indicators of compromise that help identify current or new incidents. Incident response also serves a strategic cyberdefense purpose by providing feedback to the major IT functions of (1) Architecture, (2) Engineering, and (3) Operations. Such feedback helps to identify weaknesses in enterprise security and provides short- and long-term remediation advice to address those weaknesses.

IR-01: Threat Information

In a risk assessment process, having current threat information aids in calculating risk accurately. Threat information is available from various public security forums (for example, Cybersecurity Innovation Forum).

IR-02: Incident Tracking

Incident tracking is part of the incident life cycle. It provides a structured methodology for handling incidents. Incidents may be tracked by using security information and event management (SIEM) tools. Enterprise security can perform data analytics using the collected data to identify various trends.

IR-03: Forensic Tools

Forensic tools and methodologies are used in digital crime investigations. The investigation methodology includes (1) proper data-handling procedures, (2) evidence collection without destroying it, and (3) data analysis. Forensic experts utilize toolkits that include (1) tags and labels, (2) computer hardware tools, and (3) transportation bags and supplies to protect the collected evidence.

IR-04: Computer Imaging

Computer imaging or disk imaging is a technique to make an exact copy of the original disk for forensics without destroying the evidence.

IR-05: Indicators of Compromise (IOCs)

Indicators of compromise are used by investigators to identify compromised computers on the network. IOCs can be samples of software code, commands or command sequences, network communications patterns, or any other indicators of attacker activity that can be documented and tracked as part of an investigation.

IR-06: Black Hole Server

A black hole server is used to intercept traffic believed to be malicious so the traffic does not reach its destination and so it can be analyzed to understand attacker patterns.

IR-07: Regulatory / Legal Coordination

Digital crime investigation follows a documented procedure for identification, collection (chain of custody), analysis, safeguarding, and presentation of evidence in the court of law. If these procedures are not followed per legal requirements, a court can disregard the evidence collected, which may jeopardize a case.

Asset Management and Supply Chain (AMSC)

Asset management provides for the accounting of enterprise assets, procurement information associated with them, their life cycle and changes, as well as ensuring orderly and secure disposal without compromise of enterprise data or security.

Asset management is an essential prerequisite for endpoint and server security controls to be effective because it ensures assets in the enterprise are accounted for over their life cycle, made compliant with enterprise policies when they are put into service—such as to comply with network security, endpoint security, and other enterprise policies—and it ensures enterprise data is properly disposed of or protected when assets are finally disposed of at the end of their useful lives. Finally, when dealing with high-grade threats, asset management may even have to consider supply chain issues, such as ensuring IT systems are obtained from trustworthy suppliers or properly checked for deliberate espionage activities prior to being placed into service.

AMSC-01: Asset Management Databases

An asset management database tracks enterprise assets from their acquisition through their disposal, and should include points of contact and systems administrators for all systems. The asset management database is critical to the incident response effort, because it allows incident responders to identify points of contact associated with compromised systems.

AMSC-02: Configuration Management Databases (CMDB)

A configuration management database is a database of enterprise configuration items and their configuration parameters. Such parameters might include server names and network addresses. This database supports the configuration management and change management processes.

AMSC-03: Change Management Databases

A change management database tracks changes to enterprise IT systems. It ensures changes are properly reviewed and approved prior to implementation. Unauthorized changes may be malicious and should be detected and investigated.

AMSC-04: Software Inventory and License Management

Software inventory is required to manage vendor contracts and relationships. Software inventory is required to (1) manage software licenses, (2) receive critical security patches, and (3) pass vendor licensing audits.

AMSC-05: Supplier Certification Processes

Enterprises should review their suppliers before they sign supplier service contracts. It is a common practice to vet suppliers for their security controls along with the (1) functionality assessment, (2) cost savings calculations, and (3) fit-gap analysis. It is recommended to review suppliers' controls on an annual basis. An enterprise can accomplish this review via a third-party audit report from the supplier. Representative audits include (1) Sarbanes-Oxley, (2) SSAE 16, (3) Systrust, and (3) ISO 27001 certification.

AMSC-06: Secure Disposal, Recycling, and Data Destruction

Digital and printed data must be disposed of in a secure manner, to comply with enterprise data retention policies and e-discovery regulations. Data disposal policies need to cover printed and digital media, portable media like DVDs and thumb drives, and fixed media like hard drives. Failed hard drives present an interesting challenge for secure data disposal. Backups must also be considered and policy must be set for their retention and ultimate disposal. There are many vendors in this marketplace who can handle these requirements securely.

Policy, Audit, E-Discovery, and Training (PAET)

Policy, audit, e-discovery, and training provide policy oversight of controls and audit of their effectiveness, support for legal e-discovery activities, and training of staff in proper security policies and practices. Among other things, this functional area accounts for compliance requirements and mapping security controls to meet those requirements. It also oversees the security control audit program, which is necessary to review periodically preventive, detective, and monitoring controls to verify their operation and effectiveness.

PAET-01: Governance, Risk, and Compliance (GRC), with Reporting

Governance, risk, and compliance (GRC) is the process of managing and measuring a cybersecurity program's performance. This process generally includes tracking risk mitigation efforts and reporting compliance against external requirements and regulations, such as Sarbanes-Oxley, Payment Card Industry (PCI), or Health Insurance Portability and Accountability Act (HIPAA). When automated tools are used for GRC, they can often provide reporting against key performance indicators, compliance frameworks, and other metrics.

PAET-02: Compliance and Control Frameworks (SOX, PCI, and so forth)

As explained in PAET-01, compliance is the fulfillment of legal, regulatory, or customer-driven requirements in performing a service. There are various control frameworks that were developed to meet specific compliance needs. Not all compliance security frameworks provide a complete solution for protecting an enterprise's infrastructure. For example, SOX requirements are focused on preventing fraud. As such, they focus on integrity of data and not confidentiality or availability, which are also important in a robust security program.

PAET-03: Audit Frameworks

Audit frameworks are used to audit preventive, detective, and forensic controls to ensure they are operating properly. Frameworks organize the audit process to ensure all controls are evaluated and that the business impacts of the audit results are understood. Audit frameworks should include deficiency tracking and management to ensure deficiencies identified during audit are tracked and remediated in a timely fashion.

PAET-04: Customer Certification and Accreditation (C&A)

Certification is the formal process of testing a system or software against certain predefined security criteria or security requirements. Accreditation is the formal approval process to allow a system to go into production. The federal government mandates a certification and accreditation (C&A) process via the Federal Information Security Management Act of 2002 (FISMA). Periodic C&A is required on many systems supporting US government business services.

PAET-05: Policy and Policy Exception Management

Cybersecurity policy is a contract between security and the business, and serves as the foundation for the enterprise cybersecurity program. Security policies must be developed, approved, revised and retired over their life cycle. Exceptions to security policies must be approved and tracked for periodic review and re-approval. This capability involves managing security policies and exceptions to ensure their proper approval and periodic review.

PAET-06: Risk and Threat Management

Shon Harris (2013) defines threat as "any potential danger that is associated with the exploitation of vulnerability and risk is the likelihood of a threat agent exploiting vulnerability and the corresponding impact." Risk management is a function of an enterprise's senior leadership. Robust risk management includes good practices for (1) identification of threats and vulnerabilities, (2) determination of risk likelihood and impact, (3) calculation of risk (qualitative versus quantitative), (4) recommended remediation, and (5) documentation of risk acceptance decisions.

PAET-07: Privacy Compliance

As businesses are moving toward the digitization of personally identifiable information (for example, SSN, date of birth, bank account information) and health records, privacy is getting greater scrutiny. Along with an enterprise's policies for protecting the privacy of its employees, there are state and federal laws (for example, Health Insurance Portability and Accountability Act [HIPAA], Gramm-Leach-Bliley Act [GLBA]), and industry specific standards (for example, Payment Card Industry Data Security Standard [PCI DSS]) requiring enterprise compliance. For many enterprises, meeting the privacy compliance requirements is required to do business.

PAET-08: E-Discovery Tools

E-discovery is a process initiated by an enterprise's legal department to support investigation, litigation, or evidence collection. E-discovery involves finding electronic evidence along with its meta-data (such as username, date, and timestamp) to help with a legal case. An enterprise's data retention policies and the forensic processes support the legal team in e-discovery. There are many e-discovery forensic tools in the marketplace.

PAET-09: Personnel Security and Background Checks

Personnel security and background checks are also known as human resource (HR) security. Background checks are often performed in the first phase of employee engagement during on-boarding. Background checks may include pre-employment checks such as previous employment verification, drug testing, and Internet and social media reputation. Often the recruiter, hiring manager, and HR representatives are involved in on-boarding.

PAET-10: Security Awareness and Training

The enterprise should provide cybersecurity training to its employees to ensure they are aware of their responsibilities with regard to cybersecurity. Cybersecurity training should include training on the enterprise's policies and cybersecurity threats to the organization and its business. In addition, specialized training should be provided to employees with special cybersecurity responsibilities such as executives, systems administrators, application developers, and incident responders.

References

Casey, Eoghan. *Handbook of Digital Forensics and Investigation.* Burlington, MA: Academic Press, 2009.

Conklin, William Arthur, Gregory White, and Dwayne Williams. *Principles of Computer Security: COMPTIA Security+ and Beyond, Second Edition.* New York, NY: McGraw-Hill Inc., 2010.

Harris, Shon. *CISSP All-in-One Exam Guide, Sixth Edition.* New York, NY: McGraw-Hill Inc., 2013.

■■■

Sample Cybersecurity Policy

A successful enterprise cybersecurity program begins with policy that is unambiguous, well organized, well maintained, and balances the enterprise's security needs against its business priorities. It is important to organize this policy so it is easy to write, understand, and maintain over time. Cybersecurity policy establishes the foundation upon which the enterprise's cybersecurity program is built, and represents a contract between the enterprise's cybersecurity practice and the business. Through cybersecurity policy, the business and cybersecurity agree on the ways and extents to which cybersecurity will be used in the business to implement and enforce protections of intellectual property and information system assets.

Policy is one of many documentation and institutional knowledge components that make for an effective cybersecurity program. From a documentation perspective, it is the *tip of the documentation pyramid*, as shown in Figure D-1.

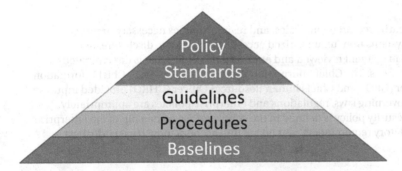

Figure D-1. *The enterprise information security policy is implemented through standards, guidelines, procedures, and baselines.*

This cybersecurity documentation pyramid consists of the following components:

- ***Policy***: High-level statement of principle or course of action governing enterprise information security.

- ***Standards***: Documents specifying standards for behavior, processes, configurations, or technologies to be used for enterprise cybersecurity.

- ***Guidelines***: Documents providing non-authoritative guidance on policy and standards for use by subordinate organizations.

- *Procedures*: Set of documents describing step-by-step or detailed instructions for implementing or maintaining security controls

- *Baselines*: Specific configurations for technologies and systems that are designed to provide for easy compliance with the established policy, standards, guidelines, and procedures

This appendix provides an example cybersecurity policy that can be used as a starting point for organizing an enterprise's policies using enterprise cybersecurity functional areas. By organizing an enterprise's policy into functional areas, policy can be well coordinated with the enterprise's personnel, budgets, technologies, IT life cycle, and cybersecurity assessments.

Consider this sample policy as a starting point for developing an enterprise's policy or policies. Do not consider the example policy as the only way to do things or the best way to do things. Standards and requirements change over time and what makes sense today will change as technologies, standards, and best practices continue to evolve. Each enterprise is different and will need to develop and evolve a cybersecurity program that makes sense for the enterprise.

The Policy

This document represents a sample cybersecurity policy for a notional enterprise requiring cybersecurity protections. This document can be used as a starting point for creating an enterprise policy that is organized using the 11 functional areas of enterprise cybersecurity.

Purpose

This security policy delineates security requirements, roles, and responsibilities necessary to protect enterprise data and information systems from unauthorized access, inappropriate disclosure, or compromise. Enterprise senior management reviewed and approved this policy that is disseminated to employees and relevant external parties. The Chief Information Security Officer (CISO), Chief Information Officer (CIO), Chief Privacy Officer (CPO), and Chief Human Resources Officer (CHRO) provided input and reviewed content to ensure governing laws, regulations and enterprise policies are appropriately incorporated. Furthermore, this security policy is defined in the context of the ownership of the enterprise (public versus private), legal regulatory requirements, and taking into account industry security best practices.

Scope and Applicability

This policy is applicable to all employees, temporary employees, contractors, and subsidiaries of the enterprise. The policy must be used to assess third-party suppliers who sign a contract to provide business services to the enterprise. This policy must also be used to assess the risk of conducting business. In accordance with enterprise policy and procedures, this policy is reviewed and adjusted as needed on an annual basis or more frequently.

Policy Statement

This policy

- complies with all legal, regulatory, and contractual obligations regarding protection of enterprise data. Where such requirements exceed the specific stipulations of this policy, the legal, regulatory, or contractual obligation shall take precedence.

- provides the authority to design, implement, and maintain security controls meeting the enterprise's standards with regards to protection of data in motion, at rest and processed by related information systems.

- ensures enterprise employees comply with the policy and undergo annual security training.

- informs employees that the enterprise monitors employee usage of information systems and hosted data without additional notice.

- requires that enterprise data be stored and manipulated on enterprise provided information systems or contracted systems that are approved for use and comply with this policy.

- implements a security incident reporting mechanism that captures incidents securely. Security incidents include policy violations, potential data breach, fraud, intrusions to information systems, and theft of hardware or data.

Compliance

Compliance lapses or failures with this policy may result in disciplinary action, such as removal or limiting access to the systems, termination of employment or contract, or unfavorable remarks in the employee performance review. The failures could have legal or regulatory ramifications with regard to federal, state, local, or international law. Compliance with the policy is conducted through executing periodic assessments by enterprise security, internal/external audits, or self-assessments.

Responsibilities

Following are the enterprise information security roles and responsibilities:

- *The Chief Information Officer (CIO)*

  - provides governance for enterprise IT systems and information with respect to security compliance with this policy.

  - publishes a common operating environment (COE) that defines the infrastructure standards incorporating security policies. Reviews and approves any low risk COE deviations or exceptions.

  - provides guidelines for on-and-off network information systems with respect to maintaining an information security plan complying with the enterprise's security policies.

- *The Chief Information Security Officer (CISO)*

  - acts as primary custodian of the information security risk assessment process. Reports identified risk to the enterprise risk committee and other key stakeholders.

  - keeps the enterprise security policy and procedures current for both digital and physical assets.

  - ensures identified system vulnerabilities are mitigated in a timely manner.

  - publishes up-to-date security standards and "gold disk" images for various infrastructure components.

  - acts as the incident lead during an active incident and is responsible for submitting a root cause report after the fact to the management.

  - enforces compliance with enterprise security policies by conducting periodic security checks and audits.

  - oversees internal and external reporting requirements (SOX, SEC, incidents, HIPAA).

  - interfaces with the legal department to support e-discovery measures as required by regulation, legislation, or litigation.

  - implements security awareness and training campaigns.

  - supports due diligence process for vetting security quality of suppliers, products, and subsidiaries during mergers and acquisitions.

- *Managers*

  - comply with enterprise's security policies by incorporating security practices, standards, and guidelines in various stages of IT development, implementation, operation, and retirement.

  - ensure annual security training is completed by the employees and non-employees (such as team members and subcontractors).

  - follow established incident reporting and escalation procedures.

  - periodically update standard operating procedures (SOPs) to ensure compliance with the enterprise policy and procedures.

- *Employees*

  - comply with the enterprise security policy and procedures.

  - complete the security training as required (for example, annual, semi-annual, and so forth).

  - follow established incident reporting and escalation procedures.

  - take reasonable care to protect their enterprise-provided equipment and access credentials.

- *Contracted third-parties, suppliers, temporary employees, and consultants*

  - must demonstrate they can meet and perform per enterprise policy and procedures.

  - provide the enterprise with required third-party audit reports as part of due care.

Policy Guidance by Functional Area

This cybersecurity policy is aligned with enterprise cybersecurity functional areas:

- Systems Administration
- Network Security
- Application Security
- Endpoint, Server, and Device Security
- Identity, Authentication, and Access Management
- Data Protection and Cryptography
- Monitoring, Vulnerability, and Patch Management
- High Availability, Disaster Recovery, and Physical Protection
- Incident Response
- Asset Management and Supply Chain
- Policy, Audit, E-Discovery, and Training

The following subsections provide cybersecurity policy guidance for the enterprise organized according to the preceding 11 functional areas.

Systems Administration

Systems administration is a critical function that provides management of sensitive enterprise information. If malicious actors compromise systems administration, they have access to enterprise data and information systems.

Systems administration activities must include the following:

- All systems administrator activities at the application, data, and operating system levels shall require authentication, and all logons to these systems shall be logged for audit.
- Systems administration protocols that are insecure or vulnerable to attack, including critical infrastructures of storage, computing, and data center management, shall only be used on isolated networks.
- Systems administration accounts shall require multi-factor authentication before administrative access is granted.
- Systems administrator activities shall be monitored for signs of inappropriate activity, and such signs shall be investigated within seven days of the occurrence.
- Systems administrator logons shall be recorded and audited weekly.
- Systems administrator access control lists shall be verified quarterly to ensure least privilege and separation of duties.
- All changes to systems administrator access control lists shall be recorded and audited weekly.

- Systems administration security configurations shall be reviewed on an annual basis, including re-validation of all policy exceptions.

- Systems administration preventive, detective, audit, and forensic controls shall be verified and tested for proper operation at least annually.

Network Security

Enterprise access to the Internet may expose enterprise data and information systems to other Internet users around the world. It is critical for the enterprise to protect the data and information systems from both internal and external malicious actors.

Network security activities must include the following:

- Network and network security infrastructure, including routers, switches, firewalls, and other components, shall be centrally managed and all logons shall be logged for audit.

- Network infrastructure administration activities shall be isolated from general business network traffic, and all administrative logons shall require credentials and multi-factor authentication.

- Networks that are publicly accessible or not physically protected, such as wireless networks and network connections in public spaces and conference rooms, shall use access control to ensure that only authorized users are permitted access.

- Networks shall have measures in place to detect and block network traffic that is known to be malicious, either through its protocols, its payloads, or its sources or destinations.

- Network traffic that is known to be malicious, either through automated or manual means, shall be blocked within one business day of detection.

- Access to enterprise networks from the Internet shall require multi-factor authentication. Access to privileged internal networks directly from the Internet shall not be permitted.

- Network traffic that is questionable and may be indicative of attacks shall be recorded and retained for 90 days to permit analysis and investigation after the fact.

- Secure network traffic shall not be excluded from analysis to identify and block malicious activity.

- Network infrastructure shall provide for basic services, including name service, host configuration, and time synchronization, and these services shall be hardened to protect them from attack or compromise.

- Network configuration changes shall require approval and shall be logged for audit and investigation, as required.

- Network security configurations shall be reviewed on an annual basis, and all network policy configurations and exceptions shall be re-validated annually.

- Network security preventive, detective, audit, and forensic controls shall be verified and tested for proper operation at least annually.

Application Security

Enterprise applications are vulnerable to attack from the Internet and attackers with insider access. Vulnerabilities and mistakes in coding and deployment of application systems are also factors. The enterprise must protect these systems from attack, and detect attacks and vulnerabilities in these systems when they occur.

Application security activities must include the following:

- Internet-facing application servers shall be protected from unauthorized configuration changes, and changes shall be logged and audited to catch the introduction of unauthorized "back doors" into these systems.

- Critical enterprise applications such as e-mail, voicemail, collaboration, and internal and external web services must be configured to prevent and detect attacks and exploits of vulnerabilities.

- For attacks and exploits that are not prevented or detected, adequate forensic logs must be maintained to permit audit and investigation after the fact.

- Communication between application components shall require authentication and shall be performed using secure protocols when performed over open networks. Where such protection is not feasible, network protection shall be utilized to protect these protocols and connections from attack.

- Applications that are sensitive to confidentiality concerns—processing data that is sensitive to breach—shall employ protection and detection to protect against data leakage.

- Applications that are sensitive to integrity concerns—potential data changes with financial or other repercussions—shall employ data integrity protections such as digital signatures and data modification audit trails to protect and detect against data changes.

- Applications that are sensitive to availability concerns shall employ high availability and rapid disaster recovery to protect them from denial of service attacks originating internally and from the Internet.

- Applications using custom source code shall have that source code analyzed using static code analysis at least quarterly, and all medium and higher vulnerabilities shall be addressed or remediated.

- Applications that are generally available on the Internet or enterprise internal networks shall be scanned for vulnerabilities using a credentialed vulnerability scanner monthly, and all medium or higher application vulnerabilities shall be addressed or remediated within 90 days of discovery.

- Applications that are found to be in violation of policy may be temporarily or permanently disconnected from the Internet and/or the enterprise network until the violation is remediated.

- Application security configurations shall be reviewed on an annual basis, including re-validation of all policy exceptions.

- Application security preventive, detective, audit, and forensic controls shall be verified and tested for proper operation at least annually.

341

Endpoint, Server, and Device Security

Endpoints such as desktops, laptops, mobile devices, servers, and other appliances must be hardened and secured using standard vendor recommended security guides/builds.

Endpoint, server, and device security activities must include the following:

- Local administrator account passwords or keys shall be unique to each endpoint. Enterprisewide endpoint management capabilities shall be considered to be critical security infrastructure and given appropriate protections.

- Enterprise endpoints and servers shall be configured from master images that are configuration-controlled and protected from tampering, changes, or the introduction of unauthorized or malicious code.

- Network-connected endpoint systems shall be configured to forward security logs— including administrator logon and security component configurations—to a central infrastructure for logging and correlation.

- All portable and removable endpoints—including personal computers, laptops, and mobile devices—shall have their built-in and removable media encrypted so it cannot be accessed without proper authentication to the device.

- Endpoint systems shall be configured for investigation of cyberincidents by installing forensic tools and configuring security logs to meet the needs of incident investigators.

- Endpoint systems shall be configured according to vendor-approved security guidelines for secure operating system installation and operation.

- Endpoint systems shall include endpoint protection to block and detect malicious software and network connectivity, as appropriate to the security posture of the system. Endpoints involved in high-security functions may be configured for more restrictive security than general-use endpoints.

- Endpoints and servers involved in operating or managing cybersecurity functions for the enterprise shall have application whitelisting installed and configured for maximum restrictiveness.

- Personal computers and mobile devices, when used for enterprise work, must include the ability to remotely delete enterprise data from the systems in the event of compromise. If this is not available, the system must include safeguards to ensure that enterprise data is not stored on the device in a persistent state.

- Security infrastructure endpoints shall include the ability to detect and alert on changes to security configuration files within one hour of them occurring.

- Servers directly connected to the Internet shall be scanned for operating system vulnerabilities using a credentialed vulnerability scanner monthly, and all medium or higher operating system vulnerabilities shall be addressed or remediated within 30 days of discovery.

- Endpoints found to be in violation of policy may be temporarily or permanently disconnected from the enterprise network until the violation is remediated.

- Endpoint server and device security configurations shall be reviewed on an annual basis, including re-validation of all policy exceptions.

- Endpoint, server, and device security preventive, detective, audit, and forensic controls shall be verified and tested for proper operation at least annually.

Identity, Authentication, and Access Management

Access to enterprise systems shall require unique network identities and authentication to systems shall use approved means. This access shall provide for unique identification of the user and non-repudiation of their activities. Accesses to data and systems shall be configured on an as-required basis according to need-to-know. Accesses and online identities that are no longer required shall be removed on a timely basis.

Identity, authentication, and access management activities must include the following:

- All production enterprise systems shall use centralized identity provisioning and de-provisioning, and centralized access management where possible. Cloud-based systems and Software-as-a-Service solutions used by the enterprise are subject to this policy as well as on premise systems.

- Identity systems shall be protected at the same or greater level as the sensitivity of the enterprise applications that they serve.

- Identity systems shall provide protective, detective, audit, and forensic controls governing all administrative changes to the identity system, all identity life cycle actions—including account provisioning, de-provisioning, and changes—and permission provisioning, de-provisioning, and changes.

- Identity systems shall alert on suspected attacker activities, including using privileged accounts on non-privileged systems and patterns of excessive logons or logon attempts that may be malicious.

- Electronic identities that are no longer needed shall be de-provisioned within 180 days.

- Access permissions that are no longer needed shall be removed within 90 days.

- Electronic identities and permissions held by non-employees shall be sponsored by at least one employee and re-certified every 90 days, or be de-provisioned.

- Electronic identities and permissions used by computer systems (service accounts) shall be sponsored by at least one employee and re-certified annually, or be de-provisioned.

- Identity systems shall support the protocols required for authentication and access control on enterprise systems, including on premise and cloud-based systems. This includes Kerberos, RADIUS, LDAP, X.509 certificates, and Security Assertion Markup Language (SAML).

- Multi-factor authentication shall be supported for access to enterprise systems and applications from untrusted networks such as the Internet, and for all uses of privileged systems administrator accounts on all networks.

- Authentication failures shall not reveal information about user names, passwords, permissions, or authentication methods.

- Failed logons shall include a delay so that no more than five failed logons can be performed in one hour (this may be implemented by a one-hour block after the fifth failed logon). More than ten failed logon attempts on a single account shall generate an alert requiring investigation before the account may be used.

- Identity, authentication, and access management security configurations shall be reviewed on an annual basis, including re-validation of all policy exceptions.

- Identity, authentication, and access management preventive, detective, audit, and forensic controls shall be verified and tested for proper operation at least annually.

Passwords, when they are used for authentication, shall be subject to the following policy requirements:

- Passwords that are actively used by users must be changed every 90 days, and the past ten passwords must be unique.

- Passwords that are internal to systems and not used interactively by users must be changed annually, and the past ten passwords must be unique.

- Passwords should be at least 12 characters long, and longer pass phrases containing spaces are encouraged. Passwords must contain uppercase, lowercase, and a number or a special character. (This complexity is to resist brute-force attacks; password length requirements will increase over time as computing power to crack passwords increases.)

- Passwords should not contain internal repetitions to allow them to meet length requirements (for example, PasswordPassword1).

- Passwords must not be displayed in clear text during the login process.

- User passwords shall not be written down on paper or stored in unencrypted computer files.

- System account passwords shall be physically protected in a locked safe. If stored electronically on network-accessible systems, such storage shall be encrypted and access-controlled. If a single electronic system contains more than 100 system passwords, user access to it shall require multi-factor authentication.

- When passwords must be generated and transmitted, such transmission shall be by encrypted means, or given verbally over the telephone. Only one-time passwords may be transmitted over insecure channels.

- Password security configurations shall be reviewed on an annual basis, including re-validation of all policy exceptions.

- Password management preventive, detective, audit, and forensic controls shall be verified and tested for proper operation at least annually.

Data Protection and Cryptography

Data protection and cryptography are essential to achieving strong authentication, non-repudiation, and the protection of confidentiality and integrity of data at rest and in transit. These capabilities are to be used to ensure enterprise data and identities are protected adequately to resist current and projected attacks.

Data protection and cryptography activities must include the following:

- Sensitive data transmissions shall be protected using Secure Sockets Layer (SSL), Transport Layer Security (TLS), Internet Protocol Security (IPSec), or equivalent secure protocols—on both internal protected networks and insecure networks such as the Internet.

- Encryption modules, algorithms, and protocols shall meet US National Institute of Standards and Technology (NIST) requirements as documented in approved Federal Information Processing Standards (FIPS) documents.

- Cryptographic algorithms shall either be rated to resist brute-force attack for a period of ten years at the time of use by an attacker with $10,000 worth of computing capacity, or attempts to brute-force attack the cryptography shall be detectable.

- Cryptography used for more sensitive operations may need to resist an attacker with $100,000 or $1,000,000 worth of computing power. (Note that as technology improves and costs drop, the amount of computing power this amount purchases will increase over time.)

- Password policy shall be set using cryptographic principles based upon the amount of entropy required and the ability of brute-force attacks to be detected or delayed. These factors shall be used to design password complexity and rotation policy so attackers have less than a 1% chance of successfully guessing a password within its usable lifetime. Passwords with longer lifetimes shall require commensurately greater complexity to resist brute-force attacks.

- Published cryptographic vulnerabilities (such as Heartbleed) shall be remediated within 30 days of publication, or compensating preventive or detective controls shall be put in place so that attempted exploits are blocked or at least detected.

- Encryption keys shall be centrally escrowed and retained for a period of seven years after the date of last use. This approach supports investigations by enterprise security, legal, or law enforcement personnel.

- All non-public enterprise data at rest shall be either physically protected in a locked facility or container, or encrypted using cryptographic keys that are separate from the data (such as a strong password or encryption token).

- Data encryption shall include adequate logging separate from the media itself to permit investigators to validate that lost media was in fact encrypted at the time of loss.

- Strong and multi-factor authentication shall use cryptographic methods to make authentication resistant to keylogging, replay, session hijacking, and brute-force attacks. These methods shall include digital certificates, one-time passwords, and secure cryptographic modules for storing persistent private asymmetric and shared symmetric keys.

- Persistent keys used for strong authentication or persistent encryption shall be protected using Hardware Security Modules (HSMs), Trusted Platform Modules (TPMs), secure elements, or smart cards that resist physical and logical attack to extract the keys.

- Session encryption (such as that used by SSL, TLS, or IPSec) does not require hardware protection, except where session compromise would pose an enterprise risk.

- Data protection and cryptography modules, algorithms, protocols, and security configurations shall be reviewed on an annual basis, including re-validation of all policy exceptions.

- Data protection and cryptography preventive, detective, audit, and forensic controls shall be verified and tested for proper operation at least annually.

Monitoring, Vulnerability, and Patch Management

Monitoring of account activity and security incidents relies on robust logging of activities and alerting that catches potentially malicious activities. In this way, the enterprise will be able to detect violations of security policies or procedures, and active attacks when they occur. Timely detection of malicious activities aids in preventing or containing malicious actions before damage can be performed. Vulnerability and patch management reduce exposure to attacks by tracking and remediating vulnerabilities in a timely fashion, and by patching systems to reduce their exposure to attack.

Monitoring, vulnerability, and patch management activities must include the following:

- Enterprise systems and cloud services delivering business-critical functions shall be monitored for performance and availability so failures can be detected within at least 30 minutes of their occurrence.

- Enterprise systems and cloud services shall forward their logs to a central system for correlation and analysis, or shall provide for in-place analysis and alerting that ties in with enterprise incident detection and investigation services.

- All log entries shall be synchronized to Coordinated Universal Time (UTC) or a clearly delineated global time zone so the times when events occur are clearly presented to investigators.

- Security audit logging must clearly tie user activity in the information system to named user or service accounts.

- Security audit logs must be protected from tampering and shall be made available to support investigations for a period of one year after the event is logged. Event logs related to public company financial activities shall be retained for a period of seven years after the event is logged.

- Networks shall be monitored to detect rogue or malicious devices connecting to them, and wireless networks shall be configured to detect attacks and rogue wireless access points.

- Cybersecurity may use detective technologies such as honeypots, honeynets, and honeytokens to detect attacker exploits of vulnerabilities and identify attacker Tools, Techniques, and Procedures (TTPs).

- System security monitoring shall feed into a central system for correlation that is monitored 24x7 to detect security incidents. Security logs shall be monitored for activities known or suspected to be malicious. Security alerts shall be generated within 30 minutes of such activity occurring.

- New applications and servers shall be vulnerability-scanned, and all medium or higher vulnerabilities shall be addressed prior to becoming operational.

- Enterprise applications that are generally available on the Internet or enterprise internal networks shall be scanned for vulnerabilities using a credentialed vulnerability scanner monthly, and all medium or higher application vulnerabilities shall be addressed or remediated within 90 days of discovery. For sensitive systems with significant business impact, this remediation window may be shorter – as little as one day.

- Servers directly connected to the Internet shall be scanned for operating system vulnerabilities using a credentialed vulnerability scanner monthly, and all medium or higher operating system vulnerabilities shall be addressed or remediated within 30 days of discovery. For sensitive systems with significant business impact, this remediation window may be shorter – as little as six hours.

- Cybersecurity shall ensure that applications and systems in violation of vulnerability remediation policy shall be disconnected from the Internet and enterprise networks until remediation is performed and validated.

- Vendor-provided patches shall be evaluated and installed as recommended by vendors. Vulnerabilities relating to missing patches shall be handled as per vulnerability policy above. When security patches cannot be installed for operational reasons, mitigating preventive and detective controls shall be employed to keep the overall risk acceptable.

- Patching is the responsibility of the system owner. System owners may use automated systems to simplify patch deployment, but limitations in these systems must be compensated for using manual techniques to ensure that security vulnerabilities are addressed in a timely manner.

- Detective controls shall be configured to detect attacker exploits of known vulnerabilities when this is technically possible.

- Internet-facing and user networks shall be penetration-tested on an annual basis to identify vulnerabilities related to real-world attacker techniques.

- Monitoring, vulnerability, and patch management security configurations shall be reviewed on an annual basis, including re-validation of all policy exceptions.

- Monitoring, vulnerability, and patch management preventive, detective, audit, and forensic controls shall be verified and tested for proper operation at least annually.

High Availability, Disaster Recovery, and Physical Protection

Enterprise IT services, systems, and data shall be protected from losses of availability related to system failure, physical destruction, and accidental or malicious incidents. Services, applications, and servers shall be configured with adequate redundancy and protection to meet business needs and ensure cost-effective service delivery in the event of accidental or deliberate incidents targeting their availability.

High availability, disaster recovery, and physical protection activities must include the following:

- Availability: Revenue-generating systems must have at least 99.99% availability. Other business IT systems must have at least 99.9% availability. Supporting infrastructure may be subject to higher availability requirements as needed by the business.

- Recovery Point Objectives (RPO) in the event of natural or man-made disaster:

  - Revenue-generating and business financial systems must be able to recover all committed transactions with customers or vendors that have financial consequences.

  - Other business IT systems must be able to recover data up into the day previous to the incident (daily backups).

- Recovery Time Objectives (RTO) in the event of natural or man-made disaster:

  - Revenue-generating business functions must be able to recover and achieve initial operating capability within seven days.

  - Business financial systems must be able to recover to initial operating capability within 45 days.

  - Other business IT systems must be able to recover to initial operating capability within 90 days.

- RTO planning shall consider the time required for rebuilding affected servers, in addition to the time required for restoring affected data.

- Major system upgrades and configuration changes must include adequate backups to "roll back" the changes within the availability, recovery point, and recovery time requirements, as previously specified.

- Backup data shall be sufficiently protected physically and logically so that natural or man-made disasters will not result in the destruction of both the primary copy and the backup.

- Backup data taken offsite shall be encrypted, and the keys to that data shall be sufficiently protected from loss or compromise so that data can be recovered even in the event of catastrophic loss.

- Theft or loss of any enterprise-furnished equipment must be reported to the incident response team as soon as possible.

- Enterprise sensitive data printed on paper or other material must be physically protected in a locked room or cabinet.

- Enterprise facilities and data centers shall include physical protection, monitoring, and detective controls to protect personnel and equipment from harm and accidents. Sensitive data and systems handling it in unencrypted fashion shall be protected using double-barrier protection and need-to-know access controls.

- Any third-party access to the facility must be approved by the data center operations supervisor and guests must be escorted during the visit.

- When automated physical access controls are used at enterprise facilities, the access logs shall be maintained for one year to support investigations by audit, security, legal, and law enforcement personnel. Logs shall be monitored 24x7 to detect intrusions and intrusion attempts.

- Backup media, replication processes, and snapshot procedures must be tested annually to verify their proper operation.

- Disaster recovery and service continuity plans must be tested using a drill, rehearsal or tabletop practical exercise every two years to ensure their effectiveness.

- Physical security risk assessments must be conducted for all data centers, server rooms, and server closets on an annual basis.

- High availability, disaster recovery, and physical protection configurations shall be reviewed on an annual basis, including re-validation of all policy exceptions.

- High availability, disaster recovery, and physical protection preventive, detective, audit, and forensic controls shall be verified and tested for proper operation at least annually.

Incident Response

A security incident is any malicious event (perceived or real) performed against the enterprise's data or information systems. An incident can originate inside the enterprise (insider threat), in external entities, or in the surrounding environment. When a cybersecurity-related incident is reported, the incident response team takes charge of the incident and matrixes in the appropriate resources from elsewhere in IT and the business to investigate and remediate the situation.

Incident response activities must include the following:

- The incident response team shall track cybersecurity threats against the enterprise, and inform cybersecurity and IT leadership of threats that pose new or previously unknown risks to the enterprise and potential mitigations for those risks.

- All information systems supporting enterprise business processes must have a documented incident response process. Incident response processes must have clearly defined roles and responsibilities. These processes may include leveraging shared services for incident response that are centrally operated by cybersecurity.

- For major incidents, a single leader must be designated for the duration of the incident, from initiation through conclusion. The incident leader is responsible for coordinating containment of the incident, reducing the impact, ensuring remediation, and keeping all the stakeholders informed of status.

- Suspected incidents shall be investigated according to the following schedule:

  - Alerts rated "critical" shall be investigated within one hour of their detection.

  - Alerts rated "high" shall be investigated within 12 hours of their detection.

  - Alerts rated "medium" shall be investigated within 24 hours of their occurrence.

  - Alerts rated "low" or "routine" shall be investigated within two business days of their occurrence.

- All incidents shall be documented to capture the originating alert or event, results of investigation, and remediation and conclusion. Confirmed incidents shall have their root cause investigated, identified, and documented. Incident documentation shall be retained for seven years following the conclusion of the incident.

- Incident investigation teams shall have the tools and permissions they need to investigate accounts, computers, and networks involved in malicious activity. They shall have the ability to directly or by request disable and remediate accounts, computers, and networks as necessary to contain and resolve the incident.

- The cybersecurity department shall be responsible for overseeing contractual, regulatory, or legal obligations related to incidents; identifying incidents with contractual, regulatory, or legal implications; and bringing to bear the appropriate resources to ensure that contractual, regulatory, and legal obligations related to those incidents are met.

- The enterprise shall have anonymous methods for employees to report security policy violations or suspected security incidents without fear of reprisal.

- Incident response configurations shall be reviewed on an annual basis, including re-validation of all policy exceptions.

- Incident response preventive, detective, audit, and forensic controls shall be verified and tested for proper operation at least annually.

Asset Management and Supply Chain

Asset management is accounting for all the assets (hardware and software) in the enterprise. It is critical that this information be kept up-to-date to support IT operation and handling of cybersecurity incidents. A supply chain management program covers both products and services to include security assessment, periodic re-assessments, and inclusion of supplier information in the asset management database.

Asset management and supply chain activities must include the following:

- All software and hardware assets shall be assigned to an enterprise system with a primary and alternate employee point of contact.

- A centralized asset management system shall be utilized to track all enterprise hardware and software assets from their acquisition through to their disposal.

- A centralized configuration and change management system shall be utilized to track configurations of enterprise hardware and software systems, track the approval of changes to those configurations, and detect unauthorized changes when they occur.

- Software licenses and software utilization in the enterprise shall be tracked so that software licenses can be matched to utilization, software license compliance can be ensured, and unauthorized software in the enterprise can be identified and remediated.

- As part of system acquisition, vendors and suppliers shall be reviewed and approved by cybersecurity, with associated risks identified and accepted, remediated, or mitigated.

- Hardware and software assets retired from service shall be properly disposed of, including the following:

  - Removal of assets from asset and configuration databases

  - Release of software licenses and termination of software and hardware support contracts

  - Sanitization or destruction of hardware persistent storage (flash and hard drive storage) to protect enterprise data

- Persistent storage media, including flash drives, portable media, hard drives, and device embedded storage (such as copiers and voicemail appliances with data storage features) shall be sanitized of enterprise data using physical destruction, data cleaning, data scrubbing, or data encryption methods such that the data may not be recovered after disposal.

- Data disposal methods shall be validated annually to ensure their effectiveness. Data encryption methods shall be validated to ensure the encryption strength is adequate to protect data for a period of ten years following disposal.

- Loss or unintended disposal of equipment or disclosure of data shall be reported as a cybersecurity incident.

- Hardware and software assets shall be inventoried annually, with all associated points of contact validated and updated as necessary.

- Hardware, software, and service provider risk evaluations shall be reviewed and updated annually, or when changes occur that materially affect the security posture of such providers (such as cyberincidents or breaches, mergers, divestitures, bankruptcies, or foreign acquisitions).

- Asset management and supply chain configurations shall be reviewed on an annual basis, including re-validation of all policy exceptions.

- Asset management and supply chain preventive, detective, audit, and forensic controls shall be verified and tested for proper operation at least annually.

Policy, Audit, E-Discovery, and Training

Security governance is paramount for the smooth functioning of the enterprise cybersecurity program. This includes the maintenance of enterprise cybersecurity policies, periodic audits of controls and protections, support for legal e-discovery activities, and training of cybersecurity personnel, employees, and contractors in proper cybersecurity practices and techniques.

Policy, audit, e-discovery, and training activities must include the following:

- Enterprise cybersecurity policy shall be approved by business leadership, with inputs from key stakeholders in the business leadership, legal, contractual, IT, and cybersecurity departments.

- A formal security forum shall be established to enable key stakeholders to discuss security matters on a regular basis and document policy changes or recommendations for enhancements.

- The enterprise shall track cybersecurity risks and their potential consequences, and shall report on those risks and their mitigation on a quarterly basis.

- The enterprise shall employ tools to provide overall cybersecurity governance, risk management, and compliance reporting so that all contractual, regulatory, statutory, and legal requirements can be met.

- The enterprise shall comply with all contractual, regulatory, statutory, and legal requirements as they are stipulated, such as Sarbanes-Oxley (SOX), Payment Card Industry (PCI), and Health Information Portability and Accountability Act (HIPAA). This may also include regulations relating to privacy of employee and customer data.

- The enterprise shall comply with all requests for e-discovery originating from the legal department. All requests shall be documented, along with the extent of the data provided in response to the request. This documentation shall be retained for seven years.

- Exceptions to cybersecurity policies shall be documented, tracked, and re-certified on an annual basis. Exceptions that are not re-certified shall be removed and the policy enforced.

- The enterprise shall comply with customer and internal requirements for information system Certification and Accreditation (C&A), as specified in customer contracts and internal Memorandums Of Understanding (MOUs).

- The enterprise shall ensure that personnel in positions of significant business and cybersecurity trust are appropriately vetted and periodically re-checked to ensure their continued suitability for such positions.

- The enterprise shall ensure all employees receive annual training on cybersecurity concerns and obligations. Employees in positions of trust, including executives and systems administrators, shall receive additional training suitable to their roles, the risks associated with those roles, and their obligations to provide for additional protection of enterprise and customer data.

- The enterprise shall audit *all* cybersecurity preventive, detective, audit, and forensic controls on an annual basis to ensure their proper design and operation.

- Policy, audit, e-discovery, and training programs shall be reviewed on an annual basis, including re-validation of all policy exceptions.

- Policy, audit, e-discovery, and training preventive, detective, audit, and forensic controls shall be verified and tested for proper operation at least annually.

APPENDIX E

███

Cybersecurity Operational Processes

To maintain an effective cybersecurity posture, the Chief Information Security Officer (CISO) should maintain a number of enterprise operational processes to include the following:

1. Policies and Policy Exception Management
2. Project and Change Security Reviews
3. Risk Management
4. Control Management
5. Auditing and Deficiency Tracking
6. Asset Inventory and Audit
7. Change Control
8. Configuration Management Database Re-certification
9. Supplier Reviews and Risk Assessments
10. Cyberintrusion Response
11. All-Hazards Emergency Preparedness Exercises
12. Vulnerability Scanning, Tracking, and Management
13. Patch Management and Deployment
14. Security Monitoring
15. Password and Key Management
16. Account and Access Periodic Re-certification
17. Privileged Account Activity Audit

While this list is not all-inclusive, it includes important processes for effective cybersecurity. These processes go beyond maintaining individual cybersecurity technologies and capabilities. Consequently, some cybersecurity processes may not be immediately obvious or considered to be absolutely essential. These processes cross over organizational and technological boundaries so, in most enterprises, such processes must be at least somewhat manual and procedural.

This appendix describes the cybersecurity processes in terms of their high-level activities, the IT teams that perform the activities, and supporting information systems. Each process is diagrammed to show the activities performed by the five major IT departments: (1) business leadership, (2) security, (3) strategy and architecture, (4) engineering, and (5) operations. In each process diagram, the major activities are ordered approximately from start to finish. In addition, interactions with supporting information sources are also shown.

Note that these processes are somewhat notional; an enterprise's implementation of the processes may vary. The objective here is to provide a starting point for identifying which cybersecurity processes an enterprise has and does not have. An enterprise's processes may be simpler or more complex as there is no one way to implement enterprise cybersecurity.

As an enterprise creates and maintains its cybersecurity processes, it is important to note that a simple process that is a little clumsy or cumbersome is more effective than an elaborate process no one follows. Enterprises need to resist the temptation to create bureaucracy for its own sake. Every activity and person involved in a cybersecurity process involves time and money. Cybersecurity processes should support the business, not stymie it.

Supporting Information Systems

In a modern IT enterprise there are many information systems, some of which support cybersecurity processes. Figure E-1 lists important cybersecurity supporting information systems. The cybersecurity department is responsible for ensuring these information systems are present and operating within the enterprise IT environment.

Figure E-1. *Cybersecurity supporting information systems.*

Similar to the cybersecurity processes, it is important an enterprise does not overthink its supporting information systems. While it might be desirable to have a sophisticated information system, a simple spreadsheet, database, or text document may be appropriate. A simple information system that is available, utilized, and actively maintained is far more useful than a sophisticated one no one actually uses.

The remainder of this section describes the information systems that are integrated with the cybersecurity processes described in this appendix. The information systems listed are not all-inclusive, and this section deliberately does not include the databases associated with specific technologies, such as firewall rules. Some of these information systems may exist in conjunction with enterprise applications or other IT systems.

Following is a brief explanation of each of these cybersecurity supporting information systems and their significance to enterprise security, as shown in Figure E-1:

- *Enterprise Risks:* This system tracks enterprise risks. It is effective when it tracks risks in terms of threats and consequences to confidentiality, integrity, and availability (CIA). For example, a risk might state "an attacker steals credit card data and causes financial damages and a regulatory violation." Mitigations then center on deploying security controls to reduce the probability or the impact of the risk.

- *Security Policies:* This system contains the enterprise security policies and standards, which are the foundation for risk mitigation.

- *Policy Exceptions:* This system addresses the fact that "for every rule there is an exception." Exceptions to policies and standards need to be tracked so they can be periodically re-evaluated and eventually mitigated. Otherwise, the enterprise runs the risk of exceptions becoming the rule and policies becoming meaningless.

- *Disaster Recovery Plans:* This system includes contingency plans for a wide range of disaster scenarios to include natural disasters and severe cybersecurity events. IT staff members need to know where the plans are and when and how to use them. These plans can be relatively simple.

- *Approval to Operate (ATO) Records:* When new IT systems are placed online, it is important to document, in part, their risks. ATO records the business decision to operate the system. System owners document and retain the performance, cost, and risk of system operation. ATO should be periodically revisited as standards and threats evolve.

- *Security Controls:* This system tracks the enterprise's active security controls. Tracking security controls is essential to being able to validate security. However, a challenge is security control lists cannot be so large that no one can comprehend them. The goal is to strike a balance of having a controls list that is sufficiently high level so it can be comprehended, while also containing sufficient detail to be auditable.

- *Asset Database:* This information system is most likely to be automated. The asset database keeps track of the IT assets in the enterprise, and allows for identifying and tracking vendors, servers, computers, networking equipment, software, and so on.

- *Configuration Management Database:* This database ties into the asset database to keep track of high-level configuration attributes of systems. This database and the asset database are essential for identifying IT assets and understanding the business impact of cybersecurity events involving IT assets.

- *Incident Records:* This system tracks enterprise cybersecurity incidents and identifies the assets involved in those incidents, threats that caused the incidents, vulnerabilities exploited, and containment and mitigation performed to resolve the incidents. These essential records track the risks associated with attacks, and help with understanding patterns of threats and vulnerabilities affecting the enterprise.

- *Security Deficiencies:* This system tracks security deficiencies identified in the course of security audits, and it tracks risks through remediation. Deficiencies are a formal artifact of the security audit process, and they should track against the affected assets and security controls.

- *Vulnerability Database*: This system tracks vulnerabilities identified through vulnerability scans and other automated methods, and tracks them against the associated IT assets. Note that while vulnerabilities are tracked, often it may not make business sense to remediate all of them. This database should track the vulnerabilities and the business decisions associated with what is done about them.

- *Accounts and Permissions*: This information will most likely be obtained from supporting information systems, such as enterprise directories and identity/access management systems.

- *Password and Key Vault*: While some enterprises track their organizational accounts and passwords in a spreadsheet, it is ideal for this information to be maintained using highly secure vault technology that provides for access controls and audit trails. These organizational accounts/passwords are the "keys to the kingdom" and should be correspondingly well protected.

- *Administrator Audit Trail*: This information system involves tracking privileged administrator activities so such activities can be audited.

1. Policies and Policy Exception Management

The Policies and Policy Exception Management process maintains enterprise policies and exceptions to those policies. Enterprises may be good at establishing cybersecurity policies and maintaining them, but managing exceptions to those policies tends to be more problematic. Enterprises need to ensure policy exceptions are formally approved, and then re-certified on a regular basis to ensure the exceptions are still valid. Security leadership needs to observe policy exceptions carefully to detect cases where the "exception becomes the rule."

The workflow for this process is shown in Figure E-2. This process is usually operated from within the "Policy, Audit, E-Discovery, and Training" functional area.

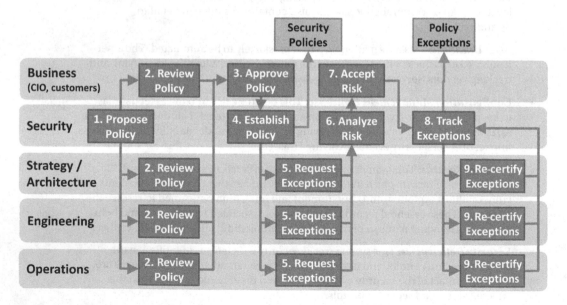

Figure E-2. *Policies and Policy Exception Management process.*

Process Overview

The Policies and Policy Exception Management process consists of the following major activities:

1. *Propose Policy*: The security team proposes that a policy be created.

2. *Review Policy*: Business leadership, strategy/architecture, engineering, and operations review the policy to ensure that it is reasonable and supports the business.

3. *Approve Policy*: The business leadership approves the policy after it has been reviewed and revised, as needed, to effectively balance risk with business needs.

4. *Establish Policy*: Once business leadership approves the policy, the security team integrates it with the rest of the security policies and establishes methods for monitoring and enforcing the policy. Note: Policies should be periodically reviewed and updated. This sub-process is not shown in the diagram.

5. *Request Exceptions*: Once the policy is established, strategy/architecture, engineering, and operations teams may find that they need exceptions to the policy.

6. *Analyze Risk*: When exceptions are requested, the security team analyzes the risk associated with the exceptions and reports that risk to business leadership.

7. *Accept Risk*: Business leadership is responsible for balancing the business value with the associated risk to make a business decision on approving the exception and accepting the associated risk. Note: If it turns out that the policy is unreasonable or unrealistic, this process may also trigger a re-evaluation of the policy.

8. *Track Exceptions*: The security team is responsible for tracking approved exceptions and ensuring that the approved exceptions are periodically re-certified.

9. *Re-certify Exceptions*: Exception requesters are required to periodically re-certify their exceptions to ensure that the exception need still exists and the risk is still acceptable. Note: Sometimes circumstances can change and an exception that was previously acceptable can become unacceptable over time.

Supporting Information Systems

The Policies and Policy Exception Management process is supported by the following information systems:

- *Security Policies*: This database is used to store the security policies involved in this process.

- *Policy Exceptions*: This database is used to store the exceptions to security policies, tied back to the related policies.

2. Project and Change Security Reviews

The Project and Change Security Reviews process involves cybersecurity in enterprise projects and changes. This process ensures, in part, that IT systems are designed and deployed with cybersecurity capabilities "baked in" to the best extent possible and that they are practical. This process should be integrated into the larger system development life cycle process. This process can also be integrated into the management gates of the enterprise IT project and change processes. Cybersecurity needs to be considered on major IT initiatives, as well as associated initiative risks and mitigations.

The workflow for this process is shown in Figure E-3. This process is often operated within the "Policy, Audit, E-Discovery, and Training" functional area.

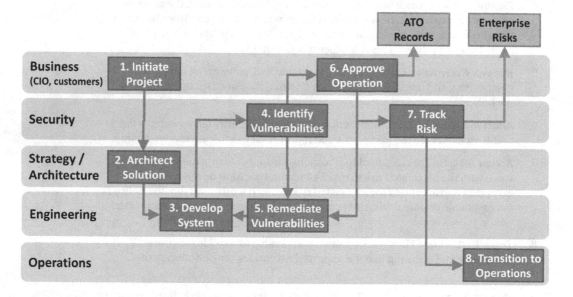

Figure E-3. *Project and Change Security Reviews process.*

Process Overview

The Project and Change Security Reviews process consists of the following major activities:

1. ***Initiate Project:*** In response to a business need, the business leadership initiates a project for a new system or an existing system change.

2. ***Architect Solution:*** In context of the overall enterprise, the strategy and architecture team architects the solution, in part, by identifying technologies and standards that comprise the solution. The strategy and architecture team factors security policies and standards into the solution.

3. ***Develop System:*** Next, the engineering team develops the system or change, taking the architecture and security standards into consideration. The engineering team designs the system by balancing performance, security, and cost requirements, as well as other constraints.

4. *Identify Vulnerabilities*: During the system design process, security reviews the proposed design and identifies vulnerabilities. Such vulnerabilities are defined in terms of threats and business consequences that result in confidentiality, integrity, or availability (CIA) losses.

5. *Remediate Vulnerabilities*: As vulnerabilities are identified, the system is engineered to reduce the potential threats and negative business consequences. Sometimes, mitigating the vulnerabilities may not make business sense.

6. *Approve Operation*: Business leadership considers the identified vulnerabilities and the corresponding business risks. If the risks are too great, engineering needs to modify the system design to acceptable risk levels. Once the business leadership accepts the risk, the leadership grants and documents the approval to operate (ATO).

7. *Track Risk*: The security team then documents the residual risks in the enterprise risk database. Documentation includes threat scenarios and the associated business impacts on confidentiality, integrity, or availability.

8. *Transition to Operations*: Once the system is approved to operate and residual risks are accounted for, the system can be transitioned to operations.

Supporting Information Systems

The Project and Change Security Reviews process is supported by the following information systems:

- *ATO Records*: These records track the enterprise approvals to operate (ATO) and the corresponding business decisions regarding the balance between business value and associated security risk.

- *Enterprise Risks*: This database tracks enterprise risks in terms of consequences to confidentiality, integrity, or availability (CIA).

3. Risk Management

The Risk Management process involves identifying and tracking enterprise risks. It is important the CISO tracks risks in terms of their business impact, not their technological impact. Risks should be technology-agnostic. Technology factors into the risk process as vulnerabilities are identified and exploited by attackers; the associated business risks can increase and possibly require additional mitigations. The risk management process involves identifying, analyzing, and tracking risks and their associated mitigating controls.

The workflow for this process is shown in Figure E-4. This process is usually operated from within the "Policy, Audit, E-Discovery, and Training" functional area.

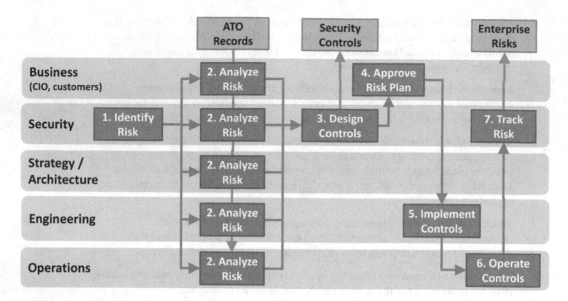

Figure E-4. *Risk Management process.*

Process Overview

The Risk Management process consists of the following major activities:

1. **Identify Risk:** The security team starts the process by identifying risk. In the event of a risk re-certification or review, this activity may involve taking an existing risk and initiating the process to review it.

2. **Analyze Risk:** Next, all departments analyze risk from their perspectives (that is, business, security, strategy and architecture, engineering, and operations). The departments evaluate the importance / consequences of the risk and potential mitigations.

3. **Design Controls:** The security team works with engineering to design controls to mitigate the risk, either by reducing its probability or reducing its impact. In some instances, the best business decision may be to accept the risk as-is without mitigation.

4. **Approve Risk Plan:** Business leadership reviews the risk and the planned mitigation measures to ensure the risk plan balances performance, security, and cost to serve the needs of the business.

5. **Implement Controls:** Once the risk plan is approved, engineering implements the controls and prepares them for production. Engineering is involved in the control design to ensure the planned controls are actually achievable.

6. **Operate Controls:** After the controls are designed and implemented, operations takes responsibility for the day-to-day activities.

7. **Track Risk:** Finally, the security team tracks the risk, along with its associated mitigating controls, via the enterprise risks database.

Supporting Information Systems

The Risk Management process is supported by the following information systems:

- *ATO Records*: Should the risk actually occur, ATO records are used to identify systems affected by a risk and the anticipated business consequences.

- *Security Controls*: Security uses this database to track the controls that are in place and how they can best be used to reduce the probability or impact of enterprise risks.

- *Enterprise Risks*: Security and operations use this database to track risks after they have been analyzed and mitigated. Security and operations report risks to business leadership and manage risks on an ongoing basis.

4. Control Management

The Control Management process involves identifying and tracking the security controls in the enterprise. Tracking controls is helpful because it allows management to track how security resources are being allocated to mitigate risks while preserving business value. A good control identifies the risk it mitigates, whether it is reducing the probability or the impact of the risk, and who is doing what to deliver mitigation. It is helpful for control management to tie into the incident management process so controls are developed to mitigate risks tied to real-world incidents and reduce the probability or the impact of future incidents. Like risk management, control management is most successful when it is done at a high level, and the actual details and implementation of the controls are left to the technical experts.

The workflow for this process is shown in Figure E-5. This process is usually operated from within the "Policy, Audit, E-Discovery, and Training" functional area.

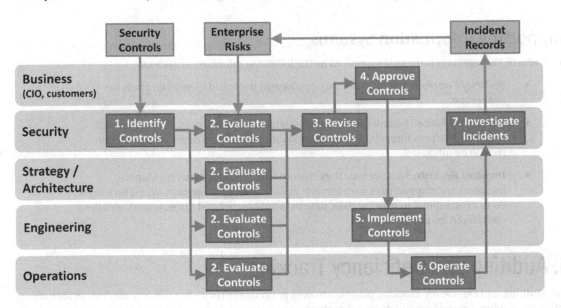

Figure E-5. *Control Management process.*

Process Overview

The Control Management process consists of the following major activities:

1. ***Identify Controls:*** The security team identifies the controls to be considered, which either come from the risk management process (in other words, identifies new controls), or a review of existing controls.

2. ***Evaluate Controls:*** Next, security, strategy and architecture, engineering, and operations consider each of the controls from their perspectives. Generally, business leadership does not need to be involved.

3. ***Revise Controls:*** The security team works with engineering to create, update, or modify the controls based on the results of the evaluation process.

4. ***Approve Controls:*** The business leadership reviews the revised controls in light of the risk and potential business impact to ensure performance, security, and cost are appropriately balanced to serve the needs of the business.

5. ***Implement Controls:*** Once the business leadership approves the revised controls, engineering implements the controls and prepares them for production. Engineering is involved in the control design to ensure the planned controls are actually achievable.

6. ***Operate Controls:*** After the controls are designed and implemented, operations takes responsibility for the day-to-day activities.

7. ***Investigate Incidents:*** During operation, the controls will generate security incidents that will require security to conduct an investigation.

Supporting Information Systems

The Control Management process is supported by the following information systems:

- ***Security Controls:*** Security uses this database to track and identify controls for evaluation.

- ***Enterprise Risks:*** The enterprise uses this database to track risks to the enterprise and their business impacts. All control evaluations are done in the context of the risks to be mitigated.

- ***Incident Records:*** Security uses these records to identify security incidents. Incidents are mapped back to enterprise risks that they encompass. When incidents do not correspond to existing risks, new risks are created and documented, and then considered for mitigation.

5. Auditing and Deficiency Tracking

The Auditing and Deficiency Tracking process involves periodically reviewing security controls to identify deficiencies when controls are not designed properly, or are not working as designed. If security controls are not being inspected and reviewed on a regular basis, such controls naturally degrade over time. Audits are essential to maintaining controls. There are multiple audit types, which follow the same general process: (1) a *self-audit* enables a team to audit itself against the documented controls and standards to assess their effectiveness and maturity, (2) an *internal audit* is performed by an internal audit team outside of the IT department and accountable to business leadership, and (3) an *external audit* is performed by an external auditor to report objective status to the enterprise's senior leadership. All audits are important.

The workflow for this process is shown in Figure E-6. This process is usually operated from within the "Policy, Audit, E-Discovery, and Training" functional area.

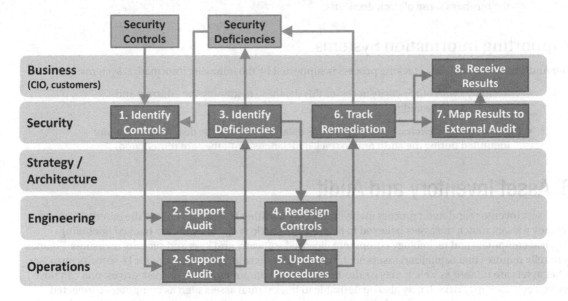

Figure E-6. *Auditing and Deficiency Tracking process.*

Process Overview

The Auditing and Deficiency Tracking process consists of the following major activities:

1. ***Identify Controls:*** The security team identifies the controls to be audited. Seldom will a single audit consider all controls; most likely an audit is a subset of all controls. Note that for internal and external audits, the process is directed by a department outside of IT, but it should still be facilitated through the security office.

2. ***Support Audit:*** Engineering and operations personnel support the audit by answering questions on the design and operation of the control.

3. ***Identify Deficiencies:*** During the course of the audit, security documents and tracks deficiencies.

4. ***Redesign Controls:*** In response to deficiencies, engineering may have to redesign or modify the controls.

5. ***Update Procedures:*** In response to deficiencies and control redesigns, operations may have to update their procedures for operating the controls or improve the execution of the procedures that are already in place.

6. ***Track Remediation:*** Security tracks the changes to the controls or their operation and works with the audit team to determine if the changes constitute adequate remediation of the deficiency. Note that not all deficiencies are resolved successfully; sometimes it may make better business sense to simply accept the deficiency.

7. **Map Results to External Audit:** For audits that are performed against an external standard such as NIST, PCI, or HIPAA, security maps the audit results from the internal controls to the requirements of the external framework.

8. **Receive Results:** Finally, senior leadership receives the audit results. In situations where deficiencies are accepted and not resolved, senior leadership weighs in on the business sense of such decisions.

Supporting Information Systems

The Auditing and Deficiency Tracking process is supported by the following information systems:

- **Security Controls:** Security accesses this database to identify the controls and procedures to be audited.

- **Security Deficiencies:** Security uses this database to track the deficiencies that are identified during the audit and to track deficiencies until they are remediated.

6. Asset Inventory and Audit

The Asset Inventory and Audit process involves tracking/auditing IT assets to ensure the enterprise assets actually present match the assets believed to be present. A wide range of assets are tracked, including physical computers and technology equipment, licensed software, and keys and security measures. Finance generally requires that capitalized assets are tracked for depreciation purposes, but for IT security purposes other assets are tracked as well. It may be desirable to track components, such as disk drives, that can pose serious cybersecurity risks. It may also be desirable to track virtual assets such as computers connected to the network or software installed in the enterprise. Assets are tracked from their acquisition through their disposal or destruction. The frequency of audits is dependent on the asset type, value, and the potential ways the asset inventory can become inaccurate or security can be jeopardized.

The workflow for this process is shown in Figure E-7. This process is usually operated from within the "Asset Management and Supply Chain" functional area.

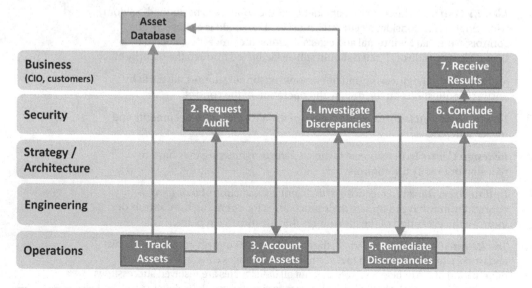

Figure E-7. *Asset Inventory and Audit process.*

Process Overview

The Asset Inventory and Audit process consists of the following major activities:

1. *Track Assets*: Operations tracks assets throughout their life cycle, from acquisition to disposal.

2. *Request Audit*: Security initiates the audit process by requesting it. The process is often done on a regular schedule, say once a year, or as a rolling audit where partial inventories are done monthly or quarterly.

3. *Account for Assets*: Under security's supervision, operations audits assets by identifying discrepancies.

4. *Investigate Discrepancies*: When discrepancies are found, security tracks them and attempts to determine if the reasons for the discrepancies are a process problem or an execution problem.

5. *Remediate Discrepancies:* When discrepancies are investigated, operations remediates the discrepancies so the actual inventory matches the asset database content.

6. *Conclude Audit:* Security concludes the audit by compiling the results of what was audited, what discrepancies were found, and how the discrepancies are remediated. This report includes valuing the cost of the discrepancies (for example, $10,000 of software was not accounted for, or $5,000 of hardware was disposed and not updated in the database). Cost values are important in making business decisions in response to the audit.

7. *Receive Results*: Senior leadership receives the audit results. Leadership makes business decisions, which might include changing processes, investing in asset management technology, or disciplining employees for not following procedures.

Supporting Information Systems

The Asset Inventory and Audit process is supported by the following information system:

- *Asset Database*: Operations uses this database to conduct the asset inventory and identify discrepancies. The enterprise maintains this database so it accurately reflects assets throughout their life cycle from acquisition to disposal.

7. Change Control

The Change Control process involves managing changes to the IT environment. This control is of interest to security for two reasons. First, changes are carefully planned to ensure they do not introduce unplanned vulnerabilities into the IT environment. Second, changes that occur without authorization or approval can be signs of deliberate attack. Because of these reasons, the change control process serves to protect against these two contingencies. The Change Control process also helps ensure smooth IT operations.

The workflow for this process is shown in Figure E-8. This process is often operated from within the "Asset Management and Supply Chain" functional area, although it is ideal for it to be operated by IT operations in coordination with security.

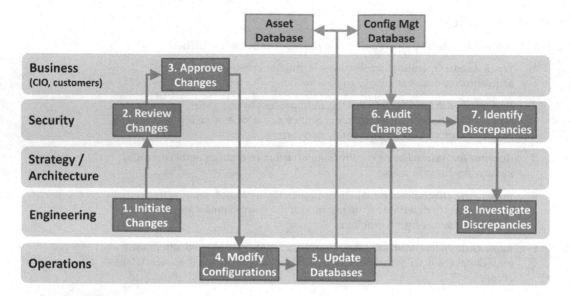

Figure E-8. *Change Control process.*

Process Overview

The Change Control process consists of the following major activities:

1. ***Initiate Changes:*** Engineering initiates this process. Ideally, changes are documented and tracked through a change management system (not shown).

2. ***Review Changes:*** Security should have an opportunity to review changes prior to their approval, with the opportunity to raise up any security concerns with the proposed change.

3. ***Approve Changes:*** By considering the business value of the proposed change with regard to operations, security risk, and cost, business leadership approves all changes prior to implementation and execution.

4. ***Modify Configurations:*** Once business approves the change, operations modifies the configuration in accordance with established procedures.

5. ***Update Databases:*** After operations completes the changes (or in conjunction with executing the changes), operations updates asset and configuration management databases to document the change. When a change control system is used, the change record is updated to reflect the completion of the change action.

6. ***Audit Changes:*** As part of the change completion process, security audits the change to ensure what was actually changed matches the documentation. Ideally, this audit is a thorough manual audit, but automated checks or abbreviated checks may be acceptable substitutes.

7. ***Identify Discrepancies:*** The audit may identify discrepancies where what was changed does not match the documentation. These discrepancies are particularly common when automated systems are used to constantly scan for unauthorized changes. When such discrepancies are discovered, the discrepancies should be treated as security incidents for investigation.

8. *Investigate Discrepancies*: When discrepancies are identified, engineering and operations work with security to investigate the discrepancies and determine what happened.

Supporting Information Systems

The Change Control process is supported by the following information systems:

- *Asset Database*: Operations uses this database and updates it when changes result in the addition or removal of IT assets from the environment.

- *Configuration Management Database*: Operations and security update this database when changes are made that affect system components and configurations. When properly maintained, discrepancies in this database may be signs of unauthorized changes including attacker activity.

8. Configuration Management Database Re-certification

The Configuration Management Database Re-certification process involves periodically auditing system configurations against the configuration management database to verify that system configurations match the databases. Ideally, this process is not necessary, but unplanned changes, debugging and troubleshooting, and attacker activity can result in configuration discrepancies that need to be resolved periodically. This process can be partially automated, depending on the maturity of the configuration management and change management systems and processes. However, security should review the changes to ensure that discrepancies are not the result of attacker activity.

The workflow for this process is shown in Figure E-9. This process is usually operated from within the "Asset Management and Supply Chain" functional area, although it is ideal for it to be operated by IT operations in coordination with security.

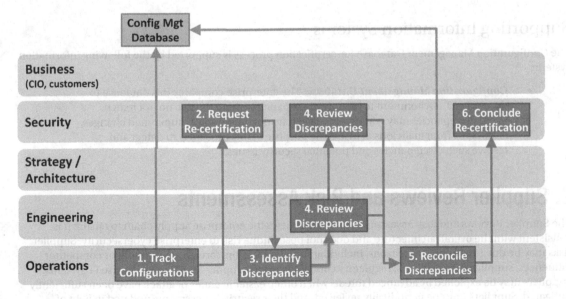

Figure E-9. Configuration Management Database Re-certification process.

Process Overview

The Configuration Management Database Re-certification process consists of the following major activities:

1. ***Track Configurations:*** Operations tracks configurations as a normal course of business and formal change control. This process may also include automated systems for detecting unauthorized changes and configuration discrepancies, which make this re-certification process simpler.

2. ***Request Re-certification:*** Security initiates the re-certification process, which is done on a routine schedule (for example, quarterly or annually), in response to an identified discrepancy, or to support other audit activities.

3. ***Identify Discrepancies:*** Operations reviews system configurations compared to the database and identifies discrepancies where the configurations do not match the database. Ideally, this process uses automated tools, and it may also involve coordination with the change control process and corresponding information systems.

4. ***Review Discrepancies:*** Engineering and security review discrepancies to determine if the discrepancies are evidence of malicious activity or represent an engineering or security risk.

5. ***Reconcile Discrepancies:*** Operations reconciles the discrepancies with what is in operation (that is, configuration management database). This reconciliation may involve either updating the database or updating the configuration so they both match. Obviously, if the configuration is to be changed, proper change control procedures must be followed.

6. ***Conclude Re-certification:*** After all discrepancies have been reviewed, security concludes the re-certification. This activity may include tracking the re-certification results to identify systemic and process problems over time.

Supporting Information Systems

The Configuration Management Database Re-certification process is supported by the following information system:

- ***Configuration Management Database:*** The enterprise compares this database to the actual IT environment to identify discrepancies where the two do not match. Such discrepancies may come from inaccurate documentation, unplanned changes, or possibly from malicious activity. The purpose of this process is to detect and resolve such discrepancies and potential security issues.

9. Supplier Reviews and Risk Assessments

The Supplier Reviews and Risk Assessments process reviews the enterprise supply chain to ensure it is consistent with the overall architecture and does not pose undue risk to enterprise cybersecurity. Supplier risks may be due to a number of reasons, including supplier location, foreign government or competitor influences, supplier vulnerabilities, regulatory compliance, and supplier access to enterprise IT systems. Suppliers may be exploited by advanced threats when other, easier avenues of attack have been sufficiently mitigated. Suppliers must be periodically reviewed, and their security assessments updated in light of evolving threats.

The workflow for this process is shown in Figure E-10. This process is usually operated from within the "Asset Management and Supply Chain" functional area, although it is ideal for it to be operated by IT strategy and architecture in coordination with security.

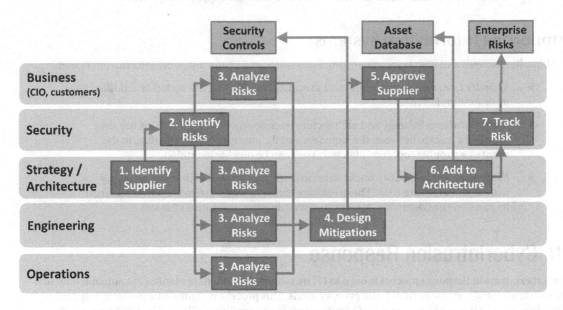

Figure E-10. Supplier Reviews and Risk Assessments process.

Process Overview

The Supplier Reviews and Risk Assessments process consists of the following major activities:

1. *Identify Supplier:* The architecture team identifies suppliers for consideration. Strategy and architecture have visibility on all major enterprise suppliers, so they can ensure suppliers and their technologies are consistent with the overall enterprise architecture.

2. *Identify Risks:* Next, security evaluates the supplier risk, considering how the supplier interacts with the enterprise (for example, do suppliers have access to enterprise networks, or supply hardware, software, or services?). Identifying risks considers a wide range of potential threat scenarios related to confidentiality, integrity, or availability, including personnel factors.

3. *Analyze Risks:* Business leadership, strategy/architecture, engineering, and operations analyze the supplier risk to understand the potential impact should it manifest itself.

4. *Design Mitigations:* Engineering collaborates with security (not shown in the figure) to design mitigations to reduce the probability or the impact of those supplier risks, if possible and warranted.

5. *Approve Supplier:* Business leadership formally approves the supplier risk mitigations by considering the business impact, risks, mitigations, and costs involved.

6. *Add to Architecture:* Strategy and architecture add approved suppliers, along with any risk assessment caveats, to the enterprise architecture.

7. *Track Risk:* Security tracks the risks associated with the approved suppliers.

Supporting Information Systems

The Supplier Reviews and Risk Assessments process is supported by the following information systems:

- *Security Controls:* Engineering tracks security controls that are added or modified to mitigate supplier risks.

- *Asset Database:* Strategy and architecture track approved suppliers. This tracking provides a linkage between the suppliers and the enterprise assets so that, in the event of a supplier problem, affected assets can be quickly identified.

- *Enterprise Risks:* Security tracks enterprise risks associated with suppliers along with other enterprise risks. These risks are characterized in terms of potential threat impacts on confidentiality, integrity, or availability of enterprise IT assets.

10. Cyberintrusion Response

The Cyberintrusion Response process is used to (1) investigate identified incidents, (2) contain the breach or intrusion, and (3) restore normal business operations. This process is central to a modern, responsive cyberdefense, and it is led by the security CyberIncident Response Team (CIRT). The CIRT works with engineering and operations to (1) investigate and resolve incidents, and (2) report the incident response status and business impact of the incident to management.

The workflow for this process is shown in Figure E-11. This process is usually operated from within the "Incident Response" functional area.

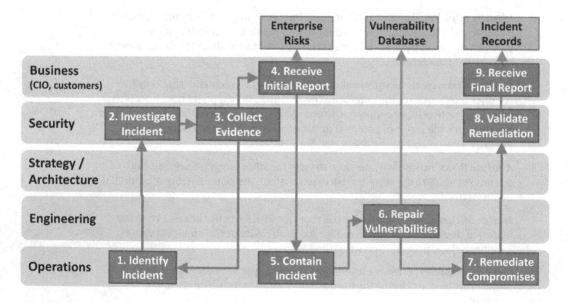

Figure E-11. Cyberintrusion Response process.

Process Overview

The Cyberintrusion Response process consists of the following major activities:

1. ***Identify Incident:*** The operations team identifies a security incident has occurred. Identification is done by reviewing and investigating alerts from monitoring systems and by conducting searches for suspected attacker activity based on known patterns.

2. ***Investigate Incident:*** Security investigates and tracks the identified incident. The investigation identifies the tools, techniques, and procedures used in the attack. The investigation's scope often expands as more hosts, accounts, and networks are identified as being involved.

3. ***Collect Evidence:*** Security collects evidence of the attack. This evidence may be used by law enforcement, but may also be of interest to auditors and regulators. It is important to follow good evidentiary procedures, even if criminal activity is not initially suspected. This investigation may also give rise to other incidents, as more information is collected.

4. ***Receive Initial Report:*** Security reports the status of the incident to business management. This status covers the business impact in terms of breaches of confidentiality, integrity, or availability, as well as the anticipated business impact due to the remediation. Business leadership, along with security, updates the enterprise risks to document how the enterprise was exploited.

5. ***Contain Incident:*** At this point in the process, the incident is understood. Operations moves forward to containing the incident. The purpose of containment is to stop the attackers from being able to operate in the environment and limit further damage.

6. ***Repair Vulnerabilities:*** Once the incident is contained, the vulnerabilities exploited by the attackers are identified and remediated as well as possible. Engineering tracks vulnerabilities that cannot be repaired immediately and considers alternative mitigating controls.

7. ***Remediate Compromises:*** Operations remediates and restores the attacked assets (such as computers, user accounts, and networks) back to normal operations. Restoration may include reimaging computers, resetting accounts, and reconfiguring networks.

8. ***Validate Remediation:*** Security validates the remediation activities to ensure the incident has been contained, vulnerabilities have been repaired, and compromised assets remediated. This activity is critical to ensure the attackers are kept out of the enterprise.

9. ***Receive Final Report:*** The IT department fully documents the incident. The report covers the business impact of the incident, as well as explaining what this incident means going forward. The report recommends actions to further strengthen enterprise defenses in the future.

Supporting Information Systems

The Cyberintrusion Response process is supported by the following information systems:

- ***Enterprise Risks:*** The IT department reviews and updates risks in the context of incident activity. Incidents may result in the identification of new risks, or the adjustment of the probability or impact of risks already being tracked. Finally, incidents may show that risk mitigation measures are not as effective as they were expected to be.

- ***Vulnerability Database:*** Incidents may identify vulnerabilities not previously known, or were known but were not remediated. During the incident response, engineering uses this database to determine if there are vulnerabilities being exploited that need to be remediated to prevent future attacks.

- ***Incident Records:*** The IT department records and tracks the results of incidents in the incident records information system. Incident records are used to identify trends and strategic challenges so resources can be allocated and prioritized to reduce the probability and the impact of future incidents. These records can also be used to assess the effectiveness of incident containment and remediation efforts over time.

11. All-Hazards Emergency Preparedness Exercises

The IT department uses the All-Hazards Emergency Preparedness Exercises process to develop and exercise procedures for emergency preparedness and disaster recovery (DR). These procedures should be generalized for all types of emergency situations (all-hazards) and should be usable for a variety of crises. The goal is to have processes worked out to handle the loss of information systems, facilities, and/or people due to a number of possible causes. Procedures should include manual workarounds, failover of applications or business processes to alternate sites or infrastructures, and restoration of data and applications from backups. For information systems, availability DR should be considered in terms of recovery point objectives (in other words, the most recent time from which data can be recovered) and recovery time objectives (that is, the amount of time required to recover). Both sets of objectives (metrics) should be considered from a business impact perspective.

The workflow for this process is shown in Figure E-12. This process is usually operated from within the "High Availability, Disaster Recovery, and Physical Protection" functional area, and frequently it may be led by departments outside of IT.

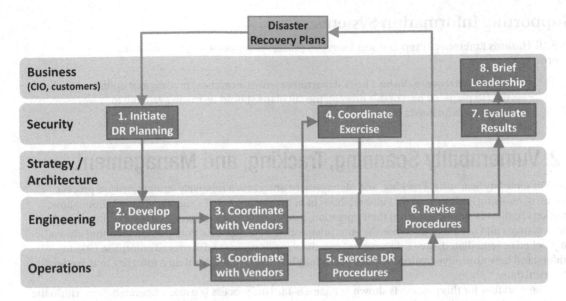

Figure E-12. *All-Hazards Emergency Preparedness Exercises process.*

Process Overview

The All-Hazards Emergency Preparedness Exercises process consists of the following major activities:

1. *Initiate Disaster Recovery (DR) Planning:* The security team ensures disaster recovery plans are maintained and periodically updated. The team initiates the exercise process on a periodic basis, such as annually.

2. *Develop Procedures:* Engineering develops or updates the DR procedures. Procedures cover a wide range of possible failure scenarios, including losses of systems, facilities, and people. Particular attention is paid to personnel factors to ensure that success is not dependent on any one person.

3. *Coordinate with Vendors:* IT DR procedures for systems are highly dependent on the capabilities of the underlying technologies. Consequently, engineering and operations develop procedures in close coordination with vendors.

4. *Coordinate Exercise:* When draft procedures are ready, the security team coordinates an exercise to occur to test and practice the procedures. The scale of the exercise is based, in part, on cost, schedule, and business impact factors.

5. *Exercise DR Procedures:* During the exercise, operations teams lead the practice of the DR procedures, as documented in the plans. This exercise can be a simple procedures walkthrough, a tabletop mock drill, or a full failover.

6. *Revise Procedures:* Based on the results of the exercise, if needed, engineering leads the revision of the DR procedures and plans.

7. *Evaluate Results:* Security compiles the results of the exercise to be reported to business leadership.

8. *Brief Leadership:* Security briefs business leadership on the results of the exercise. The results highlight the business risks posed by disaster scenarios and the parameters for recovery point objectives and recovery time objectives.

Supporting Information Systems

The All-Hazards Emergency Preparedness Exercises process is supported by the following information system:

- **Disaster Recovery Plans:** The IT department writes, exercises, revises, and updates the DR plans. As part of this process, the DR plans should be made available to everyone who needs them.

12. Vulnerability Scanning, Tracking, and Management

The Vulnerability Scanning, Tracking, and Management process is a relatively straightforward process that involves using tools to scan for vulnerabilities in network-connected systems. Vulnerabilities allow attackers to disable systems, disrupt their operation, modify data, or in the worst cases take full control of those systems and use them to access the enterprise and its data. Because vulnerabilities cannot always be patched or remediated, the IT department coordinates this process with overall enterprise risks to understand how unresolved vulnerabilities potentially impact the confidentiality, integrity, and availability of critical data.

The workflow for this process is shown in Figure E-13. This process is usually operated from within the "Monitoring, Vulnerability, and Patch Management" functional area.

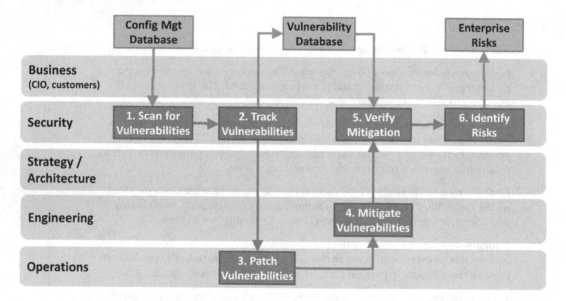

Figure E-13. *Vulnerability Scanning, Tracking, and Management process.*

Process Overview

The Vulnerability Scanning, Tracking, and Management process consists of the following major activities:

1. ***Scan for Vulnerabilities:*** The security team initiates vulnerability scans. This activity is traditionally performed by operations, but the security team ensures scanning is being conducted on a regular basis. Scanning is done using automated tools, although manual procedures can be followed as well.

2. ***Track Vulnerabilities:*** Security tracks identified vulnerabilities for remediation. Some vulnerabilities may need to be accepted; in those cases, mitigating controls should be considered.

3. ***Patch Vulnerabilities:*** For many vulnerabilities, the fix is as simple as installing a patch or performing a re-configuration.

4. ***Mitigate Vulnerabilities:*** Engineering mitigates vulnerabilities that cannot be simply patched or addressed. Mitigation may be through preventive controls that make the vulnerability harder to exploit or detective controls to catch exploits when they occur.

5. ***Verify Mitigation:*** When engineering performs mitigation, the security team is consulted to verify the mitigation will be effective and perform as desired.

6. ***Identify Risks:*** Security considers the business impacts of the vulnerabilities, their remediation, and any mitigation performed. It then uses that information to update the list of enterprise risks, as necessary.

Supporting Information Systems

The Vulnerability Scanning, Tracking, and Management process is supported by the following information systems:

- ***Configuration Management Database:*** Security uses this database to identify systems for vulnerability scanning. If necessary, scanning can be prioritized so the systems with the most business impact and criticality receive the most attention.

- ***Vulnerability Database:*** Security uses this database to track identified vulnerabilities from their detection through their resolution. Ideally, this database also tracks business decisions to accept vulnerabilities and the security controls and risks involved in their mitigation.

- ***Enterprise Risks:*** Security updates this database when vulnerabilities are accepted or cannot be mitigated. Security documents the ways the vulnerabilities affect the overall enterprise business risk posture.

13. Patch Management and Deployment

The Patch Management and Deployment process deploys patches to operational systems to address vulnerabilities, operational problems, or simple routine software maintenance. It is critical for enterprises to have a patch management and deployment process that is tightly integrated into IT operations and maintenance. In addition, this process needs to allow for the occasional deployment of unscheduled, emergency patches.

The workflow for this process is shown in Figure E-14. This process is usually operated from within the "Monitoring, Vulnerability, and Patch Management" functional area, although ideally it should be led from IT operations, with only minor allowances for security-driven patching.

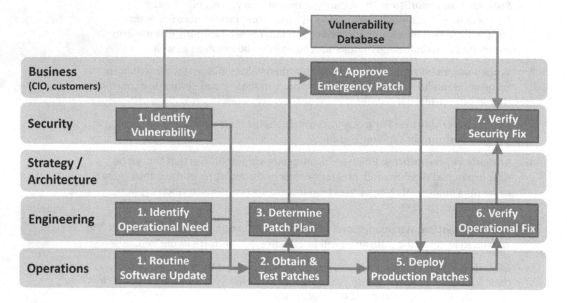

Figure E-14. *Patch Management and Deployment process.*

Process Overview

The Patch Management and Deployment process consists of the following major activities:

1. ***Identify Vulnerability, Operational Need, or Routine Software Update:*** Security identifies the need for a patch. There may be three possible patch drivers: (1) a security vulnerability, (2) an operational problem, or (3) routine software patches from the vendor. The first two possible drivers may necessitate non-routine, "emergency" patching, while routine software updates should be performed in a deliberate and scheduled fashion.

2. ***Obtain and Test Patches:*** Operations obtains the software patches and ensures their legitimacy and compatibility with the systems to be patched.

3. ***Determine Patch Plan:*** For emergency patches, engineering reviews the patches to ensure adequate testing is performed and that the operational or security risk warrants deploying the patch outside of the routine process. The patch plan includes back-out and contingency procedures.

4. ***Approve Emergency Patch:*** For emergency patches, business leadership makes the final decision to patch outside of normal procedures, evaluating the overall business risks.

5. ***Deploy Production Patches:*** Upon approval, operations proceeds with the patching either using normal operating procedures and maintenance windows, or using the emergency patch plan prepared by engineering.

6. **Verify Operational Fix:** For emergency patches in particular, engineering reviews the system post-patching to verify that the system is operating as expected.

7. **Verify Security Fix:** For security patches, security reviews the system post-patching to verify the security vulnerabilities of concern have been adequately addressed.

Supporting Information Systems

The Patch Management and Deployment process is supported by the following information system:

- **Vulnerability Database:** The IT department uses this database to track vulnerabilities requiring mitigation through patching, and to ensure the patching is performed as planned. This database is also used to track vulnerabilities deliberately not patched and any mitigating controls used to compensate for the unpatched vulnerabilities.

14. Security Monitoring

The Security Monitoring process is one of the most fundamental enterprise security processes and is a "must-have" for countering modern threats. This process involves designing alerts triggered by likely adversary activity, and then using those alerts to identify incidents in the environment. This process should be ongoing, not only to monitor systems and identify incidents, but also to continually refine the alerts to reduce false positives and search for new indicators of compromise.

The workflow for this process is shown in Figure E-15. This process is usually operated from within the "Monitoring, Vulnerability, and Patch Management" functional area, although it can also be integrated in with IT operations provided that the security aspect of it is adequately prioritized.

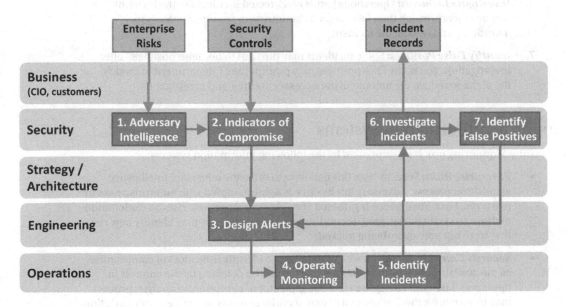

Figure E-15. *Security Monitoring process.*

Process Overview

The Security Monitoring process consists of the following major activities:

1. ***Adversary Intelligence:*** Security needs to understand the adversary threats that should be detected. The threats are considered in terms of the assets they affect and the business consequences should the threats occur. For deliberate attackers, the tools, techniques, and procedures used by the attackers are considered, if they are known.

2. ***Indicators of Compromise:*** From the threat scenarios, security can determine indicators of compromise that would indicate attacker activity or events. These indicators may be as simple as an anti-virus alert, or they may be sophisticated patterns that can be identified with a correlating log system. These indicators may also be automated indicators obtained from an external service or internally-deployed analytics technologies.

3. ***Design Alerts:*** Based on the indicators of compromise, engineering designs alerts to be triggered when those indicators are present. The alerts are designed to have a high fidelity, while also to minimize the numbers of false positives.

4. ***Operate Monitoring:*** Alerts are then passed on to IT operations that uses the monitoring capability to detect the alerts when they occur. During daily operations, the alerts are periodically tested to ensure they are functioning properly.

5. ***Identify Incidents:*** As monitoring detects alerts in the environment, security evaluates these alerts to identify incidents for investigation. A single incident may come from multiple alerts, just as a single alert may be related to multiple incidents. The difference here is that incidents are manually created, while alerts are usually automated.

6. ***Investigate Incidents:*** Operations hands off detected incidents to the incident response team, which then follows the cyberintrusion response process to investigate and resolve the incident.

7. ***Identify False Positives:*** Some incidents may turn out to be "false positives" after investigation. Too many false positives may prompt the IT department to modify the alerts to reduce the amount of unnecessary alerting and investigation.

Supporting Information Systems

The Security Monitoring process is supported by the following information systems:

- ***Enterprise Risks:*** Security uses this database to drive the adversary intelligence acquisition process. Adversary intelligence is tightly coupled with enterprise risks in two ways. First, intelligence is gathered about known enterprise risks so exploitation of those risks can be detected. Second, adversary intelligence may identify new risks that were not previously being tracked.

- ***Security Controls:*** Security uses this database to identify indicators of compromise, as the available indicators are limited to what can be detected by the controls in operation. Like with enterprise risks, the indicator of compromise analysis process may in turn drive the deployment of new security controls to enable better detection.

- **Incident Records:** As incidents are identified and investigated, security documents the incidents in this data source so the incidents can be handed off to the cyberintrusion response process and tracked through resolution.

15. Password and Key Management

The Password and Key Management process is used to manage the life cycle of cryptographic keys throughout their life cycle from creation to destruction. It is important to remember passwords are essentially keys that are easy to write down. (Cryptographic keys can be written down, as well.) Keys have life cycles driven by factors such as their cryptographic strength, usage patterns, probability of compromise, and potential attack vectors. Just because a password or a key is cryptographically "strong" does not mean it cannot be compromised in other ways. Detecting compromised keys can be extremely difficult, if not impossible.

The workflow for this process is shown in Figure E-16. This process is usually operated from within the "Data Protection and Cryptography" functional area. If it is managed by IT operations, it should be periodically reviewed by someone with cryptographic experience to ensure good practices are being followed.

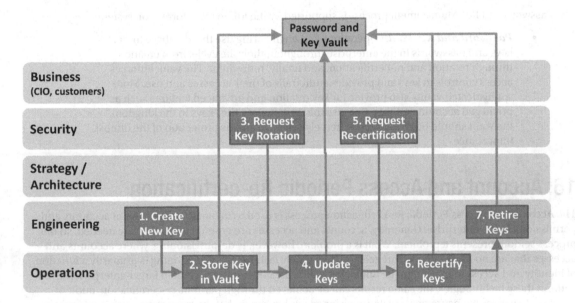

Figure E-16. *Password and Key Management process.*

Process Overview

The Password and Key Management process consists of the following major activities:

1. ***Create New Key:*** Engineering or operations creates a new key or password. Note this process primarily refers to organizational keys or passwords, although personal accounts can be managed this way if there is a compelling business need.

2. ***Store Key in Vault:*** Once the key is created, it is archived for protection. The key can be retrieved and changed when necessary. This activity may be as simple as an envelope contained in a safe, or it may be a sophisticated online system.

3. ***Request Key Rotation:*** Keys must be rotated in accordance with security policy, and this activity should be audited on a periodic basis. It is best when key rotation is performed or enforced automatically, but the process can be manual as well.

4. ***Update Keys:*** As keys are rotated or otherwise updated, operations updates the key vault to reflect the new key material or password value.

5. ***Request Re-certification:*** Security should periodically request re-certification of the keys to ensure the keys are still needed and the people responsible for the keys have access to the keys.

6. ***Re-certify Keys:*** The key re-certification activity ensures the keys are still needed, people responsible for the keys have access to the keys, and the corresponding information is up-to-date.

7. ***Retire Keys:*** Engineering retires keys at the end of their life cycle or when the system using them is retired.

Supporting Information Systems

The Password and Key Management process is supported by the following information system:

*   ***Password and Key Vault:*** Operations and engineering use this database to track keys and passwords in the enterprise throughout their life cycle, from creation through rotation and re-certification, and finally, retirement. The vault enforces access controls to keys and provides audit trails of their accesses and use. More sophisticated vaults also provide for key rotation and advanced features such as privileged account auditing. Because the vault houses the "keys to the kingdom," the vault should be considered extremely sensitive and its protection of the utmost importance.

16. Account and Access Periodic Re-certification

The Account and Access Periodic Re-certification process is used to manage the life cycle of accounts and permissions in the enterprise. Generally, accounts and accesses are granted when they are needed, so this process seldom presents a problem. What is a problem, however, is de-provisioning, where accounts and accesses that are no longer needed are released in a timely fashion. De-provisioning is primarily a function of identity and access management technologies, which are critically important in larger enterprises. Even without these technologies, the same results can be achieved through periodic re-certification/audit of accounts/accesses to ensure they are de-provisioned, and to check that the most critical privileges are not being abused.

The workflow for this process is shown in Figure E-17. This process is usually operated from within the "Identity, Authentication, and Access Management" functional area. Frequently, it will be led by an internal audit or compliance function due to its importance for regulatory compliance.

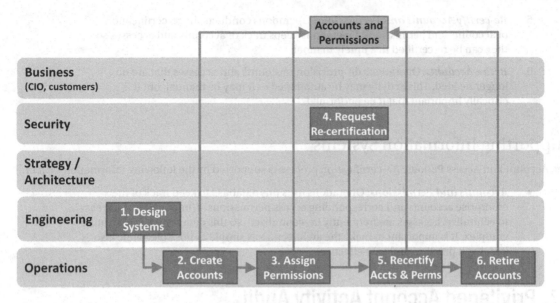

Figure E-17. Account and Access Periodic Re-certification process.

Process Overview

The Account and Access Periodic Re-certification process consists of the following major activities:

1. **Design Systems:** Accounts and accesses generally stem from systems that utilize them and the people who need access to those systems. Engineering designs and deploys systems along with associated accounts and access permissions.

2. **Create Accounts:** Once there are systems that require accounts, operations creates accounts for access to those systems.

3. **Assign Permissions:** Operations assigns account permissions for enterprise systems to allow people access. Generally, system permissions are grouped into three levels: administrators, operators, and users. Administrators have the ability to install and configure the computer, database, or application. Operators have the ability to manipulate the data of the application in a privileged way, but they cannot change the application itself. Users have unprivileged access to the application and only limited abilities to modify its data. Enterprise applications may have hundreds of roles and permissions, but they generally fall into these three categories.

4. **Request Re-certification:** As accounts and permissions are created in the enterprise, security ensures that they are periodically re-certified so that unused accounts and permissions can be removed. This activity is carefully designed so that it touches all accounts, permissions, applications, and systems. The more decentralized the enterprise is, the harder the re-certification process will be.

5. ***Re-certify Accounts and Permissions:*** Operations conducts the re-certification of accounts and permissions. Operations keeps track of accounts and accesses so they can be re-certified in a timely manner.

6. ***Retire Accounts:*** Operations de-provisions accounts and accesses that are no longer needed. This activity may be automated or it may be manual, but it is critically important that it be performed.

Supporting Information Systems

The Account and Access Periodic Re-certification process is supported by the following information system:

- ***Accounts and Permissions:*** Operations uses this database to keep track of the enterprise accounts and corresponding access permissions. While accounts are easy to centralize, accesses are frequently de-centralized, so this data source can be quite complex. It is important to make the architecture as simple as possible, while also keeping it practical and cost-effective.

17. Privileged Account Activity Audit

The Privileged Account Activity Audit process is used to audit the actions performed by the most privileged accounts in the enterprise. Accounts subject to this process should be selected using a risk-based methodology that focuses on accounts for which there are few safeguards, and where compromise of the account could result in the compromise of the entire enterprise or a significant portion of it. For these types of accounts, multiple layers of safeguards are needed, including most importantly a robust audit trail of all activities using the accounts. This audit trail must also contain safeguards so even if the accounts are compromised, the audit trail cannot be simply "turned off" without being detected.

The workflow for this process is shown in Figure E-18. This process is usually operated from within the "Systems Administration" functional area. This process is different from regular monitoring because it is an audit function, not a monitoring one, and consequently should be led by the security team.

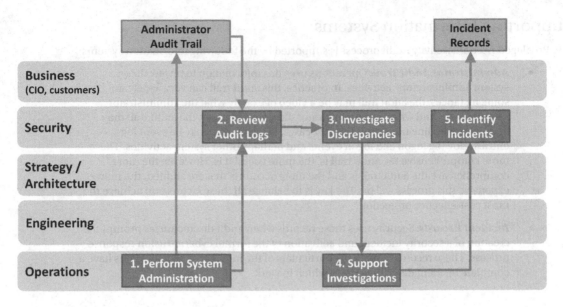

Figure E-18. *Privileged Account Activity Audit process.*

Process Overview

The Privileged Account Activity Audit process consists of the following major activities:

1. ***Perform System Administration:*** Operations performs systems administration activities that generate, in part, (1) an audit trail of all activities using the privileged accounts, and (2) alerts for security to review certain activities.

2. ***Review Audit Logs:*** The security team reviews the activity audit logs, which may reference change records and the configuration management database. Note it is helpful for operations to also get the audit logs so they can perform their own review.

3. ***Investigate Discrepancies:*** Security investigates activities that are suspicious or outside of normal patterns. Note while it is helpful to enable operations staff to conduct their own review and investigation, to properly mitigate insider threats it is necessary to have a separate team also performing these investigations.

4. ***Support Investigations:*** Operations needs to support the investigation process. While they are instrumental in supporting these investigations, it is important to ensure they are not self-auditing, either.

5. ***Identify Incidents:*** Investigations that turn up discrepancies generate incidents for follow-up by the CyberIncident Response Team, through the cyberintrusion response process.

Supporting Information Systems

The Privileged Account Activity Audit process is supported by the following information systems:

- ***Administrator Audit Trail:*** Operations uses this information to review the system administrators' activities. In practice, this audit trail can vary widely. In some instances, the audit trail may be a video of exactly what the administrator saw on screen and what the administrator did. In other cases, the audit trail may be a command line transcript. In other cases, the audit trail may be event log entries showing logon and logoff events and perhaps other system activities. The more comprehensive the audit trail is, the more useful it is. However, the more comprehensive the audit trail is and the more accounts that are audited, the more expensive this process will be. The key is to balance all these factors and achieve the most cost-effective protection.

- ***Incident Records:*** Security uses these records when audit discrepancies prompt the creation of a security incident and activation of the formal cyberintrusion response process. These records contain the particulars of the incident so that all teams have a complete incident description from which to work.

■ ■ ■

Object Measurement

An enterprise wants to protect itself from cybersecurity attacks that are constantly morphing. Consequently, successful enterprise cybersecurity is a continual improvement exercise designed to address the evolving cyberthreats. Measurement is a means for effecting this improvement.

Often, people think of cybersecurity effectiveness from a single perspective (manager, technologist, cybersecurity expert, and so on) or in terms of a function (for example, systems administration, network security, or data protection and cryptography) or a capability (such as network isolation, network traffic analysis, or digital certificates). However, measuring enterprise cybersecurity effectiveness involves multiple dimensions.

The mathematical and scientific disciplines often handle multi-dimensional quantities with entities known as *vectors*. The scientific discipline of physics uses vectors to describe many quantities to include displacement, velocity, and acceleration. To illustrate from this list of quantities, the change in position of a particle is called a *displacement*. When we go to work in the morning, we displace ourselves from our home to our place of work. This displacement can be represented as an arrow on a map drawn from home to work. Figure F-1 depicts the concept of displacement in one, two, three, and *n* dimensions.

■ **Note**   Some of the material in this appendix is adapted from Chapter 6 (Measurement) of the following book: Donaldson, Scott and Stanley Siegel. *Successful Software Development*, 2nd edition. (Upper Saddle River, NJ: Prentice Hall PTR, 2001).

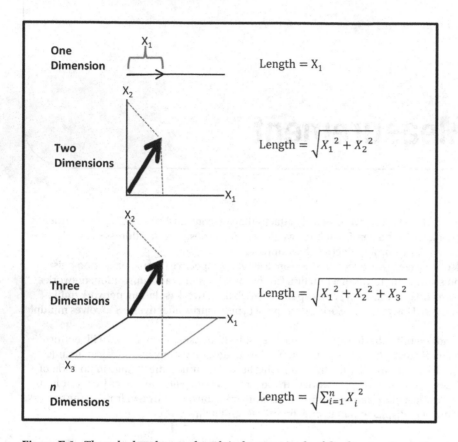

One
Dimension   Length $= X_1$

Two
Dimensions   Length $= \sqrt{X_1{}^2 + X_2{}^2}$

Three
Dimensions   Length $= \sqrt{X_1{}^2 + X_2{}^2 + X_3{}^2}$

n
Dimensions   Length $= \sqrt{\sum_{i=1}^{n} X_i{}^2}$

Figure F-1. *The calculated vector length is the magnitude of displacement.*

Simply stated, the calculated vector *length* combines multiple dimensions into a single quantity or *index*. Object Measurement (OM) uses this notion of an index to measure enterprise cybersecurity effectiveness.

Object Measurement (OM) is a generalized measurement technique that allows for the blending of multiple dimensions into an overall index.

The left-hand side of Figure F-2 depicts how OM uses the notion of a *vector* to derive an *overall index,* and the right-hand side depicts a corresponding example Cybersecurity Effectiveness Index (CSE*Index*) based on three cybersecurity functional areas.

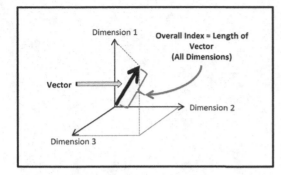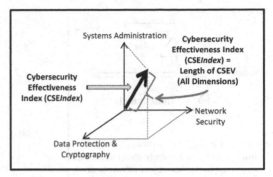

Figure F-2. *Object Measurement uses the notion of vector length to combine multiple dimensions into a single quantity called an index. This example illustrates the three functional areas being combined into a Cybersecurity Effectiveness Index or CSEIndex.*

In this example, the dimensions are defined in terms of the following cybersecurity functional areas:

- Dimension 1 = Systems Administration
- Dimension 2 = Network Security
- Dimension 3 = Data Protection and Cryptography

It is acknowledged the dimensions chosen to fold into this book's notion of a cybersecurity effectiveness index are not necessarily the same dimensions an enterprise may choose. For example, the dimensions could be defined in terms of other cybersecurity functional areas, capabilities, or other terms that make sense for a particular enterprise.

There is no one way to measure cybersecurity effectiveness. If there were, successful cybersecurity programs would have been reduced to an assembly-line process. However, there are fundamental principles whose application can increase the likelihood that enterprise cybersecurity programs will be successful.

The OM approach presented here allows an enterprise to adapt the cybersecurity effectiveness index concept to the needs of the enterprise. However, the measurement tasks cannot be onerous because they will get in the way of cybersecurity work and measurement will not be performed.

OM Index Equation

Based on the notion of vector length previously introduced, Figure F-3 depicts the general OM Index Equation, where vector dimensions are expressed in terms of object attributes.

$$OMIndex = \frac{\sqrt{\displaystyle\sum_{i=1}^{n} w_i^2 at_i^2}}{\sqrt{\displaystyle\sum_{i=1}^{n} w_i^2 (maximum[at_i])^2}}$$

where at_i = object attribute measurement
n = number of object attribute measurements
w_i = weighting factor for object attribute at_i
maximum $[at_i]$ = maximum value of at_i

Figure F-3. *The OMIndex Equation combines multiple object attributes (that is, dimensions) into a single numeric value.*

Each attribute can be weighted and there are no mathematical limits to the number of attributes. However, keep in mind that enterprise measurement programs will fail if they are too onerous. Also note the denominator is set up to normalize the OM*Index* (in other words, restrict the OM*Index* range from zero to one). Removing the denominator eliminates this normalization. Figure F-4 depicts three examples of how the OM*Index* equation can defined.

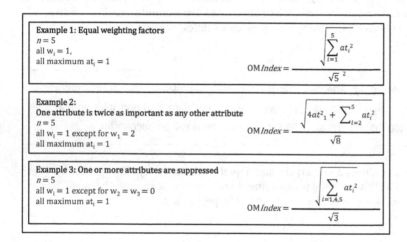

Figure F-4. *The OMIndex Equation provides an enterprise with a generalized measurement methodology that can be tailored to specific enterprise measurement requirements.*

As shown in Figure F-4, the OM Index Equation encompasses a wide range of possible OM*Index* definitions:

- Example 1 represents the case in which an object is characterized by 5 attributes.

- Example 2 represents the case in which the first attribute is considered twice as important as the other attributes.

- Example 3 represents the case in which the second and third attributes are suppressed.

The next section details the OM steps and how an enterprise can use them to measure the effectiveness of a cybersecurity program.

OM Steps

OM quantifies almost any object (such as enterprise cybersecurity functional area or capability) in terms of value scales that help tie measurement to familiar enterprise language. Figure F-5 notionally depicts OM combining multiple *value scale* measurements into an overall score (in other words, overall index).

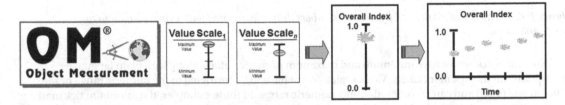

Figure F-5. *Object Measurement combines value scale measurements into an overall index that can be "unfolded" and displayed in a variety of ways to provide insight into the underlying measurements.*

OM steps include the following:

- **Step 1:** Define the questions the enterprise wants to answer.

- **Step 2:** Select appropriate object(s) to measure for collecting relevant data to answer the defined enterprise questions.

- **Step 3:** For each object, define the object characteristics to measure.

- **Step 4:** For each characteristic, create a value scale with tick marks and corresponding tick mark descriptions in plain, unambiguous language.

- **Step 5:** Measure each characteristic by (a) using expert judgment to form an opinion and matching the opinion with the appropriate value scale(s) and tick mark value(s), or (b) matching the observed data with the appropriate value scale(s) and tick mark value(s).

- **Step 6:** Substitute the selected tick mark numeric values into an appropriate OM equation to calculate an overall index.

Even though OM can measure almost anything, OM is not a measurement silver bullet. OM is applicable to efforts where multi-dimensional measurement is desired.

OM Value Scales

Value scales help associate an enterprise's vocabulary (that is, language) with measurement. The challenge is to establish value scales in a relatively painless way to make measurements based on these value scales. In the end, an enterprise needs meaningful measurements. *Meaningful* here means the enterprise uses the measurements to determine whether and where cybersecurity needs to be improved. Figure F-6 shows three types of OM value scales: discrete, binary, and sliding.

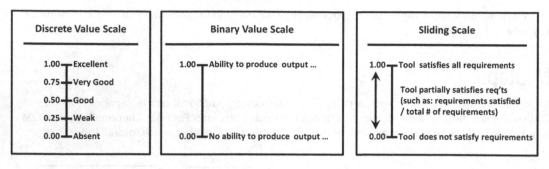

Figure F-6. *A value scale is defined by a set of numbers that is associated with expert judgment or observable data.*

Note the three scales have minimum and maximum numeric values, along with plain language descriptions on the tick mark labels. Value scales do not have to be restricted to the numeric range of zero (0.00) to one (1.00) and can accommodate any numeric range. In these examples, the minimum tick mark labels indicate not doing something, while the maximum tick mark labels generally indicate the opposite of the minimum tick mark labels. Value scales include the following types:

- ***Discrete value scales*** allow for distinct interim numeric values and corresponding tick mark labels (for example, 0.00 = Absent, 0.25 = Weak, and so on) between the minimum and maximum numeric values. When an enterprise establishes a cybersecurity improvement program, discrete value scales enable an enterprise to measure interim progress from Absent → Weak→ Good→ Very Good→ Excellent. (Note: Abbreviated tick mark labels are shown in Figure F-6 to accommodate space restrictions.)

- ***Binary value scales*** are often used to measure on/off or yes/no or desired behavior/lack of desired behavior. Generally, a binary value scale suggests the enterprise places importance on the desired behavior because, if the maximum value is not achieved, the resultant numeric value is zero.

- ***Sliding value scales*** measure a minimum numeric value, a partial numeric value based on a ratio, and a maximum numeric value. Sliding value scales are useful when measuring percent-complete values (for example, number of assessed functional areas/total number of functional areas).

The value scale tick-mark labels need to be defined in everyday enterprise language to aid in communicating measurement results. It is important to note there is *no one set of terms* (that is, numeric values and tick mark labels) that defines value scales. The enterprise decides what terms define its value scales. As described below, value scales can be defined in expert judgment language or in terms of the cybersecurity data the enterprise observes.

Expert Judgment Value Scales

Experts have their own experience-based language to describe their area of expertise to non-experts. Such language often embodies their educated guess or intuitive judgment. Figure F-7 depicts a value scale defined in expert judgment language for enterprise cybersecurity functional areas.

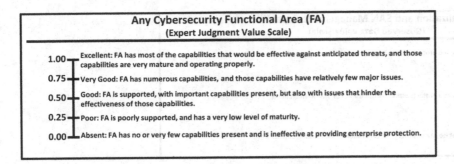

Figure F-7. *Object Measurement provides a method for defining expert judgment value scales to measure any enterprise cybersecurity functional area effectiveness.*

The expert judgment language may be somewhat "squishy," but it enables the expert to designate a particular value scale tick mark and its corresponding value as appropriate for the situation. For example, in Figure F-7, if an expert thinks a functional area is *poorly* supported and has a *very low level* of maturity, then the expert would designate 0.25 as the appropriate value for the situation.

Similarly, Figure F-8 depicts a value scale defined in expert judgment language for an enterprise cybersecurity functional area capability.

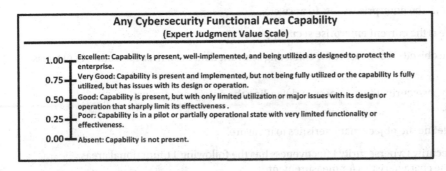

Figure F-8. *Object Measurement provides a method for defining expert judgment value scales to measure any enterprise cybersecurity functional area capability effectiveness.*

These expert judgment value scales are not *set in stone* and may be somewhat *squishy*, but they are provided as starting points for enterprise consideration. Each enterprise needs to create its own meaningful value scales.

Observed Data Value Scales

Observed data value scales are similar in structure (minimum value, maximum value, and tick mark labels) to expert judgment value scales, but tick mark labels represent observable events (also known as measurement triggers). Figure F-9 depicts an observed data value scale for a specific cybersecurity capability, Virtualization and SAN (Storage Area Network) Management, which is part of the Systems Administration functional area.

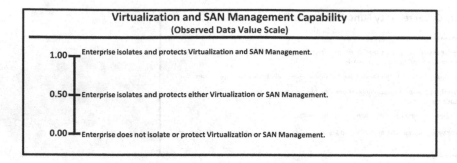

Figure F-9. *Object Measurement provides a method for defining observed data value scales to measure specific cybersecurity capabilities, which are part of specific enterprise cybersecurity functional areas.*

In this observed data capability value scale example, each tick mark label can be observed as opposed to the expert judgment capability value scale tick mark labels in Figure F-9. As is the case for expert judgment value scale definition, there is *no one set of terms* that defines observed data value scales.

Expert Judgment OM Example

Step 1: Define the questions the enterprise wants to answer.

- How effective is the current enterprise security posture?

Step 2: Select appropriate object(s) to measure for collecting relevant data to answer the defined enterprise questions.

- Enterprise Cybersecurity Effectiveness in defending the enterprise against cyberattacks.

Step 3: For each object, define the object characteristics to measure.

- Enterprise Security Cybersecurity Effectiveness has the following 11 functional areas that will be the characteristics for measurement

  - Systems Administration

  - Network Security

  - Application Security

  - Endpoint, Server, and Device Security

  - Identity, Authentication, and Access Management

  - Data Protection and Cryptography

  - Monitoring, Vulnerability, and Patch Management

  - High Availability, Disaster Recovery, and Physical Protection

  - Incident Response

  - Asset Management and Supply Chain

  - Policy, Audit, E-Discovery, and Training

Step 4: For each characteristic (that is, enterprise cybersecurity functional area), create a value scale with tick marks and corresponding tick mark descriptions in plain, unambiguous language.

- Use the Figure F-7 cybersecurity functional area value scale to define 11 expert judgment value scales shown in Figure F-10.

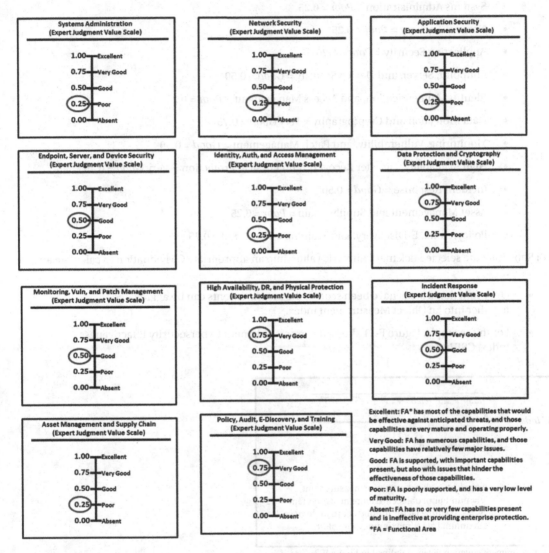

Figure F-10. *Example expert judgment cybersecurity functional area value scales with example expert judgment measurements indicated by circled values.*

Step 5: Measure each characteristic (in other words, 11 enterprise cybersecurity functional areas) by using expert judgment to form an opinion and matching the opinion with the appropriate value scale and tick mark values.

- Assume the following expert judgment measurements:

    - Systems Administration = *Poor* = 0.25

    - Network Security = *Poor* = 0.25

    - Application Security = *Poor* = 0.25

    - Endpoint, Server, and Device Security = *Good* = 0.50

    - Identity, Authentication, and Access Management = *Poor* = 0.25

    - Data Protection and Cryptography = *Very Good* = 0.75

    - Monitoring, Vulnerability, and Patch Management = *Good* = 0.50

    - High Availability, Disaster Recovery, and Physical Protection = *Very Good* = 0.75

    - Incident Response = *Good* = 0.50

    - Asset Management and Supply Chain = *Poor* = 0.25

    - Policy, Audit, E-Discovery, and Training = *Very Good* = 0.75

Step 6: Substitute the selected tick mark numeric values into an appropriate OM equation to calculate an overall index.

- Once functional areas have been scored, the measurements can be aggregated together into an Object Measurement index.

- For this example, Figure F-11 shows the expert judgment Cybersecurity Effectiveness Index, CSE*Index*.

$$CSE\textit{Index} = \frac{\sqrt{\frac{.25^2 + .25^2 + .25^2 + .5^2 + .25^2 + .75^2 + .5^2 + .75^2 + .5^2 + .25^2 + .75^2}{\sqrt{11}}}}{}$$

$$= \frac{1.6}{3.3} = 0.48$$

where at_i = object attribute measurement
n = number of object attribute measurement = 11
w_i = weighting factor for object attribute at_i = 1
maximum $[at_i]$ = maximum value of at_i = 1

Object measurement equation notation defined in Figure F-3

Figure F-11. *The expert judgment CSEIndex is calculated by substituting the selected tick mark values into the appropriate OM equation.*

- Using Figure F-7's expert judgment value scale, a CSE*Index* score = 0.48 is greater than *Poor* and less than *Good*.

- Since measurement is used, in part, to increase cybersecurity effectiveness, assume the enterprise implemented an improvement program based on the results of the above measurement. Further assume some time has elapsed after the above measurements were taken and the following expert judgment measurements were recorded after the cybersecurity improvements were implemented:

  - Systems Administration = *Very Good* = 0.75

  - Network Security = *Excellent* = 1.00

  - Application Security = *Good* = 0.50

  - Endpoint, Server, and Device Security = *Very Good* = 0.75

  - Identity, Authentication, and Access Management = *Excellent* = 1.00

  - Data Protection and Cryptography = *Very Good* = 0.75 (no change)

  - Monitoring, Vulnerability, and Patch Management = *Very Good* = 0.75

  - High Availability, Disaster Recovery, and Physical Protection = *Excellent* = 1.00

  - Incident Response = *Very Good* = 0.75

  - Asset Management and Supply Chain = *Good* = 0.50

  - Policy, Audit, E-Discovery, and Training = *Very Good* = 0.75 (no change)

- Figure F-12 shows the resulting expert judgment Cybersecurity Effectiveness Index, CSE*Index*.

$$CSE\textit{Index} = \frac{\sqrt{\begin{matrix}.75^2 + 1.0^2 + .5^2 + .75^2 + 1.0^2 + .75^2 + \\ .75^2 + 1.0^2 + .75^2 + .5^2 + .75^2\end{matrix}}}{\sqrt{11}}$$

$$= \frac{2.6}{3.3} = 0.79$$

where at_i = object attribute measurement
n = number of object attribute measurement = 11
w_i = weighting factor for object attribute at_i = 1
maximum $[at_i]$ = maximum value of at_i = 1

Object measurement equation notation defined in Figure F-3

Figure F-12. *As a result of example cybersecurity improvements, the CSEIndex increased in value from 0.48 to 0.79.*

- The question is, "What does 0.79 mean?" Using Figure F-7's expert judgment value scale, a CSE*Index* score = 0.79 is greater than *Very Good* and less than *Excellent*.

- Figure F-13 depicts the results of the above expert judgment measurement activities (left-hand side of figure) and the results of the assumed subsequent cybersecurity improvement activities (right-hand side of figure).

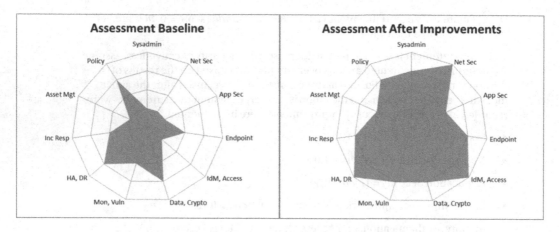

Figure F-13. *Kiviat charts (also known as spider charts) illustrate how the experts measured each enterprise cybersecurity functional area before (left) and after (right) improvements were implemented.*

- CSE*Index*, an assessment metric, can be tracked over time from assessment to assessment. Figure F-14 shows a simple line chart depicting cybersecurity assessment results over time, reflecting improvements or degradation of the enterprise's security posture.

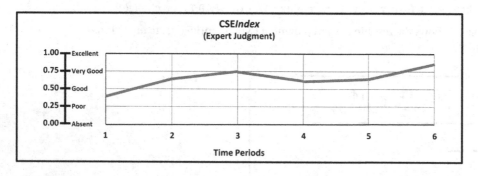

Figure F-14. *Once measured and quantified using Object Measurement, cybersecurity assessment results can be tracked over time. This type of tracking is useful to communicate the measured results of security infrastructure investments.*

The OM Index Equation provides direct linkage between the defined functional area value scale and an expert's judgment. This expressed linkage is tied to enterprise cybersecurity improvement activities. By tracking CSE*Index* over time, the expert judgment provides the enterprise a means for guiding the enterprise's ongoing cyberdefense improvement activities.

Observed Data OM Example

Step 1: Define the questions the enterprise wants to answer.

- How effective is the current enterprise Systems Administration functional area?

- This step is different from the expert judgment measurement example as only the Systems Administration functional area is being measured versus all 11 enterprise cybersecurity functional areas.

Step 2: Select appropriate object(s) to measure for collecting relevant data to answer the defined enterprise questions.

- Systems Administration effectiveness in defending the enterprise against cyberattacks.

- This step is different from the expert judgment measurement example as only the enterprise cybersecurity Systems Administration functional area is being measured versus all 11 cybersecurity functional areas.

Step 3: For each object, define the object characteristics to measure.

- Systems Administration has the following nine capabilities:

  - Bastion Host

  - Out-of-Band (OOB) Management

  - Network Isolation

  - Integrated Lights-Out (ILO), Keyboard Video Mouse (KVM), Power Controls

  - Virtualization and Storage Area Network (SAN) Management

  - Separation of Administration from Services

  - Multi-factor Authentication for Administrators

  - Administrator Audit Trail(s)

  - Command Logging and Analytics

- This step is different from the expert judgment measurement example as nine individual Systems Administration capabilities are to be measured versus the 11 enterprise cybersecurity functional areas.

Step 4: For each characteristic (in this case, the nine Systems Administration capabilities), create a value scale with tick marks and corresponding tick mark descriptions in plain, unambiguous language.

- For observed data capability measurement, use Figure F-15 cybersecurity capability value scales.

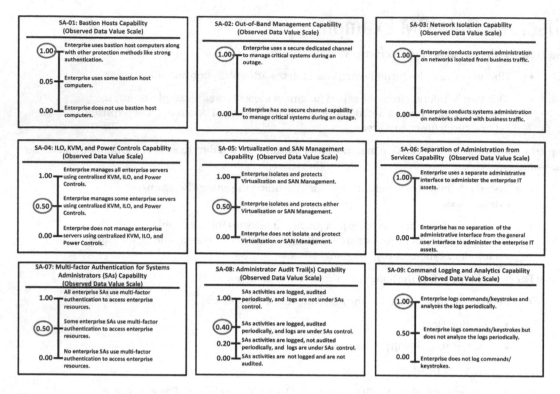

Figure F-15. *Example observed data Systems Administration capability value scales with example observed data measurements circled.*

- This step is different from the expert judgment measurement example as nine individual Systems Administration capability value scales are defined versus one expert judgment value scale being defined and used for the 11 enterprise cybersecurity functional areas.

Step 5: Measure each characteristic (in other words, nine Systems Administration capabilities) by matching the observed data with the appropriate Systems Administration capability value scales and tick mark values.

- Use Figure F-15's Systems Administration tick mark labels for this example's observed data measurements.

- Assume the following Systems Administration observed data measurements:

  - Bastion Host Capability = *Enterprise uses Bastion Host computers along with other protection methods like strong authentication* = 1.0.

  - Out-of-Band Management Capability = *Enterprise uses a secure dedicated channel to manage critical systems during an outage* = 1.0.

  - Network Isolation Capability = *Enterprise conducts systems administration on networks isolated from business traffic* = 1.0.

  - ILO, KVM, Power Controls Capability = *Enterprise manages some enterprise servers using centralized KVM, ILO, and Power Controls* = 0.50.

- Virtualization and SAN Management = *Enterprise isolates and protects either Virtualization or SAN Management* = 0.50.

- Separation of Administration from Services Capability = *Enterprise uses a separate administrative interface to administer the enterprise IT assets* = 1.0.

- Multi-factor Authentication for Administrators Capability = *Some enterprise SAs use multi-factor authentication to access enterprise resources* = 0.50.

- Administrator Audit Trail(s) Capability = *SAs activities are logged and audited periodically, and logs are under SAs control* = 0.40.

- Command Logging and Analytics Capability = *Enterprise logs commands/ keystrokes and analyzes the logs periodically* = 1.0.

Step 6: Substitute the selected tick mark numeric values into an appropriate OM equation to calculate an overall index.

- Once the Systems Administration capabilities areas have been measured, the measurements can be aggregated together into a summary rating (also known as an overall index).

- As shown in Figure F-16, the observed data Systems Administration Cybersecurity Effectiveness Index, SACSE*Index*, is calculated using the OM Index Equation.

$$\text{SACSE}Index = \frac{\sqrt{\begin{array}{c}1.0^2 + 1.0^2 + 1.0^2 + .5^2 + .5^2 + \\ 1.0^2 + .5^2 + .4^2 + 1.0^2\end{array}}}{\sqrt{9}}$$

$$= \frac{2.43}{3} = 0.81$$

where at_i = object attribute measurement
n = number of object attribute measurement = 9
w_i = weighting factor for object attribute at_i = 1
maximum $[at_i]$ = maximum value of at_i = 1

Object measurement equation notation defined in Figure F-3

Figure F-16. *SACSEIndex is calculated by substituting the appropriate tick mark value based on the observed data.*

- By combining the nine individual observed data capability measurements into an overall observed data Systems Administration Cybersecurity Effectiveness Index, SACSE*Index*, the resulting index value = 0.81.

- The question is, "What does 0.81 mean?" An abbreviated answer is that 0.81 means that Systems Administration Cybersecurity Effectiveness exactly what was observed (in other words, the observed data) as follows:

  - *Enterprise uses Bastion Host computers along with other protection methods such as strong authentication.*

  - *Enterprise uses a secure dedicated channel to manage critical systems during an outage.*

  - *Enterprise conducts systems administration on networks isolated from business traffic.*

- *Enterprise manages some enterprise servers using centralized KVM, ILO, and Power Controls.*

- *Enterprise isolates and protects either Virtualization or SAN Management.*

- *Enterprise uses a separate administrative interface to administer the enterprise IT assets.*

- *Some enterprise SAs use multi-factor authentication to access enterprise resources.*

- *Systems Administrators (SAs) activities are logged and audited periodically, and logs are under SAs control.*

- *Enterprise logs commands/keystrokes and analyzes the logs periodically.*

- With an observed data SACSE*Index* = 0.81, the enterprise's Systems Administration functional area (as defined by the enterprise) is approximately 81% of the way toward completely protecting the enterprise against cyberattacks.

- The enterprise could consider focusing on improving the following Systems Administration capabilities:

  - ILO, KVM, Power Controls

  - Virtualization and SAN Management

  - Multi-factor Authentication for Systems Administrators

  - Administrator Audit Trails

- Since measurement is used, in part, to increase cybersecurity effectiveness, assume the enterprise implemented an improvement program based on the results of the previous measurements. Further assume some time has elapsed after the measurements were taken and the following observed data measurements were recorded after the cybersecurity improvements were implemented:

  - Bastion Host Capability = *Enterprise uses Bastion Host computers along with other protection methods such as strong authentication* = 1.0. (no change)

  - Out-of-Band Management Capability = *Enterprise uses a secure dedicated channel to manage critical systems during an outage* = 1.0. (no change)

  - Network Isolation Capability = *Enterprise conducts systems administration on networks isolated from business traffic* = 1.0. (no change)

  - ILO, KVM, Power Controls Capability = *Enterprise manages all enterprise servers using centralized KVM, ILO, and Power Controls* = 1.0.

  - Virtualization and SAN Management = *Enterprise isolates and protects either Virtualization or SAN Management* = 0.50. (no change)

  - Separation of Administration from Services Capability = *Enterprise uses a separate administrative interface to administer the enterprise IT assets* = 1.0.

  - Multi-factor Authentication for Administrators Capability = *Some enterprise SAs use multi-factor authentication to access enterprise resources* = 0.50. (no change)

- Administrator Audit Trail(s) Capability = *SAs activities are logged and audited periodically, and logs are not under SAs control* = 1.0.

- Command Logging and Analytics Capability = *Enterprise logs commands/ keystrokes and analyzes the logs periodically* = 1.0. (no change)

- The resulting observed data Systems Administration Cybersecurity Effectiveness Index, SACSE*Index,* is shown in Figure F-17.

$$
\text{SACSE}Index = \frac{\sqrt{\frac{1.0^2 + 1.0^2 + 1.0^2 + 1.0^2 + .5^2 + 1.0^2 + .5^2 + 1.0^2 + 1.0^2}{\sqrt{9}}}}{3}
$$

$$
= \frac{2.74}{3} = 0.91
$$

where at_i = object attribute measurement
n = number of object attribute measurement = 9
w_i = weighting factor for object attribute at_i = 1
maximum $[at_i]$ = maximum value of at_i = 1

Object measurement equation notation defined in Figure F-3

Figure F-17. *As a result of example cybersecurity improvements, the SACSEIndex increased in value from 0.81 to 0.91.*

Figure F-18 depicts the results of the previous observed data measurement activities (left-hand side of figure) and the results of the assumed subsequent cybersecurity improvement activities (right-hand side of figure). Note: Due to the improvement activities, the SACSE*Index* increases from 0.81 to 0.91.

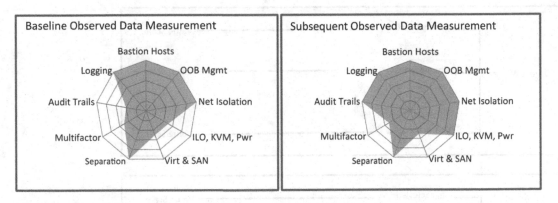

Figure F-18. *Kiviat charts (also known as spider charts) illustrate the observed data for the example Systems Administration functional area capabilities.*

- SACSE*Index,* an assessment metric, can be tracked over time from assessment to assessment. Figure F-19 shows a simple line chart depicting enterprise cybersecurity assessment results over time, reflecting improvements or degradation of the enterprise's security posture.

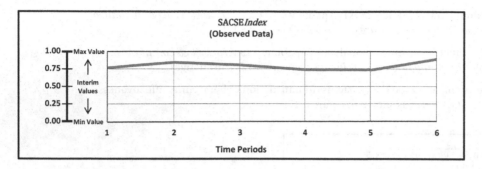

Figure F-19. *Once measured and quantified using Object Measurement, enterprise cybersecurity assessment results can be tracked over time. This type of tracking is useful to communicate the measured results of security infrastructure investments.*

The OM Index Equation provides direct linkage from the defined capabilities, via observed data, to the corresponding functional areas. This expressed linkage is tied to enterprise cybersecurity improvement activities. By tracking SACSE*Index* over time, the index and corresponding observed data value scales provide the enterprise a means for guiding the enterprise's ongoing cyberdefense improvement activities.

OM Measurement Map

To help define and visualize the value scales for each object to be measured, it is often convenient to create an OM measurement map. Figure F-20 depicts two generic measurement maps that can be used in concert with the OM steps described above (for example, Step 3, Step 4, and Step 5).

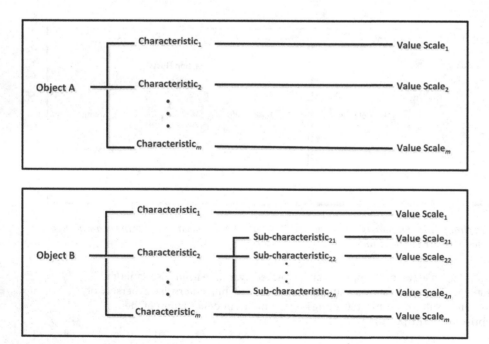

Figure F-20. *OM measurement maps help define appropriate value scales to measure an object.*

The upper half of Figure F-20 depicts Object A in terms of a number of characteristics and corresponding value scales (that is, one characteristic and one corresponding value scale). The lower half of Figure F-20 depicts Object B in terms of characteristics, sub-characteristics, and corresponding value scales (in other words, one characteristic and one corresponding value scale; one characteristic with multiple sub-characteristics and corresponding value scales). Measurement maps define the value scales at the lowest level (far right-hand side of map). Furthermore, a measurement map helps define objects in unambiguous terms and represents, in part, the scope of what is to be measured.

Figure F-21 depicts an example measurement map established for conducting an enterprise cybersecurity program assessment. As shown, the assessment is structured and scoped, in part, by the following components:

- *Risk mitigations* associated with a cyberattack sequence
- *Functional areas* defined in terms of enterprise cybersecurity capabilities
- *Security operations* associated with enterprise day-to-day security activities

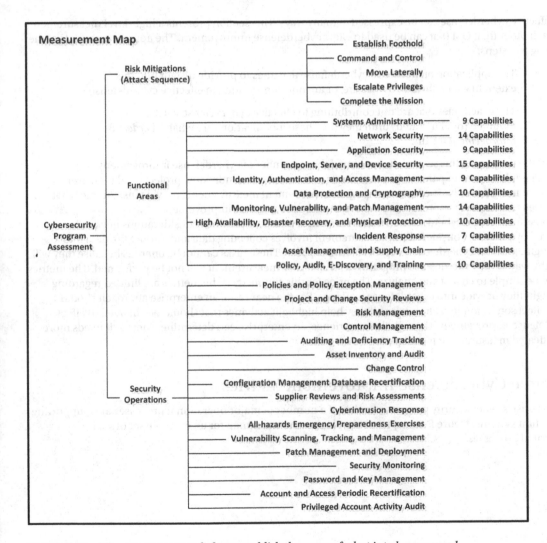

Figure F-21. *Measurement maps help to establish the scope of what is to be measured.*

Other Cybersecurity-Related Measurements

In addition to OM, it may be useful to establish other cybersecurity measurements tied to one or more aspects of an enterprise's cybersecurity program. The question is, "What attributes of the cybersecurity program are of interest to measure?" In part, the answer is tied to determining which activities contribute to *successfully securing the enterprise from cyberattacks,* an aspect that is closely tied to building an effective cyberdefense.

An effective enterprise cybersecurity program protects the enterprise in a cost-effective manner that balances technology, processes, people, budgets, and external compliance requirements, all while supporting the business mission as much as possible.

Effective cyberdefense can be expressed in many ways. This section presents a high-level measurement approach other than OM that can be used to effect cyberdefense improvement. The approach consists of the following two steps:

- The application of metrics to cyberdefense activities to provide insight into the extent to which these activities are, or are not, contributing to effective cyberdefense.

- Those activities that are not contributing to effective cyberdefense will be modified (or eliminated) until they do. These modifications are what *cyberdefense improvement* means.

For the purpose of this section, it is assumed that a number of cyberdefense improvement projects are being implemented in parallel. Improvements are measured on individual projects and then averaged over one or more projects. These average project improvement measurements provide insight into what cyberdefense areas have improved and what areas may need further improvement.

To perform actual cyberdefense program measurements, the previous considerations need to be tempered by practical considerations. Measurement involves collecting data and putting the data into a meaningful form for cyberdefense improvement purposes. These tasks cannot be onerous because they will get in the way of the cyberdefense program—in which case measurement will not be performed. The metrics need to be simple to collect and analyze. The price for this simplicity is the metrics are limited regarding the insight they provide into cyberdefense workings. For the near term, an enterprise approach should be to collect some simple metrics to see if they help highlight activities that should be changed to effect cyberdefense improvement. Through this experience, an enterprise can determine whether it needs more sophisticated measurement techniques.

Example Cyberdefense Improvement Metrics

An enterprise's cybersecurity program consists of a number of major operational processes and supporting information systems. Figure F-22 depicts a simple measurement map for an example set of such operational processes.

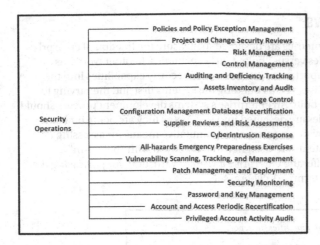

Figure F-22. Sample measurement map for security operational processes used in an enterprise.

This section presents example cybersecurity measurements for the following three security operational processes listed in Figure F-22:

- Policies and Policy Exception Management
- Project and Change Security Reviews
- Risk Management

Policies and Policy Exception Management

The Policies and Policy Exception Management process maintains enterprise policies, as well as exceptions to those policies. Enterprises may be good at establishing cybersecurity policies and maintaining them, but managing exceptions to those policies tends to be more problematic. Enterprises need to ensure policy exceptions are formally approved and then re-certified on a regular basis to ensure the policies are still valid. Security leadership needs to observe policy exceptions carefully to watch out for cases where the "exception becomes the rule."

Figure F-23 lists two example metrics that provide an enterprise quantitative means for assessing the extent to which enterprise cybersecurity policies are integrated into the enterprise business culture.

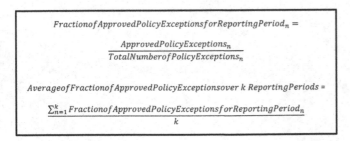

$$Fraction of Approved Policy Exceptions for Reporting Period_n =$$

$$\frac{Approved Policy Exceptions_n}{Total Number of Policy Exceptions_n}$$

$$Average of Fraction of Approved Policy Exceptions over\ k\ Reporting Periods =$$

$$\frac{\sum_{n=1}^{k} Fraction of Approved Policy Exceptions for Reporting Period_n}{k}$$

Figure F-23. These metrics provide the enterprise with a method for measuring the Policies and Policy Exception Management process.

405

Project and Change Security Reviews

The Project and Change Security Reviews process metrics are designed to measure the fraction of enterprise IT systems with "baked in" cybersecurity capabilities versus "bolted on" capabilities. In other words, as an enterprise designs and develops IT systems, it is important to integrate cybersecurity capabilities into the IT systems during the requirements and design phases versus building the systems first and then trying to "integrate" cybersecurity capabilities after they are built. An enterprise's systems development process should include activities to ensure cybersecurity capabilities are designed into systems as they are being built.

Figure F-24 lists two example metrics that provide an enterprise quantitative means for assessing the extent to which enterprise cybersecurity IT systems are designed and deployed with "baked-in" cybersecurity capabilities. These measurements offer the enterprise a visible "yardstick" for portraying the enterprise's security posture with respect to the enterprise's cyberassets.

$$Fraction of Enterprise IT Systems with "Baked in" Cybersecurity Capabilities for Reporting Period_n =$$

$$\frac{Enterprise IT Systems with "Baked in" Cybersecurity Capabilities for Reporting_n}{Total Number of Enterprise IT Systems for Reporting Period_n}$$

$$Average of Fraction of Enterprise IT Systems with Baked in Cybersecurity Cabilities over\ k\ Reporting Periods =$$

$$\frac{\sum_{n=1}^{k} Fraction of Enterprise IT Systems with "Baked in" Cybersecurity Capabilities for Reporting Period_n}{k}$$

Figure F-24. *These metrics provide the enterprise with a method for measuring the Project and Change Security Reviews process.*

Risk Management

The Risk Management process involves identifying and tracking enterprise risks. It is important the CISO tracks risks in terms of the risks' business impact, not their technological impact. Risks should be technology-agnostic. Where technology factors into the risk process is that as vulnerabilities are identified and exploited by attackers, the associated business risks can increase and possibly require additional mitigations. The risk management process should identify, analyze, and track risks, along with corresponding cybersecurity controls that help to mitigate specific risks.

Figure F-25 lists three example metrics that provide an enterprise quantitative means for assessing the extent to which identified, analyzed, and tracked risks are mitigated over time.

$$NrisksforReportingPeriod_n =$$

$$NumberofRisksIdentified, Analyzed, TrackedforReportingPeriod_n$$

$$RiskManagementEffectivenessforReportingPeriod_n =$$

$$\frac{NrisksMitigatedviaMitigatingControlsforReportingPeriod_n}{NrisksforReportingPeriod_n}$$

$$AverageofRiskManagementEffectivenesfor\ k\ ReportingPeriods =$$

$$\frac{\sum_{n=1}^{k} RiskManagementEffectivenessforReportingPeriod_n}{k}$$

Figure F-25. *These metrics provide the enterprise with a method for measuring the Risk Management process.*

These measurements, in turn, offer the enterprise a means for improving enterprise cybersecurity functional area capabilities that may be falling short in dealing effectively with these risks. For example, the enterprise may find for a given reporting period there have been successful cyberattack incidents linked to the e-mails of one or more enterprise users. As a possible starting point for mitigating the risk of e-mail security breaches, these incidents may point to a shortfall in the E-Mail Security capability of the Application Security functional area. This mitigation process would likely trigger the following enterprise upgrade to the enterprise risk management process for the E-Mail Security capability:

- The security team designs better controls for the E-Mail Security capability.

- The business leadership approves the risk mitigation plan for these improved controls.

- The engineering team implements the improved controls.

- The operations team maintains the operation of the improved controls.

- The security team tracks the extent to which the E-Mail Security breaches may have been mitigated. This tracking would show up in updates to the above metrics in subsequent reporting periods.

There is no one way to define cybersecurity metrics. It is up to the enterprise to decide what makes best sense.

APPENDIX G

▪▪▪

Cybersecurity Capability Value Scales

This appendix provides an example set of object measurement value scale definitions for 113 enterprise cybersecurity capabilities grouped by functional area. Value scales help associate an enterprise's vocabulary with measurement. There is no one set of terms that defines value scales. In the end, an enterprise needs meaningful measurements. *Meaningful* here means the enterprise uses the measurements to determine whether and where cybersecurity needs to be improved.

Figure G-1 illustrates the functional areas and the number of associated cybersecurity capabilities described in this appendix.

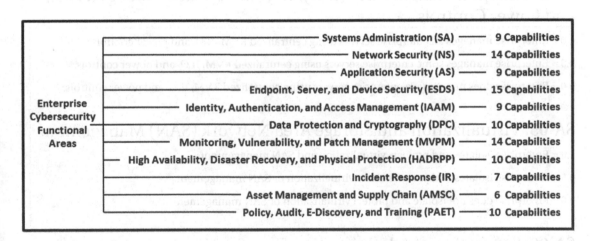

Figure G-1. *The 11 functional areas contain 113 cybersecurity capabilities.*

The following material defines example cybersecurity capability value scales that have minimum and maximum numeric values, along with plain language descriptions. The example value scales range from zero (0.00) to one (1.00), but the scales can accommodate any numeric range. For example, a value scale can range from 0% to 100%, or whatever range makes sense for the enterprise.

Appendix C and Appendix F provide additional details related to cybersecurity capabilities and value scales.

Systems Administration (SA)

SA-01: Bastion Hosts

1.0 = Enterprise uses bastion host computers to protect systems administration connections and sessions from tampering.

0.5 = Enterprise uses some bastion host computers.

0.0 = Enterprise does not use bastion host computers.

SA-02: Out-of-Band (OOB) Management

1.0 = Enterprise uses a secure, dedicated channel to manage critical systems during an outage.

0.0 = Enterprise has no secure channel capability to manage critical systems during an outage.

SA-03: Network Isolation

1.0 = Enterprise conducts systems administration on networks isolated from business traffic.

0.0 = Enterprise conducts systems administration on networks shared with business traffic.

SA-04: Integrated Lights-Out (ILO), Keyboard Video Mouse (KVM), and Power Controls

1.0 = Enterprise manages all enterprise servers using centralized KVM, ILO, and power controls.

0.5 = Enterprise manages some enterprise servers using centralized KVM, ILO, and power controls.

0.0 = Enterprise does not manage enterprise servers using centralized KVM, ILO, and power controls.

SA-05: Virtualization and Storage Area Network (SAN) Management

1.0 = Enterprise isolates and protects virtualization and SAN management.

0.5 = Enterprise isolates and protects either virtualization or SAN management.

0.0 = Enterprise does not isolate and protect virtualization or SAN management.

SA-06: Separation of Administration from Services

1.0 = Enterprise uses a separate administrative interface to administer the enterprise IT assets.

0.0 = Enterprise has no separation of the administrative interface from the general user interface to administer the enterprise IT assets.

SA-07: Multi-factor Authentication for Systems Administrators (SAs)

1.0 = All enterprise SAs use multi-factor authentication to access enterprise resources.

0.5 = Some enterprise SAs use multi-factor authentication to access enterprise resources.

0.0 = No enterprise SAs use multi-factor authentication to access enterprise resources.

SA-08: Administrator Audit Trail(s)

1.0 = SAs activities are logged and audited periodically, and logs are not under SAs control.

0.4 = SAs activities are logged and audited periodically, and logs are under SAs control.

0.2 = SAs activities are logged, but not audited periodically, and logs are under SAs control.

0.0 = SAs activities are not logged and are not audited.

SA-09: Command Logging and Analytics

1.0 = Enterprise logs commands/keystrokes and analyzes the logs periodically.

0.5 = Enterprise logs commands/keystrokes but does not analyze the logs periodically.

0.0 = Enterprise does not log commands/keystrokes.

Network Security (NS)
NS-01: Switches and Routers

1.0 = Management and operation of all switches and routers are conducted through a secure, centralized console. Logical and physical access to all the devices is restricted to a small group with "need-to-access" basis.

0.5 = Management and operation of some switches and routers are conducted through a secure, centralized console. Logical and physical access to some of these devices is restricted to a small group with "need-to-access" basis.

0.0 = Enterprise does not have secure, centralized management and operation of any switches and routers. Logical and physical access to any of these devices is not restricted.

NS-02: Software Defined Networking (SDN)

1.0 = Enterprise utilizes SDN to deploy, manage, upgrade, and retire all networking devices.

0.5 = Enterprise utilizes SDN to deploy, manage, upgrade, and retire some networking devices.

0.0 = Enterprise does not utilize SDN.

NS-03: Domain Name System (DNS) and Dynamic Host Configuration Protocol (DHCP)

1.0 = Enterprise installs security-hardened DNS with minimal features enabled (for example, DNS Security Extensions), and alerts to include Top Client, threshold DNS queries, and Response Rate limit.

0.0 = Enterprise installs Standard DNS.

NS-04: Network Time Protocol (NTP)

1.0 = Enterprise uses NTP to synchronize all system clocks to a master clock for accurate timestamping of logged events.

0.5 = Enterprise uses NTP to synchronize some system clocks to a master clock for accurate timestamping of logged events.

0.4 = Enterprise uses some capability other than NTP to synchronize all system clocks to a master clock for accurate timestamping of logged events.

0.3 = Enterprise uses some capability other than NTP (for example, Chrony, OpenNTPD) to synchronize some system clocks to a master clock for accurate timestamping of logged events.

0.0 = Enterprise does not have a capability to synchronize system clocks to a master clock. All system logs are timestamped with individual system clocks.

NS-05: Network Service Management

1.0 = Simple Network Management Protocol (SNMP) is secured by changing default "Community" string, setting permissions, and applying access filters/lists. Secure Shell (SSH) is protected by using strong passwords or generating SSH (private/public) keys for authentication, disabling root login, limiting the number of user logins or sessions, and disabling insecure protocols.

0.5 = Enterprise uses only some of the security/protection mechanisms listed above.

0.0 = Enterprise only uses standard SNMP and SHH protocols for systems administration.

NS-06: Firewall and Virtual Machine Firewall

1.0 = Firewalled network zones are set up to separate all high-risk systems (for example, Internet-facing web application servers) from low-risk internal systems (for example, database servers). Network architecture is designed to manage logically the flow of data traffic and provide visibility.

0.5 = Firewalled network zones are set up to separate some high-risk systems from low-risk internal systems. Network architecture is designed to manage logically the flow of data traffic and also provide visibility.

0.0 = Firewalled network zones are not implemented to separate high-risk systems from low-risk systems.

NS-07: Network Intrusion Detection/Network Intrusion Prevention System (IDS/IPS)

1.0 = IDS/IPS are fully implemented in the enforcement mode.

0.5 = Only IDS is implemented and IPS is in learning mode.

0.0 = IDS and IPS are not implemented.

NS-08: Wireless Networking (Wi-Fi)

1.0 = Wi-Fi is secured by setting up the following configuration: (1) changing the default administrator password, (2) using the most secured encryption available (such as WPA2), (3) using unpublished Service Set Identifier (SSID), and (4) monitoring is set up to review connection logs on a regular basis.

0.5 = Wi-Fi is secured by setting up the following configuration: (1), (2), and (3).

0.0 = Enterprise uses standard vendor-provided default configuration (including default administrator password).

(Note: This capability does not apply to an enterprise that does not use wireless networking and, therefore, does not enter into the NS effectiveness calculation.)

NS-09: Packet Intercept and Capture

1.0 = Packet intercept and capture are fully deployed to collect network traffic passing through a network segment. Packet analyzers are utilized to examine the traffic in real time and flag any malicious data packets.

0.5 = Packet intercept and capture tools are deployed to collect network traffic and to observe the throughput of the tool and network performance.

0.0 = Packet intercept and capture tools are not deployed.

NS-10: Secure Sockets Layer (SSL) Intercept

1.0 = Encrypted SSL network traffic (both inbound and outbound) is intercepted and examined.

0.8 = All encrypted SSL outbound traffic and some SSL encrypted inbound traffic are examined.

0.4 = All SSL encrypted inbound traffic and some SSL outbound network traffic are examined.

0.0 = SSL Intercept is not implemented.

NS-11: Network Access Control (NAC)

1.0 = NAC is deployed in enforcement mode.

0.5 = NAC is deployed in learning mode.

0.0 = NAC is not deployed.

NS-12: Virtual Private Networking (VPN) and Internet Protocol Security (IPSec)

1.0 = VPN is deployed with two-factor authentication solution by combining SSL and IPSec protocols for all external or remote users (for example, smart card, SMS message, PKI token).

0.5 = VPN is deployed with two-factor authentication solution for some external or remote users.

0.0 = VPN is implemented without two-factor authentication.

NS-13: Network Traffic Analysis (NTA)

1.0 = Enterprise uses NTA to analyze the volume of all network traffic.

0.5 = Enterprise uses NTA to analyze the volume of some network traffic.

0.0 = Enterprise does not use NTA.

NS-14: Network Data Analytics (NDA)

1.0 = Enterprise uses NDA to analyze (1) network traffic trends, (2) network availability, (3) planned outage impacts, and (4) network traffic with a goal to create a comprehensive model of various network threats to predict the next big network-based attack where network security policies define what *big network-based attack* means.

0.8 = Enterprise uses NDA to analyze some of the above items to achieve the goal.

0.4 = Enterprise has NDA but does not use it.

0.0 = Enterprise does not have NDA.

Application Security (AS)

AS-01: E-mail Security

1.0 = Enterprise deploys e-mail security protections such as spam filtering, e-mail block, e-mail redirect, custom malware detection signatures, scanning attachments for viruses, e-mail encryption, e-mail authentication, content filtering, and e-mail archiving.

0.5 = Enterprise deploys some of the above protections.

0.0 = Enterprise does not deploy any e-mail security protections.

AS-02: Webshell Detection

1.0 = Enterprise deploys webshell detection tools for all applications to scan for malicious code and files uploaded to the applications.

0.5 = Enterprise deploys webshell detection tools for some applications.

0.0 = Enterprise does not deploy webshell detection tools.

AS-03: Application Firewalls

1.0 = Enterprise deploys application firewalls in detection and enforcement mode to stop malicious data packets reaching all applications.

0.5 = Enterprise deploys application firewalls in detection and learning mode for some applications.

0.0 = Enterprise does not deploy application firewalls.

AS-04: Database Firewalls

1.0 = Enterprise deploys firewalls in detection and enforcement mode to stop malicious SQL data packets reaching all databases.

0.5 = Enterprise deploys firewalls in detection and learning mode for some databases.

0.0 = Enterprise does not deploy database firewalls.

AS-05: Forward Proxy and Web Filters

1.0 = Enterprise deploys forward proxy and web filters in enforcement mode for all outgoing requests from internal servers to the Internet.

0.5 = Enterprise deploys forward proxy and web filters in enforcement mode for some outgoing requests from internal servers to the Internet.

0.0 = Enterprise does not deploy forward proxy or web filters.

AS-06: Reverse Proxy

1.0 = Enterprise deploys reverse proxy to mask the internal network from all Internet users.

0.5 = Enterprise deploys reverse proxy to mask the internal network from some Internet users.

0.0 = Enterprise does not deploy reverse proxy.

AS-07: Data Leakage Protection (DLP)

1.0 = Enterprise deploys DLP in the enforcement mode.

0.5 = Enterprise deploys DLP in the learning mode and data tagging is performed.

0.0 = Enterprise does not deploy DLP tools.

AS-08: Secure Application and Database Software Development

1.0 = Secure application and database software development standards are fully utilized.

0.5 = Secure application and database software development standards are partially utilized.

0.0 = Secure application and database software development standards are not used.

AS-09: Software Code Vulnerability Analysis

1.0 = Enterprise deploys software code vulnerability analysis tools (that is, application vulnerability scanner and code reviewer).

0.5 = Enterprise deploys only the application vulnerability scanner.

0.0 = Enterprise does not deploy software code vulnerability analysis tools.

Endpoint, Server, and Device Security (ESDS)

ESDS-01: Local Administrator Privilege Restrictions

1.0 = No users have local administrative privileges on their endpoint computing devices.

0.5 = Some users have local administrative privileges on their endpoint computing devices.

0.0 = All users have local administrative rights on their endpoint computing devices.

ESDS-02: Computer Security and Logging Policies

1.0 = Enterprise records computer security logs and monitors the logs on a regular basis using pattern matching or other analytical intelligence.

0.5 = Enterprise records computer security logs, but does not monitor the logs on a regular basis.

0.1 = Enterprise implements ESDS computer security logging and log monitoring on an ad hoc basis.

0.0 = Enterprise does not have ESDS computer security and logging policies.

ESDS-03: Endpoint and Media Encryption

1.0 = Enterprise deploys endpoint and media encryption protection.

0.5 = Enterprise deploys some endpoint and media encryption.

0.0 = Enterprise does not deploy endpoint and media encryption.

ESDS-04: Computer Access Controls

1.0 = Enterprise uses computer access controls (in other words, identification, authorization, authentication, and accountability).

0.5 = Enterprise uses some computer access controls.

0.0 = Enterprise does not use computer access control.

ESDS-05: Forensic Imaging Support for Investigations

1.0 = Enterprise deploys forensic imaging policies, procedures, and tools governing what electronic data (at rest or in transmission) is recovered and analyzed to support criminal investigations.

0.0 = Enterprise does not deploy forensic imaging policies, procedures, or tools to support criminal investigations.

ESDS-06: Virtual Desktop/Thin Clients

1.0 = To facilitate endpoint security by not having to connect privately owned computers to the enterprise network, enterprise converts all these resources to virtual desktops that are kept current with latest security patches and updates.

0.5 = Enterprise converts some of privately owned resources to virtual desktops that are kept current with latest security patches and updates.

0.0 = Enterprise does not deploy virtual desktops.

ESDS-07: Mobile Device Management (MDM)

1.0 = Enterprise deploys MDM solution to allow all personally owned mobile devices to connect to the enterprise network to access enterprise data (for example, e-mail, calendaring, contacts).

0.5 = Enterprise deploys MDM solution to allow some personally owned mobile devices to connect to the enterprise network.

0.0 = Enterprise does not utilize MDM.

ESDS-08: Anti-Virus/Anti-Malware

1.0 = Enterprise deploys anti-virus/anti-malware software to protect all enterprise endpoint devices.

0.5 = Enterprise deploys anti-virus/anti-malware software to protect some enterprise endpoint devices.

0.0 = Enterprise does not deploy anti-virus/anti-malware software.

ESDS-09: Application Whitelisting

1.0 = Enterprise creates an approved list of applications allowed to execute within the enterprise; if a non-whitelist application tries to execute, it is blocked for subsequent analysis.

0.0 = Enterprise does not use application whitelisting.

(Note: Some enterprises may maintain a blacklist, which is a list of malicious applications and is generally open-ended; a key whitelist advantage is it can prevent something not previously seen.)

ESDS-10: In-Memory Malware Detection

1.0 = Enterprise deploys in-memory malware detection that analyzes system memory for malware not resident on the hard drive.

0.0 = Enterprise does not have in-memory malware detection.

ESDS-11: Host Firewall and Intrusion Detection

1.0 = Enterprise deploys host firewall, and intrusion detection systems are in full enforcement mode.

0.5 = Enterprise deploys host firewall, and intrusion detection systems are in learning mode.

0.0 = Enterprise does not deploy host firewall and intrusion detection.

417

ESDS-12: "Gold Code" Software Images

1.0 = Enterprise builds new systems using "Gold Code" software that is protected from unauthorized changes.

0.5 = Enterprise develops and uses "Gold Code" software images, but there is no protection mechanism to secure the images.

0.0 = Enterprise does not use "Gold Code" software images.

ESDS-13: Security Technical Implementation Guides (STIGs)

1.0 = Enterprise uses only vendor-recommended hardening guidelines (for example, STIGs, Center for Internet Security benchmarks) to install and maintain secure systems.

0.5 = Enterprise uses STIGs to install and maintain some secure systems and uses vendor "out-of-the-box" default configurations to install other systems.

0.0 = Enterprise uses only default installation to install systems.

ESDS-14: Always-on Virtual Private Networking (VPN)

1.0 = Enterprise uses "always-on" VPN to encrypt all network traffic, and monitoring capability exists to monitor the connections.

0.5 = Enterprise uses "always-on" VPN to encrypt some network traffic, but monitoring capability does not exists.

0.0 = Enterprise does not use "always-on" VPN capability.

ESDS-15: File Integrity and Change Monitoring

1.0 = Enterprise monitors file system changes of all networked systems to uncover, for example, malicious software, viruses, and malicious file changes.

0.5 = Enterprise monitors file system changes of critical systems.

0.0 = Enterprise does not deploy file integrity and change monitoring.

(Note: This monitoring activity generally triggers additional change activity when files may have been compromised. This change activity overlaps the Incident Response functional area and the Monitoring, Vulnerability, and Patch Management functional area.)

Identity, Authentication, and Access Management (IAAM)
IAAM-01: Identity Life Cycle Management

1.0 = Enterprise manages all enterprise user identities.

0.5 = Enterprise manages some enterprise user identities.

0.0 = Enterprise does not manage user identities.

IAAM-02: Enterprise Directory

1.0 = Enterprise uses enterprise directory to manage all users' identities, authorizations, and digital/networking resources.

0.5 = Enterprise uses enterprise directory to manage some users' identities, authorizations, and digital/networking resources.

0.0 = Enterprise does not use enterprise directory.

(Note: Enterprise directory provides administrator capabilities to manage identification, authorization, and access control for information technology resources available on the enterprise network. It is a structured methodology to organize user access across the enterprise's digital resources. This value scale is restricted to measuring the management of identification, authorization, and access control for information technology resources available on the enterprise network by means of the enterprise directory. The enterprise may use some other means for this management activity; this value scale does not address these other means.)

IAAM-03: Multi-factor Authentication

1.0 = Enterprise deploys multi-factor authentication for all enterprise resources.

0.5 = Enterprise deploys multi-factor authentication for some enterprise resources.

0.0 = Enterprise does not deploy multi-factor authentication for any enterprise resources.

IAAM-04: Privilege Management and Access Control

1.0 = Enterprise deploys privilege management and access control tools to manage high-risk user accounts.

0.0 = Enterprise does not deploy privilege management and access control tools.

IAAM-05: Identity and Access Audit Trail and Reporting

1.0 = Enterprise deploys an audit trail capability to support regulatory compliance and investigations for all user actions.

0.5 = Enterprise deploys an audit trail capability to support regulatory compliance and investigations for some user actions.

0.0 = Enterprise does not deploy an audit trail capability.

IAAM-06: Lightweight Directory Access Protocol (LDAP)

1.0 = Enterprise deploys LDAP capability with security option implemented.

0.5 = Enterprise deploys LDAP capability without security option implemented.

0.0 = Enterprise does not deploy LDAP capability.

IAAM-07: Kerberos, RADIUS, 802.1x

1.0 = Enterprise deploys Kerberos, RADIUS, 802.1x authentication protocols to support user authentication.

0.0 = Enterprise does not deploy Kerberos, RADIUS, 802.1x authentication protocols.

IAAM-08: Federated Authentication

1.0 = Enterprise deploys federated authentication services (for example, Active Directory Federation Services) for identity sharing and trust with third-party suppliers.

0.0 = Enterprise does not deploy federated authentication services.

IAAM-09: Security Assertion Markup Language (SAML)

1.0 = Enterprise implements SAML to enable federated authentication and enhanced single sign-on user experience.

0.0 = Enterprise does not implement SAML.

Data Protection and Cryptography (DPC)

DPC-01: Secure Sockets Layer (SSL) and Transport Layer Security (TLS)

1.0 = Enterprise uses SSL or TLS technology for all user and server interactive sessions to protect the communication channel.

0.5 = Enterprise uses SSL or TLS technology for some user and server interactive sessions.

0.0 = Enterprise does not use SSL or TLS technology.

DPC-02: Digital Certificates (Public Key Infrastructure [PKI])

1.0 = Enterprise deploys PKI components (for example, certificate authority, digital certificates, registration authority, keys, or users).

0.0 = Enterprise does not deploy PKI components.

DPC-03: Key Hardware Protection (Smart Cards, Trusted Platform Modules (TPMs), and Hardware Security Modules [HSMs])

1.0 = Enterprise deploys (1) smart cards to provide identification, authentication, data storage, and low-scale processing capabilities; (2) TPM microchips installed on computer motherboards to provide dedicated security-related processing; and (3) HSM devices and appliances to perform critical cryptographic functions and safeguard digital keys for the enterprise's authentication service.

0.5 = Enterprise deploys some of the above hardware protections.

0.0 = Enterprise does not deploy any of the above hardware protections.

DPC-04: One-Time Password (OTP) and Out-of-Band (OOB) Authentication

1.0 = Enterprise deploys OTP and OOB authentication services to support PKI.

0.5 = Enterprise deploys OTP or OOB authentication services to support PKI.

0.0 = Enterprise does not deploy OTP and OOB authentication services.

DPC-05: Key Life Cycle Management

1.0 = Enterprise deploys key life cycle management technology to generate, store, and destroy cryptographic keys securely.

0.5 = Enterprise deploys key life cycle management service partially.

0.0 = Enterprise does not deploy key life cycle management.

DPC-06: Digital Signatures

1.0 = Enterprise uses electronic signatures to identify each enterprise user, third-party user, and relevant processes for achieving non-repudiation and authentication.

0.5 = Enterprise uses electronic signatures to identify some third-party users and relevant processes.

0.0 = Enterprise does not use electronic signatures.

DPC-07: Complex Passwords

1.0 = Enterprise has password complexity policies.

0.0 = Enterprise does not have a password complexity policy.

DPC-08: Data Encryption and Tokenization

1.0 = Enterprise uses data encryption and tokenization to protect sensitive data.

0.0 = Enterprise does not use data encryption or tokenization.

DPC-09: Brute Force Attack Detection

1.0 = Enterprise deploys brute force attack detection via preventive controls (for example, strong passwords, password lockout, and password expiration) and detective controls (for example, multiple incorrect login attempts).

0.5 = Enterprise deploys either preventive controls or detection controls.

0.0 = Enterprise does not deploy brute force attack detection controls.

DPC-10: Digital Rights Management (DRM)

1.0 = Enterprise deploys DRM.

0.0 = Enterprise does not deploy DRM.

Monitoring, Vulnerability, and Patch Management (MVPM)

MVPM-01: Operational Performance Monitoring

1.0 = Enterprise deploys operational performance monitoring for all critical systems.

0.5 = Enterprise deploys operational performance monitoring for some critical systems.

0.0 = Enterprise does not deploy operational performance monitoring.

MVPM-02: System and Network Monitoring

1.0 = Enterprise deploys system and network monitoring for all critical systems.

0.5 = Enterprise deploys system and network monitoring for some critical systems.

0.0 = Enterprise does not deploy system and network monitoring.

MVPM-03: System Configuration Change Detection

1.0 = Enterprise deploys file integrity monitoring tools to detect configuration changes of systems.

0.0 = Enterprise does not deploy system configuration change detection.

MVPM-04: Privilege and Access Change Detection

1.0 = Enterprise deploys privilege and access change detection.

0.5 = Enterprise deploys privilege and access change logging, but active monitoring is not deployed.

0.0 = Enterprise does not deploy privilege and access change detection.

MVPM-05: Log Aggregation

1.0 = Enterprise deploys and centrally manages log aggregation.

0.0 = Enterprise does not deploy log aggregation.

MVPM-06: Data Analytics

1.0 = Enterprise deploys data analytics.

0.0 = Enterprise does not deploy data analytics.

MVPM-07: Security Information and Event Management (SIEM)

1.0 = Enterprise deploys SIEM along with MVPM 05 (log aggregation) and MVPM 06 (data analytics).

0.0 = Enterprise does not deploy SIEM.

MVPM-08: Network and Computer Vulnerability Scanning

1.0 = Enterprise deploys network and computer vulnerability scanning across all systems.

0.5 = Enterprise deploys network and computer vulnerability scanning across some systems.

0.0 = Enterprise does not deploy network and computer vulnerability scanning.

MVPM-09: Penetration Testing

1.0 = Penetration testing is performed on critical applications.

0.0 = Penetration testing is not performed.

MVPM-10: Patch Management and Deployment

1.0 = Enterprise deploys centralized patch management and deployment capability for all systems, databases, appliances, and applications.

0.5 = Enterprise partially deploys centralized patch management and deployment capability.

0.0 = Enterprise does not deploy centralized patch management and deployment capability.

MVPM-11: Rogue Network Device Detection

1.0 = Enterprise deploys rogue network device detection capability.

0.5 = Enterprise deploys rogue network device detection capability to a portion of the enterprise.

0.0 = Enterprise does not deploy rogue network device detection.

MVPM-12: Rogue Wireless Access Point Detection

1.0 = Enterprise deploys automated rogue wireless access point detection capability.

0.5 = Enterprise uses "war-driving" method to detect rogue wireless access points.

0.0 = Enterprise does not deploy rogue wireless access point detection.

MVPM-13: Honeypots/Honeynets/Honeytokens

1.0 = Enterprise deploys honeypots/honeynets/honeytokens to analyze malicious actor behavior.

0.0 = Enterprise does not deploy honeypots, honeynets, or honeytokens.

MVPM-14: Security Operations Center (SOC)

1.0 = SOC is functional and provides 24x7x365 monitoring service.

0.0 = SOC is not available.

High Availability, Disaster Recovery, and Physical Protection (HADRPP)

HADRPP-01: Clustering

1.0 = Enterprise deploys clustering for all critical systems.

0.5 = Enterprise deploys clustering for some critical systems.

0.0 = Enterprise does not deploy clustering.

HADRPP-02: Load Balancing, Global Server Load Balancing (GSLB)

1.0 = Enterprise deploys load balancing and GSLB for all critical applications and systems.

0.5 = Enterprise deploys load balancing and GSLB for some critical applications and systems.

0.0 = Enterprise does not deploy load balancing or GSLB.

HADRPP-03: Network Failover, Subnet Spanning

1.0 = Enterprise deploys automated network failover and subnet spanning capabilities.

0.0 = Enterprise does not deploy network failover or subnet spanning.

HADRPP-04: Virtual Machine Snapshots and Cloning

1.0 = Enterprise implements virtual machine snapshots and cloning for all critical servers.

0.5 = Enterprise implements virtual machine snapshots and cloning for some critical servers.

0.0 = Enterprise does not implement virtual machine snapshots or cloning.

HADRPP-05: Data Mirroring and Replication

1.0 = Enterprise deploys data mirroring and replication for all critical servers.

0.5 = Enterprise deploys data mirroring and replication for some critical servers.

0.0 = Enterprise does not deploy data mirroring and replication.

HADRPP-06: Backups and Backup Management

1.0 = Enterprise deploys backup management across enterprise.

0.5 = Enterprise manages backups on per system basis, but does not have a centralized backup status view.

0.0 = Enterprise does not deploy backup management software.

424

HADRPP-07: Off-Site Storage

1.0 = Off-site backup storage is geographically separate from the primary site.

0.0 = Off-site backup storage is within the same building or facility.

HADRPP-08: Facilities Protection

1.0 = Enterprise deploys a facilities protection plan that accounts for physical security.

0.5 = Enterprise develops a draft facilities protection plan.

0.0 = Enterprise does not have a facilities protection plan.

HADRPP-09: Physical Access Controls

1.0 = Enterprise deploys physical access controls across enterprise to slow down potential intruders.

0.5 = Enterprise partially deploys physical access controls within the enterprise.

0.0 = Enterprise does not deploy physical access controls.

HADRPP-10: Physical Security Monitoring

1.0 = Enterprise deploys physical security monitoring across enterprise.

0.5 = Enterprise collects physical security logs, but regular physical security monitoring is not deployed.

0.0 = Enterprise does not deploy physical security monitoring.

Incident Response (IR)
IR-01: Threat Information

1.0 = Enterprise collects threat information from various authoritative sources and disseminates it to analysts.

0.0 = Enterprise does not collect threat information.

IR-02: Incident Tracking

1.0 = Enterprise deploys incident tracking tools and processes.

0.5 = Enterprise deploys incident tracking tools capability to a portion of the enterprise.

0.0 = Enterprise does not deploy incident tracking tools or processes.

IR-03: Forensic Tools

1.0 = Enterprise deploys forensic tools and data handling methodology.

0.5 = Enterprise deploys forensic tools, but data handling methodology does not exist.

0.0 = Enterprise does not deploy forensic tools or data handling.

IR-04: Computer Imaging

1.0 = Enterprise deploys computer imaging tools.

0.5 = Enterprise deploys computer imaging tools capability to a portion of the enterprise.

0.0 = Enterprise does not deploy computer imaging tools.

IR-05: Indicators of Compromise (IOCs)

1.0 = Enterprise collects IOCs and makes then available for investigations.

0.0 = Enterprise does not collect IOCs.

IR-06: Black Hole Server

1.0 = Enterprise deploys black hole server.

0.5 = Enterprise deploys black hole server capability to a portion of the enterprise.

0.0 = Enterprise does not deploy black hole server.

IR-07: Regulatory/Legal Coordination

1.0 = Enterprise follows all chain of custody procedures to ensure collected evidence is admissible in the court of law.

0.5 = Enterprise follows some chain of custody procedures.

0.0 = Enterprise does not follow chain of custody procedures.

Asset Management and Supply Chain (AMSC)

AMSC-01: Asset Management Databases

1.0 = Enterprise deploys an asset management database.

0.5 = Enterprise deploys an asset management database with some assets in the database.

0.0 = Enterprise does not deploy an asset management database.

AMSC-02: Configuration Management Databases (CMDB)

1.0 = Enterprise deploys a CMDB that has a registry of all critical system configuration items.

0.5 = Enterprise deploys a CMDB with some configuration items managed.

0.0 = Enterprise does not deploy a CMDB.

AMSC-03: Change Management Databases

1.0 = Enterprise deploys change management databases to process change requests for all baselined systems.

0.5 = Enterprise deploys change management databases with some change requests processed by it.

0.0 = Enterprise does not deploy a change management database.

AMSC-04: Software Inventory and License Management

1.0 = Enterprise deploys a centralized software inventory and license management capability.

0.5 = Enterprise deploys a software inventory and license management capability, but a centralized software inventory does not exist.

0.0 = Enterprise does not deploy a software inventory and license management database.

AMSC-05: Supplier Certification Processes

1.0 = Enterprise conducts supplier certification security checks on all suppliers before contract award.

0.5 = Enterprise conducts supplier certification security checks on some suppliers before contract award.

0.0 = Enterprise does not perform supplier certification security checks before contract award.

AMSC-06: Secure Disposal, Recycling, and Data Destruction

1.0 = Enterprise deploys secure disposal, recycling, and data destruction capabilities.

0.5 = Enterprise deploys secure disposal, recycling, and data destruction capabilities for some enterprise IT assets.

0.0 = Enterprise does not deploy secure disposal, recycling, and data destruction capabilities.

Policy, Audit, E-Discovery, and Training (PAET)
PAET-01: Governance, Risk, and Compliance (GRC), with Reporting

1.0 = Enterprise deploys a GRC program that supports all aspects of risk, compliance, and mitigation life cycle.

0.5 = Enterprise deploys a GRC program limited to IT risks and does not account for regulatory compliance requirements.

0.0 = Enterprise does not deploy a GRC tool or process.

PAET-02: Compliance and Control Frameworks (SOX, PCI, and so forth)

1.0 = Enterprise deploys a security framework compliant with all legal, regulatory, and customer-driven requirements.

0.5 = Enterprise deploys individual compliance and controls frameworks to meet individual legal, regulatory, and customer-driven requirements.

0.0 = Enterprise does not have a compliance and controls framework.

PAET-03: Audit Frameworks

1.0 = Audit scope includes all critical systems, policies, standards, procedures, and baselines, supporting IT services, legal, regulatory, and customer-driven requirements.

0.5 = Audit scope is limited to legal, regulatory, and customer-driven requirements.

0.0 = Audit scope is not defined.

PAET-04: Customer Certification and Accreditation (C&A)

1.0 = Enterprise deploys a formal C&A process for all assets and services.

0.5 = Enterprise deploys a formal C&A process for some assets and services.

0.0 = Enterprise does not deploy a formal C&A process.

PAET-05: Policy and Policy Exception Management

1.0 = Enterprise deploys a policy and policy exception management capability.

0.5 = Enterprise deploys a policy and policy exception management capability without a follow-up/re-approval process on expired exceptions.

0.0 = Enterprise does not deploy a policy exception management capability.

PAET-06: Risk and Threat Management

1.0 = Enterprise deploys a risk and threat management capability.

0.5 = Enterprise deploys a risk and threat management capability to some enterprise IT processes and services.

0.0 = Enterprise does not deploy a risk and threat management capability.

PAET-07: Privacy Compliance

1.0 = Enterprise deploys a privacy compliance capability with well-documented policy and procedures.

0.5 = Enterprise deploys a privacy compliance capability to some enterprise IT processes and services.

0.0 = Enterprise does not deploy a privacy compliance capability.

PAET-08: E-Discovery Tools

1.0 = Enterprise deploys automated e-discovery tools.

0.5 = Enterprise conducts e-discovery manually.

0.0 = Enterprise does not conduct e-discovery (tools or processes).

PAET-09: Personnel Security and Background Checks

1.0 = HR performs pre-employment security and background checks on all potential employees.

0.5 = HR performs pre-employment security and background checks on some potential employees.

0.0 = HR does not perform personnel security and background checks.

PAET-10: Security Awareness and Training

1.0 = Enterprise deploys security awareness program and annual training.

0.5 = Enterprise deploys security awareness program and training to some employees.

0.0 = Enterprise does not deploy security awareness program and training.

APPENDIX H

■ ■ ■

Cybersecurity Sample Assessment

The purpose of this appendix is to bring together a previously introduced hierarchy of cybersecurity assessment concepts into three worked-out numerical examples. These worked-out examples show how an enterprise can obtain an answer to the following fundamental enterprise cybersecurity questions:

- *What is the enterprise quantitative effectiveness in defending itself against cyberattacks?*

- *How does the enterprise quantitatively improve this effectiveness?*

A cybersecurity program lends itself well to performing top-down security assessments at progressively increasing levels of detail. Each assessment level can be performed independently, or assessments can be done in progressive passes to get increasing detail focusing on the areas of greatest interest. With multiple passes, each pass would build on the findings of the previous pass to gain a greater understanding of the enterprise security posture and areas for potential improvement.

Figure H-1 depicts a top-down cybersecurity program assessment with the four levels of detail. This figure brings together into a single, concrete framework a number of important concepts described throughout the rest of the book. These concepts include the following:

- Chapter 3 introduces the 11 functional areas consisting of 113 cybersecurity capabilities, which are further detailed in Appendix C.

- Chapter 5 introduces security operations and the supporting 17 operational processes, which are further detailed in Appendix E.

- Chapter 8 introduces the concepts of effective risk mitigations by (1) defending the enterprise against the advanced attack sequence, and (2) segmenting the enterprise network, which is detailed in Appendix I (Network Segmentation).

- Chapter 11 introduces the four enterprise cybersecurity assessment levels that focus respectively on (1) risk mitigations, (2) functional areas, (3) cybersecurity capabilities, and (4) controls, technologies, and processes.

- Chapter 12 introduces the methods for measuring a cybersecurity program using the Object Measurement methodology, which is further detailed in Appendices F and G.

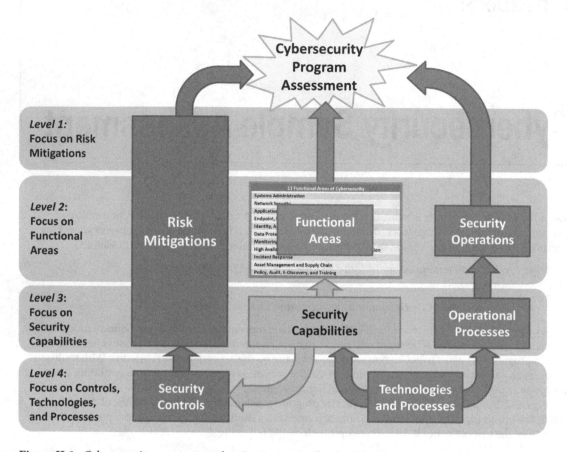

Figure H-1. *Cybersecurity assessments showing increasing levels of detail.*

Figure H-1, which is an elaboration of figures previously introduced in some of the above chapters/appendices, is the framework for this chapter's worked-out examples. Experience has demonstrated that these four levels provide a robust and flexible framework for comprehensively assessing enterprise cybersecurity. However, the approaches in this figure are hardly the only cybersecurity assessments, and each enterprise should consider what assessment methods and measurement scales make best sense for its particular situation.

Each cybersecurity assessment type analyzes enterprise cybersecurity at increasing levels of detail:

- ***Level 1 Assessment:*** Very high-level assessment that focuses on risk mitigations using expert judgment.

- ***Level 2 Assessment:*** High-level assessment that focuses on functional areas using expert judgment. It extends the Level 1 assessment results to consider the functional areas and security operations using expert judgment in addition to the risk mitigations evaluated in Level 1.

- ***Level 3 Assessment:*** Detailed assessment that focuses on capabilities using observed data. It extends the Level 1 assessment results to consider the functional areas at the capabilities level, and security operations considering individual operational processes using expert judgment. This is then combined with the Level 1 risk mitigations assessment to get a complete picture.

- ***Level 4 Assessment:*** More detailed assessment that considers controls, technologies, and/or processes using expert judgment or observed data (this level of assessment is not shown in this appendix). It considers all three aspects of enterprise security—risk mitigations, security capabilities grouped into functional areas, and security operations—at the detailed level of security controls, technologies, and processes.

The worked-out example numerical assessments in this appendix integrate the book's previously introduced concepts to illustrate how an enterprise can obtain answers to the two fundamental cybersecurity questions posed above. These answers translate into a quantitative assessment of the enterprise's cybersecurity posture and the evolution of this posture over time.

Sample Assessment Scope and Methodology

As an example of cybersecurity assessment methodology, this appendix contains a sample assessment for a hypothetical enterprise. It describes three sample assessments, showing the measurements and the index values derived from those measurements. These sample assessments consider multiple aspects of enterprise cybersecurity, including the following:

- Risk mitigations against all steps of the attack sequence

- Security capabilities in all of the functional areas

- Security operations including the 17 operational processes

These assessments analyze a single security scope consisting of the enterprise's general-purpose IT environment. The sample assessments include a Level 1 assessment focusing on risk mitigations, then continues with a Level 2 assessment focusing on the functional areas, and finally it drills down to a Level 3 assessment focusing on capabilities. Each assessment uses the Object Measurement methodology to identify the attributes for evaluation and scoring of those attributes. In each assessment, the calculated measurement index scores are combined into a single *cybersecurity program assessment index* that quantifiably represents the overall enterprise cybersecurity posture.

Level 1 Assessment: Focus on Risk Mitigations

Using the methodology of this book, the highest-level cybersecurity assessment is the Risk Mitigations Assessment. This assessment involves analyzing the Enterprise Cybersecurity Attack Sequence for the evaluated security scope (in this case, the enterprise's general-purpose IT environment). It considers how well the enterprise's cybersecurity controls are reducing the probability and the impact of attacks making it through each step of the attack sequence. When the most likely and most dangerous threats are considered in this manner, this assessment provides a good high-level evaluation of the security scope's overall cybersecurity posture. The primary advantage of this Level 1 assessment is the enterprise does not have to go into too much detail or spend too much time in analysis to obtain executive-level results.

The Level 1 assessment is an *exploratory* assessment method for evaluating an overall high-level, limited security posture. These high-level results are used, in part, to help direct further cybersecurity assessments. Because this assessment is only looking at risk mitigations, it does not account for other cybersecurity details that could be critically important.

OM Step 1: Define the Question(s) to Be Answered

In this assessment, the question to be answered for the security scope is the following:

What is the strength of the enterprise's cybersecurity when only considering risk mitigations to reduce the probability or impact of targeted cyberattacks?

OM Step 2: Select Appropriate Objects to Measure

For this assessment, the objects to measure are the five steps of the enterprise cybersecurity attack sequence:

1. Establish Foothold
2. Command and Control
3. Move Laterally
4. Escalate Privileges
5. Complete the Mission

OM Step 3: For Each Object, Define the Object Characteristics to Measure

For the five steps of the attack sequence, the enterprise's cybersecurity controls' effectiveness in reducing the probability and the impact of an attack will be evaluated using *expert judgment* as follows:

- **Probability reduction** represents the amount that attacks are less likely to succeed at the specific step of the attack sequence due to the presence of controls that disrupt, detect, delay, or defeat the attack.

- **Impact reduction** represents the amount that the impact of an attack is reduced at the specific step of the attack sequence due to the presence of controls that disrupt, detect, delay, or defeat the attack.

Based on these criteria, it is possible for the risk mitigations of a step of the attack sequence to reduce the probability of attack but not the impact, or vice versa. To receive the maximum expert judgment value, the risk mitigation controls must reduce both the probability and the impact of an intrusion.

OM Step 4: For Each Characteristic, Create a Value Scale

Expert judgments for probability and impact reduction are measured using the risk probability reduction and risk impact reduction value scales described in Chapter 12. These scales provide definitions for the terms *high, medium,* and *low* with regard to risk mitigations. Figure H-2 depicts these value scales.

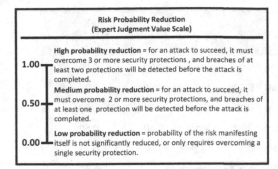

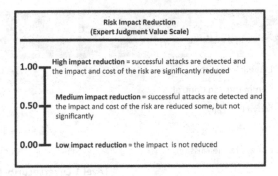

Figure H-2. *These expert judgment value scales provide definitions and values for high, medium, and low with regard to probability and impact reduction.*

Once the expert judgment value scale tick marks are defined, their values can be combined using an appropriate Object Measurement (OM) equation. Figure H-3 uses a matrix to combine them in a way that is simpler than using the full OM equation and produces similar results. The inputs to this matrix are the OM measurements for the risk probability reduction and risk impact reduction, and it converts them into a *single combined measurement.*

		RISK PROBABILITY REDUCTION VALUE SCALE		
		Low Risk Probability Reduction (0.00)	**Medium Risk Probability Reduction (0.50)**	**High Risk Probability Reduction (1.00)**
RISK IMPACT REDUCTION VALUE SCALE	**High Risk Impact Reduction (1.00)**	Good (0.50)	Very Good (0.75)	Excellent (1.00)
	Medium Risk Impact Reduction (0.50)	Weak (0.25)	Good (0.50)	Very Good (0.75)
	Low Risk Impact Reduction (0.00)	Poor (0.00)	Weak (0.25)	Good (0.50)

Figure H-3. *This simple matrix combines the expert judgment assessments of risk mitigation measures of impact and probability reduction into a single combined measurement.*

OM Step 5: Measure Each Characteristic Using the Value Scale

Figure H-4 lists the measurement values of applying expert judgment, as defined by the value scales and combined using the combination matrix, to each of the five steps in the attack sequence.

Level 1 Assessment Focusing on Risk Mitigations: Expert Judgment for 5 Steps of Attack Sequence	Risk Probability Reduction	Risk Impact Reduction	Combined Measurements
1. Establish Foothold	Low = 0.00	Low = 0.00	0.00
2. Command and Control	Low = 0.00	Medium = 0.50	0.25
3. Move Laterally	Low = 0.00	High = 1.00	0.50
4. Escalate Privileges	Medium = 0.50	Medium = 0.50	0.50
5. Complete the Mission	Medium = 0.50	High = 1.00	0.75
Level 1 Cybersecurity Program Assessment Index:			0.47

Figure H-4. *Expert judgment risk mitigation values for each of the five steps in the attack sequence.*

In the example, the cybersecurity expert performing this assessment chose the following values:

- ***Attack Sequence Step 1: Establish Foothold***

  - ***Risk Probability Reduction*** = Low = *Probability of the risk manifesting itself is not significantly reduced, or only requires overcoming a single security protection = 0.00.*

  - ***Risk Impact Reduction*** = Low = *the impact is not reduced = 0.00.*

  - ***Combined Measurement*** = *0.00.*

- ***Attack Sequence Step 2: Command and Control***

  - ***Risk Probability Reduction*** = Low = *Probability of the risk manifesting itself is not significantly reduced, or only requires overcoming a single security protection = 0.00.*

  - ***Risk Impact Reduction*** = Medium = *successful attacks are detected and the impact and cost of the risk are reduced some, but not significantly = 0.50.*

  - ***Combined Measurement*** = *0.25.*

Each value is tied to a definition expressed in enterprise cybersecurity language. This language helps to explain the underlying meaning of the numbers and preserves, in part, the content of this assessment. Future assessments may not involve the same cybersecurity expert(s), but the assessment's results can still be used to understand better how the enterprise cybersecurity posture has changed over time.

OM Step 6: Calculate the Overall Level1_*Index* Using Object Measurement

Figure H-5 depicts a measurement map for the data collected in Step 5 and shows how the data is combined to get an overall index for this assessment level.

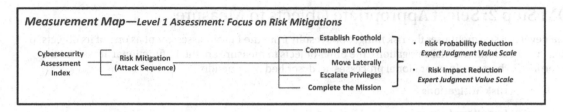

Figure H-5. *Level 1 assessment measurement map showing how assessed values are combined to get an overall risk mitigation assessment index value.*

The combined measurements are input to the Object Measurement equation as follows to calculate the overall Level 1 index value:

$$Level1\_Index = \frac{\sqrt{0.00^2 + 0.25^2 + 0.50^2 + 0.50^2 + 0.75^2}}{\sqrt{5}} = \frac{1.06}{2.24} = 0.47$$

The overall combined index score for the cybersecurity scope is 0.47, or 47%. What does a Level1_*Index* = 0.47 or 47% really mean? This result represents the enterprise's cybersecurity effectiveness as determined from the expert judgment terms defined in the value scale definitions. These terms are expressed in *enterprise language* to help increase effective communications regarding the assessment. By navigating the measurement map from left to right, the index score can be unfolded to trace back to those expert judgments.

Level 2 Assessment: Focus on Functional Areas

The second level assessment uses *expert judgment* to focus on the functional areas and security operations to obtain a more detailed assessment of the enterprise's cybersecurity within the assessed security scope. This assessment combines the Level1_*Index* with additional measurements for the 11 functional areas and security operations. The primary advantage of this Level 2 assessment is that it provides more detailed results than the Level 1 Assessment, without requiring considerably more time or detailed analysis.

Since this assessment reflects expert judgment evaluating each functional area in its entirety and without evaluating corresponding cybersecurity capabilities, processes, or technologies, this assessment is still at a high level of abstraction. The Level 2 assessment might be performed via a telephone interview or at a leadership whiteboard session. Its purpose is to get quickly to a high-level impression of the enterprise's cybersecurity posture. This impression is often used to support or validate strategic decisions about which cybersecurity areas need focus and which ones do not.

OM Step 1: Define the Question to Be Answered

In this assessment, the question to be answered for the security scope is as follows:

> *What is the strength of the enterprise's cybersecurity when considering a high-level evaluation of risk mitigation, security functional areas, and a high-level assessment of security operations?*

OM Step 2: Select Appropriate Objects to Measure

The Level 2 assessment uses the risk mitigations results from the Level 1 assessment as one of its objects to measure. In addition to risk mitigations, the other objects to measure are the 11 functional areas and the enterprise cybersecurity operational processes, as described in Appendix E:

- **Risk Mitigations**
- **Functional Areas**
  - Systems Administration
  - Network Security
  - Application Security
  - Endpoint, Server, and Device Security
  - Identity, Authentication, and Access Management
  - Data Protection and Cryptography
  - Monitoring, Vulnerability, and Patch Management
  - High Availability, Disaster Recovery, and Physical Protection
  - Incident Response
  - Asset Management and Supply Chain
  - Policy, Audit, E-Discovery, and Training
- **Security Operations**

OM Step 3: For Each Object, Define the Object Characteristics to Measure

For this assessment, the Level1_*Index* is going to be simply carried over from the previous assessment and used as an overall index for risk mitigations. For the 11 functional areas and security operations, their overall effectiveness and comprehensiveness will be evaluated using expert judgment as follows:

- ***Effectiveness*** represents the amount the functional area capabilities or operational processes are present and properly configured to support the applicable enterprise cybersecurity scope. The functional area is effective if the capabilities or operational processes it contains are mature and working properly, even if there are only a few of them.

- ***Comprehensiveness*** represents the amount the functional area capabilities or operational processes are being actively used to support the applicable enterprise cybersecurity scope. The functional area is comprehensive if it contains many of the capabilities and operational processes, even if they are not mature or working properly.

Based on these criteria, it is possible for a functional area to be effective but not comprehensive, or comprehensive but not effective. To receive the maximum expert judgment value, it must be evaluated to be *both* effective *and* comprehensive.

OM Step 4: For Each Characteristic, Create a Value Scale

Expert judgment of the functional areas and security operations will be measured using the effectiveness and comprehensiveness value scales described in Chapter 12. These scales provide definitions for the terms *high, medium,* and *low* with regard to effectiveness and comprehensiveness of functional areas. Figure H-6 depicts these value scales.

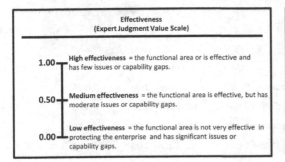
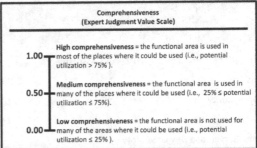

Figure H-6. *These expert judgment value scales provide definitions and values for* high, medium, *and* low *with regard to effectiveness and comprehensiveness.*

Once the expert judgment value scale tick marks are defined, their values can be combined using an appropriate Object Measurement (OM) equation. Figure H-7 uses a matrix to combine them in a way that is simpler than using the full OM equation and produces similar results. The inputs to this matrix are the OM measurements for the comprehensiveness and effectiveness of the functional area or security operations, and it converts them into a single *combined measurement.*

		COMPREHENSIVENESS VALUE SCALE		
		Low Comprehensiveness (0.00)	Medium Comprehensiveness (0.50)	High Comprehensiveness (1.00)
EFFECTIVENESS VALUE SCALE	High Effectiveness (1.00)	Good (0.50)	Very Good (0.75)	Excellent (1.00)
	Medium Effectiveness (0.50)	Weak (0.25)	Good (0.50)	Very Good (0.75)
	Low Effectiveness (0.00)	Poor (0.00)	Weak (0.25)	Good (0.50)

Figure H-7. *This simple matrix combines the expert judgment assessments of effectiveness and comprehensiveness for functional areas or security operations into a single combined measurement.*

OM Step 5: Measure Each Characteristic Using the Value Scale

Figure H-8 shows the result of this assessment and the data collected. It involves carrying over the Level 1 assessment result. Then, for the 11 functional areas and security operations, it applies expert judgment, as defined by value scales and the combination matrix, to obtain objective, combined measurements.

Level 2 Assessment Focusing on Functional Areas: Expert Judgment for Risk Mitigations, 11 Functional Areas, and Security Operations	Effective-ness	Comprehensive-ness	Combined Measurements
Risk Mitigations (carried over from Level 1 Assessment)	N/A	N/A	0.47
Systems Administration	Medium = 0.50	Low = 0.00	0.25
Network Security	Medium = 0.50	Medium = 0.50	0.50
Application Security	Medium = 0.50	Medium = 0.50	0.50
Endpoint, Server, and Device Security	High = 1.00	Low = 0.00	0.50
Identity, Authentication, and Access Management	High = 1.00	Medium = 0.50	0.75
Data Protection and Cryptography	Medium = 0.50	Low = 0.00	0.25
Monitoring, Vulnerability, and Patch Management	Low = 0.00	Medium = 0.50	0.25
High Availability, Disaster Recovery, and Physical Protection	Medium = 0.50	Medium = 0.50	0.50
Incident Response	High = 1.00	Medium = 0.50	0.75
Asset Management and Supply Chain	Medium = 0.50	Medium = 0.50	0.50
Policy, Audit, E-Discovery, and Training	High = 1.00	Medium = 0.50	0.75
Security Operations	Medium = 0.50	Medium = 0.50	0.50
Level 2 Cybersecurity Program Assessment Index:			**0.53**

Figure H-8. Expert judgment values for each of the 11 functional areas and operational processes, combined into an overall cybersecurity program assessment index.

OM Step 6: Calculate the Overall Level2_*Index* Using Object Measurement

Figure H-9 shows a measurement map for the data collected in Step 5 and depicts how the data is combined to get an overall index for this assessment level. In this measurement map, the risk mitigations index value is combined with the measurements collected for each of the 11 functional areas and security operations to get a single Level2_*Index* value.

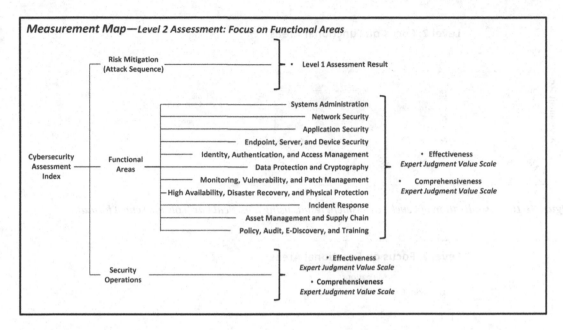

Measurement Map—*Level 2 Assessment: Focus on Functional Areas*

Figure H-9. *Measurement map showing how assessed values are combined to get an overall Level 2 assessment index value.*

The 13 combined measurements are input to the Object Measurement equation to calculate an overall index value:

$$Level2\_Index = \frac{\sqrt{\begin{array}{c}0.47^2+0.25^2+0.50^2+0.50^2+0.50^2+0.75^2+0.25^2+\\0.25^2+0.50^2+0.75^2+0.50^2+0.75^2+0.50^2\end{array}}}{\sqrt{13}} = \frac{1.90}{3.61} = 0.53$$

The overall combined Level2_*Index* score for the cybersecurity scope is 0.53, or 53%. This Level 2 assessment index represents the enterprise's cybersecurity effectiveness as determined from the expert judgment terms defined in the value scale definitions. By navigating the measurement map from left to right, the index score can be unfolded to trace back to those expert judgments.

Results Visualization and Analysis

In this assessment level, it makes sense to visualize the results as a chart so that the various functional areas can be compared to one another and functional areas that are weakest can be identified for subsequent improvement. Figure H-10 visualizes these results using a vertical bar (column) chart, while Figure H-11 visualizes these results using a spider chart. The spider chart is useful for emphasizing that all functional areas should be of approximately equal effectiveness (the target value) for the overall enterprise cybersecurity to be effective.

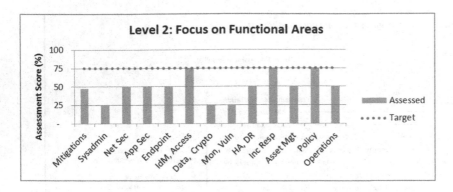

Figure H-10. *Visualization of Level 2 assessment results using a vertical bar (column) chart format.*

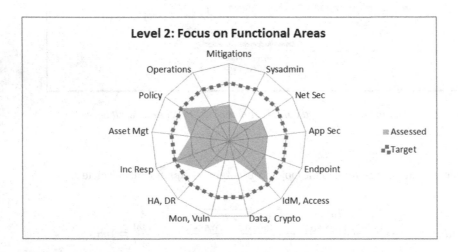

Figure H-11. *Visualization of Level 2 assessment results using a spider chart format.*

Looking at these figures, the three functional areas scoring the lowest stand out compared to the rest: (1) Systems Administration, (2) Data Protection and Cryptography, and (3) Monitoring, Vulnerability, and Patch Management. These three functional areas are the ones most likely to be exploited by a targeted attacker and thus, should be prioritized for investment and improvement.

In addition, Figures H-10 and H-11 also show a *target value* at 75%. The target value represents the enterprise's cybersecurity goal for this security scope. The target value makes it easy to see at a glance where deficiencies lie, and it helps leadership to understand the magnitude of the gap between what is present and what is desired. It is important to note the target value does not necessarily need to be 100%. Business leadership sets the target bar to an acceptable level to balance the competing interests of business expediency and cybersecurity protection, while controlling security costs and the impacts security can have on productivity.

Level 3 Assessment: Focus on Capabilities

The third level assessment uses observed data at the capabilities level to obtain a significantly more detailed assessment of the enterprise's cybersecurity within the assessed security scope. This assessment starts with the Level 1 Risk Mitigations Assessment, but then uses *observed data* to assess the 113 enterprise cybersecurity functional area capabilities (113 values), along with *expert judgment* to evaluate the 17 operational processes (17 values). These measurements are then aggregated together using the OM equation to get aggregate scores for each functional area and security operations. Finally, the 13 values (risk mitigations, 11 functional areas, security operations) are combined together to get a single Level3_*Index* value for the entire enterprise security scope.

Level 3 assessment includes a detailed analysis of the enterprise's cybersecurity capabilities and operational processes, and it uses observed data rather than expert judgment for most of its data gathering. The Level 3 assessment is significantly more detailed than Level 1 and Level 2 assessments, and it requires a commensurately greater level of effort to execute. When performed by an external assessor, it generally requires onsite visits and interviews with IT leadership involved with each of the functional areas and their capabilities. This assessment, once completed, delivers a detailed view of the enterprise's cybersecurity posture that can then be used to support detailed strategic, programmatic, and tactical decision-making.

OM Step 1: Define the Question to Be Answered

In this level of assessment, the question to be answered for the security scope is as follows:

> *What is the strength of the enterprise's cybersecurity when considering a detailed evaluation of risk mitigations, 113 functional area cybersecurity capabilities, and 17 security operational processes?*

OM Step 2: Select Appropriate Objects to Measure

The Level 3 assessment uses the risk mitigations results from the Level 1 assessment as one of its objects to measure. In addition to risk mitigations, the other objects to measure are the 113 enterprise cybersecurity functional area capabilities and the 17 enterprise cybersecurity operational processes, as described in Appendices C and E.

- **Risk Mitigations: 5 Steps**

- **Functional Areas: 11 Areas**

  - Systems Administration: 9 Capabilities

  - Network Security: 14 Capabilities

  - Application Security: 9 Capabilities

  - Endpoint, Server, and Device Security: 15 Capabilities

  - Identity, Authentication, and Access Management: 9 Capabilities

  - Data Protection and Cryptography: 10 Capabilities

  - Monitoring, Vulnerability, and Patch Management: 14 Capabilities

  - High Availability, Disaster Recovery, and Physical Protection: 10 Capabilities

  - Incident Response: 7 Capabilities

- Asset Management and Supply Chain: 6 Capabilities
- Policy, Audit, E-Discovery, and Training: 10 Capabilities
- **Operational Processes: 17 Processes**

OM Step 3: For Each Object, Define the Object Characteristics to Measure

This assessment focuses on the third level of detail, which corresponds to the risk mitigations carried over from the Level 1 assessment, the 113 capabilities within the 11 functional areas, and the 17 operational processes of security operations:

- **Risk mitigations** will be evaluated using *expert judgment* based upon their effectiveness in reducing the probability and the impact of the attack sequence.

- **The 113 capabilities** in the 11 functional areas will each be objectively evaluated using *observed data*.

- **The 17 operational processes** will be evaluated using *expert judgment* based upon the maturity and utilization of the operational processes.

For the 17 operational processes, their overall maturity and utilization will be evaluated using expert judgment as follows:

- **Maturity** represents how mature the operational process is in terms of how consistently it is performed, the quality of the data it maintains, and its ability to handle exceptions and special cases. A mature operational process is robust and reliable, uses appropriate supporting tools and technologies, and is consistently performed using documented procedures.

- **Utilization** represents how comprehensively the enterprise utilizes the operational process across the assessed scope. A well-utilized process is used everywhere it should be used, with safeguards in place to ensure it cannot be bypassed, ignored, or arbitrarily exempted.

Based on these criteria, it is possible for an operational process to be mature but not utilized, or well utilized but immature. To receive the maximum expert judgment value, it must be evaluated to be *both* mature *and* utilized.

OM Step 4: For Each Characteristic, Create a Value Scale

Since this assessment level is significantly more detailed, there are the following three types of value scales that will be utilized:

- **Risk mitigations** expert judgment values will be carried over from the Level 1 assessment along with their associated *expert judgment* value scales.

- **The 113 capabilities** in the 11 functional areas will be assessed using the *observed data* value scales that are given in Appendix G.

- **The 17 operational processes** will be evaluated using *expert judgment* of their maturity and utilization.

For the 17 operational processes, expert judgment of maturity and utilization will be measured using the maturity and utilization value scales described in Chapter 12. These scales provide definitions for the terms *high*, *medium*, and *low* with regard to maturity and utilization of operational processes. Figure H-12 depicts these value scales.

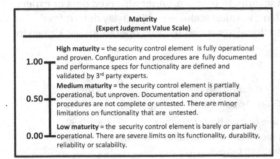
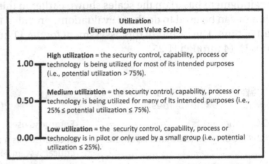

Figure H-12. *These expert judgment value scales provide definitions and values for* high, medium, *and* low *with regard to maturity and utilization.*

Once the expert judgment value scale tick marks are defined, their values can be combined using an appropriate Object Measurement (OM) equation. Figure H-13 uses a matrix to combine them in a way that is simpler than using the full OM equation and produces similar results. The inputs to this matrix are the OM measurements for the maturity and utilization of the operational process, and it converts them into a single *combined measurement*.

		UTILIZATION VALUE SCALE		
		Low Utilization (0.00)	Medium Utilization (0.50)	High Utilization (1.00)
MATURITY VALUE SCALE	High Maturity (1.00)	Good (0.50)	Very Good (0.75)	Excellent (1.00)
	Medium Maturity (0.50)	Weak (0.25)	Good (0.50)	Very Good (0.75)
	Low Maturity (0.00)	Poor (0.00)	Weak (0.25)	Good (0.50)

Figure H-13. *This simple matrix combines the expert judgment assessments of maturity and utilization for operational processes into a single combined measurement.*

OM Step 5: Measure Each Characteristic Using the Value Scale

The data collection phase of this assessment involves individually assessing each of the 113 capabilities, along with the 17 operational processes. In this example, the data collection for the capabilities uses observed data based on the scales in Appendix G, and the data collection for the operational processes uses expert judgment based on the scales shown earlier in this section. In practice, either observed data or expert judgment can be used to do these evaluations, provided that the value scales are objectively determined ahead of time. The results of this assessment for the 11 functional areas and security operations are shown in Figures H-14 through H-25.

Systems Administration (SA): 9 Capabilities	Observation (From Appendix G)	Observed Data
SA-01: Bastion hosts	Enterprise uses some bastion host computers.	0.50
SA-02: Out-of-Band (OOB) management	Enterprise has no secure channel capability to manage critical systems during an outage.	0.00
SA-03: Network isolation	Enterprise conducts systems administration on networks shared with business traffic.	0.00
SA-04: Integrated Lights-Out (ILO), Keyboard Video Mouse (KVM), and power controls	Enterprise manages some enterprise servers using centralized KVM, ILO, and power controls.	0.50
SA-05: Virtualization and Storage Area Network (SAN) management	Enterprise isolates and protects either virtualization or SAN management.	0.50
SA-06: Separation of administration from services	Enterprise has no separation of the administrative interface from the general user interface to administer the enterprise IT assets.	0.00
SA-07: Multi-factor authentication for Systems Administrators (SAs)	Some enterprise systems administrators use multi-factor authentication to access enterprise resources.	0.50
SA-08: Administrator audit trail(s)	SAs activities are logged, but not audited periodically, and logs are under SAs control.	0.20
SA-09: Command logging and analytics	Enterprise logs commands/keystrokes but does not analyze the logs periodically.	0.50
	Systems Administration Index:	**0.38**

Figure H-14. *Observed data values for Systems Administration.*

Network Security (NS): 14 Capabilities	Observation (From Appendix G)	Observed Data
NS-01: Switches and routers	Management and operation of some switches and routers are conducted through a secure centralized console. Logical and physical access to some of these devices is restricted to a small group with "need-to-access" basis.	0.50
NS-02: Software Defined Networking (SDN)	Enterprise utilizes SDN to deploy, manage, upgrade and retire some networking devices.	0.50
NS-03: Domain Name System (DNS) and Dynamic Host Configuration Protocol (DHCP)	Enterprise installs Standard DNS.	0.00
NS-04: Network Time Protocol (NTP)	Enterprise uses some capability other than NTP (for example, Chrony, OpenNTPD) to synchronize some system clocks to a master clock for accurate time stamping of logged events.	0.30
NS-05: Network service management	Enterprise uses only some of the security/protection mechanisms listed.	0.50
NS-06: Firewall and virtual machine firewall	Firewalled network zones are set up to separate some high-risk systems from low-risk internal systems. Network architecture is designed to manage logically the flow of data traffic and also get visibility.	0.50
NS-07: Network Intrusion Detection / Network Intrusion Prevention System (IDS / IPS)	Only IDS is implemented and IPS is in learning mode.	0.50
NS-08: Wireless networking (Wi-Fi)	Enterprise uses standard vendor-provided default configuration (including default administrator password).	0.00
NS-09: Packet intercept and capture	Packet intercept and capture tools are deployed to collect network traffic, and observe the throughput of the tool and network performance.	0.50
NS-10: Secure Sockets Layer (SSL) intercept	All SSL encrypted inbound traffic and some SSL outbound network traffic are examined.	0.40
NS-11: Network Access Control (NAC)	Network access control is deployed in learning mode.	0.50
NS-12: Virtual Private Networking (VPN) and Internet Protocol Security (IPSec)	VPN is deployed with two-factor authentication solution for some external or remote users.	0.50
NS-13: Network Traffic Analysis (NTA)	Enterprise uses network traffic analysis to analyze the volume of some network traffic.	0.50
NS-14: Network Data Analytics (NDA)	Enterprise has network data analytics but does not use it.	0.40
	Network Security Index:	**0.44**

Figure H-15. Observed data values for Network Security.

Application Security (AS): 9 Capabilities	Observation (From Appendix G)	Observed Data
AS-01: E-mail security	Enterprise deploys some e-mail protections.	0.50
AS-02: Webshell detection	Enterprise deploys webshell detection tools for some applications.	0.50
AS-03: Application firewalls	Enterprise deploys application firewalls in detection and learning mode for some applications.	0.50
AS-04: Database firewalls	Enterprise deploys firewalls in detection and learning mode for some databases.	0.50
AS-05: Forward proxy and web filters	Enterprise deploys forward proxy and web filters in enforcement mode for some outgoing requests from internal servers to the Internet.	0.50
AS-06: Reverse proxy	Enterprise deploys reverse proxy to mask the internal network from some Internet users.	0.50
AS-07: Data Leakage Protection (DLP)	Enterprise does not deploy DLP tools.	0.00
AS-08: Secure application and database software development	Secure application and database software development standards are partially utilized.	0.50
AS-09: Software code vulnerability analysis	Enterprise does not deploy software code vulnerability analysis tools.	0.00
	Application Security Index:	**0.44**

Figure H-16. *Observed data values for Application Security.*

Endpoint, Server, and Device Security (ESDS): 15 Capabilities	Observation (From Appendix G)	Observed Data
ESDS-01: Local administrator privilege restrictions	Some users have local administrative privileges on their end-point computing devices.	0.50
ESDS-02: Computer security and logging policies	Enterprise implements ESDS computer security logging and log monitoring on an ad hoc basis.	0.10
ESDS-03: Endpoint and media encryption	Enterprise deploys some endpoint and media encryption.	0.50
ESDS-04: Computer access controls	Enterprise uses some computer access controls.	0.50
ESDS-05: Forensic imaging support for investigations	Enterprise does not deploy forensic imaging policies, procedures or tools to support criminal investigations.	0.00
ESDS-06: Virtual desktop / thin clients	Enterprise converts some of privately-owned resources to virtual desktops that are kept current with latest security patches and updates.	0.50
ESDS-07: Mobile Device Management (MDM)	Enterprise deploys MDM solution to allow some personally-owned mobile devices to connect to the enterprise network.	0.50
ESDS-08: Anti-virus / anti-malware	Enterprise deploys anti-virus/anti-malware software to protect some enterprise end-point devices.	0.50
ESDS-09: Application whitelisting	Enterprise does not use application whitelisting.	0.00
ESDS-10: In-memory malware detection	Enterprise does not have in-memory malware detection.	0.00
ESDS-11: Host firewall and intrusion detection	Enterprise deploys host firewall, and intrusion detection systems are in learning mode.	0.50
ESDS-12: "Gold code" software images	Enterprise develops and uses "Gold Code" software images, but there is no protection mechanism to secure the images.	0.50
ESDS-13: Security Technical Implementation Guides (STIGs)	Enterprise uses only default installation to install systems.	0.00
ESDS-14: Always-on Virtual Private Networking (VPN)	Enterprise uses "always-on" VPN to encrypt some network traffic, but monitoring capability does not exist.	0.50
ESDS-15: File integrity and change monitoring	Enterprise monitors file system changes of critical systems.	0.50
	Endpoint, Server, and Device Security Index:	**0.41**

Figure H-17. *Observed data values for Endpoint, Server, and Device Security.*

Identity, Authentication, and Access Management (IAAM): 9 Capabilities	Observation (From Appendix G)	Observed Data
IAAM-01: Identity life cycle management	Enterprise manages some enterprise user identities.	0.50
IAAM-02: Enterprise directory	Enterprise uses enterprise directory to manage some users' identities, authorizations and digital/networking resources.	0.50
IAAM-03: Multi-factor authentication	Enterprise deploys multi-factor authentication for some enterprise resources.	0.50
IAAM-04: Privilege management and access control	Enterprise does not deploy privilege management and access control tools.	0.00
IAAM-05: Identity and access audit trail and reporting	Enterprise deploys an audit trail capability to support regulatory compliance and investigations for some user actions.	0.50
IAAM-06: Lightweight Directory Access Protocol (LDAP)	Enterprise deploys LDAP capability without security option implemented.	0.50
IAAM-07: Kerberos, RADIUS, 802.1x	Enterprise does not deploy Kerberos, RADIUS, 802.1x authentication protocols.	0.00
IAAM-08: Federated authentication	Enterprise deploys federated authentication services for identity sharing and trust with third-party suppliers.	1.00
IAAM-09: Security Assertion Markup Language (SAML)	Enterprise implements SAML to enable federated authentication and enhances single sign-on user experience.	1.00
Identity, Authentication, and Access Management Index:		**0.60**

Figure H-18. *Observed data values for Identity, Authentication, and Access Management.*

Data Protection and Cryptography (DPC): 10 Capabilities	Observation (From Appendix G)	Observed Data
DPC-01: Secure Sockets Layer (SSL) and Transport Layer Security (TLS)	Enterprise uses SSL or TLS technology for some user and server interactive sessions.	0.50
DPC-02: Digital certificates (Public Key Infrastructure [PKI])	Enterprise does not deploy PKI components.	0.00
DPC-03: Key hardware protection	Enterprise deploys some key hardware protections.	0.50
DPC-04: One-Time Password (OTP) and Out-of-Band (OOB) authentication	Enterprise does not deploy OTP and OOB authentication services.	0.00
DPC-05: Key life cycle management	Enterprise does not deploy key life cycle management.	0.00
DPC-06: Digital signatures	Enterprise uses electronic signatures to identify some third-party users, and relevant processes.	0.50
DPC-07: Complex passwords	Enterprise has password complexity policies.	1.00
DPC-08: Data encryption and tokenization	Enterprise does not use data encryption or tokenization.	0.00
DPC-09: Brute force attack detection	Enterprise deploys either preventive controls or detection controls.	0.50
DPC-10: Digital Rights Management (DRM)	Enterprise does not deploy DRM.	0.00
Data Protection and Cryptography Index:		**0.45**

Figure H-19. *Observed data values for Data Protection and Cryptography.*

Monitoring, Vulnerability, and Patch Management (MVPM): 14 Capabilities	Observation (From Appendix G)	Observed Data
MVPM-01: Operational performance monitoring	Enterprise deploys operational performance monitoring for some critical systems.	0.50
MVPM-02: System and network monitoring	Enterprise deploys system and network monitoring for some critical systems.	0.50
MVPM-03: System configuration change detection	Enterprise does not deploy system configuration change detection.	0.00
MVPM-04: Privilege and access change detection	Enterprise does not deploy privilege and access change detection.	0.00
MVPM-05: Log aggregation	Enterprise does not deploy log aggregation.	0.00
MVPM-06: Data analytics	Enterprise does not deploy data analytics.	0.00
MVPM-07: Security Information and Event Management (SIEM)	Enterprise does not deploy SIEM.	0.00
MVPM-08: Network and computer vulnerability scanning	Enterprise deploys network and computer vulnerability scanning across some systems.	0.50
MVPM-09: Penetration testing	Penetration testing is not performed.	0.00
MVPM-10: Patch management and deployment	Enterprise does not deploy centralized patch management and deployment capability.	0.00
MVPM-11: Rogue network device detection	Enterprise deploys rogue network device detection capability to a portion of the enterprise.	0.50
MVPM-12: Rogue wireless access point detection	Enterprise uses "war-driving" method to detect rogue wireless access points.	0.50
MVPM-13: Honeypots / honeynets / honeytokens	Enterprise does not deploy honeypots, honeynets, or honeytokens.	0.00
MVPM-14: Security Operations Center (SOC)	SOC is not available.	0.00
Monitoring, Vulnerability, and Patch Management Index:		**0.30**

Figure H-20. *Observed data values for Monitoring, Vulnerability, and Patch Management.*

High Availability, Disaster Recovery, and Physical Protection (HADRPP): 10 Capabilities	Observation (From Appendix G)	Observed Data
HADRPP-01: Clustering	Enterprise deploys clustering for some critical systems.	0.50
HADRPP-02: Load balancing, Global Server Load Balancing (GSLB)	Enterprise deploys load balancing and GSLB for some critical applications and systems.	0.50
HADRPP-03: Network failover, subnet spanning	Enterprise does not deploy network failover or subnet spanning.	0.00
HADRPP-04: Virtual machine snapshots and cloning	Enterprise implements virtual machine snapshots and cloning for some critical servers.	0.50
HADRPP-05: Data mirroring and replication	Enterprise deploys data mirroring and replication for some critical servers.	0.50
HADRPP-06: Backups and backup management	Enterprise manages backups on per system basis, but does not have a centralized backup status view.	0.50
HADRPP-07: Off-site storage	Off-site backup storage is within the same building or facility.	0.00
HADRPP-08: Facilities protection	Enterprise develops a draft facilities protection plan.	0.50
HADRPP-09: Physical access controls	Enterprise partially deploys physical access controls within the enterprise.	0.50
HADRPP-10: Physical security monitoring	Enterprise collects physical security logs, but regular physical security monitoring is not deployed.	0.50
High Availability, Disaster Recovery, and Physical Protection Index:		**0.45**

Figure H-21. *Observed data values for High Availability, Disaster Recovery, and Physical Protection.*

Incident Response (IR): 7 Capabilities	Observation (From Appendix G)	Observed Data
IR-01: Threat information	Enterprise collects threat information from various authoritative sources and disseminates it to analysts.	1.00
IR-02: Incident tracking	Enterprise deploys incident tracking tools capability to a portion of the enterprise.	0.50
IR-03: Forensic tools	Enterprise deploys forensic tools, but data handling methodology does not exist.	0.50
IR-04: Computer imaging	Enterprise deploys computer imaging tools capability to a portion of the enterprise.	0.50
IR-05: Indicators of Compromise (IOCs)	Enterprise collects IOCs and makes then available for investigations.	1.00
IR-06: Black hole server	Enterprise deploys black hole server capability to a portion of the enterprise.	0.50
IR-07: Regulatory / legal coordination	Enterprise follows some chain of custody procedures.	0.50
	Incident Response Index:	**0.68**

Figure H-22. *Observed data values for Incident Response.*

Asset Management and Supply Chain (AMSC): 6 Capabilities	Observation (From Appendix G)	Observed Data
AMSC-01: Asset management databases	Enterprise deploys an asset management database with some assets in the database.	0.50
AMSC-02: Configuration Management Databases (CMDB)	Enterprise deploys a CMDB with some configuration items managed.	0.50
AMSC-03: Change management databases	Enterprise deploys change management databases with some change requests processed by it.	0.50
AMSC-04: Software inventory and license management	Enterprise deploys a software inventory and license management capability, but a centralized software inventory does not exist.	0.50
AMSC-05: Supplier certification processes	Enterprise conducts supplier certification security checks on some suppliers before contract award.	0.50
AMSC-06: Secure disposal, recycling, and data destruction	Enterprise deploys secure disposal, recycling and data destruction capabilities for some enterprise IT assets.	0.50
	Asset Management and Supply Chain Index:	**0.50**

Figure H-23. *Observed data values for Asset Management and Supply Chain.*

Policy, Audit, E-Discovery, and Training (PAET): 10 Capabilities	Observation (From Appendix G)	Observed Data
PAET-01: Governance, Risk, and Compliance (GRC), with reporting	Enterprise deploys a GRC program limited to IT risks and does not account for regulatory compliance requirements.	0.50
PAET-02: Compliance and control frameworks	Enterprise deploys individual compliance and control frameworks to meet individual legal, regulatory and customer-driven requirements.	0.50
PAET-03: Audit frameworks	Audit scope is limited to legal, regulatory and customer-driven requirements.	0.50
PAET-04: Customer Certification and Accreditation (C&A)	Enterprise deploys a formal C&A process for some assets and services.	0.50
PAET-05: Policy and policy exception management	Enterprise deploys a policy and policy exception management capability without a follow-up/re-approval process on expired exceptions.	0.50
PAET-06: Risk and threat management	Enterprise deploys a risk and threat management capability to some enterprise IT processes and services.	0.50
PAET-07: Privacy compliance	Enterprise deploys a privacy compliance capability to some enterprise IT processes and services.	0.50
PAET-08: E-Discovery tools	Enterprise conducts e-discovery manually.	0.50
PAET-09: Personnel security and background checks	Human Resources performs pre-employment security and background checks on all potential employees.	1.00
PAET-10: Security awareness and training	Enterprise deploys security awareness program and annual training.	1.00
	Policy, Audit, E-Discovery, and Training Index:	0.63

Figure H-24. *Observed data values for Policy, Audit, E-Discovery, and Training.*

Security Operations Expert Judgment for 17 Operational Processes	Maturity	Utilization	Combined Measurements
1. Policies and Policy Exception Management	Low = 0.00	Low = 0.00	0.00
2. Project and Change Security Reviews	Medium = 0.50	Medium = 0.50	0.50
3. Risk Management	High = 1.00	Medium = 0.50	0.75
4. Control Management	Medium = 0.50	Medium = 0.50	0.50
5. Auditing and Deficiency Tracking	Medium = 0.50	Medium = 0.50	0.50
6. Asset Inventory and Audits	High = 1.00	Medium = 0.50	0.75
7. Change Control	Medium = 0.50	Medium = 0.50	0.50
8. Configuration Management Database Recertification	Medium = 0.50	Medium = 0.50	0.50
9. Supplier Reviews and Risk Assessments	High = 1.00	Medium = 0.50	0.75
10. Cyberintrusion Response	Medium = 0.50	Low = 0.00	0.25
11. All-hazards Emergency Preparedness Exercises	Low = 0.00	Low = 0.00	0.00
12. Vulnerability Scanning, Tracking, and Management	Medium = 0.50	Low = 0.00	0.25
13. Patch Management and Deployment	High = 1.00	Medium = 0.50	0.75
14. Security Monitoring	High = 1.00	Low = 0.00	0.50
15. Password and Key Management	Medium = 0.50	Medium = 0.50	0.50
16. Account and Access Periodic Recertification	Medium = 0.50	Low = 0.00	0.25
17. Privileged Account Activity Audit	High = 1.00	Medium = 0.50	0.75
		Operational Processes Index:	0.53

Figure H-25. *Expert judgment values based on maturity and utilization for the 17 security operational processes, combined using the matrix shown earlier in this section.*

OM Step 6: Calculate the Overall Level3_*Index* Using Object Measurement

For a Level 3 assessment, there are two levels of OM*Index* calculation that are performed. In the first index calculation, index values for each of the functional areas and security operations are calculated using the appropriate OM equation. The resulting index values are shown at the bottom of each of Figures H-14 through H-25. Figure H-26 depicts a compilation of these results.

Level 3 Assessment Focusing on Capabilities Combined Assessment Index for Fisk Mitigation, 11 Functional Areas, and Security Operations		Index Value
Risk Mitigations	5 Steps	0.47
Systems Administration (SA)	9 Capabilities	0.30
Network Security (NS)	14 Capabilities	0.44
Application Security (AS)	9 Capabilities	0.44
Endpoint, Server, and Device Security (ESDS)	15 Capabilities	0.41
Identity, Authentication, and Access Management (IAAM)	9 Capabilities	0.60
Data Protection and Cryptography (DPC)	10 Capabilities	0.45
Monitoring, Vulnerability, and Patch Management (MVPM)	14 Capabilities	0.30
High Availability, Disaster Recovery, and Physical Protection (HADRPP)	10 Capabilities	0.45
Incident Response (IR)	7 Capabilities	0.68
Asset Management and Supply Chain (AMSC)	6 Capabilities	0.50
Policy, Audit, E-Discovery, and Training (PAET)	10 Capabilities	0.63
Security Operations	17 Processes	0.53
Level 3 Cybersecurity Program Assessment Index:		**0.49**

Figure H-26. *This table shows the index values for risk mitigations, each of the 11 functional areas, and the 17 operational processes. Using the OM equation, these index values are then be combined into a single cybersecurity program assessment index.*

Figure H-27 shows a measurement map of the index values obtained in Step 5 and depicts how the data is combined to get an overall index for this assessment level. In this measurement map, the risk mitigations index value is combined with the measurements collected for each of the 11 functional areas and security operations to get a single Level3_*Index* value.

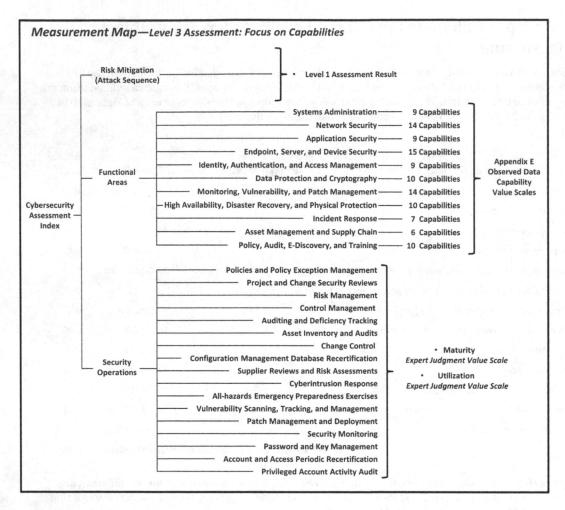

Figure H-27. *Level 3 assessment measurement map showing how assessed values are combined to get an overall cybersecurity assessment index value.*

These 13 OM*Index* values are input to the Object Measurement equation to calculate an overall index value:

$$Level3\_Index = \frac{\sqrt{\begin{array}{c} 0.47^2 + 0.30^2 + 0.44^2 + 0.44^2 + 0.41^2 + 0.60^2 + 0.45^2 + \\ 0.30^2 + 0.45^2 + 0.68^2 + 0.50^2 + 0.63^2 + 0.53^2 \end{array}}}{\sqrt{13}} = \frac{1.78}{3.61} = 0.49$$

The overall combined index score for the cybersecurity scope is 0.49, or 49%. This Level 3 assessment Level3_*Index* represents the enterprise's cybersecurity effectiveness as determined from the values assigned to the observations and expert judgments that were recorded in the assessment. By navigating the measurement map from left to right, the index score can be unfolded to trace back to those original observations and expert judgments.

Results Visualization and Analysis

Like with the previous Level 2 assessment, it makes sense to visualize the results of this assessment using a chart format. The various functional areas can be compared to one another and functional areas that are weakest can be identified for subsequent improvement. Figure H-28 visualizes these results using a vertical bar (column) chart, while Figure H-29 visualizes these results using a spider chart. The spider chart is useful for emphasizing the target value that all functional areas should be of approximately equal effectiveness for the overall enterprise cybersecurity to be effective.

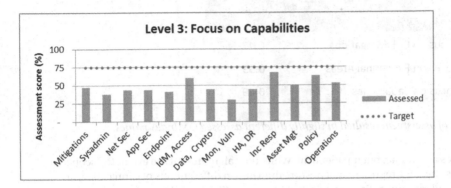

Figure H-28. *Visualization of Level 3 assessment results using a vertical bar (column) chart format.*

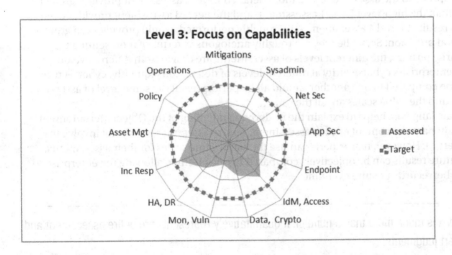

Figure H-29. *Visualization of Level 3 assessment results using a spider chart format.*

While these two charts are the same type as the charts created in the Level 2 assessment, these Level 3 charts are based upon more detailed underlying observations and capture the scope's overall cybersecurity effectiveness to a higher level of precision than the Level 2 assessment. Comparing these charts to the Level 2 assessment results, one can see that the results are very similar, but also slightly different, reflecting this difference in assessment precision. The Level 3 assessment captures the status of functional areas in greater granularity. This granularity provides clarity on which functional areas are weakest when compared to the others, or to the scope's cybersecurity target value (the dotted line).

Comparing Cybersecurity Assessment Results

The OM*Index* is a powerful tool for assessing and measuring an enterprise's cybersecurity posture, as well as modeling the potential effects of cybersecurity projects or improvements. However, it is critically important to remember the different levels of assessments, while they can all be used to calculate an OM*Index*, produce results that are not entirely analogous. For example, Figure H-30 shows the OM*Indices* calculated from each of the three sample assessments in this appendix.

Cybersecurity Program Assessment	Assessment Index
Level 1 Assessment: Focus on Risk Mitigations	0.47
Level 2 Assessment: Focus on Functional Areas	0.53
Level 3 Assessment: Focus on Capabilities	0.49

Figure H-30. *Each level of assessment resulted in slightly different assessed* OM*Index values.*

Obviously, the scores are similar, but not identical. While they all represent the evaluated scope's overall cybersecurity posture, they represent that posture drawing on different sets of source data, at different levels of detail and resolution. Each assessment level uses different value scales to rate the characteristics of the enterprise's cybersecurity, and each assessment level applies those scales at the level of granularity appropriate to the assessment. The more detailed Level 2 assessment provides greater assessment granularity than the high-level Level 1 assessment, and the Level 3 assessment provides even greater granularity in its result. A Level 4 assessment, if thoroughly performed, would provide even greater granularity and evaluation precision. So, while they are roughly analogous in terms of representing the enterprise's overall security posture, the different levels of assessments are drawn from different value scales that evaluate the enterprise's cybersecurity at different levels of detail. Consequently, cybersecurity assessments that are to be compared to one another should all be performed at the same level of assessment so the evaluated criteria and the value scales are all the same.

Enterprise value scale language helps to explain the underlying meaning of the Object Measurement numbers and preserves, in part, the content of each assessment. Future assessments may not involve the same cybersecurity expert(s). However, new experts can use the same value scales for their assessments. This ensures past and future results can be objectively compared to one another, allowing the enterprise to continuously track its cybersecurity posture over time.

Simply stated, the OM*Index* is much more than a number. It quantitatively represents the entire assessment and its observations and expert judgments.

Cybersecurity Assessments for Decision-Making

Finally, once the enterprise has assessed a security scope, it is easy to use that assessment to model cybersecurity improvements and perform *what-if* analysis and comparisons. To do this modeling, calculate the OM*Index* for the baseline security scope, and then adjust the input values to reflect desired changes to risk mitigation measures, cybersecurity capabilities, or operational processes. The OM*Index* can then be recalculated as if the improvements are already completed, and the effect on the index can be observed.

By calculating the OM*Index* before a cybersecurity improvement project is begun and after it is completed, the enterprise can estimate the project's value versus its cost, or "bang for the buck." This cost/benefit analysis reflects quantitatively the amount the enterprise's cybersecurity is expected to improve when the project is completed, versus the project's cost or effort. By modeling this calculation for different proposed cybersecurity projects, the enterprise can get an idea of which projects might be the most effective or cost-effective at improving the enterprise's cybersecurity posture. Such calculations help leaders focus on those projects that deliver the greatest potential results at the lowest costs. By comparing the cost and duration of projects with how they change the OM*Index*, the enterprise can quantify the potential value of these projects. This analysis helps business leadership make well-informed decisions regarding cybersecurity improvements compared with other business priorities.

APPENDIX I

▪▪▪

Network Segmentation

Enterprises frequently mistake complexity for "defense in depth." There are firewalls, intrusion detection systems, proxies, and packet capture—all in a single layer on the outside of the network. The enterprise states, "That's four layers of security protecting us," when the reality is that security is just one layer with four parts. Once a computer inside of the enterprise is compromised, there is nothing on the inside to provide additional protection or catch the attacker who has gotten in. Figure I-1 shows another example of defense in depth that also turned out to be inadequate when it was tested.

Similarly, in enterprise demilitarized zones (DMZ), while there is a layer of defense protecting back-end servers from Internet-facing servers, the channels connecting the two frequently allow for so much data and traffic that attackers seldom need to go any further than the DMZ to compromise the enterprise—once a machine in the DMZ is compromised, that one system can be used to access everything else that the attackers need.

So, what's missing here? The missing piece is true defense in depth. True defense in depth means that defenders get multiple chances to stop the attackers between the time when they start to attack and before they can accomplish their goal. True defense in depth slows the attackers down, channels their movement, and increases the enterprise's chances of detecting them and opportunities for stopping them.

Figure I-1. *The designers of the Titanic thought they had adequate defense in depth to protect against any possibility. [Photo credit: Dorling Kindersley/Getty Images]*

The Legacy Network

In the "legacy" network, there are generally only two "zones"—the DMZ, where Internet-facing servers reside, and the "trusted zone," where internal users and servers reside. It is ironic that enterprises build their networks so that users are right next to the servers containing the most precious enterprise data. The reality of the past several years has shown that enterprise users are the target of most attacks and ultimately the weakest link in this overall security architecture.

As shown in Figure I-2, in a legacy architecture, numerous functions all reside on the trusted network, including system administration, authentication and monitoring functions, e-mail, application servers, database servers, and virtual desktop. All these capabilities reside on the trusted network, with little or no protection separating one capability from another or providing any additional protection once an attack has gotten on the inside.

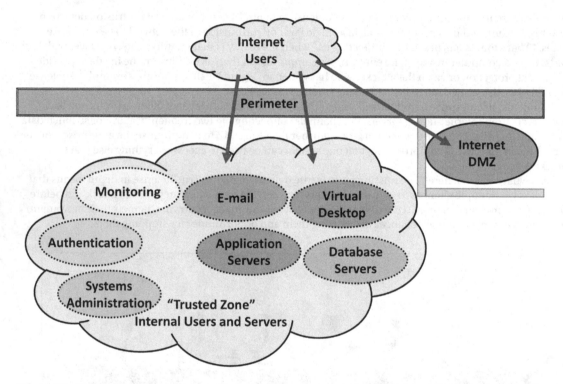

Figure I-2. *In a legacy network, Internet-facing DMZ servers are isolated, but everything else is in a single "trusted zone."*

Protecting the Security Infrastructure

Targeted attackers are not always brilliant, but enterprises should expect them to be competent. As professionals, cyberattackers will seek to get their job done as quickly and cheaply as possible, which involves taking the fastest route to compromising the enterprise and stealing its data. In an enterprise where everything is protected equally well (or poorly), the easiest way to get to anything is to take control of the systems administration channels and then use them to obtain the permissions to access everything on the network.

To thwart these attackers, the first thing enterprise cyberdefenders should do is to protect the security infrastructure and isolate it from the rest of the network, as shown in Figure I-3. This action involves taking systems administration systems, authentication systems, and monitoring systems, and then isolating them from the rest of the enterprise and making them difficult to access. With this protection in place, attackers are not just a username and a password away from complete enterprise control—they have to compromise the network first.

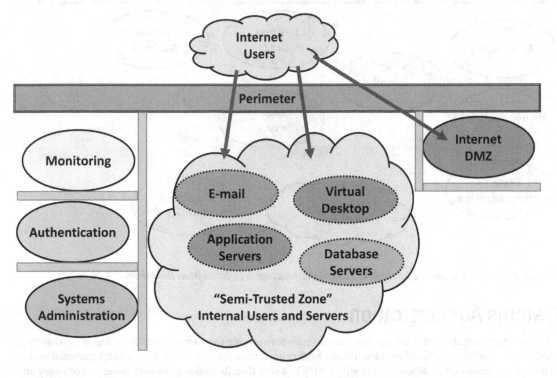

Figure I-3. *It is extremely important to protect the security infrastrucutre—monitoring, authentication, systems administration, and other security servers—from the rest of the enterprise.*

Watertight Compartments

Once the security infrastructure has been protected, the enterprise is well on its way to deploying "watertight compartments," as shown in Figure I-4. The goal of this network segmentation is to isolate enterprise capabilities around functions so there are network protections between major systems that might be attacked.

The reality is the vast majority of attacks will come from either Internet-facing servers or users. Enterprise cyberdefenses need to revolve around protecting the rest of the enterprise from these two attack vectors. After that, everything else is secondary. All things considered, the most important of these isolations is the one between internal users and enterprise IT infrastructure. If users can surf the Web or receive e-mail from the Internet, enterprises should expect that between 5% and 10% of them will be compromised every year. It is imperative to protect the rest of the enterprise from these potential attacks once they get inside the network—because they will get in, eventually. The question is about what happens once they do.

461

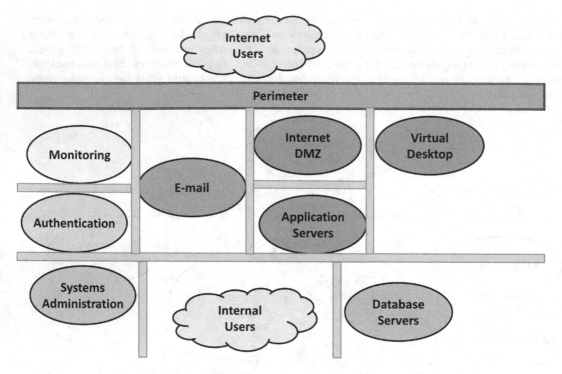

Figure I-4. *In a fully segmented network, each major function is isolated from the others.*

Systems Administration

An interesting thing about this fully segmented architecture is once the network has been segmented around functions, the traffic that should and should not be flowing across the network is both straightforward and obvious. Erroneous and malicious traffic sticks out like a sore thumb, making network defense both easy and effective.

For example, considering systems administration protocols, one can see that monitoring traffic should only go in one direction from the "monitoring" zone to the rest of the enterprise, authentication traffic should only go in one direction from the "authentication" zone, and system administration traffic should only go in one direction from the "systems administration" zone. Traffic using these protocols that does not match these patterns can be detected and investigated as a potential attack, especially in light of how targeted attacks attempt to leverage systems administration channels to take control of the enterprise. Figure I-5 depicts the patterns of legitimate systems administration network traffic.

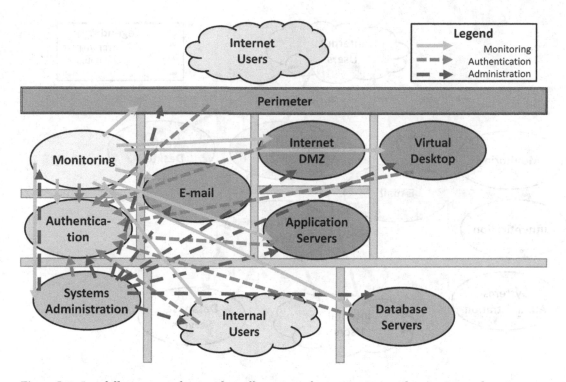

Figure I-5. *In a fully-segmented network, traffic patterns for monitoring, authentication and systems administration are well-defined. Instances of this traffic outside of these patterns is an indicator of attack.*

Applications

One can see a similar pattern of network traffic when considering the application data flow. E-mail is an interesting application because almost all systems in the enterprise need to connect to e-mail systems to be able to send alerts and notifications. Other applications have considerably simpler connectivity requirements. For example, most enterprise applications involve a front-end server and a back-end database. While the front-end server may be externally accessible, the back-end database is not generally user-facing.

Visualizing this network traffic, one can envision a picture similar to Figure I-6. Once again, the patterns of application traffic are fairly straightforward, reflecting topologies and interactions that are, at a strategic level, fairly simple. Once again, cyberdefenders can look for network traffic that does not match these patterns and investigate it as erroneous or possibly malicious. The key thing here is traffic that does not match these patterns should raise alerts and trigger investigations. Nine out of ten times the investigation reveals a misconfigured server or mistaken administrator but occasionally it reveals a real cyberattack.

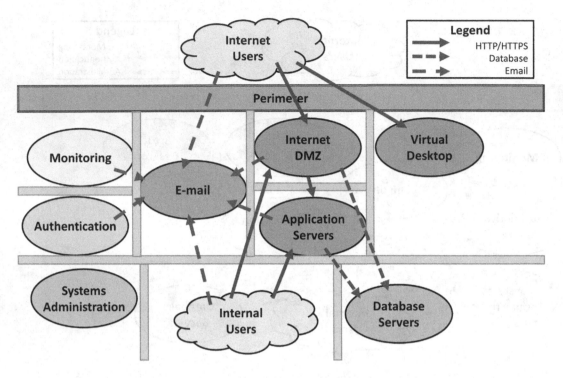

Figure I-6. *In a fully segmented network, traffic patterns for web servers, databases, and e-mail are well defined. Instances of this traffic outside of these patterns is an indicator of attack.*

Web Traffic

Similarly to how one can visualize application traffic on this topology, cyberdefenders can also envision what the web-based traffic should look like as it transits the network. With the segmented network architecture, there is only one zone that should be "surfing the Web," and that is the zone where the internal users reside. For every other zone, the only web traffic that should be occurring is patch downloads, unless they are handled by a central patch-management system. Figure I-7 shows these traffic patterns.

With this architecture, not only can the enterprise block web-surfing from its servers, but it can also alert on such communications to trigger an investigation of why a server is trying to access the Web. Cyberdefenders can then investigate if it is simply an administrator opening a browser by mistake or something more ominous. With this architecture, the enterprise has an opportunity not only to block malicious traffic, but also to alert on it and direct incident responders to the source, almost immediately.

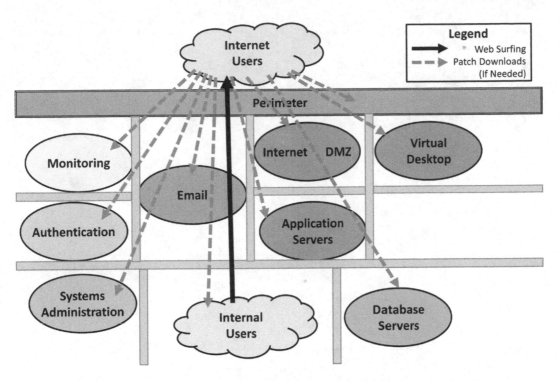

Figure I-7. *In a fully segmented network, traffic patterns for web-surfing and patch downloads are well defined. Instances of this traffic outside of these patterns is an indicator of attack.*

Network Segmentation Summary

This appendix shows how the classic network architecture is inadequate against advanced attackers. Attackers who gain a foothold in a traditional network architecture are frequently just one step away from achieving their ultimate objectives. Network segmentation can give defenders significant opportunities to repel attacks by slowing down attackers and providing opportunities to detect them and repel them before they are successful.

In a well-segmented network, legitimate network traffic follows patterns that are straightforward and easy to protect. Malicious traffic, on the other hand, follows patterns that are markedly different and can be alerted on to detect attacks when they occur. Using network segmentation, enterprises can detect and respond to attacks while they are in progress and before they can succeed.

While not a complete solution in and of itself, a properly segmented network will significantly strengthen the enterprise's security posture and give defenders the opportunity to detect and thwart today's targeted attacks.

The best defense doesn't just stop the attacker. A skilled attacker, once stopped, will go get a cup of coffee and then start figuring out how to get around the defense that stopped them. Because no defense can be absolutely perfect, the skilled attacker will eventually figure out a way to get through.

Instead, the best defense is the one that detects the attackers and alerts defenders so they can respond. Once the attackers have been detected, the enterprise can unleash the one defense that can actually defeat them once and for all. And that defense is skilled defenders.

Glossary

This glossary contains definitions of many of the cybersecurity terms used in this book, described as plainly as possible for the business reader or non-cybersecurity professional. This glossary assumes a general knowledge of information technology (IT) as it endeavors to explain cybersecurity concepts for the reader who is seeking to understand how cybersecurity fits into the overall IT picture.

In this glossary, terms that are used in definitions and are defined elsewhere in the glossary are *italicized*.

A

Access Management - Management of permissions related to computer and network resources, and applied to people, accounts, or machines. Access management oversees who can access what in an IT environment.

Advanced Persistent Threat (APT) - An advanced *cyberattacker* who penetrates a victim's network and maintains persistence within that environment to carry out cyberattacks over time. Uses advanced techniques to gain and retain access, particularly for conducting espionage or data theft.

Alert - A *cybersecurity event* that strongly indicates *malicious* behavior and generates an alarm on a detection system. The alarm indicates an *incident* is occurring and requires investigation and follow-up.

Analytics - Technology that uses pattern recognition to analyze log files or data streams for anomalies that might be indicative of *malicious* behavior. Examples include *privileged* accesses coming from an otherwise unprivileged user or network connections that do not match typical traffic patterns.

Anti-Malware - A security technology that catches *malware* by identifying its *malicious* behaviors, such as unusual network connections or attempts to change the operating system. *Anti-virus* vendors frequently label their products anti-malware when they have advanced features.

Anti-Virus - A security technology that catches *viruses* and *malware* by matching them against signatures of known *malicious* software. Its main limitation is it is unable to recognize *viruses* or *malware* that have not been added to the *blacklist* database, usually by the anti-virus vendor.

Asset Management - The process of tracking assets within an *enterprise* over their life cycle from initial acquisition through final disposal. These assets may be capital assets that are tracked for financial reasons and depreciated. Assets may also be IT assets such as computer hardware or software.

Attack Graph / Attack Tree - A method for analyzing attacks that involves creating a chart of the steps the attacker must take and tracing the relationships between those steps. Each step becomes a potential point for defending against the attacker and attempting to thwart the attack.

Attack Sequence - The steps taken by an attacker to conduct an attack. It starts with preparation and reconnaissance, and ends when the attack succeeds in compromising the *confidentiality*, *integrity*, or *availability* of the victim. It is sometimes referred to as the *kill chain*.

Audit - In *cybersecurity*, a review to verify that a *policy* is being complied with or is otherwise effective. Because audits are after the fact, they rely on logs and artifacts as evidence to show the operation of the *cybersecurity controls* enforce the *policy*.

Authentication - The process of uniquely identifying oneself to a computer. Authentication is generally performed using a username and a *password*, although *strong authentication* or *multi-factor authentication* may also be used.

Authentication Token - A *token* used for *strong authentication* or *multi-factor authentication* that produces a *one-time password* or contains a digital *certificate* and is difficult to *compromise* or duplicate.

Availability - One of the *cyberdefense* triad of *confidentiality, integrity, and availability* (CIA). Availability refers to IT services being available for use. An availability attack denies access to those services, usually through *denial of service* or *distributed denial of service* attacks.

B

Back Door - A method of accessing a computer system that is not expected or authorized. A back door might allow an *attacker* to connect to the system using an obscure network port or web address known only to the attacker. A back door frequently gives an attacker the ability to remotely control the system and run commands.

Bastion Host - A security technique that involves requiring all *privileged* accesses originate from a specific set of hardened computer systems. *Systems administrators* requiring *privileged* access would first log on to the bastion hosts, and then to the systems to be managed.

Biometrics - A method of *strong authentication* that uses biological attributes such as fingerprints, iris patterns, or facial geometry to uniquely identify a person. It can be particularly effective for physical security applications where the biometric sensors are trusted and protected from tampering.

Black Hole Server - A server configured to accept a connection from an *attacker* without actually executing any of the *attacker's* commands. It is used in *incident response* to direct *malicious* or misrouted data packets so they can do no harm.

Blacklist - A security method that involves identifying accounts, applications, networks, *passwords*, or network protocols that are explicitly untrusted. Accounts on a blacklist might not be permitted to log on. Applications on a blacklist might not be permitted to install or run. Network addresses or protocols on a blacklist might not be permitted to communicate. Blacklisting is in contrast to *whitelisting*.

Botnet - A network of *compromised* computers that are all under an attacker's central control. It can be used to conduct *distributed denial-of-service* attacks or to obtain initial entry to a victim *enterprise* through *compromised* computers.

Breach - The *compromise* of a system, networking resource, or data by an *attacker* who overcomes or defeats the established protection measures.

Brute Force Attack - An attack method that involves comprehensively trying all possible attack patterns in order to try to deduce the correct one. Most often, this attack is used to guess *passwords* or *encryption keys*. *Cryptographically* weak *passwords* and *keys* can be defeated through a brute force attack in a short amount of time.

Burndown - A *cyberattack* that destroys the victim's IT infrastructure, including servers, personal computers, and other supporting systems. This attack is akin to "burning down the house," but is in contrast to a *meltdown*, which targets just the core IT infrastructure.

C

Certificate - A *cryptographic* file that uses *digital signatures* to enable an identity to be traced back to a trusted source. Commonly used in *public key infrastructure* (PKI) for *strong authentication* or *multi-factor authentication*.

Certification and Accreditation (C&A) - A formal process for approving products or technologies to be used in an *enterprise* environment. It generally requires the products or technologies be formally reviewed and possibly tested prior to accreditation.

Change Management - The practice of managing changes to an IT environment, usually including approval processes and paths to production, and sometimes including *monitoring* to detect unauthorized changes.

Change Management Database - A database of *enterprise* changes that supports the *change management* process.

Chief Information Officer (CIO) - The senior-most enterprise IT executive. This individual is generally a corporate officer or senior executive with significant authority and reporting directly to senior enterprise leadership.

Chief Information Security Officer (CISO) - The senior-most enterprise *cybersecurity* executive. This individual is frequently a corporate officer or senior executive with accountability for *cybersecurity* matters to senior enterprise leadership. The *CISO* often reports directly to the *CIO*, but may also report outside of the *CIO's* organization.

CIA - The *cyberdefense* triad of *confidentiality*, *integrity*, and *availability*. *Cyberattacks* involve compromising one or more of these properties of IT systems, and *cyberdefenses* involve protecting them.

Cloud (Computing) - A computing model where capabilities are delivered by service providers from their facilities and data centers connected to the Internet and outside of the *enterprise's* facilities, data centers, or networks. Cloud customers purchase computing capabilities, applications, or storage as they are needed rather than purchasing individual servers, storage, or software.

Compromise - The act of taking control of a computer, *endpoint*, or *device* and modifying its configuration to suit the needs of the attacker. Frequently, compromise involves exploiting a *vulnerability* to install *malware* that gives the attacker some capability with regard to the victim.

Confidentiality - One of the *cyberdefense* triad of *confidentiality, integrity, and availability* (CIA). Confidentiality refers to the protection of data that should not be disclosed or is protected from disclosure by regulation, company *policy*, or customer requirements.

Configuration Management - The practice of tracking and managing the configuration of IT assets through their life cycles. This tracking usually includes specific parameters of the configuration such as system name and Internet address. Tracking may also include life cycle items such as baseline configurations, configuration deviations, and system release cycles.

Configuration Management Database (CMDB) - A database of *enterprise* configuration items and their configuration parameters. This database supports the *configuration management* and *change management* processes by providing an authoritative listing of all items in the *enterprise* that are subject to change and configuration of *cybersecurity controls*.

Credential - A parameter for *authentication* consisting of a user identity and a proof of identity such as a *password* or *multi-factor authentication token*.

Credential Harvesting - *Cyberattack* method that involves scanning computer memory, software code, and hard drives for stored copies of *credentials*. Generally *credential* harvesting is done to send *credentials* back to the *attacker* or use the *credentials* to further the attack.

Cryptography - *Cybersecurity* practice that includes: (1) algorithms for generating pseudo-random numbers, (2) *encrypting* data so it cannot be read by an attacker, (3) *hashing* data so changes can be detected, and (4) *digitally signing* data so its origin can be verified.

Cyber - A prefix that identifies properties related to IT systems including computers and computer networks.

Cyberattack - An attack conducted using computers and information systems to *compromise* the *confidentiality, integrity,* or *availability* of the target's information and information systems.

Cyberdefense - The act of defending computers and information systems from *cyberattack*.

Cybersecurity - The practice of protecting the *confidentiality, integrity,* and *availability* of enterprise IT assets.

Cybersecurity Control - A means of enforcing a security *policy* within the *enterprise*. Cybersecurity controls can be of multiple types to include the following: (1) preventive controls that prevent undesired behaviors, (2) detective controls that detect undesired behaviors, (3) *forensic* controls that log undesired behaviors so they can be investigated afterward, and (4) *audit* controls that search for undesired behaviors. Each control type has advantages, disadvantages, and trade-offs.

D

Data Leakage / Loss Protection (DLP) - *Cybersecurity* technology that detects and optionally blocks the transmission of sensitive data outside the *enterprise*. Generally, this technology uses pattern-matching to identify sensitive data such as social security numbers.

Demilitarized Zone (DMZ) - A section of a computer network compartmented off for protection of the IT systems contained within it. Most often, a DMZ network contains the *enterprise's* Internet-facing servers.

Denial of Service (DoS) - A *cyberattack* method that involves disabling IT systems either temporarily or permanently, denying their *availability* to the intended users.

Device - A network-connected component that has computing capabilities but is not normally called a computer. Common devices are mobile phones, tablets, network-connected sensors, and computing appliances.

Digital Rights Management (DRM) - A *cybersecurity* technology that uses *cryptography* to apply *access management* directly to data. This technology involves *encrypting* data and then only decrypting it for authorized users. DRM is supported by many common formats for documents, spreadsheets, presentations, music, and video.

Disaster Recovery - The ability of an *enterprise* to recover from a "disaster" that generally involves the dramatic loss of facilities, personnel, or other impairment of IT systems and services. Disasters may be natural—such as hurricanes or earthquakes—or they may be man-made—such as power outages, espionage, sabotage, violent crime, or warfare.

Digital Signature - A *cryptographic* technique for protecting the *integrity* of data by calculating a *hash* of the data and then *cryptographically* processing the *hash* through a trusted party. This technique makes it possible to prove the authenticity of the data, detect unauthorized changes, and achieve *non-repudiation*.

Distributed Denial of Service (DDoS) - A *denial of service* attack that uses a distributed network—usually a *botnet*—to overload IT systems with a massive surge of network traffic that the infrastructure is unable to handle.

Down Market - In the context of *cyberattacks*, the trend whereby attack methods and tools become more widely available over time. This trend is due to tools becoming commoditized and "user-friendly," and consequently accessible to an ever-expanding circle of less and less sophisticated *cyberattackers*.

E

E(lectronic)-Discovery - A legal process for retrieving evidence from electronic and computerized systems. This process is subject to legal regulations and oversight. Consequently, specific rules must be followed to protect the *integrity* of the evidence collected and its chain of custody.

Encryption - A *cryptographic* technique for protecting data so it can only be read by holders of the legitimate *key*. The effectiveness of encryption is dependent on the strength of the algorithms used, computation of strong pseudo-random number sequences, the length of the encryption key used, the distribution of the encryption key over its life cycle, and numerous other technical factors.

Endpoint - Any type of computing system, including servers, personal computers, appliances, mobile *devices* (such as tablet PCs, netbooks, and smartphones), or other network-connected *devices*. Endpoints are subject to security policies and capabilities intended to prevent their *compromise*.

Enterprise - An organization that uses computers and computer networks for personal, business, nation-state, or other purposes, and has authority over those computers and computer networks. An enterprise may range from an individual's personal computer and network up to a corporate or governmental entity with thousands or hundreds of thousands of computers connected to networks spanning the globe.

Enterprise Cybersecurity Architecture - A comprehensive framework for managing all aspects of a *cybersecurity* program, including policies, programmatics, technologies, operations, and assessments.

Enterprise Directory - A database of authorized users and computers in the *enterprise*. It can also be used to store *credential* information for *authentication* and information about access *privileges* for *access management*. It may support only internal users or users and customers. It frequently ties in with *identity management* and other *enterprise* systems.

Escalate Privileges - In a *cyberattack*, attackers obtain additional *privileges* in the *enterprise*. For example, going from regular user to *systems administrator* status on a personal computer or a file server or escalating from computer administrator to network administrator status on an *enterprise* network.

Event - An incidence of behavior that is logged and may be an indication of *malicious* behavior. *Incidents* are generated when one or more events together constitute an *indicator of compromise* and warrant investigation.

Exfiltration - The act of surreptitiously copying confidential data from an *enterprise*, preferably without being discovered.

F

Federal Information Security Management Act (FISMA) - United States legislation that specifies standards for protecting information processed by or on behalf of the US federal government.

Federated Authentication - A method of *authentication* where a service provider refers back to an issuer for identity validation. This method provides users with *single-sign-on* so they do not have to maintain separate usernames and *passwords*, and federated authentication can also support *multi-factor authentication*.

Firewall - A security capability that connects to a network and applies a security *policy* to determine what network traffic is allowed to pass and what network traffic is blocked. It can also *alert* on certain types of network traffic that might indicate an attack.

Firmware - Software installed in computer system components, such as the motherboard, networking subsystem, or hard drives. Firmware is generally programmed at the factory and seldom, if ever, modified or updated in the field. *Malware* embedded in firmware can be difficult or impossible to detect and *remediate*, and it may require replacement of the *compromised* component.

Foothold - A cyberattacker's initial entry into a target *enterprise*. It usually consists of one or more network-connected personal computers or servers that are *compromised* and have *malware* installed. The *malware* enables the cyberattacker to control the *compromised* computers or servers remotely and continue the attack using the foothold as a starting point.

Forensics - The science of investigating *compromised* computer systems to understand *attacker tools, techniques, and procedures*, and also to determine *indicators of compromise*. Forensic investigation involves analyzing logs, files, and sometimes program code to understand *attacker* activities and methods.

Forward Proxy - A network device or computer that intercepts certain types of network traffic—most often web-browsing—and applies a security *policy* to the intercepted traffic before forwarding it on (the *proxy*). Forward proxies are generally used to *monitor* web-browsing for *malicious* behavior.

G

Global Server Load Balancing (GSLB) - A method of *load balancing* between different physical sites that have separate Internet connections. This method provides geographic redundancy and *disaster recovery* capability in case one facility fails.

Gold Code - A *configuration-managed* version or configuration of software code that is generally used as a master image for software code installation on multiple computers. Gold code usually applies to operating system images and configurations or application software builds that are approved for release or distribution.

Governance, Risk, and Compliance (GRC) - Methods and tools for managing *enterprise cybersecurity* including security policies, *enterprise risks*, and compliance postures. GRC tools usually provide for management and reporting of these entities against established standards or frameworks to assist with regulatory compliance and *auditing*.

H

Hacker - A person who obtains unauthorized access to computer systems, usually by exploiting *vulnerabilities* in computer system security.

Hacking - The act of obtaining unauthorized access to computer systems, usually by exploiting *vulnerabilities* in computer system security. People who perform these acts are called *hackers*.

Hacktivism - *Hacking* conducted for political purposes, usually by an unaffiliated individual or a nongovernmental organization.

Hardware Security Module (HSM) - A *cryptographic device* used to protect *cryptographic keys* from theft. Some models can also accelerate *cryptographic* operations such as *encryption*, decryption, or *digital signatures*.

Hash - A fixed-length *cryptographic* code calculated from a document or data field such that any change to the document or data field results in the hash changing as well. The algorithm is one-way so knowledge of the hash does not lead to the original document or data being revealed. This capability is used to protect the *integrity* of documents from modification, as well as for *authentication* so *passwords* do not need to be stored unencrypted.

Health Insurance Portability and Accountability Act (HIPAA) - Legislation passed by the US Congress in 1996 that protects the *privacy* of *protected health information* held by medical practitioners, insurers, and others in the healthcare industry.

High Availability - Redundancy in an IT system so the failure or destruction of any one system component will not result in the loss of the overall service delivered by the system.

Honeypot - A system configured on an *enterprise* IT network that is attractive to *attackers*, but does not contain real production data or transactions. When attacked, the honeypot *alerts* defenders and collects information on the attacker's *tools, techniques, and procedures* and other *indicators of compromise*.

Honeynet - A portion of an *enterprise* network that is configured similarly to a core network to attract *attackers*, *alert* upon their presence, and collect information on their attack methods without risking real data, core networking resources, or transactions.

Honeytoken - Dummy data stored in an *enterprise's* databases or file servers and used to detect attacks. Honeytoken data contains patterns that can be *alerted* on if they are *exfiltrated* from the enterprise or appear on the Internet.

I

Identity Management (IdM) - A security capability that involves managing computer accounts throughout their life cycle from when they are created until they are destroyed.

Incident - A *cybersecurity* activity initiated by one or more *events* or *alarms* that indicate *malicious* behavior and warrant investigation. Incidents are investigated using *security information and event management* systems, and computer *forensics*.

Incident Response - The practice of investigating, containing, remediating, resolving, and documenting *cybersecurity incidents*, using *indicators of compromise* and performing *forensics* on *compromised* systems.

Indicator of Compromise (IOC) - An indicator that can be used to identify *attacker malicious* activity in the *enterprise*. Indicators are usually accounts, computers, network addresses, or communications patterns that are identified using *forensics* and then used to generate additional *alerts* to identify *attacker* activity wherever it is occurring.

Integrity - One of the *cyberdefense* triad of *confidentiality, integrity, and availability* (CIA). Integrity refers to having confidence that data does not change from when it is recorded until it is read. Integrity is particularly important for financial records, medical records, and transactions, but it can also apply to system configurations, log records, and other aspects of IT systems. Integrity attacks involve changing data or configurations through unauthorized means.

Intrusion Detection System (IDS) - A network security technology that generates *events* and *alerts* on network traffic patterns. These patterns may be *indicators of compromise*. A detection system is usually configured in a *monitoring* mode so it is able to detect *malicious* activity, but not respond to it.

Intrusion Prevention System (IPS) - An *intrusion detection system* that blocks network connections thought to be *malicious*.

J

No Entries.

K

Kerberos - An *authentication* protocol that uses *cryptography* to *authenticate* users' access to resources over an *enterprise* network. Accesses are granted using *digitally signed* tickets that indicate permission to access resources.

Keys - In *cryptography*, digital strings that are used to *encrypt*, decrypt, and *digitally sign* data. In general, only the holder of the key is able to perform these operations so distribution of the key can be used for *access management* or *digital rights management*. When the key is only held by one party, then data *digitally signed* by the key can be used as proof of the party's identity, or *non-repudiation*.

Keylogger - A piece of *malware* that performs *credential harvesting* by capturing keyboard input when the victim types in usernames and *passwords* to *authenticate* to systems. Usually, the keylogger has logic in it that filters out other keyboard inputs and intelligently captures logon *credentials*.

Kill Chain - The steps taken by an attacker to conduct an attack. Starts with preparation and reconnaissance, and ends when the attack succeeds in compromising the *confidentiality*, *integrity*, or *availability* of the victim. Sometimes referred to as the *attack sequence*.

L

Lateral Movement - In a *cyberattack*, moving from one computer to another where both machines are at equivalent levels of *privilege*, or using *credentials* at a single *privilege* level. Lateral movement is in contrast with *escalating privileges*, where attackers obtain additional *privileges* in the *enterprise*.

Lightweight Directory Access Protocol (LDAP) - An *enterprise directory* protocol commonly used in *enterprises* for identifying users and computers, storing their *authentication credentials*, and performing *privilege* and *access management*.

Load Balancing - A *high availability* technique that involves balancing a service load between two or more servers or nodes. This balancing ensures that as long as one of the nodes is operational the service will be delivered, and it protects against failures or maintenance causing an outage.

M

Malicious - Adjective applied to behavior, network traffic, or software intended to *compromise* the *confidentiality*, *integrity*, or *availability* of *enterprise* data and IT systems.

Malvertising - Web site advertising or advertising applications installed on computers that *compromise* computers and/or deliver *malware*. Modern *attackers* have become adept in creating advertisements that are displayed on mainstream web sites and attempt to *compromise vulnerable* web browsers.

Malware - *Malicious* software. Malware is generally characterized by one or more of the following properties: (1) it attempts to stay hidden or to persist on the victim computer after attempts to remove it, (2) it attempts to propagate from one victim computer to another, (3) it collects data from the victim and sends it to another computer, (4) it collects user *credentials* for resources and/or web sites, or (5) it *monitors* user behavior without the user's knowledge or consent.

Meltdown - A *cyberattack* that destroys the victim's IT core infrastructure—usually supporting servers and data center components—but leaves major parts of the IT environment, such as personal computers, intact. A meltdown is in contrast to a *burndown*, which destroys almost everything.

Mitigation - In *cybersecurity*, the process of compensating for *risks*, *vulnerabilities*, or *threats* by reducing either the probability of their occurrence or impact of their exploitation.

Mobile Device Management (MDM) - *Cybersecurity* technology for managing *enterprise* data stored on mobile *devices*. This technology generally works by either controlling the *device* itself or by creating within the *device* a protected data store or container for *enterprise* data. If the *device* is lost or stolen, this technology usually provides the ability to erase the *enterprise* data, or even the entire *device*, so *enterprise* data is not *compromised*.

Monitoring - Collecting log data, *events*, or *alerts* so they can be consolidated into one location for correlation and analysis in a *security information and event management* system. Monitoring can be for operational purposes—to ensure systems are performing properly—or for *cybersecurity* purposes to detect *incidents*.

Multi-Factor Authentication - *Authentication* that relies on multiple factors of identity, usually something the user knows such as a *password*, plus something the user has such as a *token* or mobile *device*, or possibly a *biometric* such as a fingerprint. Also known as *two-factor authentication* or *strong authentication*.

N

Non-Repudiation - Electronic proof of identity. Generally, non-repudiation is performed *cryptographically* by *digitally signing* a unique piece of data using a *key* that is only held by the party, thus proving the party's identity online.

O

One-Time Password - A *password* that is only used for a single *authentication* attempt. Even if the one-time password is intercepted, the *attacker* will not be able to use it for subsequent logons. Different implementations use different techniques for generating and distributing the one-time password.

Out-of-Band (OOB) - A technique for *authentication* or *systems administration* that uses a separate connection, channel, or media isolated from the primary connectivity. This approach forces the attacker to *compromise* both connections in order to intercept the *authentication* or *systems administration* activity.

P

Password - A string of characters known only to the user and used to *authenticate*, proving the user's identity to a computer system.

Patch - A software or configuration update that addresses a performance or security issue that is distributed and installed after a system is in production. Patches generally consist of updated software or configuration files, but there is no limit to how complex they can be. In complex systems, patches can have unintended consequences, so careful testing may be required.

Patch Management - The *cybersecurity* process of obtaining, testing, and distributing *patches* to resolve security issues and remediate *vulnerabilities*. This process requires carefully balancing the *cybersecurity risks* associated with *vulnerabilities* that are patched against the operational *risks* of making changes to complex systems that are difficult to test and troubleshoot.

Payment Card Industry (PCI) - A generic term for the industry involved in processing payment cards, including credit and debit cards. The Payment Card Industry Security Standards Council (PCI SSC) publishes the Payment Card Industry Data Security Standards (PCI DSS), which include security requirements for processing credit and debit card transactions.

Personally Identifiable Information (PII) - Regulated data used to uniquely identify individuals, generally including information such as home address, telephone numbers, medical and employment information, national identifier or social security number, date of birth, and bank account numbers. *Compromise* of this data can trigger disclosure requirements under state or federal law.

Phishing - A *cyberattack* technique for obtaining initial entry to an *enterprise* that involves sending *malicious* e-mails to *enterprise* users. These e-mails generally work by exploiting a *vulnerability* to install *malware* onto the victim's computer by tricking the victim into installing the *malware* by himself or herself or by tricking the victim into divulging his or her logon *credentials*.

Policy - In *cybersecurity*, a management statement of behavior to be performed within the *enterprise*. An effective policy must have four properties: (1) it must be written, (2) it must be promulgated so people are aware of it, (3) it must include consequences for non-compliance, and (4) those consequences must be enforced as fairly, completely, and ethically as possible.

Privacy - The protection of *personally identifiable information* and other data, such as *protected health information*, from unauthorized disclosure. Privacy is frequently defined and specified by government regulations that include disclosure requirements and penalties for *breaches*.

Privilege - A permission for access to an *enterprise* computer resource. *Attackers* frequently seek to obtain administrative privileges to computer systems and data. With administrator privileges, *attackers* can access and modify data at will.

Protected Health Information (PHI) - Regulated data related to personal healthcare data and activities. This data generally includes information about doctors, appointments, diagnoses, procedures, and drug prescriptions. This data is regulated by state and national law, and its *compromise* may trigger disclosure requirements or penalties.

Proxy - A network *device* that intercepts a network connection by inserting itself into the middle of what would otherwise be a direct link, usually between a user computer and a server on the Internet. This technique is used to permit the proxy to examine the data exchanged over the connection, usually for security purposes.

Public Key Infrastructure (PKI) - A *cryptographic* technology infrastructure that uses asymmetric *cryptography* to provide capabilities for *encryption*, *digital signature*, and *strong authentication* that work over an open, insecure network such as the Internet.

Q

No entries.

R

RADIUS - A network *authentication* protocol. Although it is seldom spelled out, RADIUS stands for Remote Authentication Dial-In User Service. It is used for *authentication* on many network *devices* including *routers*, switches, and *virtual private networking* systems. The RADIUS protocol includes few security features and must be carefully protected from attack.

Ransomware - A form of *malware* that *encrypts* the data stored on the victim's computer and then demands a ransom to decrypt the data. If the user refuses the ransom, the *key* is destroyed and the data is lost. More sophisticated ransomware versions are aware of backups, databases, file shares, and cloud storage. They take measures to ensure all copies of data are *encrypted* and held ransom.

Remediation - The act of restoring "normal" operation after a *breach* or *compromise* has occurred. This act generally involves removing the attacker from the environment by denying them access to computers, accounts, or *enterprise* networks, and by removing any *malware* or *viruses* installed by the attacker.

Revenge Porn – Sexually explicit media—usually pictures—posted publicly on the Internet without the consent of the subject individual. Revenge porn may be performed by a former romantic partner with the intent of embarrassing the individual, or may be performed by *hackers* who *compromise* the online accounts of celebrities.

Reverse Proxy - A network *device* or computer that intercepts network traffic originating from the Internet and destined for a server on the *enterprise* network. The reverse *proxy* applies a security *policy* to the traffic before forwarding it on, thereby masking the internal IP addresses of the networking resources, and it may *alert* or block network traffic suspected to be *malicious*.

Risk - In *cybersecurity*, the chance or likelihood that an attacker or *threat* interferes with the *confidentiality*, *integrity*, or *availability* of *enterprise* data or IT services. Normally, *risk* is analyzed based upon *threats* exploiting present *vulnerabilities* and causing an impact to an *enterprise*. In *cybersecurity*, *vulnerabilities* can be difficult to analyze and change rapidly.

Risk Management - The *cybersecurity* process of tracking and analyzing *enterprise risks* and their *mitigations*. This process considers the business impact of *cybersecurity risks* so *mitigations* can be properly prioritized and considered from a business perspective. *Risk* management is a business management function. *Risk* management may use a number of approaches to handle *risks*, including reducing them through *mitigation* and transferring them through insurance.

Rootkit - A *malware* tool that modifies the operating system of the victim machine so the tool has complete operating system access. (On some operating systems, this is referred to as "root.") The *malware* can then give the attacker complete control either locally or over a network connection, bypassing all operating system security features such as access permissions or *anti-virus* software.

Router - A networking component that routes network traffic between network segments, ensuring data is forwarded to the correct network destination.

S

Sarbanes-Oxley (SOX) - A US federal law passed in 2002 that set criminal penalties for misrepresentation of financial results at publicly traded companies. Regulations stemming from this law require that *enterprises* enact *cybersecurity controls* to protect the *integrity* of financial data and reports.

Secure Sockets Layer (SSL) - A network communications protocol that establishes an *encrypted* connection between two computers over an untrusted network. It can also include verification of one or both computers' identities. SSL has been superseded by the newer *transport layer security (TLS)* protocol, although in casual conversation both protocols are usually referred to as "SSL." SSL and *TLS* secure most Internet sessions, so there are serious business implications when *vulnerabilities* are found in these protocols.

Security Assertion Markup Language (SAML) - An open standard for performing *federated authentication*. Through SAML assertions, an *enterprise* can securely verify the identities and *privileges* of its users when they *authenticate* to cloud services.

Security Information and Event Management (SIEM) - Technology for collecting and correlating *cybersecurity events* and *alerts*, and investigating and tracking *incidents* arising from them. SIEM systems for large *enterprises* can have vast storage and computing requirements to handle all of the data collected.

Security Technical Implementation Guide (STIG) - A secure configuration document, generally for operating system initial installations. The STIG specifies security settings so the most important security features are enabled and configured properly.

Single-Sign-On (SSO) - An *authentication* technique whereby a single set of user *credentials* are usable on multiple applications. This technique reduces the need for the user to remember and maintain multiple usernames and *passwords* for different applications. *Kerberos, lightweight directory access protocol, federated authentication*, and *public key infrastructure* are common methods of implementing SSO.

Smart Card - A single-chip *hardware security module* contained in a credit card form factor that protects user *keys* for *authentication, encryption, digital signature*, and sometimes payment. Because of their security, smart cards have been used extensively in government and financial applications.

Spearphishing - A *cyberattack* technique that involves sending highly targeted *phishing* e-mails to victims within an *enterprise*. Spearphishing is distinctive because e-mails are crafted using insider information such as the names and roles of people or documents of interest to the victims. This crafting increases the probability the attack will succeed in tricking users to install *malware*, reveal *credentials*, or divulge other information.

Spyware - A type of *malware* that does not usually affect a computer's performance, but collects information about its activity and sends the information off to a remote command-and-control system. *Spyware* can collect data about web-surfing, program usage, e-mail activity, logon *credentials*, and banking or other sensitive account information.

Strong Authentication - *Authentication* that relies on multiple factors of identity, usually something the user knows such as a *password*, plus something the user has such as a *token* or mobile *device*, or possibly a *biometric* such as a fingerprint. Also known as *multi-factor authentication* or *two-factor authentication*.

Stuxnet - A famous *cyberattack* against the Iranian nuclear program. The Stuxnet *malware* targeted centrifuges used for enriching uranium and caused them to malfunction until they were ruined, while concealing the behavior until it was too late to stop. This attack impaired the Iranian nuclear program's ability to produce enriched uranium.

Systems Administrator - An individual who administers a computer system. Generally, the systems administrator has *privileges* to be able to modify all data and software on the system, including applications and the operating system. Many attacks involve obtaining systems administrator *privileges*.

T

Threat - An entity—someone or something—that can exploit an associated *vulnerability*.

Token - In *authentication*, a physical *device* used for *multi-factor authentication*. Users prove they are in possession of the token usually by generating a *cryptographic* code from *keys* stored within it. Users then enter the *cryptographic* code into the computer by typing it or through some type of electronic connection.

Tokenization - In *encryption*, the practice of *encrypting* data without modifying its format. For example, the social security number 111-22-3333 might be tokenized as 820-63-2956. Because the *encrypted* numbers are in the same format as the original values, they can be stored in the same database and handled using some of the same business logic. This formatting allows *encryption* to be retrofitted into legacy systems with less disruption and re-engineering than might otherwise be necessary.

Tools, Techniques, and Procedures (TTPs) - In computer *forensics*, identification of how *attackers* are operating: (1) the applications and other tools they are using, (2) the techniques with which they are using those tools, and (3) the procedures they are following to perform those techniques. *TTPs* are important *indicators of compromise* used to track down attackers and repel them in an *incident response*.

Transport Layer Security (TLS) - The newest version of the *secure sockets layer (SSL)* protocol, which establishes an *encrypted* connection between two computers over an untrusted network. It can also include verification of one or both computers' identities. TLS secures most web-browsing sessions, so *vulnerabilities* in its protocol can have serious business implications. TLS has almost completely superseded the *SSL* protocol in actual use, although in casual conversation both protocols are usually referred to as "*SSL.*"

Trojan Horse - Also referred to simply as "Trojan." A piece of *malware* that appears to have one purpose, but also has a hidden, *malicious* purpose. Often, free Internet applications may be Trojans. Trojans have hidden features that put up advertisements, change web-browser home pages, or record user web-surfing habits or logon *credentials,* and secretly report them.

Trusted Platform Module (TPM) - A *cryptographic hardware security module* embedded in many desktop and laptop personal computers. TPMs can be used to securely store *cryptographic keys* used for *strong authentication, encryption,* or *digital signatures*.

Two-Factor Authentication - *Authentication* that relies on multiple factors of identity, usually something the user knows such as a *password,* plus something the user has such as a *token* or mobile *device,* or possibly a *biometric* such as a fingerprint. Also known as *multi-factor authentication* or *strong authentication*.

U

No entries.

V

Virtual Private Network (VPN) - A network security technology that involves creating an *encrypted* tunnel from one host computer to another over an untrusted network. This *encrypted* tunnel is used to connect the networks at both ends so they are "virtually" connected and private from the network in between.

Virus - A form of *malware* that attaches itself to other pieces of software in order to propagate and run. A virus can be embedded into an application or computer operating system, but it is unable to run on its own. It usually includes the ability to replicate itself, and it may also have a payload to perform some type of destructive or *malicious* behavior.

Vulnerability - A flaw that allows a system to be exploited or *compromised* for *malicious* purposes. Vulnerabilities may be flaws in software code, system configurations, or security architectures. Some vulnerabilities are remediated through *patches*, while others may require significant system redesign or technology replacement. Complex environments with hundreds or thousands of computer systems can have thousands or even millions of vulnerabilities *attackers* can potentially exploit.

W

Webshell - A piece of *malware* installed on a web server that gives the *attacker* the ability to control the server from the Internet. A webshell usually consists of a customized web page known only to the *attacker* that executes commands and displays their results.

Whitelisting - A security method that involves identifying accounts, applications, networks, or network protocols that are explicitly trusted. With whitelisting, only those accounts, applications, networks, or network protocols on the approved list are permitted to operate. All other accounts, applications, networks, or network protocols are blocked and may generate *alerts* for investigation. Whitelisting is in contrast to *blacklisting*.

Worm - A form of *malware* with the ability to run and replicate itself independently. This is in contrast to a *virus*, which requires a carrier to propagate and execute. Worms usually include the ability to replicate themselves from system to system. Worms may also have a payload to perform some type of destructive or *malicious* behavior.

X

No entries.

Y

No entries.

Z

Zero-Day Exploit - A *cyberattack* that targets a *vulnerability* not publicly known or for which a *patch* is not yet available. Zero-day exploits are valuable to attackers, since they can be difficult or impossible to block. However, the use of a zero-day exploit can reveal the underlying *vulnerability* and give defenders the opportunity to *mitigate* it.

Zombie - A computer at least partially under the control of an *attacker*, or part of a *botnet*.

Zoo - It's a *cyber*zoo out there in *cyber*space, so let's all be *cyber*careful. Thanks for reading this book.

Bibliography

The documents listed in this bibliography are a selected compilation of cybersecurity references. Along with the cybersecurity references, the bibliography includes references from other disciplines, such as network engineering and software engineering.

This bibliography is not exhaustive. The entries listed here are documents and web pages that the authors consulted during the preparation of this book and believe would be of interest.

For convenience, the bibliographical entries are organized as follows:

- Books
- Frameworks
- Journal / Magazine Articles / Papers
- Threat Reports

Books

1. Carr, Houston, Charles Snyder, and Bliss Bailey. *The Management of Network Security*. New York, NY: Prentice Hall, 2010.

2. Conklin, William Arthur, Gregory White, and Dwayne Williams. *Principles of Computer Security: CompTIA Security+™ and Beyond, Second Edition*. New York, NY: McGraw-Hill Companies, 2010.

3. Donaldson, Scott, and Stanley Siegel. *Successful Software Development, Second Edition*. Upper Saddle River, NJ: Prentice Hall PTR, 2001.

4. Harris, Shon. *CISSP All-in-One Exam Guide, Sixth Edition*. New York, NY: McGraw-Hill, 2010.

5. Kahate, Atul. *Cryptography and Network Security, Second Edition*. New Delhi, India: Tata McGraw-Hill, 2009.

6. *Leading Issues in Information Warfare and Security Research, Volume One*, ed. Julie Ryan. Reading, UK: Academic Publishing International Ltd, 2011.

7. McCumber, John. *Assessing and Managing Security Risk Analysis in IT Systems: A Structured Methodology*. Boca Raton, FL: CRC Press LLC, 2005.

8. Mutch, John, and Brian Anderson. *Preventing Good People from Doing Bad Things: Implementing Least Privilege*. New York, NY: Springer-Verlag New York, Inc., 2011.

9. Peltier, Thomas. *Information Security Risk Analysis*. Boca Raton, FL: CRC Press LLC, 2001.

10. Sherwood, John, Andrew Clark, and David Lynas. *Enterprise Security Architecture, Contextual Security Architecture, A Business-Driven Approach*. San Francisco, CA: CMP Books, 2005.

Frameworks

1. "Aligning COBIT 4.1, ITIL V3 and ISO 27002 for Business Benefit." Retrieved on April 1, 2015, from `www.isaca.org/Knowledge-Center/Research/Documents/Aligning-COBIT-ITIL-V3-ISO27002-for-Business-Benefit_res_Eng_1108.pdf`.

2. Carroll, David, Marilyn Rose, and Vincent Sritapan. *Mobile Security Reference Architecture, Version 1.0*. Federal CIO Council and Department of Homeland Security National Protection and Program Directorate Office of Cybersecurity and Communications Federal Network Resilience, 2013.

3. "COBIT 4.1: Framework for IT Governance and Control." Retrieved on April 1, 2015, from `www.isaca.org/Knowledge-Center/COBIT/Pages/Overview.aspx`.

4. "Common Body of Knowledge." Retrieved on April 1, 2015, from `www.isc2.org/uploadedfiles/education/review_seminars/cbk.pdf`.

5. "Cyber Resilience Review (CRR): Self-Assessment Package." United States Computer Emergency Readiness Team, 2014. Retrieved on April 1, 2015, from `www.us-cert.gov/ccubedvp/self-service-crr`.

6. *FM 100-5: Operations*. Washington, DC: Headquarters, Department of the Army. 1993. Retrieved on April 1, 2015, from `www.fprado.com/armorsite/US-Field-Manuals/FM-100-5-Operations.pdf`.

7. "Framework for Improving Critical Infrastructure Cybersecurity, Version 1." Gaithersburg, MD: National Institute of Standards and Technology, 2014. Retrieved on April 1, 2015, from `www.nist.gov/cyberframework/upload/cybersecurity-framework-021214.pdf`.

8. "Health Information Privacy Accountability Act (HIPAA): The Security Rule." Retrieved on April 1, 2015, from `www.hhs.gov/ocr/privacy/hipaa/administrative/securityrule/`.

9. "Health Information Trust Alliance: Common Security Framework (CSF)." Retrieved on April 1, 2015, from `www.hitrustalliance.net/hitrust-csf/`.

10. "Information Technology Infrastructure Library (ITIL)." Retrieved on April 1, 2015, from `www.axelos.com/best-practice-solutions/itil/what-is-itil`.

11. ISO 27002 (August 2005–06): "Information Technology—Security Techniques—Code of Practice for Information Security Management." (ISO/IEC 17799:2005).

12. ISO/IEC 27001:2013 and ISO/IEC 27002: "Code of Practice for Information Security Management Controls." Retrieved on April 1, 2015, from `www.bsigroup.com/en-GB/iso-27001-information-security/ISOIEC-27001-Revision/`.

13. Mell, Peter, and Timothy Grance. National Institute of Standards and Technology Special Publication 800-145: "The NIST Definition of Cloud Computing." Gaithersburg, MD: National Institute of Standards and Technology, 2011.

14. National Institute of Standards and Technology (February 2006). Special Publication 800-18, Revision 1: "Guide for Developing Security Plans for Federal Information Systems." Retrieved on April 1, 2015, from http://csrc.nist.gov/publications/nistpubs/800-18-Rev1/sp800-18-Rev1-final.pdf.

15. National Institute of Standards and Technology Special Publication 800-53, Revision 4: "Security and Privacy Controls for Federal Information Systems and Organizations." Gaithersburg, MD: National Institute of Standards and Technology, 2013. Retrieved on April 1, 2015, from http://nvlpubs.nist.gov/nistpubs/SpecialPublications/NIST.SP.800-53r4.pdf.

16. "North American Electric Reliability Corporation: Critical Infrastructure Protection (CIP)." Retrieved on April 1, 2015, from www.nerc.com/Pages/default.aspx.

17. "Payment Card Industry (PCI) Data Security Standard: Requirements and Security Assessment Procedure, Version 3.0, 2013." Retrieved on April 1, 2015, from www.pcisecuritystandards.org/documents/PCI_DSS_v3.pdf.

18. "SANS 20 Critical Security Controls, v5." Retrieved on April 1, 2015, from www.sans.org/critical-security-controls/.

19. "Security Benchmarks". Center for Internet Security. Retrieved on April 1, 2015, from http://benchmarks.cisecurity.org/.

20. "Strategies to Mitigate Targeted Cyber Intrusions." Australian Government Department of Defense Intelligence and Security, 2014. Retrieved on April 1, 2015, from the www.asd.gov.au/publications/Mitigation_Strategies_2014.pdf.

21. Souppaya, Murugiah, and Karen Scarfone. National Institute of Standards and Technology Special Publication 800-124: "Guidelines for Managing the Security of Mobile Devices in the Enterprise, Revision 1." Gaithersburg, MD: National Institute of Standards and Technology, 2013.

22. "The Critical Security Controls for Effective Cyber Defense, Version 5.1." Council on Cyber Security. Retrieved on April 1, 2015, from www.counciloncybersecurity.org/critical-controls/.

Journal / Magazine Articles / Papers

1. Hutchins, Eric M., Michael J. Cloppert, and Rohan M. Amin. "Intelligence-Driven Computer Network Defense Informed by Analysis of Adversary Campaigns and Intrusion Kill Chains." Paper presented at the Sixth Annual Conference on Information Warfare and Security, Washington, DC, 2011.

2. Schneier, Bruce. "Attack Trees: Modeling Security Threats." *Dr. Dobb's Journal*, 1999.

3. Sheldon, Frederick, and Claire Vishik. "Moving Toward Trustworthy Systems: R&D Essentials." *IEEE Computer*, vol. 43, no. 9 (September 2010): 31–40.

4. Schwartz, Matthew. "Target Ignored Data Breach Alarms. InformationWeek DARK Reading, 2014." Retrieved on February 15, 2015, from www.darkreading.com/attacks-and-breaches/target-ignored-data-breach-alarms/d/d-id/1127712.

5. Talbot, Edward, Deborah Frincke, and Matt Bishop. "Demythifying Cybersecurity," Co-published by the IEEE Computer and Reliability Societies, www.computer.org/security, May / June 2010.

6. Westby, Jody, and Julia Allen. "Governing for Enterprise Security (GES) Implementation Guide." Software Engineering Institute, 2007.

Threat Reports

1. "Advanced Malware Exposed: How Advanced Malware, Zero-Day and Targeted APT Attacks Are Evading Today's Network Defenses," Milpitas, CA: FireEye, Incorporated, 2011.

2. "Advanced Threat Report," Milpitas, CA: FireEye, Incorporated, 2012.

3. "APT1: Exposing One of China's Cyber Espionage Units," Mandiant, 2013. Retrieved on February 14, 2015, from http://intelreport.mandiant.com/Mandiant_APT1_Report.pdf.

4. "Mandiant M-Trends Annual Report 2014." Mandiant, 2014. Retrieved on April 1, 2015, from https://dl.mandiant.com/EE/library/WP_M-Trends2014_140409.pdf.

5. "Verizon 2014 Data Breach Investigations Report." Retrieved on April 1, 2015, from www.verizonenterprise.com/DBIR/2014/.

6. "2015 Vormetric Insider Threat Report—Global Edition," San Jose, CA: Vormetric, Inc., 2015. (Research conducted by Harris Poll; research analyzed by Ovum).

Index

Get the eBook for only $5!

Why limit yourself?

Now you can take the weightless companion with you wherever you go and access your content on your PC, phone, tablet, or reader.

Since you've purchased this print book, we're happy to offer you the eBook in all 3 formats for just $5.

Convenient and fully searchable, the PDF version enables you to easily find and copy code—or perform examples by quickly toggling between instructions and applications. The MOBI format is ideal for your Kindle, while the ePUB can be utilized on a variety of mobile devices.

To learn more, go to www.apress.com/companion or contact support@apress.com.

Printed in the United States
By Bookmasters

Printed in the United States
By Bookmasters